Truth and Privilege

Truth and Privilege is a comparative study that brings together legal, constitutional and social history to explore the common law's diverging paths in two kindred places committed to freedom of expression but separated by the American Revolution. Comparing Nova Scotia and Massachusetts, Lyndsay Campbell examines the development of libel law, the defences of truth and privilege, and the place of courts as fora for disputes. She contrasts courts' centrality in struggles over expression and the interpretation of individual rights in Massachusetts with concerns about defining protective boundaries for the press and individuals through institutional design in Nova Scotia. Campbell's rich analysis acts as a lens through which to understand the role of law in shaping societal change in the nineteenth century, shedding light on the essential question we still grapple with today: what should law's role be in regulating expression we perceive as harmful?

Lyndsay Campbell is an Associate Professor in Law and History at the University of Calgary, and Associate Dean, Research in the Faculty of Law. She has co-edited two volumes, *Freedom's Conditions in the U.S.-Canadian Borderlands in the Age of Emancipation* and *Canada's Legal Pasts: Looking Forward, Looking Back*.

T0370937

See the Studies in Legal History series website at
http://studiesinlegalhistory.org/

Studies in Legal History

EDITORS

Sarah Barringer Gordon, University of Pennsylvania
Holly Brewer, University of Maryland, College Park
Lisa Ford, University of New South Wales
Michael Lobban, London School of Economics and Political Science
Reuel Schiller, University of California, Hastings College of the Law

Other books in the series:

Michael Lobban, *Imperial Incarceration: Detention without Trial in the Making of British Colonial Africa*
Stefan Jurasinski and Lisi Oliver, *The Laws of Alfred: The Domboc and the Making of Anglo-Saxon Law*
Sascha Auerbach, *Armed with Sword and Scales: Law, Culture, and Local Courtrooms in London, 1860–1913*
Alejandro de La Fuente and Ariela J. Gross, *Becoming Free, Becoming Black: Race, Freedom, and the Law in Cuba, Virginia, and Louisiana*
Elizabeth Papp Kamali, *Felony and the Guilty Mind in Medieval England*
Jessica K. Lowe, *Murder in the Shenandoah: Making Law Sovereign in Revolutionary Virginia*
Michael A. Schoeppner, *Moral Contagion: Black Atlantic Sailors, Citizenship, and Diplomacy in Antebellum America*
Sam Erman, *Almost Citizens: Puerto Rico, the U.S. Constitution, and Empire*

Truth and Privilege

Libel Law in Massachusetts and Nova Scotia, 1820–1840

LYNDSAY CAMPBELL
University of Calgary

CAMBRIDGE
UNIVERSITY PRESS

Shaftesbury Road, Cambridge CB2 8EA, United Kingdom

One Liberty Plaza, 20th Floor, New York, NY 10006, USA

477 Williamstown Road, Port Melbourne, VIC 3207, Australia

314–321, 3rd Floor, Plot 3, Splendor Forum, Jasola District Centre, New Delhi – 110025, India

103 Penang Road, #05–06/07, Visioncrest Commercial, Singapore 238467

Cambridge University Press is part of Cambridge University Press & Assessment, a department of the University of Cambridge.

We share the University's mission to contribute to society through the pursuit of education, learning and research at the highest international levels of excellence.

www.cambridge.org
Information on this title: www.cambridge.org/9781009017893

DOI: 10.1017/9781009039406

© Lyndsay Campbell 2022

First published 2022
First paperback edition 2024

A catalogue record for this publication is available from the British Library

Library of Congress Cataloging-in-Publication data
NAMES: Campbell, Lyndsay, author.
TITLE: Truth and privilege : libel law in Massachusetts and Nova Scotia, 1820–1840 / Lyndsay Campbell, University of Calgary.
DESCRIPTION: Cambridge, United Kingdom ; New York, NY : Cambridge University Press, 2022. | Series: Studies in legal history | Based on author's thesis (doctoral – University of California, Berkeley, 2009) issued under title: Truths and consequences : the legal and extralegal regulation of expression in Massachusetts and Nova Scotia, 1820–1840. | Includes bibliographical references and index.
IDENTIFIERS: LCCN 2021041323 (print) | LCCN 2021041324 (ebook) | ISBN 9781316510698 (hardback) | ISBN 9781009039406 (ebook)
SUBJECTS: LCSH: Libel and slander – Nova Scotia – History – 19th century. | Libel and slander – Massachusetts – History – 19th century.
CLASSIFICATION: LCC KDZ223 .C36 2022 (print) | LCC KDZ223 (ebook) | DDC 346.71603/4–dc23
LC record available at https://lccn.loc.gov/2021041323
LC ebook record available at https://lccn.loc.gov/2021041324

ISBN   978-1-316-51069-8   Hardback
ISBN   978-1-009-01789-3   Paperback

Contents

Tables

Foreword – The Osgoode Society for Canadian Legal History

Truth and Privilege is a comparative study of the forces that drove the evolution of the body of law used for disciplining wayward presses and tongues in Nova Scotia and Massachusetts in the 1820s and 1830s. The book explores the interplay among legal and constitutional traditions, political and religious controversies, publishing practices, institutional logic and personalities, as these two deeply connected places worked through the implications of responsive democratic governance. Both places prized both good character and free expression, but courtrooms were far more often the site of these conflicts in Massachusetts. Professor Campbell's research on the defenses of truth and privilege demonstrates the similarities and differences between these jurisdictions in how the tensions around assertions of legislative power and claims to individual conscience and expression played out. She explores the unfolding of legal and popular thought on acceptable justifications for publishing objectionable expression and the incentives institutions offered to draw participants, including women, into court or to keep them out.

The purpose of the Osgoode Society for Canadian Legal History is to encourage research and writing in the history of Canadian law. The Society, which was incorporated in 1979 and is registered as a charity, was founded at the initiative of the Honourable R. Roy McMurtry, and officials of the Law Society of Upper Canada. The Society seeks to stimulate the study of legal history in Canada by supporting researchers, collecting oral histories, and publishing volumes that contribute to legal-historical scholarship in Canada. This year's books bring the total published since 1981 to 114, in all fields of legal history – the courts, the judiciary and the legal profession, as well as the history of crime and punishment, women and law, law and economy, the legal treatment of Indigenous peoples and ethnic minorities, and famous cases and significant trials in all areas of the law.

Current directors of the Osgoode Society for Canadian Legal History are Constance Backhouse, Heidi Bohaker, Bevin Brookbank, Shantona Chaudhury, David Chernos, Paul Davis, Doug Downey, Linda Silver Dranoff, Timothy Hill, Ian Hull, Trisha Jackson, Mahmud Jamal, Waleed Malik, Rachel McMillan, Roy McMurtry, Dana Peebles, Paul Reinhardt, Paul Schabas, Robert Sharpe, Jon Silver, Alex Smith, Lorne Sossin, Mary Stokes, Michael Tulloch and John Wilkinson.

Robert J. Sharpe,

President

Jim Phillips,

Editor-in-Chief

Acknowledgments

This project has been with me so long it is hard to know where to begin. My interest in expression began long ago under Wes Pue's instruction at the University of British Columbia. Many years later, it was Wes who confirmed my suspicions about how important the early nineteenth-century privilege disputes were to those involved in them. My interest in the common law on expression – as opposed to the First Amendment – was fostered in the Jurisprudence and Social Policy Program at the University of California, Berkeley, where I benefitted particularly from the wisdom and experience of Harry Scheiber, David Lieberman and Tom Barnes. Both UC Berkeley and the Social Sciences and Humanities Research Council of Canada supported these studies.

Our growing legal history community at the University of Calgary has been encouraging always. Ted McCoy has my particular gratitude for his generosity with his time and energy in our various projects. Thanks are due to our library staff for their assistance with census data and other sources, and especially to Nadine Hoffman. Janet DeWolfe long ago helped comb the public archives of Nova Scotia for expression-related cases, and staff members there supported us both. Elizabeth Bouvier provided invaluable assistance over my many years of intermittent visits to the Massachusetts Judicial Archives. The archivists at the church archives in Nova Scotia and Massachusetts were invariably helpful.

I have presented papers exploring aspects of this project at many conferences, but especially at meetings of the Canadian Law and Society Association, the American Society for Legal History, the Australia and New Zealand Legal History Society, Doug Harris's Legal History Workshop on Pender Island in 2008, Bernard Bailyn's

International Seminar on the History of the Atlantic World, 1500–1825 in 2010; and the 2010 workshop on the treatise organized by Angela Fernandez and Markus Dubber in Toronto. I have benefitted from the feedback and encouragement of a positive multitude of colleagues and friends. In particular, Chris Tomlins provided detailed feedback on an early draft of this book. Tony Freyer confirmed for me what "pleading double" meant – I should have thought to ask him earlier – and supported my intellectual inquiries in many ways. Holly Brewer has been a source of great support and critical insight over the manuscript's long development. Jim Phillips and Philip Girard provided help with Nova Scotia sources and interpretations through my doctoral studies and since, and I am grateful to Philip for his careful reading and thoughtful questions in the final stages. Michael Lobban and David Lieberman let me bounce my ideas about privilege off them at a key moment. Michael's suggestion that I might like to look at *Stockdale v. Hansard* was critical, and his knack for putting his finger on soft spots has greatly strengthened the manuscript. Holly, Jim, Philip and Michael have been astute, patient and kind readers and critics, and I am very grateful to them all.

Too many friends to mention have played large and small roles in keeping me going on this project, but I have to mention, because I promised, that I am "eternally grateful" to Shaunnagh Dorsett for tracking down copyright information in Washington about the elusive first edition of *Fruits of Philosophy*. One of the absolute best things about legal history is how often the best of colleagues turn into the best of friends.

My children, Naomi and Rory Jennings, cannot remember a time when this project was not part of their lives, and in Rory's case, there has, as yet, been no such time. I am grateful to them for their forbearance and interest. My partner in all things, Cullen Jennings, has lived with libel law in Nova Scotia and Massachusetts for the majority of his adult life, has asked acute questions and supported trips and explorations of various kinds. He has been my rock always.

I

Introduction

In 1830, Thomas Cooper – a transplant from Britain, a survivor of a prosecution under the 1798 American Sedition Act, a scientist, economist, political radical, philosopher and professor in South Carolina, wrote of liberty of the press,

It forms one of the common-place panegyrics of what are called free governments. It is one of the boasts of those who admire that nonentity the British constitution. It is supposed to flourish particularly in these United States, and to form a distinguishing feature of our American governments. I hardly know in which of them to look for it.[1]

The extent to which the press and individual expression were "free" in North America in 1830 was a matter of perspective. The much younger Nova Scotian editor Joseph Howe, writing after a jury acquitted him on charges of seditious libel in 1835, pronounced,

I do not ask for the impunity which the American Press enjoys, though its greater latitude is defended by the opinions of Chancellor Kent; but give me what a British subject has a right to claim, impartial justice, administered by those principles of the English law that our forefathers fixed and have bequeathed. Let not the sons of the Rebels look across the border to the sons of the Loyalists, and reproach them that their Press is not free.[2]

---

[1] Cooper, *Treatise on the Law of Libel*, xxxiv.
[2] "Supreme Court. Hilary Term. The King vs. Joseph Howe. Trial before the Chief Justice and a Special Jury, for a Libel on the Magistrates of Halifax," *Novascotian* (Halifax), March 12, 1835.

Freedom to speak and publish were vital in Massachusetts and Nova Scotia in the early nineteenth century, in the wake of the American and French Revolutions and the repressive period that followed in Britain. Labeled the "palladium" of liberty, freedom of expression was said to protect other rights, such as freedom of religion.[3] What these freedoms entailed and protected and how they could be institutionally guaranteed in these similar and closely linked places, however, was contested. Lawyers and judges did not always agree with journalists or others about what was legally or constitutionally protected, or what limits, if any, on expression or behavior were necessary. Apprehensions about abusing freedom were weighed against the risks of restricting it. In the 1820s and 1830s, the colonies of British North America were developing their own versions of democratic governance and saw themselves as holding fast against the republicanism whose implications were being worked out south of the border. In this dynamic environment, the political and legal institutions of the Anglo-Atlantic world were remodeled in ways that involved rethinking the rights of institutions and individuals. The legal and cultural meaning of the freedoms of press and expression evolved in this context.

Legal seeds grow different ways in different climates and soils. The developing constitutional frameworks of these two closely connected places, combined with social and political pressures, caused the law of libel and the institutions through which it was expressed to evolve differently, so as to reflect prevalent understandings of the meaning and purpose of freedom of expression and of the press and to protect the two societies from apprehended harms to their own forms of democracy. The law diverged both substantively and procedurally. In Massachusetts, the place of evidence of truth in libel and slander cases was the key sticking point in criminal and civil defamation law, because individuals claimed a right to reveal their truths in the face of power, secrecy and violence. Massachusetts republicanism had to work out the balance between majoritarianism and individual rights, even as religious and social reformers seemed to be threatening political and familial authority and the American union. The place of truth in defenses in Massachusetts defamation cases twisted and turned in response to these kinds of threats, and debates around blasphemy

---

[3] See e.g. Whitman, *Trial of the Commonwealth, versus Origen Bacheler*, 28.

and obscenity were shaped by evolving views about the importance of freedom of conscience. The individual's right to express truth lay at the heart of the legal debates in this area, and courtrooms and newspapers were the fora for struggle. As the civil defamation cases I describe suggest, taking disputes to court was common for middling white people in Massachusetts. With a written constitution to be interpreted by judges, courts became a key site for determining the scope of individual rights, while the violence of the mid-1830s raised the stakes.

In colonial Nova Scotia, by contrast, libel and slander cases and debates over the role of truth were far rarer. Much more important was a commitment to designing institutions that would balance the individual's rights against the interests of society. The legal concept of privilege, of building jurisdictional immunities into the law, was essential. In Nova Scotia, individual rights were read against a strong preoccupation with altering the division of power in government to give the legislative assembly more say in political decision-making. Individual consciences and freedoms were at times infringed by the legislature, a phenomenon that was raising constitutional unease in Britain as well. British legal writers' comments on mobilizing privilege to protect expression resonated in Nova Scotia. The pressures created in Massachusetts by movements such as antislavery and Free Thought did not much ruffle religious or political life in Nova Scotia or generate legal commentary. Nova Scotians watched from a distance as Thomas Erskine and his successors made British courtrooms into the forum for defenses of individual rights. Nova Scotian courts did not attract claims over expression the way that Massachusetts courts did. Nova Scotia had only one case in the period – Joseph Howe's in 1835 – in which individual rights took center stage, and Howe framed his defense chiefly in terms of privilege. Legal doctrine, legal procedure and institutional design evolved differently in Massachusetts and Nova Scotia, two places connected by history and legal tradition but separated by a revolution and diverging in their cultural and constitutional paths.

Drawing from unpublished court records and newspaper and pamphlet accounts of legal and legislative proceedings, this study explores the adaptation of a certain body of English law in Nova

Scotia and Massachusetts in the 1820s and 1830s.[4] The most vociferous
disputes over the meaning of freedom of the press and expression in both
places occurred in the context of proceedings over objectionable texts
labeled "libels." The early nineteenth century saw the organization of
the wide variety of laws that could be used to gain redress for
troublesome expression into what we have come to know as the "law
of libel." This law was adapted to a legal and social world that bears
more than a passing resemblance to our own but was also profoundly
different. The apparatus of the state was thin, and polities were
understood to be vulnerable to collapse if the norms that bound
individual consciences were not generally shared, especially by the
lower orders. As older, more hierarchical power arrangements were
challenged by democratic impulses, the individual conscience came
increasingly to matter. The rights of individuals to hold and express
their views troubled constitutional theory and the operation of libel law
in both Massachusetts and Nova Scotia in the 1820s and 1830s, with
Nova Scotian constitutional theory being complicated, additionally, by
another layer of conflict: the question of the jurisdiction of the legislature
versus the executive, a struggle interlaced with constitutional struggles
involving similar principles but different political tensions in Britain.

   In the 1820s, Nova Scotians were feeling the distant ripples of the
considerable changes that were taking place in the British and imperial
constitutions. Cabinet government was emerging in Britain, and the
wave of repression that followed the French Revolution had produced
a strong response that was soon to bring Whig reformers to power and

---

[4] This study compares a sample of 141 cases brought in 1820 through 1840 in the
Courts of Common Pleas and Supreme Judicial Court in Massachusetts to what is
likely the entire population of slander and libel cases brought in the Supreme Court
and the Inferior Courts of Common Pleas ("ICCPs") of Nova Scotia, although the
ICCPs did not actually produce any of the cases in this study. The records of magistrates and the Suffolk Justices Court have not survived, but these bodies probably
heard few such cases anyway because even when they had jurisdiction to hear defamation cases, the monetary caps on the claims that could be made in them probably
made them unappealing – plaintiffs had to put a low value on their reputational harm.
The majority of these court records, and almost all of the unreported ones, are from
Suffolk and Worcester counties, in Massachusetts, and Halifax, Pictou and Yarmouth,
Nova Scotia, a selection of places that allows for the consideration of issues of center
and periphery. I draw as well on contemporary periodicals, church records, pamphlets,
newspapers, and catalogs and advertising drawn up by printers and libraries that offer
hints about how particular law books moved through this world. Appendix A contains
more information about sources.

liberal reforms to the political system: civic rights for Roman Catholics, the end of the rotten boroughs, limits on certain legal powers recently exercised tyrannically by the Crown, and new approaches to governance. Other constitutional forces hit Massachusetts. The Hartford Convention and New England's resistance to the War of 1812 left deep strains. The close connection between congregational churches and town government that had characterized the colonial period had received a serious blow in 1811, when a short-lived Republican government managed to pass legislation that permitted people to direct their religious taxes to the denomination of their choice. Constitutional change along the same lines would come to pass in 1833. The press was increasingly aggressive and vehement. New pamphlets appeared daily, aimed at audiences of women and young people as well as mature white men. With Jacksonian democracy and the Second Great Awakening spreading in America, Boston's brahmins on Beacon Hill faced the specter of power emerging from less rarefied addresses.

Individuals offended by expression in the 1820s and 1830s in Nova Scotia and Massachusetts could seek damages if they were prepared to pay for it. An offended person could also go to the local prosecutor or grand jury to lodge a complaint, which might, if successful, result in a fine or a few months' imprisonment or both. If the expression pertained to the legislature or a member, the legislature might exercise its powers of contempt. While few objected to civil lawsuits for slander or libel, criminal and legislative processes at times provoked concern about governmental encroachment on rights to freedom of the press and freedom of expression or "discussion," as it was often called. The prospect of legislative contempt proceedings brought the powers of the legislature, as the people's bulwark against an overbearing executive, into the discussion in ways that historians have tended to overlook in their focus on individual rights. In Massachusetts the written constitution, initially adopted in 1780, was an important element of conversations about the legitimacy of the regulation of expression. No longer new by 1820, it announced the importance of a free press but guaranteed free expression explicitly only to the members of the legislature in debate.[5]

---

[5] Constitution of the Commonwealth of Massachusetts, part I, articles XVI and XXI, printed in *General Laws of Massachusetts*.

A more extensive framework was a work in progress, the product of judicial decision-making and local activism. In Nova Scotia the constitutional framework of the period evolved against the backdrop of understandings of British law, politics and constitutional thought. These various constitutional constraints shaped the law of libel as understood in Nova Scotia and Massachusetts. Constitutional principles, however, especially the meaning of individual rights, were in turn shaped by libel and slander cases.

A vast range of other strategies for addressing problematic expression existed in both places. Editors could refuse to publish letters they received. Abolitionists, temperance advocates, unpopular politicians and others could be refused access to public spaces and pulpits or beaten in the streets. Fathers could ban pamphlets and newspapers from their homes, or try to. The acceptability of these other strategies – especially violence – affected legal and constitutional approaches to objectionable expression.

Reformers in both Massachusetts and Nova Scotia increasingly argued and assumed that the people could and should govern themselves. In Massachusetts this conviction animated contention about the boundary that protected private lives from public scrutiny, partly because Massachusetts had far more newspapers – and these were far more partisan and likely to offend – than Nova Scotia's. The question of what kinds of truths about individuals' conduct could be placed before the public came up repeatedly in Massachusetts libel cases. As abolitionists increasingly hurled insults against slaveowners, apprehension grew about the union's future. Legislative halls and courtrooms reverberated with arguments about what kinds of truths about individuals could be placed before the public: many libel cases reflected this tension. As the 1830s passed, the ground shifted somewhat to individuals' rights to speak their truth on religion and politics, as against the majority's right to silence minority opinion, whether through law or violence. Nova Scotians, however, tended to reject the republican logic of majority rights that this question assumed.

Proceedings in courtrooms provided occasions for arguing about the appropriate limits on expression as well as for gaining redress and revenge for reputational harm. Lawyers acted as champions of individual rights and of the state's interests in security and order. Seldom in either place did commentators challenge the legitimacy of civil defamation suits. The question came up in one case in

Massachusetts, but the constitution explicitly protected character and guaranteed the right to defend it in court, so not much breath or ink was wasted on this argument. How readily courts could be used, though, is important: Massachusetts courts were more accessible and inviting to defamed would-be plaintiffs than Nova Scotia courts were. Women brought lots of civil cases in Massachusetts but not in Nova Scotia. In both places, however, it was criminal libel cases that provoked the most serious commentary on rights.

Organizing the "Law of Libel"

In the early nineteenth century, jurists were reworking the law around expression. Between about 1790 and 1812, the multiplicity of legal forms pertaining to expression was organized into a body of law we have come to know as the law of libel. William Blackstone, in his *Commentaries on the Laws of England*, published in the later 1760s, reveals an enormous number of categories of objectionable expression that could attract legal attention, both civil and criminal, including oral slander; written or printed libels, pictures or signs; maliciously procuring indictments; reviling the ordinances of the church; blasphemy; profane swearing; some kinds of treason, sedition and contempt; common barratry; perjury; spreading false news; putting up an unlicensed stage-play; challenging someone to a fight; and being a common scold.[6] Few of these, however, left traces in the court records of Massachusetts or Nova Scotia in the 1820s and 1830s. A few people were charged with somehow disturbing religious services. A woman named Nancy Princess was brought more than once before the Boston municipal court on charges of being a common barrator, a scold and a disturber of the peace and for profane cursing. However, the vast majority of cases related to expression that appear in the surviving records of the courts of Halifax, Pictou, Yarmouth, Suffolk and Worcester are for spoken words (i.e. slander) or for written or printed libel. Legislative assemblies took actions in both places over "libels" that offended the dignity of the

---

[6] Civil defamation, a private wrong, is discussed at *Commentaries*, 3:123–27. These criminal offenses and others are scattered through the fourth volume, on public wrongs, organized according to who was wronged.

House or its members. These actions were more constitutionally problematic in Massachusetts.

In the late eighteenth and early nineteenth centuries, with presses multiplying and politically charged prosecutions in England and the United States drawing public attention, texts criticizing the law and procedure around it proliferated, and speeches made in controversial trials were published as pamphlets. In 1812 and 1813 three texts that we would now identify as – and which explicitly purported to be – treatises on this area of law were published: John George's *Treatise on the Offence of Libel*, Francis Ludlow Holt's *Law of Libel* and Thomas Starkie's *Treatise on the Law of Slander, Libel, Scandalum Magnatum and False Rumours*. George's was concerned mainly with defining the proper limits of political discussion and has left no trace in the law libraries or cases in Massachusetts or Nova Scotia. Holt's and Starkie's treatises rapidly became authoritative in constituting and organizing the field of libel law. Slander and libel had long been civil wrongs. Objectionable texts known as "libels" had likewise been prosecuted for centuries, but the grounds for prosecuting them, the available defenses, and the institutions that had heard these cases had shifted and changed in the turmoil of the early modern period. The law was sufficiently unclear and the oppressiveness of recent political uses of it so apparent that reformer Sir Francis Burdett in 1811 argued somewhat hyperbolically that the "supposed offence called Libel, and what is called the law upon the subject, and what I shall call the practice, is novel in its nature, is borrowed from the worst periods of our history, and hostile to every principle of the Constitution; in short, that the methods of procedure, adjudication, and punishments for Libel, are the growth of tyranny and usurpation."[7]

The task that Holt and Starkie set themselves was to draw the different threads together and rationalize a body of law and procedure that was under attack as a tool of repression wielded against those, such as Thomas Paine and William Cobbett, who criticized the government. Holt followed a Blackstonian organizational scheme, commencing with offenses against God and descending through the monarch and the branches of government down to offenses – including civil proceedings – against private individuals. Starkie's text, which superseded Holt's, began with

[7] Burdett, *Speech of Sir Francis Burdett*, 8.

civil defamation, setting out the case for the plaintiff, what had to be proven, what defenses could be raised, what punishments could be applied, and what rules for process and procedure operated. He then moved on to the criminal libel case. The purpose of these actions, he thought, was to address attempts to create disorder by weakening moral and religious constraints, undermining the people's confidence in the state or provoking individuals to violence.[8]

By 1820, the outline and most of the details of the law of libel and slander were clear. The civil case for the plaintiff was generally straightforward: it was necessary to prove publication of the troublesome matter by the defendant, reference to the plaintiff, that the matter actually was defamatory if there was any doubt, and sometimes damages. Certain kinds of oral utterances were actionable without proof of harm; otherwise some specific loss had to be proven, the assumption being that most spoken utterances were ephemeral and unlikely to cause any lasting harm.[9] Criminal prosecution was argued to reflect a somewhat different logic, as the essence of the offense, at common law, was an effort to instigate a disruption of the public peace. According to these treatises, criminal expression included the blasphemous, profane, immoral, obscene, impious, subversive, seditious, malicious or scandalous, as well as expression contemptuous of certain offices or likely to stir up strife between nations or violence within households or neighborhoods. Although criminal slander was prosecuted in Massachusetts in the eighteenth century, and although allusions to these kinds of actions left traces in confusing footnotes in early nineteenth-century law books, in neither place do criminal slander cases appear in the courts I studied.[10] In both

---

[8] Starkie, *Treatise on Slander* (1813), 485.   [9] *Ibid.*, 19–20.

[10] In eighteenth-century Massachusetts, the lower orders were prosecuted for their oral expression, including slander, usually before justices of the peace, in or out of the Sessions: Olbertson, Criminally Impolite, 74, 214. In theory, by the nineteenth century, slander – "words" in the language of the period – could be indictable if it threatened the peace and was not actionable civilly (only certain kinds of expression were: usually only impugning the plaintiff in his or her occupation, imputing a crime to the plaintiff or alleging that the plaintiff had a contagious disease). Peace bonds may have been issued instead of indictments, as more immediate remedies. Unfortunately few records of justices of the peace survive. I found only one appeal on a speech-related charge from a decision of a Suffolk justice of the peace, and it was for profane cursing and swearing, which was statutory. A Pictou grand jury indicted someone for "insulting a public officer" and "being 'an habitually wicked and

civil and criminal actions, the defense had the complicated side of the case; it was in the defenses that evolving understandings of the needs of freedom of expression and of the press were expressed.

Comparing Nova Scotia and Massachusetts

Massachusetts and Nova Scotia had similar but diverging legal orders. One was ostensibly republican, with written bills of rights (state and federal) pasted on top of older traditions. The other was a British colony with a substantial American population, working through its own legal and cultural imperatives within British constitutional traditions, which were themselves evolving. In the 1820s and 1830s, the Nova Scotian assembly was increasingly assertive in its contest with the lieutenant governor and his council, particularly over the public purse. Criticisms of legislators and councillors raised concerns about the proper shape of democratic institutions, concerns that differed from the political concerns prevalent in Massachusetts and affected the shape of arguments about expression.

Another important difference between the two places was in the commonness of using courts as fora for addressing disputes over expression. As I describe in this book, civil defamation cases were far more common in Massachusetts than in Nova Scotia, and Massachusetts offered would-be plaintiffs more tempting risk-to-reward calculations. The substantial presence of women in Massachusetts cases is an important indication of the larger place of courts there than in Nova Scotia, where women were almost completely absent. As well, Massachusetts had more lawyers, and people in some parts of Nova Scotia had very little access to either

---

malicious slanderer'" in 1835, but it seems doubtful the prosecution succeeded. Because mention of such actions was relegated to footnotes and oblique remarks by treatise writers (e.g. Holt, *Law of Libel* (1812), 190–94, notes f and g), it seems likely that these actions were forgotten and passed from use during this period. Only the offense of profane cursing and swearing was mentioned in Freeman's 1810 magistrates' manual for Massachusetts, *Massachusetts Justice*, at 65, 231–33. The rule that oral defamation could not sustain a criminal prosecution is consistent with Burn's *Justice of the Peace* (see e.g. Burn, *Justice of the Peace* (1810), 3:120–24). Sedition, however, could be uttered orally, as Henry Brougham noted in 1816, although there were no such prosecutions in Massachusetts or Nova Scotia in the 1820s or 1830s: see "Liberty of the Press," 107.

courts or lawyers, and religious, linguistic and other cultural reasons to avoid both.

Despite the different sizes of the populations (Massachusetts had four to five times as many people as Nova Scotia in the 1820s and 1830s), they had much in common. Both places were economically, legally and politically dominated by a single port city. Many New Englanders had settled in Nova Scotia in the 1760s, shortly after Halifax was founded, and many others had followed in the wake of the American Revolution. Extended families were split across the border: the young Samuel E. Sewall, soon to become a prominent abolitionist lawyer in Boston, enjoyed his time in Halifax around 1820, where he stayed with his maternal uncle, solicitor general Simon Bradstreet Robie, a direct descendant of an early governor of Massachusetts.[11] People traveled between the two places for education, religious fellowship and business, and there was much trade between them. Massachusetts had been an important source of law and civil procedure for Nova Scotia. Nova Scotians read Boston periodicals, and Bostonians reported on events in Nova Scotia. Moreover, New England's neutrality during the War of 1812 had left Nova Scotians without the suspicion of Americans that Upper Canadians often felt. Massachusetts and Nova Scotia were similar places, and they were aware of each other's experiences, fertile ground for a comparative study.

It was undoubtedly the needs and actions of newspapers and pamphleteers, their critics, supporters and persecutors, that had, for the previous three decades, been driving a small group of British lawyers to clarify and restrain the common law of libel. The texts these lawyers produced traveled across the Atlantic, at different speeds to different places, to provide guidance and frameworks for lawyers and judges called upon to consider contentious writings in newspapers. The press in Massachusetts was well established by 1820, and as in England, it was deeply involved in public life and politics. Nova Scotia, on the other hand, had few newspapers, but they multiplied between 1825 and 1840 and became much more politically engaged. Until about 1835, they seem to have been hesitant to give voice to sentiments critical of the political establishment, but after a high-profile criminal libel case that year, criticism became noticeably more direct and frequent.

[11] Tiffany, *Samuel E. Sewall*, 15–16; Beck, "Robie, Simon Bradstreet."

Both Nova Scotia and Massachusetts had an established upper crust that considered itself most fit to govern and resisted ceding political power in the face of democratizing impulses. This period was one in which the implications of republicanism, with its emphasis on the capacity for critical, responsible reasoning on the part of the vast majority of the white, male public, were being worked out in the United States. Those who held power and influence in Massachusetts often viewed the political pretensions of the masses with concern and at times contempt. Individuals who were not part of the elite, however, increasingly insisted on their rightful place as political actors and the importance of majority rule. Comparable developments were afoot in Nova Scotia, where a politically engaged middle class increasingly demanded a government accountable to the people. Responsible government – in which the executive was accountable not to a governor appointed in London but to the elected legislative assembly in Halifax – would be established in 1848, around the same time as in the Province of Canada, just over a decade after the Rebellions of 1837–38 underlined the depth of discontent especially in French Canada. During the 1820s and 1830s in both places, therefore, older political models in which a small group of people held power and addressed society's needs were challenged with assertions that the people could and should govern themselves.

Reputation was equally important in both places. Both inherited a body of law that assumed that unruly tongues were a danger to their owners and to society: intemperate speech could constitute sin, and society could suffer through destabilizing ideas, either because God might withdraw his blessing on society as a whole (an idea commonly associated with the early Puritan vision) or, more prosaically and more in keeping with common law reasoning, because angry people might resort to violence against each other or public figures. Having and keeping a good name, or "character," was also highly desirable, although not particularly rooted in Christian thought. The various threads of libel and slander law assumed that improper behavior should be kept quiet.

In a self-governing polity, however, the bad deeds of those with power were matters of deep and widespread interest. The evolution of the law of libel in Massachusetts and Nova Scotia suggests that they differed in their understandings of how much of an individual's life could be a matter of general interest. These understandings hinged on theories of governance and the nature of the prevalent disputes about public affairs. The conflicts over religion and disestablishment, abolition, freemasonry and other reform movements in Massachusetts rendered the personal far more political in Massachusetts than it was in Nova Scotia, and the Massachusetts press fanned the flames.

The Framework: "Libels," Privilege and Truth

Anglo-American writers in the late eighteenth century spoke of "libels," which were legally offensive texts. The most normative definition of a libel was "*a malicious defamation, expressed either in printing or writing*, or by *signs, pictures, &c.* tending either to blacken the memory of one who is dead, with an intent to provoke the living, or the reputation of one who is alive, and thereby exposing him to public hatred, contempt, or ridicule."[12] Libels were normally written or printed, but symbols and other forms could in theory be libels as well. In 1791, the attorney general of Massachusetts provided the Supreme Judicial Court with a definition he drew from Blackstone: "Of a nature very similar to challenges [i.e. duels] are libels, *libelli famosi*, which taken in their largest and most extensive sense, signify any writings[,] pictures, or the like, of an immoral [or] illegal tendency."[13] It was this broadest understanding of the word libel that allowed obscene publications (which generally targeted no one) to be characterized as libels in *R. v. Curll* in 1727.[14] The word libel was used colloquially as well, to label a text offensive or deserving of legal measures, even if none were taken.

A range of different actors could instigate proceedings over libels, depending on the target. Libels might attract civil suits, criminal prosecutions or contempt actions by legislatures or, theoretically, courts, although I have encountered no such cases in Massachusetts or Nova Scotia in the 1820s or 1830s. Holt's 1812 *Law of Libel* was organized into chapters on libels against Christianity, "Morality, and the Law of Nature," "the Law of Nations," "the State and Constitution," "the King and his Government," "the Two Houses of

---

[12] Holt, *Law of Libel* (1812), 50 (Holt's emphasis), cf. Bacon, *New Abridgement*, 3:490 (1740).
[13] "Supreme Judicial Court: Trial for a Libel," *Columbian Centinel* (Boston), Feb. 26, 1791.
[14] *R. v. Curll* (1727), 2 Str. 788, 93 E.R. 849.

Parliament," "the Courts of Justice," "Magistrates" and "Private
Persons."[15] Within these chapters, more specific pleas of the Crown
and of private parties in civil suits were described. Because the fulcrum
for analysis was the object – the "libel" – legal concepts and rules were
often shared across different types of proceedings: legislative contempt
proceedings were among the precedents mustered in a Massachusetts
criminal libel trial in 1836, both types of proceedings addressing
"offences against the common law of the state."[16] Statutes could be
mobilized to address particular offenses, such as blasphemy, profanity
and spreading false reports of the luminaries of the realm, although
Holt thought this last cause of action "almost obsolete," it being
preferable to treat magnates in ways comparable to humbler
citizens.[17] Treason, which also had a statutory component, could be
committed in a variety of ways, some of them written and some not.
The Houses of Parliament and courts could bring printers, editors and
others before the bar and try and sentence them for contempt based on
their expression. Although set out in law books, few of these various
types of proceedings over expression were commonly brought in Nova
Scotia or Massachusetts, or indeed even in Britain.

Because libels could be addressed through different types of
proceedings in different fora, jurisdictional conflict and risks of
double jeopardy arose. A defamatory writing could attract both
a civil action for damages and a criminal prosecution, although in
Nova Scotia and Massachusetts, defendants faced one or the other.
Both an offended legislature and the attorney general could proceed
against a person who criticized a legislature, although likewise in
practice only one did.

Constitutional protections for speech in the legislature, however,
gave rise to a fundamental jurisdictional conflict over the extent of
parliamentary privilege, a conflict that has received almost no scholarly
attention. In 1765, Blackstone explained that every court of justice had
its own laws and customs, "some the civil and canon, some the
common law, others their own peculiar laws and customs, so the
high court of parliament hath also it's [sic] own peculiar law, called

[15] Holt, *Law of Libel* (1812).
[16] *Comm. v. Whitmarsh*, Thacher's Criminal Cases 441, 450–55 (1836) ["Thach. Crim. Cas."].
[17] *Law of Libel* (1812), 151.

the *lex et consuetudo parliamenti*." Blackstone expressed Sir Edward Coke's caution that matters arising in the Houses of Parliament ought to be discussed and judged there and nowhere else. Courts were not to comment on parliamentary jurisdiction either; each House determined the proper scope of its own actions. The indeterminacy of parliamentary privilege, Blackstone said, was necessary to protect members and the "dignity and independence" of the houses from the Crown; if privileges were delimited, the Crown would be able to come up with ways to evade them and oppress troublesome members.[18] Some privileges were widely known, such as the freedom from arrest enjoyed by members of the House of Commons while the term was in session and for a certain period of time around it.

Privilege, like libel itself, was key to the constitutional disputes of the seventeenth, eighteenth and nineteenth centuries over the jurisdictions of the legislative, executive and judicial branches of government. A privilege entitled the holder to enjoy a particular liberty or bundle of liberties. The privileges of an institution such as a court or a legislature could be the foundation of disciplinary measures for contempt against those who failed to respect it or its members. Privilege could also be a shield that protected a person from legal measures – such as defamation suits – on the basis of who the person was or, in a broad sense, the circumstances under which an act was taken or expression uttered. The privileges at issue in this book are chiefly a legislative body's privilege to arrest and imprison its critics, a member's privilege of being protected against civil and criminal libel proceedings in court, and conceptual descendants of the latter, which protected other speakers and writers in other circumstances.

As writers in Nova Scotia and Massachusetts knew well, the English, and then British, constitutional struggles of the seventeenth and eighteenth centuries pitted the Crown and the judiciary against Parliament, and especially the House of Commons, that protector of the rights of Englishmen. The English Bill of Rights of 1689 protected freedom of debate in Parliament, a key privilege. Each House could discipline its own members, but no action would lie in the courts for what was said in parliamentary debate – indeed, it was a breach of the

---

[18] Blackstone, *Commentaries*, 1:158–59.

privileges of each House to publish its doings. Following the British model, most American colonial legislatures exercised judicial powers, and in the seventeenth and eighteenth centuries they disciplined and punished both their own members and "outside libelers" – importantly printers – over their characterizations of legislative proceedings and legislators.[19] The actions of legislatures were a considerable threat to the press in the colonial period, possibly more than courts in seditious libel prosecutions.[20] This history left open questions about the proper scope of the privileges of republican assemblies and Congress. As well, Americans tended to recoil at the idea that their neighbors, just because they had been elected to the assembly, could call them to account or indeed throw them in jail for criticism without the protections of a criminal trial. Even less clear were the privileges of colonial legislative assemblies such as Nova Scotia's, as they followed parliamentary practices and precedents but tended to be viewed (especially by nonmembers) as markedly less august than the British House of Commons. The question of the extent to which constitutional liberty meant guaranteeing the privileges of the legislature or, instead, protecting the individual freedoms of printers and other critics is a key point of divergence in the constitutional thought of Massachusetts and Nova Scotia. At this distance, legislative contempt actions may look like politics, not law, but this distinction reflects a perception of lines that were dimmer in the early nineteenth century than they seem now. We live in the wake of the ascendancy of courts and common law.

In the later eighteenth century, the powers of the houses of Parliament – especially the Commons – were under pressure in Britain. Luke Hansard published the first official report of parliamentary proceedings in 1774 in London, finally signaling Parliament's recognition of the public's rightful interest in its proceedings. Earlier in the century, unauthorized reports of parliamentary doings had drawn parties before the houses of Parliament to be tried and punished.[21] By the 1810s, courts were recognizing unauthorized but accurate reports of the debates of a House as providing a privilege against libel claims. Claims were being made increasingly successfully that parliamentary

---

[19] See generally Clarke, *Parliamentary Privilege in the American Colonies.*
[20] See generally Levy, *Emergence*, 14, 16–61; Clarke, *Parliamentary Privilege in the American Colonies*; Eldridge, "Before Zenger."
[21] Thomas, *Long Time Burning*, 104.

privilege was not as broad as previously thought and that individuals needed to be able to find protection in court against oppressive legislative actions, which featured angry legislators acting as prosecutors, judges and jurors in their own causes. The rise of the political press and the procedural and evidentiary protections being insisted upon in early nineteenth-century courts rendered legislative punishment increasingly problematic. The individual (typically a white man, or at least understood as such) was claiming and often acquiring increasing civil and political rights, which were understood to entail a right to speak and publish freely about matters of public importance. Any limitations on content, style or access to fora for communication had to be understood as consistent with broad public values and prevalent constitutional understandings. English cases and texts show the very concept of privilege being quietly democratized in courtrooms in the early decades of the nineteenth century, as it was reshaped from a perquisite of high personal status into a legal defense available, at least in theory, to all defendants facing libel or slander cases, in appropriate circumstances and depending on the speaker's or writer's intentions.

Privilege was an essential concept in debates over freedom of expression and the press in Nova Scotia in the 1820s and 1830s. In these decades, Nova Scotia had only a handful of prosecutions over expression, but it also had proceedings taken by the legislative assembly against newspaper printers and a recalcitrant member. These actions arose out of conflicts between the assembly and the council, conflicts that would soon result in responsible government, in which the executive was drawn from and responsible to the assembly. At stake was power generally and control over the public purse and patronage specifically. The popularly elected, increasingly assertive legislature insisted on its privileges vis-à-vis the council, and liberally inclined commentators supported claims to these privileges against the critiques of the council's supporters. Reformers' criticism was therefore muted when the legislature called its members or others to account for breaching the privileges of the assembly; it was conservatives friendly to the council who decried intrusions on freedom of expression and the press, at times magnificently misrepresenting how much more oppressive the Nova Scotian assembly was than the British House of Commons. Consistent with English tradition, a free press was characterized as an institution balanced against the other institutions of governance. In both substance and procedure, the common law needed to be shaped so as to recognize and uphold a free press. If properly established through law, it would guarantee appropriate parameters of liberty to individuals, who would, through the exercise of that liberty, keep the other institutions of governance honest and accountable. The *Novascotian* newspaper declared in 1832 that an "unshackled press" was "[a]mong the greatest privileges enjoyed under a free and enlightened government."[22]

The nature of liberty presupposed by the Nova Scotian debates was fundamentally similar to that presupposed in Massachusetts: what Michel Ducharme has called modern liberty, individuals' freedom to pursue their own ends, with the state providing legal protection for person and property.[23] It was largely in the theory of how institutional responsibilities could best be divided that the two places differed, with Nova Scotians wrestling with how to innovate while remaining loyal British subjects and not raising the specter of republicanism by flouting the common law or overly stressing the individual's right to self-expression.

American scholarship on freedom of expression tends to concentrate on a certain subset of the range of possible proceedings – court cases over libel, and especially reported criminal ones – undoubtedly largely because of the present-day importance of judicial interpretations of the First Amendment, but also because it was struggles over truth that animated libel law, certainly in Massachusetts. This book adds to the conversation about the regulation of expression in the early republic.

During the revolutionary period, the American colonies turned to the idea of fundamental, natural rights and the separation of powers, enshrined in written constitutions, to provide limits on legislative power. The Massachusetts constitution of 1780 followed – but not exactly – the English model in its treatment of expression and legislative privilege. It pronounced freedom of the press "essential to the security of freedom in a State" so that it "ought not, therefore, to be restrained in this commonwealth." Individual freedom of

---

[22] Letter to the editor, *Novascotian* (Halifax), October 17, 1832.
[23] Ducharme, *Idea of Liberty*, 25–26. Ducharme describes the different institutional arrangements the British "moderns" came up with to preserve liberty, the key point being a division of power (*ibid.* 30–32).

"deliberation, speech, and debate" was guaranteed only in the legislature: only the assembly itself could discipline its members' speech, and such speech was protected from legal action in courts. Outside the walls of the assembly, people had a right only "in an orderly and peaceable manner, to assemble to consult upon the common good; give instructions to their representatives, and to request of the legislative body, by the way of addresses, petitions, or remonstrances, redress of the wrongs done them, and of the grievances they suffer." The Massachusetts bill of rights thus provided no general guarantee of freedom of expression. Among the wrongs for which all citizens were entitled to a legal remedy were wrongs to "character" – defamation proceedings had constitutional sanction.[24] However, the constitution did not provide the legislature with the power to imprison libelous critics, an omission later interpreters thought was meant to protect the individual expression necessary in a republic and move such disputes into courtrooms.[25]

The written constitution and the role it required courts to play fundamentally reshaped individual rights in the United States, a process that took place over many years and coincided with the rise of the idea that self-governing republican citizens ought to be able to speak or publish truth without criminal sanction, at least if animated by "good motives and justifiable ends." This conviction became fundamental to conceptions of the rights of individuals and the press around the turn of the century, as newspapers multiplied and emerging party politics produced heated political and religious debates. Indeed, First Amendment scholarship has tended to focus on the fortunes of the "truth defense" as *the* marker of a commitment to free expression in American history.

In Massachusetts, despite the legislature's attempt to carve out a larger role for truth in civil and criminal defamation cases, judges were apprehensive about letting evidence of truth into the courtroom because of the risk that it would expose aspects of men's private lives that would undermine their authority both in the household and in society more broadly. Judges curtailed the use of truth through rulings

---

[24] Constitution of the Commonwealth of Massachusetts, part I, articles XI, XVI, XIX, XXI, printed in *General Laws of Massachusetts*.
[25] *Ibid.* part II, chapter I, section III, article X.

on both procedure and substantive law. On the other hand, claiming legal powers and immunities on the basis of status – that is, claiming privilege as a defense – probably sat uneasily in the popular republican conscience. Indeed, in 1808, in resisting a claim to an absolute privilege for a remark made in a legislature, counsel observed that privilege had been called "an odious plea."[26] In slander and libel cases in Massachusetts, defenses based on an inherent right to publish truth, or one's own truth, were more ideologically comfortable. The defense of "privileged communication" did come to be recognized in Massachusetts law, and the legislature had necessary privileges, but these were bounded. Offended people could turn to courts.

As this book shows, the conflicts of the 1830s show the increasing emphasis, in public discourse, on an individual's right to speak truth in Massachusetts, at times against the threat of violence. In Nova Scotia, the emphasis was on properly balancing the power among different institutions, which included building protection of the press into the common law of libel, without as much emphasis on individual rights. Differences between the two jurisdictions as to the centrality of courts and of truth are evident in civil defamation as well. The regulation of expression was fundamental to the self-understandings of these two polities, as they worked through the implications of their own versions of democracy.

Strategies and Choices: Interpreting and Applying the Law

This book is primarily concerned with the arguments that ran through three types of proceedings that could be taken against individuals whose expression caused offense: legislative contempt proceedings, criminal prosecutions over texts, and civil defamation suits. The principles governing these three types of action overlapped, and all were concerned with "libels," so it is necessary to consider them together. By 1820, all were affected by a mixture of British and more local interpretive traditions and practices. Legislators turned chiefly to the records of their own proceedings to determine the extent of their privilege, probably supplementing these understandings with personal recollections from newspapers and the accounts of travelers who had

---

[26] *Coffin v. Coffin*, 4 Mass. 1, 6 (1808).

watched Parliament or other assemblies in action. The instructions earlier governors had received and passed along provided some guidance in Nova Scotia, as did Thomas Jefferson's *Manual of Parliamentary Practice* in Massachusetts. Judges and lawyers, too, evaluated the prescriptions in the books and journals they could put their hands on, and the uptake or rejection of English common law happened case by case, rule by rule, sometimes by well-read members of the bench and bar and sometimes by those, like magistrates in rural Nova Scotia, without much legal training, who turned to texts such as manuals for justices of the peace. These texts relied on older books and were to some extent out of date. The transmission of reformist thinking from both sides of the Atlantic also influenced the evolution of law.

Strategic considerations affected the measures chosen in particular cases. If the Nova Scotia legislature wanted to silence a critic allied with the council, contempt proceedings could be much more attractive than turning the affair over to the Crown-appointed attorney general. But sometimes it was best to do nothing. Taking any proceedings over reputational harm could be viewed as an illegitimate, elitist move to avoid the cut and thrust of public debate.

Once lawyers were consulted, a number of different factors might influence the choice between civil and criminal proceedings if the objectionable text was printed or written. In neither jurisdiction do the records show evidence of private prosecutions for these kinds of cases. Most obviously, therefore, the state bore the cost of proceeding in criminal actions, which it would seek from the defendant upon conviction;[27] whereas in civil suits, the plaintiff bore the court costs up front and might recover them (aside from lawyers' fees in

---

[27] In England, individual complainants could obtain criminal informations from King's Bench to prosecute for libels without the intervention of the attorney general, after swearing that the objectionable words were false. Thomas Starkie explained that even though the defendant could not raise a defense of truth, the procedure was useful because it averted violence. The plaintiff got a chance to swear solemnly and publicly that the statements were untrue, without the defendant being then obliged to take up pistols to demonstrate his courage. Instead, the proceedings offered the opportunity for explanation and reconciliation: *Treatise on Slander* (1830), 1:cxlviii–cxlix. Similarly, Henry Brougham noted in 1816 that this manner of proceeding tended to be used for libels among men "acting in a public capacity or tending to produce a duel": "Liberty of the Press," 105. These types of proceedings did not take place in Massachusetts or Nova Scotia, where libel cases always began with an indictment brought by a grand jury.

Massachusetts) if successful. Civil suits offered the possibility of damages, which must have appealed to some plaintiffs, but others probably feared being seen as opportunists willing to sully their reputations further through the pursuit of lucre. In neither place were such suits perceived to interfere with freedom of speech or of the press. In Massachusetts, civil suits were much more commonly brought than in Nova Scotia, especially when women were involved. In that state, not only was the prospect of a windfall higher than in Nova Scotia and the costs of suit lower, but civil suits began with the attachment of the defendant's goods, chattels and lands up front for the whole amount of the claim; a defendant with insufficient assets could be jailed until trial. The strategic possibilities undoubtedly appealed to some Massachusetts plaintiffs. Nova Scotian plaintiffs could not attach assets in defamation suits but could until the mid-1820s in other suits with which defamation could be entangled. Once pre-trial civil attachment became rare in Nova Scotia, the number of defamation suits brought fell considerably.

Another factor in the calculation over civil versus criminal proceedings was the possibility of using the trial to air one's views to the public. In Nova Scotia, where truth was known to be no defense to a charge of criminal libel, there was something suspect in bringing criminal libel charges – the complainant might after all be objecting merely to the airing of the truth – but in Massachusetts, that taint probably did not bother most would-be complainants, since it was widely (though not exactly accurately) supposed that truth would exonerate the innocent. Evidentiary rules had strategic implications. Parties to civil causes could not testify under oath in either place. In criminal trials, the complainant, being a witness, could testify under oath, but the offender could not. In both places unrepresented parties could address the court unsworn, and self-represented litigants tended to be afforded considerable latitude to present their own cases. Self-representation was risky, however, in a cause of action as legally subtle as libel. Almost all criminal libel defendants and parties to civil actions had counsel in these cases, and indeed so did one complainant in a Massachusetts criminal action. The strategic risk a Massachusetts complainant faced in a criminal action was that unexpected evidence of the truth of the allegation might be brought forward by an enterprising defendant. Criminal procedure changed in 1834 to protect complainants from this kind of development, one of the ways in which truth became harder for those accused of criminal libel to deploy to their advantage. Surprise was less of a problem for plaintiffs in civil suits because truth had to be specially pleaded and because Massachusetts courts interpreted the pleas in defamation suits in a way that made truth risky to raise. One other factor that likely played a role in the decision to sue versus prosecute, which is difficult to tease out from cases, was an aggrieved person's view of the magistrate who would receive the initial complaint or the prosecuting lawyer who would conduct the case. After all, the list of potential prosecutors was short: the attorney general, the solicitor general (occasionally) and the county or district attorney in Boston's municipal court and in courts of common pleas elsewhere.[28] These various factors played out differently in different situations.

The common law contained traps for the unwary, and the propriety of various rules of law and procedure was contested, especially in Massachusetts. There, in the realm of defamation law, there was considerable uncertainty about what kind of intent a prosecutor or plaintiff had to prove before a jury could bring in a verdict of guilty. Some thought it a fundamental principle of criminal law that no one accused of a crime could be convicted without the state proving intent to cause harm. Others argued that criminal intent was present – that malice was an automatic presumption of law – if the defendant had simply intended to perform the act or omission that ultimately caused the harm, in this case the publication of the objectionable words to a third party. This was the intent requirement in civil cases. If the only intent the prosecutor or plaintiff had to prove was the intent to publish,

---

[28] *Stimpson's Boston Directory*, 1835, 9, identifies four officers of the municipal court of Boston: the judge (Peter Thacher), the attorney (Samuel D. Parker), the clerk and the crier. After 1832, Massachusetts had a district attorney for each of its four districts plus Boston, each of whom reported to the attorney general: Austin, "Annual Report," 482. I have encountered no prosecution conducted by anyone other than these officers. The law officers drew up at least a significant number of the indictments. The court clerk, commenting on upcoming cases in 1826, observed, "The Solicitor General is now at my Elbow, drawing the Indictments"; the grand jury was to convene later that day: J.H. Peirce to Austin, August 7, 1826, James Trecothick Austin papers, Ms. N-1789, Massachusetts Historical Society ["MHS"], Boston. The same papers contain a pleading letter from Alexis Eustaphieve to James T. Austin in 1824 about the prosecution of Joseph T. Buckingham, a letter that signals Eustaphieve's awareness of the vicissitudes of prosecutorial decision-making.

the defendant certainly had the more difficult case, needing to prove some other set of facts to defeat the claim for liability. Uncertainties about intent were the product of the previous centuries' English jurisprudence on civil and criminal causes of action that were based sometimes on the common law and sometimes on statutes. R.H. Helmholz has argued that intent-based arguments are evident in the pleadings of seventeenth-century English civil defamation suits but that as pleading practices changed, the arguments were still made but ceased to leave traces in the records. According to Helmholz, defendants' intentions and what effect they should have on liability were matters for juries until judges in the eighteenth century began limiting juries' jurisdiction and subjecting intention to a more fine-grained analysis.[29] Paul Mitchell observes that evidence of certain kinds of intent rebutted the presumption of malice that arose from the fact of publishing a defamatory allegation. Words spoken in grief and sorrow or in confidence and friendship had been found protected.[30] Whether or not the jury in a criminal trial could determine intent was also hotly contested in prosecutions for seditious libels in the seventeenth century and through most of the eighteenth. English reformer Charles Fox's Libel Act in 1792 gave the whole case to the jury, which in the privacy of the jury room could decide what it thought of the defendant's intentions and the other elements of the case.[31]

In the early nineteenth century in Massachusetts, the debate about the nature of criminal intent influenced the way that evidence of truth was permitted to operate in criminal libel cases. By the late 1790s, many American legal commentators were persuaded that a republican citizen could not rightly be punished for publishing the truth. At common law – and in Nova Scotia – truth was no defense to criminal libel charges because the gravamen of the offense was threatening the

---

[29] "Civil Trials and the Limits of Responsible Speech," 6–17, 20–21.
[30] *Making of the Modern Law of Defamation*, 145–46.
[31] *An Act to Remove Doubts Respecting the Functions of Juries in Cases of Libel* (U.K.), 1792, 32 Geo. III, c. 60 [aka "The Declaratory Act" or "Fox's Libel Act"]. On this statute and its origins and purposes, see Green, "The Jury, Seditious Libel, and the Criminal Law," 41–45; Lobban, "From Seditious Libel to Unlawful Assembly," 310–21. See also *R. v. Shipley* (1784), 4 Doug. 73, to which Fox's Libel Act responded, in which King's Bench, per Mansfield CJ, restricted the jury's scope to determining the facts and retained for the bench the question of guilt and the relevance of good intent.

public peace by potentially inciting the one libeled to violence, including duels. Blackstone declared that freedom of the press meant no censorship prior to publication, but that individuals could certainly be punished for abusing this freedom by publishing material that might corrupt morals or lead to violence or other harms.[32] In the United States, however, the risk of occasional violence was an acceptable price for necessary criticism. How to slot truth into a criminal libel case, however, was not entirely clear, and truth's role evolved in Massachusetts from 1808 to 1834. Initially, on the theory that the prosecution had to prove actual intention to cause harm, the defense could lead evidence of truth – in certain kinds of cases and under certain circumstances – to show good intention instead. The difficulty that then appeared was that if good intentions could exonerate a defendant from criminal liability, then falsity could be excused as well. As reformers weighed into public life, making allegations about the private lives of prominent men, this could not be borne. In 1834, evidence of truth was finally safely cabined: the prosecution would prove intent to publish, and the defendant could try to prove factual truth – along with good intentions – to rebut the charges. As well, before or at the start of the trial the defendant had to provide the Commonwealth with particulars, a list of the facts or incidents that grounded the supposedly true allegations.

Disagreement about the role of truth characterized civil defamation trials in Massachusetts as well, probably more than in Nova Scotia, although that colony's records are too spare for absolute certainty. At common law, truth was a defense to a civil cause of action, on the theory that a plaintiff should not be able to recoup damages for injury to an undeservedly pristine reputation. Unlike other defenses, however, a plea of truth had to be set out separately in the pleadings in a "special plea." In the 1830s, Massachusetts law regarding the legal inferences to be drawn from pleading of truth in civil cases diverged from that of other states in ways that made the plea riskier to Massachusetts defendants by reducing their ability to rely on other defenses. Even when the legislature abolished special pleading in 1836, judges continued to insist that for the defense to be valid, the same risky admissions and assertions had to be on the record.

[32] Blackstone, *Commentaries*, 4:151–52.

At the same time that the truth defense was emerging in Massachusetts criminal law, the defenses of privilege – absolute or qualified – were being worked out and systematized in civil and criminal cases in England. The idea that a combination of intent and context could protect a defendant against liability is deeply embedded in the history of the various forms of action that fed into the "law of libel," as it took shape in the treatises of the early nineteenth century. Paul Mitchell, in his *Making of the Modern Law of Defamation*, may take Thomas Starkie's assertions about the early nineteenth-century coherence of libel law with somewhat less salt than is necessary, but rationalizing the law around intent and malice was certainly part of Starkie's project. Mitchell argues that over the course of the nineteenth century the disappearance of the defendant's fault from the case the plaintiff had to make – which turned defamation into a tort of essentially strict liability – was the result of judges' distrust of the popular press.[33] The recognition and articulation of the qualified privilege defense, with its focus on the defendant's duty in providing the information and the hearer's interest in receiving it, made the defendant's state of mind relevant only to the plaintiff's rebuttal of the defense. Qualified privilege was a new doctrine, though, and it made cases more complicated to argue. It was a challenge both for litigants and lawyers to put forward and for judges to wrap into their reasoning.

The judges who shaped qualified privilege into a defense that marginalized the defendant's actual (presumably good) intentions were evidently cut from similar cloth to the Massachusetts judges who constrained the use of truth. In the early nineteenth century, though, privilege was still a powerful legal concept that seemed a promising approach to protecting freedom of expression. As Nova Scotian newspaperman Joseph Howe asserted of qualified privilege in 1835, quoting Thomas Starkie, "[t]he constituting a large and extensive barrier for the legal protection and immunity of those who act bona fide and sincerely according to the occasion and circumstances in which they are placed, is not only just in a moral point of view, and advisable as a measure of policy, but is absolutely

---

[33] Mitchell, *Making of the Modern Law of Defamation*, 101, 120.

necessary for the purposes of civil Society."[34] Just as absolute privilege protected proceedings in legislatures and much of what was said in courtrooms, qualified privilege protected the needs of commerce and social life and – Howe hoped – newspapers.

The last area of civil defamation law that produced a good deal of unease in Nova Scotia concerns the tort liability of newspaper editors and others who innocently republished defamatory material. The common law by the 1820s contained much scope for confusion, and Joseph Howe was concerned about rationalizing it in favor of editors. Massachusetts legal commentators paid little attention to this dimension of defamation law, as perhaps is consistent with the surprisingly frequent republication of notorious texts in that state. It seems that publishers were more concerned about profits than potential tort liability, and the law, such as it was, probably favored them.

As well as defamation, three other species of criminal libels also attracted prosecution in the 1820s and 1830s in these places, and they too were being shaped by the concerns of the period. Blackstone mentioned "instances" of "blasphemous, immoral, treasonable, schismatical, seditious, or scandalous libels" punished by English law, but not all of these varieties were in use by 1820.[35] Among the handful of criminal libel prosecutions in Nova Scotia were two for seditious libel. Rivalries among different branches of Christianity were at issue in some cases in both places, but since no single church had control of political power in either place, "schismatic" libels were far less of a problem. Blackstone's last four types of libels tended to manifest themselves as attacks on prominent individuals; however, by 1820 in Massachusetts, criminal defamatory libel proceedings seldom contained even overtones of treason, sedition or scandal regarding men holding high office. Most criminal libel cases in Massachusetts were framed as defamation, and the vast majority concerned men of middling social standing. One case of blasphemous libel was prosecuted in the 1820s and 1830s, in Massachusetts, but a new category of libel was increasingly prosecuted, especially in the

---

[34] "Supreme Court. Hilary Term. The King vs. Joseph Howe. Trial before the Chief Justice and a Special Jury, for a Libel on the Magistrates of Halifax," *Novascotian* (Halifax), March 12, 1835, quoting Starkie *Treatise on Slander* (1830), 1:cxli.

[35] Blackstone, *Commentaries*, 4:151.

early 1820s and mid-1830s: obscene libel. This offense came to be recognized and prosecuted as the sexual morals of the politically mobilized populace started to seem relevant to the integrity of public life. The newness of this varietal of criminal libel is evident in lengthy pleadings, through which counsel sought to cover all of the possible objections to their cases. Charges in the early 1820s over John Cleland's pornographic classic *Memoirs of a Woman of Pleasure* (aka *Fanny Hill*) displayed uncertainty about how much of the offending text should be reproduced in the court's records and whether or not publication to a particular person had to be proven for such a text. In the mid-1830s, the Boston clergyman and editor Abner Kneeland was prosecuted on charges derived from the comparatively new common law of obscene libel, the much older common law of blasphemous libel, and a decades-old blasphemy statute; but as the case moved tortuously through trial after trial, the state dropped many of the charges, partly for strategic and evidentiary reasons and partly because Kneeland's arguments that freedom of conscience ought to protect him from persecution for his religious opinions drew increasing public support. Criminal libel had been shaped to fit the concerns of the day.

Another constitutional current also shaped these cases. In Massachusetts, the debates of the revolutionary period and the rising status of the Jacksonian individual rendered legally and constitutionally salient the potential conflict between the majority and the individual rights-holder. If the people were the source of constitutional power, could they also interpret the constitution? Could the mob legitimately take action against expression it disliked? The treatment of violence is one of the notable differences in the legal and constitutional thought of Massachusetts and Nova Scotia in the 1820s and 1830s. Preventing violence – breaches of the peace – was the main reason English writers of treatises on libel law during the period gave for criminalizing the publication of defamation and sedition.[36] In Massachusetts, however, the risk that violence would arise from expression was a consideration to be weighed against two other factors: the violence inherent in slavery, which arguably demanded

---

[36] See e.g. Holt, *Law of Libel* (1812), 33, 54, 104; Starkie, *Treatise on Slander* (1813), 485.

sustained critical attack, and a deep commitment to the idea that truth as a matter of conscience was an ideal to be pursued at all cost. In the tempestuous 1830s, individualist understandings of constitutional rights became increasingly salient in the face of public tolerance of mob actions, especially against abolitionists, and the activities of prominent members of society both as participants in antislavery mobs and as advocates of majoritarian rationales for taking collective action against abolitionists as inciters of violence and disunion. In Nova Scotia in the same period, violence was characterized as unacceptable and not particularly important to the constitutional theory around free expression. Instead Nova Scotian understandings of freedom of the press and of expression were shaped by demands for political reform. Nova Scotian writers tended to characterize free speech for individuals as a necessary component of a particular political and institutional order, which was itself shifting into a more democratic, self-governing shape. To protect liberties, writers in this tradition looked to the legislature and hoped for sensible compromises within the common law.

This Book

Ultimately this study describes the evolution of the body of law most explicitly concerned with expression, as two places with diverging constitutional traditions worked through the implications of the democratic institutions they were developing. In Massachusetts, courts were key theatres for addressing conflicts involving reputation, through both civil suits and criminal complaints. However, with majoritarian violence targeting growing movements like temperance, antimasonry and particularly abolition, the stakes for the stability of society and the union were rising. Visions of the public's best interests were contested, and women and the lower and middling sorts were claiming an entitlement to voice an opinion on the matter. Individuals' reputations were drawn into the resulting controversies, and the law was employed strategically by people with their own personal hopes, fears and goals. Judges responded warily, by curtailing the defensive utility of truth, even as claims to a broad right to free discussion grew louder and suspicions of the judiciary's claims to impartiality in criminal cases were voiced. Privilege arguments were seldom made, but publishers nevertheless behaved as if they had the sorts of legal protections that could have been articulated in privilege defenses, and they were not prosecuted. Arguments in Nova Scotia, on the other hand, favored an understanding of freedom of the press and expression that protected the press as an institution. Individuals were understood to have the rights of Englishmen to express themselves on matters of public interest, but as the jurisdictional boundaries were being contested among colonial institutions, an idea that freedom of the press and individual freedom of expression too could be framed institutionally through the concept of privilege emerged as well. Without a written constitution, Nova Scotians could not turn to courts as arbiters of constitutional rights, and the scarcity of civil defamation suits suggests that they were disinclined to use courts this way anyway. The underlying story shows how the law's internal logic combined with the highly contingent variables of religion and morality, personalities and institutions, economics and voluntary life. The reach of freedom of expression was qualified by the peculiarities of place, time, publishing, power and personality, as well as by principles and traditions.

In Chapter 2, I take up the developments in the law pertaining to slander and various kinds of libels in the late eighteenth century and the first two decades of the nineteenth. The law and legal institutions of this period reveal the parting of ways between the unwritten and written constitutional traditions of Britain and the United States. The chapter introduces important doctrinal and political tensions in what had, by 1820, become a cohesive body of law. I move next to three challenges that transformed particular aspects of this law in the next two decades. The first, presented in Chapter 3, is the struggle over privilege, a core aspect of contempt actions and defamation cases as well as constitutional theory. The long process of working out the division of jurisdiction between courts, legislatures and the executive ultimately produced doctrinal changes in the defenses available to an individual who faced libel and slander proceedings. The second challenge, explored in Chapter 4, concerned the reorganization of sociopolitical and familial authority in Massachusetts, a preoccupation evident in debates about the truth defense. The third challenge, discussed in Chapter 5, was the tension, more pervasive in Massachusetts than Nova Scotia, between the individual's claim to a right to free expression in matters of conscience and the majority's claim to a right to impose its will, which flared in cases about religion and sexual morality. This tension increased as antislavery and other reform-oriented expression encountered violent responses. Reformers' experiences in court raised concern about judicial neutrality and fidelity to law. Finally, in Chapter 6, I turn to the use of courts themselves through a consideration of civil cases, in which individuals, through their strategic decisions, demonstrated their understandings of the invitation offered by courts as fora for disputes about reputation and expression. The last chapter draws the threads together.

2

The Common Law's Diverging Paths

The law that Massachusetts and Nova Scotia adapted in the 1820s and 1830s had been changing over the previous few decades in England and the United States. Which body – legislatures or the courts – could best determine the constitutional rights of individuals in Britain was a simmering problem. In Nova Scotia, moments of tension between the executive and the assembly foreshadowed future conflicts and echoed older ones in the American colonies, with implications for critics. Americans grappled with the implications of their new written, republican constitutions. The idea that evidence of the truth of objectionable allegations should sometimes negative criminal culpability had taken root in American jurisprudence. Obscenity was replacing blasphemy as a way of framing legal concern about expression that threatened morals. This chapter lays out the state of legal thought in these areas by 1820.

Parliament and Courts

The English constitution assumed that individuals' rights would be protected not through courts but through the proper structuring of institutions, with the powers of the two houses of Parliament balanced against each other and the Crown. Alan G. Tarr, following Robert Palmer, has observed that this logic also underlay the early American state constitutions.[1] In Blackstone's view, properly constructed

---

[1] Tarr, *Understanding State Constitutions*, 80–81.

institutional channels could address problematic expression and avoid the tyranny that would arise if the licensing of the press were left to an individual censor. The courts and legislature together would implement the mixture of common and statutory law about expression that reflected the English constitution.[2] Francis Ludlow Holt explained in his 1812 treatise, "all libels, which tend to degrade and vilify the constitution, to promote insurrection, and circulate discontent through its members, – to asperse its justice, and anywise impair the exercise of its functions; all such writings are termed seditious libels, and are visited with the peculiar rigour of the law."[3] Freedom of speech was properly limited so as to uphold stability of the institutions of government: these institutions ensured liberty, which seditious libels undermined.

Balancing the powers of the different institutions of government required protecting the institutions' jurisdiction and the liberties of the individuals who sat in them. The debates about expression in Massachusetts and Nova Scotia in the 1820s and 1830s diverged considerably on the legitimacy of claims to privilege, a claim to legal protection that could operate as shield or sword. The Massachusetts constitution considerably clarified the legislature's privileges and, moreover, made the Supreme Judicial Court ("SJC") the body that determined the outer limits of those privileges. Although the legislature and its members did have specific privileges, the idea that certain individuals could possess special, protective privileges was still suspect: a privilege could be necessary, but it could also be a corrupt remnant of the hierarchical, pre-republican past. In evaluating rights to expression, rather than discuss privileges, pleadings or procedure, American legal commentators preferred to focus on the substance of the remarks.[4] In

---

[2] See Blackstone, *Commentaries*, 4:151–52.

[3] Holt, *Law of Libel* (1812), 74–78, quotation at 78.

[4] This observation is consistent with William Nelson's observations of the changes to American pleading practices: *Americanization of the Common Law*, ch. 5. It is consistent also with J.C.D. Clark's observations about the divergence in British and American understandings of their own exceptionalism after 1783. Clark notes that by the 1830s, "British society found ways of sustaining its existing programmes of meliorative reform within the framework of the old moral order," and that English common lawyers "were increasingly bound by the doctrine of strict construction: Benthamite utiliarianism, not Jeffersonian natural rights, came to describe the truths the English saw as self-evident": *Language of Liberty*, 382, 384. In a similar vein, Barry Cahill has described how the judges of Nova Scotia at the beginning of the nineteenth century turned to rules of procedure and evidence to undercut slavery. See

American thinking, truth, not privilege, was what could make harmful expression legitimate. British commentators, on the other hand, focused on the attorney general's *ex officio* information, the composition and role of juries, and privilege, which was a claim about the context for the objectionable expression and could be raised early in litigation to stop the proceedings. In Nova Scotia, privilege was a workable way of thinking about the legal and constitutional rights of the press as well. In large part, this difference from Massachusetts arises from the different institutional tensions in Nova Scotia, where the legislature was still trying to assert itself against the executive and also where the British constitutional debates of the late eighteenth century were being interpreted and assimilated into local constitutional arguments. The institutional arrangements had to be devised so as to protect both society and the individual.

The complex evolution of privilege in Britain between about 1775 and 1840 is not well understood by scholars, who have generally overlooked the increase in the jurisdiction of the highest common law courts, led by King's and then Queen's Bench, at the expense of the House of Commons. These constitutional struggles, together with the repressive legal proceedings of the late eighteenth and early nineteenth centuries, form the backdrop to the controversies over expression in Nova Scotia that played out in the assembly and the courts. The shifting understanding of privilege also fundamentally reshaped the defenses available in libel and slander cases, as the concept of privilege was stretched to cover a wider variety of people and situations against legal actions for defamatory expression.

Privilege: The Sword of a Tyrant?

In the British constitutional tradition, it was clear that only a House of Parliament had jurisdiction to discipline a member for improper expression on the floor of the House. Regardless of what the member said, no action over the words could be brought by someone outside

Cahill, "Slavery and the Judges" and "*Habeas Corpus* and Slavery." Philip Hamburger's discussion of religious establishment makes clear the republican objections to "privileges" and "emoluments": see *Church and State*, 90–101.

the House.[5] The houses of Parliament also had a history of disciplining both members and nonmembers outside their doors – often newspaper editors and commentators – for casting aspersions on the dignity of the House as a body or its members individually.[6] Before official reporting of parliamentary proceedings began in 1774, even publishing an accurate account of what had taken place in debate was a breach of the privileges of the House and could attract contempt proceedings; the House of Commons's tolerance of journalists began to grow after its highly controversial jailing of London's mayor Brass Crosby in 1771 for his protection of a printer who had dared to publish its proceedings.[7] In contempt proceedings, the offender would be brought to the bar of the House and subjected to discipline, an apology or, at times, imprisonment.

Once reports of parliamentary debates began legally leaking into the world beyond, things got complicated. One question was whether a person could be disciplined for publishing an unauthorized report of the proceedings of a House of Parliament: in that case, the House itself was the forum for such proceedings.[8]

What if a member made defamatory allegations in debate, which were then published beyond the walls of the House? Clearly the member was protected for the speech itself, but could libel proceedings be successfully brought against the publisher? The issue was vexing.

A House could, in theory, punish the member, if so inclined; but this kind of redress was unreliable and would produce no monetary compensation in any event. Could the victim bring libel proceedings in court against the publisher? The rule gradually emerged that if the allegations were published in an official report of debates, they were protected by an absolute privilege and the offended party was out of luck. However, sometimes defamatory allegations appeared in unofficial but accurate reports of parliamentary debates – and indeed, sometimes the offending speaker published his own speech. Could the offended subject look to the court for a remedy against the

---

[5] See *An Act Declaring the Rights and Liberties of the Subject and Settling the Succession of the Crown* (U.K.), 1688, 1 W. & M. sess. 2, c. 2.

[6] See Holt, *Law and Usage of Parliament*, 25–26, 56–58, 68–69, 77; *Law of Libel* (1812), 120.

[7] Thomas, *Long Time Burning*, 104; Williams, *Eighteenth-Century Constitution*, 223–24.

[8] Holt, *Law of Libel* (1812), 129–30.

member as publisher, either civilly or criminally, or did privilege shield the publishing member? Privilege was a guarantee of liberty, but to what extent did the trappings of status and political power enable a parliamentarian to attack the reputations of other British subjects?

The varieties of punishment that a House could impose were also in some dispute. Parliament had long enjoyed the power to punish offenders of its dignity by demanding an apology or imprisoning them, usually in the Tower of London, until the end of the term (some also recalled corporal punishments such as cutting off ears, but those practices were over by this period). Was imprisonment still appropriate? Were there limits on what a House could do? Could a House imprison a nonmember? Francis Ludlow Holt, trying to make sense of these issues around the time of a major controversy, emphasized Parliament's tendency toward self-restraint in its exercise of these powers.[9]

All of these questions were underwritten by the constitutional understanding that Parliament was the highest court in the land, the king's courts therefore lacking jurisdiction to question Parliament's interpretation of the extent of its privileges. Challenging a House's authority in a court of law was one way to offend the dignity of the House and commit contempt against it. As Holt put it, "the putting the Commons to their law" was contempt, it being "to the manifest derogation of their dignity, and interruption of their proceedings."[10] For a judge faced with the task of hearing a libel suit brought against someone who had published a defamatory parliamentary speech, the safest course was to rule that such a publication was protected by parliamentary privilege and that therefore only Parliament could address any harm done by it.

The houses of Parliament had been tyrannical in the past. Judges and lawyers who had argued and acted on their view that a House had exceeded its privileges had faced unpleasant consequences, including imprisonment.[11] One perplexing affair in the background produced the linked cases of *Ashby v. White* and *R. v. Paty et al.* in 1703–5.[12]

---

[9] *Law of Libel* (1812), 126–27.   [10] *Law and Usage of Parliament*, 39.

[11] *Law and Usage of Parliament*, 71–75. As the House of Lords was the body that heard appeals from Queen's Bench, this situation left matters between the Commons and the courts at an impasse.

[12] This affair is documented in Howell's *State Trials*, 696–888, under the title "Proceedings in the House of Commons, House of Peers, and in the Queen's-Bench, in the Great Case

These cases underlined the constitutional uncertainty about the extent of parliamentary privilege and the courts' role in disputes between individuals and a House of Parliament, especially the Commons.

Constables acting as returning officers had rejected the vote of one Matthew Ashby, an indigent Aylesbury resident. At the assizes, Ashby sued the mayor (William White) and constables for rejecting his vote and was awarded five pounds' damages. However, with Chief Justice Holt dissenting, Queen's Bench arrested judgment, reasoning that jurisdiction over elections lay in the Commons so Ashby had no cause of action. Troubled by the possibility that Ashby could have a right to vote but no remedy for being deprived of it, the House of Lords reversed this decision on a writ of error. Viewing these proceedings as a great encroachment on its privileges, the members of the House of Commons resolved that they had the sole right to determine all matters related to elections, including electors' qualifications and the rights of those elected. The House resolved that Ashby and anyone else who presumed to place the rights of electors or representatives before any tribunal other than the Commons – including any lawyer involved – was guilty of a high breach of the privileges of the Commons.

Ashby's counsel, one Robert Mead, then initiated similar suits on behalf of five other electors of Aylesbury who had also been denied the vote. The House summoned Mead and the other plaintiffs, including one John Paty, to the bar and found them all to be in contempt of privilege. The plaintiffs were sent to Newgate; Mead was ordered detained but not imprisoned. Paty and the others were refused release on habeas corpus during the vacation between terms of court. They then brought their application to Queen's Bench in Hilary term, 1705. After seeking the assistance of the rest of the bench, the four impaneled judges found the imprisonment justified. Chief Justice Holt was the sole dissenter among the twelve judges. In a judgment that would become a touchstone in constitutional argument, he held that the subject's rights could not thus be sacrificed to privilege.

The Commons now ordered into custody the lawyers who had assisted the plaintiffs in seeking a writ of error. The next day the

of ASHBY & WHITE, &c. 2 & 3 ANNE, A.D. 1704, 1705." See also Williams, *Eighteenth-Century Constitution*, 224–32.

sergeant reported that the House of Lords had issued orders of protection but that he had nonetheless taken one of the lawyers into custody. Three he could not find, and one had escaped from his chambers using sheets and a rope. The House of Lords resolved that neither House could create new privileges, that subjects had a legal remedy for any breach of their rights unless they attempted to sue someone protected by the privileges of Parliament, and that the Commons lacked the privilege upon which its imprisonment of Paty and the others was based. English subjects could always bring writs of habeas corpus to test the validity of their detentions, the Commons's measures against the lawyers were pernicious, and the writ of error was "not a Writ of Grace, but of Right": the Queen was therefore obliged to issue it. The Commons did not accept these resolutions gracefully when they were presented in conference with the Lords; the precedents were thoroughly analyzed and hotly debated.

Queen Anne still had to decide whether or not to grant the writ of error. The House of Lords complained to her that the power to imprison claimed by the Commons exceeded her own power in this regard and interfered with her prerogative to demand an account of why any subject was deprived of liberty. The Lords argued that the Commons's actions endangered the certainty of law, that the subject had a right to a writ of error, and that the Queen could not refuse leave. The Queen resolved her dilemma by proroguing Parliament and thus releasing the prisoners. The affair ended with the jurisdictional questions unresolved.

The Wilkes affair of the 1760s revived dissatisfaction with the claims of the Commons. Number 45 of the *North Briton* contained criticism of a speech by George III about the Treaty of Paris, which ended the Seven Years War. The Secretary of State committed John Wilkes to the Tower of London for publishing this critique. Wilkes, however, was a member of Parliament, and he brought a habeas corpus application on the grounds that his privilege as a member protected him against arrest for any offense other than treason, felony or breach of the peace. The Commons responded by declaring that Wilkes was the author of the impugned article, that libel was a breach of the peace, and that therefore the privilege against arrest did not shield him. They resolved to expel him from the House, and the House of Lords concurred despite dissenters who strenuously opposed this new limitation on members' privileges in the face of two explicit parliamentary standing orders, as well as the implications of characterizing libel as a breach of the peace.[13] The affair thus raised the question of the Commons's jurisdiction to alter its privileges – to judge and punish a member despite the views of the electorate.

Wilkes was at the center of a storm around expression, privilege and procedure throughout this period.[14] A few years later the House of Commons expelled him twice and declared him incapable of election to Parliament. On his third reelection, the House declared his opponent elected instead.[15] A minority in the House of Lords again objected to the Commons's assertion that its privileges extended so far. Ultimately the Commons expunged the resolutions against Wilkes from its records, eliminating their precedential value as indicia of the privileges of the House.[16] Various threads in the Wilkes affair would reemerge, but Parliament's interference with the liberty of both the press and the electors was not forgotten. The name Wilkes came to stand for liberty.[17]

In the midst of the Wilkes affair, Blackstone reflected that "the principal privilege of parliament consisted in this, that it's [*sic*] privileges were not certainly known to any but the parliament itself."[18] John Rayner, in his 1765 *Digest of the Law Concerning Libels*, was uncertain whether parliamentary privilege could justify a member or anyone else in "doing a wrong Thing without Doors," such as publishing a libel, but if the Commons claimed such privileges, "they must be allowed to them; for they are to be presumed to have Wisdom to discern their own Rights, and Power sufficient to secure them."[19] However, by the early nineteenth century legal thinkers were no longer so sure.

---

[13] They warned that if libel were a breach of the peace, the Crown would be able to demand that libelers and even those who unknowingly possessed libels give bonds to the keep the peace before they were prosecuted. Suppression of the press would result. See Williams, *Eighteenth-Century Constitution*, 233–38.

[14] For a succinct review, see Hay, "Contempt by Scandalizing the Court," 440–41.

[15] Williams, *Eighteenth-Century Constitution*, 222; see also Greenwood and Wright, "Parliamentary Privilege," 423.

[16] Williams, *Eighteenth-Century Constitution*, 234–44. Jeremy Bentham's assertions about the extent to which membership in the House was controlled by members of the Lords and the monarch complicate one's sense of whose rights were actually on the line in this matter. See Bentham, *On the Liberty of the Press*, 33–34.

[17] Thomas, *Long Time Burning*, 97.   [18] Blackstone, *Commentaries*, 1:159.

[19] Rayner, *Digest of the Law Concerning Libels*, 120.

In a short book on parliamentary privilege published in 1810, shortly after his call to the bar, Francis Ludlow Holt stressed Parliament's habit of self-restraint while acknowledging its essentially unfettered power.[20] He distinguished between legal cases that challenged well-established parliamentary privileges head-on and ones in which either the privilege claim was more tenuous or the challenge incidental to a determination of the rights of a subject. The foundational privileges of Parliament included freedom of speech, freedom of the person from civil process, the right to originate money bills, and jurisdiction over its elections. It had privileges akin to those of a grand jury and privileges to enable it to punish for contempt. The Lords had additional privileges.[21] Holt in 1812 noted that the jurisdiction and privileges of the Commons "must not so wholly, in matters of penal infliction, preclude all jurisdiction of the King's courts, as to leave the subject totally at the mercy of the House, and of an uncertain law." In general, though, Holt thought the small risk that a subject could be unable to obtain a remedy for an arbitrary decision of a House of Parliament was simply a necessary cost to be borne.[22]

Parliament's jurisdiction to determine its jurisdiction – and to charge, judge and punish those who offended either House – was troubling substantively and risky to criticize. Holt was concerned about overreach by the Crown and therefore disinclined to acknowledge limits on Parliament. He did, however, review the leading cases of discipline by the Commons in a chronology that emphasized that the most extreme exercises of privilege occurred

---

[20] *The Law and Usage of Parliament in Cases of Privilege and Contempt: Being an Attempt to Reduce Them within a Theory and System.*

[21] Well-known privileges mentioned by Blackstone included freedom of speech and debate in Parliament, protection from arrest of the member and his servants, protection from entry onto members' lands, and protection against seizures of property pursuant to court orders. These protections were intended to prevent members from being diverted from "public business," so they only operated during the parliamentary session, except for the freedom of the person, "which in a peer is for ever sacred and inviolable; and in a commoner for forty days after every prorogation, and forty days before the next appointed meeting." This privilege did not, however, protect a member from arrest for "crimes of such public malignity as treason, felony, or breach of the peace; or rather perhaps in such crimes for which surety of the peace may be required": *Commentaries*, 1:159–61. As noted above, libel may have been drifting into this category.

[22] *Law of Libel* (1812), 132–33; *Law and Usage of Parliament*, 15–23, 31–32, 41–42, 94–95. On Holt, see Lobban, "Holt, Francis Ludlow."

during constitutional crises. He permitted the reader to infer that such privileges were no longer necessary. In his libel treatise published in 1812, he acknowledged that libels against the Houses of Parliament had generally been treated as breaches of privilege and addressed through contempt proceedings. Their journals therefore had more of these cases than the law reports did – not because of flaws in the common law, however, but because of Parliament's great dignity.[23] By the early nineteenth century, however, the common law courts could look more dignified than the Commons.

Holt, though discreet, was concerned about the extensive jurisdiction of the Houses of Parliament. He went back to first principles, suggesting in his 1810 text that most cases of libel against Parliament could be addressed through ordinary legal processes and presumably therefore were "not within the constitutional reason of privilege." Holt labeled verbal affronts to a House's dignity committed outside it as "fictitious" contempts, fictitious in the sense that although they might threaten the state in a broad sense, they did not endanger a House's capacity to function.[24] Holt pronounced privilege to be, in good times when the constitution was functioning properly, "like the sword of the Black Prince in Westminster Abbey ... more honourable in its rust than in its edge – more glorious in its disuse, than in its service."[25] Holt thought injustices would be rare, but he could not see how to address the risk to the individual subject. The Houses could confer on a solution, the King could advise based on the advice of the Privy Council, or Parliament could be dissolved.[26] But none of these approaches was likely to be wholly satisfactory in practice.

In April 1810, the supposedly rusty sword saw battle again over a "fictitious" libel. The Commons imprisoned a reformist member, Sir Francis Burdett, in the Tower of London for contempt over a publication that set out Burdett's arguments challenging the Commons's power to imprison the radical John Gale Jones. Retaliating, Burdett sued Charles Abbott, the Speaker of the House of Commons, for trespasses to his person and property during his arrest and imprisonment.

---

[23] Holt, *Law of Libel* (1812), 120.   [24] Holt, *Law and Usage of Parliament*, 43–44.
[25] *Ibid.* 49, cf. Holt, *Law of Libel* (1812), 135.
[26] *Law and Usage of Parliament*, 94–95, 118–19, 131–34.

Commentators weighed in on the controversy.[27] The extent to which courts would defer to parliamentary privilege – or defend the liberty of the subject – was squarely at issue.

Burdett's counsel argued at great length (the account of this argument in the report of the case is well over seventy pages long) that in a civil proceeding such as this one, the court could not be bound by a resolution of a single House of Parliament if the resolution appeared inconsistent with parliamentary law, of which the courts could take cognizance. The courts were right to refuse to inquire into the validity of a House's commitment on a habeas corpus application, but with civil proceedings, courts of law could take incidental cognizance of the privileges of Parliament because any errors courts made could be corrected on appeal to the House of Lords. Counsel argued that no sufficient cause for commitment existed, or if it did, it was not properly stated on the warrant of commitment, and the Speaker was answerable for defects in the warrant.[28]

The attorney general argued, for Abbot, that no officer could be held liable for duly issuing the process the court had ordered him to issue. The exercise of privilege could not be challenged in a court of law. The attorney general acknowledged that at times courts had to decide upon privileges when they arose incidentally – a case involving a limitation period that had expired while the defendant member was sitting was cited – but argued that the courts had never determined directly whether or not Parliament had a privilege it claimed to have. During oral argument, Chief Justice Ellenborough suggested that a direct decision on privilege was one that was "the direct and immediate fruit of the judgment of the other court," which alone had the power to issue it.[29] The attorney general, citing Paty's case, argued that the court lacked jurisdiction to intervene in Burdett's. When the attorney general referred to a 1689 case in which the Commons jailed the lord chief justice for the snub of requiring the sergeant-at-arms, as

---

[27] See e.g. Maddock, *A Vindication of the Privileges of the House of Commons*; *Mr. Blake's Speech, Relative to the Privileges of the House of Commons*; Christian, *Concise Account of the Origins of the Two Houses of Parliament*; Publicola, *Letter to the Freeholders of the County of Middlesex*; Ponsonby, *Speech of Mr. Ponsonby*.

[28] *Burdett v. Abbot* (1811), 14 East 1, 77–81, 104 E.R. 501 (K.B.). There was also an argument about the breaking down of Burdett's outer door.

[29] *Ibid.* 98.

defendant, to respond to the plaintiff's plea regarding the court's jurisdiction, Ellenborough remarked that the case "was after the Revolution, which makes such a commitment for such a cause a little alarming."[30]

The attorney general's mustering of precedent was formidable. He argued each step had been properly taken. House resolutions had properly authorized Abbot's actions. The Commons had jurisdiction to determine its own privileges and when they had been breached. Its members had duly determined that Burdett was in contempt. They had jurisdiction to order Burdett imprisoned, which they had done, and they had ordered the Speaker to carry out their decision. The Speaker had issued his warrant, which had been duly exercised. After the attorney general rested his case, Burdett's counsel responded, and then Ellenborough gave judgment.[31]

Ellenborough ruled in Abbot's favor and affirmed each House's jurisdiction to punish summarily, including by imprisonment, for breaches of its privileges; but by accepting the distinction between direct and incidental determinations of the validity of commitments he also subtly undermined the House's jurisdiction to determine its own jurisdiction, that difficult question about which Francis Ludlow Holt had been so careful. Ellenborough doubted that the court could relieve the subject on a direct habeas corpus petition unless the warrant of commitment omitted to say that the subject was being committed for contempt or appeared to be high-handed and extravagant, "beyond all bounds of reason and law."[32] However, in some cases a court might have to decide the validity of a commitment as a collateral issue, such as when the commitment was argued to justify a trespass, as indeed was so in this case. Ellenborough's ruling that the House of Commons had the power to commit Burdett for contempt of its privileges was in fact a ruling that the House of Commons had been within its jurisdiction. The warrant was sufficient and other arguments also failed. One of the two concurring justices warned of the danger that the distinction between direct and incidental challenges to the House's

[30] *Ibid.* 105.
[31] So much of what the attorney general argued was also addressed in Holt's *Law and Usage of Parliament* that I suspect that the case and the text were connected, but I do not know how.
[32] 14 East 1, 150.

privileges would erode its jurisdiction, but since he was in the minority, the distinction stood. Burdett's appeal was rejected on a writ of error in the Court of Exchequer, which held that of course the House could commit for libels, as it had been doing so for many years, and libels were an affront regardless of when they had taken place and whether or not they obstructed the functioning of the House. The people had to treat the House with a habit of "reverence and respect" for it to function.[33] Burdett's companion action against the sergeant-at-arms, mainly for bringing along at least fifty soldiers (for fear of the mob), failed before a jury.[34]

In *Burdett v. Abbot*, then, although the Commons's jurisdiction to commit a member to prison for an outside libel was upheld, King's Bench did to a limited extent take the measure of the House's jurisdiction, and the judgment in the Exchequer did nothing to disturb this aspect of Ellenborough's reasoning. The matter was hard-fought, and the implications for the increase of the court's jurisdiction were far-reaching. Ellenborough followed in Chief Justice Holt's footsteps in assuming that a subject had a right to the court's judgment, unless the claim was brought directly through habeas corpus proceedings. Ellenborough was no friend to radicals, but his training as a special pleader – and perhaps also opposition to some members of the Commons – would have made him sensitive to the difficulties that unlimited deference to that body's jurisdictional claims would pose.[35]

Francis Ludlow Holt was guardedly encouraged by this case. In 1810, he was careful about his assertions about a court's power to question the jurisdiction of a House of Parliament through its treatment of privilege claims, but his writings indicate that matters were changing. In the 1812 first edition of his libel treatise Holt included a long footnote referring the reader to previous cases on "commitments by parliament for libels and contempts," including "for a more full and comprehensive development of this subject ... the great case of Sir *Francis Burdett v. the Speaker of the House of Commons.*" Four years later, in the 1816 edition, he added twenty new

[33] *Burdett v. Abbott* (1812), 4 Taunt. 401, 444–48 (Excheq.).
[34] *Burdett v. Colman* (1811), 14 East. 163 (K.B.).
[35] Lobban, "Law, Edward." On the related expansion of courts' contempt powers, see Hay, "Contempt by Scandalizing the Court."

pages on the topic.[36] The powers and privileges of the houses of Parliament were subject to analysis, an important development.

An Alternative: Prosecuting Libelers in Court

A House of Parliament occasionally turned libels over to the government's law officers instead of acting on privilege. This approach was advantageous if getting a majority to agree to discipline the critic looked difficult but the party in power wished to be seen to be doing something. *R. v. Stockdale* arose in 1789 while impeachment proceedings were being brought against Warren Hastings, the former governor of Bengal. Charles Fox drew the attention of the House of Commons to a book that criticized the motives of certain other parliamentarians, led by Edmund Burke, in bringing these proceedings.[37] The author had died, but the attorney general prosecuted the bookseller, John Stockdale. Stockdale's counsel was the formidable Whig barrister and political reformer Thomas Erskine. Erskine argued successfully that since the House of Commons had already publicized its charges against Hastings, tearing apart his reputation after twenty years of public service, others were within their rights to defend him equally publicly, even if their language occasionally was less than temperate. Erskine argued that Stockdale was not guilty of libeling the whole House, as charged, but only of criticizing a faction within it. The jury, in acquitting Stockdale, delivered a verdict for Erskine and freedom of the press, while William Pitt's Tory government could say it had done what it could for Fox and his allies.

Pitt's government used prosecution to escape from another sticky spot in 1796. In a pamphlet, John Reeves made the ultra-Tory assertion that England was, at root, a monarchy from which had sprung the Lords and Commons; these bodies were however merely branches of the tree of state and could be lopped off and cast into the fire, leaving the tree less beautiful but nevertheless still a tree. "The Kingly Government" could go on without them.[38] This monarchist libel on

[36] Holt, *Law of Libel* (1812), 136; Holt, *Law of Libel* (1816), 132–52.
[37] *R. v. Stockdale* (1789), 22 State Trials 237 (K.B.). Hastings was successfully defended in his impeachment proceedings by Edward Law.
[38] Quoted in Beedell, "John Reeves's Prosecution for a Seditious Libel," 804.

the constitution provoked a defense of the constitutional innovations
of 1688–89 and fueled the Foxite minority's resistance to the
government's impending – draconian – treason and sedition
legislation. As A.V. Beedell makes clear, to distance themselves from
such views and to move the matter out of the Commons, Pitt and his
attorney general, Sir John Scott, engineered the prosecution. Scott,
who was assisted by Edward Law (later Chief Justice Ellenborough),
opened his case by pointing out that although the House of Commons
had resolved that the pamphlet breached its privileges, and although
the House could have proceeded against Reeves itself, it had instead
voted to submit the case to a jury.[39] The prosecution was half-hearted.
Chief Justice Kenyon did not push the jury for a conviction, reminding
them instead to consider Reeves's intentions and the whole text rather
than just the disturbing passages. Unsurprisingly, Reeves was
acquitted, although not without one of the less Tory jurors
succeeding in getting his fellow jurors to add that they found the
pamphlet a "very improper publication."[40]

There were, then, instances of prosecutions being conducted instead
of parliamentary discipline, but the Commons continued to act on its
privilege, imprisoning the radical John Cam Hobhouse for an "outside
libel" (a pamphlet addressed to Erskine) in 1819. The House
committed Hobhouse *in absentia*, without even bringing him before
the bar, and King's Bench initially refused to bring him up from
Newgate to hear his application for habeas corpus and then rejected
it.[41] Prosecution, then, was a useful strategy for a government that
preferred not to put the matter before the House of Commons, but
prosecuting also constituted no acknowledgment that there was
anything wrong with exercising the contempt power.[42]

---

[39] *R. v. Reeves* (1796), State Trials 529, 535 (K.B.).   [40] *Ibid.* 591–92, 594 (K.B.).
[41] *R. v. Hobhouse* (1820), 2 Chitty R. 207 (K.B.). Burdett's comments are contained in
the House of Commons debates of December 10 and 13, 1819, Hansard,
Parliamentary Debates, 61:989–1026.
[42] The other prosecution of this sort that I found was *R. v. Bostock*, in 1790, a case
puzzling for its triviality. The offending passage appeared in the *World* newspaper in
the midst of a couple of columns of one-sentence notes about the doings of the mighty
(including "Lady Pembroke goes to Weymouth in a few days" and "Parliament will
certainly be prorogued on the 9th of July"). The sentence was "Mr. Hastings's Trial is
to be put off to another Session, unless the Lords have spirit enough to put an end to
so shameful a business." The House of Commons took notice of this remark, resolved
that it constituted "Matter of a scandalous and libellous Nature, reflecting on the

Some, though, thought prosecution was fairer – or would be if criminal procedure were amended to eliminate its egregious bias in favor of the Crown. Discussion in the House of Commons about a petition to release Sir Francis Burdett and John Gale Jones suggests that although parliamentarians liked to think of themselves as the people's defenders against the Crown, the petitioners themselves preferred to rely on legal processes, with trial by jury and sworn testimony.[43] Likewise in 1819 in the Commons, Burdett protested vigorously, and too late, that the attorney general should prosecute Hobhouse instead. However, prosecution had the potential to be deeply unfair, especially because of the immense prosecutorial power wielded by the attorney general acting on an *ex officio* information and because of jury selection processes. The *ex officio* information was often used in politically charged cases before 1830. The attorney general himself issued the information that commenced proceedings, thus bypassing the grand jury and requiring no one to swear on oath that a wrong had actually been done. The attorney general then obtained an order from King's Bench requiring impossibly large sureties (pursuant to an 1808 statute) and committed the purported publisher – or even possessor – of the libel to prison until the next term of court. This ruinous process could then be repeated at the next term of court, with no trial being required.[44] Trials, if they took place at all, could until 1825 be conducted before a special jury, following a Crown-controlled selection process. The Crown also had the right of reply, to address the jury last. In the 1810s and 1820s, however,

Proceedings of this House," and sent the matter off for prosecution. Bostock was prosecuted a year later on an *ex officio* information and convicted. The case is mentioned in a note at the end of the *Stockdale* case, 22 State Trials 308 (K.B.). See also United Kingdom, *House of Commons Journals* (June 16, 1789), 44:463; and *R. v. Bostock* case file, TS 11/1045/4509, National Archives, Kew, Richmond.

43 Debates of the House of Commons, May 10, 1810, in Hansard, *Parliamentary Debates*, 16:950–55.

44 The 1808 statute was *An Act for Amending the Law with Regard to the Course of Proceeding on Indictments and Informations in the Court of King's Bench in Certain Cases* [etc.] (U.K.), 1808, 48 Geo. III, c. 58. For these criticisms, see Burdett, *Speech of Sir Francis Burdett*, 22; Brougham, "Liberty of the Press," 105; H [pseud.], "The Law of Libel," 432. It is possible that the determination by the House of Commons during the Wilkes affair that libel was a breach of the peace was a step in empowering the Crown to treat purported libelers this way. The *ex officio* information – though rendered somewhat less potent in 1829 – survived calls for its abolition, but after Lord Grey and the Whigs came to power in 1830 it was seldom used.

these procedures were attracting heavy criticism, and reforms were beginning.[45]

The ground, then, was starting to shift in the legal treatment of political libels in the 1810s. Despite Ellenborough's deferential language, Burdett's case stood for the proposition that sometimes King's Bench would make determinations of the House of Commons's jurisdiction. As Hobhouse learned, bringing a habeas corpus application to challenge head-on a House's jurisdiction to imprison for contempt was still impermissible, but the extent of Parliament's jurisdiction to determine its own jurisdiction was quietly beginning to waver. At the same time, reformers were raising persuasive objections to the excesses of the Crown's powers on prosecution. This focus on abusive procedure may seem, to the modern reader, "technical" and lacking in the kind of moral and ethical depth we associate with civil rights claims. It is important, however, to take seriously the commitment to protecting the individual that undergirded this focus on such matters as prosecutorial discretion, the composition and jurisdiction of the jury, the rules of evidence, the role of counsel, and indeed privilege. J.C.D. Clark has argued that British reform programs by the 1830s were expressed in terms of Benthamite utilitarianism rather than Jeffersonian natural rights and were expressed through lawyers' commitment to strict construction.[46] Nova Scotians picked up on these legal and constitutional arguments – indeed recourse to the rules of procedure and evidence enabled Nova Scotian judges at the beginning of the nineteenth century to undercut slavery.[47] Although lacking the ringing language of rights evident in American constitutional discourse, these shifts in constitutional thought marked a commitment to arranging legal and political institutions so as to properly balance the interests of the individual and society. As the forum for claims for liberty, King's Bench was on the ascendant.

Limiting Legislative Privilege in Massachusetts: *Coffin v. Coffin*

Colonial legislatures frequently punished their critics using their contempt powers. Mary Patterson Clarke, in her 1943 study of the

---

[45] Thomas, *Long Time Burning*, 175–76.   [46] Clark, *Language of Liberty*, 382, 384.
[47] Cahill, "Slavery and the Judges" and "*Habeas Corpus* and Slavery."

multiplicity of proceedings taken by offended legislatures during the colonial period, estimates that not only did assemblies discipline their own members but "scores of persons, probably hundreds" were called to the bar of legislative assemblies to account for words that had given offense. Clarke explains that the most common objectionable reflections were upon individuals, but the most heinous ones impugned the dignity of the assembly as a whole. Richard R. Johnson has argued that in the 1760s both the British Parliament and American assemblies were deeply committed to the idea of legislative supremacy, the old antagonist being the Crown, which threatened the liberties of the people. Johnson points out that earlier in the century colonial assemblies imprisoned, fined and flogged their critics and those who interfered with their proceedings, printers being particularly vulnerable. Freedom of debate was to take place inside an assembly, but criticizing it was inimical to its dignity; even a petition, if it reflected poorly on an assembly, could be judged a breach of privilege.[48]

The powers of assemblies were fundamental to American debates in the late eighteenth century. Leonard Levy identifies the 1796 privilege proceedings against William Keteltas of New York as the occasion for the first major criticism of the use of privilege to suppress criticism in the United States. To Levy's disappointment, the critique pertained to the powers of the assembly, not the rights of the individual. The assembly disciplined Keteltas for arguing that it had failed to take appropriate action about a recent unfair, politically motivated trial. The articles he published in his newspaper, in response to the assembly's actions, complained of the assembly's tyranny but addressed freedom of speech only in the context of legislative freedom of debate. Keteltas, though "an experienced politician and lawyer," did not claim for himself an individual right to criticize the government. The Keteltas affair foreshadowed Sir Francis Burdett's. A Keteltas supporter argued that jury trials were the appropriate forum for addressing seditious libels. Once liberated, Keteltas attempted to sue the speaker of the assembly, but this action failed, as had an earlier similar effort in Massachusetts.[49] As I discuss below, the 1790s saw the

---

[48] Clarke, *Parliamentary Privilege in the American Colonies*, 117, 121, 130–31; Johnson, "Parliamentary Egotisms," 351. Cf. Levy, "Did Zenger Matter?"

[49] On Keteltas, see Levy, *Emergence*, 294–96. In 1757 a Massachusetts printer who had been disciplined by the assembly unsuccessfully sued the Speaker, the messenger and

origins of the truth defense in criminal cases – that glorious shield that
social and political critics tried to use in courtrooms – but in the 1790s,
as Americans worked out their theory of republican government and
the relationship between courts and legislatures, the privileges of
assemblies were a more salient constitutional concern than the
individual's rights of critique.

The drafters of the 1780 Massachusetts constitution, while in
general following English precedent with respect to freedom of
expression and of the press, appear to have deliberately limited the
jurisdiction of the House and Senate to act against nonmembers. The
bill of rights explicitly protected free speech only in the legislature;
elsewhere, the people had rights to assemble, to instruct their
representatives, and to make requests of their legislators through
addresses, petitions and remonstrances. Liberty of the press was
referred to aspirationally: it was "essential to the security of freedom
in a State" and therefore not to be restrained. In the second part of the
constitution, the drafters set out the structure, powers and mode of
selecting the members of the legislature. The House of Representatives
and the Senate were in charge of their own elections and proceedings.
They could punish with imprisonment any nonmember who expressed
disrespect by disorderly or contemptuous behavior in their presence, or
who threatened or assaulted the "body or estate" of a member in the
town where, and when, the legislature was currently sitting. Similarly
they could punish anyone who assaulted or arrested someone they had
ordered to attend their proceedings, or who rescued anyone they had
arrested. Members were protected from arrest and legal process when
they were coming to or going from a session. These bodies could try
proceedings involving their own privileges, but no one could be
imprisoned for more than thirty days for these offenses by the
governor, council, Senate or House of Representatives.[50]
Importantly, the drafters did not mention any power to discipline
nonmembers for disrespect or contempt published outside the

the jailor. See Minot, *Continuation of the History of Massachusetts Bay*, 210–11;
Comm. v. Whitmarsh, Thach. Crim. Cas. 441, 450–52 (1836).
[50] Constitution of the Commonwealth of Massachusetts, part I, articles XVI, XIX and
XXI; and part II, chapter I, section III, articles X and XI, printed in *General Laws of
Massachusetts*.

legislature. Libels published by nonmember printers would seem to have fallen to courts.

The problem of limiting legislative privilege was clear to Thomas Jefferson, who, in February 1800, while presiding over the Senate, found himself obliged to issue a warrant for the arrest of the Democratic-Republican editor William Duane for comments the Senate had found disrespectful. The first substantive section in Jefferson's *Manual of Parliamentary Practice*, published the next year, was on privilege. After setting out the privileges that were clear in British parliamentary practice, Jefferson turned to the difficulties with the British Houses' indefinite claims, as Blackstone framed them. Jefferson described Duane's case briefly and the uncertainties it presented, pointing out the danger posed to the citizen if one branch of government could determine the law in the heat of the moment and give judgment on it.[51] And there the conundrum stood.

The key Massachusetts case regarding the jurisdiction of the assembly and the courts is *Coffin v. Coffin*, the first case in the 1808 volume of the Massachusetts law reports.[52] *Coffin* squarely addressed the jurisdictional conflict between the legislature and the court. The argument in the case highlights the deep tension between British constitutional precedents and the newer institutional organization introduced by the Massachusetts constitution, insofar as they affected individuals' ability to defend their reputational rights.

The members had been engaged in debate about appointing a second notary public for Nantucket. After the resolution passed, member Micajah Coffin approached the member who had proposed the appointment, Benjamin Russell, to ask the identity of the source on whose information Russell was acting. Russell indicated that his source was William Coffin, who was sitting elsewhere in the legislature, apparently watching the debate. Micajah offhandedly looked at William and asked "What? That convict?" When Russell responded that William had been honorably acquitted of the bank robbery to which Micajah was evidently referring, Micajah responded that an acquittal did not make William any less guilty.

[51] Jefferson, *Manual of Parliamentary Practice*, s. 3. On the Duane affair, see Dunn, *Jefferson's Second Revolution*, 170–72.
[52] *Coffin v. Coffin*, 4 Mass. (3 Tyng) 1 (1808).

No comment on William Coffin's integrity had been called for, since he was not a candidate for the office of notary. William sued Micajah for slander. Micajah's only real defense was that the suit was barred because the words were protected by the constitutional protection of free speech in the legislature. Indeed, he pointed to a resolution the House of Representatives passed afterward to protect Micajah and itself. The resolution stated that only the House could take notice of words spoken by a member within its walls on a subject the House was considering, whether in debate or individually and whether to the chair or to another member. Justice Isaac Parker told the jury that the privilege question, being constitutional, would be reserved for the consideration of the whole court, but he added that he did not think the facts would shield Micajah, as he believed the constitution gave legislators no more protection than was "necessary for their personal security and independence."

The argument before Chief Justice Theophilus Parsons and the whole court was a struggle over how far British parliamentary law applied in Massachusetts. Benjamin Whitman represented William Coffin and the rights of the individual to sue. He "hoped the practice or the claims of the British parliament would not be considered as authorities here." Whitman contrasted the unwritten British constitution with Massachusetts's written one, arguing that the rights and privileges of the houses of Parliament had been wrested from the Crown and, in the case of the Commons, from the Lords as well. In the United States, however, the judiciary was a separate, coordinate branch of government designed to provide citizens with remedies for injuries to their persons, property and characters. The court absolutely required the power to determine the jurisdiction of the House of Representatives so as to grant the plaintiff his remedy. American judges could be impeached, so the people had a remedy if the court behaved unconstitutionally or oppressively. Judges were therefore the proper protectors of individual rights. Whitman contended that the freedom of debate in the legislature referred only to speeches on the floor made by a member from his place in accordance with the rules of order. He pointed out that if the plaintiff had complained to the House for a remedy, they would have declared the conversation a private matter and referred him to the courts.

The attorney general, Barnabas Bidwell, joined Samuel Dexter in representing Micajah Coffin. Bidwell argued that although privilege had been called "an odious plea," it was not so here: this claim was for privileges conferred by the constitution on public functionaries for the overall good of the people, not for special claims for exemptions from public duties for the "ease or emolument of the individual." According to Bidwell, only the House of Representatives had jurisdiction over Micajah Coffin's speech. Bidwell cited Jean Louis de Lolme's *Constitution of England* and Blackstone's *Commentaries*. He found support in the House of Representatives's protective resolution. Samuel Dexter added that if William were an honorable man, he would be at least as pleased with an apology or Micajah's expulsion from the House as he would be with winning damages. Of course, neither outcome was likely.

Bidwell and Dexter argued, based on British precedent, that the resolution was determinative and within the House's jurisdiction. Pressed by Parsons about how far the House's jurisdiction to declare its privileges extended, Bidwell argued that its authority with respect to speech in the House while it sat was unbounded, and that only the House could determine how freedom of speech within its walls was to be exercised, whether the speech took place during debate or otherwise and whether or not it was made in accordance with the House's rules. To protect the House's independence, no other court could evaluate the propriety of its actions. Dexter suggested that members needed complete freedom to speak not only in formal debate but also in committees and elsewhere on subjects the House was considering. He warned that narrow interpretations of privilege such as Whitman had advocated could even require a court to determine whether a member had been out of order, which was clearly within the legislature's purview. Bidwell and Dexter cited an English case, *R. v. Abingdon*, in which Lord Chief Justice Kenyon told the jury that Abingdon was accountable only to the House of Lords for statements he made there about Sermon (which were not particularly connected to matters in debate) but was responsible in the courts for publishing his speech in the newspapers.[53] The line was clear, they argued.

---

[53] *Ibid.* 20–21, citing *R. v. Abingdon* (1794) 1 Espinasse 226, 170 E.R. 337 (N.P.).

Chief Justice Parsons delivered his lengthy judgment after the term ended. He reasoned that the privileges of the House were meant to protect the rights of the people to have their representatives fulfill their offices without fear of legal repercussions. Parsons did not confine legal protection to statements properly made in debate but to everything a representative said or did in his capacity as a member, whether in orderly debate or against the rules, and whether in his place or even at times outside the walls of the representatives' chamber. The House had to be in session, but the protection would extend to statements made in committee or in a convention of both Houses held in the Senate chamber. This protection applied even if the speaker's intentions were malicious. Micajah Coffin had gratuitously impugned William's character with an irrelevant allegation after debate had moved to other topics. Micajah had therefore not been acting in his role as representative and was not shielded by privilege. Parsons dexterously interpreted the protective resolution as consistent with his own view of the constitution. His interpretation required the court to assess exactly what the House had been discussing at the time of the speaking of the impugned words, a level of scrutiny of the House's affairs that would have been most unwelcome in Britain.

Decisively breaking with the British constitutional precedents, Parsons rejected the assertion that the House could declare the extent of its privileges and thus bind the courts of law. The House could declare its privileges as long as its declarations were constitutional – as determined by the judges, who were the proper arbiters of the constitutionality of claims to new privileges. British precedents were unhelpful because the Commons was understood to protect the people against the monarchy and the hereditary aristocracy. The people of Massachusetts, however, in their written constitution, had defined the powers and privileges of the House through express language and necessary implication. The legislature should not struggle to take from the people powers and privileges they had chosen not to grant. Privileges limited the rights of private citizens, rights that could only be restrained by constitutional laws. The House's resolution therefore simply elaborated known constitutional privileges. Parsons acknowledged that in some cases proceedings could take place both in the courts and in the legislature for the same matter. The case at bar fell within the court's jurisdiction, and Micajah Coffin was not entitled to the privilege he claimed.

Coffin thus signals a departure from English understandings about the conflict of jurisdiction between legislatures and courts. In Parsons's view, the written constitution, reflecting the will of republican citizens, deliberately elevated the courts into the position of constitutional arbiters. The courts could determine the limits of legislative privilege – and therefore the extent to which privilege could protect a member from defamation proceedings – because privileges had the potential to take away the rights of citizens. Some privileges were necessary to protect the proper functioning of the legislative body, but that body could not expand its privileges beyond due constitutional limits, as determined by courts. As I discuss below, this caution about privilege, and the Massachusetts courts' inclination to limit its reach, runs through court cases in which defendants attempted to raise privilege defenses.

Privilege in Nova Scotia and the Canadas

The extent of legislative privilege was a matter of considerable doubt north of the border, where assemblies were notably less ancient and august than the House of Commons and tended to be peopled with farmers, merchants and lawyers struggling for control against Crown-appointed executives. These assemblies and the people they represented emphasized their loyalty to the Crown while insisting that their claims were nothing more than the proper claims of British subjects, not manifestations of lurking republican sympathies. Assemblies' efforts to silence their critics had different implications in these political and constitutional environments. With no written bill of rights, a Crown-appointed judiciary, and a governor accountable to the British Crown, the Nova Scotian assembly walked a fine constitutional line in asserting privilege.

Certain incidents in British North American colonies before 1820 raised privilege questions. In 1803, Simon Bradstreet Robie headed an assembly committee that investigated the assembly's right to examine the journals of the council in its legislative capacity and concluded that the assembly did indeed have such a right. Over the next few years, Robie successfully led the assembly's opposition to the effort by the lieutenant governor to move control over certain road-related expenditures from the assembly to the executive. In 1806 the lieutenant governor drew protests for rejecting William Cottnam Tonge as Speaker of the assembly, an exercise of the royal prerogative that – according to a biographer of Tonge – had never taken place before in Nova Scotia, although it had in the American colonies. In 1808, the assembly (again led by Robie) protested the lieutenant governor's interference in an election, asserting that as a body founded on the same principles as the House of Commons, it alone could decide questions related to the election of its members. The assembly based this assertion on a review of its own precedents and an extensive legal opinion by attorney general Richard John Uniacke – drawn up for the lieutenant governor but included in the assembly's journals for posterity – that the *lex et consuetudo parliamenti* was part of the common law of England and thus applied to the Nova Scotia assembly. J. Murray Beck notes that ultimately the British law officers upheld the assembly's rights but rejected Uniacke's argument that Nova Scotia had inherited all of British parliamentary law.[54] Similarly in 1815 the British law officers gave the opinion that colonial legislatures lacked any more privileges than were strictly necessary to fulfill their functions and specifically lacked the power to punish "outside libellers." Nevertheless, Upper and Lower Canadian assemblies continued to imprison critics and printers through the 1830s. The fact that the law officers' opinion was communicated only to certain judges and not to the legislatures presumably reduced its influence.[55] The extent of the powers of colonial assemblies remained uncertain. By the 1820s and 1830s, privilege was a good that the increasingly assertive Nova Scotia legislature wanted for itself, even as conflicts in Britain and Massachusetts suggested the importance of limits.

Privilege As a Shield for Reports

The flipside of the privilege question, on display in *Coffin v. Coffin*, was the extent to which privilege could protect the objectionable

---

[54] NS Journals, 1807, 57–62, 103, 104–6; Tulloch, "Tonge, William Cottnam"; Beck, "Robie, Simon Bradstreet"; Beck, "Rise and Fall of Nova Scotia's Attorney General," 127; Beck, *Government of Nova Scotia*, 53–54.

[55] Greenwood and Wright, "Parliamentary Privilege," 414–15.

expression of a member of a legislature. By the English and Massachusetts bills of rights, members were protected absolutely against civil and criminal liability for anything they said in the course of legislative debate. As long as publishing the doings of a House in itself constituted contempt of privilege, an "outside libeller" was in theory liable to legislative punishment even if other legal processes were unavailable to a potential plaintiff or complainant. However, once the House began to tolerate the publication of its proceedings and then, in 1774, to pay Luke Hansard and his family to publish official versions, difficulties arose. The need to protect parliamentarians from liability for speeches in which the public was appropriately interested could come into conflict with individuals' interests in their reputations. The results were confusing.

In 1794 one Mr. Sermon, an attorney of Gray's Inn, represented by Thomas Erskine, prosecuted a peer, Lord Abingdon, over disparaging remarks Abingdon made in a speech to the House of Lords and then had printed in several newspapers.[56] The dangers of privilege were on full display. Abingdon pleaded his own cause, beginning by asserting his rank in the courtroom. He claimed that it was "the privilege of peers, situated as he was, to sit covered in court, and have a place assigned to them." He asserted that the allegations were true but called no witnesses and led no evidence. He made only one legal argument: that because he could say anything he liked in the House, he could likewise print with impunity what he had said. Rejecting this high-handed position, Chief Justice Kenyon held that although of course the court could not address a speech in the Lords, if Abingdon published a slanderous speech, "it was a libel" and, as such, punishable. Abingdon was convicted and sentenced to a substantial fine and three months' imprisonment. Speech in the Lords was protected, but a speaker could be liable for publishing an accurate but unauthorized report of what he had said.

Five years later, *R. v. Wright* raised related questions. Could parliamentary reports be the subject of libel proceedings? What if Parliament had not authorized the publication? The report in the

---

[56] *The King, on the Prosecution of Sermon, v. Lord Abingdon* (1794) 1 Espinasse 226, 228, 170 E.R. 337 (N.P.). This case is reprinted in Pollock, Campbell and Saunders, *Revised Reports*, 733.

case had been produced in anticipation of treason proceedings against
John Horne Tooke. After Horne Tooke's acquittal, the bookseller John
Wright published the report without parliamentary authorization.
Horne Tooke then applied to King's Bench for a criminal
information against Wright.[57] Erskine and one Warren argued
among other things that the House of Commons lacked the right to
publish matter that defamed an individual. Even if the Commons could
not be called to account for the publication, they could not sanction
publishing it outside of their own journals and for an audience beyond
their own members. Counsel argued that as it was a breach of privilege
to publish the Commons's proceedings without authority, it would be
extraordinary if this violation of privilege through unauthorized
publication could be set up as a defense to a libel action. How could
a text whose publication violated privilege be treated in court as
protected by it?

Erskine and Warren asserted the rights of the subject against
a House's power to call him a traitor. They argued that although
a House could report to its own members, an individual should be
able to prosecute over a defamatory report published outside the
House. King's Bench, however, refused the information and thus
blocked Horne Tooke's prosecution, because, the judges said, the
public benefitted from the publication of such matters, regardless of
the cost to the reputation of the individual, in this case a notorious
radical. Lord Kenyon remarked that although there were limits to the
jurisdiction of the House of Commons – the court would ignore an
effort to arrest counsel in the midst of arguing a case or a parliamentary
injunction to stay ordinary proceedings – "the report in question, being
adopted by the House at large, is a proceeding of those who, by the
constitution, are the guardians of the liberties of the subject; and we
cannot say that any part of that proceeding is a libel."[58] The House, by
its own law, could decide whether or not to punish a printer for an
unauthorized publication, but the court would treat the publication as
privileged, authorized or not. Justice Lawrence emphasized the
importance of the public knowing about the activities of both courts

---

[57] As noted in Chapter 1, this mode of proceeding was not used in Massachusetts or
Nova Scotia.

[58] *R. v. Wright* (1799) 8 T.R. 293, 296, 101 E.R. 1396 (K.B.).

and legislative bodies, regardless of the disadvantage to individuals. As long as Wright's account of the proceedings was "true," it was protected. Parliament's untouchability – as the guardian of the liberties of the subject – was upheld, the liberty of the press was enhanced, and a political radical was left to endure being called a traitor.

As a result of these cases, a true report of the proceedings of Parliament could not be the foundation for a libel case, even if its publication was unauthorized (although a House could impose censure if so inclined); but a peer's report of his own speech, paid for by himself, could be. A subject had no action for defamation contained in a parliamentary report but did have an action against a parliamentarian who published his allegations in a newspaper. *R. v. Creevey*, in 1813, followed the rule in Abingdon's case and held that privilege did not protect a member of the House of Commons who published an account of his defamatory speech in a newspaper in order to correct other versions of it that had been reported.[59] The trial judge had told the jury that they could infer malice from the text of the publication and that no privilege protected Creevey. King's Bench agreed. Henry Brougham's argument, for Creevey, also included overtones of a qualified privilege defense, which was emerging in civil cases around the same time and was taking shape in Francis Ludlow Holt's and Thomas Starkie's treatises.[60] Brougham asserted that malice was an essential element of the crime of libel, and that Creevey's intention to refute errors rebutted the presumption of malice that otherwise flowed from publishing a defamatory text. The argument went nowhere.

Francis Ludlow Holt attempted to explain the law pertaining to reports of proceedings in Parliament and courts. Publishing the proceedings of either House without permission was a contempt of privilege. Parliamentarians' speeches in Parliament were protected, but privilege did not protect them if their speeches were published, at least at their instigation. No libel action would lie for a true account of the proceedings of a court of justice or of Parliament, although people could be amenable to libel proceedings for the unauthorized republication of harmful statements they heard – or made – in court

---

[59] *R. v. Creevey* (1813), 1 M. & S. 273, 105 E.R. 102 (K.B.).   [60] See Chapter 3.

or in Parliament. The speeches of counsel in court, if published "with a malicious and partial intention," could likewise attract libel proceedings as well as amounting to contempt of court. Fair reports of court proceedings were privileged, unless the matter was blasphemous or obscene or otherwise mischievous. Petitions to Parliament, articles of the peace presented to magistrates, and the presentments of grand juries could not be deemed libels because these were the proper methods for airing complaints to these bodies. However, preliminary inquiries and other one-sided proceedings were not privileged.[61]

Holt's account of this rather confusing area of libel law suggests that lines were being drawn. Parliament was recognizing that the public was entitled to accurate accounts of its proceedings, but permitting parliamentary speeches and documents to be published raised the possibility that individuals' reputations might be damaged. Clearly Parliament could discipline its members for breaches of its privileges in debate, and a House could also discipline its members – and others – for outside libels that impugned the House's dignity, but nonmembers' reputations lay outside the concern of Parliament. No action would lie over a speech made in parliamentary debate, but the idea that parliamentary reports and proceedings, if published more broadly and potentially even without parliamentary authorization, might also be privileged produced new difficulties. Which institution – a House of Parliament or King's Bench – could determine whether a published report was protected? Did this determination fall within Parliament's broad jurisdiction over its privileges, or did it fall to King's Bench, which had to decide when to let legal proceedings go ahead and when to stop them? The *Abingdon*, *Wright*, *Creevey* and *Burdett* cases, taken together, suggested that courts would recognize reports authorized by Parliament as privileged, and would likely also recognize privilege for unauthorized but accurate reports published without malice, but that a report published by a member himself would probably not be considered privileged.

The most dramatic clash over defamation in official publications lay in the future, after most of the events described in this book, in the

---

[61] Holt, *Law of Libel* (1812), 129, 145–47, 163–75; Holt, *Law of Libel* (1816), 125, 160–62, 182–96.

explosive case of *Stockdale v. Hansard* and related proceedings.[62] The case brought together the dual problems of the extent of the House of Commons's jurisdiction to declare the extent of its privileges and the claim of an individual purportedly injured through defamation contained in a parliamentary report.

The House of Commons had directed the publication, for public sale, of a certain prison inspectors' report. On a shelf at Newgate, the inspectors had found a certain book, whose title and author they coyly did not provide but which they described as published in 1827 by John Joseph Stockdale, the son of the bookseller John Stockdale who had been prosecuted for publishing the defense of Hastings. The inspectors described the book as disgusting, with obscene and indecent plates.[63] Stockdale, who considered the book a serious medical text on the "generative organs,"[64] saw in this description an insinuation that he was a notorious publisher of obscene texts, and sued four members of the Hansard publishing family for damages. The House of Commons resolved that the publication was protected by privilege, which the Hansards argued blocked the claim against them; Queen's Bench, however, rejected this argument.

Legal commentators since then have suggested that rejecting the privilege claim showed the court's insensitivity to the public's need for information. The stakes, however, were much higher: Queen's Bench was asserting that the House of Commons could not unilaterally determine its own privileges. Justice Patteson explained the situation most clearly: the House could not of its own accord protect "the grossest libels" and their incursions on individual rights. Patteson observed that if the members of the House were the sole judges of the existence and extent of their powers and privileges, they could assume any new ones they wanted. There had to be a mechanism

---

[62] *Stockdale v. Hansard* (1839), 9 Ad. & E. 1, 112 E.R. 1112 (Q.B.). Related proceedings include *Case of the Sheriff of Middlesex* (1840), 11 Ad. & E. 273, 113 E.R. 419 (Q.B.) and *Howard v. Gossett* (1845), 10 Q.B. 411, 116 E.R. 158 (Exch.).

[63] See Barker, "Stockdale, John."

[64] See House of Commons (UK), *Copy of the Reply of the Inspectors of Prisons*. The book was the 1827 edition of John Roberton, *On the Generative System*. No copy of this edition seems to have survived, but extant editions reveal the book to be a practitioner's narrative of addressing various dysfunctions, along with discussions of symptoms and treatments. Its appeal must have often been more medical than erotic.

for ascertaining whether or not asserted powers and privileges were new, and, if that mechanism were courts, then the House's resolution was inoperative.[65]

The ruling that parliamentary reports were not protected by absolute privilege was addressed by statute in 1840, but the larger problem remained. In 1844, with related proceedings still ongoing, Thomas Erskine May wrote, "[t]he precise jurisdiction of courts of law in matters of privilege, is one of the most difficult questions of constitutional law that has ever arisen." Even in the early twentieth century, William Holdsworth called the question "not perhaps finally settled."[66]

The Rise of Truth in the United States

Probably the most important development in the law regarding expression in the United States was the emergence of the idea that a republican citizen had an inherent right to speak the truth without fear of prosecution. This idea acquired legal salience in the 1790s, found its legal footing in the first decade of the nineteenth century and was widely accepted by the 1820s.

Ratified in 1791, the First Amendment declared, "Congress shall make no law ... abridging the freedom of speech, or of the press." Seven years later, John Adams and his congressional allies created a federal criminal cause of action for false, seditious libels against the President or Congress.[67] The incongruity of these developments has prompted scholars to assess the constitutionality of the Sedition Act – that is, whether the First Amendment was meant to abolish "the law of seditious libel" and establish a wider version of freedom of expression than Blackstone's freedom from censorship, licensing and other prior restraints. However, because a "libel" was a text that offended, the better question is whether seditious libels were supposed to be among the types of objectionable expression against which Congress was not

[65] *Stockdale v. Hansard* (1839), 9 Ad. & E. 1, 112 E.R. 1112, 1184–85, 1192 (Q.B.).
[66] May, *Treatise upon the Law, Privileges, Proceedings and Usage of Parliament*, 113; Holdsworth, *History of English Law*, 1:192. See also Mitchell, *Making of the Modern Law of Defamation*, 194–95, 257.
[67] An Act in Addition to the Act, Entitled "An Act for the Punishment of Certain Crimes against the United States," ch. 74, 1 Stat. 596 (1798) ["Sedition Act"].

to pass laws. The First Amendment's drafters would surely not have intended to prevent Congress from passing, say, a statute regarding perjury in federal courts, even though such a measure would have restricted this speech.[68] The question is whether Americans by the late 1780s intended to protect from congressional enactments at least some of the types of libels that Blackstone labeled criminal. What kinds of laws could Congress pass regarding expression without "abridging" freedom of the press or of speech? Federalists who framed the Constitution argued strenuously that there was no federal common law, so according to this understanding, Congress could not justly claim simply to be modifying it. To be constitutional, a statute that touched on expression would have to be necessary for the exercise of a federal power and not "abridge" freedom of speech or the press, whatever that meant.[69]

Historians have reached different conclusions about what kinds of expression the First Amendment was intended to protect. Zechariah Chafee Jr., in 1942, following Thomas Cooley's 1868 *Treatise on Constitutional Limitations*, argued that the First Amendment was intended to be broadly protective of criticism and to bar both press censorship and other measures the government might use to inhibit discussion of public affairs. As long as critics did not incite their audiences to break the law, the First Amendment was intended to protect a broad liberty of expression. In *Legacy of Suppression* in 1960, revised as *Emergence of a Free Press* in 1985, Leonard W. Levy argued that Chafee was wrong. Levy concluded that there was no conclusive evidence that the framers meant the First

---

[68] Indeed, Chief Justice Oliver Ellsworth – albeit in the course of upholding the constitutionality of the Sedition Act – observed, "But, as to the constitutional difficulty, who will say that negating the right to publish slander & sedition, is '*abridging* the freedom of speech & of the press,' of a right which ever belonged to it? Or will shew us how Congress, if prohibited to authorise punishment for speaking in *any* case, could authorise it for perjury, of which nobody has yet doubted?" Quoted in Bird, Freedoms of Press and Speech, 321. See also Bird, *Press and Speech under Assault*, 66–70, arguing that Blackstone made up his view of the common law and Chief Justice Mansfield imposed it.

[69] Bird demonstrates that the points at which Supreme Court justices between 1791 and 1797 employed common law criminal concepts all took place in cases brought under obviously federal jurisdiction, such as treason, offenses against the law of nations, offenses toward federal courts, and acts taken on the high seas: Bird, Freedoms of Press and Speech, 147–54; Bird, *Press and Speech under Assault*, 90–96.

Amendment to exclude any particular aspects of the common law or prevent anything other than prior restraints. Disagreeing at least to some extent, Norman Rosenberg, in his 1986 *Protecting the Best Men*, argued that the revolutionary generation held a broader sense of what expression needed to be protected. Wendell Bird argues that the First Amendment was intended to affirm conclusively that the federal government had no power to prosecute the press for criticism of government. Based on a thorough review of the early Supreme Court justices' grand jury charges, private writings and other political and legal writings from the revolutionary period through the 1790s, Bird asserts that the Sedition Act was unconstitutional and attracted more Federalist and judicial opposition than has been recognized.[70]

Levy and Rosenberg agree that even Jeffersonians who considered the Sedition Act unconstitutional agreed that political expression had limits. David Rabban argues that the Sedition Act prosecutions convinced Americans that the criminalization of seditious libel was inconsistent with a republican idea of sovereignty, since in a republic the people needed to be able to criticize their governments. Indictments drafted in the language of sedition became seriously impolitic in the early 1800s, but criminal defamation could still be employed for attacks on the characters of individuals, whatever their station in society. Rosenberg asserts that after 1800 Jeffersonians shifted from prosecuting for attacks on government policy to prosecuting over attacks on the reputations of officials and the "best men."[71] It is clear from Levy's and Rosenberg's writings that understandings of the meaning of freedom of the press in the different states, too, had particular, local inflections.

Regardless of how much the First Amendment was intended to modify the common law, by 1798 the idea that republican citizens could not be criminally liable for publishing truth – at least on some sorts of topics – was legally salient. The argument was made in state common law cases, and courts began to wrestle with whether to admit evidence of truth and, if so, what to do with it. It is difficult to determine the moment when truth acquired the signal importance

---

[70] Chafee, *Free Speech in the United States*, 11, 18–21, 31; Levy, *Emergence*, 281; Rosenberg, *Best Men*, 53–55; Bird, Freedoms of Press and Speech; Bird, *Press and Speech under Assault*.

[71] Rabban, "Ahistorical Historian," 826–27, 854–56; Rosenberg, *Best Men*, 93.

that it had by 1820. Larry Eldridge argues that truth acquired exculpatory power in the seventeenth century. Truth became part of a defense to actions for *scandalum magnatum* or false news more than for seditious expression. Perhaps even more importantly, truth became a key factor in shaping how officials responded to disturbing expression. True statements, especially if properly expressed, became justifiable in colonies whose stability depended on popular support for political and legal institutions.[72] The thinking behind different pleas of the Crown and different available defenses washed from one expression-related cause of action to another, as both offense and defense were adapted to colonial circumstances.

In 1735, the argument that no criminal liability could flow from a libelous but true allegation was made in the famous New York prosecution of John Peter Zenger.[73] Bernard Bailyn observes that Zenger's counsel drew on the radical Whig critique offered in the 1720s by John Trenchard and Thomas Gordon in *Cato's Letters*.[74] Grounding sovereignty in the people, Trenchard and Gordon emphasized the vital importance of political criticism in improving public life and institutions and disclosing the misdeeds of the powerful. They did not, however, make any consistent appeal to truth as a good in itself, and they objected to the disclosure of private vices.[75] In 1785, English writer James Adair argued that truth ought to be a defense, or at least admissible on the question of criminal intent, at least in certain circumstances.[76] The common law remained unmodified by 1820, but individual complainants who went before King's Bench seeking informations for libels were required to swear that the objectionable words were false.[77]

Wendell Bird makes it clear that many, if not most, of the framers of the First Amendment would likely have perceived the perils in purporting to distinguish truth from falsity in political discourse. Some late eighteenth-century American legislators, writers, lawyers

[72] Eldridge, "Before Zenger."
[73] For a description of this trial, see Finkelman, *Brief Narrative*, 45–52.
[74] Bailyn, *Ideological Origins*, 52. See also Levy, *Emergence*, 41–45.
[75] See *Cato's Letters*, 1:250.   [76] See e.g. Adair, *Discussions of the Law of Libels*, vii–x.
[77] See Rayner, *Digest of the Law Concerning Libels*, 89; Adair, *Discussions of the Law of Libels*, 68–69; H [pseud.], "The Law of Libel," 435; Bird, *Press and Speech under Assault*, 41–46 (on the history of the rejection of the truth defense at common law).

and jurists, however, seized on this old idea. In 1789, Massachusetts chief justice William Cushing wrote to John Adams, reflecting on the meaning of the Massachusetts guarantee of freedom of the press and what it meant for common law seditious libel prosecutions. Cushing espoused a broad understanding of freedom of speech and of the press. He recognized that the threat of such prosecutions could shackle the press just as much as prior restraints, and he thought only false statements critical of government could be libelous: alluding to "Cato's Letters," Cushing suggested that only the guilty feared the publication of truth.[78] In 1790, Pennsylvania became the first state to provide constitutional guidance for common law criminal libel prosecutions: evidence of truth was made admissible if the matter alleged to be libelous was suitable for public comment.[79] In 1791, Massachusetts chief justice Francis Dana suggested that perhaps truth ought to be a defense to a criminal prosecution for defamatory (but not seditious) libel.[80] The argument had not been made in the case, but the line of defense was on Dana's mind.

Even though one might suppose that Americans would have agreed to a large extent with Thomas Paine's arguments about the French Revolution in *The Rights of Man*, commentators on his 1792 London trial seldom decried the injustice of prosecuting someone for simply speaking the truth about the failings of British institutions. Consistent with English law, Thomas Erskine, defending Paine, asserted not that Paine's assertions were true but that his intentions were good and political critique was vital to the nation.[81] Excerpts from Erskine's arguments were widely published in the United States. My sample of American commentary in 1792 and 1793, however, suggests that even those who approved of Paine did not characterize him as having been

[78] See Bird, Freedoms of Press and Speech, 185–88 and Bird, *Press and Speech under Assault*, 152–57. Cushing's language is also consistent with James Wilson's assertion, in a law lecture in the early 1790s, that "[t]he citizen under a free government has a right to think, to speak, to write, to print, and to publish freely, but with decency and truth, concerning publick men, publick bodies, and publick measures": Wilson, *Collected Works*, 2:1046.

[79] Rosenberg, *Best Men*, 61–66; Levy, *Emergence*, 290–91.

[80] See *Comm. v. Whitmarsh*, Thach. Crim. Cas. 441, 455–58 (1836). This trial, of a printer named Edmund Freeman, is described in "Supreme Judicial Court: Trial for a Libel," *Columbian Centinel*, February 26, 1791.

[81] Paine, *Trial of Thomas Paine*, 20.

prosecuted for publishing the truth. Many of the Massachusetts papers seem untroubled by Paine's conviction.[82] Confidence in an individual's right to publish truth on matters of political importance by no means dominated arguments around *The Rights of Man*.

Leonard Levy sees the 1798 Sedition Act as a turning point for libertarian principles, the enactment of a truth defense representing a liberal victory that Jeffersonians quickly perceived to be pyrrhic, much political critique being unamenable to proof.[83] The Act also specified that conviction required not just an intent to publish the impugned expression but an intent to defame the government, an older argument that ran through subsequent cases. The Act let the jury, under the judge's direction, give a verdict on the whole case, "as in other cases" – that is, on law and fact, rather than just on the issue of publication.[84] Andrew Hamilton had advocated this practice in *Zenger* in 1735 and it had been incorporated into English law through Fox's Libel Act in 1792;[85] however, as Levy's account shows, it was no significant concession to leave juries with the questions of intent and the libelousness of the publication when juries could easily be packed with partisans.[86]

In any case, it is clear that truth had become a central preoccupation by about 1800. The word had multiple meanings and came loaded with significance. Religions and politicians offered truths, and Americans were embroiled in controversies on both fronts. A true friend or a true

---

[82] Using the Eighteenth-Century Collections Online database (quod.lib.umich.edu/e/ ecco/), I searched for "Paine and libel" and got about 290 hits between 1790 and 1798, most of which were on point. Newspapers from all over the eastern seaboard were represented. I then read most of the articles published in 1792 and 1793 in Massachusetts and a smaller sample from the other New England states and elsewhere, reasoning that the newspapers were probably more favorably inclined toward Paine before his attack on Christianity in *The Age of Reason* was published and before the Terror began. Levy likewise detects no outpouring of libertarian sentiment in the mid-1790s: Levy, *Emergence*, 296–97.

[83] Levy, *Emergence*, 197.

[84] Sedition Act, ss. 2–3. In the prosecution of Thomas Cooper under the Sedition Act in 1800, the attorney general pronounced that truth was a defense, and even falsity could be justified if the defendant's intent was innocent: Cooper, *Account of the Trial of Thomas Cooper*, 35–36. On the passage and enforcement of the Alien and Sedition Acts, see Smith, *Freedom's Fetters*.

[85] *An Act to Remove Doubts Respecting the Functions of Juries in Cases of Libel* (U.K.), 1792, 32 Geo. III, c. 60.

[86] See Levy, *Emergence*, 282–302.

subject is one who is loyal, and loyalty is vital in politics and religion. Truthfulness was a key element of gentlemanliness in the eighteenth century.[87] Francis Ludlow Holt, while noting that the word "false" was part of the formal description of the crime of libel, described the word as merely formal, not material, an epithet for comments made "wickedly, without true cause, or justification."[88] Nevertheless, by the late 1790s, "false" had acquired a much more important valence in the United States, referring ostensibly to matters of fact. Given the Zengerian position that it should be legal to publish truth, Massachusetts jurists' earlier reliance on the concept in their understandings of the scope of freedom of the press in the Massachusetts constitution, and the salience of the word "false" in the Sedition Act, it should not be surprising that the deployment of evidence of truth became the overriding preoccupation of those concerned with libel law in Massachusetts in the 1820s and 1830s, especially as the range of truths asserted – by Free Thinkers, antimasons, abolitionists and others – multiplied and became accessible to wives, children and servants.

Evidence of Truth in Massachusetts

When Jeffersonians took power in 1800, they began prosecuting Federalists for libel. In the first years of the century, Alexander Hamilton defended New York Federalist editor Harry Croswell against a common law charge of publishing a seditious libel against Thomas Jefferson. Truth was no defense: since the offense was publishing allegations that might result in the disturbance of the peace, the truth or falsity of the matter was immaterial. True libels might even be more harmful than false ones.[89]

Contemplating the Zengerian defense of truth but not adopting it completely, Hamilton argued that truth should be admissible to prove an accused's innocent intent, as long as the text had been published with good motives and for justifiable ends. On this basis he attempted unsuccessfully to have evidence of the truth of the impugned allegation

---

[87] Olbertson, Criminally Impolite, 280–346.
[88] Holt, *Law of Libel* (1812), 280–81, quotation at 281.
[89] Starkie, *Treatise on Slander* (1813), 556–60.

admitted. Common law jurists usually said that absent particular circumstances (such as speaking the words in legislative debate) bad intent in libel and slander cases was to be inferred from publishing the offending text, so that good motives were relevant only to the punishment. Hamilton argued, however, that intent to harm had to be an actual element of this crime, a position articulated in the Sedition Act and other older lines of authority.[90] Knowing whether the allegation was true or false would help the jury determine intent. The trouble was that revealing truth could also conceivably upend private lives.

The judgment in *Croswell* was not released until 1812. The four-judge panel split evenly, leaving untouched the trial judge's exclusion of the evidence; moreover a new statute had rendered the appeal moot.[91] Hamilton's arguments endured substantially longer than the ultimate judicial opinions, but the judgments reveal some of the tensions that ran through the later jurisprudence. Chief Justice Morgan Lewis observed that letting evidence of truth enter the trial on the intent question while not permitting it to be a full defense was "a distinction for the discovery of which we are indebted to the ingenuity of our own times; there is certainly nothing to be met with in the books to rob us of the honor of it." He would have admitted evidence of truth when intent was not evident from the circumstances, but he considered that in this case actual malice was evident from the nature of the comments.

Justice James Kent took a different view: "The true rule of law is, that the intent and tendency of the publication is, in every instance, to be the substantial inquiry on the trial, and that the truth is admissible in evidence, to explain that intent, and not in every instance to justify it." Kent adopted Hamilton's argument that "the freedom of the press consists in the right to publish, with impunity, truth, with good

---

[90] *People v. Croswell*, 3 Johns. Cas. 337 (N.Y. Sup. Ct. 1804). On *Zenger* and *Croswell*, see Rosenberg, *Best Men*, 35–40, 110–14; Dickerson, *Course of Tolerance*, 21–24; Brown, "Rethinking *People v. Croswell*."

[91] The text of the statute is appended to the published version of the case. It gave the jury the right to decide the whole case, rather than just the fact of publication, and it permitted the defendant to give evidence of truth, provided that this evidence would not be a justification unless it also appeared, upon the trial, that "the matter charged as libellous, was published with good motives and for justifiable ends": *People v. Croswell*, 3 Johns. Cas. 337, 412 (N.Y. Sup. Ct. 1804).

motives, and for justifiable ends, whether it respects government, magistracy, or individuals." An intent to harm, even if the matter were true, could still sink an offender's case. The jury bore the responsibility of determining the offender's intent and whether the publication was libelous. Where the burden of proof lay was not fully clear: did the prosecution have to prove actual bad intent or was bad intent to be inferred from the fact of publication, leaving the defense to prove good intent? The other question Kent did not answer was whether good intent might save a defendant, even if the matter alleged was not proven true. Was intent really "the substantial inquiry on the trial," with truth simply a factor to be considered? Or was it really only truth, with the appropriate intention, that one actually had a right to publish? The door *Croswell* left open was that good intent might be enough to exculpate a defendant, even if the allegations were false.

Controversial political libel prosecutions took place in Massachusetts in the early 1800s, and in 1804 an unsuccessful legislative effort was made to permit those indicted for libel to give truth in evidence.[92] In 1808 – in the same term as *Coffin v. Coffin* – Chief Justice Theophilus Parsons and the Massachusetts Supreme Judicial Court decided to follow *Croswell* to a limited extent in *Commonwealth v. Clap*. Harrison Gray Otis and Thomas O. Selfridge defended William Clap, who had called an auctioneer a liar, a cheat and a scoundrel. The trial judge, Isaac Parker, had excluded evidence of a previous dispute between Clap and the auctioneer, evidence the defense wanted the jury to hear.

Parsons ruled that although truth was not a full defense, a defendant could still escape "by proving that the publication was for a justifiable purpose, and not malicious, nor with the intent to defame any man." There could, he said, be cases in which the defendant, having proved the purpose justifiable, could adduce evidence of the words' truth that would "tend to negative the malice and intent to defame." Parsons provided the first two instances in a list that would grow over the next two decades, of situations in which evidence of truth could be led on the intent question. The first was a prosecution for libel in a complaint to the legislature to remove an unworthy officer and the second was

---

[92] See Duniway, *Development of Freedom of the Press*, 147–48.

commentary on the fitness for office of someone who was standing for election or was currently sitting and would presumably stand again. True or not, a libel published "maliciously and with intent to defame" was an offense. Parsons declined to go as far as Kent by pronouncing a constitutional right to publish truth under any circumstances. If the defendant could show a justifiable purpose in publishing the matter, then its truth would be admissible to prove a lack of malice or intent to defame. Truth was not a defense per se, as it was in civil cases, but in these limited circumstances it could rebut the presumption of intent to harm.

The procedure in the courtroom under *Clap* is somewhat unclear. Probably the judge decided that the offender's purpose was "justifiable" before the jury heard the evidence of truth, although the process likely amounted simply to the defense attempting to lead the evidence, the prosecutor objecting, and the judge making a ruling on the spot, with the correctness of the decision being subject to appeal. The *Clap* rule may well have followed preexisting practice: in *Clap*, the attorney general and the solicitor general mentioned that they generally did not object to evidence of truth being led in cases involving public officers.[93] Massachusetts judges and lawyers continued to be wary about truth, but over the next two decades in courtrooms and other fora for legal and constitutional debate, the list of situations in which truth might be admissible grew, as hypotheticals and real situations multiplied.

A brief period of Republican political ascendancy from mid-1810 to mid-1812 set in motion various pieces that were still moving twenty years later, among them the idea that truth could be admissible in cases other than those concerning the reputations of men holding office or seeking election. Political and religious tensions lay at the heart of these developments. During this short period, Massachusetts had a Democratic-Republican governor, Elbridge Gerry, who had been deeply involved in the constitutional debates of the 1780s and 1790s. His first biographer, his son-in-law James Trecothick Austin, characterized Gerry as having retained the revolutionary generation's suspicion of party conflict and being somewhat out of touch with the excited party feelings that animated politics by 1810, when he ran for

---

[93] *Comm. v. Clap*, 4 Mass. (3 Tyng) 163, 163–67 (1808).

governor. Democratic-Republicans controlled both Houses of the Massachusetts assembly in 1811. Outside of government, the Harvard aristocracy, the Congregational clergy and state officeholders, including judges, were mainly Federalists.

From mid-1810 to mid-1812, under Gerry, the Democrats had their revenge for the disadvantages they had borne and the contemptuous slurs they had suffered in the press and from Congregational pulpits. In 1811 they passed a statute that permitted the citizens of Massachusetts to direct their religious tithes away from Congregationalism to religious organizations of their own choice. The Democrats expanded the franchise and chartered a state bank, preserving its stock to their friends.[94] They increased the number of Democratic senators by redrawing electoral boundaries.[95] They replaced many of the court clerks and sheriffs with their own appointees.[96] Gerry appointed Austin county attorney for Suffolk.[97] The Democrats replaced the Court of Common Pleas with a circuit court with five circuits, each with a chief justice and two puisne judges. Democrats revived the Court of Sessions and directed the appointment of a chief justice and two to four associate justices to each of these as well. Federalists were among those appointed to these new roles, but Democrats outnumbered them. Feeling the constitution was against them, they did not interfere with the Supreme Judicial Court.[98]

The Federalist press was outraged. Austin, in his biography of Gerry, delicately explains that Gerry's speech to the legislature in June 1811 prompted a highly disrespectful series of essays by one "Boston Rebel." Gerry's proclamation for thanksgiving in October inspired a similar response by someone called "Real Christian, and Old Fashioned Whig." In Austin's view, these "surpassed in intemperance of expression whatever before had been considered the limits of political severity." Eventually the governor received

[94] Austin, *Life of Gerry*, 2:335–40. The statute that so severely undercut Congregational financial security was an Act Respecting Publick Worship and Religious Freedom, ch. 6, 1811 Mass. Acts 387.
[95] According to Austin, Federalists glued Gerry's name to this practice, where it has remained; he considered it repugnant but constitutional and so signed it into law: *Life of Gerry*, 2:345–48.
[96] Austin, *Life of Gerry*, 2:341–43.
[97] "Let the People See," *Weekly Messenger* (Boston), December 20, 1811.
[98] Austin, *Life of Gerry*, 2:339–40, 343.

a threatening letter. He issued a proclamation for the detection of its author, whom he connected to the (Federalist) "incendiary writers and printers" of the state and their "more criminal employers" who were conspiring to overthrow the federal and state governments and the characters of private men and women as well. As Austin put it, such outrageous behavior "naturally drew the attention of the community to the power of the law over this delicate subject, and the protection, which the citizen might enjoy against calumny, as well as the claim he had to receive intelligence and information on matters interesting and important."[99]

In the summer of 1811, Gerry ordered his attorney general and solicitor general, Perez Morton and Daniel Davis, to examine the Boston newspapers for libels. The law officers later reported that although they had ignored libels against foreign governors and distinguished foreigners and libels by one editor against another, they had still found 236 actionable items in Federalist journals and seventeen in Republican ones. It is not clear how many indictments they actually drew up, but, according to Jeffrey Pasley, who has examined this episode, later that year the grand jury indicted on only ten. Three convictions resulted.[100]

Austin blamed Isaac Parker's defense-friendly instructions to the grand jury for the low rate of indictment.[101] Parker informed the grand jury that voters needed to be able to scrutinize the public and private character of people running for office or holding office, that the nature of government required free discussion of the men who comprised it, "and that the truth, however offensive, should be told of them." Although an attack against a private citizen could be libelous whether true or false, an attack on a public officer was not libelous if true. Although Parker purported to be explaining Parsons's ruling in *Clap*, according to the *Boston Patriot* Parker told the grand jury that truth itself was a defense, not that evidence of truth was relevant to the determination of intent. Parker did not use the words "good motives" or "justifiable ends," but after telling the grand jury to punish printers

[99] Austin, *Life of Gerry*, 2:348–49.
[100] Pasley, *"Tyranny of Printers,"* 282, Duniway, *Development of Freedom of the Press*, 153; Billias, *Elbridge Gerry*, 321–23, 426 n.55; James T. Austin to Isaac Parker, January 10, 1829, James Trecothick Austin papers, Ms. N-1789, MHS.
[101] Austin, *Life of Gerry*, 2:349–50.

who published calumny rather than truth, he invited the jurors to consider the intentions of the author if unsure whether or not a publication was libelous. An author could validly seek to convince readers of their errors, overturn prejudice, and freely "and even sharply" discuss individual politicians' characters. He could not use his position to "gratify his revengeful or malicious passions."[102] In Austin's view, this focus on the defenses rather than just the strength of the prosecution's case caused the grand jury to release the vast majority of those who stood before it. Austin must have been disappointed. Appointed that year, he may well have joined the attorney general and solicitor general in painstakingly drawing up this multitude of lengthy indictments by hand, only to convince the grand jury on ten.

A remark in the charge inspired Gerry to reflect on why the *Clap* exceptions pertained only to elected politicians, rather than judges as well. Parker told the grand jury that the needs of republican government, as guaranteed in the constitution, required the *Clap* deviation from the common law that made it safer to attack politicians than other people. Evidently intrigued – or provoked – by the newspaper's account of the charge, Gerry wrote Parker to find out if the account was accurate. After some politely hostile correspondence, in which Parker claimed not to have read the newspaper report and suggested that he did not want to incriminate himself, and Gerry disavowed any intention to bring harm to Parker, it became apparent that the printers had lost Parker's notes on his charge and probably destroyed them. The published account stood. Gerry also received his law officers' report on their stunning paucity of libel convictions. They explained that they had relied on the *Clap* rule to distinguish between cases in which truth could and could not be given in evidence. Thus informed of the *Clap* ruling's strategic importance and inspired by Parker's comments on the constitutional need for the truth defense, Gerry addressed the legislature about Parker's charge. The judges, Gerry thought, had strayed from interpreting the common law in light of the constitution into the much murkier terrain of interpreting the common law in light of "the nature of our government." He put it to the legislature that the people had just as much need for truth about judges as about politicians; the public

---

[102] "Charge to the Grand Jury," *Boston Patriot*, December 28, 1811.

needed information so it could remove the judicial "bad man" from office.[103]

In response to Gerry's urging, the House passed a bill that enabled evidence of truth to be led in any prosecution for libel against a person appointed to office by the governor and council, as long as the evidence was directed toward showing the appointee's unfitness for office. Unfortunately for Gerry, the Senate, although pronouncing sympathy with Gerry, found it lacked the time to consider the bill properly.[104] Neither the bill nor the government survived the impending election. Austin's assessment was that Gerry's "pregnant intimations" (the word "inflammatory" seems more appropriate) were delivered too late in the term to be properly understood, and that although Gerry's law officers were too wise to have mounted a full-scale attack on the judiciary, the matter increased public sympathy for the Federalists.[105]

As a result of this controversy, the door that mostly kept evidence of truth out of the courtroom opened a bit more. Parker's broad assertion that truth could be a defense and his advocacy of free discussion, combined with Gerry's argument that the *Clap* rule should extend beyond elected politicians, were significant interventions in the conversation. Gerry's son-in-law and others undoubtedly took note of the shifting terrain around public criticism, now that the bench was populated with both Democrats and Federalists. The idea that truth could play a role in a defense to a charge of criminal libel was now deeply etched into understandings of the law of libel in Massachusetts. How widely protective it was, and how it was to be weighed against bad intent, would await future developments.

Governance and the Morals of the Citizen

The roles of privilege and truth in libel cases were changing in the early nineteenth century. Another area of concern was the law pertaining to texts that did not defame specific individuals but that challenged

---

[103] Austin, *Life of Gerry*, 2:352–68; Duniway, *Development of Freedom of the Press*, 153–54; James T. Austin to Isaac Parker, January 10, 1829, James Trecothick Austin papers, Ms. N-1789, MHS.

[104] Duniway, *Development of Freedom of the Press*, 153–55.

[105] Austin, *Life of Gerry*, 2:368–69.

conventional ideas about religion and sex and, as such, were seen to threaten the ethical foundation upon which society stood. Uncertainties in this area of law demonstrate particularly well the impact of the vicissitudes of legal publishing on understandings of law in different places: lawyers and law books were unevenly distributed geographically, especially in Nova Scotia.

Blasphemous libels had long been subject to prosecution, both at common law and by statute, in Massachusetts and Britain. The idea that one could be prosecuted in common law courts over texts that stretched or violated norms around sexual expression was newer. Blasphemy entailed a verbal attack on God, key theological tenets, the authority of the Bible or the religious establishment. In some formulations apostasy – renouncing the faith – was also a form of blasphemy.[106] In 1676 Sir Matthew Hale, in holding that the common law courts had jurisdiction over blasphemy, reasoned that undermining religious faith endangered people's confidence in oaths, upon which the edifice of government depended. Hale explained that Christianity was part of the law of England, so that reproaching Christianity was subverting the law.[107] Failing to conform to the established church could be understood as seditious, although by 1800 adhering to a faith other than Anglicanism no longer drew prosecution. However, actual attacks on the established church were still blasphemous because, as Francis Ludlow Holt put it, reverence for God and religion were the main supports for honesty and indeed civil government, since they bound the consciences of those who swore oaths of office, discouraged violence, and led people to fulfill their duties and maintain the peace.[108] The French Revolution and Thomas Paine's writings touched off three decades of prosecutorial assault on radicals, in which blasphemous libel was one tool in the Crown's arsenal and protests against the tyranny of the Crown were common.[109] In the 1816 edition of his libel treatise, Holt explained

---

[106] See Levy, *Verbal Offense against the Sacred*, 205–37.
[107] Taylor's Case (1676), 3 Keb. 607, at 621, 1 Vent. 293, 86 E.R. 189 (K.B.).
[108] Levy, *Verbal Offense against the Sacred*, 324–30; Holt, *Law of Libel* (1812), 53.
[109] See Marsh, *Word Crimes*, 18–77; Booth, "Memory"; Harling, "Law of Libel"; Levy, *Verbal Offense against the Sacred*, 324–99; Thomas, *Long Time Burning*, 113–76. Marsh notes that none of the 200 nineteenth-century blasphemy trials were based on the 1698 English blasphemy statute (*An Act for the More Effectual Suppressing of*

that the law did not bar all discussion of religious issues but only indecorous, immoderate attacks.[110]

The English common law courts had slowly assumed jurisdiction over texts that were sexually explicit but not irreligious or seditious. In 1663, King's Bench found it had jurisdiction over conduct that threatened public morality; Charles Sedley, a nobleman, was prosecuted for theatrically exposing himself before a crowd on the roof of a tavern, spewing irreligion and (accounts vary) engaging in indecent acts that may have involved a toast to the King. In 1707, the court held that it lacked jurisdiction over an offense of publishing "a lascivious and obscene libel" that targeted neither the government nor any particular person; the judges thought the ecclesiastical courts should deal with such matters. The court reversed this position in 1727, faced with a sexually explicit, anti-Catholic tract published by the notorious Edmund Curll; King's Bench held that even though *Venus in the Cloister* did not target a particular person, it could still attract punishment as a libel because it subverted public morals and civil order.[111]

Until the end of the eighteenth century, obscenity unconnected to irreligion was generally not viewed as a separate branch of libel, although some legal writers thought it should be, including John Rayner, who in 1765 mentioned that prosecutions of obscene plays had been initiated but stayed because of the participants' connections.[112] After George III's 1787 "Proclamation for the Encouragement of Piety and Virtue, and for Preventing and Punishing of [*sic*] Vice, Profaneness and Immorality," successful English prosecutions of obscene libels multiplied, pursued initially by the Proclamation Society founded by William Wilberforce and later by the Society for the Suppression of Vice.[113] The legal treatises of the period bear witness to the change in

---

Blasphemy and Profaneness (U.K.), 1698, 9 & 10 Will. III, c. 32) – all were common law prosecutions: *Word Crimes*, 16.

[110] Holt, *Law of Libel* (1812), 53; Holt, *Law of Libel*, (1816), 64–65, 70.

[111] *R. v. Sedley* (1663), 1 Sid. 168, 82 E.R. 1036 (K.B.); *R. v. Read* (1707), Fortescue 98, 92 E.R. (K.B.); *R. v. Curll* (1727), 2 Str. 788, 93 E.R. 849 (K.B.).

[112] Manchester, "History of the Crime of Obscene Libel," 40–44; Levy, *Verbal Offense against the Sacred*, 308; Rayner, *Digest of the Law Concerning Libels*, 59; Adair, *Discussions of the Law of Libels*, 57–58.

[113] Thomas, *Long Time Burning*, at 113–22; Manchester, "History of the Crime of Obscene Libel," 43–44.

obscenity's legal status. Blackstone's *Commentaries* and various treatises
on pleas of the Crown published before about 1805 give no sign that
obscenity, absent immorality or public offensiveness, was considered
a criminal offense.[114] However, Holt and Starkie, in the first editions of
their libel and slander treatises in 1812 and 1813, pronounced that all
doubt had been resolved. As Starkie put it, "any immodest and immoral
publication, tending to corrupt the mind, and to destroy the love of
decency, morality, and good order" could be punished through the
temporal courts. Of course much immorality was not criminal, but
actions that could damage morality generally or affect the "mass of
society" were offenses. Plays, therefore, although oral, could attract
prosecution. Starkie tacitly acknowledged that libel law's traditional
requirement that some particular individual or institution be targeted
and that the Crown prove publication to a specified person had slipped
away for this category of text, but he continued to emphasize – without
saying so explicitly – that the crime lay in jeopardizing the morality of the
populace, not just that of the individual user of pornography.[115] The
offense was to the public, the harm self-evident. Some writers did resist
this departure from the earlier, stricter demands of libel law, which had
left the discrete individual producer or consumer alone, to be dealt with
by ecclesiastical tribunals, if at all. The 1824 edition of Hawkins's *Pleas of
the Crown*, for example, continued to insist that no writing could be
a libel unless it reflected on a particular individual and that simple obscene
ribaldry was not punishable at common law, although the culprit could
be bound over to good behavior.[116] Nonetheless, texts for secret
consumption that targeted no individual or institution and could
damage only the reader's morality (if anyone's) were increasingly
subject to prosecution as libels.

Ian Hunter, David Saunders and Dugald Williamson theorize that
pornography is best understood as a sexual practice that works
through drawing on specific cultural competencies in its consumers.

---

[114] Blackstone, *Commentaries*, 4:41–66, 151. John Tremaine's 1793 *Pleas of the Crown*
did not mention obscenity. The 1795 editor of William Hawkins's *Pleas of the
Crown* was uncertain about whether or not obscenity could be prosecuted at
common law: *Treatise of the Pleas of the Crown*, 1795, 2:130. Edward Hyde
East's 1803 *Pleas of the Crown* mentions "scandalous or open breaches of morality," as in *Sedley*, but not obscene or indecent texts (at 3).
[115] Holt, *Law of Libel* (1812), 66–67; Starkie, *Treatise on Slander* (1813), 500, 503–4.
[116] Hawkins, *Treatise of Pleas of the Crown*, 1824, 1:545, but see also 2:360.

The authors argue that pornography emerged within and in response to a religious literature of the sixteenth through eighteenth centuries that emphasized the importance of self-knowledge, self-examination and self-discipline, sexuality being one aspect of the self that required such scrutiny. As they put it, pornography developed as the profane form of a way of properly conducting the self spiritually. Before widespread literacy and the existence of cheap books, pornography circulated only in narrow, educated, affluent circles, among men who understood themselves to have the necessary self-control and taste to use it appropriately. When Edmund Curll and others made it available to the masses, the law was mobilized to attempt to curtail the consumption of pornography by those who were thought to lack the necessary cultural competencies to consume it and who would, therefore, be corrupted by it.[117] Starkie's discussion suggests that with wider literacy and cheap, widespread distribution came concern about the moral lessons that might be imbided in private moments by new readers, including women, children and servants.

Massachusetts law exhibited this concern more than did Nova Scotia's. In response to an influx of bawdy texts and the early eighteenth-century reaction to the excesses of the Restoration in England, Massachusetts passed a statute in 1712 that prohibited "composing, writing, printing or publishing of any filthy, obscene or prophane [sic] song, pamphlet, libel or mock-sermon, in imitation of preaching, or any other part of divine worship."[118] However, the first reported American obscenity case was *Commonwealth v. Sharpless*, heard in Pennsylvania in 1815. The case pertained to a "lewd, wicked, scandalous, infamous, and obscene" painting of a man and a woman. The judges agreed that an offense had been committed, even though the picture had been displayed in private, for money. If the public mind generally and the minds of youth specifically were subjected to such

---

[117] Hunter et al., *On Pornography*, 31, 40, 49–65.
[118] Schauer, *Law of Obscenity*, 8–9. The statute was "An Act against Intemperance, Immorality and Profaneness, and for Reformation of Manners," ch. 6, 1711–12 Mass. Prov. Laws 679, 682 (s. 19). Schauer notes that there were no reported cases under this statute until 1821. It appears that the case to which he refers is *Comm. v. Holmes*, 17 Mass. (16 Tyng) 336 (1821), but *Holmes* was entirely a common law case – indeed, the court noted specifically that this was not an offense created by statute. Cases may well have been brought under this statute at some point, but *Holmes* was not among them.

texts, the moral bonds that held society together would disintegrate.[119] As Americans worked through the implications of their new constitutional experiment, this was a danger to be taken seriously. A few years later, the first of such cases would be heard in Massachusetts as well, as I discuss in Chapter 5.

Conclusion: Law in Transition

Between the 1780s and 1820, legal thought around privilege and truth was diverging in the United States and Britain, with implications that would play out in Massachusetts and Nova Scotia. In Britain, concerns about the extent to which the constitution exposed the subject to capricious imprisonment by Parliament and the Crown ran through debates around punishing libelers. English constitutional theory was unclear about what could be done if the Commons, as the guardian of the liberties of the subject, turned out to be tyrannical. *Burdett v. Abbot* shows King's Bench wrestling with these difficulties and opening the door just a bit to allowing individuals to ask the court's help to determine the jurisdiction of the Commons. In Nova Scotia the question of the extent to which the assembly enjoyed the privileges of the House of Commons became increasingly contentious later in the 1820s. In the United States, after a troubled colonial history of punishment by prickly legislatures, courts were establishing their role as arbiters of constitutional rights, backed by a written constitution established by the sovereign people, or at least the portion of them that counted politically. Consistent with the theory that elected bodies held power through the exercise of the people's will, in *Coffin v. Coffin* the Massachusetts SJC cabined the legislature's jurisdictional claims and kept the conflict in the courtroom.

English arguments about criminal libel prosecutions tended to focus on procedural and institutional matters, such as the *ex officio* information and jury selection. Evidence of truth was to be confined to civil cases, as truth could still lead to a breach of the peace. Nova Scotia inherited this approach. In the United States in the 1790s, though, the idea that publishing truth should not be punishable became salient. The first decades of the nineteenth century saw

---

[119] *Comm. v. Sharpless*, 2 Serg. & Rawle 91 (Pa. S.C. 1815).

Massachusetts legal commentators working out what role evidence of truth should play in a libel trial, and whose reputational interests could justly be compromised by the public disclosure of true but uncomplimentary allegations. The list started with politicians and kept growing. The key doctrinal difficulty concerned the interplay between truth and intentions: some thought malicious intention was key to criminal liability, but the prospect that people with good intentions who published untruths might end up escaping liability was a specter to vanquish.

The common law on immoral, irreligious and obscene expression was evolving in the early 1800s, as courts and legal commentators came to accept that sexually explicit texts that did not target religion and were consumed in private might still be a danger to public morality. The divergence of the law in Massachusetts and Nova Scotia in this area was very much influenced by the range of ideas and texts that circulated in these places, a matter I explore in Chapter 5.

The next chapter explores the quiet transformation of the concept of privilege in the early decades of the nineteenth century, the process through which a legal entitlement attached to status turned into a qualified defense for individuals and the press, especially in Nova Scotia, even as the reach of legislative privilege continued to be contentious. The qualified privilege defense also made it to Massachusetts, but to the republicans of the early decades of the century who sought to protect individual rights of expression, privilege seemed less promising than truth.

3

The Transformation of Privilege

Introduction

In 1832, David Lee Child, a young Massachusetts lawyer and legislator accused by the House of Representatives of breaching its privileges, argued that the House was relying on a body of English law that "one of the greatest English lawyers" had described as "unknown to many and comprehended by few." Those few were tyrannical parliamentarians. Child asserted that this power had

cast some of the foulest stains on the pages of English history. The House of Commons at last swallowed up all the co-ordinate branches, usurped the jurisdiction of the courts, and drenched the kingdom with blood. To this day its power remains uncertain and wrapped in awful mystery. Cases of extreme hardship, if not of oppression, might be cited, which have occurred within the last few years.

This power, he said, was put forward especially sternly around the "time of the formation of our excellent constitution."[1]

Privilege was cast in an entirely different light three years later in Halifax, when the editor and emerging politician Joseph Howe, facing seditious libel proceedings, claimed that a broad privilege protected freedom of the press, as long as newspapers properly fulfilled their duties to the public. In Chapter 2, I discussed the divergence in constitutional fundamentals around expression that

---

[1] Child, *Report of the Case of Alleged Contempt*, 43.

occurred after the American Revolution. The idea of privilege operated differently in constitutional and legal thought in Nova Scotia and Massachusetts in the 1820s and 1830s, as institutions evolved to address tensions between the individual and the state. Legal publishing practices shaped the arguments made, and ideas washed back and forth between legislatures and courts and between civil and criminal law, as individuals were brought "before the bar" in courts and legislatures. In Nova Scotia, the imperative to increase the power of the legislative assembly made privilege a more palatable concept – both in the context of legislative proceedings and in courtrooms – than it was in Massachusetts. There, as I discuss in subsequent chapters, battles over expression took place in courts, where individuals increasingly insisted on an individual right to express their truths.

Legislative Privilege in Nova Scotia and Massachusetts

Before the late 1820s, editors seldom challenged the dignity of the Nova Scotian assembly, possibly partly due to apprehensions of discipline, but also the people as a whole may not yet have decided to subject public life to scrutiny. By the late 1820s, however, the dynamics were changing as newspapers multiplied and took sides in the colony's main political tension: between the elected assembly and the lieutenant governor's appointed council, which exercised legislative and executive functions.

Nova Scotia's experience of privilege reveals threads similar to those in Britain and Massachusetts, with the concept being used both in the assembly and in court. Committees of privilege established by the legislature to assess challenges turned to their own journals and the records they had of the British House of Commons and other colonial legislatures, with which they exchanged journals. A handful of incidents of discipline by the Nova Scotia assembly over expression show the tensions around privilege. As well, for reformers, the concept was promising for increasing the assembly's jurisdiction, especially in budgetary matters. As the assembly increasingly vigorously opposed the council, it punished conservative newsmen, who waved the flag of free expression in protest. The contrast to Massachusetts approaches to privilege was sharp.

In this climate, privilege offered a way of thinking about freedom of the press as protecting expression through properly structured institutions and procedure. In keeping with British constitutional thought, Nova Scotian arguments about the law of libel turned on privilege, procedure, the rights of the jury, and the republication of secondhand news, which generally could not be checked for accuracy. The concept of privilege was mustered, with mixed success, to protect the politically engaged press. Nova Scotia had few libel and slander cases, unlike Massachusetts, where courts were a forum for vehement assertions of individual rights and where arguments around privilege were rare and far less important than arguments around truth, which focused on the substance of the allegation, rather than the context. Privilege did have its place in Massachusetts, though: this chapter concludes with the recognition by Chief Justice Lemuel Shaw of the "privileged communication" defense, meant to protect unflattering but necessary communications, usually in business.

Newspapers, Legislative Privilege and Allegations of Smuggling

The "libels" addressed in the legislative assembly and courtrooms in Nova Scotia generally came off the presses of local printers. In 1820, all five of Nova Scotia's newspapers – all weeklies – were published in Halifax. One of the early voices of "improvement" was the printer Anthony Henry Holland. After likely working as a printer in Maine for William W. Clapp, in about 1812 Holland moved to Halifax. He began publishing the *Acadian Recorder* in 1813. Unlike the other three newspapers then being published in Halifax (John Howe's *Royal Gazette*, William Minns's *Weekly Chronicle* and John Howe Jr.'s *Halifax Journal*), the *Recorder* aspired to promote improvements in agriculture and the economy and to examine political principles and the characters of public men and measures. The *Recorder* was the first paper to print the assembly's proceedings regularly.[2]

Anthony Henry Holland and his brother Philip John Holland, who, with Edward A. Moody, took over the *Recorder* in the mid-1820s, had

---

[2] Tratt, "Holland, Anthony Henry." The Maine paper was the *Gazette of Maine, Hancock & Washington Advertiser*. Clapp, who moved on to publish Boston newspapers, is one of the many links between Massachusetts and Nova Scotia.

a number of experiences with libel and the regulation of expression. Anthony Henry was reprimanded by the assembly in 1818 for publishing two pieces of satire aimed at a representative of Pictou district.[3] Three years later, Philip was both prosecuted and sued for attacking, with a stick, another newspaper publisher, Edmund Ward. The Hollands and Ward, who had been printing the conservative *Free Press* since 1816, had an ongoing editorial feud. Rescued by provincial treasurer Michael Wallace, Ward explained that he had expected an attack because he had previously been horsewhipped by another young man, George Young, the son of John Young, an advocate for agricultural improvements. James W. Johnston represented Ward, while Samuel George William Archibald (made one of the province's first King's Counsel in 1817) represented Holland. Since Philip Holland had already been fined forty shillings for breaching the peace, the issue was damages, not guilt. Archibald blamed the incident on Ward, suggesting that Ward had left Bermuda after a battle with the governor that involved a trial and now irrationally took on Young and the Hollands. The *Free Press* had been founded to provide the "news and nonsense" that its sober predecessors had not supplied. The paper, Archibald said, "was ushered into the world after a learned prospectus which promised every thing that was chaste, learned or critical – in fact every thing except that which the paper had since contained." Philip Holland, by contrast, was "as quiet a man as ever lived – a sober, cool-headed Dutchman" provoked by Ward. Probably entertained but unconvinced, the special jury awarded Ward nine pounds three pence in damages, not the two copper coins Archibald recommended.[4]

By the mid-1820s, dissatisfaction was building. The assembly and council were frequently at odds. Two particularly contentious issues were appropriations for the Presbyterian academy at Pictou – meant to provide higher education for young men who could not in good conscience swear their commitment to the Anglican creeds required at King's College, Windsor – and road-building, which was important

---

[3] NS Journals, 1818, 29–30, 38; Buggey, "Mortimer, Edward"; Akins, *History of Halifax City*, 185; Tratt, *Survey and Listing of Nova Scotia Newspapers*, 42.

[4] "Supreme Court – Case of Edmund Ward v. P. J. Holland for Assault and Battery," *Acadian Recorder* (Halifax), October 27, 1821; Edmund Ward v. Philip Holland (NSSC Halifax, Mich. 1821).

in Nova Scotia, not only because people needed roads but because they needed the money that the government paid them for doing the work. This tension provided the context for political criticism, which prompted the legislature to discipline its critics. Critics, in turn, challenged the colonial legislature's constitutional powers and privileges as they touched on both expression and money.

In March 1827, assembly member Thomas Chandler Haliburton, frustrated by the council's refusal to increase funding for common schools, referred to the councillors as "twelve dignified, deep read, pensioned, old ladies, but filled with prejudices and whims like all other antiquated spinsters." Haliburton described consulting these "Sybiline oracles" on his school bill. Recounting this experience, he told the assembly that two-thirds of the councillors had never left the Halifax area and the others had only the most superficial knowledge of the province beyond. Haliburton described three councillors as tending to dismiss the idea of helping the poor and seeming even to doubt that Nova Scotia had any. He claimed that the council had rejected his bill without reading it. After concluding with his dismay at the ignorance of the proceedings, he added that he intended no disrespect.[5]

Haliburton's comments were reprinted by George Young in his three-year-old newspaper, the *Novascotian*. Scandalized, the council asked the assembly to discipline Haliburton if he alone was responsible and Young if he had misstated the debates. The assembly's initial response was to brush off the council's inquiry (while providing assurances of respect) by resolving that freedom of expression in the assembly required protection and claiming to have no knowledge of exactly what Haliburton had said or how accurate most of it was.[6] When the council expressed dissatisfaction, the assembly reconsidered. This time, it announced that it highly disapproved of the publication, and that if the newspaper report was accurate, it was "a gross indecorum and unwarrantable imputation" on the eminently respectable council. Haliburton was called upon and admitted speaking and publishing the words. The assembly resolved that his conduct was reprehensible, and the Speaker called him to the bar and

---

[5] "School Bill," Supplement to the *Novascotian*, March 29, 1827.
[6] "In Council," *Novascotian* (Halifax), April 5, 1827; NS Journals, 1827, 130–34; Patterson, *History of Pictou*, 372; Cuthbertson, "Place, Politics and the Brandy Election," 9; Beck, *Joseph Howe: Conservative Reformer*, 45.

reprimanded him. Informed of these doings, the council pronounced itself satisfied. Young, in his columns, indicated that if he had known how unpleasant the matter would be, he would have suppressed the report of the debate. He published in full the council's self-defense, in which it denied all Haliburton's allegations of caprice and inattention. Young gratefully noted that Haliburton had taken full responsibility for the speech.[7]

The assembly's willingness to defer to the council lessened considerably in the late 1820s, not coincidentally just as a reformist press was gaining momentum. By 1840 Halifax had about seven weekly newspapers, and about three were published in other towns. Organized political parties did not yet exist, but newspapers were contributing to the emergence of political alliances. Nova Scotia's newspapers were similar to a certain, decorous segment of the much more varied Massachusetts press.[8] They generally pronounced their intention to avoid American-style vituperation and respect common decency in their discussions of politics, to protect the sanctity of private life, and not to insult religion or morality. Like some Massachusetts writers and editors, Nova Scotians sometimes moved defamatory allegations offstage somewhat, by alluding to events without providing enough specificity to constitute a direct attack on character. Nova Scotia newspapers and the more upper-crust Massachusetts ones both pronounced "private character" off limits, but Nova Scotian writers tended to be more scrupulous than their Massachusetts counterparts about emphasizing that the behavior they were decrying really was relevant to public affairs.

Newspapers were undoubtedly the most important Nova Scotian institutions of the sort that Jeffrey McNairn has described, in the Upper

---

[7] NS Journals, 1827, 139; "In Council," *Novascotian* (Halifax), April 5, 1827; "Provincial Legislature," *Novascotian* (Halifax), April 5, 1827.
[8] A very few papers committed to moral and religious causes and to literary pursuits appeared (often briefly) in Nova Scotia in these decades. Unlike Massachusetts, Nova Scotia did not have party organs or a "penny press," with its breezy, slangy language nestled within refined syntax and proper grammar and its snide comments on the social lives of the upper crust, its stories of crime and marital infidelity, and its personal abuse of politicians. No Nova Scotian newspapers directly appealed to the poorer classes, but their moral and literary "improvement" tended to be a goal of the more reformist newspapers. On the American penny press, see Cmiel, *Democratic Eloquence*, 60–61 and Horowitz, *Rereading Sex*, 130.

Canadian context, as leading to the development of a sense of a cohesive "public" whose opinion had to be attended to.[9] The field for political expression opened significantly with the appearance of the Pictou *Colonial Patriot* in December 1827 and Joseph Howe's acquisition of the *Novascotian* the next month. Initially edited anonymously, the *Patriot* was by March 1829 being openly edited by Jotham Blanchard, who had attended the Pictou Academy and studied law in Pictou with S.G.W. Archibald's brother-in-law. Committed to improving education, promoting temperance and scrutinizing the government, the *Patriot* revelled in the reformist spirit afoot in Britain, quoting Henry Brougham and the *Edinburgh Review* in its first issue. In the third, it invited a disgruntled reader who had called its editor a radical to read the London papers or the debates of the British House of Commons which would seem "the very hot-houses of democracy."[10]

Joseph Howe's publishing career began when he was thirteen and started working in the *Royal Gazette* print shop, run by his half-brother John Howe Jr., one of Joseph Howe's many relatives in publishing in New England and Nova Scotia. In 1827, Joseph Howe and a cousin took over the *Weekly Chronicle* and renamed it. Howe sold that interest a year later and bought the *Novascotian* from George Young.[11] Howe published extensive articles on provincial and imperial politics as well as public addresses on improving themes – lectures to the Mechanics' Institutes, for example, and advice on education and domestic life. Howe's concern about freedom of the press was evident from the beginning: the *Novascotian*'s masthead proclaimed "The free Constitution which guards the British Press – Sir James Mackintosh." However, the freedom of the press was not always at the forefront of Howe's mind, at least in the early days of his publishing career, when he found himself embroiled in the conflicts between the council and the assembly.

The heat was rising. In a letter to the *Patriot* of February 1828, a correspondent, one "Dodington," objected strenuously to the

---

[9] McNairn, *Capacity to Judge*. McNairn also stresses the importance of voluntary associations, which proliferated in Nova Scotia in the 1820s and 1830s.

[10] Patterson, *History of Pictou*, 369; Dunlop, "Dickson, Thomas"; Editorials, *Colonial Patriot* (Pictou), December 7 and 21, 1827; "Education," *Colonial Patriot* (Pictou), December 7, 1827; "Temperance," *Colonial Patriot* (Pictou), December 7, 1827.

[11] Tratt, *Survey and Listing of Nova Scotia Newspapers*, 41–43.

assembly's receptiveness to the council's rebuke over a speech by Haliburton that lampooned the council for refusing to pass a bill on education, presumably his "pensioned old ladies" speech of almost a year earlier. Haliburton's observations, Dodington thought, were indecorous, but freedom of speech was one of the most valuable privileges of the House and could only be constrained by the assembly itself. For the council to presume to direct the assembly in its treatment of its members' speeches in debate was unconstitutional. The British House of Lords could defend the Crown's prerogative if the Commons encroached on it, but the Lords' legislative power was limited. Importantly, to protect the people's control over the public purse, the Lords could not originate an appropriations bill or amend a money bill of any kind. The implication, of course, was that the council was obliged to pass the assembly's money bills as long as they did not in some way offend the constitution. In a subsequent letter Dodington argued that since education did not concern the Crown, the council was constitutionally obliged to pass measures for funding education that the assembly had passed.[12]

Although the power to control money bills was not among the canonical privileges belonging to a legislative body, it was the most important of the privileges and powers insisted upon by the Nova Scotian assembly in the 1820s and 1830s.[13] The colonial situation made the situation complex. Criticism of the assembly and its claims could inspire retaliation, which in turn brought into question the assembly's powers of punishment. These intertwined issues surfaced in two incidents, one involving an allegation that a member of the assembly was a smuggler and the other the taxation of brandy.[14]

---

[12] Dodington [pseud.], letters to the editor, *Colonial Patriot* (Pictou), February 8 and 15, 1828.

[13] Maitland calls it a "so-called privilege": Maitland, *Constitutional History of England*, 310. Core privileges included control over elections, freedom of speech in debate, freedom from arrest while the assembly was in session and for a certain time on either side, and control over members. Many other powers were also raised at different times.

[14] On these two events, see generally Morison, "Brandy Election"; Cuthbertson, "Place, Politics and the Brandy Election"; and Beck, *Joseph Howe: Conservative Reformer*, 58–80. The House's proceedings appear in its *Journal and Proceedings* for 1829 and 1830. The *Acadian Recorder*, *Free Press*, *Novascotian* and *Colonial Patriot* related these events as they unfolded and reflected on them afterward.

In late February of 1829, John Barry, a representative from Shelburne and generally a supporter of the council, was excluded by the assembly for seeming to imply that another member, one Colonel Freeman, was a smuggler. Barry had been attempting to introduce a petition from Patrick Gough, a Liverpool County resident, who was complaining of the hardships of militia duty and the peremptory dismissal of his efforts to obtain a medical exemption, by Freeman among others. Barry had been agitating to change the militia law to reduce the maximum distance that men could be required to go for duty, since poor men had to walk, sometimes for several hours. One of the Liverpool members, seeking the petition's rejection, called Gough a smuggler and suggested that he was shirking his duties. In response, Barry read the closing of a letter Gough had written to Freeman, a commanding officer of the Queen's County militia. Gough signed it "your old friend and partner." Barry's stress on the word "partner" and his body language seemed to insinuate that Freeman was just as much a smuggler as Gough, although Barry later protested that he had meant that Gough was just as respectable as Freeman.

Several minutes later, Freeman, having ordered the galleries cleared, rose to accuse Barry of calling him a smuggler. The Speaker, S.G.W. Archibald, refused to let Barry explain what he meant, and the assembly demanded that Barry apologize to Freeman. Barry said he would apologize to the House itself for breaching decorum and even to Freeman for wounding his feelings, but he would not apologize for calling Freeman a smuggler as he had not done so. Minutes later he reiterated that he would apologize to the House but not to Freeman. The House then suspended Barry until he framed his apology in terms of the House's order. Barry had, over the previous few days, been trying to introduce petitions from people outside his own constituency who wanted the militia law changed. Suspiciously, these petitioners' own representatives, some of whom were implicated in the petitioners' complaints, succeeded in having these petitions rejected unheard. Any potential concerns about the right to petition were, however, overshadowed by the measures taken against Barry.[15]

---

[15] In a letter to the editor of the *Free Press* on February 9, 1830, one "Lucius" suggested that ultimately all the erroneous rulings on the Barry affair would be wiped off the assembly's journals, as in the *Wilkes* case, so that they would not set precedent. He was wrong.

The *Acadian Recorder* and *Free Press* were sympathetic to Barry, and Holland regularly published lengthy letters of self-justification from Barry in the ensuing months. Several difficult questions arose. One was whether Archibald has misstepped in dictating an apology without giving Barry a chance to explain, and another concerned the assembly's power to exclude duly elected members. Edmund Ward, in the *Free Press*, argued that, following the precedent in the Wilkes case, Archibald's first duty as Speaker had been to ask Barry to explain his words. If the explanation was insufficient, the assembly's options were to reprimand him, to commit him, or to declare his seat vacant and hold an election immediately. He could not be told what to say. By suspending Barry, the assembly was leaving Shelburne County unrepresented and unconstitutionally dictating who could sit in the assembly. Barry himself argued that the assembly's journals revealed no precedent in which an apology had been required; Haliburton had merely been reprimanded for his outrageous comments about the council. Indeed, neither Holland nor Burdett had been required to apologize either.

Barry's Shelburne constituents may well have lost out on allocations for roads and bridges while Barry was suspended in March 1829. Although one member tried at points to get the assembly to content itself with reprimanding Barry or else to accede to Barry's petition to have his seat vacated so an election could be held, the assembly did neither. Barry claimed they resented his stance on the militia bill and the Pictou Academy. Personalities undoubtedly mattered as well. Toward the end of the month the assembly's committee of privileges, having reviewed their own journals and those of the Commons and Lords, reported that it would be improper to vacate Barry's seat. Similar instances were rare, and the committee thought the assembly had acted moderately in not jailing Barry for contempt. Shelburne would have been appropriately represented if Barry had behaved himself. The committee nudged the assembly to consider renewing Barry's suspension in the next legislative session.[16]

On April 1, the assembly rejected another petition from Barry, in which he proposed to impeach Freeman and another member, James DeWolf, by accusing them of smuggling while they were members of

---

[16] NS Journals, 1829, 491.

the assembly and justices of the peace. Philip Holland published the petition in the *Acadian Recorder*, with an explanatory letter from Barry in which he declared himself willing to be sent to "the coldest vault in the common gaol of *this* County" in the name of freedom of speech.[17] He soon got his chance.

Frustrated with his suspension, on Saturday, April 4, Barry shocked the assembly by appearing. As he described it afterwards, he advanced to the bar, bowed "in the *most respectful manner* of which I was capable," and seated himself after explaining, over the uproar, that in his constituents' interests he was determined to take his seat. When Barry again declined to proffer the necessary apology, the assembly resolved that he be taken into custody, again over a proposal that he simply be reprimanded instead. The sergeant-at-arms took Barry into custody but having no instructions to convey him anywhere in particular, placed him in his wife's custody, at home, across the street. Barry saw deceit and conspiracy behind the assembly's moves. The assembly received petitions from Shelburne over the next few days asking that Barry's seat be vacated, but the committee of privileges again concluded that the assembly could do so only on its own initiative and not on a member's own request or his constituents'. Barry had attacked private character, repeated his allegations in newspapers, violated the assembly's orders, and committed "an indecent and gross insult to the Speaker, and in the Assembly." The committee thought Barry deserved expulsion, but since that was what he wanted, his suspension should continue. In the next session he could make amends.

Not only did Philip Holland publish Barry's accounts, but on April 7, Edmund Ward, in the *Free Press*, incorporated into an editorial some commentary from a New Brunswick paper. The author pronounced that well-informed people thought Barry had been improperly prevented from explaining himself. The assembly's actions were inconsistent with constitutional principles and had compromised its dignity, probably out of personal animosity. The next day the assembly resolved that Holland and Ward had breached the assembly's privileges by publishing "remarks derogatory to this

---

[17] John A. Barry, "To the Freeholders of the Township of Shelburne," *Acadian Recorder* (Halifax), April 4, 1829.

House, and containing reflections on the Privileges of this House." The printers were brought to the bar and reprimanded by Archibald, who refused to let them respond and warned them that they were subject to legislative discipline for any observations they made during the upcoming recess. Before bowing and leaving, Ward retorted that he would provide an "ample review" of the assembly's measures when the session closed. Holland, in a subsequent editorial, said he thought himself justified in giving Barry a platform to explain himself, in the name of fulsome, independent reporting. Positioning himself as a defender of freedom of the press and the constitution, Ward published his account and returned to the topic the following winter, promising nonetheless to avoid improper allusions to individuals and remarks incompatible with the dignity of the House and the respect it deserved. He even quoted Chief Justice Holt's (disputed) assertion in Paty's case that Parliament's authority was circumscribed by law.

The *Halifax Journal* guardedly observed, "it is a dangerous thing medling [*sic*] with the liberty of the Press, and never ought to be resorted to by Public Bodies, except in extreme cases" – which this evidently was.[18] In the *Novascotian*, Joseph Howe pronounced his admiration for the assembly but nevertheless suggested that it should defend the free press, where its true hope for vindication lay. He warned darkly that "if Editors are brought for offenses to the Bar of the House, Legislators may depend upon this – that they will be brought, individually and collectively, to a bitter expiation before the bar of the public." The assembly referred these remarks to the Committee of Privileges as well, but nothing was done. Ward and Barry perceived personal relationships and promises operating behind the scenes.

On Saturday, April 11, matters came to a head, focusing attention on the assembly's power to imprison. Philip Holland published Barry's account of the events of the previous Saturday. Among other offenses, the letter accused the Committee of Privileges of uttering falsehoods; took specific aim at Haliburton; noted the discipline of Holland and Ward; thanked Ward for his "fair and impartial view" of the proceedings; and accused the Committee of Privileges of a "*base* and

<hr>

[18] "Mr. Barry Again," *Colonial Patriot* (Pictou), April 22, 1829, reprinted from the *Halifax Journal*.

insidious attempt ... to foist the odium of the late occurrences in the House on [Barry's] shoulders."[19] When this article was read to the assembly, they brought Barry in, obtained his admission of authorship, and ordered the Speaker to issue his warrant to commit Barry to jail. What happened next was subject to different interpretations. Some said a large crowd formed and rescued Barry. Ward and Barry said that once Barry left the assembly, he denied the warrant's legality and refused to accompany the sergeant-at-arms. A slight scuffle took place, a few people present separated the parties, and Barry escaped and hid for a few hours before returning home. In this version, the real violence arose after Barry disappeared. Members walking to Government House for dinner were attacked, one member received a cut on his head, and something was thrown through a window into Archibald's chambers. The military was called out to quell the violence. That Monday, the assembly finally expelled Barry and ordered him detained until the end of the session less than a week later. The assembly also pronounced Barry unfit to serve in the legislature, the sort of prospective declaration that had ended badly for the Commons in the Wilkes case and which the Nova Scotia assembly ultimately overlooked once Barry was reelected. He turned himself in and wrote voluminous, self-involved epistles to the *Acadian Recorder* for the next few weeks from prison, in which among other things he compared himself to England's John Wilkes.[20]

The *Free Press*, supported by the *Acadian Recorder*, energetically challenged the legality of Barry's imprisonment. Ward asserted that no law lay behind the long-assumed power of the House of Commons to imprison British subjects. In this revision of history, Ward asserted that Parliament was "extremely careful" about "how it tamper[ed] with the liberties of the subject," and its authority to control anyone other than its members and officers had never been satisfactorily determined. Ward cited a Bahamas case from 1817 to 1818 in which the

---

[19] John A. Barry, "To the Freeholders of the Township of Shelburne," *Acadian Recorder* (Halifax), April 11, 1829 (Barry's emphasis).

[20] NS Journals, 1829, 551–53; John A. Barry, "To the Inhabitants of the Province of Nova Scotia," *Acadian Recorder* (Halifax), April 25, 1829; John A. Barry, letter to James R. DeWolf, *Acadian Recorder* (Halifax), April 25, 1829; John A. Barry, "To the Inhabitants of the Province of Nova Scotia," *Acadian Recorder* (Halifax), May 2, 1829.

assembly attempted to arrest the attorney general for writing something that offended the assembly. The attorney general challenged his detention on habeas corpus and was discharged by the judges. Ultimately Earl Bathurst informed the governor that the King had never intended to permit colonial assemblies to imprison his subjects – even members of the assembly (which the attorney general was not) – for "what they might term a breach of privilege." Ward printed the governor's messages.[21]

Before the lieutenant governor cooled matters down by dissolving the assembly, it also jailed "Frederick Major, the Elder" for taking part in Barry's rescue, even though Major was already facing criminal charges for the same activities. The assembly brought Philip Holland back in for publishing Barry's lengthy account of the House's doings and its faults. Holland was discharged when he disavowed any intention to be disrespectful and indicated that Barry had led him to think that he had obtained legal advice that the letter was not libelous – and most importantly because of a death in the family. The assembly allocated £500 to finding the culprits in the riot. Ultimately the grand jury dismissed the riot as the unpremeditated work of mere "boys." Not everyone was convinced, however – some perceived the machinations of the council in the background. The Halifax oligarchy, Brian Cuthbertson observes, relished the undignified light in which the affair cast the assembly.[22]

Barry and Major were ordered released one week after the riot, April 18, at the end of the session. Barry won reelection in Shelburne and returned to the assembly when it next met, in February 1830, when another privilege dispute exploded. This one – the "brandy dispute" – began with claims about the assembly's control over money bills and, as it unfolded, raised questions about its jurisdiction over expression.

---

[21] "Nassau, N. P. Sept. 2, 1817," *Free Press* (Halifax), April 21, 1829; "Halifax. Tuesday, April 14, 1829," *Free Press* (Halifax), April 14, 1829; Editorial, *Acadian Recorder* (Halifax), April 18, 1829. Howe asserted that the governor dissolved the assembly (releasing the attorney general) because he believed the commitment was oppressive, though not illegal: "The Assembly," *Novascotian* (Halifax), April 16, 1829. This view is hard to square with Bathurst's response. The Bahamas incident is discussed in Johnson, *Race Relations in the Bahamas*, 96–99 and Craton and Saunders, *Islanders in the Stream*, 221–24.

[22] Cuthbertson, "Place, Politics and the Brandy Election," 13.

These events reinforced the importance of the idea of privilege in Nova Scotia.

In 1828, an editorial in the *Colonial Patriot* had predicted that the challenges facing Lower Canada would soon arrive: Nova Scotia would be called upon to pay its own expenses and would have to decide whether or not to "make over to her office holders in perpetuity the greatest portion of her revenues, and render them independent of all controul and influence in the domestic administration of her affairs." Joseph Howe had previously accused Jotham Blanchard of radicalism, but Howe's confidence in the governor general and the upper house waned with these events.[23]

The brandy dispute pitted the council, heavily influenced by merchant interests, against the assembly, accountable to a broader population in need of roads, bridges and schools. Much of the province's revenue came from duties on imports, which were unpopular with merchants, who believed their revenues fell as duties rose. Toward the end of the legislative session, the assembly was concluding the passage of its supply bills. Legislators discovered that a small portion of a tax – fourpence per gallon – on foreign brandy had gone uncollected since 1826 owing to a statutory provision that rendered it nugatory.[24] The assembly passed a bill that would have required collecting this missing tax. Nova Scotia had a well-established practice of the two houses appointing committees to confer about each separate tax the assembly proposed. Then, having determined the council's position, the assembly would draft a bill that satisfied both

---

[23] "Canadian Affairs," *Colonial Patriot* (Pictou), December 7, 1827; Editorial, *Colonial Patriot* (Pictou), June 18, 1828; Beck, *Joseph Howe: Conservative Reformer*, 31–32, 45–69. This dispute unfolds on the pages of the NS Journals, 1830, 1st sess., starting March 4, 1830 and in issue after issue of the *Novascotian*, *Colonial Patriot*, *Free Press* and other local papers. See also Cuthbertson, "Place, Politics and the Brandy Election" and Morison, "Brandy Election."

[24] Why it went uncollected is somewhat mysterious. There are allusions to poor statutory drafting, but there are also hints that the fourpence was deliberately made not payable because of fears of reciprocal tariffs being placed on Nova Scotian goods. Although the cost would ultimately be passed to the consumer, the importers appear to have been obliged to remit the duty upon importation – probably when they took it out of the warehouse – before they actually sold the products, which left them out of pocket for a period of time. Archibald claimed that after the 1829 revenue bill expired, the warehoused brandy was released and was "running in floods through the streets": "Halifax, Friday, April 16, 1830," *Free Press* (Halifax), April 16, 1830.

houses. In this instance, time being short, council received the supply bill and appointed a three-person committee of merchants and customs collectors to consider it.[25] Thus advised, the council explained to the assembly that Nova Scotia's taxes were already too high and that this additional tax would unduly harm trade, but that it would accede to keeping the revenues the same as in 1829.

The assembly, however, refused to consider the council's position, interpreting it as unconstitutional meddling with the power over the purse they enjoyed as a Nova Scotian House of Commons. The *Free Press*, supporting the council, explained that there was more to the British practice than immediately met the eye. There, the government proposed resolutions to cover the upcoming year's expenditures. The Commons then passed the measures it thought appropriate and submitted these to the Lords, whose choice was to agree or disagree. The Commons would reject any proposed amendments as a breach of their privileges. However, the Lords' amendments might nevertheless make it into subsequent legislation. Conferences between committees of the two houses were also held to settle differences; if agreement was impossible the bill was dropped. The Commons thus did constrain government spending, but the Lords had some input. The *Free Press* did not acknowledge the institutional differences inherent in the colonial situation: the colonial government would not fall if a revenue bill failed to pass. When the interests of the assembly and council were opposed, the council's upper hand was frustrating to members who sought benefits for their constituents. On the other hand, the council and lieutenant governor were responsible for coordinating the imperial and colonial customs regimes, so placing the assembly fully in charge would have been problematic.[26]

The old Revenue Act expired at midnight on April 1, 1830, and merchants – possibly including council members – removed their goods from their bonded warehouses and threw them on the market tax-free.[27] The assembly's effort to send a slightly altered version of the bill back to the council so that the revenues would not be entirely lost was

[25] NS Journals, 1830, 1st sess., 729, 754.
[26] See A Constitutionalist [pseud.], letter to the editor, *Free Press* (Halifax), May 4, 1830.
[27] Patterson, *History of Pictou*, 381.

rejected as a breach of procedure – the same bill could not be sent to the council twice – as well as commercially ill-advised.

On April 5, the assembly resolved itself into a committee of the whole for discussion, and S.G.W. Archibald, having left the Speaker's chair, launched into a long, eloquent attack on the council, claiming for the assembly the exclusive privilege of drafting revenue bills and denying that the council could even suggest changes. He did not think that a small excess duty on a product people could spare was an excessive burden. Archibald also suggested that the council had been duplicitous in some of its dealings with the assembly.

Archibald's frustration undoubtedly emerged in part from his own unsuccessful efforts to position himself as the next chief justice, an office that two members of council, attorney general Richard Uniacke and Brenton Halliburton, also wanted and that Halliburton ultimately obtained. Archibald's argument was the opposite of the one he had made when the Prince Edward Island (PEI) assembly made similar demands in 1827: then, as chief justice and president of the council, Archibald advised them to follow Nova Scotia's practice of conferences. In 1827, Archibald observed that PEI's first lieutenant governor had been officially instructed to refer to the royal instructions for Nova Scotia, the first of which – from 1756 – specifically deprived the assembly of certain privileges that, the instructions said, had proven unmanageable in the American colonies. One of these was unilateral control over money bills.[28] Evidently, as a PEI

---

[28] Aristides [pseud.], *Free Press* (Halifax), May 4, 1830. The text, aside from emphasis added in the *Free Press*, matches Labaree's rendition in *Royal Instructions to British Colonial Governors*, 1:112–13. This debate between the council and the assembly appears in the PEI Journals, 1827, on May 5, 1827. The explicit instruction that the council was to have the power to frame money bills also appeared in other colonial instructions of the period, including those given to James Murray and Guy Carleton for Quebec in 1760 and 1768 respectively, and to the governor of North Carolina in 1754: "Instructions to Governor James Murray," 8; "Instructions to Governor Carleton," 307; "Instructions for Our Trusty and Wellbeloved Arthur Dobbs," 1111–12. (Evarts Boutell Greene outlines some of the underlying disputes in *Provincial Governor*, 122–23.) The PEI instructions, however, did not tell the governor to follow scrupulously every word of the instructions for Nova Scotia (or Georgia, also noted) but simply to refer to them and to guard against giving any powers or privileges to the PEI House of Assembly that had not been given to assemblies in other colonies. The council's case was therefore stronger in Nova Scotia than in PEI, making Archibald's flip-flop really quite egregious.

commentator noted sardonically, Archibald's views had "undergone some slight modification" since 1827.[29]

Critics of the assembly argued that the brandy tax should have been severed from the rest of the statute so that the rest could have passed, blamed personalities and the grinding of personal axes, and accused the assembly of bad faith in trying to raise taxes and depart from a workable system for raising and appropriating revenue. Joseph Howe, however, was deeply impressed with Archibald's defense of the assembly and published the debates in the *Novascotian*, although he apparently tempered the tone of Archibald's speech. Offended, the council called the assembly's attention to publications "purporting to be the reports of the Debates in the House of Assembly" that reflected indecorously on the council. Calling Archibald's language unparliamentary and citing authorities, the council informed the members that it was their duty to punish the offending member or members. The council was especially angry about Archibald's allegation that the council had been duplicitous in its dealings with the assembly and about allegations of corruption leveled by another member, David Dill, who had remarked that a council member had already taken advantage of the situation by removing brandy from a warehouse. The council resolved that the *Novascotian* contained "gross, scandalous and libellous" charges against the council and its members that breached the council's privileges. The council demanded that the assembly discipline its members if they had actually said such things and Howe if they had not. The council declared that it would be justified in breaking off all communication with the assembly until satisfaction was received but it forbore from doing so because of the probable impact on the province.[30]

The assembly was more resolute and probably more sensitized to encroachments on its privileges than it had been when T.C. Haliburton

---

[29] "Prince Edward Island, May 4. Disturbance in Nova-Scotia," *Free Press* (Halifax), May 11, 1830. Archibald later wrote to the colonial secretary, George Murray, relating the assembly's views, which Murray thought could not be "supported upon any Constitutional grounds." He also thought the council had behaved badly. See Murray to Officer Administering the Government, Jun. 5, 1830, Nova Scotia: Despatches, Letters from Secretary of State, Sept. 30, 1823–Aug. 1, 1832, pp. 270–75, CO 218/30, National Archives, Kew, Richmond.

[30] NS Journals, 1830, 1st sess., 743–44; "Halifax, Tuesday, April 13, 1830," *Free Press* (Halifax), April 13, 1830; "In Council," *Novascotian* (Halifax), April 15, 1830.

criticized the council. The assembly defended its actions, pointing out the council's role in the financial troubles that now faced the province, as the council had rejected £25,000 in revenue to avoid £700 in taxes that had only failed to be collected in the past because of a mistake. The assembly reiterated its privilege claims with respect to money, that it was the sole judge of what taxes free British subjects should have to bear.[31] The majority also resolved not to consider the council's resolutions about Archibald and the debates in the assembly (ultimately the council, in turn, also refused to consider their rejection). Rebuffing an initiative to discipline Archibald and Dill, the assembly resolved that it had "the highest esteem for the talents, integrity and ability, of the Honorable Speaker, whose public conduct has secured him the confidence of this House, and of the Country."[32] They took steps to collect what revenue they could, but an impasse had arisen: the council's president and provincial treasurer, Michael Wallace, acting for the absent lieutenant governor, prorogued the legislature on April 13. Matters settled down – and the tax passed – after a hotly contested election in the fall held because George IV had died. Reformers including Jotham Blanchard were elected; John Barry and other supporters of the council were not.

The jurisdiction of the assembly to punish its critics was uncertain in these controversies. The *Acadian Recorder* had given Barry a platform for self-defense, and it now supported Archibald and the assembly against the high-handed council. The *Novascotian* and the *Colonial Patriot*, as advocates of political reform, took the same side. Howe thought the assembly was entirely justified in its response to Barry's attack on individual members of the assembly and his charges of deliberate falsehood, and he criticized Ward's views of the assembly.[33] The *Patriot* reminded its readers that the council "yet [held] the reins of government in their unworthy hands." Every free man in the province was advised to object to the council's effort to call the assembly to account for the exercise of freedom of speech within it.[34] Only Edmund Ward and the *Free Press* took the council's side in both disputes. Ward's Toryism was Nova Scotian Toryism. He

---

[31] NS Journals, 1830, 1st sess., 746–47.   [32] *Ibid.* 748.
[33] "The Assembly," *Novascotian* (Halifax), April 16, 1829; "Domestic Politics," *Novascotian* (Halifax), April 23, 1829.
[34] "Freedom of Speech," *Colonial Patriot* (Pictou), May 1, 1830.

deplored using the military to repress civil dissent. He opposed restrictions on the civil rights of British and Irish Catholics. He characterized Nova Scotian politics as having fallen from their previous golden harmony through the efforts of T.C. Haliburton, the Pictou Academy and the nefarious Presbyterians. He hoped His Majesty's government would formally clarify the extent of the assembly's powers. He positioned himself as the defender of a free press against an overbearing legislature and its Speaker. He had nothing to say about freedom of speech in the assembly.

One observer astutely remarked that not much law seemed to govern the doings of the assembly, and Barry himself commented on the apparent arbitrariness of parliamentary law.[35] Five elements of this lengthy drama relate to the relationship between privilege and expression in Nova Scotian constitutional thought: the council's call to reprimand Archibald, Dill or Howe, Barry's suspension for failing to apologize satisfactorily for his comment on Freeman, the reprimands of Holland and Ward and the contemplated discipline of Howe for his warnings, Barry's commitment without imprisonment, and the imprisonment of Barry and Major in connection with Barry's "rescue."

The council's effort to instruct the assembly in parliamentary procedure and to dictate that it demand that it punish whoever was responsible for the attacks attributed to Archibald and Dill undoubtedly encroached on even the most restrictive understandings of the powers of an assembly. When Archibald was elected Speaker in 1827, he promised "[t]o preserve, inviolate the privileges of the House" but also to guard against encroaching on Crown prerogative or the rights of "other branches of the Legislature," that is, the council. As was standard practice, he asked the lieutenant governor for freedom of speech in debate, freedom from arrest, and free access for himself to the lieutenant governor as required. The lieutenant governor "cheerfully" agreed, "conformably to ancient usage, the Laws of the Land, and the Royal Instructions."[36] The council was certainly within its rights to pronounce itself offended and probably even to break off

35 Clytus [pseud.], letter to the editor, *Novascotian* (Halifax), April 23, 1829; John A. Barry, "To the Freeholders of the Township of Shelburne," *Acadian Recorder* (Halifax), March 14, 1829.
36 NS Journals, 1827, 7–8. Cf. Murdoch, *Epitome of the Laws of Nova-Scotia*, 1:65.

communications, but instructing the assembly about unparliamentary expression and demanding specific actions seems excessive.

Barry's suspension for failing to deliver the requisite apology for his slur on another member is more problematic. J. Murray Beck, who sympathizes with Barry, thinks the assembly should not have made this demand, since its members must have known Barry would not be able to bring himself to do so, but this is not the question.[37] Reprimands by the Speaker to members not permitted to explain themselves seem to have been normal practice in Nova Scotia; demands for apologies were not.[38] Archibald could have avoided interfering with the rights of the Shelburne voters by simply reproving Barry and moving on, an approach Joseph Howe thought would have been preferable because it was "familiar," even though he did not question the constitutionality of the assembly's course of action; he thought giving Barry a chance to explain would have been a good idea as well.[39] As to the "outside libellers" – Holland, Ward and Howe – accused of publishing what Francis Ludlow Holt called "fictitious contempts," the assembly's reprimands of Holland and Ward certainly struck Ward as constitutionally objectionable, but the restrained responses of the *Patriot* and the *Novascotian* probably suggest that their editors and correspondents thought such discipline unwise but consistent with the practices of the House of Commons and therefore constitutional. Even if *Burdett v. Abbot* seemed antique, the House of Commons had imprisoned Burdett's colleague John Cam Hobhouse for a critical pamphlet only a decade earlier.[40] The assembly's alternative was to ask the lieutenant governor to have the attorney general, Richard Uniacke, initiate a prosecution. Uniacke, however, sat on the council and was an unreliable defender of the dignity of the assembly. Even if he had been inclined to pursue the matter assiduously, prosecutions

---

[37] Beck, *Joseph Howe: Conservative Reformer*, 59.
[38] The PEI assembly – as shown in incidents after the Barry controversy – allowed its members and others to explain themselves and then dictated the terms of required apologies. See PEI Journals, 1831, 58; PEI Journals, 1832, 6; PEI Journals, 1837, 34. Adopting a procedure similar to Nova Scotia's, the New Brunswick assembly in 1837 imprisoned a printer, James A. Pierce, who libeled a member, without giving him a chance to explain or apologize: NB Journals, 1837, 311.
[39] "The Assembly," *Novascotian* (Halifax), April 16, 1829.
[40] *R. v. Hobhouse* (1820), 2 Chitty R. 207 (K.B.). See Cochran, "Hobhouse, John Cam, Baron Broughton."

take time and juries might sympathize with persecuted printers. The assembly's only real choice was between legislative discipline and letting Ward, Holland and Barry say what they liked and fighting back through a different paper (such as the *Novascotian*). The assembly was not ready to entrust its dignity to the mercies of printers, probably especially given the well-informed critics who corresponded with the *Free Press*.

Beginning in 1831, the New Brunswick and PEI journals show instances of suspending offending members and others – committing them to the custody of the sergeant-at-arms who then kept track of them for a while.[41] Since Barry was a member of the assembly and subject to its discipline, his commitment for failing to acquiesce seems unremarkable. The more difficult question was the assembly's power to imprison, whether for libel or at all. Colonial assemblies were modeled after the House of Commons, but as the brandy dispute demonstrates, their constitutional situation was different. An 1815 opinion of the British law officers and the 1817–18 Bahamas case related by Edmund Ward both indicated that colonial assemblies could not imprison their critics, but the Nova Scotia and New Brunswick assemblies – quite possibly happily unaware of these opinions – did so anyway, as did Canadian legislative bodies.[42] Howe told his readers that there was no question that colonial assemblies had all the powers of Parliament.[43] One commentator

---

[41] In 1837, the PEI assembly suspended three members for refusing to acknowledge misrepresenting the assembly's debates in a public meeting to demand a court of escheat: PEI Journals, 1837, 23–27, 34–35. In 1831, the New Brunswick assembly committed a constable to the custody of the sergeant-at-arms for serving a summons on a sitting member: NB Journals, 1831, 58–60. In 1832 they followed the same process regarding parties alleged to have been involved in challenging a member to a duel: NB Journals, 1832, 16. They acted likewise for another episode of assault and abusive language aimed at members in 1836: NB Journals, 1836, 28–29, 133–34.

[42] On the law officers' opinion and Canadian measures, see Greenwood and Wright, "Parliamentary Privilege," 414–15 and generally. In 1829, the New Brunswick assembly imprisoned a man who had assaulted a member and used "threatening and abusive language" toward him with respect to his vote in the House: NB Journals, 1829, 90. In 1837, they specifically rejected a proposal simply to commit printer James A. Pierce to the sergeant-at-arms for libel, choosing to imprison Pierce instead: NB Journals, 1837, 311. In 1839 they imprisoned a law student who, although disavowing any disrespectful intentions, declined to explain why he had tricked the doorkeeper into serving a legal document on a sitting member: NB Journals, 1839, 2nd sess., 310–11.

[43] "The Assembly," *Novascotian* (Halifax), April 16, 1829.

asserted, optimistically, that even the House of Commons had stopped imprisoning critics. Reporters were now given seats so that they could deliver their opinions on parliamentarians every day, and parliamentarians would not think of interfering.[44]

Burdett v. Abbot made it clear that King's Bench would not consider a habeas corpus application from someone imprisoned by a legislative body. The Nova Scotia Supreme Court followed King's Bench's lead when John Barry brought a habeas corpus application: two judges in chambers refused to grant the writ and thus allow the validity of his imprisonment to be tested.[45] When instructing the grand jury about indicting those suspected of attempting to rescue Barry, Justice Brenton Halliburton asserted that these two judges had already ruled that the warrant properly stated that Barry was guilty of contempt and that the assembly had the power to commit members guilty of contempt or disobedience of its rules. Halliburton now pronounced the same opinion. "Such powers are incident to all superior Courts and legislative Bodies; they could not perform their duties unless they possessed them; they are not privileges conferred upon them to increase their power and dignity, but they are inherent rights, essential to their existence, and to the due discharge of their respective functions." The grand jury, therefore, could legally indict for rescue, if the evidence warranted the charge.[46] This grand jury, as noted, declined.

Uncertainty around the assembly's power to imprison continued for more than a decade.[47] In 1832 Nova Scotia lawyer and legal scholar Beamish Murdoch suggested that the laws that governed the provincial assembly were not necessarily analogous to those of Parliament but depended instead on the "constitution and usage" of Nova Scotia.

---

[44] An Enquirer [pseud.], letter to the editor on the laws of Parliament, *Acadian Recorder* (Halifax), May 23, 1829. The *Stockdale v. Hansard* affair made it clear that this assertion of the Commons's restraint was greatly overblown.

[45] John A. Barry, "To the Inhabitants of the Province of Nova Scotia," *Acadian Recorder* (Halifax), April 25, 1829.

[46] "Supreme Court," *Novascotian* (Halifax), April 23, 1829. The journals of the assembly for the next four sessions give no sign Barry appealed. In *Hill v. Weldon* (1845), 5 N.B.R. 1 at 30 (S.C.), Barry's case was referred to in argument in terms that suggest that it never went beyond the Nova Scotia Supreme Court.

[47] The case that probably finally closed the door on imprisonment by assemblies is *Kielley v. Carson* (1842), 4 Moore 63, 13 E.R. 225 (J.C.P.C., on appeal from Newfoundland).

Parliament was governed by the *lex parliamenti*, or its own precedents, while a colony was regulated by "the common law and colonial usages." Murdoch observed that although the council had never arrested anyone for contempt of its privileges, the assembly had "often done so." He added that the Lower Canadian legislative council had recently arrested two newspaper editors. Among the tasks of sergeants-at-arms, as Murdoch enumerated them, was summoning and arresting parties. Murdoch said nothing about jailing anyone, although the Lower Canadian editors had in fact been jailed.[48] Murdoch's caution was justified, especially with respect to imprisoning nonmembers, but being unable to jail Barry when he took his seat despite being suspended would have placed the assembly in an awkward position. The Supreme Court's deference to the assembly was practical and politically necessary, as well as consistent with *Burdett v. Abbot*; overriding the assembly's measures could only have attracted criticism for embarrassing the assembly, whose measures had already attracted plenty of disgust. Better to let the matter rest. Barry could enjoy his cell for a few more days.

Nova Scotian reformers' desire to bolster the powers of the assembly caused them to insist that its powers were similar to those of the House of Commons. The Commons, however, had even recently shown a tendency to tyranny where critics were concerned, tendencies most loyal Nova Scotians hesitated to acknowledge. Handing critics to the attorney general for prosecution could produce unpredictable results, as Halifax's magistrates learned when they sought to prosecute Joseph Howe in 1835. All legal measures to suppress criticism were fraught with difficulty.

The extent to which the Nova Scotian assembly enjoyed the privileges of Parliament was a matter of contention in this period, as these two disputes demonstrate; but the larger point is that privilege – a legal entitlement that could act as sword or shield and that was attached to status or to membership in certain bodies – was a well-known, respectable constitutional concept in Nova Scotia. With reform of political institutions in the air, Edmund Ward's warning that the assembly would use its privilege to violate individual rights to free expression could be discounted as obsequiously supporting the

---

[48] Murdoch, *Epitome of the Laws of Nova-Scotia*, 1:64, 67, 81.

council and ignoring Nova Scotians' British constitutional inheritance. In Massachusetts, however, parliamentary privilege was more problematic, as the episode discussed next shows.

Legislative Privilege in Massachusetts

David Lee Child's censure for commenting, in his newspaper, on a dispute in which he was involved as a member of the state House of Representatives was not the first privilege controversy in Massachusetts. Concern about the punitive reach of offended legislatures arose in the tempestuous first decade of the century, as Federalists and Republicans struggled for preeminence. In Massachusetts in 1805 – before *Coffin* and *Clap* – a committee of the House of Representatives, determining not to rescind a certain printing contract despite the unflattering portrait of Thomas Jefferson the printer had published in a newspaper, pronounced that everyone had a right to "publish truth from good motives, and for justifiable ends." The committee considered libelous reflections the purview of juries, not the House, because the House could not evaluate a libel's truth, as it lacked the capacities of a judicial body. The committee warned that threats from the House could interfere with public access to information and that the House might be tempted to rule in cases that did not impair its privileges, which would blur the line between judicial and legislative bodies. The House adopted this report, but in 1823 it nonetheless required two printers to apologize for an objectionable item, and special committees of the House in 1824 and 1827 censured the publishers of "certain newspaper items relating to its proceedings."[49]

David Lee Child was a young lawyer, politician, journalist and reformer. Known to history mainly because of his remarkable wife, the writer and abolitionist (Lydia) Maria Francis Child, David himself contributed much to the development of libel law. A Harvard graduate called to the bar in Suffolk in 1825, he was elected to the state House of Representatives in 1826 and served most years until 1832. On July 4, 1826, he delivered an oration to the Republicans of Boston about the

---

[49] See Duniway, *Development of Freedom of the Press*, 149–50, 161 n.2.

excellence of American institutions, premised on the need for pure-minded scrutiny.[50] Not everyone appreciated Child's spirit.

From 1828 until early 1832 Child edited the *Massachusetts Journal*, founded to be distinguished and respectable and to provide readers with an account of the doings of Congress. The *Journal* supported John Quincy Adams and Henry Clay and opposed Andrew Jackson. Maria Child, having met David in 1824 and married him in 1828, assisted with the newspaper, which in turn published her stories and articles. The young abolitionist William Lloyd Garrison worked there briefly as a journeyman printer.[51]

David Lee Child used the paper as a platform to advance societal improvement. In January 1832, while a member of the state House of Representatives, Child stated in the *Journal* that the *Daily Commercial Gazette* had misdescribed a procedural dispute between himself and the Speaker, William Calhoun.[52] Offended by the *Journal*'s version, Calhoun demanded that the House discipline Child. The gist was that Calhoun, who Child thought unduly controlled the House and its record-keeping, first ignored and then overruled Child's motion to adjourn, when the members were packing up at the end of the day's contentious debate, instead pushing through other motions. When the clerk asked whether he should include the ruling on Child's motion in the House's journal, Calhoun shrugged the matter off, rather than telling the clerk to relate the whole proceedings fully and impartially. Child asserted that absent other motions on the floor, a motion to adjourn took precedence. In the *Journal*, Child tersely noted that not only had his motion been declared out of order but that Calhoun had managed to ensure that no record of his ruling appeared in the journal. This short note implied that Calhoun wielded undue influence over both the clerk and the pliable House, a theme Child had evidently raised before. Not only the Speaker but also the other members disliked the light cast on them.

[50] Reference department, Massachusetts State Library, email message to author, April 19, 2007; Suffolk Common Pleas Record Book, p. 240, MJA; Child, *Oration*.
[51] *Massachusetts Journal* founding documents, Massachusetts Journal papers, Ms. S-665, MHS; Papers related to the criminal prosecution of Theodore Lyman, Jr. by Daniel Webster, 1828–76, Ms. S-416, MHS; L.M. Child, *Appeal*, xiii, xix.
[52] Child published an extensive report of these proceedings in *Report of the Case of Alleged Contempt*, from which this account is drawn.

The House formed a committee to consider disciplining Child. When the committee recommended censure, Child argued strenuously that the House lacked jurisdiction to discipline for an outside libel. He observed that the Massachusetts constitution specified the privileges of the legislature and its members, and punishing for libel was not on the list. He pronounced the "the English law of privilege" to be "repugnant to many particular provisions and to the whole spirit of our constitution." Child argued that English parliamentary law was unlimited, oppressive and unknown to courts. He argued that Massachusetts's precedents, as assembled by the committee, actually showed the House's tendency to tyranny, and the wisdom of earlier Americans who had tried "to erect a barrier against its abuses." In England, parliamentary privilege was the people's shield against the Crown, but because the United States was founded on the consent of the people, any increases to legislative privilege had to be carved from the people's liberties. The Massachusetts constitution was meant to guard against such encroachments. Massachusetts precedents were inapplicable, either on their facts or because they arose during the revolutionary period when matters were much more tense than they were in 1832.[53]

Child reviewed the House's proceedings on libels by nonmember printers since the revolution. He noted that the Senate's clerk had failed to find a single case of this type in the Senate records. Child outlined five episodes, in none of which the legislature had actually even attempted discipline. Arguing for a strict reading of the House's privileges, Child likewise denied the House's constitutional jurisdiction to imprison members. He quoted Chief Justice Parsons's views of the inapplicability of British precedent. He argued that the House's proper response to calumny was to turn the matter over to the government's law officers for prosecution. He argued that he had not, in fact, been out of order but rather that the Speaker had improperly and oppressively silenced him.[54]

The House ultimately ruled that Child's publication was disrespectful to the House and unjust to the Speaker. Disagreeing about demanding an apology, the members settled on pronouncing Child deserving of censure. Submitting a lengthy protest against the

---

[53] *Ibid.* 40, 43, 50.   [54] *Ibid.* 53–68.

Speaker and the House, Child resigned his seat. In a final gesture of contempt, the House tabled his protest, neither accepting nor rejecting it but ensuring its omission from the House's records.

Legislative contempt actions for outside libels, then, did take place in Massachusetts, despite the colonial precedents, despite *Coffin* and despite Child's warnings about the oppressive dangers of British precedent. It was evidently hard for the Massachusetts House of Representatives to accept that it could not discipline Child for using his newspaper to offend the House. Child's arguments about the limits of legislative power were philosophically and constitutionally sound, but Congress, too, adopted a different approach – it preferred the arguments Joseph Story would make the following year in his *Commentaries on the Constitution of the United States.*[55] In the post-revolutionary republican setting, however, parliamentary privilege was more dubious than it was in Nova Scotia, where reformers were keen to increase the assembly's power at the expense of the council. British parliamentary precedents were a less valuable currency in Massachusetts, and parliamentary tyranny a more resonant threat. Whether guided by principle or discretion, the Massachusetts House pulled back from the edge at the end: in not demanding an apology it avoided courting Child's defiance, which could have led to a public showdown in – and with – the Supreme Judicial Court. Legislative privilege rested, maligned and uncertain.

The Emergence of the Qualified Privilege Defense in Massachusetts and Nova Scotia

Well before the term "qualified privilege" was employed, the common law recognized situations in which circumstances blocked a defamed person from suing or prosecuting over a nonmalicious assertion. The qualified privilege defense as we know it took shape in England through a series of early nineteenth-century judgments that reflected changing social needs and the work of legal commentators. The defense was made in an 1835 Nova Scotia case and probably also earlier. In Massachusetts, however, although the defense was recognized in 1831, its uptake was confused, entangled with the tort

[55] Story, *Commentaries*, 1833, 302–10.

of malicious prosecution and the evolving defense of truth, which, as I discuss in the next chapter, was more frequently made and more controversial. Because the truth defense was unavailable in criminal cases in Nova Scotia and also because well into the 1830s lawyers in Massachusetts relied on American versions of the first edition of Thomas Starkie's treatise on slander and libel, Starkie's later theorization of an extensive qualified privilege capable of protecting a wide range of communications was less important in Massachusetts than in Nova Scotia, to which Starkie's second edition, of 1830, made its way. As well, Massachusetts legal commentators were already thinking of expression as an individual right to be upheld in court, subject to content-based limits. Nova Scotians were more receptive to the qualified privilege defense because they already thought about their institutions through the lens of privilege.

The emergence of the qualified privilege defense strongly recalls Jürgen Habermas's arguments about the development of the western European public sphere in the later eighteenth century, in which ideas could be rationally discussed regardless of the status of the speaker and, eventually, could be conveyed to the state as public opinion. Habermas sees the public sphere as manifest in salons, coffee houses and newspapers, which stood apart from both the state and the private sphere of economic exchange and social labor. A key element was the emergence of an institutionalized literary sphere, with interpretive power held by everyone with access to texts, such as paintings, plays and books. Privilege defenses assume that information and opinions need to circulate in particular spheres and that in some circumstances people may or should speak. In 1830 Starkie argued that a defense of qualified privilege was available even to newspapers if they circulated ideas the public needed, but he relied on cases in which reference letters and literary criticism had been found privileged. Likewise Francis Ludlow Holt devoted many pages of his 1812 libel text to the law's protection of literary and theatrical criticism.[56] The legal categories themselves – emerging in English jurisprudence and traveling to North America in law books – therefore reflected evolving European

[56] Habermas, *Structural Transformation*, 30–43; Starkie, *Treatise on Slander* (1830), 1: lxxxiv–cxix, 1:305–315, 2:255–57; Holt, *Law of Libel* (1812), 181–87. See also Calhoun, "Introduction: Habermas and the Public Sphere," 10–13.

distinctions between the private and the public and tensions around the proper role of rational, public communication in a state that imagined itself as characterized by personal liberty.

Qualified Privilege, Inchoate

The vicissitudes of legal publishing are part of this story of how legal and social needs blended with legal and constitutional traditions in the evolution of common law defenses in slander and libel cases. The case law upon which Holt and Starkie attempted to impose order through their treatises of 1812 and 1813 included a variety of instances in which a combination of circumstances and intentions had been held to protect defendants from liability. Ultimately Starkie's treatise was more influential, probably because it set out the elements of the case for both sides, theorizing carefully about defenses. Holt's treatise, arranged – following Blackstone – on the social rank of the plaintiff or complainant, left the defenses unsystematized. In Starkie's 1830 second English edition, he elaborated a more expansive theory and framework for protecting the press than he had in 1813. It was, however, his first edition that was glossed by American legal writers and published in New York in 1826 and 1832. Massachusetts lawyers also used Starkie's 1824 London evidence treatise and its several subsequent American editions.

In their first editions in 1812 and 1813, Holt and Starkie both described the elements of what would come to be called the qualified privilege defense. Both cited a footnote in which Chief Justice Ellenborough, in 1808, referred to a defendant's defamatory assertion in a business situation as a "privileged communication." The parties were engaged in selling beer to publicans. The plaintiff, Dunman, a beer dealer, and the defendant, Bigg, a brewer, were connected through a third party, Leigh, who provided surety and whom the brewer had promised to tell if the dealer was in arrears. The brewer told Leigh "in very opprobrious terms" that the dealer, who owed the brewer money, had adulterated the beer and then returned it as unmerchantable. Ellenborough held that because of the relationship, even if the defendant brewer's allegations were "intemperate and unfounded," as long as he believed them true he could not be said to have acted maliciously and with intent to defame the beer dealer. Ellenborough said he thought the brewer's statement was a "privileged communication" but rather than nonsuit the plaintiff, he left it to a jury to determine the brewer's intentions. This commercial context could raise the presumption of a valid defense, but actual malice could rebut it.[57]

Organizing his 1812 text according to the type of insult done to the plaintiff, Holt unsystematically demonstrated that sometimes defendants escaped liability for defamatory allegations. In discussing libels with respect to a person's calling or profession, Holt explained that allowing businesspeople to communicate confidentially and freely benefitted society. When two people did business with the same solicitor and one wrote the other confidentially criticizing the solicitor over matters in his charge, no libel action lay. The socially important issue of reference letters for servants received the same treatment: even false allegations by the employer were protected unless the former servant also proved malice. Outside of the business context, similar protections could exist for confidential communications. Quietly cautioning one's wife's elderly uncle about one's wife's brother's bad propensities was acceptable if done from the right motives, but not if done simply to gain a larger legacy for one's wife. Confidential communications arising from friendship were protected, as were the rulings made by religious groups pursuant to their disciplinary proceedings, even if conveyed to the group generally. Publicly ridiculing a literary composition or its author was also not libelous. Holt quoted Lord Ellenborough who, in another 1808 case, pointed out that if authors and their works were not open to criticism, the errors of the first person to write on a subject would be preserved in perpetuity. Ellenborough added, however, that reflections on the writer's personal character would not be protected. Other cases Holt cited showed that a newspaper editor or theater visitor could comment on public entertainment as long as no malice was present, a proposition Holt developed further in his 1816 second edition, again quoting Ellenborough.[58]

---

[57] *Dunman v. Bigg* (1808), 1 Camp. 269, 170 E.R. 953 (K.B.), quoted in Starkie, *Treatise on Slander* (1813), 241–43, and in Holt, *Law of Libel* (1812), 190.

[58] Holt, *Law of Libel* (1812), 180–89; Holt, *Law of Libel* (1816), 203–7, 270. The allusion to Locke and Filmer is from *Carr v. Hood* (1808) 1 Camp. 355, 170 E.R. 983 (K.B.). The New York edition of 1818 is based on the 1816 edition.

In his 1813 treatise, Thomas Starkie also analyzed these aspects of the law. Starkie, however, theorized about why these defendants were not liable. He reasoned that either they actually lacked malicious intent or else for policy reasons the law drew this presumption, conclusively in the case of impartial and true reports of court and legislative proceedings. If a defendant's "public or private" duty made speaking imperative, the public interest might demand that the speech be absolutely protected, regardless of the defendant's intentions, because too many "inconveniences and perplexities" would arise otherwise. In other cases, the court would presume innocent intention from the circumstances but the plaintiff could rebut the presumption on the evidence. Like Holt, Starkie included character references and book reviews as examples.[59] According to Paul Mitchell, the character reference issue was acutely important to the employing class in the later eighteenth century, as servants' insistence on tips from guests was increasing their independence and decreasing their deference: disgruntled employers claimed the threat of a poor character reference was one of the few tools they had. Mitchell suggests that it was in these cases that the courts introduced the idea that defendants had only to prove these special circumstances and not their own innocent intent – the former servant had the harder job of proving the employer's actual ill will.[60] This treatment of intent was the same for civil and criminal cases.

Starkie was prolific. His treatises on criminal pleading and evidence published up to 1824 all contain similar explanations of the pleas and evidence in defamation cases. In his 1824 evidence text (reproduced in American editions in 1826, 1828 and 1830) he reiterated that expression could deserve protection if the defendant had uttered or published the words in discharging some "legal or moral duty to society." In general, proving malice was a necessary element of the plaintiff's case, but since people were presumed to intend the natural consequences of their actions, this initial step ("legal malice") was usually easy. If the objectionable words were not obviously injurious or had been uttered in circumstances that on their face suggested a lack of malice, then the plaintiff had to prove the circumstances that made

---

[59] Starkie, *Treatise on Slander* (1813), 198–99, 223–24, 231–32, 556.
[60] Mitchell, *Making of the Modern Law of Defamation*, 146–50.

them injurious (e.g. describing someone's recent marriage would not usually be defamatory, unless the person was already married to someone else). The burden then shifted to the defendant. If the defendant had borne a legal duty to speak, proving the occasion barred the action completely. The words of judges, witnesses and parties to legal actions (but not lawyers) were protected this way – ill will in such cases was irrelevant. However, if the defendant's duty had only been moral, then the plaintiff had to prove that the defendant had used the occasion as a cover for venting ("actual") malice. Starkie discussed examples in which a defendant had laid a claim to land which caused a loss to the real owner; character references; a wife's newspaper advertisement that could have been read as suggesting that her husband was bigamous; a communication about a serjeant to his corps's governing committee; and, generally, words "delivered by way of admonition or advice ... or spoken in confidence and friendship." Starkie thought fair criticism of literary works was protected on similar principles. His discussion of the prosecutor's pleas in a criminal case followed the same reasoning: the defendant could rebut the initial legal inference of malice by showing a lack of intent to publish the libel or by leading evidence showing he was fairly and honestly discharging a duty to society or honestly pursuing a legal claim.[61]

A theoretical framework based on duty and intention, of course, is unlikely to reach gratuitous insults made in legislative debate. Starkie did not work through this aspect of his theoretical framework for privilege until his 1830 slander and libel treatise. In the first edition he alluded to uncertainty in the law over whether correct reports of judicial or legislative proceedings could furnish a full defense to civil or criminal actions, reviewing the problematic cases discussed in Chapter 2. Recognizing an absolute privilege that protected the publication of accounts of certain libel trials also raised tricky policy issues. Referring in his 1824 evidence treatise to recent criminal proceedings against Mary Carlile, sister of England's radical publisher Richard Carlile, Starkie remarked that "the publication of such an account [of a trial] will not be justifiable if it contain matter of a scandalous, blasphemous or indecent nature."[62]

---

[61] Starkie, *Practical Treatise on Evidence* (1824), 2:863–67, 881.   [62] *Ibid.* 2:876.

Privilege in Massachusetts

Privilege played a modest role in libel law in Massachusetts. Lawyers and judges were instead preoccupied with evidence of truth, which individuals loudly proclaimed themselves to have a constitutional right to speak and publish. Claims of absolute privilege, like Micajah Coffin's, were seldom made or discussed. Occasionally in Massachusetts a qualified version of privilege was found: although the circumstances might tend to excuse the defamatory allegation, proof of the defendant's actual ill will would rebut the defense. The key difficulty arose from the interface between the logic of experience and the rules of pleading. It seemed sensible that speaking falsely of someone generally reflected nefarious intent, while speaking truth suggested the opposite. In civil proceedings, evidence relevant to a privilege defense could be introduced under the first plea a defendant would normally make, the general denial. For much of the 1820s and 1830s, however, evidence of truth was inadmissible unless a truth plea was specifically set out in a "special plea," to notify the plaintiff that the facts underlying the allegations would be revealed. In criminal cases, at common law truth defenses were not allowed at all, but as I discuss in Chapter 4, Massachusetts law was shifting during this period to permit it to enter the courtroom under an unstable, ever-expanding set of circumstances. Qualified privilege defenses therefore seemed a way for defendants to sneak evidence of truth into their cases without assuming the difficulties of raising it directly. No privilege claims were properly raised as defenses in the criminal cases in my sample; truth was the central preoccupation of these cases. However, the civil cases touching on privilege show Massachusetts judges and lawyers grappling with current sociocultural needs, a general republican aversion to privilege, evolving understandings of the nature of malice and its place in defamation cases, arguments in English law books, and most importantly how to reconcile privilege and truth. Many Massachusetts commentators were uncomfortable with the possibility that false statements might be excused by the circumstances of their publication and the speaker's honest though misinformed intentions. Qualified privilege did emerge in Massachusetts, but it did not seem to offer the kind of potential to protect the press that Thomas Starkie and Nova Scotia's Joseph Howe envisioned for it.

The vicissitudes of legal publishing and how they shaped the circulation of legal ideas are a factor in the differences in how these legal ideas were taken up in Massachusetts and Nova Scotia. In the second edition of Starkie's slander and libel treatise, published in 1830, he expanded his conception of qualified privilege in a way that offered broad protection for the embattled English press. I return to this revised theory below. However, in the 1810s and 1820s, the idea that privilege could protect the expression of all ranks of society in their business or other dealings was barely appreciable in Massachusetts legal thought. Massachusetts jurists were already preoccupied with the redemptive possibilities of truth. By the time Starkie's more expansive theory of privilege arrived on Massachusetts bookshelves, the belief in the well-intentioned individual's right to speak or publish truth was too central to dislodge.

Tracking the appearance and use of Holt's and Starkie's various treatises sheds light on the important role of books as information vectors. Before the mid-1820s, case citations and records from libraries and catalogs show few signs of Holt's or Starkie's views. The first American edition of Holt's *Law of Libel* appeared in 1818 and was based on the second London edition of 1816. Starkie's *Treatise on the Law of Slander* did not appear in an American edition until 1826, and the second American edition, in 1832, was also based on Starkie's 1813 first edition, rather than on the intervening 1830 London edition. Starkie's 1824 evidence treatise appeared in three American editions, in 1826, 1828 and 1830, before a new London edition was published. All of these American editions were almost exactly the same as the originals, with footnotes to American cases that multiplied and lengthened from edition to edition.

Cases were always the main authorities counsel cited in court, with references to digests, abridgements and guides to pleading also common. Treatises were less commonly cited and almost always by counsel – judges mainly cited cases. Starkie's more usefully organized text gradually superseded Holt's. In Massachusetts, the first citation to either Holt or Starkie is to "Holt on Libel" – evidently the 1818 American edition – in 1822.[63] The next year Harrison Gray Otis

---

[63] *Maffit's Trial*, 19, citing Holt, *Law of Libel* (1818), 279.

cited one of the earlier English editions of Holt.[64] In 1824, Daniel Davis, the solicitor general of Massachusetts, in an instruction book for justices of the peace, referred readers to "Starkie on slander, and Holt upon libels."[65] Prosecuting four years later, Davis cited both Holt and Starkie, probably the 1816 English edition of Holt's treatise and the 1813 edition of Starkie.[66] The American edition of Holt was cited in an 1824 case, the report of which was published in 1826.[67] This edition was also referred to by counsel in 1825 in *Commonwealth v. Blanding*, the case in which "Starkie on Slander" – evidently the 1813 London edition – first appeared in a Massachusetts reported judgment.[68] In 1827, Starkie's evidence treatise was cited by counsel.[69] For this citation and for an 1828 citation of "Stark. on Slander," it is unclear which edition was being used because the pagination in the American versions is almost identical to the 1813 English original.[70] By the mid-1830s, though, citations to Holt's treatise had become rare, and Starkie's slander text prevailed. Starkie's evidence treatise was also cited periodically in libel and slander cases, either the 1824 English edition or the American editions based on it.

Although some judges and lawyers, therefore, had access to the early English editions of Holt's and Starkie's treatises on libel and slander, these texts' prevalence seems to have risen in the 1820s, once Massachusetts booksellers started to sell versions printed in the United States. Massachusetts booksellers' catalogs and surviving library catalogs show no signs of texts by either Holt or Starkie before 1826.[71] The 1818 American edition of Holt first appeared in the

[64] Otis, *Letter to the Hon. Josiah Quincy*, 13, citing a proposition from pages 30 and 31 of both the 1812 and 1816 editions but not the 1818 edition.
[65] Davis, *Practical Treatise* (1824), 467, cf. 474.
[66] Whitman, *Report of a Trial*, 11–13 The page numbers cited correspond best to these volumes, but many of them seem scrambled.
[67] *Clark v. Binney*, 19 Mass. (2 Pick.) 113, 114 (1824).
[68] *Comm. v. Blanding*, 20 Mass. (3 Pick.) 304, 307, 310, 315 (1825); Holt, *Law of Libel* (1818), 171; Starkie, *Treatise on Slander* (1813), c. 11.
[69] *Hix. v. Drury*, 22 Mass. (5 Pick.) 296, 301 (1827); Starkie, *Practical Treatise on Evidence* (1824 & 1826), 2:877–78.
[70] *Sibley v. Marsh*, 24 Mass. (7 Pick.) 38, 39 (1828); *Treatise on Slander* (1813 & 1826), 55. *Harding v. Brooks*, 22 Mass. (5 Pick.) 244, 251 (1827) probably cites the 1826 edition.
[71] Nothing by Holt or Starkie appears in the 1814 estate catalogs of the libraries of Samuel Sewall or Theophilus Parsons, although Parsons did have a book called "Digest of the Law of Libels," said to have been published in quarto form in

Harvard law library catalog in 1826,[72] and the first surviving
advertisements for Starkie that I have found date to 1827; the first
American edition was published in 1826.[73] The number of copies of
"Starkie on Slander" being advertised at an annual book wholesalers'
auction declined from 1827 to 1829, quite possibly because the book
was the 1826 edition, for which demand was dissipating.[74] Starkie's
treatise on criminal pleading was advertised in 1828.[75] The other
references to these texts in journals and library catalogs suggest that
these books were eventually drawn into the Massachusetts legal market,
with Holt being accepted first.[76] Massachusetts legal audiences, then,
read Holt's Blackstonian approach to libel law and Starkie's early
thinking, well after Starkie himself had articulated a broader
understanding of privilege in the second English editions of his libel
and evidence treatises.

London in 1763 (p. 19): *Catalogue of the Library of Sewall*; *Catalogue of the Library of Parsons*. An 1823 Boston book auction catalog lacked any law books but Blackstone's *Commentaries*: *Catalogue of Books to be Sold at Auction*.

[72] Harvard University, *Catalogue*, 1826.

[73] Joseph Cunningham advertised no libel treatises among his law books in 1827, but "Starkie on Slander" was advertised by Hilliard, Gray & Co. and Collins & Hannay at the Boston Trade Sale the same year: Cunningham, *Catalogue of Law Books*; *Boston Trade Sale*. Hilliard, Gray & Co. also advertised "Starkie on Slander" in 1828 and 1829: Cunningham, *Second Boston Trade Sale*; Cunningham, *Second Catalogue of the Third Boston Trade Sale*.

[74] Thirty copies of "Starkie on Slander" were listed in 1827, ten in 1828 and five in 1829: *Boston Trade Sale*; Cunningham, *Second Boston Trade Sale*; Cunningham, *Third Boston Trade Sale*.

[75] Cunningham, *Second Catalogue of the Second Boston Trade Sale*.

[76] The 1834 catalog of the Harvard Law Library had the 1816 second English edition of Holt but no longer the 1818 American edition. Regarding Starkie's libel and slander treatise, the 1830 second English edition and the 1832 second American edition were the first editions to appear in the Harvard Law Library catalog, in 1841: Harvard University, *Catalogue*, 1826; Harvard University, *Catalogue*, 1834; Harvard University, *Catalogue*, 1841. Hilliard, Gray & Co. of Boston advertised "Holt's Law of Libel" in 1831 and 1832 but not Starkie: *Catalogue of Law Books*, 1831 & 1832. By 1837, Boston's Little & Brown, who had bought Hilliard & Gray's stock of law books, were offering to sell and ship to other states and the "British Provinces" both the 1818 American edition of Holt and the 1832 second American edition of Starkie: Little & Brown, *Catalogue of Law Books*. In an 1834 speech made at his inauguration as Royall Professor of Law at Harvard, Simon Greenleaf recommended "Starkie on Slander" to law students for private reading, but said it was not part of the regular curriculum: "Sketch of the Law School at Cambridge." The *American Jurist*'s comprehensive, over sixty–page review of law books in 1834 did not mention any libel texts: "Characters of Law Books and Judges."

What, then, of nascent qualified privilege cases in Massachusetts, those in which circumstances and intentions arguably ought to have relieved defendants from liability? The argument was seldom made. Perhaps, as in England, people seldom sued in such situations, because they accepted the fundamental ethical insight that sometimes we all have a duty to speak, and if we do it appropriately, no legal recourse should follow. In any case, when defendants did find themselves sued, the argument was rarely made and appears to have succeeded only twice.[77] In the first of these cases, Chief Justice Parker's judgment protected the integrity of church disciplinary proceedings, while stirring into defamation law some ingredients from malicious prosecution. In the conceptually clearer second case, in 1831, Chief Justice Shaw recognized and upheld a defense of "privileged communication," either absolute or qualified by the absence of malice. Shaw's articulation of these defenses was essentially the same as Starkie's from 1830, but in Massachusetts the law bore the stamp of jurists' preoccupation with truth. Even though truth ostensibly had to be specially pleaded in civil cases until the demise of special pleading later in the 1830s, evidence of truth was nevertheless allowed to slip into claims for the qualified version of the privileged communication defense: satisfying the Massachusetts legal and ethical imagination required acknowledging that a smidgeon of truth had to be accommodated.

Privilege in Massachusetts Courts

Given the colonial history of legislative privilege and *Coffin v. Coffin*, it should be no surprise that Massachusetts judges and lawyers were suspicious of privilege claims. According to Norman Rosenberg, American petitions to legislatures – unlike their English counterparts – were vulnerable if they contained falsehoods or signs of bad faith. Rosenberg says most American courts rejected privilege claims for periodicals that "published libelous falsehoods" about political leaders or private citizens.[78] Rosenberg's assessment

[77] Depositions and other documents in case files likewise reveal no traces of the evidentiary groundwork being made for such arguments.
[78] *Best Men*, 122 (contra *Lake v. King* (1669), 1 Lev. 240, 83 E.R. 387 (K.B.), on petitions), 133.

tellingly demonstrates how the question of truth became entangled in privilege arguments in Massachusetts.

One difficulty in explaining the history of qualified privilege in Massachusetts is that lawyers, judges and court reporters were often confused and seldom took the defense seriously. Privilege-type arguments, usually not identified as such, were usually secondary to the main defense, truth. Snippets of Starkie's 1813 analysis were tossed in, and elements of the tort of malicious prosecution turned up as well.

The mid-1820s saw three civil defamation cases and one case of criminal libel in which elements of a qualified privilege defense were made on appeal in the Supreme Judicial Court, only once successfully. *Clark v. Binney*, decided in 1824, arose from an official inquiry into allegations naval agent Amos Binney had skimmed some personal profit off a naval contract.[79] Binney published a pamphlet in response, in which he described Clark's testimony in the inquiry as fanning the flames of calumny and propagating "groundless and base insinuations" against himself. His main defense was truth, which the jury rejected. His second approach, which the writer of the headnote ignored, was that the pamphlet was protected by the occasion and circumstances of its making because it was an account of the inquiry. Considering this argument, Justice Levi Lincoln Jr. noted that since the jury had found the allegations untrue, no circumstances that could have justified them appeared in the record – and anyway, only accurate accounts of judicial proceedings, with "just and fair comments upon the testimony of the witnesses," were protected. Binney's counsel, James T. Austin, also evidently argued that the public's need for information justified Binney in publishing his account. The report of the judgment is confused on this point, containing an implication that Binney himself was seeking information through his publication, which surely makes no sense. What is clear is that Lincoln rejected whatever argument Austin made and dismissed the appeal. The case thus shows elements of what would become a qualified privilege defense, but they were entangled with and undermined by the failure of the truth defense. Besides, it was probably hard to convince judges that self-serving pamphlets were dispassionate providers of information the public

---

[79] *Clark v. Binney*, 19 Mass. (2 Pick.) 113 (1824).

needed. Although Clark's counsel referred to the 1818 American edition of Holt's *Law of Libel* (on different issues), Starkie was not cited.[80]

The sole successful privilege-type defense of the mid-1820s came later in 1824, when Chief Justice Parker ruled that the circumstances protected the defendants, William and Seneca Congdon. The Congdons had lodged a complaint with Ezekiel Remington's Baptist church, asking it to discipline him over false testimony and other acts inconsistent with good Christian character.[81] This type of proceeding was vexing to courts because they had to balance protecting individual reputation with protecting churches.[82] The Congdons did not belong to Remington's church. It appears from the court file that the church ultimately excluded Remington from fellowship.

The Congdons did not plead truth; instead the argument and the trial judge's reasoning imported elements of malicious prosecution into a privilege framework. The trial judge instructed the jury that a complaint against a church member "in the way of Church discipline" was excusable in law if the person laying the complaint had probable cause, a key element in a defense to a malicious prosecution action.[83] The church's decision to uphold the complaint provided this proof. Remington could have rebutted the defense by proving that the defendants were motivated by actual malice but did not do so. The jury found for the Congdons.

The brief report of the argument on appeal suggests that Remington's counsel denied that a qualified privilege-type defense could arise on these facts. He argued that since the Congdons had not pleaded truth, Remington needed only to prove publication, from which the law would infer malice. Counsel acknowledged that there

---

[80] *Ibid.* 118. Lincoln had tried a peculiar version of a privilege defense in 1812 as well, in *Dodds v. Henry*, 9 Mass. (8 Tyng) 262 (1812). He argued unsuccessfully that a registered voter ought to be protected by a privilege if the voter impugned the honesty of an elected official – a town clerk – running an election.

[81] *Remington v. Congdon et al.*, 19 Mass. (2 Pick.) 310 (1824).

[82] See King, "Law of Slander in Early Antebellum America," 18–21.

[83] The second edition of Starkie's libel treatise was called *A Treatise on the Law of Slander and Libel, and Incidentally of Malicious Prosecutions*. This text discusses reasonable or probable cause only in the context of malicious prosecution cases, defamation by counsel in the course of legal proceedings, and slander of title, in which someone has challenged the plaintiff's title to land (1:276–91).

were "some exceptions, as in giving the character of a servant &c., but this case does not come within these exceptions."[84] According to counsel, there was thus no need for proof of actual malice, and admitting evidence on probable cause – of the church's finding of guilt – wrongly opened a backdoor to evidence of truth.

Observing that malicious prosecution was the proper remedy for improper complaints made in courts, Chief Justice Parker imported the logic of malicious prosecution into this defamation action. Since the plaintiff had voluntarily committed himself to the church and its discipline, the complaint would be protected unless Remington proved that the Congdons acted from actual malice. Because the church had sustained the complaint and no evidence of malicious motives had been introduced, the appeal was dismissed. Parker found it acceptable that some evidence of truth had found its way into the courtroom under the auspices of probable cause, despite the lack of a special plea. By contrast, Starkie's framework of duty and honest intention – based on Ellenborough's reasoning – made less space for truth and would have been more difficult for the Congdons to employ: since they and Remington belonged to different churches, they bore no duty to report his actions.[85] By focusing on intent and probable cause rather than duty, Chief Justice Parker allowed evidence of truth to wiggle into a privilege framework. He also muddied the distinction between the torts of defamation and malicious prosecution.

Parker further confused the law in *Commonwealth v. Blanding* in 1825, a judgment that outraged the legal community and prompted statutory change because of Parker's ruling that evidence of truth had been properly excluded.[86] Blanding had arranged to have printed in a newspaper an account that accused an innkeeper of being at fault in the death of a patron who had left the inn drunk. The article referred to the findings of a coroner's inquiry. When Blanding was prosecuted for

---

[84] *Remington v. Congdon et al.*, 19 Mass. (2 Pick.) 310, 312 (1824).

[85] Another emerging element of the concept of privilege – the idea that the recipient of the communication needed to have a genuine interest in receiving it – could have been noted but was not. In *Treatise on Slander* (1813), 262–63, Starkie mentioned this element in connection with *Barbaud v. Hookham* (1804), 5 Esp. 109, 170 E.R. 754 (K.B.), but neither in 1813 nor in the 1824 evidence treatise and the American versions that followed it did Starkie suggest that both interest and duty had to be present. That combination came later.

[86] *Comm. v. Blanding*, 20 Mass. (3 Pick.) 304 (1825).

libel, the trial judge excluded evidence of the inquiry, evidence that presumably would have gone to the cause of death and the truth of Blanding's account. Citing the 1818 American edition of Holt, Blanding's counsel argued that the inquiry was a judicial proceeding, and a fair statement of it, even accompanied by defamatory inferences, was not a libel. The attorney general, Perez Morton, observed in response that the report could have been protected if it had been addressed to the court of sessions when the innkeeper sought to renew his liquor license but that Blanding's newspaper account was indeed libelous.

Citing several cases as well as "Starkie on Slander" but not using the word "privilege," Parker noted that circumstances could protect defendants when certain public interests outweighed the potential harm to the character of an individual. He mentioned speech in legislatures and courts but thought these protections could be rebutted by proof of malice. In English law, though, proof of malice was only relevant for barristers; otherwise these privileges were absolute. In Massachusetts as well, *Coffin v. Coffin* in 1804 had proceeded from the assumption that legislative debate was absolutely privileged. Parker discussed the case law on privilege in an offhand, casually muddled way. He returned at the end to truth: these cases showed, he said, that the common law had other ways of protecting expression that alleviated any possible hardships flowing from the rule that truth was no defense in criminal libel cases. Parker did not bother to provide the simple reason why a coroner's inquest was, in fact, not protected by privilege: the proceedings were more like a preliminary inquiry than a trial so could bias potential jurors. The privilege framework was evidently not worth exploring even when the analysis was straightforward.

The fourth case from the mid-1820s that included privilege arguments enhanced the confusion further and demonstrated the difficulties that the entanglement of privilege and truth produced for defendants. In November 1825, a young, self-supporting schoolteacher named Sophia Bodwell sued a local notable, Benjamin Osgood, over allegations that she was unfit to teach school because of her bad sexual reputation. Osgood made these allegations in a formal complaint to the town committee that appointed public school teachers. Before laying this complaint, Osgood obtained "certificates" – probably sworn statements – from neighbors about Bodwell's conduct.

Pleading truth was risky in Massachusetts, as the defendant was taken to be admitting uttering the words and was also thought to be increasing the plaintiff's injury by repeating the allegations. Osgood's lawyers decided instead to run a privilege-type defense under the general issue. However, the trial judge, Samuel Putnam, turned Osgood's efforts against him. Putnam did not put a privilege-type defense to the jury but instead focused on intent. He told the jury that Osgood could escape liability if he proved that he had published the charges believing them true and honestly intending to cause Bodwell to be removed from the school "for a want of chastity."[87] Putnam told the jury that Osgood's failure to plead truth after gathering the certificates might suggest that he knew the complaint was false when he made it and that his intentions were in fact malicious. In a nutshell, because of Putnam's understanding of how intent operated, Osgood's failure to plead truth undermined his qualified privilege defense.[88] Losing, Osgood appealed.[89]

Osgood's lawyers argued that the jury should not have been instructed that it could infer malicious intent from Osgood's failure to plead truth, and that no action lay – regardless of malice or falsity – because this was a formal complaint properly lodged with the appropriate authority. This was a claim of absolute privilege, although that expression was not used. Upholding Putnam's decision (as the full court practically always did), Justice Samuel Wilde focused on intent and mangled the privilege argument beyond recognition.

Osgood's counsel had laid the evidentiary groundwork to argue, in effect, both that Osgood's speech was absolutely privileged and that, even if it was covered only by a qualified privilege, he had lacked malice and so should still succeed. They contended that Osgood had a duty "to his children and grandchildren, and to the preservation of public

---

[87] Rather than Osgood proving that duty justified protecting the expression and Bodwell then having to prove malice, Osgood simply had to prove good intent.
[88] This approach did not fit with the newer approach to intent (legal malice and actual malice) and was reworked in the early nineteenth century, both through the privilege framework and in the law around the truth defense.
[89] *Bodwell v. Osgood*, 20 Mass. (3 Pick.) 379 (1825).

morals" to lay the complaint. He had acted deliberately to gain information before proceeding.

The inference Putnam invited the jury to make from the absence of a truth plea placed Osgood and his lawyers in an impossible position. In Massachusetts, if the jury rejected the truth defense, the special plea was taken as evidence of actual malice. As a result, pleading truth and failing to prove it undermined a qualified privilege defense. But thanks to Putnam's logic, not pleading truth after doing some investigating also constituted evidence of malice and had the same result. Osgood's own thoroughness undermined his qualified privilege defense, whether or not he also ran the risks of a truth plea. Having investigated, truth was basically the only defense he had.

Samuel Wilde, for the full court, followed Putnam's logic. Wilde reasoned that if Osgood had been so diligent, he ought to have been willing to present the evidence that convinced him of Bodwell's sexual conduct. If the evidence was not sound enough to put to a jury, Osgood's complaint was likely unfounded and therefore libelous. Wilde reasoned that the jury must have concluded that Osgood had known the allegations against Bodwell were false. Osgood's counsel had attempted a defense that had come into English law and was articulated in Starkie's treatises, but Putnam and Wilde would not consider it.

Wilde's judgment demonstrates the impact of the intermingling and compounding uncertainties around both truth and privilege. Wilde's acknowledgment that a defendant could escape liability by proving good intentions and honest belief in the matter's truth was consistent with *Clap* in 1804 and some older case law, but as I discuss in Chapter 4, this approach was becoming doubtful: actual truth was poised to supersede good intentions plus honest belief in truth as the only available defense. In the same sentence, after a semicolon, Wilde acknowledged that at times "the occasion of the publication would prevent the legal inference of malice."[90] However, intentions and belief were at most secondary to the analysis of "the occasion of publication"

[90] *Bodwell v. Osgood*, 20 Mass. (3 Pick.) 379 (1825). This logic echoes Justice Charles Jackson's observation that a defendant could "show that he was not actuated by malice, by proving that the words were spoken privately or confidentially, or in the course of legal proceedings; and this will excuse him, whether the words were true or not": *Jackson v. Stetson*, 15 Mass. (14 Tyng) 48 (1818).

that was evolving into a qualified privilege defense. In Starkie's framework, the burden was on the plaintiff to prove actual malicious intention, not the defendant to prove the opposite. As Wilde's and Putnam's views suggest, though, there was something ethically troubling about denying that meaning well was a valid defense. They were suspicious of Osgood, who seemed to be claiming a right to make extremely damaging allegations in the town hall without being willing to attempt to prove them in court. The privilege framework's prioritization of the institutional context for the remarks was unsatisfying when what one really wanted to understand was the truth and the motives.

In *Bradley v. Heath* in 1831, the new chief justice of the Supreme Judicial Court, Lemuel Shaw, finally cleared up some of the confusion and established the defense of "privileged communication" in Massachusetts.[91] Ebenezer Heath, a Brookline selectman, had been in charge of ensuring that no one voted improperly in a town election. The pleadings suggest that Benjamin Bradley did something suspicious at the ballot box, and Heath on the spot and also possibly afterward announced that Bradley had put in two votes for one office. Bradley sued Heath for slander. At trial in Supreme Judicial Court before Samuel Putnam, Heath did not enter a special plea of truth. Bradley proved the speaking of the words; Heath proved that he had borne a duty to scrutinize the voting and that Bradley's conduct had attracted his suspicion. Putnam instructed the jurors that if they believed that Bradley's conduct had induced Heath to say what he had said, then Heath had spoken without malice and they should find for him, which they did. Bradley appealed.

Bradley's counsel argued that since truth had not been specially pleaded, Putnam should have excluded the evidence about Bradley's conduct at the ballot box, because it tended to show Heath's words to be true. Bradley's counsel acknowledged that circumstances could protect defamatory expressions but argued that this case did not fall within the recognized categories.

Dismissing the appeal, Shaw deemed Heath's words a "privileged communication." Unlike Lincoln, Parker, Wilde and Putnam, he carefully identified principles that could protect expression:

[91] *Bradley v. Heath*, 29 Mass. (12 Pick.) 163 (1831).

Where words imputing misconduct to another are spoken by one having a duty to perform, and the words are spoken in good faith, and in the belief that it comes within the discharge of that duty, or where they are spoken in good faith, to those who have an interest in the communication, and a right to know and act upon the facts stated, no presumption of malice arises from the speaking of the words; and therefore no action can be maintained in such cases, without proof of express malice. If the occasion is used merely as a means of enabling the party uttering the slander to indulge his malice, and not in good faith to perform a duty or make a communication useful and beneficial to others, the occasion will furnish no excuse.[92]

Either the speaker's duty or the audience's interest could render the communication privileged and rebuttable by proof of actual, "express" malice. Shaw reasoned that Heath had borne a duty to notify the assembled citizens at the election if he saw someone put in two ballots, so that the matter could be investigated and rectified. The voters had a legitimate interest in receiving this information from Heath, as they had a real interest in the conduct of the election. Heath's assertion was therefore a privileged communication. A bit of evidence of truth could slip in, because the defendant's conduct could legitimately be introduced (but of course this evidence did not have to go so far as to show that Bradley submitted two ballots – perhaps he just turned his back or seemed to fumble the papers unnecessarily).

Thus far the analysis sounds like Starkie's. The authorities cited by Heath's counsel and by Shaw himself suggest that Shaw was combining the ruling in an 1825 English case, *Bromage v. Prosser*, with threads Starkie had articulated in his 1826 evidence treatise and in his 1813 slander treatise or one of its American offspring. *Bromage v. Prosser* elaborated Starkie's understanding of the two different kinds of intent that operated in defamation cases, with the shifting burden of proof, and rejected the trial judge's simpler approach, which resembled that of Putnam and Wilde in *Bodwell v. Osgood*.[93] Shaw also, however,

---

[92] *Ibid.* 164–65.
[93] *Bromage v. Prosser* (1825), 4 B. & C. 247, 107 E.R. 1051 (K.B.). The defendant, based on a conversation with another person about the reliability of the plaintiff bankers' notes, had told yet another person that the bankers had defaulted on some payments. Justice Bayley overruled the trial judge's reasoning on intent. The trial judge told the jury that if the defendant had not spoken from actual ill will, he should escape liability. The plaintiff applied for a new trial, arguing that since the occasion did not justify the speaking of the words, malice was to be inferred from the

followed Parker in reiterating that probable cause could play a role in a privileged communication defense, as it had in *Remington v. Condon*, when an allegation had been laid before an authority. Acknowledging that a bit of evidence of truth could thus slip in, Shaw assured his readers that nevertheless normally truth had to be specially pleaded.[94] Probable or reasonable cause, therefore, which played a necessary role in malicious prosecution (the plaintiff proving its absence), could sometimes be part of a defense to a slander or libel case as well.

One more privilege argument was made at a sentencing hearing in 1835 on facts that show the considerable difficulties that arose from the law's intense preoccupation with truth. A Congregationalist temperance reformer named George Cheever had been convicted of defamatory libel for publishing a temperance tale about a Unitarian deacon in Salem who employed demons to work in his rum distillery. A real Salem Unitarian deacon named John Stone saw himself in the story. Cheever, who represented himself, quoted Starkie's 1824 evidence treatise, arguing that the occasion and circumstances of publication afforded a prima facie presumption that he intended not to disparage Stone but to discharge a duty to society, a presumption that he evidently thought should mitigate his punishment.[95] Cheever argued that the evil of intemperance was propagating wildly, that he had the opportunity to combat it, and that in intending to do so he had entirely lacked actual malice, circumstances that rendered his tale

---

defendant's uttering of defamatory allegations, and his actual intentions, good or malicious, were irrelevant. Bayley explained that legal malice simply meant "a wrongful act, done intentionally, without just cause or excuse." This malice differed from "malice in fact," that is, actual ill will. In many cases legal malice was evident from the fact of uttering the defamatory words. The plaintiff would have to prove actual malice "in actions for such slander as is primâ facie excusable on account of the cause of speaking or writing it, as in the case of servant's [sic] characters, confidential advice, or communications to persons who ask it, or have a right to expect it." Bayley ordered a new trial so that the qualified privilege defense could be considered.

[94] Evidence of truth or falsity also crept into English cases against masters who gave unfavorable references for servants. However, it was the plaintiff servant who had to prove falsity (and actual malice), rather than the master who had to prove truth. See *Rogers v. Clifton* (1803), 3 Box. & Pul. 587, 127 E.R. 317 (C.P.); Starkie, *Practical Treatise on Evidence* (1833), 2:462; Starkie, *Treatise on Slander* (1830), 1:293–94.

[95] Cheever, *Defence in Abatement*, 14–16. Cf. Starkie, *Practical Treatise on Evidence* (1824), 2:863.

privileged, even if aspects of the life of the central character did bear a striking resemblance to the life of John Stone.[96]

Perhaps if Cheever had consulted the second London edition of Starkie's evidence treatise or the 1834 American edition based on it, he would have discovered a useful parallel to his own circumstances in an evocative footnote. A man named Greenwood sued a clergyman over a sermon that included a story, purportedly from a book of martyrs, "that one Greenwood, being a perjured person and a great persecutor, had great plagues inflicted on him, and died by the hand of God." The Greenwood listening in his pew felt defamed and asserted that "in truth he never was so plagued." The trial judge told the jury that the clergyman would not be liable over a story delivered with no intention to slander, so the suit failed.[97] John Stone and Greenwood evidently faced similar situations with outspoken clergymen. Nonetheless, there is no sign that the privilege argument helped Cheever at all: Shaw sentenced him to a month in jail and costs of prosecution and required him to post a bond with sureties for two years of good behavior.

In Massachusetts, then, the doctrine of privileged communication had arrived by 1831 through *Coffin v. Coffin*, *Remington v. Congdon* and *Bradley v. Heath*. Unless plaintiffs could prove defendants' actual malice, defendants would be protected for assertions made under circumstances that imposed a legal or moral duty on them, or that they made in justly pursuing their own interests, or that they made to a person who had an appropriate interest in receiving the communications. Even though the defense would be raised under the general issue, under cover of probable cause, on the right facts, a defendant could lead some evidence of truth. Although privilege claims were possible in Massachusetts, truth was never forgotten.

Thomas Starkie's Qualified Privilege Defense

In the second edition of his slander and libel treatise, published in 1830, Thomas Starkie articulated an expansive argument for the existence of a defense of qualified privilege that would protect

---

[96] Cheever, *Defence in Abatement*, 17–21.
[97] Starkie, *Practical Treatise on Evidence* (1833), 2:463, note (d).

honest, though possibly mistaken, expression. The dedication – to the memory of Lord Ellenborough – was less ironic and fawning that it may seem. Ellenborough – originally Edward Law – defended Warren Hastings in his impeachment proceedings, prosecuted treason and sedition cases in the 1790s, and became attorney general in 1801. Trained as a special pleader, Law fell out with the Whigs over his opposition to war with France in the 1790s and became more conservative as he aged.[98] He was harsh in criminal libel proceedings, including two of William Hone's for blasphemy in 1817.[99] However, Ellenborough also decided key civil cases, such as *Dunman v. Bigg*, brought by the beer dealer. In *Burdett v. Abbot*, Ellenborough acknowledged that King's Bench could occasionally make determinations about parliamentary privilege.

Starkie's 1830 text began with a deeply considered introductory "Preliminary Discourse," more than 160 pages long in which he explored the acceptable limits on expression. Through a sober display of learning, references to Roman and civil law, great (even ponderous) length, and a reassuringly moderate tone, Starkie tethered his argument for the law's liberalization firmly within legal and constitutional tradition. The great challenge was to foster the press's enormous capacity for good without also protecting its harmful propensities. Fully acknowledging the importance of individual character, Starkie emphasized the constitutional importance of free expression. Ultimately he assured his readers that society would be more stable with a free press and broad but bounded freedom of expression for all classes than it would be under a system that repressed dissent until it burst into violence. Governance would be more responsible and honorable if those with power knew they were being watched by a literate public who would expose bad behavior.

Starkie canvassed the history of laws about speech in other times and places. He considered the informational needs of business, and he reviewed key principles: justifications for compensation, the place of truth, and – importantly – when and why utterances that might be defamatory and even false nevertheless deserved protection. Asking hypothetically whether it would be better to permit all true

---

[98] Lobban, "Law, Edward." Starkie's first edition was also dedicated to Ellenborough.
[99] See Thomas, *Long Time Burning*, 156–59.

communications to be published regardless of damage to character or, on the other hand, to criminalize the publication of all defamation, true or false, Starkie opted for the first option – but he argued that the law contained wise compromises that reduced the harm associated with either of these stark choices. One such compromise was criminalizing written, but not most oral, defamatory communications. Another was allowing the circumstances of the communication and the parties' interests to provide a shield against liability. Starkie concluded by reminding his readers that the common law's great strength lay in its rootedness in reason and "convenience." Citing the powerful authority of Lord Coke, Starkie urged them to consider how the law served society, to preserve precedent without blindly applying it. English jurisprudence, he concluded reassuringly, was founded on just and equitable principles, informed by a spirit of moderation and liberality, which to a significant degree made the people the guardians of their own liberties. These extensive liberties supported public safety and promoted the community's moral and political interests.

Starkie's second edition provided a principled interpretive framework for balancing the harms of slander and libel against freedom of expression and the press. Like the first, this edition was arranged around the case to be made by each side. The second edition shifted the analytical framework, however. The first edition began with an analysis of the plaintiff's loss and an explanation of the kinds of losses for slander that did not require proof of damage. The second edition stepped back analytically, emphasizing that the civil action lay for willful communications made without lawful justification or excuse. Starkie in 1830 thus positioned the nature of the communication and the circumstances around its making as foundational to the analytical framework.[100]

The footnotes to Starkie's Preliminary Discourse contain a one-sided conversation with de Lolme's *Constitution of England* and John Borthwick's "very able and excellent work" on libel and slander in Scotland, published in Edinburgh and London in 1826. Borthwick was more guarded and conservative than Starkie about the value of free expression, but nevertheless, as Paul Mitchell has

---

[100] Starkie, *Treatise on Slander* (1830), 1:2–6.

observed, Borthwick – who drew on Holt and on Starkie's first edition – influenced Starkie. It seems to have been Borthwick who first made extensive use of the word "privileged" as an umbrella term for defenses arising when people were duty-bound to comment on others' characters. These situations, Borthwick said, gave the defendant

the advantage incident to cases which are termed *privileged*, because, when an action is brought for language employed by individuals so placed, the law affords the benefit of a presumption in their favor, which, in some cases, will of itself exclude the action, and in other cases also be effectual, though, in the latter class of cases, it may be removed by a proof of malice adduced by the complainer.[101]

Classifying privilege cases, and footnoting lightly, Borthwick began with the absolute cases: parliamentary debate, judges' and magistrates' speech from the bench, expressions of witnesses testifying in court, and "impartial and correct accounts of the proceedings in Parliament, or in the courts of justice," a privilege that Borthwick thought was too broad in England and rightly narrower in Scotland. He then moved on to "cases in which the defender's plea of privilege may be set aside by proof that he has acted maliciously." Unusually, the first privilege of this type was drawn from Blackstone: Borthwick thought barristers were protected for words relevant to the cause and grounded in their clients' instructions, even if these amounted to groundless aspersions on character; but if they propounded their own untruths or spewed irrelevant falsities, even on their clients' instructions, they were liable.[102]

Borthwick's second privilege rebuttable by proof of malice was for litigants who made allegations – even heated and partial ones – in support of their causes, and, to a lesser extent, for witnesses. In English law, the allegations underlying unsuccessful criminal prosecutions could be actionable through the tort of malicious prosecution. Massachusetts records, however, disclose malicious prosecution actions over paternity claims and proceedings for violating liquor statutes; there may have been others. Borthwick may

[101] *Ibid.* xliii; Mitchell, *Making of the Modern Law of Defamation*, 152–53; Borthwick, *Treatise on the Law of Libel and Slander*, 198.
[102] *Treatise on the Law of Libel and Slander*, 198–214, citing *Commentaries* 3:29.

well have drawn Starkie's attention to the overlap in these causes of action, since in the second edition, but not the first, Starkie outlined the policy problems that would arise from allowing anyone who had been unsuccessfully prosecuted to retaliate through a libel action. He explained that malicious prosecution required the plaintiff to prove both the defendant's malice and lack of a probable or reasonable cause for the prosecution.[103]

Borthwick's third kind of privilege rebuttable by proof of malice was for character references, and his fourth was for literary and theatrical criticism. His fifth arose from the interest that either the defendant or the person the defendant addressed had in learning of the defamatory matter, a diverse category of privilege that covered reports to those who needed to know of the malfeasance of agents, employees, parishioners, clergy and the perpetrators of crimes. Borthwick led off this discussion by referring to Lord Ellenborough's 1808 decisions in *McDougal v. Claridge* and *Dunman v. Bigg*, footnoting Starkie's 1813 slander and libel treatise as well. Starkie in 1813 had noted that "interest" was a basis for a qualified privilege defense; Borthwick elaborated on this discussion through his discussion of Scottish cases, although the law he cited circumscribed privilege (in ways that protected the powerful) far more than Starkie would in 1830. Indeed, Borthwick argued that sometimes privilege would not be enough: the Scottish "defender" would also have to plead and prove the truth of the matter. In Scottish law, Borthwick said, the truth strengthened the qualified privilege, and, on its own, either might fail to eliminate liability, although truth by itself could mitigate damages or reduce the fine in criminal cases. Starkie completely severed truth and falsity from privilege.[104]

More expansively than Borthwick, Starkie articulated broadly protective principles at the beginning of his chapter on "malice in fact." This actual ill will had to be proven by the plaintiff whenever "the author of the alleged mischief acted in the discharge of any public or private duty, whether legal or moral, which the ordinary exigencies of society, or his own private interest, or even that of another called

---

[103] Starkie, *Treatise on Slander* (1830), 1:276–91.
[104] Starkie, *Treatise on Slander* (1813), 241 (contra Mitchell, *Making of the Modern Law of Defamation*, 152–53); Borthwick, *Treatise on the Law of Libel and Slander*, 239–40, 244, 251–56.

upon him to perform." Thus were ordinary communicative needs
balanced against the risk of wanton slander that an absolute privilege
might otherwise protect. Starkie analyzed the character reference cases
and the protection of literary criticism. He reasoned that these cases
showed a general principle that occasion could be a defense, absent
malice, when a public duty required it. Interest – one's own or
another's – could operate similarly. Confidential communications
supposed by the speaker to be true, and admonitions or advice were
therefore protected.[105] Unlike Borthwick – and Chief Justice Shaw in
Massachusetts – Starkie made no room for proof of truth in his
qualified privilege defense, unless it slipped in under the guise of
occasion, a possibility he did not acknowledge. Defendants
frequently adduced evidence of the circumstances under which they
made their problematic allegations, but most plaintiffs, in rebuttal,
were confined to proving malice or unnecessarily broad publication.
Except for the character reference cases, the truth or falsity of the
allegations would have been collateral and not addressed unless it
was specially pleaded.

Borthwick's categories were useful, but Starkie was more
sympathetic to the press and more concerned with the introduction
of evidence – with who had to prove what. Starkie was also precise
about tricky concepts like malice and intent. The tools Starkie devised
for the defense of the press were, therefore, fashioned from the raw
materials of the common law, rather than from a principled
commitment to truth and republican government, the preoccupations
of American legal and constitutional thinkers. Starkie reiterated his
qualified privilege framework in the second edition of his evidence
treatise in 1833, and it was further recognized in English law in
1834.[106] Although this defense migrated to Massachusetts, it was
overshadowed by the truth defense, with elements of the qualified
privilege analysis sometimes mustered to support the argument that
what really should save a defendant was honest belief in truth and not
only truth itself.[107] Norman Rosenberg has judged it ironic that by the
1840s, American lawyers advocating for greater freedom of the press

[105] *Treatise on Slander* (1830), 1:292–93, 315, 320–21.
[106] Starkie, *Practical Treatise on Evidence* (1833), 2:462; *Toogood v. Spyring* (1834), 1
C. M. & R. 181, 149 E.R. 1044 (Exch.).
[107] See discussion of the prosecution of David Lee Child in Chapter 4.

were looking to English law and American courts were rejecting qualified privilege defenses.[108]

The development of the qualified privilege defense, therefore, took place incrementally over a couple of decades, out of the view of more flamboyant legal reformers like Henry Brougham and Sir Francis Burdett (not to mention Jeremy Bentham), who focused on the abuses made possible by English criminal procedure, the corruption of juries, and the lack of protection for truth in English libel law.[109] The word "privilege" was slippery and perhaps too Tory-sounding to be much use in Massachusetts. However this conservative resonance may well have been exactly what made the term useful for Starkie in advancing a more protective framework for expression. In Halifax in 1835 Joseph Howe made qualified privilege an important component of his defense when he faced seditious libel proceedings over a letter in the *Novascotian* that criticized local government. The rights of the press were asserted alongside contention about political institutions. As it turned out, in Nova Scotia the judicial acceptance of privilege was undermined more by a shortage of precedent than by too much.

English Libel Law in Nova Scotia

Prosecutions for libel were far less common in Nova Scotia than in Massachusetts in the 1820s and 1830s.[110] In the Nova Scotia cases local concerns were filtered through English law and legal debates, sometimes with a sprinkling of American thought. Prosecuting for seditious libel, for example, was contentious but not anathema in Nova Scotia.[111] Truth was no defense, but the jury and the *ex officio* information were discussed, as was the liability of those who

---

[108] *Best Men*, 132–33, 160.
[109] See Brougham, "Liberty of the Press" and Burdett, "Speech of Sir Francis Burdett."
[110] My Massachusetts sample – reported cases, the full run of cases in Supreme Judicial Court in two counties (Suffolk and Worcester), selected years in Common Pleas in those counties, and other cases I found through newspapers and pamphlets – disclosed prosecutions on thirty-three indictments. My Nova Scotia research disclosed five, all in Halifax. It is unlikely that more than perhaps one or two lurk in the records of other counties or districts or have been lost. Massachusetts's population was about five times Nova Scotia's.
[111] On seditious libel prosecutions associated with the American Revolution, see Cahill, "Sedition Trial of Timothy Houghton"; Cahill, "Treason of the Merchants"; and Clarke and Phillips, "Rebellion and Repression."

innocently reprinted defamatory texts, usually news items. In this environment, a place could be made for privilege.

In the 1820s and 1830s, Nova Scotia saw two prosecutions for seditious libel and one for a defamatory libel.[112] Cases in New Brunswick and PEI also drew illuminating commentary. Seditious libel proceedings had fallen into disrepute in the United States after the partisan trials of the late 1790s and early 1800s. The British seditious libel trials of the late eighteenth and early nineteenth centuries had likewise been highly controversial. Echoes of American and English concerns were heard in the Nova Scotian cases, unsurprisingly since not only did news circulate but many of the senior members of the legal profession had been trained in Britain or Massachusetts.[113]

Criminalizing sedition, like criminalizing blasphemy and obscenity, meant assuming that political stability could be threatened by assertions that questioned the people's confidence in fundamental institutions and beliefs. On April 19, 1820, the *Nova-Scotia Royal Gazette* reported on the trial of a young man named William Wilkie for "a malicious and scandalous libel, aspersing almost all the constituted authorities in this Country."[114] The screed in question, *A Letter to the People of Halifax*, published early in 1820 and sold cheaply, attributed financial and other kinds of mismanagement – and graft – to the public officers at most of the public institutions in the city: the police office, the magistracy, the workhouse, the poorhouse, the jail, the court of commissioners, a road commissioner, the judiciary,

---

[112] Thomas Forrester was prosecuted in 1824 for a criminal defamatory libel for a letter he wrote under an assumed name to certain London insurance underwriters, in which he alleged that the Halifax-based consignees, auctioneers and surveyors who assessed and then put up for auction a cargo of shipped goods that had been damaged in a storm were conspiring to defraud the underwriters. With Archibald prosecuting, Forrester was convicted and fined £100, but the accounts are too sparse for any observations about arguments made in the case. See Sutherland, "Forrester, Thomas"; Beck, "Archibald, Samuel George William"; Longworth, *Life of S.G.W. Archibald*, 32–35. There was also one obscene libel case, discussed in Chapter 5, and one true bill for libel in Yarmouth, but it seems not to have gone to trial.

[113] On the judiciary, see Greco, "Superior Court Judiciary," 47–55. S.G.W. Archibald was educated in Massachusetts and then apprenticed to Simon Bradstreet Robie: Lynch, "Early Reminiscences," 199. Younger members were largely training locally. See Moody, "Crawley, Edmund Albern"; Bell, "Paths to the Law," 37–39.

[114] "Supreme Court," *Royal Gazette* (Halifax), April 19, 1820.

special juries, the lieutenant governor's council, the assembly, the militia and physicians, all in twenty-one pages. Local chronicler Thomas Akins, writing in 1839, says the proceedings were viewed as a tyrannical and cruel response to a "very paltry offence" committed by a lesser member of a respectable family. Wilkie's views of Halifax's municipal governance were not new, but his language offended.[115]

Wilkie was prosecuted on an indictment found by the grand jury, not on an *ex officio* information issued by the attorney general. The availability of this controversial and oppressive legal weapon in Nova Scotia is a matter of dispute. It was used in 1831 in New Brunswick, but in the volume of the *Epitome of the Laws of Nova-Scotia* published in 1833, Beamish Murdoch doubted its availability. In 1835 S.G.W. Archibald, as attorney general, suggested it was a prosecutorial option.[116]

How aware Nova Scotians were of the English controversies over the *ex officio* information and other aspects of the law and procedure around libel is difficult to determine, since awareness may have come through idiosyncratic channels, such as education in England, letters and travels. Reports of notable trials were sometimes copied into Nova Scotian newspapers, and the *Edinburgh Review* published regular, critical, strongly Whig commentary on parliamentary reform, the abolition of slavery in the Empire, and legal and constitutional controversies. C. Duncan Rice has called this journal "the most distinguished periodical of its time, in any language." The *Review* was being published in New York as well as London and Edinburgh by about 1812, and by 1813 an American edition was being sold in major cities along the American eastern seaboard. In 1816 Henry Brougham – a founder of the *Review* and member of the House of Commons – published an extensive critique of libel law which included a scathing attack on the *ex officio* information.[117]

---

115 Akins, *History of Halifax City*, 195. See also Cahill, "Sedition in Nova Scotia: R. v. *Wilkie*."
116 "Case of Libel," *Novascotian* (Halifax), January 27, 1831; Murdoch, *Epitome of the Laws of Nova-Scotia*, 4:181–82; "Supreme Court. Hilary Term. The King vs. Joseph Howe. Trial before the Chief Justice and a Special Jury, for a Libel on the Magistrates of Halifax," *Novascotian* (Halifax), March 12, 1835.
117 Rice, "Enlightenment, Evangelism, and Economics," 127; Brougham, "Liberty of the Press." *Comm. v. Blanding*, 20 Mass. (3 Pick.) 304, 307, 309 (1825) cites Brougham's review.

The Halifax *Royal Gazette* seemed at least somewhat familiar with
English criticisms but confident that Wilkie was treated justly. The
paper praised the moderate comments of Crown prosecutor S.G.W.
Archibald (not yet either Speaker of the assembly or attorney general)
and his reflections on the dangers of Wilkie's critique which
demonstrated a novel "licentious spirit." The British attorney
general's control over the selection of trial jurors was attracting
much criticism, but Wilkie could challenge any jurors he pleased.[118]
The law officers probably judged the *ex officio* information
unnecessary – and it should have offended a Massachusetts-trained
lawyer – but in any case, they avoided it in *Wilkie* and again in *Howe*
in 1835.[119] The *Gazette* assured its readers that Wilkie had been
permitted to defend himself, that he acknowledged his authorship
of the libel, and that his commentary had been even more offensive
than the original pamphlet. The "venerable Chief Justice," Sampson
Salter Blowers, charged the jury on the "shameful" publication's
dangers but told them that if they believed in good conscience that
Wilkie's intention was innocent and aimed at the public good, they
should acquit him. Barry Cahill assesses Blowers's charge as applying
Fox's Libel Act, which left to the jury not only the question of
publication (which was admitted) but also the finding of
libelousness and the ultimate verdict. Blowers's references to
innocent intent and public good, though, probably reflect his
Massachusetts training and ongoing familiarity with legal

---

[118] "Supreme Court," *Royal Gazette* (Halifax), April 19, 1820.
[119] One puzzle is why Wilkie was prosecuted by Archibald, rather than by either
Richard John Uniacke, the attorney general, or Simon Bradstreet Robie, the solicitor
general. Hypotheses both principled and personal suggest themselves. Robie, the
solicitor general, was Speaker of the assembly, which Wilkie attacked; defending it
might have been awkward. Moreover, Robie may have disapproved of the prosecution on principle: around this time Lieutenant Governor Lord Dalhousie accused
Robie of holding Yankee principles and being disposed to disregard the Crown's
prerogative rights. Uniacke was on the lieutenant governor's council, which Wilkie
also attacked. Uniacke had also lost out to John Albro as deputy grand master of the
local freemasons, and Albro, formerly a tanner and butcher but now a successful
merchant, was the target of particular opprobrium in Wilkie's pamphlet.
Prosecuting Wilkie might have meant defending Albro, which perhaps lacked appeal
for Uniacke. See Wilkie, *Letter to the People of Halifax*, 18–19; Cahill, "Sedition in
Nova Scotia: *R. v. Wilkie*," 472; Bunting, *History of St. John's Lodge*, 350; Harland-
Jacobs, *Builders of Empire*, 177–80; Dunlop, "Albro, John"; Macdonald, *Annals
North British Society*, 132.

developments in that state.[120] Twelve years earlier, the Massachusetts Supreme Judicial Court had ruled that evidence of truth could be led in some political cases, on the ground that knowing the allegation's truth or falsity would help the jury determine criminal intent. Nevertheless, the jury quickly convicted Wilkie, and Blowers sentenced him to two years at hard labor but added that he could apply after a year to the lieutenant governor for the remission of the second half of his sentence.[121] The *Gazette* was impressed with the justness, moderation and lenity of the trial, which nonetheless would show the licentious and unruly that their efforts to disturb the peace would come to nothing.

English approaches to privilege, American rhetoric around truth, and the murky common law on second publication all appeared in the arguments S.G.W. Archibald and Charles R. Fairbanks made, as they defended Anthony Henry Holland in an unreported civil case from 1821. Holland was sued by Simon Fraser, a Scottish immigration promoter who arranged the transportation of Scots pushed off their farms who sought new opportunities in Nova Scotia. Fraser had arranged a schooner to take a load of immigrants from the Inverness area to Pictou. The ship was provisioned and sailed. After a week or so, it had trouble in high seas and put back into port. A British officer, acting pursuant to a statute meant to protect passengers like Fraser's, examined the provisions and found them wholly inadequate and suspiciously arranged. For example, a cask that purported to be filled with bread had bread only at the ends, with rotten potatoes and straw in the middle. Rotten fish hid between beef and pork. Since Fraser himself had already left for Nova Scotia on a different ship, the ship's owner had to pay for proper provisions before the ship sailed. Once it arrived in Pictou, the ship's master, Primrose Smith, went before a Pictou magistrate, Robert Patterson, and swore an affidavit describing the events, ostensibly to warn other immigrants but

[120] See *Comm. v. Clap*, 4 Mass. (3 Tyng) 163, 169 (1808). William H. Laurence's review of lawyer William Young's library makes it clear that the legal texts available in Nova Scotia in the early decades of the nineteenth century were published on both sides of the Atlantic and also included continental writings: Laurence, "Acquiring the Law."

[121] Cahill, "Sedition in Nova Scotia: *R. v. Wilkie*," 486. Cahill thinks Wilkie was probably released upon agreeing to leave Nova Scotia.

possibly also to deflect his own legal risk.[122] John Howe Jr. printed the affidavit in the *Halifax Journal*. Beneath the text, Howe asked the public to let Fraser reply before judging him, which he shortly did. Anthony Holland, however, copied the affidavit from the *Journal* directly into the *Acadian Recorder* without Fraser's rejoinder. Fraser sued Holland and the magistrate, but not Howe, for libel. The case was tried before a special jury, and Holland covered it in the *Recorder*.[123]

Through this period, Archibald regularly represented Holland in court on various matters. In this case, one (dubious) defense was that Holland's publication was protected because it was a correct account of judicial proceedings. English law by 1811 was not yet completely clear that reports of pre-trial legal proceedings were not privileged because of their tendency to prejudice a jury. Indeed, commentary from a few years later suggests that uncertainty remained about liability over true reports of pre-trial proceedings and even trials in superior courts. Smith's affidavit represented only one side's view of the situation on the ship, but evidently the argument seemed worth a try.[124]

Archibald and Fairbanks also made what was in effect a qualified privilege defense, although they did not use that term. They pleaded that Holland should be absolved of liability because he was

accustomed and authorized to print and publish such articles of foreign and domestic intelligence, and such information on subjects of general and public interest and such true and correct accounts of Judicial proceedings and investigations as come to the knowledge of the said Anthony H. Holland and were and are proper to be published and made known to the public.

The occasion and circumstances, together with the interest people had in news, justified the publication, as long as Fraser did not prove actual malice. The argument was innovative: nothing in Starkie's first edition or the case law it cited would have extended this kind of defense to newspapers.

---

[122] See also Campey, *After the Hector*, 55–57, 251; Patterson, *History of Pictou*, 242–43; Bumsted, *People's Clearance*, 114.

[123] "The Press," *Acadian Recorder* (Halifax), May 5, 1821; Letter to the editor, *Acadian Recorder* (Halifax), April 13, 1822.

[124] *R. v. Fischer* (1811), 2 Camp. 563, 170 E.R. 1253 (K.B.), per Ellenborough C.J.; Letter to the editor, *Colonial Patriot* (Pictou), June 4, 1828.

Representing Fraser, James W. Johnston, John George Marshall, William Hill and William Sawers sought to prove Holland's malice by contrasting his actions to John Howe's. Howe testified that he had published the article to encourage would-be immigrants to investigate the provisioning for their journeys. He had thought he owed Fraser the opportunity to respond. If he had not heard from Fraser he would have published the affidavit, but he would not have copied it if Holland had published it first. He thought Holland should have published Fraser's response. Archibald, however, asserted that Holland had been duty-bound to publish a well-merited caution to ship owners and emigrants in the form of this honest man's justly indignant affidavit. The silver-tongued Archibald hoped the article had been read in English and Gaelic, not only in Nova Scotia, "but also in the Highland hills, that the echo of it had sounded round their mountains and their lakes to warn those desirous of emigrating against the frauds of the like kind in future."

Archibald and Fairbanks also pleaded that Holland could legally copy an article that had been published elsewhere, as long as he lacked malice. The liability of second publishers of defamatory allegations was a vexing topic during this period of multiplying newspapers. Starkie in 1813 explained that a person repeating a slanderous statement could be justified if, at the time he spoke, he named his source and repeated the words verbatim. The doctrine originated in a Star Chamber case for *scandalum magnatum*. Six men stood charged with propagating two different "false and horrible Scandals." Each blamed someone else for originating the rumor. All were fined, but those at the beginning of each chain, who were unable to pin blame on some other identifiable person, paid the largest fines.[125]

The rule probably makes sense in its context, since the purpose of *scandalum magnatum* was to discourage the circulation of false rumors about the mighty. It fit awkwardly with defamation law, however, which aimed to compensate those whose reputations had been besmirched. Deep tensions ran below the surface of the ensuing case law: should libels be treated like slander? Was the essence of the wrong of slander the defendant's actual malice or the fact of publishing a false – or simply

---

[125] Starkie, *Treatise on Slander* (1813), 249; *The Earl of Northampton's Case* (1612), 12 Co. Rep. 132, 77 E.R. 1407 (Star Chamber).

injurious – report?[126] Was the plea of repetition actually a kind of plea of justification by truth?[127] Starkie considered the basis for the republication defense doubtful. One possible rationale was that it was better to identify and sue the original speaker, but of course sometimes that is impossible and repeating a rumor tends to strengthen it. Starkie rationalized the rule by postulating a rather unlikely scenario that allowed him to frame the defense in terms of malice: the person repeating the rumor could have friendly motives and be repeating it in order to give the defamed person an action. The rule, Starkie thought, should therefore be understood as creating a prima facie presumption in the defendant's favor, which could be rebutted by evidence of actual malice. A defendant forfeited the protection of the rule by increasing the injury by using "more forcible terms, or by reducing the slander to writing or print."[128]

This defense, in Starkie's reading and on the English authorities, pertained to slander, not libel, so should not have helped Holland.[129] The Scottish writer Borthwick concurred with Starkie that translating

---

[126] Counsel argued this point in *Davis v. Lewis* (1796), 7 T.R. 17, 1 B. & P. 529, 101 E. R. 832 (K.B.).

[127] The language of justification on the basis of truth runs through the old cases but is difficult to understand. The cases do not seem to suggest that it was the truth of the hearsay statement "A said X about B" that was at issue – there was never a suggestion that the speaking of the words was the proposition whose truth was relevant but only, ever, the truth of the assertion about B. The injury to B's reputation needed a remedy, whether or not it was true that A had defamed B first. My best guess, therefore, is that the logic underlying this defense is that if the defendant named the original speaker when uttering the defamatory remarks, the plaintiff was thereby given the knowledge necessary to sue both speakers. The original speaker then had the opportunity to enter a truth defense. If the plaintiff failed to take the opportunity to sue the original speaker, then the second speaker, perhaps, was rightly absolved of liability. Kenyon LJ explained the rule in these terms in *Davis v. Lewis* (1796), 7 T.R. 17, 1 B. & P. 529, 101 E.R. 832, 833 (K.B.). However, the possibility that the defendant was motivated by malice in repeating the defamatory allegation complicated this logic, since jurists also said that malice was the essence of the wrong. Starkie's bifurcation of malice into legal malice (intent to perform the injurious act) and actual malice (ill will toward the plaintiff) caused him, I think, to frame this rule as he did, as raising a rebuttable inference in the defendant's favor.

[128] Starkie, *Treatise on Slander* (1813), 249–53.

[129] The thread of almost all of the cases is slander: see *Crawford v. Middleton* (1685), 1 Keb. 377, 83 E.R. 1004 (K.B.); *Davis v. Lewis* (1796), 7 T.R. 17, 1 B. & P. 529, 101 E. R. 832 (K.B.); *Woolnoth v. Meadows* (1804), 5 East 463, 102 E.R. 1148 (K.B.). *Maitland v. Goldney* (1802), 2 East 426, 102 E.R. 431 (K.B.) was actually a libel case, and while the argument was made that this defense was therefore inapplicable, the judges preferred to ground their rejection of the defense on the lack of specificity in the defendant's pleadings. The judges agreed that the defendants, in repeating the slander,

oral rumor into printed form rendered the printer liable, even if he disclosed his source. Borthwick pointed out, however, that in Scottish law printers had been allowed to escape liability by giving up the author and showing that they had published the libelous text on the author's orders. Borthwick observed that when the English radical William Cobbett was convicted of publishing a certain letter, "he was not called up for judgment, 'having redeemed himself by giving up the author of the libel.'" Starkie, in treating this issue in the 1830 edition of his slander and libel treatise, ignored these cases and argued that the defense was of very limited application. He acknowledged that the *scandalum magnatum* statutes demanded imprisoning the propagators of these rumors until they revealed the authors. He fell back on his earlier reasoning, suggesting that a person who repeated slander in order to allow the innocent defamed person to sue was not liable.[130]

Despite the legal uncertainty, however, the defense was pleaded at least once in Massachusetts in the early nineteenth century, and printers seem to have enjoyed the benefit of the defense or practices derived from it.[131] The second publisher does not even seem to have had to identify the source at the moment of publication. The case that mentions this practice was related by Boston's municipal court judge Peter Oxenbridge Thacher in 1836. Thacher explained that in 1801, one John Lillie, the editor of a Boston newspaper, was convicted of a libel against Chief Justice Dana. Lillie appealed to the whole court, arguing that the indictment was flawed. His appeal was postponed until February 1802, "to give the defendant an opportunity to divulge the author." At that term, Lillie produced the original writing "and an indictment was returned against John Vinall, Esq. as the author." Then Vinall was tried but acquitted: the jury was not convinced he was the author. After relating these facts, Thacher added that Lillie had been sentenced to a fine, costs and imprisonment.[132] It certainly sounds as if

had to name the speaker and give enough information to give the plaintiffs a cause of action against that person, including quoting the words exactly.

[130] Borthwick, *Treatise on the Law of Libel and Slander*, 301; Starkie, *Treatise on Slander* (1830), 1:338–39.

[131] It was pleaded in *Jackson v. Stetson*, 15 Mass. (14 Tyng) 48 (1818), but the case went in a different direction.

[132] *Comm. v. Whitmarsh*, Thach. Crim. Cas. 441 (1836), 460–65. William J. Snelling in the early 1830s also said he could have avoided a libel prosecution by giving up his source: *Exposé of the Vice of Gaming*, 48.

Lillie was not sentenced until the jury rejected the claim that Vinall was the author. Similarly, as an aside in an 1828 jury charge, Justice Marcus Morton explained that one way a defendant might rebut a presumption of malice was to show "that he had received certain information, and had given his authority, and had stated the information correctly as he had received it." Oral rumor could thus probably be safely transformed into writing in Massachusetts, unless the printer was actually malicious.[133]

In arguing that Holland, as a second publisher who had divulged the author, should not be liable, Archibald and Fairbanks implicitly argued that a rule pertaining to slander should be extended to libel. Fraser's lawyers followed Starkie's reasoning in arguing that Holland's decision to omit Fraser's explanation was evidence of malice, which would rebut either the second-publisher defense or a qualified privilege–type defense, both of which Archibald and Fairbanks were advancing.

A more important argument, at least to the *Recorder*, was truth. Archibald – educated in Massachusetts between 1792 and 1796[134] – argued truth, but he did not follow Starkie by asserting simply that Fraser could not collect damages for harm to an undeservedly good reputation. Instead, Archibald told the jury that freedom of the press implied a right to publish the truth about public matters, although not private lives or discreditable transactions that people were entitled to keep quiet. Sounding remarkably like a Massachusetts lawyer, he announced, "there are truths in which the public are concerned and which ought to be published and read, and whenever the case requires it, and [if] the printer does his duty the law should protect him or *the Liberty of the Press is but a name!*"[135] If true, Holland's account deserved to be published in America and all over the United Kingdom. Since truth defenses were allowed in civil cases, truth and

[133] Whitman, *Trial of Commonwealth versus David Lee Child*, 102.
[134] Beck, "Archibald, Samuel George William." Beck remarks that S.G.W., born in 1777, apparently changed his third given name from Washington to William in order to better his chances in Nova Scotia, but his family's sympathies were apparent in his original name. His paternal grandfather had come from Londonderry, northern Ireland, and his mother, Rachel Todd, was from Massachusetts.
[135] *Recorder*'s emphasis.

the liberty of the press could be linked together, and Archibald did not miss the opportunity.

Holland's witnesses recounted the inadequate and deceptive provisioning of the ship. Fraser's counsel and witnesses put forward alternative interpretations: there was less bread than the inspectors demanded but more oats, which the passengers preferred; a bit of pork had gone off but had nevertheless been sold for a good price. Overall, the tale of woe and fraud had been concocted by ship's master, the silly, drunken, malicious Primrose Smith. What, if anything, the judge, Brenton Halliburton, told the jury about Holland's arguments about privilege and republication is unclear. Halliburton told them that truth was a bold defense that required very solid proof, and, in the *Recorder*'s view, implied that Fraser should win. Nevertheless, the verdict was for Holland. Halliburton suppressed the bursts of applause in the courtroom and ordered Fraser to pay costs.

Fraser v. Holland shows Holland's lawyers' awareness of the legal protection afforded to "true and correct accounts of Judicial proceedings and investigations." The logic of qualified privilege was there, but the term "privilege" was not, at least in the pleadings. This absence is unsurprising for a libel case in the early 1820s and may also suggest that Archibald had a Massachusetts lawyer's aversion to the word, to accompany his association of truth with freedom of the press. Nova Scotian legal thought thus shows influences from both England and Massachusetts.

During the 1820s and 1830s, as calls for political reform increased in Nova Scotia, the English law of libel was a regular and growing minor theme for journalists. Early in the 1820s a few prominent English libel trials were noted, normally without much editorializing. Thomas Erskine's death inspired tributes. An article in the *Free Press* argued that it was absurd that reporting on coroners' inquests was illegal, and made fun of judges' fears that if such proceedings could be published, those sent to trial by coroners would have already been convicted by the press before they reached the courtroom.[136] The *Acadian Recorder* in 1824 cited Richard Phillips's 1811 *On the Powers and Duties of Juries*, which was highly protective of free expression and the press, reminding jurors that they were guardians

---

[136] "The Judges and the Journals," *Free Press* (Halifax), March 2, 1824.

of liberty and advising them that criminal intention was necessary for convictions for criminal libel.[137] For Phillips, actual malice was part of what the plaintiff or Crown had to prove at the outset. He and others who made this argument often turned for authority to Fox's Libel Act, which gave the whole case to the jury, including the determination of intention. This argument had rhetorical appeal and resonated with the *Clap* idea (1808) that evidence of truth could be introduced to negative the inference of malice drawn from the fact of publication, but Phillips's views had been superseded by the shifting burden of proof in the privilege framework that Ellenborough and Starkie had developed and whose logic dominated the case law by the 1820s. In this framework, the plaintiff had to prove actual malice only if the defendant proved the circumstances in which privilege could arise – otherwise the fact of intentional publication was sufficient, even in criminal cases. As I describe in Chapter 4, the idea that malicious (criminal) intention had to be proven by the prosecution and could be negatived through evidence of honest belief in truth got quashed in Massachusetts as well.

Later in the 1820s and through the 1830s, prominent English and Irish libel cases inspired more Nova Scotian commentary. Pieces on the importance of a free press appeared, along with complaints about how the press was portraying particular issues. Howe regularly published articles on the freedom of the press and indeed sent a tribute to freedom of the press to his readers to enhance their Christmas celebrations in 1833.[138]

Howe, Blanchard, the Hollands (especially Philip) and their correspondents periodically assessed specific aspects of libel law and commented on cases and incidents from New Brunswick, PEI, Newfoundland and the Canadas, where political unrest was growing. As the *Patriot* noted, bad law filtered from one colony to another.[139] Problematic aspects of libel law included the distinction between attacks on private and public character, the role of juries, reports of legislative proceedings, the meaning of malice, liability for

[137] "Phillips' Exhortation or Advice to Jurors," *Acadian Recorder* (Halifax), February 28, 1824, referring to Phillips, *On the Powers and Duties of Juries*, 226–59.
[138] "Christmas Stanzas," *Novascotian* (Halifax), December 25, 1833 supplement.
[139] "Palmer v. Haszard," *Colonial Patriot* (Pictou), July 22, 1829.

republication of defamatory reports, the lack of protection for reports of pre-trial proceedings, and the requirement of unanimous verdicts in criminal cases.[140] Alexander Lawson, in his *Yarmouth Herald*, advocated Phillips's understanding of the jury's role in determining the intent necessary for libel convictions. In 1830, Jotham Blanchard published an excerpt from a Scottish paper that firmly opposed the core premise of seditious libel, that individuals degraded the government by attacking officeholders. The writer insisted that although private lives were "sacred," officials acting in their public, institutional capacities should be thoroughly scrutinized.[141] The *Patriot* also took issue with the guilty verdict in an 1829 PEI civil libel suit, in which the chief justice charged the jury on the distinction between legal and actual malice: the *Patriot*'s writer insisted on Phillips's view that the plaintiff had to prove actual intention to injure. The case concerned a newspaper's liability for publishing a speech made in legislative debate. The attorney general had criticized a controversial lawyer and political figure named James Bardin Palmer. James Douglas Haszard published the speech in his newspaper. Sued by Palmer, Haszard admitted publication but denied maliciously libeling Palmer, arguing and proving that the text was "a correct report of a speech in Parliament." The judge, however, followed *R. v. Creevey*, which he said he had heard handed down in England. Creevey's effort to correct a circulating account of his speech by publishing his own version in his own newspaper was held to be unprotected. The law had since been clarified, but the PEI judge reasoned that if Creevey could not publish his own speech assailing someone's reputation, neither could a printer. The judge told the jury they could reduce damages if they felt the report was fair and Haszard had lacked actual malice. They awarded Palmer a single shilling. Relying on Phillips, the *Patriot*'s writer insisted that since the jury had told the judge they found that Haszard lacked actual malice, Haszard should have escaped liability. The *Patriot*'s writer did

---

[140] See e.g. "Sir Robert Peel and the Press," *Novascotian* (Halifax), November 2, 1831; "Unanimity of Juries," *Novascotian* (Halifax), February 14 & 21, 1833; Letter to the editor, *Colonial Patriot* (Pictou), June 4, 1828; "Lord Brougham's Evidence on the Libel Laws," *Novascotian* (Halifax), October 29, 1834.

[141] "Golden Rules for Jurymen. By Sir Richard Phillips," *Yarmouth Herald*, December 22, 1837; "Freedom of the Press," *Colonial Patriot* (Pictou), April 3, 1830. Lawson trained with Blanchard and began publishing the *Yarmouth Herald* in August 1833: McKay, "Lawson, Alexander."

not argue that a fair report of proceedings in the assembly was absolutely privileged, regardless of malice.[142]

The *ex officio* information was a topic of concern as well. In the late 1820s, before the brandy rebellion, Blanchard supported the Lower Canadians' right to select their own Speaker and admired the Upper Canadian journalist and political reformer William Lyon Mackenzie. Not only was Blanchard assailed in newspapers and at one point burned in effigy, but in August 1830 the *Patriot* announced that proceedings for seditious libel were to be launched against it. Blanchard said he was always aware of the attorney general's power to file an *ex officio* information against him but was sure no jury would be sufficiently ignorant of constitutional rights to convict him. He was disappointed in Nova Scotians for associating criticism of government with disloyalty to the nation, a doctrine which he said had been laid to rest thirty years earlier in Britain. He hinted at the possibility of revolution. Neither the court records nor the surviving issues of the *Patriot* give any sign that this matter went anywhere. If a prosecution did begin, it rapidly came to a halt, and undoubtedly not because the *Patriot* repented. In the fall of 1830, Richard John Uniacke died and S.G.W. Archibald succeeded him as attorney general.[143] Around the same time, the Brandy Election, which swept reformers, including Blanchard, into office, would have made such a prosecution politically untenable, even if Archibald was willing and able to prosecute his former student.

In 1831, a New Brunswick prosecution, brought on *ex officio* information against a newspaper printer and his correspondent, disturbed the patrons and editors of the *Novascotian* and the *Colonial Patriot*. In a letter to John Hooper's *British Colonist*, Thomas Gardiner called the members of the province's legal establishment such names as harpies, beasts of prey and wretches and "reflected not only on their public and professional but on their private

[142] "Palmer v. Haszard," *Colonial Patriot* (Pictou), July 22, 1829; Holman, "Palmer, James Bardin"; *R. v. Creevey* (1813), 1 M. & S. 273, 105 E.R. 102 (K.B.).

[143] "Mr. Murdoch and the Editor of the Novascotian," *Colonial Patriot* (Pictou), April 10, 1830; "The Colonial Advocate," *Colonial Patriot* (Pictou), December 3, 1833; Patterson, *History of Pictou*, 374–77, 379–80; "Disloyalty, Prosecution, Constitution, &c.," *Colonial Patriot* (Pictou), August 14, 1830; Untitled notice, *Colonial Patriot* (Pictou), January 8, 1831.

characters, as men destitute of feeling, and sacrificing every principle of virtuous conduct to mercenary considerations." The judge, Ward Chipman, who had spent the 1810s studying law in London, told the special jury that the *ex officio* information was an ancient, legitimate and unobjectionable mode of proceeding. Such attacks were an abuse of the freedom of discussion. When the jury decided that Hooper had lacked evil intent in publishing the article, the attorney general discontinued the proceedings against him. Gardiner, the writer, was convicted, although because he was poor (an organist) he received a "lenient sentence," a thirty-pound fine with sureties for good behavior.[144]

Howe, confident in the power and good sense of juries, saw the verdict as recognizing that printers should not suffer for their correspondents' views. A few more such decisions, Howe thought, would give the press the protection he asserted that it enjoyed "at home" in Britain. The *Colonial Patriot* reprinted Howe's assessment. The *Patriot* also seemed pleased with the results of another New Brunswick case, in which a special jury insultingly awarded a farthing in damages to a former customs inspector who sued the editor and publisher of a St. Andrews paper over an article that accused him of malfeasance in his office.[145]

The potential liability of printers for unknowingly republishing libelous material continued to bother Howe and Blanchard. In May 1832, Blanchard called a correspondent to the Pictou *Observer* a "blockhead" for supposing that an editor was responsible for all the opinions in his paper. Blanchard announced that his newspaper was open to all views, especially if they came from known correspondents.[146] Blanchard and Howe seem to have thought authors should usually be punished more severely than the editors and printers who published their views, because any actual malice was normally borne by the original author, with the editors and

[144] "Case of Libel," *Novascotian* (Halifax), January 27, 1831; "In the Exchequer," *Colonial Patriot* (Pictou), March 26, 1831; Buckner, "Chipman, Ward."
[145] "Libel," *Novascotian* (Halifax), January 27, 1831; "Libel," *Colonial Patriot* (Pictou), January 29, 1831; "Spearman v. Stubs," *Colonial Patriot* (Pictou), March 19, 1833.
[146] Untitled editorial, *Colonial Patriot* (Pictou), May 26, 1832.

printers simply giving the text publicity. Of course if they too bore malice, their punishment should be adjusted accordingly.[147]

The English rule that a defendant could escape liability for slander by giving up the source and repeating the words exactly as they had been spoken – which Starkie thought lacked a clear basis in principle – was eliminated from English law in 1829 in *De Crespigny v. Wellesley*, which also clarified that the defense did not extend to libel, because written and printed texts could travel beyond the circles in which the dubiousness of the original allegation was known. One simply had a duty not to promulgate defamation. The impact of this case on readers across the Atlantic, however, was probably minimal, at least for a while, in part because of the case's timing. The second edition of Starkie's libel treatise was in press when *De Crespigny* was released, and Starkie noted it in an appendix but did not incorporate it into his main text. It was not until the 1843 edition of Starkie's libel treatise that *De Crespigny* was mentioned in the American editor's footnote.[148] On the confusing question of second publishers, then, commentators in both Nova Scotia and Massachusetts tended to do their own theorizing.

Qualified Privilege in Joseph Howe's Libel Trial

In presenting a set of resolutions for constitutional reform in the assembly in 1837, Joseph Howe, who had recently been elected for the first time, demanded on behalf of colonials around the world who, like him, wished to live and die as British subjects, "the blessed privilege of her constitution and her laws."[149] Nova Scotian law, with a bit of adjusting, could be a similar blessing. Howe's 1835 libel trial has been analyzed by several historians and is the stuff of lore and bus tour narrations in Nova Scotia, where it is celebrated as a key

---

[147] See "What is a Libel?" *Novascotian* (Halifax), September 4, 1833.

[148] *De Crespigny v. Wellesley* (1829), 5 Bing 293, 130 E.R. 1112 (C.P.); *M'Pherson v. Daniels* (1829), 10 B. & C. 263, 109 E.R. 448 (K.B.); Starkie, *Treatise on Slander* (1830), 2:427; Starkie, *Treatise on Slander* (1843), 1:301–3. For a discussion of the history of this defense, see Mitchell, *Making of the Modern Law of Defamation*, 123–31.

[149] Longley, *Joseph Howe*, 40.

moment in the history of both the press and the career of a revered and loved political figure.[150]

On January 1, 1835, Howe published the second of two letters critical of the magistrates who governed Halifax.[151] The first passed without comment, but the second provoked the magistrates into action. The Halifax magistrates had caused discontent for years over how they ran institutions and collected taxes. By refusing to deliver financial records, the magistrates frustrated the grand juries who were supposed to provide oversight. Howe, who served on the 1832 grand jury, was intimately familiar with the magistracy's ability to deflect criticism and avoid having its finances assessed. The *Novascotian* and other newspapers had for years published the grand juries' reports. The December 1834 report attracted vociferous criticism. Howe also published the critical letters that came his way. The one that led to his trial accused identifiable magistrates of reprehensible irresponsibility, incompetence, self-dealing to the tune of thousands of pounds, and general self-interestedness in the conduct of their offices. Howe's correspondent alleged that the magistracy had for thirty years unfairly taxed Halifax and unjustly taken £30,000 from the people. The writer suggested that an unnamed magistrate had taken funds from an institution for the poor and that the Court of Sessions had annually taken £1,000 from the poor to benefit "men whose services the Country might well spare." The writer alluded to great unrest afoot about the year's assessment.

Attorney General S.G.W. Archibald proceeded by indictment, perhaps out of a distaste for prosecutions of the press, perhaps because Howe was a friend, or perhaps most likely because of the oppressive connotations and questionable legality of the *ex officio* information.[152] Archibald's junior, James Gray, told the court that he was glad Archibald had not proceeded on information, as the indictment was "more consonant to the principles of public liberty."

[150] See Beck, "A Fool for a Client"; Cahill, "Sedition in Nova Scotia: *R. v. Howe* "; Cahill, "*Howe* (1835)"; Chisholm, "The King v. Joseph Howe"; Campbell, "Licence to Publish." Howe published updates on his case in the *Novascotian* throughout the period, with a full report on March 12, 1835. It was also published as a pamphlet, *Trial for Libel, on the Magistrates of Halifax*, and much of it is set out in Howe, *Speeches and Public Letters*, 1:22–88.
[151] The People [pseud.], letter to the editor, *Novascotian* (Halifax), January 1, 1835.
[152] On the 1835 grand jury, see Cahill, "Tale of Twelve Magistrates," 553–58.

The indictment, whose text survives only through the record of Howe's argument, began in the language of seditious libel. It alleged that Howe published the letter, being "greatly disaffected" with the government "and wickedly, maliciously and seditiously, contriving, devising and intending, to stir up and excite discontent and sedition." However, Archibald and Gray focused on the defamation of the magistrates and avoided talking about sedition. Gray advised the special jury that they merely had to determine whether the publication was libelous and whether Howe had published it, which he did not deny. Good motives or a lack of intention to injure would be irrelevant. Truth was no defense, because defamation should not be published whether true or false. Gray assured the jury that because the magistrates had been defamed as a body rather than as individuals, they could not have brought a civil action, in which truth could have been raised. He suggested that Howe could not have proven truth anyway because of the broad, longstanding allegations in the letter. Complaints should properly have been addressed to the lieutenant governor, not the newspapers. Acknowledging that the prosecution was unpopular, Gray urged the jury to do justice between the parties.

Local lawyers were pessimistic about Howe's chances but lent him books. Like Wilkie, he defended himself in court, arguing for six hours, with Beamish Murdoch joining him at the counsel table. Howe explained that he preferred to avoid spectacles like this but thought the press had to learn to defend itself; "simple principles of truth and justice" should prevail. Defending himself also gave him the opportunity to express his intentions. Being accused, he could not give sworn testimony. The Crown did not ask for the name of the writer, and Howe evidently did not wish turn the person over himself.[153]

Howe emphasized his devotion to the British constitution. He suggested generously that Archibald was acting only out of duty and disliked persecuting the press. He said that Archibald, as Speaker, had declined to act when members of the assembly had demanded a response to attacks in the *Novascotian*. Archibald reciprocated in

---

[153] Howe, *Speeches and Public Letters*, 1:23. Beck, in "A Fool for a Client," 31, says the letters were written by Howe's friend George Thompson, about whom little is known.

closing his case, referring to Howe as a "personal friend," noting his own obligation to uphold the law and the public peace, and pointing out that he had avoided the notorious *ex officio* information. Archibald too emphasized the importance of a free press.

Howe's defense ran on two interwoven tracks. One was an argument that Fox's Libel Act empowered the jury to judge both fact and law and that, in law, he could not be convicted without actual malicious motives. The fact of publication was insufficient to prove criminal intent. Relying on the indictment, he argued that the Crown had to prove he intended to undermine the government (sedition) rather than simply to asperse the magistrates. Gray presented a correct explanation of legal malice, but Howe told the jury that the Crown had to prove actual malice. He suggested that the magistrates, in prosecuting rather than suing, were avoiding having to confront the truth of the multitude of allegations of their malfeasance. Of course, substantiating these allegations would have been difficult if not impossible because of the magistrates' own record-keeping. Howe was able to score rhetorical points by lamenting his legal inability to prove truth without the difficulty of having to do so.

Howe's second line of defense was a qualified privilege argument. He asserted that as a newspaper editor and former member of the grand jury, he bore a duty to Haligonians and Nova Scotians to reveal what he knew, as they had an interest in knowing about the magistrates' misdeeds. Howe based his argument on the second London edition of Starkie's libel and slander treatise, from 1830, which explained and expanded the defense of qualified privilege, arguing that it provided broad protection to those who commented on matters of public interest.

Unlike Massachusetts, where American editions of Starkie's first edition were sold and cited, Nova Scotia had English editions. The Loyalist influx in the 1780s had brought many New England lawyers to Nova Scotia, but between 1820 and 1840 the Nova Scotia bar became strongly native-born and melded New England legal traditions with those of other groups, particularly the Anglo-Irish.[154] English law dominated. Legal publishing and bookselling were in their infancy in Nova Scotia in the 1830s, with Murdoch's four-volume

---

[154] Girard, Patriot Jurist, 89–90, 131–38.

landmark *Epitome* only recently in print. John George Marshall's guide for justices of the peace would be published in 1837. Booksellers mostly sold law books by special order, and most law books in the province were published in London.[155] In 1835 the Nova Scotia barristers' library had Holt's libel text but not Starkie's. Halifax lawyer William Young had both. Richard John Uniacke's library lacked Holt but had the 1830 English edition of Starkie – perhaps it was en route to him when he died that year.[156]

Howe quoted extensively from Starkie's introduction. In asserting his duty to publish the letter, Howe argued that he had known from previous experience that the magistracy was "the most negligent and imbecile, if not the most reprehensible Body, that ever mismanaged a people's affairs." He told the jury that in English law a person prosecuted for criminal libel had the "privilege" of explaining to them his praiseworthy motives, honorable intentions and the circumstances that demanded his action. Leaving aside his other argument about the Crown having to prove bad intent, Howe explained that the fact of publication raised a legal inference of malice and required the accused person to rebut that inference by showing that he was innocent from ignorance or that "some public exigency" justified his action. The circumstances of a communication could give rise to an exemption (absolute or qualified) from criminal responsibility. A large protective barrier against libel actions was necessary for the public good. As long as the speaker's intentions and beliefs were good and consistent with the demands of the occasion, the defense would succeed, even if the information circulated was untrue. As Howe put it, quoting Starkie, "the continual and casual publication of erroneous opinions cannot be placed in competition with the splendid advantages which flow from permitting full and fair discussion on every subject of interest to mankind, as connected with religion, politics, philosophy, and morals." As long as the law could

[155] See Laurence, "Process and Particulars" and "Acquiring the Law"; Macleod, "Library of Richard John Uniacke." On publishing and reading in Quebec and Nova Scotia from the mid-eighteenth century to about 1830, see Eamon, *Imprinting Britain.*
[156] *List of Books Belonging to the Estate of the Late Hon. R.J. Uniacke*; William Laurence, email message to author regarding the catalog of the library of William Young, January 28, 2006; *Catalogue of Books, in the Law Library at Halifax.*

distinguish between publications animated by a sincere, honest desire to do right and malicious attempts to injure society or individuals through blasphemy, sedition or defamation, society's needs were served.[157]

After extensively cataloging the many ways in which the magistrates had failed to live up to their obligations and declaring his pure intentions, Howe asked the jury whether he had not served the community's interests in publishing the letter, activated only by virtue in the face of overwhelming public necessity. He was not asking, he said, for "the impunity which the American Press enjoys" but the impartial justice he was due as a British subject. "Let not the sons of the Rebels look across the border to the sons of the Loyalists, and reproach them that their Press is not free." In Boston a few years earlier, David Lee Child had raised the specter of British parliamentary tyranny; Howe characterized the Americans as having gone too far in liberating the press. British law, he thought, got the balance right. In this logic, privilege was democratized: a defense with its roots in freedom of speech behind the closed doors of the Houses of Parliament became translated into a claim that ordinary printers were entitled to keep watch over politicians and inform the masses of any failures to abide by their public responsibilities.

Archibald's charge to the jury was much shorter than Howe's and graceful enough, though less sparkling than those for which he was known. He argued that this broad qualified privilege defense was unknown to law, despite his own arguments in Holland's defense fourteen years earlier. Chief Justice Halliburton followed Gray and Archibald in his presentation of the law, rejecting the argument that privilege applied in these circumstances. However, enabled by Fox's Libel Act, the jury ignored Halliburton's views and, after ten minutes of deliberation, acquitted Howe.

Howe's report of the trial celebrated the vindication of the free press through that fundamental English institution, the jury. The crowd shouted with joy, and friends congratulated him. Howe thanked the court for the courtesy of allowing him to deliver his whole argument uninterrupted. Crowds bore him home, and for the next two days "[a]ll

---

[157] On Howe's arguments, see Campbell, "Licence to Publish" and "Starkie's Adventures in North America."

the sleds in Town were turned out in procession with banners; and all ranks and classes seemed to join in felicitations on the triumph of the Press." A lawyer would have pointed out that the qualified privilege defense had not been accepted into Nova Scotia law, but Howe saw the jury as the true guarantor of rights.

The Aftermath

Howe claimed to have established for Nova Scotians a freedom to publish, from good motives, information about public measures that the public needed to have. The legal existence of the qualified privilege defense was recognized – although inapplicable on the facts – in an 1840 case. Edmund Ward, now publishing a New Brunswick paper, warned the public against one Duncan who had moved to Halifax, calling him a swindler. Duncan, in response, wrote to the *Acadian Recorder*, denying the charge and calling Ward a swindler, a cheat and prone to quarreling. Ward sued the *Recorder*'s proprietors, now Hugh Blackadar and John English. James W. Johnston, the solicitor general, acted for Ward. James B. Uniacke defended English and Blackadar, arguing for the importance of liberty of the press. While denying Uniacke's argument that the reciprocal mudslinging made the assertions unactionable, Johnston acknowledged that "[p]ersons might give opinions of others, without fear of legal consequences, as for example, when they were legally acting – such as a person giving a character of a servant, a relative or a commercial correspondent, stating opinions of a third party, a reporter furnishing proceedings of the house of parliament or courts of law."[158] Privilege defenses had made it to Nova Scotia.

Howe seems to have assumed that if one jury had recognized the proper nature of freedom of the press, subsequent similar prosecutions would likely fail too. He had argued intent, and he had escaped liability for his correspondent's opinions: things had turned out correctly, given his understanding of the proper constitutional understanding of the place of the press. Vindicated in court, he continued to press for political reform. Newspapers seem to have become emboldened about airing political combat. Before 1835, critiques often began

[158] Quoted in Mullane, "Sketch of Lawrence O'Connor Doyle," 187.

with invocations of the "privilege" of free discussion and were framed as wise advice to the government or the world in general.[159] After Howe's trial, these invocations disappeared and attacks became more direct. Real names had started to appear in the *Colonial Patriot* in the late 1820s but did not displace pen names and initials. By the mid-1830s, real names appeared much more frequently, especially when tempers ran high and libel suits seemed a risk. In both Nova Scotia and Massachusetts, the publication of an author's real name could signal that both the newspaper and the author anticipated an engaged, public argument. These arguments proliferated in the later 1830s in Nova Scotia.

Howe continued to be interested in libel law after his trial, especially the responsibility of editors for their correspondents' allegations. In November 1837 he explained the legal theory that had governed his handling of a potentially defamatory letter. He said he had published the letter without the author's name because the author had agreed to take responsibility for it. Without that commitment, Howe would have named him. Howe claimed to be following the practices of editors in England, Ireland and Scotland. He felt that the public or a grand jury would have exonerated him for publishing the letter, but that he would have needed to call on the writer for support.[160] These comments reflect Howe's sense that the writer of a libel was the one chiefly responsible for it and that a jury – although not necessarily a judge – would exonerate a publisher on the basis of his lack of malice.

This was not a position Starkie would have taken, and it was becoming problematic in Massachusetts, where Chief Justice Shaw held in 1834 that false statements could not be saved by innocent intent. Boston judge Peter Thacher told a jury in 1833 that republishing a libel was as great an offense as the original publication, since it could do even more damage. A conservative English writer

---

[159] See e.g. a letter to the editor contained in Editorial, *Colonial Patriot* (Pictou), February 1, 1828.

[160] Mr. Sheriff Harrington," *Novascotian* (Halifax), November 8, 1837. Howe reasoned similarly in an editorial note at the end of John Joseph Marshall, "No. 2. To W.Q. Sawers, Esquire, Chief Justice of the Inferior Court of Common Pleas, and President of the Sessions in the County of Guysborough," *Novascotian* (Halifax), May 16, 1839.

objected that protecting the publisher if the author were disclosed would promote calumny and might frequently deprive those wronged of any effective remedy.[161]

Despite the law, though, Howe's view was consistent with the practices of Massachusetts publishers, who often behaved as if they believed that only the original author was potentially liable. Indeed, the frequency with which work that had been judged libelous was republished in Massachusetts requires noting. Editor Charles Greene reprinted *Deacon Giles' Distillery* before Cheever was even tried – and indeed, charges against the newspaper and editor were dropped. Joseph Whitmarsh sold Cheever's tract after he went to jail. After Charles Knowlton's conviction for obscene libel over his birth control book, both Knowlton and editor and printer Abner Kneeland continued to sell it. Samuel T. Armstrong, the state's lieutenant governor, printed the parts of two newspaper articles for which Kneeland had been jailed for blasphemy and posted them on the walls of a public reading room, to discourage readers from signing the petition for Kneeland's release. Kneeland himself published a pamphlet containing the offending text. Being prosecuted for republishing a libel was apparently not an important threat. Either the risk of further prosecution was minimal, the benefits of taking a stand for freedom of expression were substantial or the profits to be made from scandal were too tempting to forgo. Despite Howe's disparagement of the "impunity which the American press enjoys," on the question of republication by printers he seems to have shared their spirit. Although he urged favorable interpretations of the law, his confidence was fundamentally rooted in juries. Libel law continued to be a risk for the Nova Scotian press in the 1840s, and arguments about doctrine continued to be made, but the dogs of newspaper war had been loosed.[162]

---

[161] *Comm. v. Snelling*, 15 Pick. 337, 32 Mass. (15 Pick.) 337 (1834); Locke, *Trial of Moore & Sevey*, 69–70; H [pseud.], "Law of Libel," 442–43.

[162] R. Murray Beck discusses the libel actions brought against Howe's successor at the *Novascotian*, Richard Nugent, when Nugent indiscreetly tangled with various people, including a Halifax legal functionary named William Q. Sawers: Beck, "Nugent, Richard." The journals of the assembly and the council reveal that efforts to introduce legislative changes to libel law in March 1844 foundered over competing views of how much protection the press deserved.

Conclusion: Privilege and Institutions

The Nova Scotian legal world – like that of Massachusetts – was characterized by borrowings and adaptations, even as lawyers and judges often denied that change was taking place. The British constitutional struggles over repressive prosecutions affected Nova Scotian legal strategies, with Howe extolling the wisdom of juries and Archibald avoiding the *ex officio* information. In both places legislatures relied on privilege to protect their "dignity" and that of their members, but actions for contempt of privilege were more important and repressive in Nova Scotia, as a reformist legislature exerted itself against critics who sided with the overbearing council. It was council supporters like Edmund Ward who flew the flag of freedom of expression and reformers who found themselves – at times awkwardly – supporting the assembly. In Massachusetts, David Lee Child invoked the oppressive history of the British House of Commons as a cautionary tale; for loyal, nonrepublican Nova Scotians, its bad deeds called for a bit of whitewash. Uncertainty about exactly what the British authorities thought were appropriate powers for colonial legislatures complicated debates further.

The defense of qualified privilege or privileged communication emerged to address specific political and legal concerns but was reinterpreted, first by Starkie and then by others in Nova Scotia and Massachusetts, to meet other needs. Massachusetts was already immersed in content-oriented arguments about truth, so privilege arguments were seldom made, and concerns about truth drifted into them too. In Nova Scotia, where truth was no defense to criminal libel, privilege was a more promising foundation for a defense. Another factor was the vicissitudes of legal publication, which brought Thomas Starkie's 1830 analysis to the desks of Joseph Howe's legal friends in Nova Scotia but not to Massachusetts lawyers.

Other aspects of the law of defamation also troubled Nova Scotia and Massachusetts, and at times practices in both places evolved, unheralded, in ways inconsistent with the English common law. The murky common law on republishing defamation was particularly unsuited to North American conditions and was reinterpreted and ignored even more than other aspects of libel law, and – perhaps as a result – such publications were seldom the subject of legal action in Massachusetts or Nova Scotia.

Privilege is fundamentally a claim about jurisdictional boundaries and reflects an understanding that properly constructed institutions – legislatures included – are key to protecting freedom. The Nova Scotian approach to rights and institutions is part of a long British constitutional tradition, which, as David Lieberman observes, has centered on the idea that in order to preserve political freedom, governmental structures have to frustrate the abuse of political power.[163] Philip Girard has observed that Beamish Murdoch – chronicler of Nova Scotian history, legal advisor to Joseph Howe and author of the *Epitome of the Laws of Nova-Scotia* in the early 1830s – conceived of freedom as rooted in governmental structures, rather than in the rights of individuals. An 1832 review of the first volume of Beamish Murdoch's *Epitome* quoted Murdoch's identification of the most valuable parts of English laws, which Murdoch said had been adopted in Nova Scotia: "Habeas Corpus – the freedom of the Press – the trial by Jury – the Representative Branch of legislature [*sic*] – the viva voce examination of witnesses."[164] Similarly, Jeffrey McNairn explains that Upper Canadian Reform leader Robert Baldwin saw freedom of the press as "a social rather than an individual right." It protected a public right of discussion rather than an individual right to speech, and it was celebrated as liberating the mind and society and protecting the integrity of government. Daniel Hulsebosch has noted the common law's older function as an apparatus for resolving disputes rather than a cohesive body of substantive doctrines, which it was increasingly becoming in the early republic.[165] All of these insights into constitutional sensibilities resonate with the understandings of freedom of expression and of the press that were articulated in Nova Scotia in the 1820s and 1830s. In a system of properly structured and balanced institutions, the law would protect the press, which could then advocate for institutional reform, which would in turn protect individual liberties. A free press was a key institution: ordinary newspaper editors and contributors would keep public actors honest. A correspondent to the *Novascotian* in the winter and spring of 1835–36 submitted a series of essays on "the use and freedom of the press,"

---

[163] Lieberman, "The Mixed Constitution and the Common Law," 317.

[164] Review of Murdoch's *Epitome*, *Novascotian* (Halifax), May 3, 1832; Girard, "Themes and Variations," 126.

[165] McNairn, *Capacity to Judge*, 141; Hulsebosch, *Constituting Empire*, 287–88.

which described why and how a free press supported good governance. Joseph Howe's concern was that legal rules and practices respect and support this institution, as they evolved with the other institutions of governance in Nova Scotia.

As I describe in the next chapters, Massachusetts commentators, working with a written constitution and a tradition of bringing disputes to court, were formulating different, more individualistic understandings of these rights. The implications of republicanism for balancing the individual's interests against those of society were still a work in progress. Tempers were rising over antimasonry, temperance and other reform movements, but the most important issue was abolition. Claims to authority produced dramatic confrontations over expression, which, in courtrooms, focused on the role of truth.

4

Truth, Privacy and Authority

Introduction

In 1822 Massachusetts newspaper editor Joseph T. Buckingham, defending himself on criminal libel charges, pronounced that he had published

> nothing but truth and that truth, and good intention justify the publication, a doctrine, which, however novel in the practice of courts, is one which corresponds with the wishes, the feelings, and the good sense of every man in the nation.[1]

Truth had long been a defense in civil cases, but the idea that it should be a defense in criminal cases was contested. In the 1820s and 1830s, it was popularly, but not fully accurately, believed that in Massachusetts, a free state governed by republican principles, individuals had the right to publish truth – at least on "public" matters – if their motives were good and their ends justifiable. With structures of social and political authority being contested, however, people disagreed about what was true, what was public, and what constituted good motives and justifiable ends. As well, if majority will was the basis of constitutional legitimacy in a republic, was the majority entitled to dictate what an individual could say and to enforce its opinion by

---

[1] *Trial: Commonwealth vs. J. T. Buckingham*, 20.

force? The threat of majoritarian violence is an important part of the backdrop to the libel proceedings in Massachusetts. In Nova Scotia, where people far less often faced prosecution for libel, the common law was understood to bar reliance on truth in criminal libel proceedings. Public discourse focused on structure more than content – on the proper arrangement of institutions, including "the free press," rather than the right of the well-intentioned individual to express truth.

A Challenging Time

The debates over the place of truth in Massachusetts law took place as structures of political, religious and familial authority were being seriously challenged and the consequences for the future of the country and the souls of its populace seemed dire.

The financial strength of Congregationalism was undercut in 1811 during a brief Republican interlude in government. This process culminated in constitutional change in 1833 to eliminate religious establishment. Upstart religious persuasions like the Methodists and Universalists benefitted, while the orthodox Congregationalists and the Unitarians were destabilized. The advocates of antimasonry, temperance, abolitionism and other reform movements challenged orthodoxies of all kinds.

Burgeoning associational activity seemed to be undermining local authority. Leonard Richards has observed that after the War of 1812 large organizations developed, often headquartered in Washington or New York, with goals as diverse as building canals and spreading Christian texts. In 1829 the Unitarian divine William Ellery Channing expressed concern that the moral and religious sensibilities of individuals who joined reformist organizations might well be railroaded by the driving force of the organization – the organization was a kind of mob, without the violence. These organizations reduced the influence of local elites in various spheres of life, including the home. Temperance manuals, abolitionist newspapers, household advice books, birth control guides and similar literature found audiences in wives, young people and servants, thereby threatening to undermine paternal authority. An essential question in libel cases was whether the matter was public or private. As Laura Edwards has argued regarding the South, these words were labels that described not a place or a sort of person but claims that a matter was not subject to outside intervention.[2] Saying a matter was private was declaring that the speaker or writer should not have presumed to address it. Speaking truth about individuals who endeavored to position themselves as authorities without the usual social background checks could seem like a public service. The means and ends of those who sought to change arrangements of power might well be challenged by those who wielded it. In Massachusetts the place of truth in slander and libel cases evolved against the backdrop of debates over moral, legal and social power.

Disputes about the role of truth took place in both civil and criminal proceedings in Massachusetts. A statute passed in 1826 addressed truth in both contexts. The interpretation of the law was the product of legal conversations among a fairly small number of participants. As in Nova Scotia, the same names appear in case after case in Massachusetts, and individual personalities left their mark. Justice Charles Jackson, for example, was responsible for a peculiar rule in Massachusetts civil pleading that applied mainly, if not wholly, to defamation suits. Perez Morton and Daniel Davis were at the end of their careers as the state's law officers, while James T. Austin and Samuel Parker were on the rise. As chief justice, Isaac Parker muddled distinctions that Theophilus Parsons had attempted to clarify. Parker's successor Lemuel Shaw and municipal court judge Peter Oxenbridge Thacher were generally more acute than Parker, although Shaw in one notable case cobbled together a procedural rule through remarkable leaps of legal logic. In Worcester, Pliny Merrick, Rejoice Newton and a couple of other local lawyers appeared in case after case.

Many of the participants in these cases – libelers and libeled – were interconnected as well. Probably the most important link among participants in several cases is abolitionism. Although some did consider abolitionist expression indictable as having the potential to incite violence in the South, none of these libel cases pertained to abolitionist speech.[3] However, abolitionists appeared in them

---

[2] Richards, *"Gentlemen of Property and Standing,"* 60–62, 165–69; Channing, "Remarks on Associations," in *Works of Channing*, 139–43; Ryan, *Empire of the Mother*, 16–26; Edwards, "Status without Rights," 385–86. See also Grossberg, *Governing the Hearth*, 4–5, 25–29.

[3] See "Abolitionist Publications," *Boston Daily Advocate*, November 16, 1837.

anyway. David Lee Child, William Joseph Snelling, Doctor Abner Phelps, Reverend Moses Thacher, Ellis Gray Loring and Samuel Sewall were all founding members of the New England Anti-Slavery Society, led by William Lloyd Garrison, which was founded in the winter of 1831–32, in a ground floor room of the African Meeting House, off Belknap (now Joy) Street in Boston – in the heavily racialized area of Boston referred to as "Negro Hill" (and variants thereof).[4] These men were mainly social reformers from within the religious mainstream. Many were orthodox Congregationalists. Child and Sewall, classmates at Harvard, were Unitarian, as was Loring. Abner Phelps was one of the best-known members of the Suffolk antimasonry committee.[5] They and other reformers were linked through their causes and through libel cases. These cases often do not look "political," but they were.

For both ideological and strategic reasons, Massachusetts had far more civil and criminal cases for slander and libel than did Nova Scotia.[6] Truth was a factor. In the 1830 edition of his slander and libel treatise, Thomas Starkie noted the tension in the common law about whether the essence of the wrong addressed by slander (but not libel) actions was the malicious attack on the individual or, on the other hand, the utterance of untruth.[7] These two rationales were intertwined, but early nineteenth-century Massachusetts legal

---

[4] On the racial geography of Boston, see Horton and Horton, *Black Bostonians*, 1–6.

[5] Garrison, *William Lloyd Garrison*, 277–79. "Every one of the twelve [original members] was strongly Orthodox while the three dissenters were Unitarians by conviction or affiliation. They were also the only lawyers": *ibid.* 280. Child, Loring and Sewall were lawyers. On Phelps, see Vaughn, *Antimasonic Party*, 115. See also Clarke, "The Antislavery Movement in Boston," 375; Tiffany, *Samuel E. Sewall*, 12 (George B. Emerson and Samuel J. May were also in that class).

[6] My Nova Scotia sample contains 5 criminal prosecutions (1 for obscenity) and 23 civil suits. My Massachusetts sample contains 35 criminal prosecutions (11 for obscenity and blasphemy) and 106 civil defamation suits. When population and the comprehensiveness of the sampling are considered, it is clear that Nova Scotians turned to libel law far less frequently than did their counterparts to the south. See Appendix A and Chapter 6 for a discussion of sampling. Chapter 6 explores the strategic dimension of this difference in civil proceedings.

[7] Starkie pointed out that Blackstone considered falsity to be part of the definition of slander. *Scandalum magnatum*, too, was a cause of action that penalized only falsehoods. Starkie suggested that the distinction did not really matter much but that it was better to think of truth as a "ground of collateral justification or excuse." See *Treatise on Slander* (1830), 1:5–7.

commentators, following the trajectory established in the previous century, tended to assume that falsity was the crux of the problem, asserting that the core of free expression and freedom of the press was the right to utter truth, with certain important qualifications. Starkie, on the other hand, aimed to frame the common law so that it did not inhibit ordinary conversations or honest opinions on legitimate topics but, at the same time, sanctioned publications aimed maliciously at public or private mischief.[8] The question for Starkie was how to draw protective lines around context and circumstance, rather than leave editors and others to defend themselves through a content-based individual right to speak truth. For Starkie, truth simply eliminated the right to damages in civil suits; the bundle of factors concerning circumstances, duties, interests and intentions that combined into privilege defenses were more important.[9] In Massachusetts, as reform movements and religious splinter groups multiplied, and with mob violence on the rise, the individual's right to speak truth became increasingly salient – and increasingly threatening to those in authority.

Truth in Civil Suits

Massachusetts

In both civil and criminal actions in Massachusetts the admissibility and relevance of evidence of truth was contentious. The most important problem in civil suits in the 1820s and 1830s concerned

---

[8] Starkie, *Treatise on Slander* (1813), 6–7.
[9] John Borthwick argued that Scots law properly made truth even less significant. Truth was not even available as a defense in a civil suit if the context for the utterance was a private matter in which the audience had no legitimate interest, gave rise to a qualified privilege or was a moment of "temporary excitement" – it could only mitigate damages (it could also reduce the fine in criminal proceedings, but no more): *Treatise on the Law of Libel and Slander*, 244–56. At times – especially, it seems, when the defendant was powerful or the attack was published in the newspaper – truth was not even admissible to mitigate damages, even when the "defender" was protected by a privilege as well: *ibid.* 256–60. Starkie, while engaging with Borthwick, ignored these limitations on the use of truth. For Starkie, the truth of the defamatory allegation, if proven in a civil case, entirely eliminated the right to damages. Borthwick heartily disagreed and devoted many pages to reconciling the arguments of various Scottish judges that, notwithstanding the views of Blackstone and English law, the use of truth should be limited even in civil cases: *Treatise on the Law of Libel and Slander*, 244–79.

the plea of justification, that is, that the truth of the objectionable assertion justified its publication. Andrew King has argued that early nineteenth-century judges "demanded stricter adherence to the rules of special pleading in order to professionalize the bar." King thinks courts attempted to control the increasingly uninhibited communication of an increasingly disorderly social world by insisting that lawyers follow technical rules of pleading; however, by mid-century the movement to liberalize pleading had reached defamation cases. Morton Horwitz argues that lawyers in the early nineteenth century increasingly agreed that substance should trump form – they saw focusing on the correctness of pleadings as avoiding questions of substantive justice. Increasingly, too, American courts faced the question of how much they should attempt to adjudicate abrasive expression in a political world in which barbs and arrows were commonplace.[10] Massachusetts judges' concerns about the pleading of truth must be understood within this larger context of changing attitudes to expression, to pleading and to publicizing evidence of truth.

The common law presumed that attacking others' characters was unacceptable and that harmful truths should be decorously and generously concealed rather than aired.[11] In the understanding of writers like Starkie and Holt, truth was a defense to a civil suit, not because people were entitled to speak the truth about one another but because they were not entitled to recover damages for harm to undeservedly good reputations. The issue was damages, not the jury's interest in a fulsome understanding of the case, which was unnecessary and indeed undesirable. While most grounds of defense were argued under the defendant's standard "general denial" plea, truth was specially pleaded because it was a separate consideration. In this plea, the defendant admitted uttering the words but claimed to be justified by their truth. The defamatory assertion was repeated in the plea, which, at common law, was supposed to increase the harm and therefore the damages awarded. The legal logic conflicted with normative understandings, however: in Massachusetts, it was generally considered desirable, and certainly excusable, to speak

---

[10] King, "Law of Slander in Early Antebellum America," 43; Horwitz, *Transformation of American Law*, 24–25, 29–30.
[11] See Shuger, "Civility and Censorship," 101 and generally regarding the evils to be addressed through censorship in early modern England.

truth. A line of cases on the special plea of truth shows – as the criminal cases also do – a sense that a defendant's well-founded belief in the truth of the words should at least reduce the plaintiff's entitlement to damages, if not exonerate the defendant completely. The eventual legislated demise of special pleading signals, therefore, not just a growing generalized dislike of the privileging of form over content or a desire to reduce the professional caché of skilled special pleaders but a more specific frustration with judges' refusal to allow truth the exculpatory power it was supposed to have.[12]

The cases that turned on issues around pleading reveal both the trouble with truth and the trouble with special pleading. Civil suits in Massachusetts began in the Court of Common Pleas, where the parties entered their pleas and judgment was entered, more often without a trial than with one. An appeal to the Supreme Judicial Court frequently followed, with a jury trial there, sometimes after the pleas were amended. Truth was perilous to plead. The admission of publication in the truth plea contradicted the general denial, which, standing alone, could cover many different arguments about the flaws in the plaintiff's case. Under this plea, the defendant might, for instance, deny publishing the impugned words at all, deny their reference to the plaintiff, deny that they meant what the plaintiff said they meant, or raise privilege-type defenses. Repeating the defamatory allegation on the court's records could be considered evidence of malice, which could rebut a privilege defense or aggravate the damages. The admissions and assertions in the truth plea could undercut these other various lines of defense unless the pleas were read separately.

To mitigate this risk, until special pleading was abolished in 1836, defendants who contemplated a truth defense applied to "plead double" when they first appeared in Common Pleas – or at least, they certainly did in Worcester, whose meticulous court clerk kept better records than did Suffolk's. Pleading double was made possible under an early eighteenth-century English statute[13]: if permitted, it required the court to consider the evidence pertaining to each plea separately. As

---

[12] On the dispute over double pleading and pleading generally, see also King, "Law of Slander in Early Antebellum America," 39–42.
[13] *An Act for the Amendment of the Law and the Better Advancement of Justice* (U.K.), 1705, 4 & 5 Anne, c. 16.

Worcester lawyers understood it, if the application to plead double was granted, which it normally was, the defendant should be able to enter the truth plea while maintaining the general denial.

Trouble arrived in 1818. A Suffolk slander case, *Jackson v. Stetson*, showed the perils of pleading truth and cast doubt on the protection afforded by pleading double. The defendants, Sally Stetson and her husband, entered three pleas: a general denial; that Sally had heard the defamatory allegations from a third party, whom they named; and that the allegations were true. They did not apply for leave to plead double.

At trial in Supreme Judicial Court, Patty Jackson led no evidence that Sally Stetson had actually spoken the words, relying on the admissions in the second and third pleas. Instead of taking the pleas individually, the judge observed that the second two pleas were inconsistent with the first – that is, that the Stetsons' pleas of innocent repetition and justification on the basis of truth were incompatible with denying that Sally had made the statements at all. Justice Charles Jackson's instructions to the jury encouraged them to treat the admissions and assumptions underlying each plea as evidence on the others. As a result, the plaintiff did not have to prove that Sally had spoken the words. As well, the judge told the jury that if the truth plea failed, then any defenses that might have otherwise arisen under the general issue that were rebuttable by proof of malice (e.g. that the words were spoken confidentially) would be automatically defeated, since repeating a false allegation in court was proof of malice. He added that a failed truth claim also aggravated the injury.

The plaintiff succeeded on all three counts, and the defendants moved for a new trial on the grounds that the judge had misdirected the jury. James T. Austin represented the plaintiff and Benjamin Whitman the defendants. The appeal on the law to the whole court addressed two issues: 1) whether the admissions in the second and third pleas ought to have been treated as evidence pertinent to the first, and 2) whether after finding the allegations false, the jury ought to have treated the repetition of the claim in the pleadings as proof of malice sufficient to rebut any possible defenses under the general denial. Writing for the whole court, Jackson reasoned that although it might not actually be improper to plead the general issue alongside a truth plea, in most cases they would be logically inconsistent. He reasoned that once it was clear that the defendant had spoken the defamatory words and that they were false, the only remaining question was the defendant's motives. The jury would naturally interpret the defendant's deliberate, formal avowal of the truth of the words as an indication of malice.

Moreover, even if the Stetsons had pleaded double, it would not have helped. Jackson said pleading double was not very important, that permission was given as a matter of course, and that it made sense for a jury to consider the case as a coherent whole, taking into account any relevant admissions made on the record. Ordinarily, under the general issue, a plaintiff would have to prove the time, place and circumstances around the speaking of the words, but if the defendant alleged truth, the plaintiff did not have to prove these matters, although doing so might increase the award of damages. Thus did pleading truth increase the defendant's risk, even with permission to plead double. The trial verdict stood.

Jackson's judgment was logically sensible and attuned to how juries undoubtedly interpreted cases: they heard all the evidence, evaluated the defendant's intentions and considered whether the plaintiff deserved to recover damages. The bar, however, was unhappy. A lengthy footnote attached by a later editor to the case of *Jackson v. Stetson* indicates that lawyers viewed this ruling as inconsistent with the established practices around double pleading. It placed additional risk on defendants. Nevertheless, the ruling was upheld soon afterward in another contentious slander case, *Alderman v. French*.

The defendant French had accused the plaintiff of committing adultery with a specific woman. There were several counts. The defendant entered a general denial of all the counts, along with a special plea that alleged certain facts pertinent to the first count and concluded with the assertion that he, the defendant, was justified in speaking the words. This special plea was not a plea of truth but of other facts that must have gone to the circumstances and malice. At Common Pleas, the plaintiff successfully argued that the special plea was bad because it failed to directly aver that the words spoken were true or that the plaintiff had committed adultery: because it did not assert truth, it was not a valid special plea.

The failed special plea was the defendant's downfall at trial in the Supreme Judicial Court. The plaintiff tendered only the now-abandoned special plea as evidence on the first count and did not attempt to prove the other counts. The judge ruled that the failed special plea proved the speaking of the words. He refused to let the defendant attempt to prove the facts alleged in the special plea in mitigation of damages. The defendant moved to withdraw the special plea and plead truth instead, but the court refused. The defendant attempted to introduce a deposition to show that the words were not spoken maliciously, but the judge ruled that the necessary malice was evident in the fact that the words were actionable. The defendant tried to introduce evidence of a general rumor of the adultery, but the judge would not permit this evidence to be admitted either. Unsurprisingly, the jury found for the plaintiff. The defendant applied for a new trial.

Justice Charles Jackson again wrote for the whole court. The judgment was long and expansive, as if Jackson knew he was breaking with authority even as he asserted that the matter had never really been considered properly before. Upholding the trial judgment, he ruled that the special plea had been bad and that the plaintiff could use the assertions in it as evidence to undermine the general denial.

If the only fact that could have been considered proven by the truth plea had been publication, which raised the inference of legal malice, the consequences of Jackson's judgment would have been less significant, as defenses like second publication and qualified privilege would have remained available. However, repeating the assertion on the court's record was also typically understood as proof of actual malice, which would aggravate damages and could rebut these other defenses. The net result was that in general, defendants who pleaded truth put all their eggs in that basket.

Other perplexing points arose. There was consensus that because a plaintiff claimed to have had a good character before the allegations were made, the defendant should be able to introduce evidence that the plaintiff's character was not so good (likewise, the plaintiff could introduce evidence of having enjoyed an unusually good character that was thus more severely injured). Often, however, the line between evidence of general character and evidence of truth was a fine one: if there were rumors in the neighborhood that the plaintiff was a horse thief and the defendant's accusation was of stealing a particular horse, could the evidence of the rumor be led even if the defendant did not attempt to prove that the plaintiff had stolen that specific horse?

And what impact did evidence of truth have on damages? In an 1807 case, *Larned v. Buffinton*, Chief Justice Parsons distinguished between general evidence of character, which could be used to mitigate or increase the quantum of damages, and evidence introduced under a truth plea. Parsons also reasoned that the evidence adduced to support an unsuccessful truth plea could not be used to mitigate damages if repeating the allegation on the court record showed malice. Timing could be critical. A defendant who claimed to have spoken in the heat of passion or to have been honestly mistaken but who nonetheless knowingly repeated the allegation on the pleadings could not look to the evidence introduced under the truth plea to mitigate damages. On the other hand, if the plaintiff's own actions had led the defendant to believe in the truth of the allegations and it was only after the pleas were entered that the defendant had realized that the allegations were false, then the evidence of what the plaintiff had done could be considered on the damages question. This logical ruling stood awkwardly beside the common law rule that a failed truth plea would aggravate the damages. At one point in *Alderman v. French* Jackson observed that if French, though unable to prove the truth of the words, showed that he had believed the words true because of Alderman's own misconduct, damages should be mitigated. In the final paragraphs, however, Jackson called Parsons's distinction dubious and restricted the introduction of such evidence to situations in which the defendant admitted making a mistake, rather than allowing it to be considered in connection with damages more broadly. Confusion remained, but the idea that evidence that suggested that the allegations were true could be used to mitigate damages was doubtful, especially if truth was pleaded.

On March 3, 1827, the Massachusetts governor approved a statute passed by the legislature in late 1826 that made evidence of truth admissible in all criminal libel cases and truth a justification for a defendant with good motives and justifiable ends. The second section of that statute aimed directly at overruling *Alderman v. French*.[14] It provided that in civil actions for libel and slander in

[14] An Act Relating to Prosecutions for Libel, and to Pleadings in Actions for Libel and Slander, ch. 107, 1826 Mass. Acts 493. Rufus Choate and Leverett Saltonstall in the early 1830s asserted that this was the purpose of s. 2: *Trial of William Beals &*

which the defendant pleaded both the general issue and truth, the truth plea was not to be "held or taken as evidence" that the defendant had published the words. As well, such a plea, if it failed, was not to be held to be proof of malice. It was the jury's job to decide, based on the case as a whole, whether the special plea was made with malicious intent, "any law or usage to the contrary notwithstanding." However, instructed to provide self-contradictory instructions to juries and already wary of the truth defense, judges did not accept this legislative directive with grace.

In July 1826 Sarepta Hix issued a writ against Joel Drury over an allegation of theft. The case began in September 1826 and was continued from term to term until March 1827, when the new statute came into force. At this point, defense counsel applied to plead double, but Hix's counsel objected, possibly because the application was usually made the first time the parties appeared in court, rather than just as the case was about to be heard. The judge at Common Pleas refused the application and gave judgment for Hix. In Supreme Judicial Court, Drury elected to waive the general issue and proceed only on the defense of truth, arguing that Hix had in fact entered his house and stolen a large bundle of yarn. Drury's counsel also argued, though, that even if Hix had not stolen the yarn, her own suspicious actions (entering the empty house, giving contradictory explanations) should at least mitigate the damages, per *Larned v. Buffinton*. Chief Justice Isaac Parker, however, instructed the jury that if they did not believe Hix had stolen the yarn, they had to infer malice from the truth plea and could not consider Drury's beliefs in mitigation of damages: entering a truth plea would necessarily aggravate damages if the jury did not believe the evidence and the general issue had been waived. The jury found for Hix.

On appeal, Drury's lawyers argued that the new statute implied that it was the jury's job to evaluate the whole case and decide whether the special plea had been made maliciously, which, of course, they said, it had not been, so the damages should not have been increased. They argued that although the statute referred to a situation in which the general issue and special plea of justification had both been pleaded, it

---

Charles Greene, 16. The editor of the *Massachusetts Reports* who wrote the long, critical footnote to *Jackson v. Stetson* made the same point.

should still protect Drury, even though he waived the general denial – it would have made no sense, they argued, to have denied making the allegations when he fully intended to admit speaking them because he had believed them true. His decision to rely strictly on truth should not be held against him; it did not aggravate Hix's damage any more than entering both pleas would have done.

This sensible argument was rejected by the whole court. Rather than extracting from the second section of the 1826 statute the broad principle that the failure to prove truth as pleaded could not by itself aggravate the damages, the court held that the case did not come within the statute because the general issue had been waived. Accordingly, the influence of Hix's actions on Drury's belief could not mitigate the damages. Malicious intent would be inferred from the fact of pleading truth and the damages increased accordingly. The court called the relevant part of the 1826 statute a great departure from English practice and the practice of the Commonwealth. Pleading truth would remain risky.

One of Sarepta Hix's counsel on the appeal to the whole court was a Worcester lawyer named Pliny Merrick. A couple of years later, Merrick defended John Howe II for calling a Congregational minister named Samuel Russell a liar. The case may reflect uncertainty about how to handle truth pleas – or at least a complex set of them – in this legal environment. On Howe's first appearance in Common Pleas, Merrick duly applied to plead double. They succeeded on demurrer, and Russell appealed. When the trial began at Supreme Judicial Court, Merrick applied to add a ninth special plea, which was inconsistent with the other eight. The parties then agreed to waive all the special pleas and let the defendant advance, under the general issue, any matter that he otherwise might have specially pleaded in justification. These matters were various incidents that justified Howe in calling Russell, a liar – that is, they were evidence of truth and of Russell's own contributions to Howe's beliefs.[15] Like Drury, Howe evidently had no intention of denying speaking the words. Howe won, and Russell's application for a new trial on the basis of interference with the jury failed. The strange procedure adopted in this case – and especially the fact that it was inconsistency among the truth pleas that inspired it – may suggest

[15] *Trial of an Action in Favor of the Rev. Samuel Russell*, 4, 21–27.

underlying unease among judges and lawyers about how to deal with these pleas.

The legislature tried again to overrule the judiciary when it consolidated the state's statutes in November 1835. Among the general provisions about litigation, it enacted that a truth plea in a civil suit, even if unsupported by the evidence, would not "in any case be of itself proof of the malice alleged in the declaration." The statute also decreed that if a defendant made more than one plea, no "averment, confession, or acknowledgement" in one of the pleas could be used to undercut any other plea.[16]

In April 1836 the legislature abolished special pleading. Defenses were to be given in their entirety under the general issue, with courts at liberty to establish rules to make sure parties provided notice of what they intended to prove and argue.[17] The Supreme Judicial Court, however, continued to be wary of evidence of truth and to require that the truth defense be on the record in other ways. The burden of proving truth remained with the defendant.[18] In 1838, the court ruled that the notice of a special matter to be given in evidence under the general issue – truth, that is – which was to be filed with the general issue did not require the "technicality" of a special plea but did have to "contain as distinct an allegation of the grounds of the defence as would be stated in a special plea."[19] Most importantly, this notice could not simply allege improprieties and problematic conduct without committing the defendant to prove that the allegations against the plaintiff were in fact true – the notice could not simply suggest that the plaintiff was partly at fault. The notice was not sufficient unless the assertions in it, if pleaded specially, would be good on demurrer. The obligation to set out the "substantive matter of the defence" of truth thus survived the abolition of special pleading. The facts that could underlie a truth plea – such as evidence of Sarepta Hix's surreptitious entry into the Drury home – could only be introduced pursuant to a notice that explicitly alleged that the defamatory allegation was true. For the judges, the defense remained truth, not something like contributory negligence – although juries

---

[16] Rev. Stat. Mass. 1835, c. 100, ss. 18 & 19.
[17] An Act to Abolish Special Pleading in Civil Actions, ch. 273, 1836 Mass. Acts 1000.
[18] *Sperry v. Wilcox*, 42 Mass. 267 (1840).   [19] *Brickett v. Davis*, 38 Mass. 404 (1838).

may have seen things differently. The new statute, of course, pertained to the interpretation of pleas alone. The court did not say that the notice had to contain an admission of speaking or publishing the defamatory words, the admission that had caused so much trouble with conflict between the pleas, but of course the 1835 statutory changes had (it seems) nullified the effect of that admission. The judges may have finally recognized that resistance was futile on that point.

Judges, then, continued to resist the idea that evidence of the plaintiff's bad conduct should be allowed to seep into the trial unless the defendant committed to proving the allegations true. Even though the legislature seemed willing to let juries make allowances for a plaintiff's honestly held mistaken impressions, the Supreme Judicial Court insisted on shaping the rules of pleading and practice to prevent juries from considering the plaintiff's behavior in assessing the defendant's liability, especially if the defendant asserted that the allegations were true. Statutory changes likely reduced the risks of offering to rely on truth, but judges continued to resist the idea that juries should consider the plaintiff's own actions. The end of special pleading in Massachusetts, then, signals not just the lawyers' preference for content over form but a resistance to the judiciary's constraints. In Massachusetts the end of special pleading in defamation cases reflected less a broad preference for content over form than a commitment to opening up the courtroom to more of a particular kind of content, evidence of truth.

Nova Scotia

Truth caused no comparable problems in Nova Scotia during this period. As in Massachusetts until 1836, the truth defense was specially pleaded in civil suits. The surviving Nova Scotia records disclose only two truth defenses made in civil cases during the 1820s and 1830s.[20] The plea was made by S.G.W. Archibald and Charles Fairbanks in defending Anthony Henry Holland against Simon Fraser: a great deal of evidence about the insufficient provisioning of the *Ann*

---

[20] The pleadings have not survived for most of the Nova Scotia cases of the period, but it is clear that in seven other Halifax cases no truth plea was made.

of Banff was introduced to convince the jury of Fraser's dangerously parsimonious ways.[21] Justice Brenton Halliburton told the jury that "clear and unquestionable proof" was necessary when such a "bold" plea was put forward. The *Acadian Recorder*'s reporter inferred that Halliburton thought that Holland's evidence did not fully prove the truth of everything in the objectionable affidavit and that Fraser should win. Nonetheless, whether because of this line of defense or another, the jury acquitted Holland, to resounding cheers.

The following year, in 1822, Archibald again defended Holland, this time in a suit over a letter Holland published that suggested that a western county postmaster named William Bowes had been intercepting newspapers and renting them out before giving them to their proper recipients.[22] John Howe Jr., who was Nova Scotia's Deputy Postmaster General, fired Bowes and refused to reinstate him unless he could clear his name. The case showed the theatrics of courtroom strategy. Without pleading truth in advance, Archibald led certain evidence about Bowes's suspicious acts with newspapers that passed through his hands. Bowes's counsel, James W. Johnston and Richard J. Uniacke Jr., could have objected to the introduction of this evidence but did not. After Archibald finished introducing this evidence – perhaps over Justice James Stewart's raised eyebrows – Johnston rose and pointed out that although he could have protested against this admission of this evidence, his client "was anxious that a strict investigation should take place." Johnston said he had taken the precaution of having some witnesses present (not as many, the jury could infer, as might have been available if proper notice had been given) who could rescue Bowes's character. These witnesses then explained the circumstances around the renting out of some of the papers that passed through Bowes's hands, all of which suggested that he had behaved with perfect propriety. The fact that some people who had not given permission had also had their papers rented out went disregarded. If Archibald and Holland had actually set out these incidents in truth pleas, rather than springing them on Bowes, both Bowes and the judge would have had to address them fully. But these

[21] "The Press – Colonel Simon Fraser v. Anthony H. Holland for a Libel," *Acadian Recorder* (Halifax), May 5, 1821.
[22] "Supreme Court. Hilary Term: Action for Libel," *Free Press* (Halifax), January 22, 1822.

allegations were not pleaded. The jury awarded Bowes fifty pounds in damages, so the explanations must have been convincing, even though they did not address the improprieties of which Holland's witnesses complained.

The truth defense, then, may have worked in Holland's first case but it failed in his second. *Bowes v. Holland* suggests that in Nova Scotia the defense could be set up even without the plea if the plaintiff did not object; the importance of actually raising the available objections must always be kept in mind. Johnston apparently realized that Bowes's character would be redeemed more effectively by a win based on the jury's belief in his integrity than on a win based on the exclusion of evidence of truth. Appearing to be caught off guard by Archibald but still able to defend his client probably strengthened Johnston's hand by drawing the jury's sympathy.

Johnston's response to Archibald's stunt in *Bowes v. Holland* – allowing the evidence to be led despite the lack of a truth plea – would have been out of place in Massachusetts. Massachusetts lawyers often gave notice that they might plead truth (by seeking permission to plead double) and then did not do so, but when they acted for plaintiffs they were alert to exclude evidence of truth unless it was pleaded. Truth was much more of an electrified rail in Massachusetts than it was in Nova Scotia, despite the essentially similar law.

Truth in Criminal Cases

Truth was no defense to a criminal libel prosecution in Nova Scotia in the 1820s and 1830s. In Massachusetts, however, the role of truth was the central controversy in this area of law during the period: was evidence of truth only admissible to show the good intentions of a certain subset of defendants or would truth instead be recognized as a full defense to criminal proceedings? My sample contains no seditious libel prosecutions: these proceedings had been discredited after the partisan prosecutions of the early 1800s, being perceived as incompatible with a political system that depended on open disagreements among political actors.[23] The good reputations of citizens, however, were another matter, and libel prosecutions

---

[23] See Rabban, "Ahistorical Historian," 852–53; Post, "Defaming Public Officials," 543.

continued throughout the 1830s. Norman Rosenberg has argued that in the United States civil suits became more important than criminal actions, and by the Jacksonian period both were less important than newspapers as fora for airing political differences.[24] Indeed, in Massachusetts few criminal libel prosecutions arose from obviously partisan conflicts or were brought by the "best men," in Rosenberg's language, but they were often political nonetheless, as representatives of upstart religious persuasions and moral and social reform movements brought and defended claims. The goodness of their intentions and the propriety of publicizing certain matters were central considerations in these cases. The development of the law around evidence of truth lurched this way and that, as judges adapted it to cabin the threat these people posed to the existing structures of religious, political and familial authority.

Dangerous Apothecaries and Methodist Preachers

Discussion at the 1820 Massachusetts constitutional convention of explicitly recognizing a truth defense reflected and generated approaches to the topic that resonated through the 1820s and 1830s. More than 460 delegates attended, including Chief Justice Isaac Parker, who presided; justices Charles Jackson, Joseph Story and Samuel Wilde; other prominent members of the bar, including John Davis, Josiah Quincy, James T. Austin, Daniel Davis, Perez Morton, Levi Lincoln, John Adams, Daniel Webster and Lemuel Shaw; and other men of local prominence. The delegates fairly briefly considered a constitutional amendment that would have permitted anyone accused of a criminal libel against a "public" figure to introduce "evidence in support of his allegations" – that is, truth. The amendment would also have empowered the jury to decide both fact and law. Boston lawyer George Blake argued that the "odious" common law of libel operated in Massachusetts, that judges had "unlimited power in relation to the punishment of offenders" and that the truth of the allegation aggravated the offense. He and William Austin of Charlestown, both Republicans, defended the resolution, pointing out that the common law had a history of being

[24] Rosenberg, *Best Men*, 120, 130–52.

altered to impair freedom of the press and that the legislature had already had plenty of time to amend the common law if so inclined.

Among those opposing the amendment were Isaac Parker, Charles Jackson and Salem lawyer Leverett Saltonstall. They expressed confidence in the correctness of the common law as it currently stood, asserting that the amendment would merely establish constitutionally what was already common law and that the legislature could enact any necessary changes. Jackson, who had already decided *Jackson v. Stetson*, argued that the proposed amendment was both too narrow and too wide. He believed that currently one could "always publish the truth from right motives and for justifiable ends" and that the proposed amendment was too narrow in extending only to public figures. He thought the law should also protect reports on other situations, such as an apothecary vending poisons in the guise of medicine. On the other hand, the resolution seemed to establish a right to publicize any truth at all about a public officer, for any reason, including malicious ones, even if the matter had nothing to do with public life. The resolution failed and the *Clap* rule remained, but Jackson's two observations – that it had to be legal to report a dangerous apothecary and that the private lives of public officers had to be protected – resonated throughout the 1820s and 1830s.[25]

Jackson's proposition that certain issues might justify publication of truth underlay the prosecution of Joseph T. Buckingham in 1822 over an article he published in the *New-England Galaxy*. More diverse and controversial than the Nova Scotia press, the Massachusetts press included political and religious papers, as well as literary periodicals and the penny press, a breezy genre aimed at poorer people entertained by the social lives and misbehavior of the wealthy and respectable. At least twenty-four newspapers were published in Boston in 1830, and in mid-1833 a journal reported that at least seventy-six periodicals were being sold there.[26]

---

[25] *Journal of Debates and Proceedings in the Convention of Delegates*, 5–8, 243–44.
[26] See "Boston Books," *Spirit of the Age* (Boston), July 25, 1833 and Gregory, *American Newspapers*, 268–83 (Gregory's coverage does not include literary magazines). On literary periodicals and the penny press, see Cmiel, *Democratic Eloquence*, 60–61 and Horowitz, *Rereading Sex*, 129–30.

Travelers like Alexis de Tocqueville described the centrality of newspapers in Americans' lives. The news was usually delivered with the political or religious spin of the newspaper's editor, alongside a lot of advertising.[27] Most Boston dailies ran at least two columns in each issue about a political or religious controversy. Sparring letters laid issues before "the public" for judgment, often assailing views expressed in other newspapers. Articles on books, manners, domestic help and childrearing were aimed at women readers, for whom separate publications were also increasingly published. News was often reprinted from elsewhere or came from the courts or other local sources. The papers varied in their commitment to decorum and their willingness to engage in heated, partisan – and personal – debate, with some, such as the antimasonic papers, being particularly vitriolic. Henry Wadsworth Longfellow thought American newspapers appalling, partisan and deliberately provocative.[28] Of course, where some saw candor, others saw licentiousness.

Joseph Buckingham's *New-England Galaxy* was one of the more decorous, respectable Boston papers, although it was not uniformly conservative. The young Joseph Howe was an avid reader. He admired Buckingham's "spirit of fearless enquiry," despite the number of enemies it attracted and the occasional want of goodwill accompanying Buckingham's wit. Buckingham was no brahmin, but he nevertheless disdained political partisanship, believing that truth would prevail through "manly and temperate" political and religious discussion. Looking back in the early 1850s on his career in publishing, he reflected that some "licentiousness" – "caustic applications, bitter satire, unchristian reproach" – characterized the popular press of his earlier years, but he ascribed it to publishers pursuing financial stability by appealing "to the aristocratical sensibility of one class," and "the jacobinical prejudices of another."[29]

Despite this supposed distaste for licentiousness, Buckingham and other Massachusetts editors were more likely than Nova Scotian ones to make obviously defamatory allegations. For example, a poet named

[27] Tocqueville, *Democracy in America*, 92–94.
[28] "The Political Press," *Boston Recorder*, November 17, 1830.
[29] "The New-England Magazine," *Novascotian* (Halifax), May 2, 1833; Buckingham, *Personal Memoirs*, 1:78–80 and 2:120–21. On Buckingham, see Kornblith, "Becoming Joseph T. Buckingham."

R.S. Coffin complained of Buckingham's reprinting of an article that described Coffin, "the 'Boston Bard,'" as living in drunken poverty and misery in New York. (Coffin also wrote a pamphlet decrying the miserliness of New Englanders, who defamed him and failed to support his poetic endeavors.)[30] It was the Reverend John N. Maffit, however, who first brought Buckingham into court.

Maffit, a charismatic, young, originally Irish, itinerant Methodist clergyman, sued over an article that suggested that he had deceived his listeners about his past as a tailor and, moreover, did not really believe what he preached but enjoyed his access to the ladies. Buckingham, defending himself in court, opened by pronouncing truth his talisman and his sword, declaring he had published nothing but truth, and claiming that truth plus good intentions justified publication in the eyes of all men of good sense, even if the doctrine were new to courts. Under *Clap*, evidence of the truth of the allegations should have been inadmissible because Maffit held no public office and was not running for one. James T. Austin, prosecuting, acknowledged as much but nonetheless agreed to the admission of this evidence. The judge, Josiah Quincy III, who had lived through the furor of 1811 and attended the constitutional convention, issued a formal ruling, despite *Clap*, that the evidence could be admitted. He told the jury to acquit Buckingham if they found the article true and published with good motives and for justifiable ends – he said he thought the constitution required this result. Accordingly, evidence of Maffit's conversations with young women behind closed doors was admitted, as were confidential remarks he had made about his faith. Quincy, a Unitarian, evidently decided that the popular Methodist preacher's integrity was important enough to justify admitting evidence of the truth.[31] Buckingham was acquitted.

Quincy's ruling drew an open letter of protest from the old Unitarian Federalist Harrison Gray Otis, who had defended Clap. Otis reproached Quincy for unnecessarily exceeding his jurisdiction by following James Kent's judgment in *Croswell*, rather than *Clap*.

---

[30] Coffin, *Epistle to Joseph T. Buckingham*; Coffin, *The "Boston Bard" to the Citizens of Boston*.

[31] *Trial: Commonwealth vs. J. T. Buckingham*, 5, 6–7, 28–30; *Maffit's Trial*, 4; Buckingham, *Personal Memoirs*, 105–9; Otis, *Letter to the Hon. Josiah Quincy*, 6–7; Kimball, *Reflections Upon the Law of Libel*, 8; "Quincy, Josiah."

Otis warned that true libels would be even more likely than false ones to lead to disturbances of the peace. Otis thought it appropriate to limit the use of truth to cases involving men who occupied or sought public stations, and he thought it should only cover discussion of qualities that pertained to their fitness for office. Personal character defects were off limits. According to Otis, "all history shews that the greatest benefits have been sometimes conferred on nations, by statesmen and generals whose private characters were far from irreproachable." As well, the *Clap* assumption that the prosecution had to prove actual intent to harm (which made truth relevant) was misplaced: mere intent to publish was safer. Otherwise people claiming good intent would act as censors of others, giving their targets no chance to defend themselves. A person had no more right "to condemn, and punish, by a public exposure in the press" than to convict without trial and commit to the pillory. The proper response to vices that broke no law was to draw a veil over them. Otis recognized the difficulty in determining what was irrelevant to public life, but he was sure his distinction was "obvious and sound." In Otis's view, freedom of the press had never given a person the right to defame anyone else "but was thought valuable and worth contending for, only as the means of informing and enlightening the public, on questions of general concern."[32] This view was consistent with the language of the Massachusetts bill of rights, but more individualistic sensibilities prevailed.

Otis was right: a broader right to publish truth did permit some to judge others. Otis, however, was concerned about attacks on men in the higher ranks of society, whereas men like Maffit – challengers to religious and social orthodoxies – also experienced the consequences of this expanded commitment to truth. As the cases played out, the privacy interests of the class that concerned Otis tended to find protection, but the characters of Maffit and others like him were exposed to public scrutiny.

Libel Cases: Patterns of Prosecution

The records of the courts of Boston – but not Worcester – suggest a growing reliance on the law of criminal defamation beginning in the

---

[32] Otis, *Letter to the Hon. Josiah Quincy*, 6–8, 15, 31–34, 39, 44, 62.

later 1820s and probably tapering off in the later 1830s. This uptick correlates chronologically with the rise of reform movements and breakaway religious factions. From 1819 through 1826, the municipal court of Boston heard three prosecutions for obscene libel and four for defamatory libel, two of which emerged from the same original indictment. One of the obscene libel cases and two of the defamatory libel cases targeted Lorenzo Turner Hall for articles he published in the *Boston Castigator* and the *Independent Microscope* in 1822 and 1824, in which he vividly exposed the location of brothels and suggested that an engraver and a naval agent were corrupt. Hall was convicted and sentenced to jail every time, and his sole appeal was dismissed.

The other two defamatory libel cases were brought against Joseph T. Buckingham. The first concerned Reverend John Maffit. The second was brought in 1824 on the complaint of Boston's Russian consul: he objected to being lampooned in the *Galaxy* for his childrearing practices and literary and artistic pretensions, and he disliked the insinuation that he had been involved in a fight at a ball. In these proceedings, Peter Oxenbridge Thacher, who had succeeded Quincy in the municipal court, held that the consul, although a figure in the world of politics, literature and law, was not a "public man," such that evidence of truth could be adduced against him under *Clap*. The public had no cognizable interest in the ball, even though at least 200 people attended it. Good motives and justifiable ends might justify publicizing news of a fugitive escaping justice for an infamous crime, but the ball was off limits, making evidence of truth inadmissible to rebut the presumption of malice. While Thacher followed *Clap*, his escaping fugitive joined Jackson's dangerous apothecary in the bestiary of hypotheticals that might justify the admission of evidence of truth.

These prosecutions of Buckingham and Hall, along with two obscenity cases, were brought by James T. Austin, the Suffolk county attorney appointed by Elbridge Gerry just over a decade earlier. Other editors and texts escaped his gaze, or he ignored them, and libel prosecutions remained rare in Suffolk in the 1820s. The municipal court heard none in 1830. By 1835, Austin was attorney general and Samuel D. Parker had taken over as Suffolk's attorney: that year there were three cases, but 1840 saw none. The records of the Supreme Judicial Court in Suffolk, which heard appeals (by new trial) throughout the period, also suggest a prosecutorial bump in the early 1830s. The record books reveal two criminal defamatory libel cases in the 1820s but one in 1832, three in 1833, one in 1837 and one in 1839, along with one prosecution for blasphemous libel.[33] In Worcester, on the other hand, after two obscene libel cases in 1820 and 1821, the Supreme Judicial Court heard only two more libel cases during the period, both for defamation, and Common Pleas heard none in 1820, 1825, 1830 or 1835.

A disproportionate number of the cases in this sample involved either religious challengers – Universalists or Methodists – or reformers who campaigned against freemasonry, slavery, intemperance, sexual impropriety or gambling. I trace here the development of the law on the role of truth in criminal libel cases, paying particular attention to cases involving these sorts of people, who posed an acute problem for the respectable, self-regarding citizens of Boston. When reformers appeared in criminal court, they lost almost every time. The law was shaped largely by their arguments and the fears they activated. To make this point, while also tracing the doctrinal changes, I keep score on these cases, contrasting the failures of these reformers and religious challengers to the successes of those they opposed. Lorenzo Turner Hall may have been a reformer of a sort, but not much can be determined about him, so I leave him aside. Buckingham's victory in the Maffit case is therefore the first of these. Score: 0 for unorthodox preachers; 1 for the mainstream press.

James Blanding and Statutory Change

In 1825, two years after Harrison Gray Otis warned that reformers would claim the protection of truth as they sat in judgment over others, his prophecy came true. The Supreme Judicial Court in Bristol County entertained the first of the criminal libel cases in my sample over attacks on people who manufactured, sold or drank alcohol. As historians such as Alice Felt Tyler and Ian Tyrrell have explained, temperance was among the first of the major reform movements in

---

[33] The 1828 prosecution of Theodore Lyman Jr. for a libel on Daniel Webster does not appear in the record books because the Commonwealth stayed the charges. Other cases may also have ended this way, but probably most such cases would have been mentioned in newspapers or in pamphlets.

Massachusetts. Heavy liquor consumption both was, and was
constructed as, a large, longstanding problem. Alcohol was blamed
for a great deal of disorderly and criminal behavior. At first, the
temperance movement aimed at improving the behavior of the
northeast's lower orders after the War of 1812. That initiative having
failed, in the mid-1820s the movement was taken up by evangelically
inspired reformers seeking to improve all ranks of society. Waves of
prosecutions for violating liquor licensing laws took place in Boston's
municipal court in the early 1820s. Concerned about such matters as
the souls of the vulnerable, the productive efficiencies offered by
a sober workforce and a desire for personal upward mobility, women
and men pledged abstinence and sought crackdowns on unlicensed
sales and, ultimately, the end of licensing altogether.[34] In 1833,
nearly every Massachusetts county jailor reported that the largest
single category of crime for which he detained prisoners was
intemperance and drunkenness. A newspaper correspondent in 1835
claimed that one-quarter of Massachusetts criminal prosecutions were
for violations of license laws.[35]

In 1825 James Blanding, the editor of the Providence, Rhode Island
Gazette, faced a jury in Bristol for printing a letter that accused
a Massachusetts innkeeper, Enoch Fowler, of being responsible for
a man's death from intoxication and warning readers not to frequent
the inn. The court records of 1825 and 1826 suggest an ongoing local
conflict: Fowler's license was attacked in court, and he accused others
of purveying liquor without a license.[36] Even if Fowler's own actions
fueled the situation, though, Blanding's language of "liquid poison"
suggests that he was no friend to alcohol.

---

[34] Tyrrell, *Sobering Up*, 61–63, 91–98; Tyler, *Freedom's Ferment*, 308–50. Robert
Abzug recounts one scholar's opinion that in 1825 the average American over the
age of fifteen drank about seven gallons of alcohol each year, which was equivalent to
almost forty gallons of alcoholic beverages. By 1850, largely as a result of the
temperance movement, that American was drinking a mere 1.8 gallons of alcohol
a year: *Cosmos Crumbling*, 82. See also Miller, *Larger Hope*, 514–25; Abzug,
Cosmos Crumbling, 79–104; Novak, *People's Welfare*, 172–88.

[35] "Chapter of Crime," *Spirit of the Age* (Boston), March 6, 1834 (there was no report
from Berkshire). "The License Law and the Temperance People," *Boston Morning
Post*, March 5, 1835.

[36] See *Goff v. Fowler*, 20 Mass. (3 Pick.) 300 (1825) and the record books of the
Supreme Judicial Court at Bristol.

The judge refused to permit Blanding to adduce evidence from a coroner's inquiry that, by showing the truth of the claim, would also (it was hoped) have shown Blanding's lack of criminal intent. The arguments in the case blended recognized legal and constitutional precedent with principles that had been advanced as hypotheticals in earlier debates. Blanding's counsel, as well as demonstrating an awareness of English debates over libel law (and arguing that a report of a coroner's inquiry was protected), argued based on *Croswell* that freedom of the press "consists in publishing with impunity, truth with good motives and for justifiable ends, whether it relates to men or measures." He noted that Charles Jackson had adopted the same language at the 1820 constitutional convention and had suggested that an apothecary vending poison in the guise of medicine would also be protected – one would have a duty to inform. The attorney general, Perez Morton, argued that true libels could produce breaches of the peace and that Blanding's allegations could rightly only have been made to the court of sessions on a license renewal application. Freedom of the press, Morton argued, meant only freedom from prior restraint.

Chief Justice Parker, hearing the appeal about the excluded evidence, upheld the lower court's verdict. Parker suggested that the principles underlying *Clap* could be extended to other situations. Nevertheless, the public interest required that people "not arraign their neighbors, exposing them to partial trials in forms not warranted by the constitution or laws" and imposing on them heavier punishment than the law would have imposed for the offenses they had supposedly committed. Parker warned that although legal processes were accepted and did not inspire revenge among their targets, unlawful revenge, duels and assassinations would become common "if private intermeddlers, assuming the character of reformers" were permitted to make public accusations and to justify themselves "by breaking into the circle of friends, families, children and domestics, to prove the existence of errors or faults which may have been overlooked or forgiven where they were most injurious." The constitution protected character as well as the liberty of the press, and the press was protected only from prior restraints on what it could publish. Criticism of "public men," even in their "private characters" was acceptable as necessary for republicanism, but the line had to be drawn there, or else society would collapse in violence. Certain narrow privilege-type defenses provided all the additional protection necessary in the absence of a wide-ranging truth defense.

The coroner's jury had held that the deceased died of intoxication in Fowler's inn. Blanding's jury convicted him for alleging that Fowler had "administered the *liquid poison*" that caused the man's death and for warning others. Parker acknowledged that cases might arise in which newspaper warnings could prevent greater evil, referring to Jackson's dangerous apothecary and adding his own hypothetical, "cases of gross swindling" – but Blanding's situation was different, since statutes provided a regulatory environment for punishing an innkeeper for malfeasance. Blanding's conviction stood. Score: 0 for reformers and representatives of upstart religions; 2 for those who disapproved of them (one of these having been a newspaperman, in Maffit's case, and one the complainant).

A New Statute: The Clap Rule under Pressure

The *Blanding* ruling was frustrating. The American Temperance Society was founded in Boston in 1826, and by the early 1830s temperance meetings were a regular feature of Massachusetts life.[37] James T. Austin, addressing the Massachusetts Society for the Suppression of Intemperance in 1830, urged the legal suppression of "places of resort" that sold alcohol. Some, however, thought reformers demanded too much. In 1833, the *Spirit of the Age* remarked dryly upon its "daily fortune to notice, with a regularity more exact than that of the steamboat," the sixth meeting of the "respectable Anti-Intemperance Society." The next month the *New-England Galaxy* – no longer edited by Buckingham – expressed the view that a beneficial reduction in alcohol consumption had taken place in the previous decade but that once former-alcoholics-turned-temperance-crusaders took over the movement, its ambitions had become too extreme; their demands for pledges of total abstinence intruded too far into families' private affairs.[38]

---

[37] Abzug, *Cosmos Crumbling*, 82, 90; Tyrrell, *Sobering Up*, 87–91.
[38] "Where Intemperance Begins," *Boston Recorder*, June 16, 1830; "Temperance Meeting," *Spirit of the Age* (Boston), July 4, 1833; "The Temperance Crusade," *New-England Galaxy* (Boston), August 31, 1833.

In March 1827 the new slander and libel statute passed into law, thanks at least in part to the efforts of Buckingham's former counsel Samuel Knapp and a liberal-minded lawyer named Andrew Dunlap.[39] As noted above, the second section took aim at the rule in *Alderman v. French*. The first section loosed New York's approach to truth on Massachusetts, stating

[t]hat in every prosecution for writing and publishing any libel, it shall be lawful for any defendant upon trial of the cause, to give in evidence in his defence, the truth of the matter contained in the publication charged as libellous: [p]rovided, always, that such evidence shall not be a justification, unless on the trial it shall be further made satisfactorily to appear, that the matter charged as libellous was published with good motives and for justifiable ends.[40]

With this statute, the creeping growth of situations in which judges recognized or hypothesized that evidence of truth could be admitted while still preserving the proper line between public and private life ended. Truth officially became a defense, rather than just a factor relevant to a finding of good intent. Now "good motives" and "justifiable ends" rather than the appropriateness of the public's interest in the plaintiff's character became the snare for the unwary. The statute was interpreted as establishing that truth could be a defense if good motives and justifiable ends were established. It left unanswered the question of whether a lack of criminal intent could still save a defendant, pursuant to *Clap*. If criminal intent was still a core issue, false statements made innocently might still be excused. Otherwise, a defendant would not escape unless the allegations were true, regardless of intention.

The possibility that a lack of bad intent might yet save someone accused of an allegation that turned out to be false survived the only two overtly political prosecutions in the period, of Theodore Lyman Jr. in 1828–29 in Suffolk and David Lee Child in 1832 in Middlesex. Lyman was one of a group of sometime Federalists who opposed the reelection of John Quincy Adams because of his support for Jefferson's

---

[39] Dickerson, *Course of Tolerance*, 33; *Law of Libel. Report of the Trial of Dr. Samuel Thomson*, 7.
[40] An Act Relating to Prosecutions for Libel, and to Pleadings in Actions for Libel and Slander, ch. 107, 1826 Mass. Acts 493.

Embargo Acts of 1807 and 1808. Lyman supported Jackson instead. The article Lyman published really attacked Adams, but Lyman lumped Daniel Webster in with the Federalists who, Lyman suggested, had conspired in 1807 and 1808 to break up the union and reannex Massachusetts to Great Britain. Webster, finding himself labeled a traitor by a Jacksonian, objected heartily.

Austin received the complaint and recommended taking it directly to the Supreme Judicial Court, rather than the municipal court. It was prosecuted by Daniel Davis, the solicitor general and a veteran of Elbridge Gerry's 1811 campaign against the Federalist press. Davis apparently offered to discontinue the proceedings if Lyman would offer a frank acknowledgment of his error, but Lyman refused.[41]

The defense argued that there were now two ways to defend against a libel prosecution: the older *Clap* approach, "to deny the act and the malice, and to put the prosecutor to the proof of both," and the newer truth defense, "to assert the truth of the matter contained in the supposed libel, and that it was published from good motives and justifiable ends." Webster's commitment to the union was not in question, and Lyman's counsel did not attempt a truth defense. Instead, they took the first path, arguing that the jury could consider all the evidence in determining whether or not Lyman's intent was malicious. Davis, who had prosecuted Clap, argued that it was the height of legal absurdity that falsity could be given in evidence to prove good intent. It was truth, he argued, that disproved malice, without which there was no libel.[42]

Parker charged the jury on the importance of a free press but also on the press's legal obligation to respect private character and not circulate falsehood against either private or "public" men. Following *Clap*, Parker stated that the inference of malice drawn from the publication could be rebutted by proof of "an honest purpose and an innocent design." The jury could not reach a verdict, and in November 1829 Davis discontinued the proceedings, reasoning that justice did not require another trial.[43]

---

[41] Whitman, *Report of a Trial*, 26–27; Benton, *Notable Libel Case*, 96.
[42] Whitman, *Report of a Trial*, 15–19, 61. This case also contained the only fair comment defense in my sample: *ibid*. 68; Benton, *Notable Libel Case*, 99.
[43] Whitman, *Report of a Trial*, 72; Benton, *Notable Libel Case*, 102–3. The arguments and reasoning in the *Clap* line of cases are inconsistent on which side bore the burden

Origen Bacheler: Serving the Public Good by Debating the Unorthodox

The Methodist John Maffit is the first representative of religious unorthodoxy in my sample to appear in a Massachusetts courtroom in a criminal libel case. In the second such case, an outspoken orthodox newspaper editor, Origen Bacheler, was prosecuted in Boston's municipal court in March 1829 for what was actually an attack on the Universalists' *Trumpet* newspaper. The municipal court judge, Unitarian deacon Peter Oxenbridge Thacher, had to deal with both the suspect Universalists and the dogmatic, argumentative and poorly self-represented Bacheler and his truth defense.[44]

The *Trumpet* had published an obituary of a young man, George Beals, whom it characterized as a having lived a model life, free of profanity and drink, and modest and genteel in deportment. Beals, it said, did not adhere to any particular religion but died believing that he had lived well, that God was above the Devil, and that he had nothing to fear from death. Bacheler, however, in his *Anti-Universalist* newspaper, asserted that Beals had been a habitually profane Universalist who – fortunately – had experienced a deathbed conversion and died in grace. It was likely the young man's father who complained to James T. Austin about Bacheler's depiction of his son.

Bacheler argued that Beals was really defamed not by the *Anti-Universalist*'s account but by the *Trumpet*'s, in its depiction of the deceased's insipid state of mind on facing death. Representing himself, Bacheler called the deceased's friends and relatives to prove his habitual profanity. Austin denied that Bacheler could possibly have had good motives and justifiable ends in exposing the beliefs and character of one who had died so young and in stirring up the feelings of the living to promote religious controversy. Bacheler, on the other hand, asserted that the press could not be restrained on

---

of proof with respect to intent. The question likely did not matter much in practice, since juries ultimately decided.

[44] "Died," *Trumpet* (Boston), January 10, 1829; "Veracity of the Trumpet," *Anti-Universalist* (Boston), January 21, 1829; Bacheler, *Review of the Trial of Origen Bacheler*; Whitman, *Trial of the Commonwealth, versus Origen Bacheler*.

religious matters and that the *Trumpet*'s lies were of great public importance.[45]

Bacheler persuaded Thacher. He suggested to the jury that inappropriate eulogizing of the dead would not stimulate the living to virtue. It seemed acceptable to him, in the name of legitimate controversy and freedom of religion and the press, for Bacheler to correct errors and "seize the opportunity to inculcate a religious or moral truth." But, like the question of George Beals's propensity to swear, the question of intent was, in the end, for the jury. The next day the jury acquitted Bacheler, presumably finding the article true and his motives good. They did, however, ask Thacher to tell Bacheler that they did not approve of what he had done.[46] Score: 0 for reformers and representatives of upstart religions; 3 for those who disapproved of them (two newspapermen and one complainant).

David Lee Child: The Lawyer As Reformer

David Lee Child, introduced in Chapter 3, had recently become both a lawyer and a legislator when, in the lead-up to the 1828 federal election, he found himself defending two libel cases, one civil and one criminal. The civil case arose after years of public concern about financial malfeasance in the state prison.[47] Child had appeared before a legislative committee as counsel for the prison's warden. When Child published his findings about the prison, its superintendent, Samuel Johnson, sued him, while the governor and others moved to reform the institution. Child prevailed in Common Pleas but lost before a jury in Supreme Judicial Court in November 1828. Johnson was represented by Lemuel Shaw and James T. Austin, soon to become chief justice and attorney general, respectively. Child's truth defense failed, but damages were small.

The criminal prosecution – the second overtly political prosecution in my sample – arose from an article Child published in the *Journal* in March 1828. The article contained an allegation that John Keyes, who

---

[45] Whitman, *Trial of the Commonwealth, versus Origen Bacheler*, 22–25, 28, 46.
[46] *Ibid.*, 45–47. Being very much aggrieved by the jury's admonition and the treatment meted out to him in court, Bacheler then published a sixty-seven-page pamphlet in which he laid his case before the public: Bacheler, *Review of the Trial of Origen Bacheler*, 3–4.
[47] D.L. Child, *Report of the Case of Alleged Contempt.*

represented Middlesex in the Massachusetts Senate, had acted corruptly as chairman of the Committee of Accounts. The committee had advertised for sealed proposals for the state printing contract. Child alleged that before the seals were broken Keyes proposed that the contract should be given to the proprietors of the *Boston Statesman*, a Jacksonian paper, as long as their proposal did not exceed others' by more than $500. The *Statesman* had held the contract for the previous two or three years.[48]

Like Theodore Lyman's prosecution, this case went straight to Supreme Judicial Court. Child was prosecuted at the October 1828 term in Middlesex by Daniel Davis. Davis began his remarks by observing that candidates for election could expect to have their characters "ripped and torn all to pieces by lawless writers for the public press," but he assured the jury that Child had more talent, integrity and standing in the community than other editors. Davis succinctly defined a libel and stated his assumption that the defense would be truth. He told the jury that the law imputes malicious intent from acts that harm others, but that the presumption of malice could be rebutted by proof of innocent intent. Malice, he added, was inferred from a false libel, but the presumption could be rebutted by proof of absence of malice.[49] In opening, Davis thus followed *Clap* in his explanation of the role of truth, and he left open the possibility that a false libel published with good intentions could be excused.

One of Child's lawyers, William Gardiner, told the jury that as the editor of a respectable journal, Child was bold in airing public issues but was not given to vulgar slander, exposing domestic life to the public or heaping scurrilous abuse on his opponents. Gardiner suggested that Keyes, in prosecuting for political criticism, was offending republican principles. This was a public matter properly brought before the public, especially since an election in which Keyes was a candidate was on the horizon. Gardiner denied that Child's decision to write about the events a few months after they occurred, in the lead-up to the election, indicated malice – this was, Gardiner

[48] Whitman, *Trial of the Commonwealth versus David Lee Child*, 3–4, 7. See also *Review, of the Report of the Case.*
[49] Whitman, *Trial of the Commonwealth versus David Lee Child*, 9–10.

said, exactly the right time to air information about a candidate for
office.[50]

In opening argument Gardiner presented a progressive narrative in
which freedom of the press in the United States became broader than
anywhere else in the world but still in need of improvement in the name
of republican liberty. He reasoned that the English formulation of
freedom of the press as freedom from prior restraint left unanswered
the vital question of what content libel law forbade. Gardiner
described the oppressive history of English libel law and the peculiar
position of juries, instructed to infer malicious intent from the fact of
publication but in fact empowered to judge intent along with the rest of
the case under Fox's Libel Act. He noted that in cases not involving the
government, judges had ameliorated the law's severity, such as by
shielding authors against hostile book reviewers. Gardiner urged the
court to rethink common law principles, to enable the public to
scrutinize freely the conduct of officeholders and candidates by
allowing newspaper editors to disclose what the people needed to
know.[51]

Gardiner then turned to American law. Even the Sedition Act made
bad intent part of the offense, made truth a defense and gave the whole
case to the jury. He reviewed the law since the Revolution, building up
to the recent statutory change in Massachusetts that allowed truth to
be given in evidence in libel cases and be a sufficient defense, if
published with good motives and for justifiable ends. Gardiner tried
to align the defenses of privilege and truth into a more protective shield
for the press. He argued that truth was not indispensable; an editor's
intent to inform the people of his honest belief in the misconduct of
a public official protected him because the essence of criminal libel was
criminal intent. Even falsity could be excused if published with good
motives and for justifiable ends. Without using the word "privilege,"
Gardiner described the English scenarios in which honest intent saved
the defendant: character references for servants, literary criticism, and
letters to friends warning of a merchant's impending bankruptcy. *Clap*,
Gardiner observed, left the defendant's intention the key question for
the trial and permitted truth to be admitted as evidence on this point.
Gardiner also cited the privilege cases *Remington v. Congdon* and

---

[50] *Ibid.* 10–16.   [51] *Ibid.* 17–21.

Bodwell v. Osgood, arguing that without proof of actual malice, complaints made to competent authorities could not be the subject of legal proceedings, a point noted in *Blanding* and made more clearly in *Thorn v. Blanchard* from New York. The public was the proper tribunal for complaints like Child's. Gardiner argued that people had a constitutional right to publish the truth about anyone or to publish whatever they honestly and on reasonable grounds believed about a public official, as long as they had good motives and justifiable ends.[52]

Gardiner went on to describe the circumstances and prepare the jury to hear the evidence that Child's allegations were true and that, even if they were not, his innocence was nonetheless clear. Keyes and other witnesses were heard. Richard Fletcher mounted a learned closing for the defense (although Davis called him out for citing Jeremy Bentham). He reviewed the evidence and continued to insist on the importance of a free press to free Americans and that intention was the crux of the case.[53]

In closing, Davis called newspapers "the star chamber of the mob." He told the jury that the questions for them were whether a libelous statement had been published against Keyes and whether it was true. If it was false, it was malicious. Some witnesses had testified that the allegations were untrue. Davis denied that a false statement published ignorantly or on reasonable grounds could be excused: "if the allegations were false, and of a criminal nature in their accusations, they were malicious and libellous." The new statute meant that only a true statement could be excused, and it must also be made with good motives and justifiable ends. No false statement could be justified, regardless of intent. Although, per *Clap*, truth could be given in evidence to show good motives and justifiable ends, falsehood could not.[54]

In English law, evidence of truth could not be led in criminal cases; privilege arguments turned on circumstances and intentions. Massachusetts courts, having opened the door to truth, had to address falsity. The end has not yet come for the argument that

[52] *Ibid.* 22–29; *Thorn v. Blanchard*, 5 Johns. 508 (NY CE, 1809).
[53] Whitman, *Trial of the Commonwealth versus David Lee Child*, 29–32, 62–79.
[54] *Ibid.* 79–82, 86–87.

malicious intention was essential for a criminal conviction, but it was
in sight now that truth was a full-fledged defense. Justice Marcus
Morton spoke of the importance of a free press and of informing the
public about the characters of people running for office. Freedom of the
press, he said, meant the right to publish truth with good motives and
for justifiable ends – but not to publish "falsehood, calumny, and
slanders." Although the jury could judge both law and fact, they
should only depart from the law as laid down by the judge unless it
was obviously wrong to abide by it. He told the jurors he thought
Child's words libelous but to make up their own minds. If the words
were true – not necessarily literally but generally so in charging Keyes
with corruption in the course of these events – then Child was justified
in publishing them. Morton carefully reviewed the evidence. He
instructed the jury that the law inferred malicious intention from the
publication, and that if the truth defense failed, the necessary intent
would be proven from the publication itself.[55] Morton allowed,
however, that in some cases, the publication's falsehood might "not
be inconsistent with innocence of all malicious intent," and sometimes
the circumstances could rebut the inference of malice. One such
situation was innocent republication, in which the defendant gave the
authority for the allegation and repeated it exactly; but Child had made
no such defense. The next morning the jury returned a verdict of
guilty.[56]

Child's appeal fell apart before it was properly filed, so that the
arguments his counsel should have made – on whether good motives
could still save a defendant – never reached the full court. Gardiner and
Fletcher did not apply for a new trial until several weeks after the term
ended. Essential to this kind of application was the trial judge's report
of how he had handled the disputed issues, in this case the evidence and
his instructions on intent. Usually the report was a couple of
handwritten paragraphs. Unfortunately, by the time Morton started
drafting his report, months had passed, pamphlets had been published
and his recollections were no longer certain. Gardiner and Fletcher sent
him a draft, which departed substantially from what he remembered
saying (and, apparently, was enormously long and alleged forty-six
errors). Morton therefore described the proceedings briefly, omitting

---

[55] *Ibid.* 89–98, 102.   [56] *Ibid.* 102–3.

all of the controverted evidence. Fletcher and Gardiner applied to the full court in the fall of 1830 for an order requiring Morton to draw up the report they required, but the judges refused. Child's application for a new trial and arrest of judgment was based only on this very brief report. Child did win in the end, but not on the question of intent: two years later judgment was arrested over the indictment's failure to refer adequately to certain facts without which the matter could not be libelous. Successful appeals on the law are extremely rare in my sample, and Child's was the only successful appeal in a criminal case.

Some were alarmed about the risks Morton's ruling posed for the political press, since regardless of editors' intentions, they would be liable if their allegations turned out to be false. One writer noted that Keyes had declined to stand for reelection and postulated that Morton, an honest judge though a Jacksonian, had simply erred in his instruction to the jury.[57] Score: 1 dubious victory (Child's belated one) for reformers and representatives of upstart religions; 3 for those who disapproved of them (two newspapermen and one complainant).

Truth and Strategy: William Wesson's Efforts to Silence His Colleagues

The scorekeeping must pause briefly for an exploration of the impact of the 1826–27 statute on the legal strategies and outcomes evident in civil and criminal proceedings based on the complaints of a young Congregational minister, William Wesson. In 1824 two more senior ministers, Thomas Holt and John Fiske, orally told people in Worcester County that Wesson had committed adultery with a "girl of ill fame" and had been warned that if he again attempted to preach, his character would be exposed. Holt and Fiske said they had a handbill with details ready to print. Two other respected clerical colleagues, Thomas Snell and Daniel Tomlinson, had prepared the handbill. In it, Snell and Tomlinson claimed to possess a copy of a letter from Wesson, dated November 1823, in which he responded guiltily to a letter accusing him of visiting a Boston brothel the previous May. Wesson's letter asked them to keep quiet and to forgive his

---

[57] *Review, of the Report of the Case*, 16.

misdeeds. Wesson's Hardwick congregation had dismissed him in 1824 for other reasons, at which point Wesson agreed not to seek another ministerial position in exchange for the silence of the other four ministers. When he sought to return to the pulpit anyway, the four took action.

Wesson began a slander suit against Holt and Fiske in 1825. In Common Pleas they pleaded truth – that in May of 1823 Wesson had committed adultery in a "house of ill fame" in Boston. Depositions in the court files indicate that during a ministerial convention in Boston (whose agenda included suppressing immorality), Wesson, a married man, had been seen more than once entering and leaving "Miss Pearce's" infamous brothel at the corner of Garden and Southack streets on "The Hill." "The Hill" or "Negro Hill," as it was also known, was a small, racially mixed area proximate to the West End on the north side of Beacon Hill, where about one-third of Boston's 1,900 African Americans lived and worked, where homes and shops were packed close together and where venues for drinking, sex and gambling were readily available.[58] A minister's wife who lived across the street deposed to having seen Wesson enter and leave the brothel. The next day another minister who lived nearby saw Wesson on the street and followed him, subsequently seeing, through a window of the same house, the torso of a man in dark clothes with his arm wrapped around a woman. Holt and Fiske prevailed on demurrers in Common Pleas in August 1825.

Wesson also pursued a criminal libel prosecution against Snell and Tomlinson over the pamphlet. The ministers were indicted in October 1825, and the case was continued to April 1826. At that point, Snell and Tomlinson submitted to the court a "statement of facts" that informed the prosecution of the events that justified their actions: that, in the self-incriminating letters quoted in the handbill, Wesson had agreed not to preach again and that they had not published the handbill until he again offered himself for the ministry. These kinds of facts would have been specially pleaded in a civil case.

---

[58] Bacon, *Rambles*, 141–43; *Plan of the City of Boston*; Hales, *Map of Boston*; Whitehill, *Boston*, 70–71; Hobson, *Uneasy Virtue*, 13–14; Horton and Horton, *Black Bostonians*, 1–3.

In April 1826, Solicitor General Daniel Davis admitted that Snell and Tomlinson could establish most of these particulars but challenged the "competency of the evidence" of the truth of these facts. Davis said that if the evidence could go to the jury, Snell and Tomlinson should be acquitted; otherwise they should be tried. Since the new statute was not yet in effect, Davis must have assumed that the impugned evidence would persuade the jury that Wesson, in resuming preaching, had turned into the clerical equivalent of a dangerous apothecary – truth plus good motives and justifiable ends would be proven – but Davis must also have thought the clergy were not obviously covered by the *Clap* exception (Thacher's ruling in *Buckingham* notwithstanding). Then the lawyers waited. The indictment was continued to October 1826 and then April 1827, when Davis discontinued the proceedings because of the passage of the new statute and the court's indication that it would apply to this case.

In a strange twist, in Supreme Judicial Court in October 1826, Wesson won his civil cases, despite Fiske's and Holt's truth defenses. A jury awarded him damages of fifty dollars against each of them, rather less than the five thousand pounds (each) he sought. The sum was not quite insultingly small. Perhaps the jurors felt sympathetic to Wesson or suspicious of prominent ministers who tried to prevent other men from preaching. Presumably no witness had seen Wesson in the act, but it seems unlikely that the jury was convinced by the story Wesson's witnesses were constructing in their depositions, that, while walking around Boston trying to track down a young relative, he and another, nameless man of a similar size wearing similar clothes were accosted by a denizen of Miss Pearce's, and that it was the other man who accepted her advances and was observed. This tale would not have stood up well against Wesson's supplications for pardon and mercy in the correspondence quoted in the handbill. Davis may have had understandable reservations about putting Wesson on the stand as complainant in the criminal case if evidence of truth were admissible. In a civil case, however, neither party could testify. The truth defense thus failed Fiske and Holt but saved Snell and Tomlinson, not at trial but through Davis's discretionary decision to stay the proceedings.

Wesson and his accusers being clergy of the same denomination, the score remains unchanged.

Frederick S. Hill and the Burdens of Disclosure

A procedural difficulty emerged once truth became a defense, or part of one. Snell and Tomlinson advised the prosecution of the particulars of their truth defense, but they did not have to: in criminal cases, unlike civil suits, defendants could surprise prosecutors with unexpected evidence. In a case called *Commonwealth v. Hill*, James T. Austin took the first step to ease this prosecutorial inconvenience – and again, a reformer lost.

By April 1830, Frederick S. Hill was editing the *New-England Galaxy*. Hill was no friend to the antimasonic movement, which had gathered much momentum in the wake of the kidnapping and presumed murder of William Morgan in upstate New York in 1826, just after he finished his exposé of freemasonry. Antimasonry was a centralized crusade that linked evangelical Christianity with an egalitarian suspicion of secret societies, influence and privilege. Chiefly a political, rather than a moral, reform movement, antimasonry appealed especially to the lower and middling orders of society, such as small retailers, less prominent lawyers and physicians, tavernkeepers, skilled artisans and farmers. Bruce Laurie argues that the very indifference of the conservative elite of Massachusetts to the needs of the toiling majority made it a fertile ground for antimasonry and later third-party movements.[59]

Hill's is the first case in my sample that involved antimasonry. In 1830 he published an article applauding the Salem selectmen's decision to refuse to permit a group of antimasonic "itinerant mountebanks" to present their views in a hall they had rented without disclosing their purposes. One of the ejected antimasons, Avery Allyn, complained.[60]

James T. Austin argued in the municipal court that the new statutory truth defense necessitated a rule that a defendant who intended to prove truth be required to provide a "bill of particulars" of what would be proven, with specific times and places, and be prevented from leading any evidence at trial that had not been

---

[59] Vaughn, *Antimasonic Party*, 1, 13–22; Laurie, "Spavined Ministers," 100, 118. See also Bullock, *Revolutionary Brotherhood*.

[60] On this case, see "Anti-Masonry," *New-England Galaxy* (Boston), April 30, 1830; "Our Indictment!" *New-England Galaxy* (Boston), June 18, 1831; "Anti-Masonry," *New-England Galaxy* (Boston), June 25, 1831.

particularized. Hill's lawyer, Mr. Prescott, successfully argued that such a procedure would be unprecedented, that surprise was simply a risk the prosecution took in deciding to bring an indictment. Particulars were required for a charge of barratry (repeated vexatious litigation), but, as Prescott pointed out, in these cases the prosecution furnished particulars to the defense, not the other way around. Prescott observed that the Massachusetts bill of rights protected a person from being "compelled to accuse or furnish evidence against himself'" and permitted every subject "to produce all proofs that may be favorable to him."

Peter Thacher ruled for Hill and also denied Austin's motion to postpone the case to gather evidence. The antimason Allyn had brought the case and should have known, Thacher thought, that Hill would have the right to put forward a truth defense, which might open up Allyn's past to investigation. Thacher commented that he knew "of no law or usage which authorizes the Court, in any criminal case, to require the Defendant before trial to disclose how he means to defend himself at his trial, or to give notice thereof to the prosecutor." At trial, a defendant could rely on any available evidence. Austin discontinued the proceedings, and whatever hopes the antimason held of vindication in court were disappointed. Hill announced in the next issue of the *Galaxy* that he would henceforth always speak of Allyn as "The Vagrant." Score: 1 limited victory for reformers and representatives of upstart religions (Child's); 4 for those who disapproved of them (three newspapermen and one complainant).

Tempers Rising

My sample suggests that the early 1830s brought an uptick in criminal libel prosecutions in Suffolk. One factor appears to have been a generational shift. Samuel D. Parker became county attorney for Suffolk in 1832, when James T. Austin became attorney general, replacing Perez Morton, who had been appointed in 1810, around the time that Austin became Suffolk's attorney.[61] James Blanding, alone in my sample, was prosecuted by Morton, by then in his

---

[61] The timing of Austin's appointment emerges from the cases and from Parker to Austin, July 6, 1832, James Trecothick Austin papers, Ms. N-1789, MHS.

seventies. Like Morton, Daniel Davis – who argued *Clap* and remained solicitor general through Elbridge Gerry's rise and fall – brought few libel cases. With the Worcester county attorney, Rejoice Newton, Davis conducted an obscenity prosecution in Supreme Judicial Court in 1821. In 1827, once truth became a defense, Davis, then well into his sixties, discontinued the prosecutions of Thomas Snell and Daniel Tomlinson. Davis prosecuted Theodore Lyman Jr., discontinuing those proceedings in 1829. He prosecuted David Lee Child in 1828 and defended the state in Child's 1830 appeal. In 1832 the office of solicitor general was abolished and Davis retired.[62] Austin and Parker held their appointments through the end of the 1830s, conducting all of the libel prosecutions in Suffolk for the rest of the 1830s and evidently bringing new enthusiasm to the work.

Reform causes, too, were gathering momentum in the later 1820s and early 1830s in Boston, shaping the environment in which libel law operated. David Lee Child and Maria Child became deeply involved in antislavery. In the winter of 1828–29 Maria Child published her *First Settlers of New-England*, a children's book that included theories of racial equality and suggested that interracial marriage was acceptable. In the fall of 1829, William Lloyd Garrison called her the "first woman in the republic." She reached a huge audience with her homemaking advice book, *The Frugal Housewife*, first published in November 1829. It ultimately went through thirty-three American editions, as well as English and German ones. Child published her first antislavery story in her *Juvenile Miscellany* magazine in the fall of 1830, and each subsequent issue contained an antislavery story. She published the first American manual on childrearing, her *Mother's Book*, in June 1831; it ultimately went through eight editions. Not everyone was impressed, however. A tale called "My Wife's Novel" was published in 1832. The story, attributed to Edward Everett (who became governor of Massachusetts in 1835), attacks a young woman who, with her husband's encouragement, embarks on a career as an author, which leads to financial and social embarrassment for them both. The characters and plot strongly resembled the Childs and their careers.[63]

---

[62] Davis, *History of the Judiciary of Massachusetts*, 285.
[63] L.M. Child, *Appeal*, xiii–xiv; Austin, "Collection As Literary Form," 160–62. On L.M. Child's life, see Karcher, *First Woman in the Republic*. See also review of *The*

David Lee Child became involved in a third libel case in the late 1820s, which emerged from a battle with William Beals and the other editors of the *Commercial Gazette*. In July 1829, the *Gazette* published two satirical poems, one of which depicted Child as fiendishly violent, a man who beat his wife and sister, tortured farm animals, attempted to murder another youth at Harvard, and violently abused his students when he taught school. The second poem suggested Child opposed prison discipline, sympathized with thieves, had slandered Justice Samuel Putnam and certain respectable women, and deserved jail for his libels. Child sued, losing in Common Pleas but prevailing before a jury in Supreme Judicial Court. Unusually, the full court allowed the defendants' appeal and ordered a new trial on the odd grounds that evidence of provocation should have been admitted to mitigate damages. Child appears then to have dropped the case.

As described in Chapter 3, Child touched off legislative proceedings for a libel against himself in January 1832 through his representation, in the *Massachusetts Journal* (which he stopped editing soon afterward), of a procedural dispute he had with the speaker of the Massachusetts House, William Calhoun. Child's version of the events suggested that Calhoun ruled a pliable House with a heavy hand. The House ultimately pronounced Child deserving of censure. He resigned his seat in protest, never to return.

As Maria Child's popularity was reaching its zenith and David Lee Child's political reform efforts were attracting opposition in some quarters, the couple's engagement with antislavery was deepening. When William Lloyd Garrison was tried for libel in Baltimore for an article he published in late 1829, David Lee Child defended him in the *Journal*. Neither Garrison nor Child thought that the heirs of the American Revolution could justly condemn Nat Turner and his followers for rising up against slaveholders and other white people in August 1831.[64] It was an unpopular opinion. Both Childs espoused antislavery views in print. David joined Garrison and others in founding the New England Anti-Slavery Society in the winter of 1831–32. Its constitution was adopted January 6, 1832 in the

---

Token: A Christmas and New Year's Present, edited by Samuel G. Goodrich, *New-England Magazine*, 1 (July–December 1831): 356.

[64] Karcher, "Introduction," in L.M. Child, *Appeal*, xx–xxviii; Garrison, *Brief Sketch*.

African Meeting House, on the Hill. In a speech on the NEASS's first anniversary, David argued that American slaveholders were the worst in the world.[65] Months later, Maria Child published the first edition of her *Appeal in Favor of that Class of Americans Called Africans.* Social distancing and the mass cancellation of subscriptions to the *Juvenile Miscellany* ensued, and she ceased editing that journal. Her *Mother's Book* rapidly disappeared, and even sales of *The Frugal Housewife* fell off. James T. Austin supposedly threw the *Appeal* out the window with a pair of tongs. Maria Child and Louisa Loring organized the first antislavery fair in December 1834. Child continued her very public antislavery activities throughout the rest of the decade, while her husband left legal practice. Their abolitionist contemporary John Greenleaf Whittier observed that David's "outspoken hostility to the peculiar institution greatly and unfavorably affected his interests as a lawyer."[66]

David Lee Child's work as a lawyer also affected the development of the law around evidence of truth through his defense – with Samuel Sewall – of William J. Snelling, another early member of the NEASS. Snelling had succeeded Joseph T. Buckingham and Frederick S. Hill in the editorship of the *New-England Galaxy.* In 1831, while purporting to guard "the sanctuary of private life," Snelling published a life of Andrew Jackson, in the spirit of exposing character flaws he felt the public needed to understand.[67] That spirit did not serve Snelling well in Massachusetts.

Snelling participated in the American antigambling movement of the mid-1830s.[68] In 1833 he was publishing letters and articles about gamblers and gambling establishments. One result was three libel prosecutions over articles he published in the *Galaxy.* The first arose from a May article in which Snelling very deliberately accused police court judge Benjamin Whitman "of disgracing his office, of perverting

---

[65] D.L. Child, *Despotism of Freedom.*

[66] L.M. Child, *Appeal,* xiv, xliv–xlv; Ceplair, *Public Years,* 5–10; Whittier, biographical introduction to L.M. Child, *Letters,* ix.

[67] Snelling, *Brief and Impartial History,* iv. Snelling's father was Josiah Snelling Jr., after whom Fort Snelling, in Minnesota, is named. The younger Snelling, who in his early twenties lived among the Dakota, gained lasting acclaim for his writing on Native Americans: Reichardt, "Snelling, William Joseph."

[68] Gamblers were lynched in St. Louis and in Vicksburg, MI in 1833 and 1835, respectively: Waldrep, *Many Faces of Judge Lynch,* 27–35.

law – which, bad as it is, is yet worse in such hands – of doing injustice on his seat, of descending from his official dignity, of suffering personal feeling to interfere with the discharge of his functions."[69] Alcohol was part of the problem. Unfortunately for Snelling, Whitman was one of the most highly regarded older lawyers of the period. He had argued *Coffin v. Coffin* in 1808, had sat in the police court since its founding in 1822, and was an elder in the eminently respectable Congregational Old South Church.[70]

The problem of the defense surprising the prosecution with unanticipated evidence arose again in this case, which ultimately produced a ruling that broke with constitutional tradition by requiring the defense to supply particulars to the prosecution. Ultimately Austin got this order from the relatively new chief justice, Lemuel Shaw. The manner in which Sewall and Child defended Snelling contributed to making the Commonwealth lawyers' demands for particulars persuasive, especially to Shaw.

Over a four-day trial in municipal court in July 1833, Snelling was prosecuted by the new Suffolk attorney, Samuel D. Parker, and defended by Child, while other newspaper editors watched the trial closely. Parker, in opening, noted that the grand jury had found this indictment itself – Whitman had not laid a complaint. Parker argued that such libels endangered the stability of the state, even if true, and asserted that instead of addressing the public about Whitman, Snelling should have petitioned the Senate. Opening for the defense, Child proposed to prove the charges true and published from good motives and for justifiable ends. Citing *Blanding*, Child asserted that it was wholly proper for Snelling to comment on the conduct of a public

---

[69] *Comm. v. Snelling*, Thach. Crim. Cas. 318, 318 (1836); *Trial of William J. Snelling*, 3 (quoting the article). See also "Our Trial," *New-England Galaxy* (Boston), July 13, 1833; "Trial of William J. Snelling," *New-England Galaxy* (Boston), July 13, 1833; "Trial of William J. Snelling," *New-England Galaxy* (Boston), July 20, 1833; "Snelling's Trial," *Boston Morning Post*, July 11, 1833; "Trial of William J. Snelling," *Boston Morning Post*, July 11, 1833; "Trial of William J. Snelling," *Boston Morning Post*, July 12, 1833; "Trial of William J. Snelling," *Boston Morning Post*, July 13, 1833; "Trial of William J. Snelling," *Spirit of the Age* (Boston), July 18, 1833; "Libels," *Boston Daily Advocate*, July 13, 1833; Thomas W. Phillips to James T. Austin, November 19, 1833, James Trecothick Austin papers, Ms. N-1789, MHS.

[70] Davis, *History of the Judiciary*, 207–8, 227; Old South Church Records, 1817–1854, Congregational Church archives, Boston; and see Warren, *History of the American Bar*, 318–19.

officer. Child enumerated instances of Whitman's supposed failures to dispose properly of cases before him, including his refusal to take steps against some dangerous people Snelling had crossed in his antigambling campaign. Child began calling witnesses to show the truth of Snelling's allegations. When he then tried to introduce evidence of yet more episodes of misconduct, Parker objected that since the new incidents had not been mentioned in Child's opening address and were not evident in the libel itself, the prosecution had no opportunity to prepare to meet them. Thacher permitted Child to add some new allegations and the evidence to support them but ruled that no further allegations could be added. At least some of these new allegations appear to have involved allegations of drunkenness off the bench, but Child did not attempt to prove that Whitman was intoxicated in court. Thacher ruled that the defense could be restricted to specifications set out at the beginning of the case for the defense.[71]

Thacher's charge to the jury favored Whitman, presenting Snelling as a zealous young man of considerable ability unjustly attacking an older man mercifully exercising his legitimate discretion on the bench. Ignoring the pre-1826 decisions that had expanded the range of situations that might justify introducing evidence of the truth of defamatory allegations, Thacher read the requirement of good motives and justifiable ends in the new statute as imposing on the defendant who mounted a truth defense the need to prove that the public needed the information. Otherwise, the follies of youth might be raked up or "the sanctuary of domestic life ... invaded by publishing the faults of a child or other near relative, and only to justify a refined malice." If the public had no just interest in the information and Snelling was animated by actual malice, the defense would fail.[72] Thacher's attention then shifted from Snelling's intentions to the instances Child had amassed to show misconduct, suggesting that if Whitman appeared lenient toward Boston's malefactors, he was probably erring on the side of being too humane, making the allegations false. The jury convicted Snelling, and he was sentenced to a fifty-dollar fine plus costs of $25.98 and sixty days' imprisonment.

---

[71] *Comm. v. Snelling*, Thach. Crim. Cas. 318, 319–20 (1836).   [72] *Ibid.* 323–24.

Snelling appealed. Samuel Putnam presided over Snelling's trial in the Supreme Judicial Court in late December 1833, which took more than a week.[73] This time the new attorney general, James T. Austin, joined Parker, and Franklin Dexter and Samuel Sewall took over from David Lee Child. The trial involved forty witnesses for the defense alone.

As in *Hill*, the prosecution sought an order requiring the defense to particularize by providing the details of every episode they intended to prove true. This time Austin got his order. The defense had four hours to set out the case. The incidents of alleged magisterial malfeasance included not only Whitman's actions in various proceedings before him but also instances in which he had been too intoxicated to perform properly on the bench. Snelling's counsel announced their intention to prove "that he has, for years together, drank [*sic*] a pint and a half of gin *per diem*. We shall show that he has been seen inebriated on his bench. We do not mean to say that he gets drunk every day; but we expect to show the continued habit of hard drinking."

Parker opened, insisting that "the greater the truth, the greater the libel" and that most of Whitman's so-called errors were legitimate exercises of his discretion. Snelling's malice, Parker argued, was manifest: he had called Whitman a fool and an old woman, which, Parker said, "unsexe[d]" Whitman and indeed was "the most flagrant insult that anger and malignity could devise." Parker suggested that Snelling intended to incite a mob against Whitman. At one point he spoke of Whitman being the one really on trial.

Part way through Sewall's opening address, as he began to lay out the cases that he said showed Whitman's improper sympathies for those before him, Parker and Austin attempted to have the entire truth defense thrown out. Parker objected that improper motives could not be inferred from legitimate exercises of discretion, even if the decisions had been wrong. Austin said no evidence of truth could even be led until Snelling's lawyers first showed that the publication had been made with good motives and justifiable ends. Dexter insisted that the incidents did support the allegations, that it would be unjust to

---

[73] "Libel Case," *Boston Morning Post*, January 6, 1834. The details of these proceedings are taken from the pamphlet *Trial of William J. Snelling*, which displays a certain tilt toward Snelling's side and may well reflect notes he took while listening.

reject the defense simply because the specifications might be less exact than a special plea in a civil suit, and that Snelling was entitled to lead evidence of truth before showing good motives and justifiable ends. After considering the matter overnight, Putnam decided in Snelling's favor. Austin, according to the reporter, made further objections but was overruled.

Sewall completed his opening address by briefly describing the incidents in the particulars and what they would show. Witnesses then began to testify, about Whitman's refusals to issue restraining orders to protect Snelling, his failure to permit some complaints to be fully presented, his altering of the records of what he had done, his confused, uncomprehending mien on the bench, his sometimes unsteady gait, and the occasional smell of liquor about him. This time the evidence of alcohol consumption went in. Whitman's adult children, an estranged daughter-in-law, a grandchild, domestics and other observers presented a great deal of evidence on how much alcohol was kept in his house (not more than two gallons of gin), how much Whitman drank and how it affected him. A number of witnesses testified to having seen him drunk on the bench and lurching through the streets in the daytime. The daughter-in-law, who had been turned out of the house, testified that Whitman was frequently drunk and abusive to his grandchildren and to herself. Although Whitman fed and clothed the children, she complained that they were often "lousy, and with their knees out." Mary Hall, who had worked as his cook and chambermaid, said he kept liquor in a closet, drank about a gill (four fluid ounces) at least seven or eight times a day and staggered to bed; she said she would not have testified if the defense had not compelled her to do so. Her husband, Lorenzo T. Hall, sometime editor of the *Boston Castigator*, spoke of his high regard for Whitman but also of seeing him drunk.

Prosecution witnesses presented circumstances to explain why Whitman had exercised his discretion as he had in these various cases, most suggesting that his drinking was not excessive and others emphasizing Whitman's great care of his grandchildren and the daughter-in-law's animus. One observed, "Judge Whitman drinks more freely at dinner than most people do now-a-days. He is one of the old school, but is not at all intemperate." Whitman himself testified, noting at the outset that his son had served in the military under Snelling's father. Asked about one incident after another, he described his considerations, saying he had not known about the danger to Snelling. Whitman alluded to rumors that his resignation was imminent. He wept on the stand.

The lawyers were disturbed. Closing for the defense, Dexter acknowledged that if he had known how the evidence would come out, he and Sewall might not have included the alcoholism incidents in their particulars. He asserted, however, that the public needed to know these facts. He reviewed the various cases of Whitman's apparent malfeasance, and he pointed out that the many witnesses to intoxication had no reason to lie. Recalling situations mentioned in *Blanding* and the constitutional convention, Dexter compared Whitman to a physician "being a quack, and selling poison. If true, the fact proves the motive." Whitman's intoxication affected the public. Snelling's motives were meritorious: he was attempting to clean up public life. Although the "old woman" comment was admittedly indiscreet, Snelling's motives and ends were good in using a newspaper to place his concerns before the public.

Austin, however, was venomous:

Is there not great cause to complain of the whole course of this defence – of these inflammatory specifications – of the inflamed language of the opening counsel for the defendant – of the character of the witnesses – of discarded children – domestics – witnesses from the purlieus of Judge Whitman's court, who have been convicted before him – gathering from those hells Mr. Snelling has described, the most infamous of the wretched? Judge you, gentlemen, which party has most right to complain!

Insisting, as Parker had, that it was really Whitman who was on trial, Austin doubted that there was "a particle of evidence on which this judge could be found guilty." Austin ran through the instances of purported judicial misconduct and asserted that the evidence showed Whitman's intentions to have been honorable and humane and his decisions to have been valid exercises of judicial discretion. Austin pronounced himself surprised that defense counsel would even mention intoxication, defying the evidence of the witnesses and asserting that "[a]ll persons, who have had connection with Judge Whitman for twenty years, state, that they have never had any suspicion of him." He declined to discuss the matter further, suggesting that if the testimony did not satisfy the jurors nothing he could say would. Austin thus invited the respectable men of the jury to entirely discount the sworn evidence of the defense witnesses on the strength of his categorical denial of their credibility. The topic was too unseemly; the witnesses to Whitman's intoxication were to be disbelieved out of hand with no consideration of the possibility that Whitman was, in fact, regularly too impaired to do his job. Austin asserted that Snelling's goal was to drive Whitman from the bench by publicly humiliating him, which was an unjustifiable end. Snelling's bad motives were to be inferred from the language Snelling used, of promising to hunt down Whitman like a bloodhound, calling him an old woman, and "persisting in the charge of intemperance."

Charging the jury, Samuel Putnam declared that the article was definitely a libel. He did not, he said, regret the investigation Snelling had sparked; the difficulty was the truth defense. Through the trials, the lawyers had disagreed on what the jury had to decide about the particularized incidents of malfeasance: Parker had said they had to agree on each allegation's truth in order for it to be considered proven; Dexter had said they simply had to agree overall that Whitman was unjust, perverted the law, was influenced by personal motives and disgraced the bench; Austin had insisted that they had to agree on the truth of at least one particularized event in order to exonerate Snelling. Putnam explained that Snelling's allegation was that Whitman was unjust, a perverter of the law and a disgrace to the bench. Dexter was correct: if the jurors believed that Whitman had intentionally perverted the law even once, Snelling deserved acquittal. Putnam reviewed the instances, reminding the jury for each that the question was not whether Whitman had made a mistake but whether he had intended to pervert the law. Reasoning like Parker and Austin that Whitman was also on trial, Putnam told the jury that Whitman, like Snelling, was "innocent till he is proved guilty." Putnam said he thought intemperance would disgrace a judge. He left it to the jury to consider the explanation that certain witnesses had advanced, that Whitman's unusual gait, which some had read as a sign of impairment, was actually caused by "infirmity of his limbs," rather than alcohol. Putnam reminded the jury that Snelling had to prove that the libel was true and that his motives were good and his ends justifiable.

After deliberating for eight hours, the jury returned to the courtroom saying they agreed that the article was a libel but disagreed on Snelling's motives. Putnam then said that preparing the public for Whitman's impeachment would constitute an improper motive. After another half hour's deliberation, the jury brought in a verdict of guilty with a recommendation of utmost lenity, which apparently tempered the joy of the reprobate court-watchers in attendance. The sentence was not lenient for these kinds of cases, however: three months' imprisonment and costs of prosecution. Dexter and Sewall moved to arrest judgment. Whitman resigned about a week later.[74]

The main grounds of Snelling's appeal were that he should not have been required to notify the prosecution that he would raise a truth defense or to supply particulars that constrained his defense. Chief Justice Shaw, for the court, upheld Putnam's decision. Purporting to unearth a long-held common law truth of the need for both sides to inform one another and ignoring any concerns about a criminal defendant's constitutional rights, Shaw cobbled together (out of procedures imposed on the prosecution in common barratry cases and a recent embezzlement case, and on both sides in civil cases generally) a justification for permitting the prosecution to require the defense to provide, either orally or in writing, the incidents of supposed misconduct upon which the defense would be based. Shaw explained that otherwise Whitman would have been in the impossible position of needing to prepare to defend every decision he had made in over ten years on the bench. This judgment imposed on criminal cases the same kind of procedure that judges were refusing to give up in civil defamation cases. Two years later, this ruling was one of the planks in an argument, in the *Boston Morning Post*, that judges were corruptly insinuating an aristocratic agenda into republican institutions. This ruling would disable a defense lawyer from drawing out evidence of previously unknown instances of intoxication from unwilling witnesses who had been compelled to testify. There was no way to get such people to come forward before the trial, so if their knowledge could not be drawn out by compelling them to testify under

---

[74] "Libel Case," *Boston Morning Post*, January 6, 1834; "Judge Whitman," *Boston Masonic Mirror*, January 11, 1834.

oath, their knowledge would stay in the shadows where the aristocratic interests wanted it to stay.[75] Score: 1 limited victory for reformers and representatives of upstart religions; 5 for those who disapproved of them (three newspapermen and two complainants).

One of Snelling's three cases cannot be counted because he did not fight it. This case is the only criminal case in my sample that concerned a woman. As part of Snelling's antigambling agenda, he published a story of a young man named Munroe whose gambling habits led to his downfall, remarking in passing that he "married a strumpet." Snelling subsequently explained that he had been referring not to the real wife but to another woman who was evidently calling herself "Mrs. Munroe." Snelling said he apologized to the real wife, Susan Munroe, who died before he was indicted later the same month. Thacher imposed a sentence of six months' imprisonment and $21.85 in costs, and Snelling appealed. The Supreme Judicial Court lifted the sentence of imprisonment but imposed a fifty-dollar fine and $25.09 in costs.[76] The score remains: 1 limited victory for reformers and representatives of upstart religions; 5 for those who disapproved of them (three newspapermen defendants and two complainants).

As described in Chapter 3, concerns about truth percolated into privilege-type defenses in Massachusetts. In *Commonwealth v. Child*, William Gardiner, focusing on the idea that an innocent mind should set a person free, attempted to fold elements of the emerging privilege defenses into his argument around truth. Gardiner noted that Chief Justice Parker in *Blanding* had referred to a broad right to complain about public officers, and he noted similar language in *Bodwell v. Osgood*.[77] Parker in *Blanding* and Marcus Morton in *Child* acknowledged that circumstances did exist in which no libel case would lie, but the situations were unsystematized in Massachusetts, at least until *Bradley v. Heath* in 1831. Because truth and good intentions were linked from *Clap* onward, judges and lawyers always had to face the possibility that falsehoods would be excused if intentions and circumstances were the bases of defense. In the remaining *Snelling* case Shaw finally closed that door.

---

[75] "Power of the Judiciary," *Boston Morning Post*, August 20, 1836.
[76] "More Libels," *New-England Galaxy* (Boston), July 20, 1833.
[77] Whitman, *Trial of the Commonwealth versus David Lee Child*, 27–29.

Snelling published the other troublesome article a week before the Whitman piece. This one alleged that a dentist and an innholder were gamblers and cheats, and that they had recently won a lot of money gambling and indeed had rigged a horse race by betting $1,000 that a certain horse would lose and then dosing it with ipecac to make sure. Samuel Parker again prosecuted Snelling in municipal court and Child defended him. Citing *Bodwell v. Osgood*, Child proposed to prove not that the allegations were true but that Snelling had believed them true, on the basis of information from a "professional bonesetter," S.C. Hewitt. Child said that after the article appeared, Hewitt turned on Snelling and went to the grand jury. According to Snelling's account, at trial Hewitt equivocated badly and, though threatened with perjury, did not provide the evidence Snelling needed.

Parker cited *Jackson v. Stetson* in arguing that people should not be allowed to publish libels and then excuse themselves by blaming irresponsible or absent third parties. Thacher held that although Snelling's beliefs might be relevant to the penalty, the defense was truth, not belief in it. The jury took half an hour to convict Snelling. Parker then told the court that Snelling had asked to publish an explanation, which the complainants preferred over seeing him imprisoned, so sentencing was deferred. Ultimately, though, Thacher imposed a sixty-day sentence, to be served after the one imposed in the Whitman prosecution, plus costs of prosecution. In total, Thacher sentenced Snelling to 180 days in jail, a fifty-dollar fine and costs of $95.51.[78]

Represented again by Child before Samuel Wilde and a jury at Supreme Judicial Court, Snelling lost. On appeal to the full court, Child insisted that actual malice was necessary for a libel conviction and that Wilde had erred in excluding the evidence of Snelling's respectable source and honest belief in truth, which should have gone to the jury to rebut the inference of malice raised by the fact of publication.

[78] "Libels," *Boston Daily Advocate*, July 13, 1833; Snelling, letter to the editor, *Boston Morning Post*, July 16, 1833; Untitled note, *New-England Galaxy* (Boston), July 13, 1833; "More Libels," *New-England Galaxy* (Boston), July 20, 1833; "Matters and Things in General: Excissorized [*sic*]," *New-England Galaxy* (Boston), July 20, 1833; "The Gallery of the Municipal Court," *New-England Galaxy* (Boston), July 20, 1833; Snelling, *Exposé of the Vice of Gaming*, 46.

Chief Justice Shaw, sitting with Putnam and Wilde, entertained Child's "full and elaborate argument" about "the nature of crime in general, and the offence of libel in particular." Of course, Shaw said, malice was the essence of libel, but what was required was legal malice – purposely doing the act that caused the harm. Individuals were not to make themselves judges of others, to try others' characters outside of courtrooms. Shaw settled the uncertainty about whether actual malice was an essential element of criminal libel, with evidence of truth admissible to rebut the inference that would otherwise be drawn from the fact of publication. Mere innocent intent was not enough to exonerate a defendant. The statute had not changed the old law, he said, but merely added a new defense. However, truth had to be proved before the question of motives and ends was addressed. In passing the statute, the legislature had not intended to encourage the promulgation of untruths, however well intentioned. Finally, Shaw also ruled that Child was wrong in drawing from civil cases the inference that evidence of the complainants' general bad character (which Wilde had also rejected) was admissible in criminal cases as well: in civil cases, that evidence could mitigate damages, but in criminal cases its only role would be to lure the jury into improper inferences.

This case marked the end of the line in Massachusetts for the argument that actual bad intent was necessary for a conviction for criminal defamatory libel, or at least that good intent might be a defense. Reformers like Snelling were not to escape that easily. In theory, privilege arguments remained available in criminal cases, but only one appears in my sample, made by a self-represented temperance reformer, George Cheever, in what was essentially a sentencing hearing, when the point was moot. Truth had become the only real game in town. Score: 1 limited victory for reformers and representatives of upstart religions; 6 for those who disapproved of them (three newspapermen and three complainants).

Snelling was ultimately sentenced to three and a half months in prison, a fifty-dollar fine, and costs of prosecution that must have exceeded $200. He stopped editing the *Galaxy* and was also barred from grand jury service.[79] He pronounced himself persecuted and

---

[79] "Beauties of Judge Law," *Boston Investigator*, February 5, 1836, quoting the *Boston Morning Post*.

ruined but entirely satisfied with Child, who impressed Snelling with his ability to control his temper in the face of "the interruptions, obstructions and embarrassments thrown in his way by others." Unrepentant, Snelling compiled his accounts of his antigambling efforts – minus the libelous pieces but including plenty of other names and bad deeds – into an *Exposé of the Vice of Gaming* and published them to pay his legal costs.[80]

Moore and Sevey: *The Reformer As Complainant*

In the July 1833 term, Peter Thacher and one of Snelling's trial juries heard another libel prosecution, which highlighted libel law's role in reifying a line between private and public to support patriarchal authority.[81] Like the *Hill* complainant Avery Allyn, Samuel D. Greene, was an itinerant antimason, formerly a teacher and publican.[82] In April 1833, Charles Moore and Edwin Sevey reprinted in their *Boston Masonic Mirror* an article from an upstate New York paper that suggested that Greene was dishonest and had tried to use insolvency laws to defraud his creditors.[83] The *Mirror* aimed to dissuade New Hampshire voters from favoring antimasonry in an upcoming election. Greene later lamented not having been able to get a bill of particulars to help the prosecution fend off an attack on his whole life, an order that became available only after Snelling's appeal in the spring of 1834. Samuel D. Parker had also beaten this drum in November 1833 in *Guild*, discussed below, before he and Austin finally convinced Shaw to come to the aid of the prosecution.

Greene – alone among complainants in my sample – had his own lawyer, Benjamin Franklin Hallett, to help Parker rebut the truth

---

[80] *Exposé of the Vice of Gaming*, 3, 49.
[81] Parker gave the *Moore and Sevey* jury only a brief review of the law because, he said, they had already heard another libel case that term, which had to be one of Snelling's. See Locke, *Trial of Moore & Sevey*, 5.
[82] See Greene, *Broken Seal*, 15–25.
[83] The discussion of this case draws primarily from two pamphlets, Locke, *Trial of Moore & Sevey* and Greene, *Appeal of Greene* and also on contemporary reporting in the *Boston Morning Post*, *Boston Daily Advertiser*, *Boston Masonic Mirror* and *Boston Daily Advocate*. Greene wrote about the Morgan affair in *The Broken Seal*. On the *Moore and Sevey*, *Clough* and *Guild* cases, see also Bussiere, "Trial by Jury," 170–86.

defense.[84] Perhaps Greene and Hallett feared that Parker would follow
Austin's lead in *Hill* by discontinuing the prosecution when faced with
a wide-ranging attack on Greene's character or perhaps they feared
institutional bias against antimasons.[85] Hallett figures largely in
reformist and Jacksonian politics during the period and especially in
the antimasonic movement. He was a young newcomer to the Boston
bar when he defended the generally pro-masonic Buckingham in the
Maffit prosecution in 1822. Within a few years, though, Hallett was an
antimasonic crusader. When the antimasonic party was organized, he
became editor-in-chief of its mouthpiece, the *Boston Advocate*. From
1827 to 1831 he edited the *Boston Daily Advertiser*, advocating for
antimasonry and temperance and printing abolitionists' views. By
July 1833 he was back at the *Advocate*. When antimasonry subsided,
Hallett in 1836 became a Democrat, but not before dabbling with
Garrisonian abolitionism, anti-Catholicism, and Whiggery. Arthur
Schlesinger Jr. calls Hallett "[a]n energetic and thick-skinned
politician ... [who] could be no more ignored than trusted." William
Preston Vaughn labels Hallett "the most notable (if not notorious)" of
the antimasonic leaders. Charles G. Greene, the Jacksonian editor of
the *Morning Post*, called Hallett "the 'soldier of fortune,' who had
'fought for, and betrayed, every party and faction that has arisen since
his entrance into political life.'"[86]

Moore and Sevey was complicated to argue and took seven days.[87]
Greene had apparently been one of the first to identify the masons who
abducted and probably murdered William Morgan in upstate
New York, and much of the evidence on both sides was rooted in
that explosive affair. Parker and the defense attorneys, Fletcher and
Simmons, wanted to limit the evidence about the Morgan affair and
focus on Greene and his creditors; Hallett, on the other hand, wanted
the court to understand that the defense's key witness, Johnson
Goodwill, was one of the "Morgan conspirators," whom Greene

[84] The uniqueness of this situation was emphasized in "Court Calendar," *Boston Daily Advertiser*, April 11, 1839.
[85] Elizabeth Bussiere discusses judges' efforts to curtail antimasonry's impact on juries in "Trial by Jury."
[86] Schlesinger, *Age of Jackson*, 173–74; "Hallett, Benjamin"; Vaughn, *Antimasonic Party*, 117.
[87] Thomas W. Phillips to James T. Austin, November 19, 1833, James Trecothick Austin papers, Ms. N-1789, MHS.

claimed to have exposed, provoking a sustained campaign to damage his reputation and make him fear for his life. In support of his own good character, Greene presented himself as a representative of religion, a sometime editor of the Boston *Antimasonic Christian Herald* and one who had worshipped in good standing in a Presbyterian church in upstate New York before being driven out by the masons. He had found welcome and protection in Boston's respectable, orthodox Congregational Park Street Church, which around that time was experiencing the ministry of the famed Presbyterian evangelist Charles Grandison Finney. The threads of antimasonry, evangelicalism and scandal were knotted together.

The defense argued that the impugned article was true and had been published with good motives and for justifiable ends. Much evidence was adduced about Greene's relations with creditors and supposed creditors years before. Closing the case, Fletcher argued that, as newsmen, Moore and Sevey had a duty to warn the public about a partisan public lecturer like Greene, so that if what they said was true, they should be acquitted. The press could not "tamper with private reputation," but when a person like Greene put himself forward to the public, "everything concerning him may be truly stated, be it for good or for evil. It is just as proper to point out defects in the bad, as to praise the worthy." It would be wrong to rake up the long-past bad deeds of someone pursuing his own private ends, but if that person sought to influence the community, it was right to expose him. "I put it to any man," Fletcher argued, "if any one comes pretending to be a teacher or a minister in his family, and is likely to exert a dangerous influence, if he would not wish to be put on his guard. Such is the duty of the public press. There is no plainer maxim in reason, or in law."[88] Fletcher suggested that the words "antimasonic" and "Christian" were incompatible. Greene traveled about propounding his views, advocating ousting masons from public offices, jury boxes and churches, and promulgating division and dissent. He deserved to be thoroughly investigated.

Judge Peter Thacher thought that the evidence supporting the truth defense ought to be as probative as the prosecution's evidence on a criminal charge would have to be. The defense's task was not to

---

[88] Locke, *Trial of Moore & Sevey*, 58.

raise a reasonable doubt or even to prove truth on a balance of probabilities. Once convinced the defendants had published a libelous article, the jury had to be fully persuaded of its truth before acquitting. On the other hand, Thacher accepted the newspaper editors' good intentions in airing their suspicions about a character like Greene. Dubious characters deserved investigation. Thacher advised the jury that "to profess to be a teacher, a guide and instructor of mankind, in religion, morals, or government, is to assume a high character, and carries with it a claim to superior sanctity." Thacher's comments echoed instructions he had given a grand jury less than a year earlier: "If any one, under the assumed garb of truth, honesty, religion, or patriotism, engage in the commission of a fraud, it is the right of any citizen to strip the imposter of his mask, and to put the public on guard."[89] The jury acquitted Moore and Sevey, and within a couple of weeks they were advertising a pamphlet describing the trial. Score: 1 limited victory for reformers and representatives of upstart religions; 7 for those who disapproved of them (four newspapermen and three complainants).

Recall James T. Austin's categorical refusal to address the allegations of drunkenness made against police magistrate Benjamin Whitman. Like Buckingham's prosecution over the Maffit allegations, the *Moore and Sevey* case signaled that the characters and backgrounds of reformers, in religion, morals or politics, could be scrutinized far more closely than those of other people. If reformers initiated libel proceedings to clear their names, they would have more difficulty than would, say, a consul or a police magistrate, in showing that bad motives and unjustifiable ends lay behind attacks on them, because investigating their characters was beneficial to society. As long as the jury accepted the evidence of truth (or some of it), the defendant would tend to be acquitted, regardless of the intrusiveness of the libel. In *Moore and Sevey*, the evidence of truth came from Goodwill, who, as one of the supposed Morgan conspirators, was said to have a longstanding vendetta against Greene. Goodwill's credibility went unimpeached because doing so would have necessitated testimony about his possible involvement in the unsavory Morgan affair. Wary that considering religious and political affiliations would lead to

---

[89] *Ibid.* 70–71; Thacher, *Charge to the Grand Jury, December 1832*, 21.

doubts about the integrity of judges and juries as well as witnesses, Thacher was determined to keep antimasonic politics out of the courtroom.

Guild *and Influences on the Jury*

The drumbeat of systemic corruption continued, with Benjamin Franklin Hallett at the center. One case, which introduces a thematic thread I pick up again in Chapter 5, concerned the place of individual conscience in the courtroom, and the propriety of excluding people from juries on the basis of their beliefs. A *Moore and Sevey* juror, Ebenezer Clough, was unsuccessfully prosecuted for embracery – attempting to influence a juror – for putting an antimasonic pamphlet into the hands of a masonic fellow juror.[90] Four years earlier, Peter Thacher had refused Origen Bacheler's effort to have both witnesses and jurors excluded if they did not believe their bad deeds would be punished in the afterlife – the theory was that such beliefs, which Universalists held, made oaths useless. Both Thacher and James T. Austin considered Bacheler's approach dangerous for justice.[91] This time, though, Thacher acceded to Hallett's request that jurors be asked if they were masons. The *Masonic Mirror* and the *Galaxy* objected strenuously. One commentator warned this practice would lead to Jacksonians getting Federalists excluded, or members of the Trinitarian Old South Church ousting the testimony of Unitarians from "Judge Thacher's Society in Brattle Street."[92]

Moore and Sevey spawned another libel prosecution as well. Two jurors had been uncertain about acquitting the editors, and Hallett tried, unsuccessfully, to turn this indecision into grounds for a new trial. Aaron Guild was prosecuted over a letter Hallett published in the *Advocate* in which Guild claimed to have overheard a juror named

---

[90] Untitled editorial, *Boston Daily Advocate*, July 30, 1833; "Municipal Court," *Boston Masonic Mirror*, August 17, 1833; "Trial of Ebenezer Clough," *Boston Masonic Mirror*, October 19, 1833.

[91] Whitman, *Trial of the Commonwealth, versus Origen Bacheler*, 4–9; Bacheler, *Review of the Trial of Origen Bacheler*, 33.

[92] "Judge Thacher's Triors," *Boston Masonic Mirror*, October 19, 1833; One of the People [pseud.], "The Case of Mr Clough, and Hon Judge Thatcher's [*sic*] Law in the Case," *New-England Galaxy* (Boston), October 19, 1833; "Trial of a Juror," *New-England Galaxy* (Boston), October 19, 1833.

Thomas French describe spending the whole night abusively "damning it into" the holdout jurors that Greene had contradicted himself. French would have succeeded, Guild said, if not for Hallett's efforts. For these allegations of pro-masonic coercion (which so nicely flattered Hallett-as-lawyer), Guild was prosecuted for criminal libel.[93]

Prosecuting, Samuel D. Parker noted that the law was defective in not (yet) requiring the defense to particularize in a truth plea, but he acknowledged not needing particulars in this case. Hallett mounted an aggressive defense on all elements of the charge and tried to prove the truth behind the words French had allegedly spoken: that he had indeed misbehaved in the jury room. Parker, however, insisted that the real question was the truth of Guild's statement: had French spoken the words Guild attributed to him? As Parker wanted, Thacher excluded other jurors' evidence about French's influence in the jury room, reasoning that it was irrelevant to whether or not French had bragged about it. Thacher suggested that such evidence might have been admissible in a civil case, but not here. French, as complainant, could swear on oath that he said no such thing, and Guild, as a party, was barred from testifying and no one else had overheard French's supposed boasts. With this ruling, the truth defense had little chance of success.

Another line of defense concerned the propriety of drawing an inference of malice from publication. Hallett as editor had done the publishing, argued Hallett as defense counsel, so malice should not be imputed to Guild. Citing *Bromage v. Prosser*, Thacher distinguished legal malice from actual malice, with legal malice established by proof of publication. Thacher smoothly left the question of Guild's and Hallett's respective roles to the jury. He moved on to the question of whether or not the words actually defamed French and specifically whether they meant, as the charge said, that French had "work[ed] all night to control, abuse, influence and ill treat" the jurors, and to illegally urge them to rule against their beliefs "by indecent, improper and profane language." Thacher painted a word picture of the thoughtful, respectful deliberations of an idealized jury room,

---

[93] For details of these proceedings, see Locke, *Trial of Moore & Sevey*, 76–78 and the *Boston Masonic Mirror*, the *Boston Morning Post*, and the *Boston Daily Advocate* from July through November 1833.

explaining why such conduct would be "indecent." He then added that if the jury thought that Guild's characterization meant only that the conversation was time-consuming and heated, then the state had not proven the defamatory innuendo.

Twice the jurors returned to court with a special, limited verdict and were sent back to their room. Finally, Thacher accepted it: the jury found that Guild had published the text in question and that although his motives were not justifiable, he lacked the malicious intent to hurt French. Hallett, representing Guild, moved to acquit, and Parker moved to sentence. When these motions were argued a month later, Thacher ruled that the verdict required a new trial. Parker then stayed the proceedings. Hallett and Guild clearly lost on the interlocutory motion to admit the evidence of improper jury-room behavior by a masonic sympathizer; but the ambiguous ruling on malice favored Guild, and a discontinued prosecution is a victory of sorts. The score will remain unchanged, at 1 limited victory for reformers and representatives of upstart religions; 7 for those who disapproved of such people (four newspapermen and three complainants).

Cheever, Whitmarsh *and* Thomson: *The Pattern Continues*

The subversive potential of the truth defense to damage the characters of the respectable had been contained: the prosecution was now entitled to particulars, the simple absence of actual malice was no defense, and the "good motives and justifiable ends" requirement was understood to justify more searching scrutiny of the characters of religious and moral reformers than of more conservative and respectable people. Reformers continued to do poorly in court, and the truth defense continued not to help them much.

George Cheever was a young orthodox minister who, by 1832, was a pastor in Salem, where he busied himself with assailing Unitarianism. Although a Garrisonian at this point, he got into trouble over his temperance advocacy.[94] Cheever was prosecuted over a story he published in January 1835 in a temperance newspaper called the

[94] York, *George B. Cheever*, v, 81–82; Upham, *Salem Controversy*. See also Mackey, "Reverend George Barrell Cheever," 323–25. In 1834 Cheever converted from colonizationism to abolitionism, welcoming the English abolitionist George Thompson to his pulpit and becoming an official in the Salem Anti-Slavery Society.

Salem Landmark, "Inquire at Amos Giles's Distillery," eventually
a monumentally successful, if not wholly original, temperance tract,
which he later published under such titles as *The Dream* and *The True
History of Deacon Giles's Distillery*. It told of a deacon who owned
a distillery from which he also distributed Bibles. When his workers
refused to work on the Sabbath, he hired demonic replacements. The
pamphlet laid at the deacon's feet all of the destruction of individuals
and families that temperance reformers linked to alcoholism. John
Stone, a Unitarian deacon who ran an Essex distillery, saw himself
and his family in certain details of Cheever's story and complained.[95]

Distilling alcohol was a major industry in Salem, but efforts were
afoot to restrict it.[96] Cheever infuriated the alcohol interests, and the
rivalry between Unitarians and orthodox Congregationalists
increased. Charles Greene, in the *Boston Morning Post*, decried the
"revolting" attack on "Mr. Giles." Greene reprinted the story, saying
readers wanted to know why Cheever had received "a public
chastisement": he was beaten in the street by a group of mariners,
one of whom worked at times in the distillery and resented being
characterized as a devil. One pleaded no contest to assault
proceedings, but the rest had their charges dropped. Criminal libel
proceedings against Ferdinand Andrews, the printer of the *Salem
Landmark*, and its editor, Congregational minister Dudley Phelps,
were also dropped.[97]

Cheever was prosecuted in Common Pleas in Salem in June 1835.
Austin prosecuted, assisted by Leverett Saltonstall. Peleg Sprague and
Rufus Choate defended Cheever. Choate apparently argued that
Cheever had been doing his duty by reporting the evils of alcohol and
that his account was true of distillers in general and therefore of Stone
in particular. Testimony about the impact of alcohol was admitted.
Austin, in closing, told the jury that there was no question that the
"Dream" was libelous; the only question was whether the fictional
Giles was really Stone. A jury convicted Cheever, and he entered an

[95] Cheever, *True History*, 3, 7–8; York, *George B. Cheever*, 72. Cheever reprinted this
story and "Deacon Jones's Brewery" in *Dream*, *True History* and other temperance
texts.
[96] See Tyrrell, *Sobering Up*, 231–35.
[97] "The Rev. Mr. Cheever," *Boston Morning Post*, December 9, 1835; "Salem Police,"
Boston Morning Post, February 19, 1835.

appeal. Evidently unfazed, around this time he published another, similar temperance story called "Deacon Jones' Brewery."[98]

In the Supreme Judicial Court later in 1835, Cheever changed his plea to no contest. At his sentencing hearing in December, Cheever made a speech that contained three interesting though legally irrelevant arguments. He asserted that his story was protected by a qualified privilege and that it was a fair comment – that an editor of a public newspaper could comment fairly and candidly on a place or type of public entertainment, as long as the editor was not motivated by actual malice. Cheever also made an unusual truth defense. He denied that the pamphlet referred to any single person but asserted that it was true that alcohol caused a variety of social ills and ought to be banned. The "liberty of the press," he said, was "a mockery" if a person who wished to attack an evil like alcoholism could not describe its true harms without risking legal proceedings for harming the reputation of someone who sold alcohol. If one could not legally print the stories of real life, he said, "our Temperance Reports are the most libellous productions in the world." However, because Cheever had pleaded no contest, Chief Justice Shaw did not have to consider these arguments and probably ignored them. He sentenced Cheever to thirty days' imprisonment, $130 in costs of prosecution, and the requirement that he post a bond of $1,000, with sureties, to keep the peace for two years.[99]

Supported by his friends, Cheever served his month in jail and was released around one o'clock on a morning in early January 1836. He resumed preaching a few hours later.[100] Score: 1 limited victory for reformers and representatives of upstart religions; 8 for those who disapproved of such people (four newspapermen and four complainants).

Later in the 1830s a more iconoclastic reformer named Joseph Whitmarsh tangled with libel law. Whitmarsh had various reform ties. 1836 found him selling *Deacon Giles' Distillery*. A year later he

[98] "Deacon Jones' Brewery: Or, the Distiller Turned Brewer – A Dream. By the Author of 'Deacon Giles' Distillery'," *Temperance Recorder* (Halifax), October 2, 1835, reprinted from the *New York Observer*.

[99] "Case of Mr. Cheever," *Boston Morning Post*, November 18, 1835; Cheever, *Defence in Abatement*; Untitled, *Boston Morning Post*, December 7, 1835.

[100] "Mr. Cheever's Enlargement," *Boston Investigator*, February 5, 1836.

was still advocating total abstinence from intoxicating drinks and railing against the Tremont Theater as a hotbed of vice. In 1837 he was peripherally involved in a civil libel suit brought by a Garrisonian with antimasonic sympathies, Reverend Moses Thacher, over an allegation of adultery. Around this time, though, Whitmarsh seems to have reversed his earlier support for Garrison and decided abolitionists should be avoided, since if their cause was bad nothing would come of it, and if God approved of it, it would succeed without their help. By 1838 he had been excommunicated by the antislavery First Free Church of Boston. By 1842, Whitmarsh was railing against all religion, all scripture, all societies.[101]

The year 1836 found Whitmarsh publishing a newspaper, the *Illuminator*, which opposed sexual misbehavior and exposed the secret sexual misdeeds of powerful men. In it, he alleged that the editor of the *Standard*, an anti-Catholic "literary" newspaper, ran a brothel – or at least accommodated carousing and sexual trysts – in its office in its off-hours. The two newspapers' offices were on the same floor of the same building. Anti-Catholic sentiment was growing in Boston. Like freemasonry, the Church of Rome was characterized as bearing dark secrets, holding secret rites and demanding the obedience of its devotees. Presumably alluding to Rebecca Reed's *Six Months in a Convent* and Maria Monk's *Awful Disclosures* – key texts in the genre – Whitmarsh speculated that the doings in the *Standard*'s office resembled those that were rumored to take place in convents.[102]

Whitmarsh was prosecuted by Samuel D. Parker and defended by Benjamin Franklin Hallett, who may have contributed to the production of *Six Months in a Convent*.[103] Hallett's central argument was one that was being advocated strenuously in contemporary newspapers, a matter I take up further in Chapter 5:

---

[101] *Review of the Case of Moses Thacher*, 13; Whitmarsh, *To the Members of the "First Free Church"*; Phelps, *Sabbath*, 9–10.

[102] Editorial, *Illuminator*, March 30, 1836. I am grateful to Vincent Golden, Curator of Newspapers and Periodicals of the American Antiquarian Society, for his description of these periodicals: email to author, September 11, 2006. The case file at the Massachusetts Judicial Archives contains the extract from the *Illuminator*. On these texts and the growth of the anti-Catholic movement, see Billington, *Protestant Crusade*, 32–119 and Schultz, "Introduction."

[103] Schultz, "Introduction," xii–xiii.

that the common law of libel had never been received in Massachusetts, as it had not been applied before the state constitution was adopted in 1780 and was inconsistent with the guarantee of freedom of the press in the Declaration of Rights. Unconvinced, for the pre-1780 period Peter Thacher, in municipal court, found precedents in the instances of legislatures – in their "judicial character" – disciplining printers for "libels" that were contempts on the privileges of the legislature. Since 1780, libel had been treated as indictable. Whitmarsh was convicted and his motion to arrest judgment was unavailing. He was fined twenty dollars and probably also costs of prosecution.

Whitmarsh's first appeal to Supreme Judicial Court produced a hung jury, in November 1836. The case was retried a year later. Justice Samuel Wilde told the jury that the common law regarding institutions that Massachusetts did not have had not been introduced, but that courts were bound to administer the law if it had been received, acted upon and not repealed by the legislature. Hallett's arguments notwithstanding, the jury deliberated for an hour and returned with a verdict of guilty.[104] Score: 1 limited victory for reformers and representatives of upstart religions; 9 for those who disapproved of such people (four newspapermen and five complainants).

1:9 is the final score in cases with reformers and the religiously unorthodox on one side and, on the other, newspapers or the more traditionally respectable. Not much is known of Lorenzo Turner Hall, who sought to expose corruption, but his two convictions for defamatory libel and one for obscene libel seem likely to reflect the same dynamic. The dropping of criminal libel charges against the Essex printer Ferdinand Andrews and the editor and Congregational minister Dudley Phelps for printing George Cheever's temperance tale underlines Cheever's vulnerability as a crusader.

Of course, not all the criminal libel cases in my sample pitted reformers against the more respectable. One other case had reform types on both sides: the founder of one unorthodox school of medicine, Samuel Thomson, was prosecuted by a rival in 1839 for "warning" the public against this other "botanical physician" interloper. Although

---

[104] "Court Calendar," *Boston Daily Advertiser*, November 17, 1837; Editorial, *Boston Daily Advocate*, November 17, 1837.

Peter Thacher accepted that a desire to warn the public would constitute good motives and justifiable ends, the truth defense failed to convince the jury. Benjamin Franklin Hallett failed (again) to convince Thacher that there was no law of criminal libel in Massachusetts and that the jury should determine the law according to conscience. Thomson appealed but ultimately pleaded guilty at Supreme Judicial Court, where he was sentenced to a fifty-dollar fine and costs.[105] Instead of reformers, other cases involved Joseph Buckingham, the Russian consul Alexis Eustaphieve, Thomas Snell, Daniel Tomlinson, William Wesson, Theodore Lyman and Daniel Webster. As well, *Commonwealth v. Stockwell and Sessions* (1827) concerned an allegation that a trader and innholder had violated postal legislation; ultimately the governor pardoned them. Samuel Parker dropped the case against Edward Stearns when the complainant and defendant, both minors, settled their dispute. Two other cases involved newspapermen prosecuted on the complaints of other newspapermen: juries convicted Benjamin F. Bond (who was fined twenty dollars), and acquitted Edward C. Purdy. These last four cases entailed no important legal rulings on libel law.

The Efficacy of Truth

A disproportionate number of criminal defamatory libel cases in Massachusetts in the 1820s and 1830s involved representatives of moral or social reform or of upstart religious persuasions who tangled with the more respectable. The role of truth in a defense was shaped by the dynamics of these cases. With a reformer, William Snelling, in the dock, the procedure in criminal libel cases was altered so that in these cases – unlike most if not all others – the prosecutor became entitled to demand from the defense a list of the particular, allegedly true facts that underlay the libel. The defense would then be barred from proving any other facts, even if the evidence was unavailable until the witnesses were compelled to attend at court to testify under oath.

Before 1827, evidence of truth was admissible only in "public" cases concerning allegations about "public" men, originally in the electoral

---

[105] *Law of Libel: Report of the Trial of Thomson.*

context. There was, however, a certain shakiness to this rule. Judge Josiah Quincy III and the state prosecutors Austin and Davis let evidence of truth be led anyway in different circumstances, and, in and out of court, men like Charles Jackson and Isaac Parker articulated an ever-growing list of hypothetical situations in which the public interest could justify admitting such evidence. From 1826 to March 1834, uncertainty reigned about whether truth was admissible simply on the question of intent – to rebut the presumption of malice that arose from the fact of publishing defamation – or whether the defendant had to prove both truth and good intentions. However, the possibility that Child, Snelling and others like them would go free on the basis of their good intentions, despite publishing falsehoods, was intolerable to Chief Justice Shaw and most if not all of the other judges of the period. In 1834, Shaw settled the question: the malice element in criminal libel could be proved by proof of publication of a defamatory text, and truth would only save a defendant if it was, in fact, true. Good motives and justifiable ends had to be proven as well.

One legal innovation that Peter Thacher rejected was to treat the complainant (the antimason Samuel D. Greene) as a party and bar him from testifying. Thacher's commitment to standard practices in criminal procedure extended this far: he rejected the Commonwealth lawyers' various suggestions that he treat defendants as prosecutors and complainants as parties or even defendants.

A legal conundrum that went unresolved during the period was whether the defendant was required to prove completely all of the facts alleged in a truth defense or whether proving some of the facts, along with good motives and justifiable ends, would be enough. To convict, a jury did have to agree on the defendant's guilt on at least one count in the charge, but it was not clear whether they had to agree on any or all of the defense's particulars. (No one spoke of burdens of proof or the level of doubt or certainty the jury had to entertain.) The fact that the problem was resolved behind closed doors in the jury room made the uncertainty on this point bearable, but it surely arose because reformers kept turning up on both sides of the cases.

How often did truth save a defendant? Answering the question is harder in criminal cases than in civil ones, because court records, even after 1834, do not necessarily reveal that the defense was raised, and prosecutors sometimes let the evidence in despite the law. There is no

indication that any effort was made to attempt a truth defense in either
of the prosecutions of Lorenzo Hall for defamatory libel in the early
1820s or in Joseph T. Buckingham's prosecutions over libels against
the Russian consul, and in none of these cases were the *Clap* criteria for
admitting evidence of truth met. Of course, neither were they met in the
Maffit case, but evidence of truth was admitted anyway, and
Buckingham was acquitted. Blanding was convicted when evidence
of truth was excluded. The charges against Snell and Tomlinson were
dropped once the truth defense was established by statute. Before
1827, then, the defense was rarely possible, but it did succeed in the
Maffit case, and the prospect that it would be raised in the Snell and
Tomlinson case (in which so much evidence was available that Wesson
had visited a brothel) inspired Daniel Davis to drop the charges.

Between 1827 and 1834, it was possible to raise the truth defense in
any criminal libel proceeding, as was done in at least six of the ten cases
in my sample. Origen Bacheler and his fellow newsmen Charles Moore
and Edwin Sevey were acquitted, the prosecution against Frederick
Hill was dropped after Thacher refused to make an order for
particulars, and the charges against Aaron Guild were likewise
dropped when the jury failed to agree on a verdict. David Lee Child
and William Snelling were convicted despite their truth defenses,
although Child's appeal on a flaw in the pleadings was ultimately
successful. The defense helped, but it helped printers and editors
more than it helped reformers.

After orders of particulars became part of the procedure in 1834,
truth pleas were less often made, but the cases, too, were less fiery. The
charges were dropped in two of the seven cases brought in this period,
and there is no sign that a truth plea was contemplated in either – these
are the prosecutions of a minor, Edward Stearns, for depicting another
youth as conceited, and of Phelps and Andrews, who had published
Cheever's *Dream*. Reformer Joseph Whitmarsh did not plead truth; he
and printer Benjamin Bond were both convicted. In Whig editor Edward
Purdy's case, truth was pleaded, but the particulars were delivered late
and were withdrawn by consent. Apparently identity – "reference to the
plaintiff" in legal terms – was "so imperfectly established" that the
jurors acquitted Purdy without leaving their seats.[106] The temperance

[106] "Libel Suit," *Boston Morning Post*, February 17, 1835.

crusader George Cheever and the founder of the botanical school of medicine Samuel Thomson raised truth defenses but were convicted anyway. In the 1820s and 1830s, then, cases could succeed or fail in a variety of ways. Truth defenses sometimes helped, but they were by no means a safe bet, and they did little to save reformers.

Conclusion: Power, Privacy, Truth and Motives

The considerable concern in Massachusetts – but not Nova Scotia – about the dangers of evidence of truth in this period is part of the story of new religious groups and reform initiatives rising alongside other challengers to older structures of authority, and about those with authority shaping law to protect themselves. Politically, Jacksonians had undermined Boston's old Federalist establishment, a dynamic operating in the *Lyman* case. Voices advocating for labor interests were beginning to be heard. On the religious front, Eldridge Gerry's Democratic-Republicans had undercut the financial security of Congregational churches in 1811; constitutional change in 1833 finally eliminated establishment. Upstart religious persuasions like the Methodists and Universalists benefitted, while the orthodox Congregationalists and the Unitarians were destabilized. Into this environment came David Lee Child, William J. Snelling, Moses Thacher, George Cheever and Joseph Whitmarsh. It was not simply the possibility of personal public humiliation that made the respectable wary of reformers' "truths" in the early 1830s in Boston. It was also not, strictly speaking, that the respectable necessarily disagreed with the reformers' goals, although of course at times they did. David Lee Child's revelations about corruption and mismanagement in public institutions drew respect as well as satire. Alcohol, slavery and gambling were major problems, but opinions differed about what to do about them, about whether emotionally inspired legislated solutions were likely to work better than calm, gradual, conciliating appeals to a higher moral sense that might have less dramatic economic, political and personal effects.[107]

---

[107] See e.g., "Impracticable Schemes of Reformers," *Boston Morning Post*, July 10, 1835.

Reformers also undermined authority structures in households. As Mary P. Ryan and Leonard L. Richards have emphasized, wives and young people, as well as more mature men, joined voluntary associations and brought home reading material. Michael Grossberg has described families being transformed in the early republic, with strongly patriarchal arrangements giving way to greater parity in relations between spouses and generations and lighter legal controls over servants. The family shifted from "a community of interests governed by a publicly accountable patriarch" to a collective of members with distinct responsibilities and rights, governed by family law.[108]

These changes could be wrenching and threatening. The *Masonic Mirror* printed a story in 1833 about a young temperance society member in New Hampshire who tried to poison his father, an alcoholic, because he believed the world would be better off without him.[109] Reformers and unusual religious figures like the itinerant Methodist John Maffit were a force in reshaping family dynamics. Domestic advice books were another, crossing the threshold of the home and pushing aside older forms of authority. One of the most successful of these was Maria Child's *Frugal Housewife*, which was widely distributed throughout the country and had run to seven editions by 1832. When David Lee Child appeared before the courts in the early 1830s, he probably seemed an emasculated figure, a lawyer whose wife was supporting their household by describing how she managed on the pittance he earned. New texts on birth control, particularly Robert Dale Owen's *Moral Physiology* and Charles Knowlton's *Fruits of Philosophy*, gave people – especially women – some control over their own reproduction, which must have preempted conversations with clergy about how to bear the blessings of fertility.

In the 1820s, women in the northeast were beginning to speak in public and to organize for a variety of causes, including ultimately temperance and abolition. Even though these activities were obviously political and economic, they were understood as taking place in

---

[108] Ryan, *Empire of the Mother*, 16–26; Richards, "*Gentlemen of Property and Standing*," 60–62; Grossberg, *Governing the Hearth*, 4–5, 29.
[109] "Shocking," *Boston Masonic Mirror*, March 16, 1833.

private – that is, as not entailing an unseemly intrusion into male terrain – as long as the women were volunteers who presented themselves as members of families or representatives of their social classes.[110] Norms began to change, however, in the early 1830s in the wake of the highly controversial public lectures of a particularly notable Englishwoman, Frances Wright, whose place in these events will be explored in Chapter 5. Facing a backlash and wary of being perceived as followers of Wright, by the end of the 1830s, although women continued to be informed about politics and to lobby, petition and join organizations, they increasingly came to feel that home and church were the proper spheres for their actions. In this environment, with so much gendered contestation over what was private and what public, combined with deep fears that attacking slavery would break up the union and that reform causes could destabilize religion, politics and the economy, the notion that a person guided by "good motives and justifiable ends" had a right to publish truth raised considerable concern.

In hearing arguments about the proper role of truth, both under the *Clap* test and in the context of justifying motives and ends, courts became fora for debates over what was justly public and what was private and thus not subject to outside scrutiny. Was Benjamin Whitman's drinking a matter of public concern? William Snelling thought so; James T. Austin vehemently disagreed. In a dynamic that remains familiar to us, disagreement about how much information the public needed about which people – which men – in order to govern itself well were fundamental to the debates over the place of truth and falsity in the courtroom. Once Snelling's cases had been decided – once Lemuel Shaw had tamed the difficulties the truth defense posed for prosecutors and had put an end to arguments that actual malicious intention was necessary for a conviction – the arguments over how to negotiate private–public tensions in the courtroom in criminal libel cases abated. On the civil side, special pleading disappeared, but truth defenses remained constrained by procedural rules that made them risky to raise. In the 1830s, then, the truth defense was shaped to contain its subversive potential in the interests of the respectable.

[110] Boylan, *Origins of Women's Activism*, 12.

Truth was a defense in civil defamation cases in Nova Scotia, but it produced little concern. Plaintiffs could present themselves as willing to bravely prove defendants liars, but defendants could characterize plaintiffs as grasping for financial gains that would have been unavailable if criminal proceedings had been launched instead. In William Bowes's lawsuit, S.G.W. Archibald and James W. Johnston played a kind of strategic game when Archibald raised a truth defense without pleading it and Johnston met it anyway, or at least well enough to persuade the jury; truth defenses were too rhetorically and strategically fraught in Massachusetts for such gambits.

Nova Scotians were focused on reforming their political institutions, especially the relationship between the executive and the assembly. Moral reform causes had scarcely appeared, and white society generally understood the most important of them – abolition – to be a problem for other people elsewhere. The religious landscape in Nova Scotia addressed diversity in a different way, with politics and religion entwined most visibly through access to higher education. In this environment, individual itinerant clergymen like John Maffit posed little real concern.

By about 1832, antiabolitionist violence was increasing in American cities. The wording of the Massachusetts constitution provided limited explicit protection for an individual's freedom of conscience, but those who sought political and religious change insisted that conscience was meant to be protected in a more fulsome way. New arguments emerged in and around libel cases. Harbingers had already been felt: Origen Bacheler had sought to have Universalist witnesses disqualified for their beliefs, and jurors had been asked about their attitudes to antimasonry in *Guild*. In a republican system of government, the majority's views, it seemed, should carry the day, but what did this mean for the individual who held unpopular views? Majoritarian violence combined with the rise of the "Free Thought" movement spurred new emphases in the constitutional conversation in Massachusetts, particularly in Boston. These tensions ran high through cases over sexual and religious expression in the 1830s. It is to these matters of individual conscience that I turn next.

5

The Individual Conscience and Blasphemous and Obscene Expression

In Massachusetts, the mid-1830s brought an increase in argumentation, both in and out of courtrooms, about the meaning of the constitutional guarantees of freedom of conscience, discussion and the press. The very existence of criminal libel was attacked in the mid-1830s, and judges convicting reformers upheld it on dubious grounds. These arguments arose especially in prosecutions for blasphemous and obscene libel, over the expression of ideas that some thought threatened the moral foundations of society. Violence against individuals with unpopular views gave urgency to the arguments. Concerned to protect existing authority structures, judges were reluctant to recognize such people's rights of conscience and expression, and many commentators approved: rights to free speech had limits in a republic, and majority opinion could be backed by force if necessary. Nova Scotia did not see similar controversies, mainly because its political struggles seldom pitted the individual against the majority over matters of conscience. In Nova Scotia, where no one was legally obliged to contribute directly to the support of a church, contests over religion had to do with access to political power, largely through higher education. Courts were seldom sites for constitutional arguments about individual rights.

This chapter traces the shifts in the 1820s and 1830s in the law that purported to regulate expression related to morality and belief. The early 1820s, in Massachusetts, saw a burst of legal interest in John Cleland's pornographic classic *Memoirs of a Woman of Pleasure*, commonly known as *Fanny Hill* and first published about 1749. Through these controversies the law of obscene libel took shape. Different social tensions and vectors for spreading legal doctrine produced differences in the uptake of the law of obscene libel in Nova Scotia. In the early 1830s, explosive controversies in Boston arose over new texts and practices that some saw as immoral and irreligious, in that they promoted and justified less strict rules around sexual morality. As antiabolitionist violence grew, religious and moral reformers' demands to speak their truths to majoritarian power placed a new stamp on arguments around libel law. These debates played out quite differently in Nova Scotia, where majoritarianism was a more dubious constitutional principle and abolitionism and Free Thought were other people's problems, but the reality of political revolution came closer to home with the Upper and especially Lower Canadian rebellions of 1837–38.

The Backdrop: Establishment and Disestablishment

The idea that law and religion together maintained social stability was a core premise behind the law of defamation and the legal protection of churches and religion. The dynamics of the relationship between these forces was different in Massachusetts and Nova Scotia because the money flowed differently. Officially, the Church of England was established in Nova Scotia, but people were never taxed directly to support it, and since other Protestants had freedom of worship, dissent proliferated. Pushing aside Indigenous communities, groups of European immigrants settled in different regions. Anglicanism, the religion of power and education, dominated in peninsular Halifax and ran most strongly northwest to Annapolis and Windsor, home to the Anglican King's College. In 1827, Anglicans in Nova Scotia were outnumbered by Presbyterians. Roman Catholics came third and Baptists fourth. Baptists dominated in Shelburne (which then included Yarmouth), Scottish Presbyterians in Pictou, and Catholics in Cape Breton.[1] When Halifax was founded, civil disabilities were imposed on Catholics, but by around 1800 they could vote if otherwise qualified, and by 1827 they could nominate candidates and sit in the

---

[1] See Untitled, *Colonial Patriot*, April 12, 1828.

legislature. More disturbing than Catholics were the democratic impulses of Protestant dissenters, especially the Pictou Presbyterians, who energetically sought permanent funding for their academy, which provided an educational alternative to the Anglican King's College. Various sects challenged Anglicans' claims to a monopoly over the issuance of marriage licenses. The spread of subversive moral and religious ideas did not attract much concern.[2]

Religious establishment was better financed in Massachusetts. Massachusetts and Connecticut towns had long hired and maintained a minister, who was, naturally, Congregational. Article II of Part I of the 1780 Massachusetts constitution declared that "all men in society" had both a right and a duty "publicly, and at stated seasons, to worship the Supreme Being, the great creator and preserver of the universe." No one's manner of worship was to be interfered with unless it endangered the peace. Article III authorized the legislature to compel towns and other civic bodies to tax their citizens for the support of "public Protestant teachers of piety, religion and morality" and to require citizens to attend public worship regularly, as long as services they could, in good conscience, attend were available. Officially all Christian sects were equal.

Baptists objected loudly to being taxed to support religion, and Universalists challenged the rules around corporate structure and ordination that cut them off from public support.[3] In 1811 Democratic-Republicans, briefly in power and responding to the torrents of abuse that had flowed their way from Congregational pulpits, legislated to allow people to choose the organization that received their religious taxes, whether or not it was incorporated and regardless of how its clergy were ordained.[4] Some towns, including Worcester, gave up on collecting such taxes, leaving churches to rely on their members for support.[5]

Later in the 1810s, Congregationalism split into a more orthodox Trinitarian majority and a more liberal Unitarian minority.

---

[2] Cuthbertson, *Old Attorney General*, 78–103; Garner, *Franchise and Politics*, 140–44; Fingard, "The 1820s," 264–66.

[3] Curry, *First Freedoms*, 163–73; Cushing, "Notes on Disestablishment"; Miller, *Larger Hope*, 170–71, 297.

[4] An Act Respecting Publick Worship and Religious Freedom, ch. 6, 1811 Mass. Acts 387.

[5] Lawes, *Women and Reform*, 12.

Controversies and rivalry erupted within towns, undergirding several
of the defamation actions described in Chapter 6. Congregationalists
began to reconsider their suspicion of disestablishment and join
Baptists and other dissenters in favoring voluntarism. In the 1820s,
while opposing establishment, Congregationalists, Baptists, Protestant
dissenters and evangelicals generally agreed that Christianity should
nevertheless infuse governance.[6]

By the end of the 1820s, an equality of Protestant sects within a state
whose citizens voluntarily supported their churches was looking
appealing. Despite the objections of prominent Unitarians – and
perhaps the disapproval of certain judges – the eleventh amendment to
the state constitution was ratified with overwhelming public support in
November 1833, superseding Article III.[7] Enabling legislation regarding
church membership and taxation became effective April 1, 1834.[8] All
members of a religious society, incorporated or not, were guaranteed the
right to elect their clergy and support them. Membership in a religious
society became voluntary, and no religious society could impose
financial obligations on nonmembers. Neither "Christian" nor
"Protestant" appeared in either the constitutional amendment or the
enabling legislation. All sects and denominations were equal. Citizens
could legally avoid churches altogether, or attend services without
becoming full members and liable for church tithes. Those who
connected fidelity to traditional orthodox Congregationalism to
loyalty to the Commonwealth saw danger to the hierarchies of
authority upon which social stability rested.[9] Abner Kneeland and
other Free Thinkers elicited strong resistance from legal actors
determined to curb the most radical implications of disestablishment.

The Emergence of Obscene Libel: *Fanny Hill* in Worcester and Boston

Previous chapters have shown the common law of defamation being
adapted to fit new sociopolitical circumstances in Massachusetts and
Nova Scotia in the early nineteenth century. The law of blasphemy, on

[6] See Hamburger, *Church and State*, 112–26, 133, 180–89.
[7] Editorial note, *Revised Statutes of the Commonwealth of Massachusetts*, 52–53; Dunlap, *Speech*, 134–35.
[8] An Act Relating to Parishes and Religious Freedom, ch. 183, 1834 Mass. Acts 265.
[9] See "Political Atheism," *Boston Recorder*, December 1 and 8, 1830.

the other hand, was used only once in the 1820s and 1830s, in Massachusetts, and then left in ignominy. The almost brand-new common law of obscenity blossomed and flourished. These criminal causes of action targeted expression that threatened moral and religious principles considered foundational to social and political obligations and stability.

By about 1810, English writers accepted that obscene libels could be prosecuted in common law courts, although, as I describe in Chapter 2, disagreements remained about whether the prosecution had to prove publication to an identifiable individual and whether a text that reflected on no one in particular could attract prosecution. These uncertainties and concern about how explicitly to describe such a text appear in the early prosecutions for obscene libel in Worcester and Boston, as lawyers' hands and minds were drawn into this work. In Nova Scotia, on the other hand, a charge over an obscene libel seems to have been laid only once, in Halifax, on facts that did not raise these issues. Possibly, Nova Scotian magistrates' attention was not drawn to the same sorts of texts, but another factor may be that the available law books provided little guidance on how to draft a charge for an obscene libel even if one came along. Although some writers have speculated that nuisance law was used in regulating expression, no nuisance cases over expression appear in the records of either place.[10]

The emergence of obscenity law in Massachusetts in the late 1810s and early 1820s focused on *Fanny Hill*. By 1800, an extensive erotic canon was available to those who could afford it. If kept out of the public eye, these books seem not to have troubled Americans or their English contemporaries. Enterprising American printers, however, were finding ways to produce such texts cheaply for wider audiences. Horowitz recounts a tale which ends with sheets of paper with *Fanny Hill* printed on one side being used, around 1814, to line the covers of volumes of court records and writings of Cotton Mather. She speculates that some Boston journeymen or apprentices got caught printing these sheets and that, paper being expensive, their master used the illicit sheets to line the boards.[11]

---

[10] Richard B. Kielbowicz suggests that antiabolitionist mobs believed, probably wrongly, that the law of nuisance justified their attacks on the abolitionist press: "Law and Mob Law," 575–84.

[11] Horowitz, *Rereading Sex*, 29–34.

Concerned about increasingly visible signs of vice, prosecutors took action. The first Massachusetts *Fanny Hill* prosecutions took place just before Boston police, under the new mayor and former municipal court judge Josiah Quincy, began to systematically target prostitutes and brothels – and other vices, such as idleness, drinking and carousing – especially on the Hill, on Beacon Hill's north side.[12]

An 1815 Pennsylvania case, *Commonwealth v. Sharpless*, suggested that obscene libels could draw prosecution in American states.[13] Prosecutions in Worcester and Suffolk between 1818 and 1821 show lawyers grappling with incorporating this view into Massachusetts law. None of the indictments in these cases referred to a statute, such as one from 1711 that aimed at material perceived to offend either religion or morality.[14]

Massachusetts's first obscene libel prosecution was probably the one brought against Peter Holmes in Worcester. Holmes's indictment charged that in July 1818 he "unlawfully, wickedly, maliciously and scandalously, did utter, publish and deliver" *Fanny Hill* to three named individuals at West Boylston. Although in other libel proceedings the objectionable words and their meanings had to be clearly specified in the indictment, the lawyer who drafted the indictment for Holmes was evidently unsure about how much of a narrative devoted to the pleasures of the flesh he should include. The indictment had two counts pertaining to the publication of the book to each recipient. They differed in that, for each transaction, the first count described the material as "a certain lewd, wicked, scandalous, infamous and obscene print on paper, representing a man, in an obscene, impudent and indecent posture with a woman, and which said lewd, wicked, scandalous, infamous and obscene print, on paper, was contained in a certain printed book ... intituled 'Memoirs of a Woman of Pleasure.'" The second count simply referred to "a certain lewd, wicked, scandalous, infamous and obscene printed book, intituled 'Memoirs of a Woman of Pleasure,' (which said printed book is so lewd, wicked and obscene that the same would be offensive to the

---

[12] See Hobson, *Uneasy Virtue*, 11–13; Lane, *Policing the City*, 6.
[13] 2 Serg. & Rawle 91, 103 (Pa. S.C. 1815).
[14] An Act against Intemperance, Immorality and Profaneness, and for Reformation of Manners, ch. 6, 1711–12 Mass. Prov. Laws 679, which prohibited lewd and profane songs and written texts, especially when they also mocked religious texts or exercises.

Court here, and improper to be placed upon the records thereof; wherefore the Jurors aforesaid do not set for the same in the Indictment . . .)." [15]

Holmes was convicted at Common Pleas and, after two trials, at Supreme Judicial Court in October 1820. His grounds of appeal to the full bench reveal the novelty of the case. Holmes challenged the courts' jurisdiction, the indictment's omission of verbatim passages and descriptions of the postures of the man and woman in the book, and the possibility that presenting a text to a single person could constitute publication at law. Holmes's lawyer argued that the offense was unknown to Massachusetts law and that the counts were too uncertain to found a verdict. Chief Justice Parker dismissed most of the objections out of hand, mainly considering the jurisdiction issue. He imposed a $200 fine plus costs of prosecution ($134.75) and ordered Holmes to post recognizances and keep the peace for two years.

The Suffolk indictment against three Boston auctioneers for selling *Fanny Hill* in May 1819 was more breathless and enraged, more graphic and less succinct than the one that faced Holmes. [16] The text, it charged, contained

amongst other things divers wicked false feigned impious impure bawdy & obscene matters wherein are represented the most gross & filthy scenes of lewdness & obscenity & in terms & impressions not fit or proper to be received or mentioned in any language or in any Court of Justice & most manifestly tending to scandalize & debase human nature & to destroy & totally deface all those fundamental principles & notions of modesty decency, & virtue which

[15] Two obscene libel prosecutions brought against Stillman Howe, also in Worcester, were based on similar indictments. Late in 1819, Howe was charged with selling *Fanny Hill* to one Ebenezer Perry at Holden in October 1818 and with selling the book to Perry and four others in November 1819. In April 1820, different Supreme Judicial Court juries acquitted Howe in the first case but convicted him in the second; he was sentenced to one day of solitary imprisonment and six months of hard labor. The records of the second case indicate that Howe was initially tried and convicted by a Worcester lawyer and justice of the peace, Rejoice Newton, as may well also have happened in the first proceedings, but the records are not clear. Since Newton, as a county attorney, was one of the lawyers who argued *Holmes* at the Supreme Judicial Court, it seems reasonable to suppose he may have had a hand in drafting all of these indictments.

[16] *Comm. v. Thomas Boardman, Jun., Charles Willis, Jun. and John Minchin* (Mar. 1820, Mun. Ct. Bos.).

are proper & necessary to be kept up & preserved in all civil societies, by the publishing of which said libel last above mentioned they the said Defendants have most unlawfully wickedly & impiously attempted & as much as in them lay endeavoured to spoil & corrupt the morals of all the good citizens of said Commonwealth & to debauch, poison and infect the minds of all the youth of this Commonwealth and to bring them into a state of wickedness, lewdness and brutality to the high displeasure of Almighty God, to the scandal & reproach of the christian religion, & in contempt of the laws of said Commonwealth to the great offence of all civil governments, to the evil & pernicious example of all others in like case offending & against the peace.

The Suffolk drafter, likely James T. Austin, was clear about the harm this text posed to society, but, like his Worcester counterpart, was unsure how much of *Fanny Hill* to include in the indictment: one count set out a long, explicit passage, in which Fanny witnesses an act of intercourse. Although libel indictments, like civil pleadings, often contained some counts that quoted the objectionable expression exactly and others that set out only its general gist, no subsequent cases contained such graphic passages.

Documents in the court file suggest that the books were being held as security for money the auctioneers had lent to a local printer and that they were not meant for sale. Austin thought the auctioneers should be punished to the extent of their gains, likely a small sum. When the case came to trial in May 1820, the auctioneers declined to contend with the Commonwealth. Each was fined $100 plus costs of prosecution and was sentenced to thirty days in jail; unlike Holmes, they were not required to post security for good behavior.

Even though the *Holmes* appeal was still outstanding, the jurisdictional and drafting issues probably seemed clearer by the time Thomas Farnam, a Boston silversmith, was prosecuted by Austin in March 1821 in the Boston municipal court for selling *Fanny Hill*. Farnam's indictment was less indignant and vehement than the auctioneers', perhaps reflecting knowledge of the more restrained, shorter Worcester indictments that had sufficed in *Howe* and seemed likely to withstand appeal in *Holmes*. As in the key 1727 English *Curll* case,[17] neither Boston indictment identified a particular person to whom the material had allegedly been published, but both Worcester

---

[17] *R. v. Curll*, 2 Str. 788; 93 E.R. 849 (1727).

ones did, more closely tracking standard pleading practices for libel. In any event, Farnam also did not contend with the Commonwealth and was fined only twenty dollars and costs of prosecution.

Publishing an obscene text that defamed no specific person was considered an indictable common law offense by 1820 in Massachusetts. Uncertainties around how to describe an obscene text and whether it was necessary to prove that the text had actually fallen into someone's hands were being resolved – indeed, the decision that obscene passages should not grace legal records spread into civil defamation as well.[18] At this point Boston's and Worcester's prosecutions over *Fanny Hill* ended. Perhaps the flow of texts was stanched, or perhaps the prosecutorial eye turned to the Hill or elsewhere. The only other obscene libel case I have found in the early 1820s in Boston was of Lorenzo Turner Hall, late in 1822, for publishing in his *Boston Castigator* "a certain immoral, wicked and obscene and mischievous libel" that purported to advertise the excellent services available at three local brothels, whose locations were provided. Hall undoubtedly intended merely to direct police attention to these establishments, but he was convicted by a jury and sentenced to jail for six months.

Obscenity in Nova Scotia

The history of obscene libel in Nova Scotia suggests an absence of the relevant kinds of texts. While *Fanny Hill* and its kin were probably known in Nova Scotia in the 1820s and 1830s, they left no trace in the legal records. Probably they were kept in private collections, away from those considered corruptible. The only imprint of *Memoirs of a Woman of Pleasure* that purports to have been published in Halifax was undoubtedly published elsewhere: its supposed publishers, "G. Fendon for W.H.S. Fillman," were not Haligonians, and indeed "G. Fendon" is remarkably similar to the "G. Fenton" adopted by one of the original London publishers, Fenton Griffiths, who sold it from his shop on the Strand in 1749.[19] Also, Halifax printers could spell Nova Scotia.

---

[18] Cf. *Peter Fay v. Temple Parker* (Mar. 1825, Worc. C.P.), concerning an allegation of incest.

[19] This book was published as John Cleland, *The Memoirs of Fanny Hill, A Woman of Pleasure. With Plates, Engraved by a Member of the Royal Academy. Written by*

If *Fanny Hill* had come to the attention of a Nova Scotian justice of the peace in the late 1810s or early 1820s, he might have turned to one of the many recent editions of Burn's *Justice of the Peace*, a widely used text advertised for sale in five volumes in Halifax in January 1824.[20] However, neither this edition nor earlier London ones mentioned prosecuting for obscenity. *Curll* (over *The Nun in Her Smock* and *The Art of Flogging*) stood for the proposition that offending religion constituted offending the common law. The 1836 edition of Burn mentioned in passing that "prophane or obscene publications" were indictable misdemeanors. However, citing Hawkins's *Pleas of the Crown*, the writers also noted that Hawkins claimed to have heard a King's Bench judge say that "a writing full of obscene ribaldry" that reflected on no specific person could not attract prosecution but that its author could be bound to good behavior "as a scandalous person of evil fame." By 1836, then, Burn's manual seemed to acknowledge that indictments for obscene libel could be drafted but provided little guidance. Nova Scotian judge John George Marshall's 1837 manual for justices of the peace tracked Burn almost verbatim. Marshall did not even cite *Curll* as an example of a prosecution for a text that was both obscene and irreligious.[21] Perhaps some Nova Scotian magistrates bound over to good behavior "scandalous persons of evil fame" who sold texts like *Fanny Hill*, but no records of such actions appear to have survived.

The books that could have helped more than Burn's were marketed to lawyers and judges rather than to justices of the peace. Holt's 1812 and 1816 London and 1818 New York editions listed, as misdemeanors under the topic of "obscene exhibitions," indecent pictures, writings and other representations.[22] Sample indictments

---

Herself. Halifax, Novia Scotia [*sic*]: G. Fendon for W.H.S Fillman, 1820. See also Stern, "*Fanny Hill* and the 'Laws of Decency.'"

[20] *Weekly Chronicle*, January 2, 1824. On the legal knowledge of justices of the peace, see generally Phillips, "Low Law Counter Treatise?" Thomas McCulloch numbered magistrates wanting "Bunn's [*sic*] Justice" as among those whose lowbrow tastes were influencing the new Pictou library's acquisitions around 1822: Harvey, "Early Public Libraries in Nova Scotia," 434.

[21] Burn, *Justice of the Peace* (1810), 1:322; Burn, *Justice of the Peace* (1836), 3:361, 892; Marshall, *Justice of the Peace*, 71, 247. Marshall was Chief Justice of the Inferior Court of Common Pleas on Cape Breton.

[22] Holt, *Law of Libel* (1812), 63–64; Holt, *Law of Libel* (1816), 72–75; Holt, *Law of Libel* (1818), 83–84.

for seditious and blasphemous libels and for selling an obscene print were provided in Archbold's *Pleading and Evidence in Criminal Cases*, first published in 1822 in London and frequently reprinted there and in New York.[23] Starkie indicated that immoral and obscene texts were criminal if they tended to subvert public morality.[24] In 1833, Nova Scotia's Beamish Murdoch, citing Archbold, pronounced it a misdemeanor to publish "obscene or profane books, prints, &c."[25] Justices of the peace in the outlying parts of the province tended not to be legally trained, and lawyers were strongly concentrated in Halifax, especially in the 1820s (further afield the numbers grew with time). Their choices in legal texts may have contributed to the absence of obscenity cases in the records from outside Halifax.

When guides to the law or model indictments were available, indictments for obscene libel could be drafted with some confidence. Accordingly, early in 1833 in Halifax, John H. Flohr was prosecuted for "obcenity" in the Supreme Court.[26] No captivating tale of the travels of *Fanny Hill* can be told here, however. Flohr, age sixty-five and a former military man, was prosecuted over the appearance in his garden of a sign "with indecent words about Mr. David Fletcher." Convicted and fined, Flohr wrote a long letter to the *Novascotian*, denying all knowledge of the sign and offering $100 to the one who could identify the culprit. A miniature tempest and a reciprocal libel suit ensued, Fletcher suing Flohr, but no additional light was shed on obscenity law.

Blasphemy Law's Diverging Threads

Nova Scotian newspaper commentary in the 1820s and 1830s reveals little interest in using law to control or eliminate texts dangerous to

---

[23] See e.g. Archbold, *Pleading and Evidence* (1822), 285, 294–95 and see e.g. Jervis (ed.), *Archbold's Pleading and Evidence* (1835), 407–10. "Archbold's *Pleadings*" appears in the estate of R.J. Uniacke: *List of Books Belonging to the Estate of the Late Hon. R.J. Uniacke*, #42b, vol. 1769, MG 1, Nova Scotia Archives ("NSA").

[24] Starkie, *Treatise on Slander* (1813), 503–4; Starkie, *Treatise on Slander* (1830), 2:155–59.

[25] Murdoch, *Epitome of the Laws of Nova-Scotia*, 4:163.

[26] The only surviving court record is the grand jury's record of Flohr's indictment for "obscenity" in December 1832. See also the flurry of letters to the editor of the *Novascotian* published on June 5, 1833.

Nova Scotian religious or moral commitments. There were calls for action about gambling, the seduction of young women, Sabbath observance, houses of ill fame and riotous grog shops. Opinion was divided over whether theaters were "improving" or harmful. However, no one acknowledged the temptations of obscene, irreligious or immoral texts. Even an agitated writer to the *Halifax Journal* in 1824, appalled by a parody of a Christian hymn that had appeared in another newspaper, felt that the proper censure was public reproof in the newspaper – no demand for a prosecution was made. Two weeks later, the author wrote again, disgruntled that his reproof had drawn the response that the parody had been written by Alexander Pope and therefore did not deserve the critique.[27]

Blasphemous libels, although well established as objects of prosecution in Britain and Massachusetts, do not appear to have attracted prosecution in Nova Scotia in the 1820s and 1830s. Thomas Paine's *Age of Reason*, William Hone's *Sinecurist's Creed* and other controversial texts prosecuted in England during the period may have been rare in Nova Scotia. As well, however, Nova Scotian legal writers ignored the expanding reach of common law blasphemy that English prosecutors were embracing. A 1758 Nova Scotia statute criminalized willful blasphemy against any member of the Trinity; denying, cursing or reproaching "the true God, his Creation or Government of the World"; or denying, cursing or reproaching the canonical scriptures of the old and new testaments. Note the absence of reference to the final judgment and the Anglican church. As punishment, the statute rather mildly imposed two separate hours in the pillory or three months' imprisonment for each instance. In treating blasphemy in their legal texts, both Beamish Murdoch and John George Marshall referred only to this statute, despite – or perhaps because of – the recent, highly charged, common law blasphemy prosecutions in England, which depended on an understanding of blasphemy that also protected the Church of England and Trinitarians. Murdoch and Marshall also refrained from mentioning Blackstone's assertion that profane scoffing, contempt and ridicule were illegal.[28] They evidently thought

---

[27] X [pseud.], letters to the editor, *Halifax Journal*, January 19 and February 2, 1824.
[28] *An Act for Punishing Criminal Offenders*, S.N.S. 1758, c. 20, s. 1 [this is the citation that appears in Murdoch and Marshall, but by my count, it is chapter 27]; Murdoch, *Epitome of the Laws of Nova-Scotia*, 4:136; Marshall, *Justice of the Peace*, 71.

Nova Scotia, with its range of Christian commitments, could do without a broad, severe version of blasphemy law.

Unitarianism formally offended in Nova Scotia, but in other respects the Massachusetts 1782 Blasphemy Act took a harder line on religious disagreement and mockery. Under the act, it was an offense to deny, curse or contumeliously reproach God. Denying Jesus or the Holy Spirit was no offense, but cursing or reproaching either of them was: polite Unitarians had nothing to fear. The act also criminalized denying God's "Creation, Government, or final Judging of the World," a potential difficulty for Universalists and Free Thinkers. The act specified the canonical texts, and it prohibited not only cursing or contumeliously reproaching them but also casting contempt or ridicule upon them. Massachusetts offered more punishment options as well: imprisonment for up to twelve months, the pillory, whipping, sitting in the gallows with a rope around one's neck, or bonds for good behavior.[29]

The differences in blasphemy law in Massachusetts and Nova Scotia reflect their religious politics. The Anglican elite's efforts to link loyalty to Anglicanism in Nova Scotia were widely seen as repellent. Thomas Chandler Haliburton, a reform-oriented Anglican member of the assembly, severely objected to portrayals of Protestant dissenters, and specifically Pictou Presbyterians, as disloyal subjects.[30] As well, Nova Scotians were aware of but did not directly face the radical challenges to political power and Christian belief that Massachusetts perceived in the views of Baptists, Universalists and deists – not to mention the "infidels" Fanny Wright, Robert Dale Owen, Charles Knowlton and Abner Kneeland, who challenged organized Christianity and conventional views of sexual morality.

An 1829 controversy over skating on the Sabbath suggests the relatively narrow range of apprehended threats to the souls of Nova Scotians and, at the same time, hints at prevalent attitudes to the law's proper role in enforcing religious commitment. In the winter of 1828–29, magistrate John Marshall – who wrote the magistrates' manual – saw Henry Crawley out skating on a Sunday in Sydney, on Cape Breton Island. Crawley was in his early thirties, the son of

[29] An Act Against Blasphemy, ch. 8, 1782 Mass. Acts 27.
[30] Haliburton's speech is reprinted in Patterson, *History of Pictou*, 339–40.

a prosperous naval captain and surveyor general and thus the sort of person who knew or should have known that he was setting an example to youth and others. Marshall charged and convicted Crawley with violating the statute that banned amusements on the Sabbath. Crawley appealed to the Supreme Court, where solicitor general S.G.W. Archibald and Justice Brenton Halliburton took the perhaps surprising position that the statute was based on an overly puritanical seventeenth-century English one and could safely be disregarded. Archibald referred to Blackstone's view that innocent recreation on the Sabbath was fine, and Halliburton commented that these matters should be governed by "the pulpit," not the law. Uproar followed, not only about the risk to social stability if the state ceased to support religion but also on the ground that provincial magistrates were surely right to enforce a provincial statute, regardless of its antecedents. Joseph Howe, in the *Novascotian*, agreed with Halliburton and Archibald. Objectors wrote to Philip Holland of the *Acadian Recorder*, hinting that the youthful Howe had no business weighing in on such serious matters. "A Christian of the Old School," an astute legal mind from Digby, reviewed the provenance of the English statute and pointed out that in a prosecution over Thomas Paine's *Age of Reason*, even Thomas Erskine had insisted that Christianity was an essential component of the polity. And "surely," the correspondent added, "Mr Erskine was sufficiently *liberal*."[31]

Newspaper correspondents debated whether skating in order to go somewhere necessary on Sunday would be proscribed for being enjoyable and observed that judges, lawyers, sheriffs, magistrates, physicians and even the occasional governor were known to undertake unnecessary errands that day. Boys were warned against thinking that boisterous sledding would be tolerated by more sober persons marching to church. However, it seems doubtful that either boys or their respectable elders changed their ways. Whether out of liberalism or prudence, Haligonians preferred to let social pressure manage this issue, even in the face of one of their own statutes.

---

[31] A Christian of the Old School [pseud.], letter to the editor, *Acadian Recorder* (Halifax), February 28, 1829, italics in original. I suspect this correspondent was the judge Peleg Wiswall. See also Vindicator [pseud.], letter to the editor, *Acadian Recorder* (Halifax), March 21, 1829.

Boston in the 1830s, faced with more profound moral dangers, took a different approach to law.

The Stakes Rise in Massachusetts

As I described in Chapter 4, the various reform movements that shook Massachusetts beginning in the mid-1820s shaped the evolution of the truth defense in criminal libel cases by raising the specter of truths about the wrong sorts of people being aired publicly, while subordinate members of households evaluated these truths, evading or even rejecting traditional patriarchal authority. A right to speak truth, though absent from the text of the state constitution, was understood to be threaded by constitutional necessity into the fabric of the common law. However, by early 1834 judges had largely neutralized the risk that truth would free the wrong sort of person in criminal libel cases. In the crucible of disestablishment and increasingly vocal opposition to intemperance and especially slavery, another argument was increasingly made in public debate. Against a backdrop of violence and social pressure to be silent, individuals asserted a right to believe what they wished and to express those beliefs publicly. Some denied that criminal libel was legitimately part of Massachusetts law. Courts had tamed the truth defense, and, in cases framed as blasphemous, obscene and defamatory libel, they took a similarly dim view of these broad claims about conscience and law.

The Red Harlot of Babylon

The electrifying, radical lectures that a young British woman named Frances Wright began in the late 1820s to deliver to immense public audiences in the United States were pebbles that sent ripples in all directions. Wright and her Free Thought colleagues raised the stakes around free expression on matters of conscience, stakes that rose further as Garrisonian abolitionism took root in Boston. Wright challenged the fundamentals of capitalism, religion, slavery and patriarchy, as well as behavioral norms for women. She and her allies significantly shaped the religious climate of Massachusetts in the 1830s. Distancing themselves from Wright and her beliefs, American women reoriented their engagement with public life. For her critics,

Wright's name became metonymic for all the ideological novelty seeping into Massachusetts culture and threatening its supposed internal harmony.

Raised in wealth in the intellectual tumult of early nineteenth-century Britain, Wright was drawn to the promise of American freedom and dismayed by slavery and the grueling plight of women in marriage. In 1821 she published an account of her travels in the United States. She subsequently worked to establish a small colony, Nashoba (which failed), that would prepare former slaves for freedom and free its members from the constraints of marriage. She came to believe that racial mixing was inevitable and acceptable. In mid-1828 she joined Robert Dale Owen in editing what became the *Free Enquirer*, "promulgating the principles of infidelity, and writing against marriage," as one critic put it.[32] With Owen and others, she published the *Free Enquirer* in New York City until 1830. She and Owen opened their Hall of Science in the spring of 1829, where debates and speeches took place and books were sold. Across the street, perpetually taunted, stood the evangelical New York Tract Society. The two movements agreed on some issues, such as antislavery, but the *Free Enquirer* crusaded against private property and women's legal disabilities, and it commended Richard Carlile's birth control tract.

Wright's public lectures in various cities over the winter of 1828–29 drew immense crowds. Toasted in some quarters and maligned in many more, she condemned the conditions that promoted inequality, focusing on capitalism, the banking system, the "'professional aristocracy' of priests, lawyers and politicians"; the institution of marriage; and the educational system, which she and Owen proposed to replace with universal public education, including boarding schools. They opposed Sabbatarianism and the evangelical preoccupation with preventing "lust-driven sin." In particular, Wright defended open inquiry and attacked organized religion, clerical dominance and the irrationality of evangelical revivalism. Despite concerted efforts by Boston's merchants and clergy to get the public to shun her, she spoke in Boston on July 30, 1829 to a full house that included respectable, educated women.[33]

---

[32] "Miss Frances Wright," *New-England Galaxy* (Boston), August 8, 1828.
[33] Ginzberg, "Hearts of Your Readers," 201–2; Eckhardt, *Fanny Wright*, 1–2, 180–99; Horowitz, *Rereading Sex*, 48–52; Schlesinger, *Age of Jackson*, 183.

Female exhorters were known among some evangelical denominations, especially in the North, and not all newspapers were shocked by Wright's appearances, although the scale of her intervention was new. Wright became a flashpoint in battles over religion, political power and marriage, an embodiment of heresy on all three fronts at once. She personified "infidelity," the label commonly applied to her. Wright and the Free Thinkers from 1825 to 1835 antagonized and galvanized the clergy and its supporters, uniting the orthodox and the evangelical against a common enemy. Her very name became an epithet to be hurled at anyone protesting traditional power arrangements in politics, religion, labor or the home. Progressive women too, including Maria Child and Angelina Grimké, distanced themselves from Wright. Wright was an outlier in Free Thought too, as it was largely a male movement that linked intellectual freedom with masculinity and characterized women – prominent in churches – as the clergy's main dupes, despite also advocating for education and women's equality. With Wright's dramatic, public challenge to sexual morality and marriage, Free Thought as a whole could be, and was, tarred with conflating religious and sexual infidelity. In mid-1831, a year after Wright moved back to Europe, Wright's great friend and supporter the English writer Frances Trollope marveled at how quickly Wright's name had disappeared from the newspapers. "Last year," Trollope commented, "I hardly ever looked at a paper without seeing long and repeated mention of Miss Wright. Her eloquence and her mischief, her wisdom and her folly, her strange principles and her no principles were discussed without ceasing. Now her name appears utterly forgotten."[34] Trollope was wrong: Wright's "infidelity" clung to Free Thinkers and women who presumed to speak in public. Throughout most of the rest of the nineteenth century, women's activists shaped their philosophy around a Protestant ethos, trying to avoid charges of "immorality, unfemininity, and, tellingly, 'Fanny Wrightism.'"[35]

With disestablishment looming and the various Protestant sects competing for members, Boston roiled with religious argument that sometimes began elsewhere. Free Thinker Abner Kneeland had engaged in a confrontational debate with the orthodox in Philadelphia in 1824

---

[34] Quoted in Eckhardt, *Fanny Wright*, 224.
[35] Ginzberg, "Hearts of Your Readers," 208–9, 218.

over eternal punishment, and Origen Bacheler and Robert Dale Owen had a lengthy, public epistolary debate in 1831.[36] Even "liberal Christians," such as the Universalist Linus S. Everett, were horrified by the free inquirers' assault on marriage and by Wright's suggestion that the "amalgamation" of whites and blacks would be acceptable. Moreover, in 1831, Robert Dale Owen published a defense of birth control, *Moral Physiology; or, A Brief and Plain Treatise on the Population Question.* Owen saw contraception as the best solution to the looming population problem. He did not anticipate an increase in prostitution because, he thought, with birth control, young women who had been led astray would have other economic alternatives. The text ran through at least six editions in 1831 and more would follow.[37]

Horrified, Everett the same year published his *Exposure of the Principles of the 'Free Inquirers'*, which purported to educate the public about the real principles of five people, led by "foreigners," who had infiltrated America and, relying parasitically on its freedoms, were spreading the poison of "infidelity." Modern infidelity, Everett argued, was "a disgusting compound of *vanity, obscenity, indecency,* and *impudence.*"[38] Its emissaries were Robert Owen, his son Robert Dale Owen, Frances Wright, her associate Robert L. Jennings, and Abner Kneeland, whose prosecution for blasphemy lay in the near future. Everett had evidently not yet heard of a young doctor in western Massachusetts, Charles Knowlton, who had published, in 1829, an enormous book denying the fundamentals of Christianity and would soon publish a small, cheap, much more popular "how-to" guide to birth control, *Fruits of Philosophy*, which quickly attracted prosecution for obscene libel.

Efforts to Stem the Tide

Commentators on America in the 1830s observed that individuals feared that speaking their minds would make them pariahs or worse.[39] Activist women sought to avoid being charged with "Fanny

---

[36] Kneeland and McCalla, *Minutes*; *Articles of Faith*, 8–9; Bacheler to Owen, January 22, 1831, in Bacheler, *Discussion of the Existence of God*, 4–6.
[37] Horowitz, *Rereading Sex*, 58–61, 67–69, 76–77.   [38] Everett, *Exposure*, 41.
[39] See e.g. Hamilton, *Men and Manners*, xvi–xviii; Tocqueville, *Democracy in America*, 116–20; Cooper, *Treatise on the Law of Libel*, xxxv–xxxvi.

Wrightism," a label that imputed moral and religious corruption to a woman who dared to participate in public controversies, especially by speaking in public. Public speeches by Angelina Grimké and other abolitionist women drew much criticism, from not only newspaper commentators but also from the clergy. In an 1837 public letter, the Congregational General Association of Massachusetts chastised women for departing from their proper spheres of influence, for eschewing a posture of vulnerability – which, they said, evoked benevolence in men – for a posture of authority, which made men defensive. Sarah Grimké replied in a public letter to Mary S. Parker, president of the Boston Female Anti-Slavery Society, emphasizing women's equal access to understandings of God's purposes and their equal duty to serve God. Women's presence in antislavery ranks proved an opening for tarnishing the movement with sexual innuendo, and the antislavery movement soon fractured over its commitment to women's equality. Other women felt the onslaught as well: one writer argued that even if the religious convictions of the English Quaker preacher Anna Braithwaite were entirely correct and sincere (which the paper doubted), she had "forfeited all the claims of her sex to gentle treatment, by her boldness, her defence of her trade without argument, her evident wish to make a noise in the world, and be thought an extraordinary woman."[40]

Men too were told to be silent, which provoked them and their supporters into demanding legal and extralegal recognition for freedom of speech and conscience. William Lloyd Garrison thought attacks on his character increased after he began to take on the American Colonization Society in print around 1830. When he could find nowhere to speak but the Boston Common, he took up Abner Kneeland's offer of Julien Hall in late 1830. Doors were barred to abolitionist speakers. Ministers refused to announce abolitionist activities from the pulpit. A Washington, DC libel suit hastened the demise of *The Genius of Universal Emancipation*, which Garrison coedited, and in 1831 prominent southerners asked Harrison Gray

[40] "Pastoral Letter: The General Association of Massachusetts to the Churches under Their Care," *New England Spectator* (Boston), July 12, 1837, reprinted in part in Ceplair, *Public Years*, 211–12, along with Grimké's reply; Williams, "Female Antislavery Movement"; Abzug, *Cosmos Crumbling*, 212–28; "Female Preaching," *New-England Galaxy* (Boston), July 18, 1838.

Otis – Boston's mayor – to use law to restrain Garrison's press. The canny Otis, Rosenberg notes, advised them that such steps would alienate northerners and let abolitionists draw on the public memory of sedition prosecutions to justify themselves. The stakes rose with Nat Turner's Rebellion in August 1831. In 1832, Peter Thacher charged a grand jury that it was deeply inappropriate to send abolitionist tracts to the South; "grave and decent discussion" among serious men, he asserted, was the proper way to address the imperfections of political and legal systems.[41] Southerners, furious about what they perceived as a seditious northern conspiracy to undermine slavery and thereby the union, attempted to block the circulation of antislavery views. In December 1835 Andrew Jackson unsuccessfully called for a federal law to achieve this end. Southern postmasters in 1835 declined to deliver such texts. In the 1830s, thousands of petitions to end slavery were presented in Congress and left to lie on the table forever by the outraged members. On the floor of the United States House of Representatives one southerner asserted southern gentlemen bore a duty to God and honor to kill any abolitionist they could lay hands on in the South.[42]

Violence was a prevalent threat. Trials for rioting took place a few times a year in the Boston municipal court in the 1820s and 1830s. A theater was sacked in the winter of 1825–26.[43] In 1833 William Snelling publicly complained that police magistrate Benjamin Whitman was, among other things, ignoring Snelling's requests for legal protection from the threats he was receiving. George Cheever was attacked for his temperance tract. Newspapers reported regularly on mob violence in Massachusetts and elsewhere. Abolitionist speech, however, was the target that inspired both the most violence and the most emphatic defenses of freedom of conscience. The "flood tide" of mob violence faced abolitionists between 1834 and 1836. Leading these riots were usually "gentlemen of property and standing," who

---

[41] Garrison, *Brief Sketch*, iv; May, *Some Recollections of Our Anti-slavery Conflict*, 16–18; Rosenberg, *Best Men*, 150; Thacher, "Incendiary Publications," 66. See also Thacher, *Charge to the Grand Jury, December 1832* and Boston Female Anti-Slavery Society, *Annual Report*, 29–32.

[42] Nye, *Fettered Freedom*, 32–69; Miller, *Arguing about Slavery*, 76–77, 97–111, 144 and generally.

[43] "Theatre," *Free Press* (Halifax), January 3, 1826.

perceived danger to the union in the flow of abolitionist texts flying recklessly from New York publishing houses into the hands of the unedified multitude and their own families. Violence was visited on those who criticized the American Colonization Society's goal of removing free African Americans from the United States or who sought to educate African American children. By about 1837 in Boston, with antislavery established and the financial Panic of 1837 tempering the output of abolitionist presses, this violence appears to have tapered off.[44]

In the mid-1830s, assertions of a right to speak the truth in Massachusetts shifted somewhat into assertions of a right to express one's own mind on matters of conscience. The linking of abolitionist speech with freedom of expression that Harrison Gray Otis had prophesied came to pass.[45] As John Quincy Adams told the House of Representatives in December 1836, "You suppress the right of petition; you suppress the freedom of the press; you suppress the freedom of religion; for in the sentiments of many respectable men, fanatics if you please to call them, they are found to act under a sense of duty to their God."[46] Commitments to revealing the truth of conscience drove embattled abolitionists into alliance with other proponents of free discussion, who professed an individual right to expound their views regardless of the cost to social order or the will of the majority.

Scholars have identified a thread in American popular constitutionalism that justified such collective violence. E.P. Thompson and George Rudé have demonstrated that mobs in the Anglo-American and continental traditions have, at times, acted with deliberate political ends, under self-imposed constraints fashioned out of their sense of their traditional, customary or constitutional rights. Pauline Maier has argued that mobs in eighteenth-century America were a common, if not always entirely legitimate, part of the political system, serving needs a community's legal system could not meet. According to Larry Kramer, mobs were accepted as a necessary

[44] Richards, *"Gentlemen of Property and Standing,"* 12, 24–43, 48–62, 71–73, 144–50, 155–57, 167–68; Ryan, *Empire of the Mother*, 41–43.
[45] See also Rosenberg, *Best Men*, 149–50; Curtis, *"People's Darling Privilege,"* 217–41; and see generally Miller, *Arguing about Slavery*.
[46] Quoted in Miller, *Arguing about Slavery*, 198.

check on power. Mobs claimed legal rights based on constitutional arguments that assumed that "the people" were the final arbiters of the meaning of constitutional rights. Maier argues that as the nineteenth century progressed, however, the threat that mobs could pose to institutional stability and individual safety looked increasingly great, so that such public upheavals came to look illegitimate.[47] This dynamic was taking place in Massachusetts in the 1830s.

The frequency of violence in America generally and Boston in particular, along with constitutional sensibilities around majority rights and the obligations of comity in a federal union (which made antislavery protests unseemly), appalled some commentators. Peter Thacher told a Boston grand jury in 1831 that violence was never a proper response to theaters, gaming houses or houses of ill fame.[48] This view prevailed in Nova Scotia as well, where commentators voiced a distinct aversion to violent means to achieve ends: that was what Americans did. Violence occurred in Nova Scotia around this time, but there was no prevalent sense – among the respectable anyway – that constitutional rights could justify it, a view Nova Scotians seem to have shared with propertied Englishmen.[49] Violence had sometimes erupted in Maritime Loyalist communities in the 1780s over the distribution of land. Election-related violence took place around Pictou in 1830 and Sydney in 1832, and the Canso area saw hostility between Catholics and Protestants in 1833. The Nova Scotia scholarship does not suggest, however, that this violence tended to be seen as constitutionally legitimate. When Nova Scotian editors looked south, as they often did, they deplored American violence without perceiving rights claims behind it. They were unsympathetic to those who advocated or embraced violence to force constitutional and political change in other British North American colonies. The destruction of a Halifax brothel in the late summer of 1838 attracted only condemnation in the newspapers and the attribution of unprincipled, personal motivations. Even when a Halifax mob in 1829 was somehow involved in John Barry's escape from the assembly's sergeant-at-arms, after the assembly's constitutionally

[47] See Thompson, *Customs in Common*, 185–258; Thompson, *Making of the English Working Class*, 67–87; Rudé, "Gordon Riots,"; Maier, "Popular Uprisings," 71, 82–84; Kramer, *People Themselves*, 25–27. See also, Kielbowicz, "Law and Mob Law."
[48] Thacher, *Charge to the Grand Jury, December 1831*.
[49] Hamburger, *Church and State*, 216.

questionable decision to imprison him, the public discussion that followed contained no claims that the crowd had a right to free him. The different backdrops with respect to the legitimacy of collective violence shaped the claims for an individual right to speak the truth of one's conscience that were made in Massachusetts and Nova Scotia.

Charles Knowlton, Medicine, Free Thought and "Infidelity"

Several libel prosecutions drew the objection that rights to conscience and expression were being suppressed in Boston in the mid-1830s. Abner Kneeland's ordeal by prosecution began with his indictment for obscenity and blasphemy in December 1833 and ended with his release from jail in 1838. Attitudes to his rights claims shifted over time as Samuel D. Parker and James T. Austin refused to lower the sword of prosecution that hung over Kneeland's aged head while one uncertain jury after another failed to convict him. Kneeland's experiences were entangled with those of others: of Charles Knowlton, a doctor in western Massachusetts prosecuted at least three times in various parts of the state over his book on birth control; of George Cheever, prosecuted in Essex for taking on the rum industry; and of William Beals and Charles Greene, sued by the master of an academy over allegations of cruelty to a child. Objecting heartily to all of these encroachments on free expression was Charles Greene of the *Boston Morning Post*, who asserted, with Benjamin Franklin Hallett, that juries had the right to find – and should find – that the common law of libel had never been incorporated into Massachusetts law and was inconsistent with the state constitution. They were good arguments, but the Supreme Judicial Court rejected them in *Whitmarsh* in 1837. The 1830s ended with the judges hanging onto all three variants of criminal libel, while the ground moved under their feet as Bostonians reckoned with the implications of the death of the abolitionist editor Elijah P. Lovejoy at the hands of an antiabolitionist mob in Alton, Illinois in November 1837.

Historians have observed that in the early nineteenth century claims to religious and medical knowledge had a similar dynamic: while the regular clergy moved against challengers, practitioners of "official medicine" tightened licensing requirements in the face of new movements that offered personal choice and control over health. Samuel Thomson, for example, who was prosecuted for libel by a rival in Boston in 1839, was a self-educated practitioner of "botanical" medicine who extended his practice from New Hampshire into Essex County after 1800. Abner Kneeland sold Thomson's book in Boston. Other movements for taking charge of one's physical, spiritual and moral health – including temperance – also grew in the 1830s.[50] At their Hall of Science, Frances Wright and Robert Dale Owen offered for sale Richard Carlile's *Every Woman's Book* and Owen's *Moral Physiology*, pathbreaking texts that provided physiological information and contraceptive advice.[51]

According to its prospectus, the first edition of Charles Knowlton's *Fruits of Philosophy* was a small book, about seventy-two pages long, printed on "forty-eighths."[52] No copies are known to have survived. The second edition apparently expanded the anatomical information. It began with a philosophical "proem" that justified contraception, suggesting that humans were entirely right to try to remedy the difficulties that could arise from satisfying their perfectly natural appetites.[53] Whereas Robert Dale Owen had recommended coitus

---

[50] Wiebe, *Opening of American Society*, 161–64; Wiebe, *Self-Rule*, 19–20; Hatch, *Democratization of American Christianity*, 28–29; Abzug, *Cosmos Crumbing*, 163–64.

[51] Himes, *Medical History*, 224.

[52] The prospectus survives in the court file for Knowlton's Taunton, Bristol County prosecution in 1832. A "forty-eighth" was one forty-eighth of a standard, uncut piece of paper, so was about 2.5 inches wide and slightly more than that in length. The second edition, published in 1833 (and preserved at the Houghton Library at Harvard University), was the same size. It is about half an inch thick and covered in plain, brown binding with no writing on it. According to Horowitz, *Rereading Sex*, 75, the first edition was published anonymously, "By a Physician," in 1832 in New York, possibly at the press of the *Free Enquirer*. The copyright records held at the Library of Congress, however, disclose that the first edition was copyrighted in the District of Rhode Island on December 16, 1831. Horowitz cites a copy in the Lilly Library at Indiana University at Bloomington, but the dimensions of that book do not match those given in the description in the prospectus that Knowlton was hawking in 1832. The Indiana book, which has a "Proem" that matches at least the first couple of pages of the 1833 edition, may be a copy of the "spurious" edition that Knowlton mentioned was printed about 1832, or it may be a later edition. Its title page is gone. I am grateful to Shaunnagh Dorsett for finding the copyright information for the first edition, and to Shawn C. Wilson, the Library and Archives Public Services Manager at the Kinsey Institute, for describing the Indiana text to me in an email of September 9, 2015 and sending photographs.

[53] Knowlton, *Fruits of Philosophy*, 5–14. Knowlton remarked that the second edition – the target of the Greenfield prosecution – was so unlike the first that he thought it necessary to secure copyright for both: *Recent Excitement in Ashfield*, 19.

interruptus, Knowlton, arguing that sexual appetites demanded to be sated, described a douche made of well-known ingredients that could prevent pregnancy. Knowlton attempted, reasonably successfully, to market the book to adults only: according to the prospectus, it would be sold by subscription only and not for less than fifty cents. Norman Himes attributes great importance to Knowlton's book, commending its detail and completeness. Knowlton's method was cheap, harmless, reasonably reliable, would not cause sterility and "involved no sacrifices during coitus." It placed control of fertility into the woman's hands.[54]

Between January 1832 and March 1835, Knowlton was prosecuted three times for *Fruits of Philosophy* in proceedings in Taunton, Lowell and Greenfield that signal a willingness by prosecutors and judges, and possibly one defense lawyer, to contort the law to make it fit Knowlton and his book.[55]

The first prosecution arose from Knowlton's efforts to sell subscriptions for the first edition to three men in Taunton in January 1832. In April, a Supreme Judicial Court jury convicted him, apparently on a directed verdict once he admitted writing the book. The judge must have determined it was legally obscene. Knowlton was fined fifty dollars and costs. He said that the proceedings astonished him and that the prosecutor regretted commencing them and actually returned the costs to him after the trial. Knowlton later recounted being told by a lawyer that the judge must not have thought to apply the statutory truth defense to the case. If so, the judge's understanding of the place of the truth defense was broadly consistent with Thomas Starkie's assertion that it would be absurd to admit evidence of truth in cases of libels against religion or morality. The idea that truth should excuse an immoral publication would likely have struck contemporaries as ludicrous and legally wrong.[56]

---

[54] Himes, *Medical History of Contraception*, 227–29. See also Riegel, "American Father."

[55] On these proceedings, see the case files and Horowitz, *Rereading Sex*, 75–85; Riegel, "American Father"; Knowlton, *Recent Excitement*; Knowlton, *Two Remarkable Lectures*; "The Days of Witchcraft Returned," *Boston Investigator*, January 4, 1833; Knowlton, letter to the editor, *Boston Investigator*, January 11, 1833; Letter to the editor, *Boston Investigator*, February 8, 1833; Knowlton, letter to the editor, *Boston Investigator*, September 25, 1835. See also Putnam, "Excommunication"; Lane, *Historical Sketches*, 110–11; Howes, *History of Ashfield*, 163.

[56] See Starkie, *Treatise on Slander* (1813), 561–62.

Before Knowlton's Taunton trial, a complaint was also laid against him in Common Pleas in Lowell, Middlesex County, which was followed by an indictment in June 1832. He was accused of offering *Fruits of Philosophy* for sale, again through the prospectus. In language echoing the earlier Worcester *Fanny Hill* indictments, *Fruits* was said to be "lewd, wicked, scandalous, infamous and obscene." It "purport[ed] to describe among other things certain processes and to give certain directions, by means whereof men and women may practice carnal copulation, and hinder and obstruct the ordinary issues and course of nature." As in the earlier Taunton trial and the later Greenfield one, the details were said to be too lewd and obscene to put before the court or place in its records.

Uncertainty about whether or not it was necessary to identify the recipient of the libel is evident in the Lowell indictment: one of the counts identified the buyer but the other did not. More remarkably, Knowlton said he was charged on the basis of the prospectus alone. The prospectus's wording suggests that he understood himself to be reasonably safe in marketing the book by subscription. Convicting someone of publishing obscene libel for soliciting orders through a prospectus was a stretch for the law of libel, since the prospectus was not, itself, alleged to be objectionable. The court may well never have seen the actual book. Knowlton later complained that his incompetent (or perfidious) lawyer gave the court a copy of Owen's *Moral Physiology*, presumably to demonstrate what sort of book Knowlton's was. Knowlton did not think the judge read it, since the court immediately adjourned for dinner. No opportunity to test these legal issues arose, however. At his lawyer's urging, Knowlton pleaded guilty in December 1832 and was sentenced to hard labor in Cambridge for three months, starting January 1, 1833.

Although most of the Boston papers ignored the case, Abner Kneeland, who sold such books, did not. Kneeland declared that "a man" had been sentenced "for publishing a book – in other words, for disseminating knowledge – alias, 'for publishing the idea of destroying the fecundating property of the sperm by chemical agents.'" Kneeland warned that such coercive tactics would ultimately encourage the dissemination of knowledge. Knowlton responded by letter from jail. He was pleased to be noticed by Kneeland and especially by Kneeland's comparison of the proceedings to the Salem witch trials. The letter explained the misunderstandings *Fruits of Philosophy* sought to correct and how its remedies would permit people to regulate their fertility. Knowlton claimed that various commentators disapproved heartily of the prosecution and were appalled at the infringement of liberty of the press and the blow to scientific knowledge. A Providence correspondent to the *Boston Investigator* wrote a couple of weeks later comparing *Fruits of Philosophy* to Paine's *Common Sense* and deploring the public suppression of truths known at least to some in medicine. The writer lamented the lack of concern for personal liberty. Kneeland published two lectures Knowlton delivered upon his release from jail, pointedly emphasizing in the title that Knowlton had been imprisoned "for publishing a book." Unbowed, Knowlton continued to warn against superstition; that humans, like other animals, were nothing but matter; and that the pangs of conscience humans experienced when they acted badly were signs not of a deep-seated awareness of future punishment but only of their education. By April, the pages of the *Investigator* showed considerable support for Knowlton.

Over a year later, in August 1834, Knowlton and his medical associate, Roswell Shepard, were indicted in Greenfield, Franklin County for selling the second edition of *Fruits of Philosophy* in nearby Ashfield. Evidence in the case file suggests that a third man was also selling the book. The book was described as objectionable in that it described female anatomy in detail and explained how to prevent pregnancy. The counts identified the recipients of the books.

Ashfield was in a state of religious turmoil. Its population had peaked in 1820 at about 1,800 people but was declining, owing to out-migration. In 1830 it had four churches, two Baptist, one Episcopal and one Congregational. In 1833, on the eve of disestablishment, the longstanding Congregational pastor left and was replaced in May by Reverend Mason Grosvenor, whose tenure was much less peaceful. In the summer of 1834, in a public meeting that accompanied a series of sermons, Grosvenor attacked "the infidelity and Dr. Knowlton as the leader of it."

In 1829, Knowlton had published his magnum opus, *Elements of Modern Materialism*, in which he denied the existence of a soul or spirit, arguing that our essence lay in our brains and that the idea of an afterlife was a sham. Well over 400 pages long, it sold poorly, but

Knowlton later attributed the Greenfield prosecution over *Fruits of Philosophy* to the religious beliefs he had expressed in *Modern Materialism* and to his position on the local temperance movement.[57] By that time Knowlton was finding himself labeled an "infidel," discursively linked in Ashfield to Owen, Wright and Kneeland, whose troubles in Boston had begun: a pamphlet of prosecutor Samuel Parker's arguments was circulating in Ashfield.

Knowlton said Grosvenor, at the public meeting, quoted, out of context, from both *Modern Materialism* and *Fruits of Philosophy*. Ashfield was warned that young men would shun its daughters as wives because of the town's openness to "infidelity and licentiousness." Grosvenor refused to let Knowlton speak, and resolutions were passed to suppress infidelity and *Fruits of Philosophy*. Knowlton later protested that the citizens had been ignorant of the book and that in fact their former pastor had purchased it a year earlier, being recently married. Knowlton thought Ashfield had been unconcerned about the book until after Grosvenor attended a certain ministerial meeting in the summer of 1834, when Abner Kneeland's long ordeal with blasphemy law was underway. Grosvenor's refusal to let Knowlton defend himself, and his "severe sermon against the doctor," sparked a defense by a prominent church member, that member's excommunication and his subsequent restoration to the church. According to the later town historian who recorded the episode, "there was not a person of calm nerves in the whole town." Knowlton accused Grosvenor of a campaign to slur and silence him, of slandering his wife and discouraging his patients from patronizing him.

In a pamphlet of October 1834, *A History of the Recent Excitement in Ashfield*, Knowlton attributed the Ashfield prosecution not to the information in *Fruits of Philosophy* but to his religious beliefs. He positioned himself as one whose religious freedom, freedom of expression and right to publish were being assaulted by repressive clergymen. He said his religious beliefs had been "all the cry in Ashfield" until other ministers at the convention reminded Grosvenor "that every man has a right to enjoy his own religious opinions" and suggested prosecuting Knowlton for obscenity instead. He observed that after this convention, "all at once, in different parts of the county,

---

[57] Horowitz, *Rereading Sex*, 74; Knowlton, *Recent Excitement*, 1–4.

(as I am informed) 'licentiousness' was coupled with the term infidelity." He also noted an increased demand for his book from the "Church-and-State clergy," hinting that this demand arose both because they were gathering evidence and because they were curious about the useful information it contained. He noted that others who were circulating his book were not being prosecuted: their religious beliefs were not controversial.

Knowlton claimed he had obtained a legal opinion that *Fruits of Philosophy* could not be suppressed, that the common law did not reach books about common medical issues: the law, he said, "bans obscene books but not simply immoral ones," there being insufficient agreement on what "immoral tendency" meant. It is possible – even probable, given the book's evident popularity – that many others quietly agreed with him on contraception but disliked his religious views. He and his business partner were tried twice in Common Pleas in Greenfield, in November 1834 and March 1835, but neither jury reached a verdict, and in August 1835 the district attorney dropped the case.

Committed to an overall increase in happiness in the world, Knowlton seems not to have appreciated how deeply the orthodox clergy believed that a woman who transgressed sexual norms should pay for her indiscretions for the rest of her life and beyond. Knowlton believed the earth faced an unsustainable population explosion, and he thought young men sought out prostitutes because they were wretched without sex but could not yet afford the costs of childrearing. He thought the straightforward physiological information he was presenting would lessen these harms and save women and men from the cost to health and finances of frequent unplanned pregnancies. He did not think ignorance alone kept women virtuous. He attached as an appendix to the second edition of *Fruits of Philosophy* an extract from the *Boston Investigator* that argued that women were unjustly slandered by the idea that fear of pregnancy was the only thing that restrained them from indiscriminate sexual adventurism.

In July 1835, the church dismissed Grosvenor.[58] Knowlton, however, stayed in Ashfield.[59] His religious views did not prevail in

[58] Putnam, "Excommunication," 5–6.
[59] Shepard moved to Rochester, New York, where he tried his hand at editing and then moved to Ohio: *Portrait and Biographical Record of Shelby and Moultrie Counties,* 380; "Liberal Convention," *Boston Investigator,* August 19, 1836.

his time, but Americans do seem to have taken the chance to control their fertility, rejecting the necessity of a link between sexual licentiousness and religious infidelity. By the fall of 1835, the *Investigator* was advertising a book called "Dr. Knowlton's Work on Physiology," and fertility rates declined dramatically in the middle of the nineteenth century.[60]

Abner Kneeland's Trials Begin

In January 1834, Free Thinker Abner Kneeland first stood trial for what Peter Thacher called "obscene, impious and blasphemous libel" over three articles Kneeland published in the weekly *Boston Investigator*. Continuing for more than four years, Kneeland's legal ordeal would become a touchstone in arguments about liberty of conscience in Massachusetts.[61] The forces of conservatism mobilized against a lone, older man with unpopular views, and no one emerged unscathed.

Kneeland had long edited and published religious newspapers. In Charlestown, while still a Universalist, he edited *The Gospel Visitant*. In Philadelphia, he published the weekly *Christian Messenger* from 1819 to 1821, the monthly *Philadelphia Universalist Magazine and Christian Messenger* from 1821 to 1823, and the weekly *Gazetteer* in 1824. He apparently started another Universalist newspaper in New York in 1828, the weekly *Olive Branch and Christian Inquirer*, but it seems not to have survived his fallout with, and expulsion from,

---

[60] Horowitz, *Rereading Sex*, 85; Grossberg, *Governing*, 156–57. Ryan, *Empire of the Mother*, 104, citing Paul David and Warren Sanderson, "The Effectiveness of Nineteenth-Century Contraceptive Practices: An Application of Microdemographic Modelling Approaches," in *Seventh International Economic History Congress, Edinburgh, 1978: Papers on 'B Themes' by the International Economic History Association* (Edinburgh: Edinburgh University Press, 1978), 67–68. According to Marvin McInnis, fertility information for nineteenth-century Canada is difficult to come by, but his work suggests that at least by 1861, one of the most important variables in determining whether a county in Canada West or East had a high marital fertility rate was the proportion of the population that was English-speaking with American roots: McInnis, "Population of Canada," 401–2. Knowlton's advice may well have spread northward.

[61] This case has received considerable scholarly attention. See Levy, *Blasphemy in Massachusetts*; Commager, "Blasphemy of Abner Kneeland"; Burkholder, "Divinity School Address"; French, "Liberation from Man and God"; French, *Trials of Abner Kneeland*; Gallaher, "Abner Kneeland."

the Universalists in 1829. He became associated with the *Free Enquirer* and then moved to Boston, where he began lecturing with the First Society of Free Enquirers. In 1831 he founded the *Investigator*, which attacked all versions of Protestantism while supporting Andrew Jackson and commemorating Thomas Paine and his *Age of Reason*.[62]

The *Investigator* reported on Robert Dale Owen, Richard Carlile and the misdeeds of the clergy, with tales of Methodists embroiled in seamy sexual exploits appearing more often than their numbers would seem to warrant. It attacked the subordination of women through marriage and advocated their equality. It also cautiously opposed slavery and advocated a national system of education, the abolition of imprisonment for debt and the improvement of the working classes. The society held Sunday meetings and Wednesday dances, at which men, women and children were welcome, the unmarried free to consort as they wished. The *Investigator* at least once announced a ball on a public fast day – while the pious fasted, the Free Inquirers would dance.[63] Kneeland's approach to sex and marriage fueled his enemies' fire.

Kneeland's ongoing public disagreements with the Universalists were the context for his prosecution. In the late 1820s and early 1830s, Thomas Whittemore's Universalist *Trumpet* newspaper featured ongoing jousting not only with Free Thinkers but also with more conservative Christians, such as Lyman Beecher and Origen Bacheler. The Universalists opposed Sabbatarian legislation, state fast days and sectarian education, and they objected to calls by the orthodox to exclude them from public offices, standing on their rights to freedom of conscience and free exercise of religion. Universalists were leaders in the effort to bring full disestablishment to Massachusetts.[64] Kneeland and the Universalists shared many views but not all. The text at the core of the prosecution was Kneeland's statement describing how his beliefs differed from the Universalists'.

---

[62] Schlesinger, *Age of Jackson*, 356–57; Horowitz, *Rereading Sex*, 70–71; Miller, *Larger Hope*, 188–91. Kneeland's career in publishing has been pieced together from the records in Worldcat, www.worldcat.org.

[63] Horowitz, *Rereading Sex*, 71; French, "Liberation from Man and God," 208. See e.g. "Ball at Julien Hall – Fast Day Evening," *Boston Investigator*, April 20, 1832.

[64] Miller, *Larger Hope*, 170–74.

The complaint was filed by Lucius M. Sargent, an Episcopalian Boston lawyer, author of popular temperance stories, and sometime newspaper essayist aggrieved by the *Investigator*'s reviews of his fiction.[65] Three excerpts from the *Boston Investigator* of Friday, December 20, 1833 served as the basis of the prosecution. Two had been cribbed from the *Free Enquirer* and one was by Kneeland himself. The first passage, by Voltaire, mocked the notion of the virgin birth, making fun of a Frenchman who, "though he be too stupid to understand the laws of evidence, or too illiterate to apply them to history, firmly believes that Jesus Christ was begotten without any testicles at all." The second item ridiculed prayer, suggesting that if Christians were correct, God must listen to endless, contradictory pleas "that are every moment ascending up, or down to him." Heretically, the article declared, "the old gentleman is more a subject of pity, than General Jackson was during his late visit." In the third passage, a letter to Thomas Whittemore, Kneeland set out four points of faith on which he differed from the Universalists. Tellingly, on the issue of the *Investigator* in the court file, someone has circled these three passages and also one more: an advertisement for *Fruits of Philosophy*, which added that copies were available at the *Investigator*'s office. A connection between "infidelity" and "licentiousness" was evidently on the mind of the person who brought the case together, likely Samuel D. Parker or an assistant.

The indictment charged Kneeland with publishing a "scandalous, impious, obscene, blasphemous and profane libel," and with contravening the 1782 Massachusetts blasphemy statute, whose wording the indictment exactly tracked. As the proceedings wore on and public concern about mob violence and freedom of conscience rose, the Commonwealth's case gradually narrowed, as its lawyers dropped plank after plank in their argument.

Samuel Parker, the son of an episcopal bishop, opened the case before a packed courtroom. Parker explained that Kneeland was charged under both the blasphemy statute and the common law. The statute, he said, was constitutional because Christian obligations were built into it in 1780 and had survived the 1820 constitutional revisions.

[65] Miller, *Larger Hope*, 191; Commager, "Blasphemy," 31. See also Sargent, *Temperance Tales*.

Because the statute was contemporaneous with the constitution, and because the common law had been adopted except where explicitly changed by statute, both were obviously valid, a "no one has ever questioned this" line of reasoning more persuasive to the judiciary than to critics. Parker ignored the recent constitutional amendment that was about to end obligatory state support for religion. He cited Starkie's 1813 slander and libel treatise for the proposition that obscene and blasphemous libels were offenses at common law. He also cited the 1816 second English edition of Holt's *Law of Libel* on these common law offenses.[66]

Parker reminded the jury of the oaths they had sworn before God, that religion was the foundation of all they held dear and that Kneeland's crime was "his open, indecent and wilful, public attempt to deprive the community of this solemn security, by ridiculing and denying that God." Kneeland, he said, was worse than Hume, Gibbon, Voltaire and others because only certain men, of "sound understanding," read their works, but Kneeland's paper was cheap and his views were "so easily read – so coarsely expressed – so industriously spread abroad." They were "sent into a thousand families," presumably regardless of the wishes of the household patriarch. Parker assured the jury that Christianity was in no real danger from "Robert Owen, Fanny Wright, or Abner Kneeland, or any of their conceited disciples." Kneeland could reason candidly and fairly as much as he pleased, but Christianity was not to be "debauched" with vulgarity and scoffing, because upon it rested the safety of the state. Rights of conscience, Parker said, protected one's religious feelings from insult and one's other sensibilities from "offensive and disgusting obscenity." Liberty of discussion protected sincere, decent, moderate expression. Liberty of the press was to be fully supported but not allowed to protect licentiousness or character assassination, or seditious, obscene, malicious or blasphemous libels. All creeds were to be tolerated, if pitied, but publishing and vilifying God was criminal because it uprooted truth and virtue, the safeguards of obligation. There was to be no religious persecution, but the law was to be upheld to protect people's beliefs. Malice could be inferred from

---

[66] *Report of the Arguments of the Attorney of the Commonwealth*, 179–87; Levy, *Verbal Offense against the Sacred*, 415.

the text without proof of the defendant's actual intentions. Republishing another's composition was prima facie evidence of intent to publish it. A proprietor or editor of a newspaper was responsible for libels inserted without his knowledge. Parker offered to read the libel, but Andrew Dunlap, for Kneeland, agreed that Parker could be spared this step, as it was correctly set out in the indictment.[67] After this two-hour address, Parker called his sole witness, who gave evidence about the provenance of the various articles. Parker rested his case.

Kneeland was defended by Andrew Dunlap, a "rabid" Democrat and former state attorney general, who was well regarded in the federal courts, where he commonly practiced.[68] After calling several witnesses, Dunlap argued for fourteen hours over three days.[69] His argument was eloquent, learned, devout and provocative, perhaps too much so. Dunlap spoke respectfully of all religions and was highly favorable toward Catholics. He argued that the case fell outside the statute, that the statute violated the state constitution, that the common law offense did not exist and that the law on blasphemy was incompatible with the federal constitution. The argument rested squarely on republican principles: the rights to freedom of religion, conscience, press and speech guaranteed through the Revolution and the Massachusetts constitution, and the inapplicability of English law, long associated with religious persecution. The first two articles were coarse, not blasphemous, and the third was a genuine, calm, constitutionally protected statement of "disbelief in the belief of the Universalists, in the divinity of Jesus Christ, and in the doctrine of the resurrection." Dunlap pointed out that Christian sects differed over the virgin birth and that critics like Swift and Voltaire had been similarly ribald. He pointed out that in more tolerant New York, a headline referring to Kneeland's prosecution announced, "The Holy Inquisition Re-Established in Boston."

The third article – Kneeland's statement of his beliefs – required the most careful defense. Kneeland had four points of disagreement with

[67] *Report of the Arguments of the Attorney of the Commonwealth*, 188–96.
[68] Schlesinger, *Age of Jackson*, 358; Levy, *Verbal Offense against the Sacred*, 415. See Untitled, *Boston Morning Post*, Feb. 19, 1835; "Death of Mr. Dunlap," *Boston Morning Post*, July 31, 1835.
[69] Dunlap, *Speech*, 47–175.

the Universalists. First, he said, "Universalists believe in a God which I do not; but believe that their God with all his moral attributes (aside from nature itself) is nothing more than a mere chimera of their own imagination." Second, unlike the Universalists, he believed that the story of Christ was a fable. Third, unlike the Universalists, he did not believe in miracles: stories about them were either accounts of natural events or tricks. Fourth, Kneeland denied the resurrection of the dead and eternal life and asserted that all life ended in the individual's eternal extinction.[70] Dunlap's explication of the first point took him into deep exegetical water: had Kneeland actually denied God and revealed himself as an atheist, or had he only denied the Universalists' understanding of God? The first would contravene the statute; the second would not (after all, most Bostonians agreed that the Universalists misunderstood God). Dunlap denied Kneeland was an atheist, claiming he believed humans were religious beings and was merely clarifying his position. Dunlap took the jury on a learned excursion through English and French grammar. When Thacher interrupted to press him on whether the Universalists' god was not, indeed, the single god of all, Dunlap politely said that this was a question for the jury and told the jury to disregard Thacher on this matter. Dunlap canvassed how different learned writers had talked about God. When Thacher asked what god Kneeland actually did believe in, Dunlap declared that a matter for Kneeland's own conscience. Kneeland's other three statements, Dunlap said, were not caught by the statute, as in the absence of contumelious reproach, which Kneeland had not printed, only denying God outright violated the statute. Dunlap raised the specter of a multitude of sects using blasphemy law to persecute those with different beliefs.

Dunlap turned to the blasphemy statute, telling the jurors that they could assess its constitutionality, as well as judge if it had been offended. The statute, he said, was logically incoherent and unconstitutional. Unless "God" referred to all gods, non-Christians who swore oaths by their gods would automatically commit blasphemy. The references to Jesus Christ, the Holy Ghost and Holy Scripture could be read as imposing Trinitarianism on the state and

---

[70] Kneeland's theological assertions were quoted in the indictment. See also *Comm. v. Kneeland*, Thach. Crim. Cas. 346 (1834).

making Unitarians blasphemers. This statute, unlike others, he pointed out (and unlike Nova Scotia's), criminalized denying God's final judging of the world, which made Universalists blasphemers. The statute also threatened biblical scholarship by banning casting contempt or ridicule on the canonical scriptures.

Finally Dunlap turned to the common law – "the rank growth of a Monarchy."[71] Blasphemy law was intended to support the Church of England. Dunlap thought people agreed that the law of obscene libel was constitutional and necessary for the protection of morals, but blasphemy law was not. He denied that the testicles piece was obscene and also argued that Kneeland should not be held responsible for it because he had not approved its inclusion in the newspaper. He distinguished between attacking morality or specific individuals and attacking points of belief. He denied that Christianity was part of the common law and reminded the court that federal law excluded the common law of crime. He argued that blasphemy law was incompatible with the federal power over naturalization, because it could ensnare many immigrants. The Massachusetts constitution, and especially its recent amendments, enshrined freedom of conscience and religious equality for all. Chronicling the long history of religious persecution of Christians, Dunlap urged the jury to protect all faiths.

Samuel Parker then closed the Commonwealth's case, drawing the jury's attention back to Kneeland and away from the state's impoverished commitment to freedom of conscience. He presented himself as a hardworking prosecutor, constrained by law, limited time and the need to check infidelity – and, unlike Dunlap, not given to flights of oratory or clever displays of erudition. He was glad, he said, to hear that Kneeland was not an atheist and that Dunlap denounced Kneeland's doctrines, but he suggested that Dunlap must therefore be a hypocrite and a mercenary. Parker would not further tax the jury's patience but "place before [them], as men, as husbands, as fathers, as christians and as Jurors, a most serious and shocking charge" against Kneeland. If the prosecution failed, "impious and disgusting publications" could multiply, and the results could be fatal to "thousands of human beings, young and old, male and female, married and single, rich and poor." Dunlap's long address was

[71] Dunlap, *Speech*, 116–17.

unprecedented, unnecessary and tedious. Kneeland had violated the statute. Notwithstanding Dunlap's strained interpretation, Kneeland was an atheist who had denied God, the scriptures and other aspects of faith and had heaped contumely on Christianity. The blasphemy statute was constitutional. Unitarian and Universalist jurors could and should enforce it. He denied that the jury could "blot this law out of the Statute Book" if they thought it unconstitutional. He told the jury to judge Kneeland, not the other thinkers Dunlap had cited. What if the prosecution failed? "Do you wish to see the Boston Investigator in every family, such obscenity and impiety in the hands of your wives, your sons and your daughters? If so, shut up your meeting-houses and churches, and go to Julien Hall, where all the mysteries of infidelity will be developed to you." If Kneeland were not stopped, infidelity would break up families and corrupt young men and women, leading to crime and prostitution. If Dunlap's federal naturalization law argument were right, polygamy and murdering aged parents would also be tolerated in the United States. The blasphemy statute offended neither the federal constitution nor federal naturalization laws: the state's constitution governed its own laws, and federal power did not reach that far. He closed: "Good men and true, stand together. Fear God – do justice – honor the law. So may God help you in the hour of your trial!" – their trial, not Kneeland's.[72]

Thacher's jury charge strongly favored the prosecution. He assured the jury that Kneeland was responsible for everything in the *Investigator*, regardless of his actual choice of all the pieces. Kneeland was charged with publishing an "obscene, impious and blasphemous libel" that violated both the common law and the blasphemy statute. Defining blasphemy, Thacher assured the jury that Kneeland was not being tried for his beliefs and that the law backed no particular sect. Blasphemy law protected good order and the sanctity of oaths. Consistent with his refusal to bar Universalist witnesses in *Bacheler* in 1829, Thacher explained that only atheists could not testify and only atheism offended the law and the constitution. Acknowledging that it fell to the jurors to determine the publication's obscenity and impiety, he informed them that the state constitution protected freedom of religion. The first principle of all

[72] *Report of the Arguments of the Attorney of the Commonwealth*, 197–216.

religion was the existence of God; the blasphemy statute restrained and punished those who offended that principle, protecting the peace as well. The division between Trinitarians and Unitarians was not a problem for blasphemy law. Thacher, unlike Parker, addressed the recent constitutional changes, acknowledging that a statute that depended on the old Article III would have been virtually repealed by the recent amendments. However, Thacher reasoned that the new provisions merely established that the clergy must depend on voluntary support. The citizen enjoyed freedom of conscience, and "the name of the Supreme Being, and reverence for religious institutions, still stand in capitals upon the front of the constitution." Blasphemy law was untouched. Thacher was unconvinced by Kneeland's circumlocutions and his disavowals of atheism. Kneeland's newspaper circulated among "thousands of the poor and laboring classes of the community" who deeply needed the consolations of religion. Emphasizing that he was supporting religious freedom, Thacher underlined the coarseness, scurrility and irreverence in the first two articles.[73] He concluded that if the jury believed Kneeland had published his statements "unwittingly, not knowing the force of words, and devoid of an evil intent," they should acquit him. However, if they believed that knowing the power of words and intending to promote atheism, he

has, by this publication, blasphemed the holy name of God, and denied him – that he has reproached Jesus Christ, by representing his history as a fable, and his miracles as the tricks of an imposter – and that he has contumeliously reproached the Holy Scriptures – thus endeavoring, in his malignity, to disseminate his impious sentiments among the poor and ignorant, and to deprive them of the faith and hopes of religion, the sole consolation of the miserable, both in life and death, – you must find him guilty. Judge his cause with charity, but let your verdict be the voice of wisdom and truth.[74]

Unsurprisingly, Kneeland was convicted and sentenced to three months in jail. He was ordered to provide sureties to ensure he kept the peace for two years. He appealed.[75]

---

[73] Thacher, "Charge to the Jury," 271–87.
[74] *Ibid.* 287–88; cf. *Comm. v. Kneeland*, Thach. Crim. Cas. 346, 390 (1834).
[75] "Mr. Kneeland," *Spirit of the Age* (Boston), January 30, 1834.

Supreme Judicial Court juries failed to reach verdicts in May and November 1834 before finally convicting Kneeland in November 1835, a decision Kneeland appealed to the full bench, which heard the case in March 1836 but did not deliver a verdict for two years. Andrew Dunlap defended Kneeland in his first Supreme Judicial Court trial but after that Kneeland represented himself. By February 1835 Dunlap was seriously ill, and he died the following summer.[76] Samuel Parker prosecuted in November 1834 but then passed the torch to James T. Austin. The two slogged grimly on, arguing to the end about the dependence of civilized society on religious faith and warning of the dangers posed by Kneeland and his associates. Gradually, the case narrowed. Parker abandoned the obscenity charge in May 1834. When Austin took over, he decided to rest the case on the statute alone, not the common law. He conceded that denying that the scriptures were the word of God did not necessarily constitute blasphemy.[77] In November 1835, Austin gave up on the first two counts: now the case rested on the question of whether the first sentence of Kneeland's statement of belief, in the excerpt he had written himself, contravened the blasphemy statute. Had Kneeland denied God, or had he merely denied the god of the Universalists, or were these the same thing? Justice Samuel Wilde advised the jury to give the passage its obvious grammatical construction. He informed them that the willful denial of the existence of any god other than the material universe itself (Kneeland had at points said he was a pantheist) would constitute a violation of the statute, which, Wilde said, was constitutional. Finally the Commonwealth prevailed, and Kneeland was convicted and sentenced to sixty days' imprisonment.

Before his first Supreme Judicial Court trial in May 1834, Kneeland and his publisher, John Quincy Adams, published Kneeland's defense of himself and Dunlap's speech, warning of the danger to freedom of religion posed by the alliance of church and state upon which Thacher insisted. The drumbeat of freedom of conscience and expression (or "discussion") had begun. Arguments around these rights mingled with

---

[76] Untitled, *Boston Morning Post*, February 19, 1835; "Death of Mr. Dunlap," *Boston Morning Post*, July 31, 1835.

[77] This was prudent, since Unitarians denied that a large part of the scriptures were holy writ, and Free Inquirers simply extended the denial to the scriptures as a whole.

arguments about the common law's legitimacy, about interpreting the
constitution, and about the role of juries. In court, Dunlap shortened his
arguments and finished in one day. Parker again characterized them as
excessive. He spent more energy on liberty of the press this time, arguing
that it meant only the absence of prior restraint and was fully consistent
with punishing for blasphemy. Just as the freedom to keep firearms was
not freedom to commit murder, freedom of the press did not protect
a liberty to publish just anything at all, regardless of consequences. The
law rightly interfered with Kneeland's intemperate attacks on society's
foundational beliefs. Indeed, Parker argued, Kneeland and Fanny
Wright were persecuting the faithful, not the other way around. As to
the argument that blasphemy law violated the separation of church and
state, Parker noted that it had recently become fashionable to challenge
the constitutionality of statutes, but nevertheless Christianity was
embedded in the common law; he devoted much time to rebutting
Thomas Jefferson's contrary argument. Parker reviewed English and
American case law recognizing blasphemy as a crime, and he cited
a multitude of law books. Both the statute and the common law
against blasphemy were constitutional. He warned the jury
strenuously that making law was the job of the legislature and the
governor: other roads led to tyranny, the rule of men, not law.
Liberally quoting Fanny Wright, Robert Dale Owen and Charles
Knowlton, especially their attacks on marriage and advocacy of
contraception, Parker warned the jury of the mortal peril society
faced: "Atheism, Infidelity, and revolutionary and ruinous principles."[78]

In his charge, Samuel Putnam informed the jury that they could
decide both law and facts in criminal cases, but he thought they were
bound by the judge's description of the law unless they knew it to be
erroneous. He gave reasons for upholding the constitutionality of the
statute. He asserted that decent discussion was the acceptable way to
promulgate one's opinion, and that reverence toward a Supreme Being
could be required by law because it did not infringe religious freedom
but instead protected believers' freedom of conscience.[79]

The trial ended in a hung jury, with Charles G. Greene, the editor of
the *Boston Morning Post*, holding out. An opponent called Greene

[78] *Report of the Arguments of the Attorney of the Commonwealth*, 220–69.
[79] Putnam, "Charge to the Jury," 289–91.

a "personal and political friend" of Dunlap's, placed irregularly on the jury by Dunlap. Greene had admired Dunlap's address in municipal court and continued to be convinced by his arguments. Publicly attacked for his dissent in May 1834, Greene responded at length in his columns, commenting on Boston's intolerance toward those who dared to think for themselves. It was not Kneeland's principles that were at issue, Greene said, but his constitutional rights. Greene was persuaded that all religious groups were equal, which this statute made impossible. The people had enacted a constitution that did not enable the legislature to establish a state religion. As a juror, Greene was entitled to judge the law, as Putnam had acknowledged.[80]

Throughout, Kneeland continued with his publishing, dances and meetings, flying the flag of freedom of conscience. The legal proceedings attracted tremendous attention, and, over the next four years the tide of public opinion gradually shifted in his favor. His ideas were contested, but so was his right to express them and the propriety of applying the "English" common law in Massachusetts. Boston's elite looked down their noses at the vulgarity of Kneeland's following, even as they feared his influence on his followers' moral, religious and political (i.e. Jacksonian) propensities. As well, the violence against unpopular expression in these years (largely but not entirely abolitionist) shaped the environment in which claims to freedom of expression were made by Kneeland and others.

Beliefs and Violence in the Mid-1830s

Over the next year and a half, conflict over belief raged in Boston, in courtrooms and on the streets, and the law's capacity to respond appropriately both to expressions of belief and to violence was increasingly called into question. William Snelling was jailed for alleging that police magistrate Benjamin Whitman had been too drunk to function and had failed to recognize and respond to the threats Snelling brought before him. Charles Knowlton was indicted in Ashfield in the summer of 1834. The previous summer, Benjamin

---

[80] *Report of the Arguments of the Attorney of the Commonwealth*, 269; Untitled re Kneeland proceedings, *Boston Morning Post*, January 24, 1834; Charles G. Greene, "Abner Kneeland's Case," *Boston Morning Post*, May 26, 1834; Untitled editorial, *Boston Morning Post*, May 22, 1834.

Franklin Hallett and the antimasons had challenged the integrity of the courts through *Moore and Sevey, Clough* and *Guild,* as questions were vetted about jury biases and the admissibility of evidence of conspiracies. In May 1834, objecting to attacks on himself for failing to concur in the *Kneeland* jury's verdict, Greene declared that in Boston, a man could only be accounted wise and respectable if he followed the views of the majority and the rich. Free expression was condemned as much as in the days of George III if it contradicted prevailing opinion:

> To be sure they do not *directly* imprison and whip you, and confiscate your property, but they gratify their malice in a different manner – they belie your character, your acts, and your motives – they attempt to deprive you of the *enjoyment* of liberty, and might as well put you in prison – they take from you *the means whereby you live*, and might as well confiscate your estate – they do not scourge you with a whip, but with what is worse, *a slanderous tongue.*

Greene, of course, denied being afraid of "this dictatorial spirit"; liberty was worth more than a reputation maintained under such terms.[81]

Majoritarian anti-Catholicism was a violent force in the United States in the 1830s, as Protestant mobs mobilized against the Roman church's supposed constraints on spiritual liberty, as embodied largely in Irish immigrants. In August 1834, a mob – unimpeded by police or fire trucks – burned down the Ursuline convent in Charlestown, an event with class aspects as well, as upper-class Bostonians sent their daughters there to escape the public school system's Congregationalism. Some thought the prominent orthodox clergyman Lyman Beecher had incited the riot in a violently anti-Catholic sermon the day before, although he condemned the riot the following Sunday, and plans for the riot were afoot before the sermon. Beecher's defenders insisted on his freedom of expression. Hallett saw scope for profit and led efforts to publish Rebecca Reed's inflammatory, anti-Catholic *Six Months in a Convent* shortly afterward. Mob attacks on Catholic churches in New England multiplied.[82]

James T. Austin took over for Parker in *Kneeland* in November 1834, appearing before Samuel Wilde. What was argued

---

[81] Untitled editorial, *Boston Morning Post,* May 22, 1834, emphasis in original.
[82] Hamburger, *Church and State,* 200–17; Billington, *Protestant Crusade,* 35–90; Lane, *Policing the City,* 30–31.

is somewhat less certain because Austin did not publish his speech and Kneeland printed much of his pamphlet before the trial but changed what he said to respond to Austin. Kneeland thought Austin "was more moderate, less abusive, and displayed by far greater talent" than Parker, but Kneeland still felt misused, depicted as intellectually deficient at some points and as guiltier than a murderer or a pirate at others.

This time Austin based the Commonwealth's case on a narrower understanding of the blasphemy statute. Kneeland, now defending himself but often reading from Dunlap's speech, continued to assert that he was not morally responsible for publishing articles inserted in the paper without his knowledge. He denied the blasphemousness of the first article and pointed to biblical exegesis on the virgin birth. He explained that the second article was satire, well known in theological and philosophical debate, and that even if the worst possible interpretation were given to it, it was not contumelious, reproachful or otherwise blasphemous. Regarding the third article, Kneeland explained that he was a pantheist, not an atheist, and he presented a copy of his philosophical creed, which he had published in July 1833. He insisted that the impugned statement was not a denial of God but simply a statement of unbelief, which was different. He claimed he had merely exercised the rights and privileges of every American citizen, regardless of religion. He emphasized the history of Christian biblical critique. He asked the jury for sympathy for his rights and his age. He warned that more prosecutions could follow and remarked that the attorney general had recently been called upon to prosecute the publisher of an article written by a group of well-regarded Christians for the same offense – presumably blasphemy. He said he was more embarrassed for Massachusetts than for himself and his family, and he predicted, correctly, that posterity would view this trial as persecution.[83] This jury too failed to reach a verdict.

In the winter of 1834–35 Boston liberals began shifting from general denunciations of infidelity to specific attacks on Kneeland and his activities. Doctor Samuel Gridley Howe called on the owners of the Federal Street theater, where Kneeland and his followers met, to "remove" the Free Thinkers or face citizen action by the "watchmen

[83] Kneeland, *Speech of Abner Kneeland*, 310–41.

and sentinels of society," together with exclusion from social circles and economic sanctions.[84] Delivered against a backdrop of collective violence, these threats of extralegal action were undoubtedly ominous.

After this trial, probably in the winter or spring of 1835, a pamphlet alleging judicial partiality appeared, written by "A Cosmopolite" – David Henshaw – a leader of the Massachusetts Democratic party and a friend of Dunlap's.[85] Henshaw tore into the two Commonwealth attorneys, especially Parker; the three judges, especially Thacher; and the arguments that supported Kneeland's conviction. Henshaw accused Parker of making "a most abusive speech" about Kneeland. Thacher, Putnam and Wilde were all charged with pushing juries to convict Kneeland. Putnam, although "not personal and offensive against the defendant was, we think, as unsound in his law as Judge Thacher, and quite incorrect in many of his statements." Thacher, in publishing his jury charge, was trying to influence the subsequent proceedings. Unitarians would regret these proceedings, Henshaw implied, for they too brought Christianity's truths into contempt: theirs was "a bastard sort of faith, a kind of mongrel christianity ... in reality, little short of pure Deism." Their numbers, he said, included the judges, at least one prosecutor, and the former governor, who he thought had ordered the prosecution. Henshaw said a Boston grand jury had recently received a complaint against the Unitarians' *Christian Examiner* for denying the divinity of Jesus.[86] Henshaw could have been prosecuted for libel for this abusive and indecorous attack, but such a step would have been highly impolitic.

As well, Henshaw forcefully articulated core arguments in Kneeland's favor. The obscenity charges were a sneaky attempt to avoid open debate about blasphemy. Hand-wringing about Kneeland corrupting the poor and laboring classes was hypocritical: the "rich and lazy classes" would read his works in private. The constitution of 1780 was not the constitution of 1834: the words, the social context and the people's beliefs had changed. The argument that the common

---

[84] French, "Liberation from Man and God," 216–18.
[85] Schlesinger, *Age of Jackson*, 358; "Henshaw, David, 1791–1852."
[86] A Cosmopolite, *Review of the Prosecution of Kneeland*. I have found no record of these proceedings, but bills rejected by the grand jury would not appear in my Boston sample. It was likely the same affair Kneeland referred to. Henshaw's review was likely written before Dunlap died since it does not mention his passing.

law included Christianity was wrong historically and had no place in Massachusetts in any case, where people could not be prosecuted for their beliefs or lack thereof. Freedom of religion was inherent in the original constitution, and the recent abolition of state support for "protestant" ministers simply made all support voluntary. "The Judiciary alone ... appear insensible to this advance of a liberal age, and hang with tenacious grasp upon the obsolete code of a dark and bigoted era." It was preposterous to suppose that one could not ridicule prevailing beliefs – "Judge Putnam's '*God we worship*,' and Mr Austin's '*God of the statute*'" – because tender feelings might be wounded. Moderation and decency were not required. Henshaw objected strenuously to Putnam's assertion that it would be worthwhile to put down the infidel's creed, even if it were true, because it was so inimical to order and morality: it was "monstrous" that a man could be prohibited "from seeking and promulgating a creed that is TRUE!"[87] Henshaw finished his argument by accusing the judges of overstepping the line between judge and jury. Juries, he argued, could expect a judge to explain the law, but ultimately they could decide whether or not a law was right and constitutional. Henshaw accused the various judges of pressuring juries to believe that they could do no more than administer the law that the judges gave them.

Around the time of Henshaw's critique, while Samuel Parker was busy in Boston prosecuting over strangely inconsequential publications in which rival printers attacked one other and one teenager made fun of another's pretensions as a library clerk, George Cheever was attracting legal attention over his efforts to call to account the distilling interests in Essex. On January 31, 1835, Cheever published his "Inquire at Amos Giles's Distillery" in the *Salem Landmark*. A Unitarian deacon who ran a Salem distillery thought the story was about himself and complained. In early February Cheever was beaten in the streets by one of the deacon's workers and some mariner friends; one pleaded no contest but the charges against the others were dropped. The orthodox *Boston Recorder*, edited by Nathaniel Willis and at times others, hesitated to comment on the facts before the trial for fear of a lawsuit, noting that Cheever's piece,

---

[87] All emphases are Henshaw's.

while criticizing Unitarianism, was doing a marvelous job of advertising the distillery.[88] Cheever's efforts to argue that his tale of the harm done by alcohol was true and therefore statutorily protected were unsuccessful. He was convicted in June 1835 and spent the fall awaiting sentencing, one more casualty of the law's distaste for the expression of criticism.

During the summer of 1835, in the wake of another riot – involving Irishmen outside a "colored boarding house" on Ann Street[89] – the *Boston Morning Post* revealed its editors' dislike of moral reformers, commitment to the press and disgust with the law of libel, especially as it was playing out in Cheever's and Kneeland's cases. A correspondent called Common Sense argued that the common law of libel was unconstitutional, having been introduced to Massachusetts in 1808 by Theophilus Parsons, presumably in *Clap*.[90] The law, the writer thought, was the product of Star Chamber, created during the reign "of James or Charles of England." It punished truth: "the greater the truth the greater the libel." The American Revolution was meant to throw off not only British political power but also English legal and political institutions, including the common law. These "odious bonds" had been broken most completely with regard to libel law and to ecclesiastical law, the original tool for persecuting people for blasphemy. The constitution protected the press; no statute authorized prosecuting over any publication at all, "however false, impious, and disgusting." The common law rule that truth was no defense to criminal libel was evidence that the common law of libel was unconstitutional, notwithstanding that Massachusetts had modified it by statute. The "all grasping" judiciary would never reform itself, but juries owed it to the republic to stand up for what was right.

---

[88] "The Outrage at Salem," *Boston Recorder*, February 20, 1835.
[89] "Municipal Court," *Boston Morning Post*, July 10, 1835.
[90] Common Sense [pseud.], "The Criminal Law of Libel," *Boston Morning Post*, July 22, 1835. According to Peter Thacher, the first libel prosecution actually took place in 1791: a printer, Edmund Freeman, was prosecuted for libel for suggesting that a local lawyer and legislator had, among other things, murdered his wife, verbally abused his daughter and neglected the Sabbath. It was in this case that Francis Dana first suggested that perhaps truth ought to be a defense to a criminal prosecution for libel in Massachusetts: *Comm. v. Whitmarsh*, Thach. Crim. Cas. 441, 455–58 (1836). See also "Supreme Judicial Court: Trial for a Libel," *Columbian Centinel*, February 26, 1791.

Neither the state nor the federal constitution permitted these
infringements on the freedom of the press: the only legitimate
limitation on the "paramount natural law" was that one must not
use one's own rights to invade those of one's neighbors. Juries
needed to defend the press's constitutional liberty. While civil
defamation was legitimate, criminal libel was not.

In August, after two mistrials, the obscenity charges against
Knowlton and Shepard were dropped, and Ashfield settled down. In
Boston, however, tensions around expression continued. While
Kneeland awaited his third trial in Supreme Judicial Court, the
Morning Post's Charles Greene and his partner William Beals were
sued by a schoolteacher, Alfred Pike, over a piece that alleged that Pike
cruelly neglected a young girl in his care. Beals and Greene won on
demurrer at Common Pleas in Essex in September 1835. In November,
a Supreme Judicial Court jury awarded Pike the insulting sum of one
dollar in damages and twenty-five cents in costs. He had claimed
$10,000. Greene published a pamphlet with the details too awful to
print in the newspaper.[91]

The stakes around free expression rose in the face of majoritarian
arguments that violence could legitimately be used to defend the union
against abolitionist speech. In the late summer of 1835, antiabolitionist
rallies were held in "[a]lmost every major city and town in the nation."[92]
Britain's abolition of slavery in the Empire, effective August 1, 1834,
added fuel to American fires. In August 1835, 1,500 prominent citizens
met in Faneuil Hall to denounce antislavery for imperiling the union and
to rally themselves to meet the awful prospect of the English abolitionist
George Thompson – credited by Henry Brougham for bringing about
emancipation in the Empire[93] – addressing the Boston Female Anti-
Slavery Society ("BFASS"). Among the leaders in denouncing
Thompson were lawyers Harrison Gray Otis and Richard Fletcher.[94]
The *Boston Recorder* approved of the resolutions passed at the meeting,

[91] The printers' motion for a new trial a year later was ultimately unsuccessful. See *Trial of Beals and Greene*; "Alfred W. Pike vs. Charles G. Greene," *Boston Investigator*, December 11, 1835; and coverage in the *Post*.
[92] Richards, *"Gentlemen of Property and Standing,"* 15–16.
[93] Clarke, "The Antislavery Movement in Boston," 381.
[94] *Ibid.* Fletcher defended Child in the Keyes prosecution and later supported abolition in the District of Columbia and ending the domestic slave trade: L.M. Child, *Selected Letters*, 60, n.2.

which claimed "freedom of individual thought *and expression*" and accepted that antislavery societies could exist in the North but condemned "*such* societies as the south has any right to complain of." Unless states stayed out of other states' affairs, they imperiled the union. Enough agitation already existed, with controversy raging over petitions in Congress and abolitionists' use of the mails to send their materials south. One resolution also "deprecate[d] all tumultuous assemblies, all riotous or violent proceedings, all outrages on person and property, and all illegal notions of the right or duty of executing summary or vindictive justice in any mode unsanctioned by law."[95]

Events played out otherwise. When the BFASS women met in late October, Thompson had left the city, so no one was able to collect the $100 reward the *Commercial Gazette* offered, to enable Thompson to be "taken to the tarkettle before dark." Instead, a crowd that William Lloyd Garrison numbered in the thousands broke up the women's meeting and captured Garrison, taking his clothes but not his life, thanks to the intervention of the sheriff and another man, who took him to the jail in the city hall for his own protection. Garrison said almost every daily newspaper had approved of the mob, except for Hallett's *Advocate* and another paper called the *Reformer*. The mayor had not formally called for order, no military force had opposed the mob and no arrests had been made. A writer in the *Boston Recorder* criticized Garrison for deliberately inciting violence to draw support from those who disapproved of it. One editorial called for the rioters to be prosecuted, but not much came of that, probably because, as abolitionist lawyer Samuel Sewall alleged, the instigators were "[t]he merchants connected by business with the South." Sewall had braved the crowd to protect Garrison and the BFASS women.[96]

A justice system more useful for prosecuting clergymen and editors than violent rioters struck many as seriously flawed. Others, while not exactly excusing the rioters, blamed their targets. Antiabolitionist mobs were particularly likely to benefit from this reasoning, probably partly because of their cause – the preservation of the union and their

[95] "Public Meeting in Boston," *Boston Recorder*, August 28, 1835 (*Recorder's* emphasis); "Faneuil Hall Resolutions," *Boston Recorder*, August 28, 1835.
[96] Garrison, "Triumph of Mobocracy," 374–88; "Mr. Garrison's Policy," *Boston Recorder*, October 23, 1835; Untitled editorial, *Boston Recorder*, November 13, 1835; Tiffany, *Samuel E. Sewall*, 45–52.

less-trumpeted desire to maintain profitable commerce with the South – and partly because these mobs tended to be composed of men more respectable than those who assaulted George Cheever. Opinions consistent with the rationale behind sedition law and the law of criminal defamatory libel were voiced: troublemakers were not to stir up violence by promulgating incendiary opinions and proposals about defects in the political system. A correspondent to the *Boston Morning Post* deplored the paper's recent criticism of the country's institutions and people. While lamenting the mob that attacked the BFASS and Garrison, the correspondent called Garrison's *Liberator* "perfectly demoniacal," with its "unqualified slanders," "raving bigotry" and so on. Abolitionists wanted to kindle a conflagration, regardless of the carnage that might ensue, all in the name of God. God, however, preferred that people pursue peace.[97]

In the late summer and early fall of 1835, William Ellery Channing, the famous Unitarian divine, was preparing a text condemning slavery while seeking a path that would not end in conflagration. It was published in early December. Channing called slavery "radically, essentially evil." He spoke explicitly of fundamental human rights and cautioned against the despotism of the majority, which might protect the institution for its own ends. The drama unfolding in the West Indies demonstrated that slaveholders, with their intimate knowledge of slaves, would be the only suitable judges of how to proceed with emancipation, although Channing sketched out a plan. Immediatist abolitionists, despite their blameless and sincere commitments, enraged southern slaveholders and endangered slaves further. Appealing to those who could not know better, abolitionists sent out their fiery orators "to gather together young and old, pupils from schools, females hardly arrived at years of discretion, the ignorant, the excitable, the impetuous, and to organize these into associations for the battle against oppression." Channing lumped African Americans into this "mixed and excitable multitude." He deplored mobs, which he said claimed to represent "the People," even as they usurped the law, the expression of the people's actual sovereign will. Antiabolitionist mobs were turning abolition into the

[97] "The Liberator," *Boston Morning Post*, November 20, 1835.

cause of freedom.[98] Free expression needed protection. After an antiabolitionist riot in Cincinnati in 1836 Channing criticized the newspapers for failing to censure mob violence and for tending to denounce all discussions of slavery out of a fear of exasperating the South.[99]

Others agreed. While disapproving of abolitionists, the Congregationalist *Boston Recorder*'s editors consistently expressed dismay at the law's inability to deal with mob violence and, like Channing, perceived that the supposedly respectable majority could be turning abolitionists into martyrs to freedom. Commenting in 1836 on a murder elsewhere, a writer observed that some people seemed to believe that if a mob killed someone who deserved death, it was not murder. "The reasoning is, that 'the will of the people is law:' and, if it be 'the will of the people' that a man should be deemed worthy of death and killed without trial, it is therefore right to kill him." In fact, the will of the people was not law until it was expressed in laws compliant with the constitution. A mob was not "the people," and inflicting death without legal sanction was murder.[100] When Garrison numbered the *Recorder* as being among those responsible for the attack on him, its editor claimed to have been urged by friends to prosecute him for libel, but said he probably would not, owing to expediency and the optics of attacking Garrison. The editor preferred to leave the matter to the grand jury.[101] No libel prosecution appears to have been forthcoming.

"Judge Lynch" and Other Judges

Judges continued to reject claims for the protection of conscience over the fall and winter of 1835–36. Some thought the judges were properly shoring up true religion and social order; others saw partiality. Some thought the law was failing to deal with the Garrisonian threat to

---

[98] Channing, *Slavery*, 105–7, 116, 131–36, 143–45. Others too have argued that by the winter of 1835–36 in Boston, the causes of antislavery, freedom of conscience and freedom of the press had become tightly linked in claims to a broad, individualized right to freedom of conscience and expression that courts were wrongly refusing to recognize. See Rosenberg, *Best Men*, 150.
[99] Channing, "The Abolitionists: A Letter to James G. Birney," in *Works of Channing*, 744–47.
[100] "Murder by Mobs," *Boston Recorder*, May 20, 1836.
[101] "Another Libel," *Boston Recorder*, December 4, 1835.

union and commerce and that stronger, collective measures were therefore appropriate; others insisted that rights of conscience and expression were under assault on all sides, and that the law was insufficiently committed to upholding them. Judge Peter Thacher drew criticism at least twice. In October 1835, he barred a Free Inquirer from testifying under oath in the prosecution of a young man accused of stealing money from Abner Kneeland at the witness's house. The frustrated would-be witness complained to the *Investigator* that to testify, one had to believe in "the genuine bonafide god of the statute of this Commonwealth; or, if you please, Judge Thacher's god." Free Inquiry was spreading so quickly that soon no one would be eligible for jury duty, and "Judge Lynch" would end up presiding. The young man was convicted anyway, but the would-be witness thought the affair recalled the Inquisition.[102]

The second episode began with William Snelling being elected foreman by his fellow grand jurors. Thacher, however, ruled that Snelling was barred from serving on the grand jury at all because his earlier libels were "scandalous crimes." The *Post* and *Investigator* thought Snelling had been convicted of a nonexistent offense and denied that Thacher had such jurisdiction over the grand jury. The legislature rejected both Snelling's petition for redress and a bill, promoted by Thomas Whittemore and the Universalists, to abolish the disqualification of witnesses for their religious beliefs.[103] The majority would hold the line on the type of belief that made a person too untrustworthy to participate in the legal system. With temperance-related contention widespread as well, concerns about legal actors misusing or exceeding their jurisdiction extended to county commissioners who refused to issue any liquor licenses at all, rather than simply evaluating the character of each applicant, as the governing legislation required them to do. Defenders of the press asserted that many in Boston did not want an unrestrained press and

---

[102] Edward H. Whitaker, letter to the editor, *Boston Investigator*, October 2, 1835; "Judge Thacher," *Boston Investigator*, October 9, 1835; *Comm. v. William Barnard* (Mun. Ct. Bos., September 1835).

[103] "Beauties of Judge Law," *Boston Investigator*, February 5, 1836; "Disqualification of Witnesses," *Boston Investigator*, February 19 and 26, 1836; "Competency of Witnesses," *Boston Investigator*, March 11, 1836.

engaged in mob actions and libel prosecutions in the name of the common good; a corrupt justice system supported them.

In mid-November 1835, before Samuel Wilde, a jury finally convicted Kneeland. He began his address by comparing his prosecution to the witchcraft trials and the persecution of the early Quakers. He reviewed the contradictions in previous judges' statements, explained his religious convictions, and laid out his view of the facts, the law and the constitution. Quoting a grand jury address by Justice John Jay in New York, he argued that the freedom of the press protected every conceivable kind of political or religious discussion, even the opinions of infidels. Wilde disagreed, assuring the jury that the blasphemy statute was constitutional, that in its obvious grammatical construction, Kneeland's text denied the existence of any god, and that denying the existence of any god except the material universe would contravene the statute.[104]

About two weeks later, on December 4, George Cheever's appeal came before Chief Justice Shaw. Deciding not to contend with the Commonwealth, Cheever spoke for himself. As noted in Chapter 3, he made a privilege argument and also pointed out that social criticism was endangered if anyone whose lived experience showed the criticism to mirror reality could bring legal action against the critic. It was unjust, he argued, to blame antiabolitionist riots on antislavery literature, to judge the tendency of a publication by its results. He observed pointedly that an account of respectable Boston men engaged in a riot could not be libelous if it was true. Even respectable distillers should be held accountable for the harm they did. He pointed to the incongruity in his being assaulted in the street and prosecuted for libel by the same attorney – Austin – who dropped the charges against two of the three men who assaulted him. Nevertheless, Cheever was sentenced to thirty days in jail and costs and was required to post a $1,000 bond to keep the peace for two years. All was not lost, however: he published his speech, *Deacon Giles* became a highly popular temperance tract, the deacon's distilling business declined

---

[104] Kneeland did not publish a pamphlet of his argument this time, but he provided an account in the *Investigator* and later included some of these remarks in a pamphlet. See Kneeland, *Speech before the Full Bench*, 377–82; "Freedom of Speech and Liberty of the Press," *Boston Investigator*, November 20, 1835; "Court Calendar," *Boston Daily Advertiser*, April 3, 1838.

and eventually a temperance organization took over the distillery's premises.[105]

These proceedings against Charles Greene, Kneeland and Cheever – coming on the heels of Garrison's near-lynching and interwoven with incidents that rendered the judges' impartiality suspect – bolstered Greene's sustained campaign against the constitutionality of libel law in the *Boston Morning Post*. He was supported by correspondents to his paper and Kneeland's. The *Post*'s writers were not Free Inquirers and had never liked Cheever – his attacks on Unitarians and alcohol were too violent and too extreme – but these prosecutions struck them as outrageous. Critics labeled it inconsistent to support prosecuting Kneeland but object to prosecuting Cheever. Well into the spring of 1836, Greene published articles and editorials that argued that the law of libel was unconstitutional. Kneeland reprinted excerpts in the *Boston Investigator*, along with his own editorials and correspondence. Other newspapers such as Hallett's *Advocate*, the *Daily Advertiser*, the *Mercantile Journal* and the *Salem Advertiser* participated in the debate. Essentially, the critique was that the 1780 state constitution stipulated that freedom of the press was not to be restrained and that judges who purported to curb the press's "licentiousness" were simply imposing their own preferences. The appearance of the oppressive, Blackstonian common law of libel since the Revolution was illegitimate because the constitution had only preserved the parts of the common law in use in 1780, which, these critics argued, did not include criminal libel. Christianity was not part of the common law. Juries should apply their own knowledge of the constitution and judge both law and fact.

One of Kneeland's correspondents asserted that whether or not slavery could be abolished, "nothing but the demon of oppression" could deny the right to discuss it, "and the mobocratic violence which would deprive any one of this right, erects a despotism, friend Kneeland, of the same stamp that would deprive *you* of the unquestionable right to discuss the subject of religion." The correspondent thought Garrison was theologically wrong but "foully belied and persecuted" and, like other abolitionists, "patriotic, republican and just." A letter in the *Boston Recorder* announced that its writer had joined the American Anti-Slavery Society largely, if not wholly, in defense of the right to free

[105] York, *George B. Cheever*, 78; Untitled, *Boston Morning Post*, December 7, 1835.

expression, which was assailed by "[m]obs, demagogues and newspapers, without number." Northerners were only too happy to comply with southern demands to enact laws to suppress free expression. The writer declared that because of the abolitionist society's defense of freedom of discussion in the face of brutal efforts to suppress it, "if the Society be suffered to fall, the right of free discussion will fall with it."[106]

Mob violence was a conceptual and strategic problem for those who disapproved of slavery but feared that Garrison and his allies were endangering the union (and economic relations). They hoped to cabin northern criticism while preventing the abolitionists from aligning their cause with liberty of conscience and expression. The feat could not be managed, in part because abolitionists could not be persuaded that their ideals should yield to states' rights and commerce and in part because of the prosecutions of Kneeland and Cheever for their ideas. By the winter of 1835–36, the Free Inquirers' and abolitionists' difficulties with the legal system and in holding public meetings had aligned – if not allied – them in the cause of free discussion, despite their differences on theology and antislavery strategies.[107] Others were joining them in this alliance. The legal system itself was part of the problem, as it showed itself suspiciously corruptible in the antimasonry cases, committed to a particular system of belief, and unable to address even small-scale collective violence.

Kneeland's Appeal

In March 1836, Kneeland argued his appeal and again published a pamphlet. His lack of counsel, Shaw explained, rendered the case murkier than it might have been.[108] The case raised now-familiar

---

[106] Charondas [pseud.], letter to the editor, *Boston Investigator*, December 18, 1835; "Gerrit Smith, Esq. – Anti-Slavery Society – Boston Recorder," *Boston Investigator*, December 11, 1835, reprinting letter of December 4, 1835.

[107] The 1837 report of the BFASS chronicles the suppression of their organizational efforts by the Unitarian and Congregational clergy. As they contemplated constructing a building for free discussion, someone asked if Kneeland could speak there, and there was great applause when the answer was yes: Boston Female Anti-Slavery Society, *Annual Report*, 16–17.

[108] Kneeland, *Speech before the Full Bench*. He sought both an order for a new trial and an order to arrest judgment, which led to some confusion, but once the court held the statute constitutional, the application focused on the motion for a new trial. Notes in the case file indicate that Kneeland put forward several grounds to support this

arguments. Kneeland said in his opening that Austin had refused to agree in writing not to proceed on the first and second counts in the appeal, so Kneeland had prepared a defense that would cover all of the problematic writings. Austin told the full court that although he did plan to proceed only on the last article, the other two provided context and aggravated the offense. The judges conferred and decided to consider "the whole."

Kneeland argued that denying the virgin birth did not violate the statute and asserted his right to join other theologians, some of whom he cited, in debating the immaculate conception; he defended his tone, saying that ridicule and satire were common in theological controversy. He argued that the second article was an acceptable comment on prayer, another topic of theological debate. He asserted that the third article was a statement of disbelief in the god the Universalists believed in, rather than an outright denial of God – a statement of his own beliefs rather than an attempt to influence others. He explained his meaning, wording and punctuation. He argued that the other statements in the third article, which were serious and thoughtful, did not constitute a willful denial of God or contumelious reproach; if mere disbelief in these other theological premises constituted blasphemy then the Unitarians would be at risk before an orthodox jury, Catholics could be convicted by Protestants, and so on.

On the constitutionality of the blasphemy statute, Kneeland argued that the framers of Article II had intended to protect all sentiments, religious, irreligious or otherwise. He claimed the freedom of the press protected him as well. Finally, he argued that the federal Constitution and laws destroyed the validity of the blasphemy statute, since "[t]he

---

motion: 1) that the judge had wrongly instructed the jury that the publication amounted to a denial of God; 2) that the verdict was against the evidence, the law and the constitution; 3) that the facts did not constitute an offense because the 1782 statute contravened the state constitution and the federal law of naturalization; 4) that the indictment failed to aver that the publications were falsely or maliciously published and was otherwise imperfect, informal and insufficient; and 5) that it did not appear that Kneeland had been indicted by a Sussex grand jury, which he had been, although the indictment did not say so. This ground was not mentioned in the reported case. According to the reported case, the first point of appeal on the motion for arrest of judgment was that the facts alleged in the indictment did not constitute an offense under the statute or the common law.

oppressed of every political sentiment, and the persecuted of every religious faith" would not be able to take refuge in Massachusetts under such a law. Since Christians claimed the right to assail the faiths of Muslims and Jews, then members of those faiths had to be able to do likewise to Christians.

The attorney general may have been tiring of the battle. Kneeland thought Austin's argument was "almost too puerile to merit a reply": it seemed "more like 'giving up the ship,' than like defending the fortress." Austin thought all discussion was protected if done decently; Kneeland pointed to the absence of any such language in the constitution and the protection of freedom of the press. Austin asserted that it was illegal to discuss the possibility that God did not exist; Kneeland denied that any doctrines were off-limits for discussion. Kneeland accused Austin of deliberately misrepresenting him in asserting that Kneeland's god had no intelligence; Kneeland avowed that his god "embraces all the intelligence in the universe." Austin argued that the blasphemy statute should be held constitutional because it had never before been challenged, had been on the books so long and had recently been reenacted; Kneeland noted that witchcraft was also still on the books. Austin asserted that the constitution permitted a man to worship but did not permit him to abstain from worship; Kneeland asked for the constitutional provision that said that. Austin's most astonishing point, Kneeland thought, was that an atheist could have no conscience; Kneeland looked him in the eye and pronounced, "Judge not, that ye be not judged" before explaining that everyone of common sense had a conscience. Kneeland thought that reputational slander should be punishable civilly but that no criminal cases over expression "on general subjects" should be possible. Kneeland indicated that if lost, he would seek to appeal to the Supreme Court of the United States.[109]

Another two years passed before judgment was given. Shaw attributed the delay to "intrinsic difficulty" of some of the issues and "a difference of opinion among the judges on some of those questions." Perhaps, too, the judges hoped the fires would die down if they said nothing for a while, especially as by this point newspapers in Boston

---

[109] Kneeland, *Speech before the Full Bench*, 415–18.

and farther afield were regularly criticizing them while arguing about the constitutionality of criminal libel.

Joseph A. Whitmarsh and the Constitutionality of Libel Law

The cry against the constitutionality of libel law was now raised by Benjamin Franklin Hallett in his defense of the iconoclastic, vehemently anti-Catholic editor Joseph Whitmarsh. In May 1836, Whitmarsh was indicted for an article in his anti-vice newspaper that alleged that the editor of a rival newspaper facilitated its offices' use as a place of sexual assignation after hours. Before the municipal court jury was impaneled in June, Hallett moved to quash the indictment on the grounds that it set out no charge known to the statute or common law of Massachusetts. After hearing argument by Hallett and Samuel Parker, Thacher, in July, dismissed the motion and the jury convicted Whitmarsh.

The *Advocate* and the *Post* took the opportunity to assess libel law's constitutionality. If the English common law of criminal libel was not part of the law of Massachusetts when the constitution was adopted, it was, arguably, not legitimately part of the law, being repugnant to the rights and liberties guaranteed in the new constitution. Peter Thacher upheld the constitutionality of libel law through an extensive yet oddly unconvincing disquisition on its history in Massachusetts, beginning with the first English settlers. The *Post*'s commentator pointed out that the settlers had carefully taken steps to be bound not by the common law but by their own laws, with biblical rules as backup in case of gaps.[110] Thacher cited Lord Coke for the proposition that when the settlers arrived, "the common law of England punished, as offences against the state, every libel made either against 'a private man, or against a magistrate, or public person,'" and he quoted Coke's rationale at length. However, although he cited incidents of the prerevolutionary assembly bringing proceedings against libelers for violations of its privileges, he cited no successful libel prosecutions brought by the Crown in a court. The only prerevolutionary precedent Thacher cited that was initiated by the attorney general took place in 1768, but the grand jury rejected the indictment,

---

[110] The *Post*'s extensive critique ran for two days. See "The Law of Libel," *Boston Morning Post*, August 17 & 18, 1836.

making the case a curious piece of evidence for the proposition that the common law of criminal libel was in force – Thacher evidently sympathized with the council's view that the fault lay in the grand jury, not the law. The members of another grand jury, in 1769, drew up and found their own bills of indictment against the governor and other colonial officers, after the attorney general refused to participate in such subversive drafting; the court interposed to order the clerk not to issue warrants or summons on the basis of the bills, and the attorney general entered a nolle on each count. Thacher concluded this unpersuasive discussion of prerevolutionary criminal libel precedents by inviting the reader to continue the research. The *Post*'s correspondent did so and found no better evidence. The idea that legislative contempt actions could be precedents for court cases struck the writer as absurd. The legislature in 1768 had told the aggrieved to look to the "common course of law" – not "the common law" – for a remedy; this instruction was no evidence of the existence in Massachusetts of the common law of libel.

The rest of Thacher's precedents were equally dubious as evidence that the common law of criminal libel was in force in Massachusetts in 1780, as they all came after the Revolution. The first was Edmund Freeman's trial in 1791. Thacher noted that three of the four judges had been members of the original state constitutional convention and that Justice Increase Sumner drew his definition of libel from Hawkins's *Pleas of the Crown*, which, Thacher added, would have been improper if the law of libel had not been adopted in Massachusetts. The judges all agreed that libel was an offense and drew their law from English authorities. Thacher thought the law of libel must have been recognized, because neither defense counsel nor the judiciary even hinted that it was not (the *Post*'s commentator saw conspiracy here). An enormous footnote described the 1799 proceedings against Abijah Adams for his attack on the Massachusetts legislature for its condemnation of the Virginia resolutions on the federal alien and sedition acts. Adams argued that the English common law no longer operated in the United States, but Chief Justice Dana admonished Adams that this argument was novel and that the common law was the "birthright and best inheritance" of Americans, as evidenced in passages from their constitutions. Most of these passages excluded the parts of the common law that were not in use or were inconsistent with the constitutional liberties these documents guaranteed, but Dana addressed this important logical gap through bluster and question-begging, not argument. Thacher also cited more recent events, including *Clap, Blanding* and the wording of the 1826 statute, to show that the common law of criminal libel was part of the law of Massachusetts. It had existed "time out of mind," Thacher asserted, and was "established by the highest evidence known in law" – which apparently did not include a single successful prerevolutionary prosecution or even a grand jury indictment.

Thacher went on to hold that the Declaration of Rights did not nullify the common law of libel, defining the liberty of press as the right to write and publish what one pleased, subject to prosecution for abusing this liberty. The constitution, in Thacher's view, balanced the whole community's needs and entitlements. All rights had limits. Citizens had no right "to calumniate individuals, and to scatter among the people, treason, sedition, and obscenity." Citizens' redress was not only civil, as Hallett had argued it was (an entitlement the constitution explicitly protected); they had to be able to summon the state to their aid. Thacher denied Hallett's motion and entered a conviction.

The *Post*'s commentator was outraged. The reasoning behind punishing libels – a threat to the peace – made no sense, since slander was not criminalized. More importantly, the writer argued, the English common law courts exercised "an authority as absolute and arbitrary as the British Parliament exercises within its sphere of action." American governance, the writer argued, rested on an entirely different principle: that the people, through the constitution, had prescribed "well-defined orbits" for legislatures and courts. Neither the actions of Parliament nor those of the English common law courts were valid precedents. The only valid offenses were those created by statute. Dana, Parsons and the rest of the judiciary and bar had unconstitutionally imposed the English common law on Massachusetts.

Maybe these arguments had some effect. Whitmarsh's first Supreme Judicial Court jury, in November 1836, failed to reach a verdict. He was finally convicted a year later and fined twenty dollars.

Law's Failure? An Abolitionist Mob

In Massachusetts in the mid-1830s, profound disputes over belief and the law's relationship to it led to widespread criticism about the legitimacy and sufficiency of legal proceedings. Defenses of the legal system often seemed opportunistic and self-interested, not principled. The British abolitionist George Thompson wrote Garrison after his mobbing, declaring that mob supremacy was overrunning key elements of American legal and social order, including freedom of speech and association, personal liberty, property rights, trial by jury and the judiciary's prerogatives. Thompson linked antiabolitionism to Missouri's anti-Mormonism, "the Anti-Anti-Masonic fury," "anti-Temperance," "anti-Cheever" and many other "antis."[111] Abolitionists themselves engaged in collective action in Boston on August 1, 1836, when a Baltimore slavecatcher's effort to reclaim two women, traveling as Eliza Small and Polly Ann Bates, was foiled in Shaw's courtroom. Shaw had concluded that the women's detention by the captain of the ship was illegal but had not yet given an order for their release when, seeing the slavecatcher rise to initiate a new seizure of the women, who were sitting nearby in the courtroom, the crowd burst into action and spirited the women away.[112] Shaw's efforts to stem the human tide were ignored, and one of the white abolitionist women present chided the slavecatcher. Shaw seems to have been less upset than most of Boston's newspapers, which were stunned by the assertiveness of the African American crowd and the white women and unsure about even attributing agency to them – they blamed Samuel Sewall, the women's lawyer, for leading the impressionable African Americans into wrongdoing. Charles Greene saw imminent social breakdown in the women's treatment of the slavecatcher. White women were told to find "more amiable employment," although not by Hallett, who seemed impressed. Murmurs were heard of a need to

---

[111] George Thompson to William Lloyd Garrison, *Liberator* (Boston), November 7, 1835, reprinted in Garrison, *Selections from the Writings*, 390–400.

[112] This account is drawn from Levy, "Abolition Riot" and *Law of the Commonwealth*, 72–78; as well as Tiffany, *Samuel E. Sewall*, 62–66; "Supreme Judicial Court," *Boston Morning Post*, August 2, 1836; Untitled editorial, *Boston Morning Post*, August 3, 1836; Untitled note, *Boston Morning Post*, August 4, 1836; "The Slave Rescue Again," *Boston Morning Post*, August 5, 1836; "The Slave Rescue," *Boston Morning Post*, August 15, 1836; "Supreme Judicial Court," *Boston Investigator*, August 5, 1836; "Rescue of the Slaves," *Boston Recorder*, August 12, 1836; "Case of Two Women Claimed as Slaves," *Boston Daily Advocate*, August 2, 1836; "An Assault in the 'Upper Class,'" *Boston Morning Post*, August 30, 1836; Untitled re lynching, *Boston Morning Post*, August 31, 1836. See also Campbell, "The 'Abolition Riot' Redux."

keep African Americans from attending court or assembling. Most of the newspapers expressed concern about the lack of involvement of the sheriff – Charles Pinckney Sumner – in assisting the slavecatcher in his efforts to mobilize law.

Few newspapers saw this mob as the product of an environment in which collective action was a standing option and courts' impartiality was suspect; instead they rallied to the defense of law. Indeed, one newspaper declared that a mob could have stepped in: if "the respectable property owners in State Street" had anticipated the violence, "five-hundred men could have been rallied to the Court ... prepared to sustain the supremacy of the laws." Individual acts of violence were generally considered more objectionable – a *Post* writer expressed concern a month later, after lawyer Samuel Sewall was attacked with a horsewhip in his office for bringing the legal proceedings to free Bates and Small. However, collective violence was acceptable if it showed the sovereign will of "the people" prevailing.

Fall 1837: Murder in Illinois, Rebellion in the Canadas

Another anti-Irish riot took place on Broad Street in Boston in June 1837,[113] and efforts to quell undesirable expression continued. Following a meeting in Brookfield in July, the General Association of the Congregational clergy published a public letter counseling women that their public activities were imperiling their modesty by pulling them from the home, where their true power could properly be exercised, where they advanced religion through their unostentatious influence and won their husbands' respect through dependence.[114] The abolitionist Sarah Grimké's response, based in scripture and addressed to the president of the BFASS, was that God had called both men and women to carry out the divine will. This letter and others were published in 1838 under the title *Letters on the Equality of the Sexes, and the Condition of Woman.*

[113] Lane, *Policing the City*, 33.
[114] "Pastoral Letter: The General Association of Massachusetts to the Churches Under Their Care," *New England Spectator* (Boston), July 12, 1837, reprinted in part in Ceplair, *Public Years*, 211–12.

Over a few days in mid-November 1837, news of two disturbing events broke in Boston newspapers. First, with Kneeland still awaiting judgment, Whitmarsh was convicted. Second, Boston learned of the recent murder of abolitionist editor Reverend Elijah Lovejoy by an antiabolitionist mob in Alton, Illinois, an event that, as others have noted, confirmed the connection between freedom of the press and abolitionism.[115] The claim that majoritarian violence in a republic was justified because the majority's views must prevail aroused vehement responses from individuals who asserted that in this republic, individuals were entitled to express what they knew or believed about science, religion and politics – and that courts should recognize this individual right rather than siding with majoritarian power. The constitutionality of criminal libel – so useful for those who disliked critique like Kneeland's – continued to be contested as an illegitimate English import, before judges whose lack of impartiality continued to draw murmurs of concern.

Justice Samuel Wilde told the *Whitmarsh* jury that the common law had been received, except for the parts inconsistent with "the very object and intent of the government here established" – parts pertaining to church establishment and other institutions that never (he thought) existed in Massachusetts. Samuel D. Parker was brief but "extremely severe upon that portion of the American press, which has denied the existence of the criminal law of libel."[116] The jury took about an hour to convict Whitmarsh.

In the *Advocate* Hallett objected to Wilde's insistence that determining the law was not the jury's job. The bench and bar were having remarkable difficulty proving the existence of a body of law under which they had been punishing people for decades. The jury was simply spineless.[117] Greene and the *Post*, unfazed by Parker's "severe" remarks, began preparing a lengthy attack on the supposed criminality of libel, but this extensive critique was not published until December 22. Lovejoy's murder and its aftermath took the spotlight.

Many people – including those who opposed slavery – deplored both the mob and Lovejoy for inciting it. Republicanism, announced

---

[115] See e.g. Dickerson, *Course of Tolerance*, 116–29.
[116] "Supreme J. Court," *Boston Morning Post*, November 18, 1837.
[117] Editorial, *Boston Daily Advocate*, November 20, 1837.

one Congregationalist minister from his pulpit on November 30, granted people the liberty to do and say what "the prevailing voice and will of the brotherhood will allow and protect." Winslow declared, "It is in vain that you plead for the prosecution of *law*, when the power is wanting to *execute* that law. What is law but a dead letter, in a republic, unless enforced by a standing army stronger than the people, when the prevailing will of the people is against its execution?"[118] The will of the majority would rightly prevail.

Within weeks of Lovejoy's murder, William Ellery Channing and more than 100 others proposed to hold a meeting in Faneuil Hall, but the mayor and aldermen refused to let them use the building, expressing concern that heated, partisan opinion rather than "calm wisdom" would be vented: outsiders might infer that the resolutions expressed majority opinion in Boston. Greene was outraged and pointed to other times when the building had been used to discuss one side of a controversy. Before the Revolution, the hall was used "on the very 'exciting' question whether the citizens should pay their postage or commit treason." Others responded that the meeting was intended to express the community's outrage against this assault on the press, not to meddle with partisan issues. The Massachusetts Anti-Slavery Society pointed out that Faneuil Hall "was built for the grand object of AGITATION – to keep up a perpetual EXCITEMENT – the excitement of free speech against gags and padlocks – the excitement of liberty in conflict with slavery – the excitement of equal rights against aristocratic usurpations. Its name, its history, is EXCITEMENT."[119]

Channing wrote a public letter, urging Bostonians to recall their commitment to liberty, even in the face of threats of violence. Insisting on their right to meet to express their abhorrence of mobs and the violent repression of expression, Hallett and others called a meeting elsewhere to consider the refusal of the use of Faneuil Hall.[120]

---

[118] Winslow, *Rejoice with Trembling*, 25–28.
[119] "Most Extraordinary!" *Boston Morning Post*, December 2, 1837; Francis Jackson, Ellis Gray Loring and Edmund Quincy, "To the Public," *Boston Morning Post*, December 5, 1837; Massachusetts Anti-Slavery Society, *Sixth Annual Report*, 43.
[120] Massachusetts Anti-Slavery Society, *Sixth Annual Report*, 44–46.

The city's representatives (who faced an election) changed course. On December 8, 1837, Faneuil Hall's doors were opened. Channing and Hallett were among the meeting's leaders. James T. Austin's speech, however, drew great applause. According to the Massachusetts Anti-Slavery Society, his speech was "in the highest degree inflammatory, ferocious, and mobocratic." Austin declared that "Lovejoy died as a fool dieth." He compared the Alton rioters to the conductors of the Boston Tea Party. Freeing the enslaved, he declared, would be tantamount to breaking open a menagerie. Austin compared a prospective Missourian uprising against abolitionists to American patriots rising up against Britain and its taxes. Abolitionist Wendell Phillips defended Lovejoy, insisting that the British government had lacked the right to tax the American colonies, whereas Lovejoy did indeed enjoy the right to speak.[121]

Paeans to Lovejoy's memory were composed. Hallett declared, "Free discussion now has her martyr." He pronounced it humiliating that Boston "in all except the shedding of blood" had been as dishonored as Alton.[122] In these columns, Lovejoy was compared to New England's seventeenth-century Quakers and witchcraze victims and to William Morgan, the ill-fated ex-freemason.

The front pages of the *Post* on December 22 and 23, 1837 bore a letter from "A Friend to the Constitutional Rights of the Citizen" to the *Whitmarsh* jurors, who were addressed by name.[123] The letter was a remarkable attack on the postrevolutionary judiciary's imposition of the English common law of libel on Massachusetts. "Friend" devoted much print to debunking the argument that the common law naturally flowed to Massachusetts as its birthright. Many of the early settlers were not English and if they had been, they would have disavowed its laws. "Friend" argued that libel was addressed only under a 1692 statute that criminalized lies and libels directed at particular individuals and also the circulation of false news. The fine was twenty shillings for the first violation, with sureties for good behavior. No penalty was specified for subsequent offenses. If the

---

[121] *Ibid.* 46–49.
[122] "Liberty Murdered," *Boston Daily Advocate*, November 20, 1837; Untitled editorial, *Boston Daily Advocate*, November 21, 1837.
[123] *Boston Morning Post*, December 22, 1837 and December 23, 1837. Beals and Greene published it in a pamphlet as well.

defendant could not pay, up to three hours in the stocks or whipping were alternatives. Proceedings were to take place before a justice of the peace.[124] "Friend" pointed to an incident in 1716 in which the governor rebuked the assembly for refusing to pass a bill prohibiting people from making and publishing libels and slanderous pamphlets, which would have been unnecessary if the common law of libel had been operational.

"Friend" had not heard Wilde's charge and mainly targeted Thacher's. "Friend" shredded the prevalent arguments for the existence of the common law of criminal libel, perhaps laying out arguments for an appeal, but none was forthcoming. Only the legislature had ever had power to make law for Massachusetts, and the constitution had abrogated the 1692 statute, the only one ever passed. Contrary to the constitution and the principles of republican government, in *Freeman* in 1791 Increase Sumner had wrongfully imported the English common law of libel, using the "silly and false reasons, usually given by law pedants, from black letter Coke, Hawkins and Blackstone, down to our pitiful drivellers." "Friend" reasoned that the state constitution was more protective of the press than the federal one, because the state constitution protected every person who wanted to use the press, whereas the federal constitution only prohibited Congress from passing a law *"abridging* the freedom of the press, that is making it less free than it then was." The writer tied the judges' overreach in *Whitmarsh* to their reasoning that Kneeland's beliefs were irreligious, not religious, and therefore not constitutionally protected. The judges were behaving like the federal legislators who reasoned that although the people had a right to petition Congress for redress of grievances, antislavery petitions could be ignored because slavery was not a grievance.

According to "Friend," the framers of the state's constitution wanted the people to be free to "express any opinion upon any subject, whether true or false, right or wrong." They were "philanthropists of Jefferson's day, and of Jefferson's school." Jurors could judge both fact and law and should demand to see the statute that made an action criminal. "The bench and bar will resist this

[124] An Act for the Punishment of Criminal Offenders, ch. 18, 1692 Mass. Prov. Laws 51, 53 (s. 7).

course – they are Englishmen in all their legal education, and modes of legal practice and argument." It was the jury's job to read, understand and apply a constitution or a statute – to be American and to "Americanize our judicial proceedings." The bench, in its pride, would resist, of course, not wishing to be caught out in their errors. Juries, although humble and plain, would ultimately detect this error and correct it. "Friend" was wrong, of course: the common law as presented by the judges endured.

Looking back on the Faneuil Hall meeting, Wendell Phillips recalled his puzzlement, as a lawyer, about the "abnormal power" of the mob, a phenomenon outside of American constitutional theory and for whose "irregular actions" there was no check or balance. The place of collective action in a republic in which sovereignty lay in the people was a conceptual challenge, and not everyone was confident that the courts, enforcing properly passed, constitutional laws, could establish order. British North American editors often observed American violence with an appalled yet smug delight in republicanism's evident flaws. In 1835, a column in the *New-England Galaxy* said Canadian papers presented the United States as the worst country in the world, with no law or justice, no authorities able "to prevent the burning of every city in the Union," and so many people slaughtered weekly that the principal papers kept records.[125]

During the fall of 1837, however, serious violence broke out in the Canadas. Followed closely by papers in both Nova Scotia and Massachusetts, this violence provides another window on these places' understandings of the legitimacy of politically motivated violence. In mid-November, Hallett's *Advocate* noted the sacking of the office of the radical, frequently republican-sounding Montreal *Vindicator*, correctly predicting further violence to come. In late November and early December, the *Post* devoted much more space to the unfolding unrest in the Canadas than to the Lovejoy affair, hoping the rebels would throw off the British yoke. After the Upper Canadian rebellion was quashed, the *Post* reported with excitement on the escape to Buffalo of its leader, William Lyon Mackenzie, and on a public meeting that followed.[126]

[125] Bartlett, "Persistence of Wendell Phillips," 114; W. [pseud.], "Our Country," *New-England Galaxy*, August 22, 1835.
[126] Untitled note, *Boston Daily Advocate*, November 15, 1837; "Mr. Mackenzie," *Boston Morning Post*, December 19, 1837.

The Nova Scotia newspapers had been watching discontent grow, especially in Lower Canada, for over a decade. Their responses to the Canadian rebellions and to Lovejoy's murder show a mixture of attitudes to the republican note in Canadian calls for political reform, to the conceptual constitutional challenge inherent in majoritarian violence, and to seeing Lovejoy as a martyr to free expression.

Responding to Lovejoy's death, the antislavery *Yarmouth Herald* quoted a New York paper horrified by the "outrage" on liberty of the press, free discussion and the blame a St. Louis paper cast on Lovejoy. Yarmouth, with its proximity to Maine, its large Baptist population and its residents' American connections, may well have been more republican than Halifax. The Halifax *Wesleyan* – less sympathetic to American dilemmas – reprinted an article called "Evils of Democracy" from the Upper Canadian *Christian Guardian*. Demonstrating the perils of rebellion, Lovejoy's death portended an American slide into anarchy, as the lower classes became increasingly destitute (the recession of 1837 was the unstated backdrop). These disturbances were more frequent than "in any other civilized country," and, unusually, they were "abetted, and often perpetrated, by that class of the community termed 'respectable.'" It was far preferable to be governed by Britain; the *Guardian* warned that Mackenzie's path would end in destruction and more deaths like Lovejoy's in Upper Canada.[127]

The *Yarmouth Herald* reprinted a Saint John, New Brunswick article noting an anti-British spirit in the United States in the wake of the rebellions. The inhabitants of Buffalo, "[n]ot content with affording every assistance to bands of robbers on the Niagara frontier," held public meetings declaring their resolve to commit reprisals on British property as compensation for the destruction of the American steamer *Caroline*, which Mackenzie and other rebels had used in their flight. The writer complained that at Rochester, the lieutenant governor's wife was "brutally insulted," when

---

[127] "Mob Law and Bloodshed!" *Yarmouth Herald*, December 8, 1837; "Evils of Democracy," *Wesleyan* (Halifax), April 9, 1838. R.H. McDonald observes that the Pictou and Yarmouth papers were friendlier than Halifax ones to the US and notes the many ties between Yarmouth and the US: "Nova Scotia Newspapers," 2, 11.

Americans stopped her carriage looking for her husband. The writer doubted the American government's assurances that it would suppress these activities if it could.[128] Not only republicanism but republicans posed a danger north of the border.

Joseph Howe, like the *Yarmouth Herald*'s editor Alexander Lawson, sympathized with many Canadian grievances. Elected to the legislature in 1836, Howe had been advocating for political reform. Week after week he reprinted in the *Novascotian*, with little if any editorial comment, excerpts from the Montreal *Vindicator* and other newspapers' reports of the rising tensions. Finally declaring that civil war had arrived, Howe announced that the only likely outcomes were either independence or the minority continuing its "long enjoyed ascendancy" over the majority through British military power. He blamed both unsound British policy and French Canadians for the violence.[129] To those who then accused him of disloyalty, he insisted that he was, as always, committed to improving Nova Scotia by legal and constitutional means, but the British deserved criticism and would get it.

Howe's concerns were with British North American constitutional structures. Less inclined than Lawson or American writers to see freedom of the press as an individual right and unsympathetic to republicanism, Howe reported on Lovejoy's murder in offhandedly succinct terms. Calling slavery "a great curse," Howe observed:

The Cincinnati Journal gives an account of an anti-abolition mob, and murder of a clergyman, at a place called Alton, in Illinois, for the goodly reason, that the said Clergyman and his friends were about to set up a Press, for the diffusion of religion, and it may be abolition views and intelligence.[130]

This was just one more violent American mob. Howe would not reflect on the importance of a free press for disseminating unpopular views in a republic. He focused on reforms of British institutional structures in the colonies.

One other incident prompted commentary on mob violence. In August 1838 the *Novascotian* reported that "[l]ynch Law – which was heretofore a thing to talk of, by way of contrast, to show how

---

[128] Untitled, *Yarmouth Herald*, March 10, 1838.
[129] "Civil War in Lower Canada," *Novascotian* (Halifax), December 6, 1837.
[130] "Murder in Illinois," *Novascotian* (Halifax), December 13, 1837.

free we were from the evil – has come to our own doors."[131] On
a Wednesday night a sailor was ill-treated in a brothel. Sailors,
soldiers from the local garrison and others returned the next two
nights and sacked that house and four others nearby. When the
soldiers were recalled to barracks, Haligonians, apparently of "the
lower character," took over, while a great crowd watched the
destruction with more approval than alarm. The police prevented
further rioting on the Saturday night. Charges were laid against
several men. A defense lawyer argued that others besides his clients
contributed to the damage, and made a majoritarian argument that if
the law would not touch these houses, the crowd's will should obviate
his clients' guilt.

Despite the rescue of John Barry in 1829, the 1830 Pictou election
rioting and other riots around Canso in 1834, the *Novascotian*
declared that this disorder was the first of its kind to disgrace Nova
Scotia. Presumably the difference was the argument that it was justified
by law's failure. The writer hoped the jury would respond
appropriately:

[L]et it not be said, that in any matter, any part of a British community should
so *far forget the character which should be their glory*, that peace and order,
and the sacredness of property and person, and respect for law, – should ever
give place to the cruel and most dangerous insanity, of a tumultuous crowd
setting itself up as the dispenser of justice, or vengeance.

Other newspapers likewise blamed the sailors and soldiers, regardless
of any provocation or how much the brothels had deserved
elimination. Britishness required privileging the laws protecting
property over the public will. Nova Scotia should not follow the
example of those who departed so far from British principle as to
look to the mob to step in when courts neglected their work.

The judge cautioned the jurors to set aside any biases they might
have. Violence of the American and, lately, Canadian kind was to be

---

[131] "Halifax, September Term: Court of Quarter Sessions. Trial for the Late Riots and
Destruction of Property," *Novascotian* (Halifax), September 20, 1838. See also
"Disgraceful Outrages in Halifax," *Pearl* (Halifax), September 7, 1838;
"Disgraceful Outrages," *Yarmouth Herald*, September 10, 1838; "Outrages,"
Novascotian (Halifax), September 6, 1838 and several articles in the *Novascotian*
of September 27, 1838.

avoided. Collective action not only endangered peace and property but
could lead to bloodshed. To let a mob suppress such houses "would be
to pull down the bulwarks of the Constitution and to destroy all peace
and prosperity." When the jury acquitted most of the accused men, the
judge cautioned them nevertheless to behave properly and avoid future
misconduct. Only one conviction followed: of a "coloured man"
named Clarke, probably a resident of one of the houses, who had
assaulted a soldier, quite possibly in self-defense.

As well as probably displaying racism, the responses to the brothel
riot signal the complicated, apprehensive constitutional environment
in Nova Scotia. Clearly many Haligonians sympathized with the
brothel rioters. The jury, if bothered at all by this outbreak of
majoritarian violence, was inclined to pin its concerns on the only
person of color implicated in the events and leave it at that. The
representatives of the respectable classes – the judge and the
newspaper editors – urged Nova Scotians to reject violence and look
to legal processes. Majoritarian violence, a peril of republicanism, was
threatening the United States and making inroads in the Canadas.
Better to seek reform of the existing political institutions and to
protect the press through the common law, as described in
Chapter 3, than to pit individuals against majorities, the conundrum
of republican sovereignty. Nova Scotians did not declare, as did the
editor of the *Boston Recorder* in late December 1837, that the liberty of
the press was

the PERSONAL LIBERTY OF THE CONDUCTER OF THE PRESS, IN A GIVEN CASE, TO
PUBLISH HIS OWN SENTIMENTS, OR THE SENTIMENTS OF OTHERS, ACCORDING
TO THE DICTATES OF HIS OWN CONSCIENCE, AND HIS BEST JUDGMENT OF WHAT
THE PUBLIC GOOD REQUIRES, without being subjected to the censorship of the
government; of individuals; of party; of a mob; or of any combination
whatever.

The newspaper was the private property of the "conducter," who had
a right to determine its content according to his sense of the public
good, even if others objected.[132] Alexander Lawson, in Yarmouth, was
sympathetic to calls for freedom of the press and freedom of
conscience, but Nova Scotian discourse in general tended to deplore

[132] "The Liberty of the Press," *Boston Recorder*, December 29, 1837.

violence, to urge faith in legal institutions and orderly constitutional reform, and to downplay the tension between the individual and the majority.

Coda: Kneeland Finally Loses

In the spring of 1838, aligning itself with the orthodox and many Unitarians – and over the reluctance of those with "heterodox ideas – utopians, abolitionists, Transcendentalists" and others – the Supreme Judicial Court upheld the state's right to use the law to punish Kneeland for his views. Others too had experienced this threat. James T. Austin had threatened the biblical scholar George Noyes with prosecution for heresy. Samuel Parker remarked in 1834 that a prosecution had been brought under the blasphemy statute approximately every five years since it had been enacted. In 1835, David Henshaw claimed a Boston grand jury had received a complaint against the Unitarians' *Christian Examiner* for denying the divinity of Jesus.[133]

Shaw (a Unitarian, a Whig and a minister's son) wrote for himself, Wilde, Putnam, and Charles A. Dewey. Where possible, he deferred to tradition, the jury and the trial judge, Wilde. Shaw upheld the statute but read it more liberally than Austin did. We may even discern a caution to trial judges to instruct the jury properly on the intention requirements for blasphemy, which were (as both Shaw and Morton made clear) more than simply the intention to publish the text.

Shaw's interpretation of the constitutionality of the 1782 blasphemy statute revealed both a determination not to unsettle past practices and a concern not to constrain freedom of conscience quite as much as Austin was urging. Shaw was unperturbed by the banality of Austin's argument that it was too late to question the statute's constitutionality, that no objections to it had been raised at the 1820 constitutional convention, and that it had recently been included in the revised statutes. Freedom of the press meant merely the absence of prior restraint, such as licensing, and did not bar prosecution after

---

[133] Levy, *Verbal Offense against the Sacred*, 419–23; *Report of the Arguments of the Attorney of the Commonwealth*, 209; A Cosmopolite, *Review of the Prosecution of Kneeland*, 355.

publication. As to the argument based on Article II, pertaining to the duty or liberty to worship, Shaw held that full inquiry and free discussion for "honest and fair purposes," including the discovery of truth, were protected. Rejecting Austin's argument and almost accepting Kneeland's, Shaw held that the law "does not prevent the simple and sincere avowal of a disbelief in the existence and attributes of a supreme, intelligent being, upon suitable and proper occasions." A man might do so when asked about his beliefs under oath, or inadvertently in the heat of debate, or confidentially to a friend, or even "publicly, with the honest purpose of eliciting a more general and thorough inquiry, by public discussion, the true and honest purpose being the discovery and diffusion of truth." Interpreted this way, the blasphemy statute was constitutionally acceptable. The statute fit with the constitution as a whole, especially Article III – which Shaw relied on even though it had been repealed and replaced[134] – and the preservation of the sanctity of oaths and of peace and security.[135] The legislators' intention was not to "prevent or restrain the formation of any opinions or the profession of any religious sentiments whatever, but to restrain and punish acts which have a tendency to disturb the public peace."

Kneeland's most challenging argument was that he had not offended the statute, properly construed, essentially because he had been honestly stating his beliefs rather than attempting to vilify God. Shaw reviewed authorities and found one common idea: "that the wilful denial of God, and of his creation and government of the world, with an intent and purpose to impair and destroy the reverence due to him, is the offence intended to be prohibited." Wilde's short account of his instructions to

---

[134] To recap: the new Article III was ratified before Kneeland was charged. It eliminated the language in which the people empowered the legislature to impose public support for religious societies and attendance at religious worship. The amendment began with the premise that the public worship of God was desirable and imposed voluntarism on all religious societies, making them all equal. Before the enabling legislation was passed, Kneeland was tried in municipal court and once in Supreme Judicial Court. Both the constitutional amendment and the legislation were in force well before his final trial in Supreme Judicial Court. Shaw's reliance on the repealed Article III is hard to understand in legal terms but consistent with its treatment by the editors of the 1836 *Revised Statutes*, who left the old Article III in the main text of the state constitution and, in marginalia, referred the reader to the Articles of Amendment appended to the end.

[135] See *Revised Statutes of Massachusetts*, c. 130, s. 15 (1836).

the jury raised the concern that had given the impression that Kneeland could be convicted simply for denying the existence of God, even if his intention had not been willfully blasphemous. Indeed, Austin had argued that regardless of intent or occasion, simply disavowing belief in God would offend the statute (as in criminal defamatory libel, in which legal malice was inferred from the words published). Shaw recognized that at times one could justly be expected to state one's honest beliefs, and such explanations could not be criminal. However, the majority got over its concerns about Wilde's instructions: he said he had told the jury that the "wilful" denial of the existence of any God other than the material universe itself would violate the blasphemy statute. That single word, "wilful," gave Shaw and the majority confidence that the jury had been fully and properly instructed on intent and would not have inferred blasphemous intent from Kneeland's words alone. Surely, they reasoned, if the instructions had been flawed, exception would have been taken at the time – even by a self-represented defendant. Shaw thus somewhat clarified and liberalized the law while rejecting, on dubious grounds, the argument that it was fundamentally unconstitutional. Kneeland would go to jail for sixty days.

Marcus Morton (the only Jacksonian on the bench[136]) would have ordered a new trial. He was concerned that Kneeland's lack of counsel had prejudiced him. Like Shaw, though, Morton was uneasy about the destabilizing possibilities in arguments that statutes were unconstitutional and preferred to find a constitutional interpretation of the Blasphemy Act. Article XVI said, "The liberty of the press is essential to the security of freedom in a state; it ought not, therefore, to be restrained in this Commonwealth." Morton thought the language protected oral expression as well as printed, that it did not protect absolutely everything that might possibly be printed, and that although the framers had probably been thinking mainly of prior restraints, he could think of other ways of improperly restraining the press and invading its rights and liberties that would also be constitutionally prohibited. The framers had not, however, intended to prohibit all legislation applicable to the press, for if they had, they would have used the language of absolute protection that they gave to legislative

---

[136] Levy, *Verbal Offense against the Sacred*, 422.

debates in Article XXI. Morton concluded that while Article XVI "scrupulously" protected truth and free discussion on both sacred and profane subjects, along with "the dissemination and inculcation of all honest opinions," the legislature could still punish violations of others' rights and disturbances of the peace committed through "malicious falsehoods or obscene or profane publications or exhibitions." According to Morton, then, truth deserved special protection, but on the whole, although freedom of the press went beyond simply barring prior restraints, it did not provide a broad license to print just anything at all.

Morton then turned to the last clause of Article II: "No subject shall be hurt, molested, or restrained, in his person, liberty, or estate, for worshipping God, in the manner and season most agreeable to the dictates of his own conscience; or for his religious professions or sentiments; provided he doth not disturb the public peace, or obstruct others in their religious worship." The first part of the sentence, Morton reasoned, protected complete liberty of worship for all faiths, including Jews, Muslims and Deists – but not atheists. The provision protected not just holding these beliefs but also professing them. Unlike Shaw, Morton observed that the public worship provision, Article III, did not seem to have been entirely consistent with Article II but in any case had now been abrogated. Returning not to atheism per se but to expressions of nonbelief, Morton noted that the various sects routinely called each other irreligious, so that the distinction between religious and irreligious sentiments was hard to draw: the word "religious" had to be construed carefully. Article II protected "*all* sentiments and professions *concerning* or *upon the subject* of religion; and guaranties [*sic*] to every one a perfect right to form and to promulgate such opinions and doctrine upon *religious* matters and *in relation* to the existence, power and providence of a Supreme Being, as to himself shall seem just." For a legislature to attempt to control or dictate people's beliefs would be futile, unjust and productive of hypocrisy. Suppressing particular views would imply a lack of confidence that truth would prevail, ultimately leading "to skepticism and infidelity." The legislature was to guard every citizen's right to hold and promulgate any opinion, on any subject, which could entail punishing those who "wantonly and wickedly" invaded others' enjoyment of these rights. A law "punishing malicious falsehoods or obscene, profane or blasphemous language, used with the malicious intent to injure others" would be constitutional.

The key, then, was motive. Facts and honest opinions could legitimately be communicated, with a great deal of latitude given to the manner of expression. "But if the object be to calumniate, or wantonly or maliciously to cause pain or injury to others, by wounding their feelings or corrupting their principles, then it is an abuse of that freedom and the proper subject of criminal legislation." In Morton's view, to render the blasphemy statute constitutional, it had to be read as requiring a "corrupt and malicious intent." To offend the statute, a defendant required a "wicked and injurious intent to infringe others' rights, destroy their peace of mind or disturb society's good order." And of course, the beliefs thus offended were those set out in the act.

Had Wilde properly charged the jury on malice? Morton agreed with Shaw that Wilde had accurately construed Kneeland's statement of belief as denying the existence of God. However, Morton thought Wilde had misdirected the jury into believing, wrongly, that a mere denial of God was enough to render Kneeland guilty of blasphemy. Simply using the word "wilful" was not enough to convey the intent requirement. Unable to see conclusive evidence of blasphemous intent in Kneeland's language, Morton would have ordered a new trial. Neither judge addressed the argument based on federal law at that time, but separate proceedings on that head came to an end a few days later. The start of Kneeland's sentence was postponed because his wife was expecting a baby soon, who died. The court could not be persuaded – although Kneeland tried – to treat four years of proceedings as adequate punishment. Kneeland went to jail and wrote energetically and aggrievedly for the next two months, while he and his wife grieved the loss of their baby apart.[137]

Prominent Universalists criticized the verdict, even though they disagreed with Kneeland's views. Before judgment was issued, William Channing told the abolitionist lawyer Ellis Gray Loring that he intended to talk to Shaw about how shocking it would be to see

---

[137] Kneeland, *Review of Trial, Conviction, and Final Imprisonment*, 494–505. His last pamphlet is his longest, at more than 130 pages.

a person punished for his opinions.[138] After the verdict, Channing and Loring drew up and circulated a petition for pardon. It attracted the signatures of 150 citizens, including William Lloyd Garrison, Ralph Waldo Emerson, Theodore Parker and George Ripley. Maria Child pronounced herself pleased with it. The petition may well have been doomed by these signatures, of "transcendentalists, abolitionists, and come-outers," who were "little better than Abner Kneeland himself." Reverend Samuel Kirkland Lothrup, pastor at Peter Thacher's Unitarian Brattle Street Church, refused to sign, preaching a sermon in response and circulating a counterpetition. Kneeland told his friends not to sign the first petition, since it implied guilt and since, he said, it arose from the Unitarians' newfound desire to escape the odium of responsibility for his conviction, even though they had started the business. Samuel T. Armstrong, a former lieutenant governor of Massachusetts and now mayor of Boston, printed the offending passages and posted them on the walls in a public reading room, urging the public not to sign the petition; a newspaper correspondent observed that this too was publishing blasphemy. Another writer observed that Austin would not dare prosecute Armstrong.[139]

Kneeland served his time and emerged unrepentant, but perhaps because of financial difficulties he subsequently moved to Iowa to start a Free Thought community, which failed to prosper. He died in 1844, but the *Boston Investigator* lived on.[140]

Conclusion: Dangers, Strategies and Rights

Many threads run through these disputes over immoral and irreligious expression, threads that suggest how law was shaped and operationalized in two different cultural and constitutional environments. First, these cases hint at the importance of backstage steps in the transmission and crafting of legal knowledge. Although blasphemy was an old prosecutorial weapon, the actionability of

---

[138] Levy, *Verbal Offense against the Sacred*, 419.
[139] Kneeland, *Review of Trial, Conviction, and Final Imprisonment*, 520–22, 530, 547; Child, *Selected Letters*, 78; Miller, *Larger Hope*, 192; McCoy, Banned in Boston, 22; Schlesinger, *Age of Jackson*, 358–59; Commager, "Blasphemy," 40.
[140] "The Infidel Kneeland," *Yarmouth Herald*, April 26, 1839, and see Gallaher, "Pantheist"; Bonney, "Salubria Story."

obscenity was less certain in 1818 when Peter Holmes was indicted over *Fanny Hill*. Through cases from Worcester and Boston in the 1820s and 1830s, lawyers adapted indictments to reflect their evolving understanding of the legal elements of these cases. By the time Abner Kneeland was tried, obscenity was clearly indictable, but blasphemy charges had become troubling, as they recalled a repressive pre-republican past. Some commentators were indignant that allegations of obscenity and blasphemy had been folded together. Some thought undue sensitivity was being displayed to a certain plain, scientific word for an ordinary male body part; but another concern was that if blasphemy were to be prosecuted, it should stand alone for all to see and discuss. The common law on obscenity blossomed during the period, supplemented in Massachusetts by statute[141]: the treatise-writers' concern that a book had to be published to at least one identified person in order to be considered a libel was abandoned. Indictments were sanitized so as not to purvey objectionable text.

Knowledge about drafting indictments and conducting prosecutions was conveyed through books. In Halifax, as in Boston and Worcester, books on law and pleadings were available to assist a lawyer or justice of the peace to draft an indictment, but a magistrate outside Halifax with no legal training might have opted to hold a person to good behavior rather than venture into drafting an indictment without guidance. Indicting for blasphemous libel might have been manageable with the assistance, first, of Burn's manual for justices of the peace and, later, of Murdoch's and Marshall's texts, but the range of prosecutable views was narrower than in England and the punishments were light. The major sects were Trinitarian, and the tensions among them were political rather than theological; Fanny Wright and Abner Kneeland were far away. Indicting for obscenity was even more uncertain than indicting for blasphemy. These material conditions affected what the law was called upon to do and how it could do it.

The relationships among law, religion and morality were far more contested in Massachusetts than in Nova Scotia. In overruling a conviction for a clear violation of one of the province's own statutes on the grounds that a law punishing someone like Henry

---

[141] See *Revised Statutes of Massachusetts*, c. 130, s. 10 (1836).

Crawley for skating on a Sunday was too puritanical, the Nova Scotia Supreme Court signaled that, at least with respect to harmless recreation, it would not weigh in on a matter of conscience. Contention between Presbyterians and Anglicans was causing enough difficulty on the political and constitutional front. The critics who observed wryly that judges, lawyers, doctors and others sometimes traveled unnecessarily and indulged in recreation on the Sabbath were probably not wrong either. Law is not self-activating, and it is often easier to ignore a statute than to endure the political consequences of trying to repeal it.

In Massachusetts, disagreement on matters of conscience spread out in a number of directions. Although for women the propriety of standing up publicly for a cause was fraught by association with Frances Wright, the calls by Garrison and abolitionists to take up the torch for the enslaved as a matter of fidelity to Christian principle was making antislavery a matter of conscience and faith, a profound challenge to the view that accommodating slavery was simply a commercially beneficial part of the constitutional bargain. A great deal of concern runs through the Massachusetts cases that a mixture of sexual knowledge and atheism would be transmitted both to the lower classes and to wives, sons and daughters who might read a newspaper like the *Boston Investigator* or Charles Knowlton's *Fruits of Philosophy*. The democratization of medical – particularly sexual – knowledge was dangerous. *Fanny Hill* could corrupt a vulnerable reader's moral framework, upon which the family's integrity rested. *Fruits of Philosophy* deeply disturbed those who believed that it was only the fear of bearing a child outside marriage that kept single women virtuous. If the fear of punishment in the afterlife were removed, restraints would be further loosened – hence the connection Charles Knowlton noted between "infidelity" and "licentiousness." The combination of irreligion and lower-class agitation that were understood to have produced the horrors of the French Revolution provided a cautionary tale invoked repeatedly in Abner Kneeland's case. Courts saw themselves charged with upholding morality so as to keep public order intact and, through it, government. The backdrop of religious disestablishment made the stakes high.

In the mid-1830s, these cases, as well as other forces such as resistance to the growing temperance movement and objections to majoritarian violence, rendered salient the importance of insisting on individual rights to freedom of conscience and expression. The Unitarians' unease about the conspicuous display of ideological prejudice and repression evident in Kneeland's prosecution was part of a larger shift that took place as people began to assert that individuals must have a right to express unpopular views – political, religious or otherwise – even against an oppressive, potentially violent majority. With this view came troubling murmurs that courts were showing partiality to certain views in interpreting the common law and in deciding who could testify and who could not. Courts seemed to see the unorthodox as trouble-makers bent on fomenting unrest and possibly disrupting the union. Violence, which was prevalent, went more or less unaddressed, while reformers went to jail.

In December 1835, one of Kneeland's correspondents, Gerrit Smith, explained that he wanted to join the American Anti-Slavery Society in part because it was "now so far identified with the right of free discussion, on account, not only of its manly defense of that right, but still more on account of the lawless and brutal endeavors to hinder its exercise of it, that if the Society be suffered to fall, the right of free discussion will fall with it."[142] David Henshaw was outraged at the prospect that truth could ever be suppressed in the name of social order. Glossing Smith's letter, Kneeland himself pronounced, "We wish to make men as free in every sense of the word, as the air they breathe: free to think free to speak, and free to write on all subjects; free to publish their thoughts to the world, only let them publish the truth, or what they believe to be the truth, with good motives, and for justifiable ends." Not just truth, but what people believed to be true required protection.

The Massachusetts debates described in this chapter pivot on the necessary limits of constitutional rights vested in individuals. Chapter 4 described judges cabining evidence of truth in order to protect certain people's reputations and interests and expose others'. In *Kneeland* and *Whitmarsh*, judges rejected arguments that common law criminal libel and the blasphemy statute were unconstitutional: individuals could not have unlimited rights to attack doctrines upon

---

[142] "Gerrit Smith, Esq. – Anti-Slavery Society – Boston Recorder," *Boston Investigator*, December 11, 1835.

which social order seemed to rest. In *Kneeland*, both Shaw and Morton made one concession to the pressures of the present in acknowledging that the jury had to be sure of a defendant's actual blasphemous intentions; the simple intention to publish a statement that advanced propositions contrary to the blasphemy statute was not enough for a conviction. Probably the unhappy prospect of seeing Unitarians and Universalists prosecuted for blasphemy was on their minds.

When Hallett, in *Whitmarsh*, raised the constitutional question he was shut down, but claims for individual rights had been made, and doubts about the courts were in play. Whether or not the common law of criminal libel had been applied in Massachusetts courtrooms before 1765, it was, indeed, too late to challenge it by 1837, given the judiciary. The judges' impartiality in these cases was doubtful and to a limited extent was questioned, although not usually by the "respectable," who reflexively insisted that judges were impartial and courts were competent, even while suggesting that a mob could usefully back up the courts' authority. The judges' political conservatism did lead to legally murky decisions. Judges took steps to neutralize the courtroom impact of antimasonic conspiratorial thinking.[143] Chapter 4 showed reformers losing libel case after libel case, including one – against William Snelling – in which the defense was ordered to supply particulars to the prosecution, while various participants argued that it was really the complainant who was on trial. In *Kneeland*, Shaw disregarded the new constitutional provisions and cited the old text, which had been repealed. Knowlton went to jail apparently on the basis of a prospectus alone for a book promulgating information that was evidently very welcome to couples overwhelmed by the prospect of recurring pregnancies. Peter Thacher disqualified atheists as witnesses and upheld the constitutionality of criminal libel law despite a startling absence of evidence that it had actually been used in Massachusetts courtrooms before 1791. Prosecutions conspicuously failed over episodes of violence against abolitionists and other reformers.

Perhaps a tool used so often inevitably reveals nicks in its edges. Perhaps courtroom actors' preference for aligning themselves with the "respectable" majority came not just from their mostly Whig political

[143] See Bussiere, "Trial by Jury."

sympathies and their Unitarian or Congregational affiliations but also from the embeddedness of their decisions in the day-to-day life of their communities. Boston's judges did not enjoy the splendid, awe-inspiring social distance of the assize judges in Douglas Hay's "Property, Authority and the Criminal Law." The judges were an integral part of social, religious and commercial life, and perhaps it is unsurprising that they were disinclined to disturb it. In the next chapter I take up the implications of the extraordinary ordinariness of defamation actions in Massachusetts and examine the similarities and differences in court usage in Massachusetts and Nova Scotia. In Massachusetts, more than in Nova Scotia, incentive structures brought middle-class, white women, as well as men, into courtrooms to complain of defamation. In both places, court usage in the cultural and commercial centers – Halifax and Boston – differed from court usage in the smaller towns of Pictou, Yarmouth and Worcester. The civil cases show the place of courts in these societies more generally and allow us to step back and consider courts as sites for arguments about speech on broad social issues and constitutional theory. It is, therefore, to the civil cases that I turn last.

6

Private Defamation Suits

Courts in Everyday Life

Previous chapters have examined courts as sites for arguments about constitutional rights pertaining to expression, which they were to a much greater extent in Massachusetts. These arguments tended to arise when the individual was targeted by the state. This chapter moves the lens to cases people brought against each other, mobilizing the courtroom to achieve their personal goals, such as redress or revenge. Like criminal libel cases, civil defamation suits were far more common in Massachusetts than in Nova Scotia. Massachusetts women were far more often parties. In various ways, that state offered better incentives to would-be plaintiffs, thus reinforcing the centrality of courts as fora for disputes.

The Cases

This research draws from 105 Massachusetts civil defamation cases that appear in court records from 1820 to 1840. About three-quarters of the cases come from Worcester or Suffolk, and the rest are from other counties. One additional Worcester case was begun with the wrong writ so cannot be identified as either slander or libel. Of the 86 slander cases, 30 are from Suffolk, 29 are from Worcester and 27 are from other counties. Of the 19 libel cases, 12 are from Suffolk, 2 from Worcester and 5 from other counties. The Nova Scotia records disclose at least the beginnings of 23 civil defamation suits. None are from Yarmouth. The two Pictou cases are both for "words," meaning the offending statements were oral. Of the 21 Halifax cases, 9 are for libel, 6 are for slander, and 6 cases are styled "trespass on the case" for defamation and external clues do not reveal whether the objectionable words were oral or written.

Civil defamation suits appear to have been similarly common in Suffolk, Worcester and Halifax until about 1825 after which Nova Scotia cases became rare, while Massachusetts cases remained common. The Nova Scotia sample is substantially comprehensive for Halifax, Pictou and Yarmouth. The Massachusetts cases are comprehensive for the Supreme Judicial Court ("SJC") for Suffolk and Worcester, as far as the record books reveal, but civil cases began in Common Pleas ("CP"), which I sampled for certain years. CP in Suffolk and Worcester together heard sixteen civil defamation cases in 1825, eight per county, or about one case for about 7,770 people in Suffolk and one for 10,544 in Worcester. The Nova Scotia Supreme Court ("NSSC") in Halifax heard two cases in 1825, or one for 12,438 people.[1] Afterward, Nova Scotia cases all but disappear, dropping from seventeen from 1820 to 1825 to four over the next fifteen years. In 1835, for example, Suffolk had six civil defamation cases, Worcester had five, and Halifax, Pictou and Yarmouth had none.[2]

---

[1] The US census of the midpoint year, 1830, put the Massachusetts population at 610,408, with 62,163 people in Suffolk and 84,355 in Worcester. Nova Scotia in 1827 had 123,844 people, with 24,876 in Halifax (14,439 in the peninsula and 10,437 in the district) and 13,949 in Pictou district. Yarmouth was part of Shelburne County (population 12,018). See *Colonial Patriot*, April 12, 1828.

[2] Appendix A explains the sampling. If neither party appeared, the clerk who compiled the Massachusetts record books did not indicate the claim. After 1820, Pictou, saw sixteen "trespass on the case" actions in the NSSC and five in the Inferior Court of Common Pleas ("ICCP") from 1832 through 1838, but probably few if any of these were for defamation. In 1835, Pictou had one trespass on the case suit in ICCP and one in NSSC, but there is no reason to think either was for defamation. Two of the four post-1825 Nova Scotia defamation suits, all from Halifax, are also styled as trespass on the case, but since there were only two to four trespass on the case actions per year, likely no more than one or two defamation suits lurk unidentified in the records. The ICCP heard no defamation suits in Halifax. Until 1834, the NSSC did not sit in Yarmouth, which was included in Shelburne County, but there are no evidently speech-related cases in either place from 1820 to 1840. After 1834, Yarmouth had one trespass on the case action in NSSC. Yarmouth's ICCP records have not survived, but only three civil trials took place there from 1835 through 1839: NS Journals, 1841, A22–102.

Other than the much greater number of cases in Massachusetts than in Nova Scotia, the most salient difference between the two places pertains to the presence of women. One woman was a party (a plaintiff) in Nova Scotia. Of the Massachusetts cases, 28 had women as parties, including one brought by a woman using the wrong writ (25 plaintiffs, 12 defendants). Almost all of the women defendants were sued by other women, alone or with their husbands. Nova Scotia, therefore, had far fewer civil cases overall, and women rarely participated as parties. I doubt that there was less objectionable expression in Nova Scotia, although newspapers were more temperate and less numerous. We must consider structural factors. To begin exploring courts' invitation to potential plaintiffs, particularly women, I turn to a set of intertwined cases from Hampshire County, Massachusetts.

Writs and Strategies: *Miller v. Parish*

In the November 1828 term, in CP, nineteen-year-old Jennett Miller sued a lawyer named Daniel Parish, aged about thirty-three, over his allegation that Miller, contrary to the beliefs of her maternal uncle Hiram Bagg, was readily available for sex. Parish did not say he had committed sexual intercourse with her but he implied that he might have, perhaps a safer stance for one who was about to be married. The case was part of a complex web of legal and social transactions involving Miller, Bagg, Parish, a local sheriff and at least three or four other men. It was interconnected with two other slander suits and a number of debt claims that show courts being used both to address reputational injuries and, probably, to tie up property as other debt claims were disputed.

Jennett Miller's mother had died, and her father had remarried. She lived with Hiram Bagg and his family, and so did Daniel Parish, until the summer of 1828. None of these parties was new to legal action, even Miller who had successfully sued at about age seventeen for unpaid-for millinery work.[3] Parish had sued several clients for unpaid legal bills.

[3] *Jennett Miller v. John Miller* (CP Hampshire, Nov. 1826). These cases are all found in the CP record books for Hampshire County.

In March 1828, Miller, Parish and his brother attended a party at the home of Daniel Hewitt, a sheriff. According to the account Miller must have given to her uncle Hiram, Parish threw her out of the sleigh on the way home and attempted to sexually assault her. Over the next few months, relations disintegrated, with Bagg telling neighbors about Parish, and Parish saying Miller's account was an unlikely story because Miller had been hanging on him and kissing him in the sleigh and had on other occasions hidden under the woodshed and called out to him from under the window. According to Miller's pleadings, he said that if he had done anything with her, it was no more than she wanted. Bagg was also complaining about Parish's actions as a lawyer for two other men, with whom Bagg evidently had unsettled business. Parish moved out of Bagg's house.

Two writs were entered on August 3. First, Bagg sued Parish for labor, room and board. Second, probably because being a party would have barred Hiram Bagg from testifying, his brother Linus, acting as Miller's guardian *ad litem*, sued Parish for defamation. On August 4, Parish, on behalf of one Horace Miner, issued a writ against Hiram Bagg for defamation for alleging that Miner had forged a promissory note.

These were writs of attachment. Once the plaintiff had sworn out the claim before the court clerk, the clerk ordered the sheriff to attach the defendant's goods to the value of the plaintiff's claim to ensure the defendant would appear at the next court term and to safeguard property out of which the plaintiff could recover damages. If the defendant lacked sufficient property, the sheriff was to "take and keep" the defendant. Some property could not be attached, and sheriffs seem to have had some discretion about how to handle the property – one sheriff put a woman's household goods in her boarder's custody in order to prevent a subsequent creditor from seizing them – but sheriffs who failed to secure sufficient property could be liable for the plaintiff's damages, so they must have been cautious.[4] Property attached in other Massachusetts defamation cases included livestock, timber, a sleigh and land.

---

[4] See *Revised Statutes of Massachusetts*, c. 90, ss. 24–38, 58–62 (1836); *Massachusetts Sheriff*, 37–38, 62–64; Dane, *General Abridgement*, 79, 81, 84–85; *Buckingham v. Billings*, 13 Mass. R. 82; Cushing, *Practical Treatise on the Trustee Process*, 1.

Linus Bagg and Jennett Miller claimed damages of $1,000 for defamation, and Hiram Bagg claimed $200 for housing Parish. Parish's client, Miner, claimed $3,000. Attachments covered the full claim, even though successful Massachusetts plaintiffs were lucky to recover even one-third of their defamation claims. Miner's claim was likely secured against Bagg's land, but Parish evidently lacked property so was arrested by his erstwhile party host, Sheriff Hewitt. Someone posted a bail bond for him.

These three cases were heard in CP in November 1828. The Baggs' suits against Parish were decided on the pleadings, with Hiram Bagg winning and Linus Bagg and Miller losing. Appeals were entered, setting the parties up for jury trials in SJC. Horace Miner prevailed before a jury, which assessed damages of a mere $27.50 against Hiram Bagg, who appealed. The Baggs and Miller were represented throughout by a lawyer named J.C. Bates, but Parish represented not only Miner but also himself. Parish must have been financially pressed: he was also successfully sued for $169 on an unpaid debt in the same term of court, a judgment he also appealed.

Parish retaliated. On October 31, he issued a writ of attachment against Hiram Bagg, claiming $4,000 in damages over Bagg's allegations that Parish had not only assaulted Miller intending to rape her but had also tried to rape a young woman called Eunice Marsh in Bagg's store, when Bagg left them alone for a few minutes. Parish also objected to allegations Bagg had made about how Parish behaved as a lawyer. The case was entered in court in the November term and, as usual, put forward to the next term – March 1829 – for hearing.

Since the SJC sat in Hampshire in April and September, the first three cases were still pending when Parish's slander suit against Bagg was heard in CP. Bagg, again represented by Bates, won on the pleadings against the self-represented Parish, who appealed. Another case was also heard this term: Horace Miner sued Hiram Bagg for $100 for failing to settle up in a compromise they had reached over two other suits, both of which involved Sheriff Hewitt as a nominal party and pertained to what Hewitt had done with property he had taken. Miner, however, was nonsuited for failing to appear (perhaps he had fallen out with Parish), and Bagg, represented again by Bates, was ordered to recover costs, which he did: the court record notes execution on May 16.

The April term of SJC, in which all four outstanding cases were addressed, went much better for Hiram Bagg than it did for Daniel Parish. Parish failed to appear when called to defend against Bagg's action for labor and lodging, and Bagg was ordered to recover over $200 in damages and costs. The three defamation cases were all heard by juries. The jury found Bagg not guilty of defaming Miner by alleging he had forged a promissory note. Execution for costs was issued on this judgment too.

Parish, still self-represented, won his slander suit against Bagg for alleging that Parish had assaulted Miller and Marsh, had turned traitor to his clients and was stirring up litigation. At this point, Bates and Bagg added a truth plea: that Bagg's allegation was justified because Parish had in fact assaulted Miller and attempted to rape her. The jury awarded Parish the insulting sum of five dollars plus costs of $1.25. Execution was issued – apparently he did want the money.

Miller's suit against Parish is the only one that became a reported case; the complex web of intertwined debts and strategic retaliation disappears unless the records of CP are consulted. Parish lost to Miller and Linus Bagg before the jury. Still self-represented – and of course unable to testify – he entered a truth plea: that he was justified in his allegations about Miller's sexual availability because Miller had, in fact, fawned and hung about him and kissed him on the way home from Hewitt's, and that she had knocked under his window at night and called to him from under a woodshed. Parish apparently thought that if the jury believed Miller had behaved suggestively they would doubt he had assaulted her, or would blame her for whatever had happened. The evidentiary record is unclear, but a deposition sworn by Parish's brother supported Parish's version of Miller's conduct. Hiram Bagg probably testified for Miller. The jury awarded her $300 in damages.

Finally retaining a lawyer, J.H. Ashmun, Parish appealed, moving to arrest judgment on the basis that the counts in the pleadings upon which the verdict was based were bad. Bagg and Miller had pleaded that Parish's words contained the innuendo that he had engaged in sexual intercourse with Miller. Ashmun did not object to this inference (even though Parish had actually been cagey on the point) but argued that fornication by an unmarried woman, punishable only by fine, was not a sufficiently serious offense to make alleging it actionable per se as

slander. The court overruled the motion, and Miller was ordered to
recover $307.35 in damages and costs of $160.12. Execution was
issued on September 28, but documents in the court file indicate that
she recovered only $234.58, from someone whose name might be
Samuel Clark, possibly a relative of Parish's bride, Jerusha Clarke:
another knot in the community's web of debt.

Did this suit salvage Miller's reputation? Was it damaged in the first
place? She was not actually raped in a snowy tussle outside on a March
night in the presence of witnesses. Neighbors may well have considered
Parish's conduct distasteful and unchivalrous at best. Soon Miller was
married and had children. Parish, unlike Bates and Ashmun, did not
draw praise from later town historians. This very public, reported case
may well have demonstrated his unsuitability for the bar.[5]

Hiram Bagg and Daniel Parish may have been involved in more
cases simultaneously than most people were, but defamation suits
intertwined with other cases were common in Massachusetts,
especially in Worcester. Of the thirty-one Worcester cases, five
involved allegations related to perjury, and a few cases refer to
religious proceedings. Such connections are less evident in the Suffolk
records, perhaps because people were less intimately interconnected in
the city, but the court files are also thinner and actions in the Justices'
and Police Courts have not survived. The strategic possibilities of
defamation were less attractive in Nova Scotia. The opening gambits
in these Hampshire cases – writs of attachments issued for increasing,
indeed fancifully large, sums of $1,000, $3,000 and $4,000 – were
likely impossible in Nova Scotia; no actions in my dataset began with
this writ.[6] Moreover, according to Beamish Murdoch, in 1824 Nova
Scotia restricted writs of attachment to cases involving absent or
absconding debtors, having found that widespread use of this writ
was ruining businesses and families: creditors used it strategically to
gain priority by locking up the debtor's assets, if there was any hint that
the debtor might not be able to pay, or even if the creditor simply

[5] On these lawyers, see Rice and Brewster, *History of the Town of Worthington*, 105–6;
Massachusetts Register and United States Calendar, 54; Williams, *Biographical
Encyclopedia*, 448.
[6] James Muir notes that attachments were not available in actions based on more
"subjective" claims, such as slander or assault, in the 1750s and 1760s: *Law, Debt,
and Merchant Power*, 52. I have found no statutory changes until 1824.

needed the money.[7] The possibility of attaching assets in Massachusetts and the evident lack of such an avenue in Nova Scotia is a significant difference in the strategic possibilities offered by defamation suits. It may be, as well, that the 1824 change in procedure reduced the frequency of strategic debt claims and, as a consequence, retaliatory defamation claims, even though the writ of attachment had not been available in such cases.

Actionability

The argument that Daniel Parish's words were not actionable points to another strategic consideration. Although libel proceedings could be brought over any text intelligible to the eye, only certain kinds of spoken words were actionable per se, without proof of special damage (interfering with existing rights or identifiable future benefits): words that tended to harm a plaintiff's practice of a profession, office or trade; words accusing a plaintiff of committing a crime; words imputing to the plaintiff a serious, contagious disease; and words impugning a plaintiff's title to land (e.g. by alleging bastardy).[8] Rules about actionability shaped what appeared in court: we must be cautious about reading slander suits as showing their participants' dearest values and vulnerabilities.

Different kinds of slander suits have been brought in different places at different times. In reviewing 239 reported American slander cases from 1800 through 1830, Andrew King has found that 28 percent pertained to allegations of theft, 5 percent to forgery, 23 percent to false swearing and 17 percent to sexual immorality. My Nova Scotia sample does not permit this kind of breakdown, but accusations of dishonesty certainly dominate. Overall, of the Massachusetts slander cases for which the underlying allegation is clear, just over 40 percent are for theft, but of the cases from outside Worcester and Suffolk (which are mostly reported) only 21 percent are for theft. Theft allegations may have been easily made but also easily settled so that

---

[7] See Murdoch, *Epitome of the Laws of Nova-Scotia*, 3:132–34. *An Act to Restrain the Issuing Writs of Attachment in Certain Cases*, S.N.S. 1824, c. 7 was continued several times and remained in effect throughout the period.

[8] Starkie, *Treatise on Slander* (1830), 1:10. The last two categories do not appear in any Massachusetts or Nova Scotia cases.

they seldom led to reported cases. Two cases arose from allegations of forgery, a proportion roughly similar to King's.[9]

Actionability undoubtedly shaped plaintiffs' strategic decisions.[10] Only four Massachusetts slander cases, of the eighty-two for which the substance of the allegation is clear, pertained to allegation of perjury or false swearing, a proportion considerably lower than King's. According to Mark Steiner's figures, around 20 percent of the men whom Abraham Lincoln represented in slander cases in Illinois somewhat later in the century sued over accusations of false swearing.[11] In Illinois, swearing falsely was actionable per se, whether or not the allegation pertained to judicial proceedings.[12] Massachusetts plaintiffs, however, always carefully established that the allegation was falsely swearing to material facts under oath in specific proceedings, that is, perjury. The category was narrower and the claims rarer.

As *Miller v. Parish* suggests, legal constraints also had the potential to shape claims regarding sexual improprieties. Chief Justice Parker, in holding that fornication by an unmarried woman was a serious offense, even if she could not be jailed for it, ensured that fornication allegations were actionable as crimes, without proof of special damages, as they also were in Illinois but were not in England or, likely, Nova Scotia.[13] Over 25 percent of the Massachusetts cases

---

[9] The figures are as follows. Suffolk: 5 sexual improprieties; 17 theft/larceny/being a scoundrel; 4 fraud/cheating employer; 1 sexual impropriety and theft together; 1 mutiny; 1 perjury; 1 lying/being incompetent on the job (total 30). Worcester: 7 sexual improprieties; 9 theft; 4 perjury-related (1 for suborning); 1 theft and perjury together; 1 being a bankrupt bigamist; 1 forgery; 2 drunkenness; 1 murder; 1 poisoning animals; 1 imputing dishonesty to a minister; 1 wasting an estate (total 29). Other counties: 10 sexual improprieties; 1 sexual improprieties and lawyerly misconduct (Parish's); 6 theft; 3 fraud (2 re an election); 1 imputing dishonesty to a minister; 1 forgery; 1 bribery; 4 unidentifiable (total 27). Not all of these allegations were, of course, actionable, and some cases ended on the pleadings. The Worcester case that used the wrong writ would have been a slander allegation for sexual improprieties.

[10] Mary Beth Norton notes that when Maryland, in 1671, eliminated the per se actionability of allegations that "scandalized" the good name of all but government officials, women's participation in slander suits dropped: "Gender and Defamation in Seventeenth-Century Maryland," 8.

[11] Steiner, *Honest Calling*, 87–91.

[12] *Ibid.* 86–87, citing An Act Declaring Certain Words Actionable, 1822 Ill. Laws 82.

[13] Only one Massachusetts woman, Mary Hayden, alleged she had lost her fiancé because of the allegations.

arose from allegations of sexual improprieties, a proportion somewhat larger than King's for reported cases (17 percent). However, the Massachusetts data reveal fewer of these cases in Suffolk and more among the cases from the other counties (over 35 percent), more of which are reported, which may suggest that other factors were in play, such as the unusually large number of women involved as parties to appeals to the full bench in Massachusetts, a phenomenon I discuss below. States' differences in their treatment of allegations of fornication may shed additional light on why King finds a lower proportion of such cases in the reported cases than exist in the Massachusetts dataset.[14]

Structural Factors

Jennett Miller sued at least twice before she was twenty. Courts were evidently available to her and her uncles as they conducted their affairs. However, access – and attitudes – to courts and lawyers were not uniform across Nova Scotia and Massachusetts in the 1820s and 1830s, and this variability probably had gendered effects.

Courts open to defamation suits sat four times a year in Boston, Halifax, Worcester and Pictou throughout the period, but remote Yarmouth, at the southwest tip of Nova Scotia, was less well served. The ICCP sat once each year in two towns in Yarmouth district, but until 1834 its litigants had to go to Shelburne to attend NSSC; beginning in 1834, the NSSC sat in Yarmouth in June.[15]

---

[14] See King, "Law of Slander in Early Antebellum America," 1. The *Revised Statutes of Massachusetts*, c. 130, ss. 1, 4& 5 (1836) provided that the maximum punishment for adultery and for lewd and lascivious association or cohabitation was imprisonment for three years or a $500 fine. Fornication by the unmarried could draw two months' imprisonment or a $30 fine. Starkie considered the English common law rule deeply unfair to women and pointed out that although the reputations of "mechanics" in their trades were protected, the prospects of a woman of any rank could be ruined with impunity, unless she could show that a particular fiancé had fled or other specific consequences. See Starkie, *Treatise on Slander* (1830), 1:196–202. In Nova Scotia, fornication appears not to have been an offense, although adultery was criminal and punishable by fine or imprisonment: Murdoch, *Epitome of the Laws of Nova-Scotia*, 4:135–38. Some sexual slander claims by women would presumably have therefore been kept out of court.

[15] See Appendix A for an explanation of courts and their jurisdictions. *An Act Respecting the Trial of Issues in the Supreme Court, and for Regulating the Times of Holding the Circuits of the said Court in the Several Counties and Districts of this*

Worcester County was mostly rural, but it was connected to Boston and Providence, Rhode Island by turnpike, canal and railroad, in a commercial network that intensified in the 1830s. From Halifax, a road to Pictou adequate for carriages had been completed by about 1810, and a small commercial carriage that took about two days was running weekly by around 1820. Although still taxing, service improved in the 1830s.[16]

Courts in Suffolk and Worcester both did a brisk business, but court usage varied in the three Nova Scotia jurisdictions. From 1835 through 1839, Halifax had 102 trials, Pictou had 69, and Yarmouth had three, a surprisingly small number.[17] Travel around the Yarmouth area was difficult, as was getting to Halifax, either by land or sea. Another factor, though, was the availability of two other, more compelling fora for resolving disputes. The first was a priest, Jean-Mandé Sigogne, who ministered to the large, French-speaking Acadian population.[18] Regulations he introduced in 1799 required settling disputes internally as far as possible. According to Joseph Howe, who "rambled" around Nova Scotia in 1828, at least 500 Acadian families in the area were governed by the refined, educated Sigogne, who ministered to the area for over forty-five years. He also acted as their sole lawyer, learning from a friend, Judge Peleg Wiswall of Digby, how to draft deeds, wills, mortgages, notes and other legal documents,

---

Province, S.N.S. 1834, c. 4; *An Act for the Better Regulating the Manner of Holding the Inferior Court of Common Pleas and General Sessions of the Peace, in the District of Yarmouth and Argyle, in the County of Shelburne*, S.N.S. 1817, c. 24, as amended. Phillips and Miller note the importance of the distance and road quality in shaping litigants' choice of court in Nova Scotia: "Too Many Courts and Too Much Law," 129.

[16] Lincoln, *History of Worcester*, 282–83; Taylor, *Transportation Revolution*, 37–38; Patterson, *History of Pictou Nova Scotia*, 264–65, 391–92; Evans, "Stage Coaches," 109–12

[17] NS Journals, 1841, A22-102. In 1838, Pictou's population was 21,518 and Yarmouth's was 9,189. The population of peninsular Halifax (the city) was 14,422, and of Halifax district 14,148. I am grateful to Dani Pahulje and Peter Peller of the University of Calgary for compiling these statistics.

[18] In 1827, Shelburne County, which included the Yarmouth district, was 40.5 percent Baptist (4,872 people) and 11.0 percent Catholic (1,326): *Colonial Patriot*, April 12, 1828. The records of the clergy who served the various denominations in the area speak to the strong regionalization of the francophone Catholic population. See Brown, *Yarmouth, Nova Scotia*, 337–38; Campbell, *History of the County of Yarmouth*, 123–24.

and keeping the records. Howe thought nowhere in the province were there so few quarrels or lawsuits. Sigogne also ministered to and assisted the substantial Mi'kmaq population in the area.[19] Reputational disputes among the Mi'kmaq and Acadians were unlikely to end up in court.

Another large group in the Yarmouth area also got by without courts: the Baptists. Upon becoming members of churches, adherents to certain "covenantal" Protestant denominations, including Baptists and Congregationalists, promised to take prescribed steps to address their conflicts. Excellent records of two decades of the doings of the First Baptist church in Yarmouth area have survived.[20] Not much discipline occurred in the early 1820s, but after 1826 the church's fortunes seem to have improved; its membership increased, and its disciplinary proceedings became numerous, involving both men and women. Most discipline was for offending the church, by skipping meetings and worshiping elsewhere, or for disreputable behavior like drunkenness or sexual impropriety. The church may not have absolutely prohibited litigation, but in several cases elders tried to resolve disputes that had produced litigation or were heading that way. One man was subjected to proceedings because his bad feelings against another man owing to a court verdict were interfering with his covenantal obligations – in Massachusetts such feelings could produce allegations of perjury and then defamation claims. The church's authority may well have been buttressed by one of its elders also being, by 1835, a justice of the peace.

The dictates of covenantal theology, although likely reducing litigation in the Yarmouth area, did less to discourage litigation in Massachusetts because the threat of expulsion from fellowship was less troubling. As disestablishment took hold, Congregationalists, Unitarians and Baptists competed for members and did less disciplining.[21] Religious hegemony was equally unavailable in

---

[19] Pothier, "Sigogne, Jean-Mandé"; d'Entremont, "Father Jean Mande Sigogne, 1799–1844," 105–10; "Western Rambles," *Novascotian* (Halifax), October 9, 1828.

[20] Zion United Baptist Church, Yarmouth Co., NS, Records 1815–31, D1900, 401/392–93, and Records 1831–42, D1900.401/6, Acadia University Archives ("AUA"). See also Goodwin, *Into Deep Waters*, 42–74.

[21] See Hamburger, *Church and State*, 195. In the 1820s and 1830s, for example, Boston's Old South Church did more disciplining than did Park Street Church: see CR III: Old South Church, Boston, Records, 1817–54, and Park Street Church,

Halifax.[22] Neighbors with different religious outlooks could draw Congregationalists or Baptists into court.[23]

Defamation suits are complex, and almost all were conducted by lawyers, with whom Boston, Worcester and Halifax were fairly well supplied. Loosening educational requirements in the early nineteenth century opened the bars of Suffolk and Worcester to the nonelite. In 1830, Suffolk had one lawyer for every 426 people and Worcester had one for every 1,096 people. Peninsular Halifax had a slightly lower density of lawyers than Boston in the 1830s, with about one lawyer for every 500 people, or one lawyer for about 800 people in Halifax city and district combined. In the mid-1830s Pictou had about one lawyer for every 2,700 people, and Yarmouth about one lawyer for every 4,000 people.[24] Just as particular lawyers influenced criminal libel actions, they also influenced which civil suits were brought and what arguments were made and avoided.

Either the Suffolk clerks did not consistently identify the attorneys who appeared in the cases or else self-representation was more common there than in Worcester, but some names are notable. Future chief justice Lemuel Shaw and James T. Austin represented

Church Clerk Minutes, vol. 22, 1809–34, Congregational Archives, Boston. On church membership and discipline, see also Lawes, *Women and Reform*, 26–44, 200; Moir, *Early Presbyterianism in Canada*, 72–84.

[22] Peninsular Halifax in 1827 was about 42 percent Anglican, 25 percent Catholic, 20 percent Presbyterian, 8 percent Methodist and 5 percent Baptist: *Colonial Patriot*, April 12, 1828. Baptists did discipline their members. See First Baptist Church, Halifax, N.S., Records 1827–41, D1900.121/1, Acadia University Archives; Granville Street Baptist, Halifax, Minutes 1836–44, No. 41B, MG 4, NSA.

[23] The presbyteries and synods of Pictou Presbyterianism, while addressing offenses against morals, sometimes recommended recourse to legal arbiters when legal questions arose. See Presbyterian Synod records, Presbyterian Church of Nova Scotia 1817–60 and Minutes of the Presbytery of Pictou, Presbyterian Church of Nova Scotia (Secession Synod of N.S.) July 2, 1829–June 15, 1840 and June 30, 1840–June 25, 1844, both at United Church Maritime Conference Archives, Sackville, New Brunswick.

[24] See Gawalt, Massachusetts Lawyers, 118–20, 225; Chroust, *Rise of the Legal Profession*, 163, 207. Peninsular Halifax had about 30 lawyers for 15,000 people in 1830 (1 for every 500 people, or 1 for every 833 of the 25,000 people in the city and district combined). By 1838, Halifax city had 38 lawyers for 14,422 people (1 for every 480 people, or 1 for every 752 of the 28,570 people in the city and district combined). Pictou had 5 lawyers in 1833 and 8 in 1838, for a population that grew from 13,949 in 1827 to 21,518 in 1838. Yarmouth had 1 lawyer in 1833 and 4 in 1838. Its population was part of Shelburne County (population 12,018) in 1827 but numbered See *Belcher's Farmer's Almanack 1833*, 52–53; *Belcher's Farmer's Almanack 1838*, 21–23.

the state prison employee Samuel R. Johnson in his suit against David Lee Child for allegations of fraud and embezzlement, and Austin also defended the prominent naval agent Amos Binney. Samuel D. Parker represented at least four, much more obscure, plaintiffs and one defendant. Abraham Moore represented three plaintiffs and one defendant, traders and a housewright; one of his plaintiffs won forty dollars before a jury, one lost and one was nonsuit; his defendant was acquitted.[25]

In Worcester, several names appear repeatedly. Pliny Merrick represented two plaintiffs and seven defendants. Rejoice Newton represented two plaintiffs and three defendants. John Davis represented five plaintiffs and one defendant. Charles Allen represented two plaintiffs and three defendants. Aaron Brooks Jr. represented four plaintiffs and one defendant. Other lawyers represented one, two or three parties, a mixture of plaintiffs and defendants.

Merrick, Newton and Davis all had strong links to public law and public offices in Worcester and more broadly, and Charles Allen practiced with Davis. Merrick trained with Levi Lincoln Jr. just before Lincoln became state governor in 1825. Merrick and Newton both held the post of county attorney for Worcester, Newton resigning in 1824 and entering into practice with Lincoln's brother William in 1826. The duo, who were brothers-in-law, trained many Worcester lawyers. Merrick became county attorney in 1824, and Levi Lincoln appointed him district attorney for the Middle District, which included Worcester, when the state was divided into districts in 1832. Merrick held this post alongside his civil practice until he became a judge in 1843. Both Merrick and Newton served in the state legislature in the late 1820s and early 1830s. John Davis practiced with Levi Lincoln in 1823–24 and subsequently with Allen and then Emory Washburn, who also appears in the defamation cases. Davis served in the federal House of Representatives from 1824 to 1834 and was governor of Massachusetts from 1834 to 1836.[26]

Their defamation client bases overlapped but were somewhat different. Davis's clients included three Congregational ministers, an

---

[25] See Green, *Account of the Lawyers of Groton*, 33, 45–47.
[26] Lincoln, *History of Worcester*, 200–12, Lawes, *Women and Reform*, 110–11; Hurd, *History of Worcester County*, xxxii–xxxvii.

established physician, and a "yeoman." Davis's political prominence did not translate into consistent success with juries. At least once he took a case opposed to his personal interests: he represented Charles Goodrich, a much-resented young Congregational minister detested by the prominent uncle and aunts of soon-to-be-governor Levi Lincoln. Nonetheless, prominence in law and politics evidently went together. Lincoln represented only one party in my sample, Mary Knowlton, who won an astonishing $1,200 in 1821.

Rejoice Newton's and Pliny Merrick's clients were less prominent, and two of Newton's were older women. He also defended Charles Goodrich's antagonist. Merrick and Newton may have attracted their clients in part through being public prosecutors. Merrick's flip from freemasonry to antimasonry and his moderation on temperance may have helped as well.[27] Charles Allen and Aaron Brooks Jr. had a similarly mixed group of clients. Brooks, who had trained briefly with Lincoln, represented two young women plaintiffs; he appeared twice with Aaron Bigelow and once with Newton and Washburn. Allen appeared once with Merrick and once with Davis. These lawyers' defamation clients were less illustrious than John Davis's, but like his, the results of their cases were mixed.

Nova Scotia's lawyers were unevenly distributed, and business was not uniformly good. In 1820, 25 of Nova Scotia's 38 lawyers practiced in Halifax. By 1840, Halifax had 42 lawyers and the rest of the province 75. Nova Scotia lawyers worked hard to fortify their fortunes through family connections and political appointments, and in the later 1820s young lawyers had to be willing to leave Halifax to seek their fortunes. The vast majority of Beamish Murdoch's clients in the mid-1820s, when he was a young Halifax lawyer, were "smaller merchants and 'mechanics,' leavened by a few farmers and mariners and their widows." Lawyers gradually tried to build their practices with repeat clients and work they preferred.[28] Massachusetts lawyers may have been able to choose their work somewhat, but lawyers in both places probably generally just took the problem that came with the client.

---

[27] Merrick, *Letter on Speculative Free Masonry*; Vaughn, *Antimasonic Party*, 127; Tyrrell, *Sobering Up*, 105–7.
[28] Girard, *Lawyers and Legal Culture*, 62–63, 66–70, 87, 99–101; Bell, "Paths to the Law."

As in Massachusetts, two or even three lawyers often appeared on the record in Halifax cases, which may be a result of formalities, the complexity of the case or a desire to expose younger colleagues to unusual, interesting suits. Three Nova Scotia lawyers appeared frequently. William Q. Sawers appeared in at least four cases, all in 1820 and 1821 (before he took up plum judicial posts and antagonized Pictou temperance reformers[29]); James W. Johnston appeared in ten, nine in the early 1820s; and Samuel G.W. Archibald appeared in eleven (and also prosecuted at least three and probably all five of the criminal libel cases between 1820 and 1840, once with Johnston).

Born in 1777 in Truro and educated in Massachusetts, Archibald married into the influential Dickson family and was studying law in Halifax with Simon Bradstreet Robie when Robie began to assert the assembly's rights against the council. Archibald held various offices and was first elected to the assembly in 1806. In 1817 he was one of the colony's first two lawyers to be appointed King's Counsel. He was speaker of the Nova Scotia assembly from 1824 to 1841. He became acting attorney general in 1830 after Richard J. Uniacke died and was fully installed in 1832. Although preeminent in the Halifax courtroom, Archibald's defamation clients were mostly a middling lot. He acted regularly for Anthony Henry Holland throughout the 1820s and both sued and defended others in defamation suits, including merchant Thomas Forrester and a couple of Holland's neighbors.

Fifteen years younger than Archibald, James W. Johnston was born in Jamaica, the grandson of a Scottish Loyalist. Moving, as a young lawyer, to Halifax in 1815, he entered into partnership with Simon Bradstreet Robie and must have been in the social milieu when Robie hosted the young Samuel Sewall around 1820. Johnston married

[29] Overlooked even by the *Dictionary of Canadian Biography*, Sawers is remembered mainly as the obnoxious antagonist of proponents of political and institutional reform. In the early 1820s he often appeared in uncontested debt cases in Halifax's ICCP. His 1824 appointment as chief justice of the ICCP for the Eastern District and president (*custos rotulorum*) of the Sessions was controversial. Despite being commended for his handling of the Canso Riots in the mid-1830s, he infuriated Pictou's temperance-minded grand juries by impeding their efforts to limit liquor licenses. Fury followed his 1835 appointment as *custos rotulorum* and supervisor of the police establishment in Halifax. In 1842, Richard Nugent, of the *Novascotian*, labeled Sawers "'a rapacious attorney, doing a small business,' who had pursued 'a tortuous, pettifogging and vexatious course' to gratify 'a spiteful malignity'"; Sawers successfully sued him for libel. See Beck, "Nugent, Richard."

Amelia Almon, the daughter of an influential Halifax doctor. Johnston led a faction that split from Halifax's respectable St. Paul's Anglican church and founded a Baptist church in 1827. He was active in establishing and promoting higher education as well as commercial pursuits. He became solicitor general in 1834 and succeeded Archibald as attorney general in 1841. He clashed with Joseph Howe over political reform in the later 1830s.[30] Like Archibald, Johnston represented a range of clients, and he opposed Archibald in five defamation suits, the bar being so small. Overall, then, Massachusetts and Nova Scotia lawyers had similar types of clients in defamation suits, but the small bar and the concentration of power and influence in Nova Scotia made a few lawyers particularly prominent.

Access to lawyers and courts, a married woman's need for her husband's sign-on in civil suits, care responsibilities, shortages of cash, clerical pressure and other structural factors probably differentially affected women. Being less involved in commercial relationships, women probably were also less likely to want to use defamation claims strategically. These factors were less inhibitory to Massachusetts women with grievances, and the actionability of allegations of sexual improprieties opened courtrooms to them. However, in the 1820s the law also showed signs of receptivity to a woman's right to pursue paid labor and her need for a good character for that purpose. I next turn to the parties and their allegations.

The Suits

Nova Scotia

Table 6.1 shows the civil defamation cases in the Nova Scotia sample, all of which took place in the NSSC.

In Nova Scotia, middling white men mostly sued each other over allegations of dishonesty. The Mi'kmaq and African-descended populations of Nova Scotia are undetectable in the records, which are admittedly thin.

---

[30] Sutherland, "Johnston, James William."

TABLE 6.1 Civil defamation cases in the Nova Scotia sample. Dates are of trials. "L" means libel.

Dates	Causes of action	Allegations	Plaintiffs	Defendants
1820–25 (17 cases: 15 Halifax, 2 Pictou)	4 newspaper libels 2 epistolary libel (one letter, two plaintiffs) 3 slander 1 slander + malicious prosecution 5 "defamation" 2 "words" (Pictou)	1 ministerial bigamy 2 fraudulently inadequately provisioning a ship (same ship) (2L) 1 self-dealing postmaster (1L) 1 theft 1 theft and breaking and entering 2 theft and absconding (same letter/ plaintiffs) (2L) 9 unclear (1L)	1 Church of Scotland clergyman 2 immigration promoter (sued twice re same ship) (2L) 1 deputy postmaster (1L) 2 youths (absconding brothers) (2L) 1 married woman, prominent family 1 mechanic (likely blacksmith) 1 probable cabinetmaker 8 unclear (1L)	1 radical Presbyterian leader 1 innkeeper/farmer 2 newspaperman/businessman (both Holland) (2L) 1 magistrate (1L) 1 prominent merchant 2 farmers 2 might be a JP (one JP, two plaintiffs) (2L) 7 unclear (1L)

(continued)

TABLE 6.1 (*continued*)

Dates	Causes of action	Allegations	Plaintiffs	Defendants
1825–30 (2 cases, both 1825)	1 slander 1 "defamation"	1 theft & murder 1 unclear	1 innkeeper/farmer 1 unclear	1 farmer 1 unclear
1831–35 (2 cases)	1 "defamation" 1 slander	1 theft 1 unclear	2 unclear	1 farmer 1 unclear
1836–40 (2 cases)	2 newspaper libels	1 deceitfully manufacturing obscenity allegations (1L) 1 being a swindler (1L)	1 newspaperman (Ward) (1L) 1 unclear (Fletcher) (1L)	1 retired military man (1L) 1 newspaperman (1L)

As in Massachusetts, these actions often look like aspects of ongoing disputes among neighbors and those with commercial dealings. Several cases arose in the area between "Dutch Village," on the northwestern edge of Halifax, and the area north of the Sackville Bridge at the head of Bedford Basin, and somewhat west. John Heffler, James Doyle, Henry Mixner or Maxner, John Goff and other men with the same surnames appear as parties and witnesses in these cases and in many others for debt and trespass in the record books of the early 1820s. Anthony Henry Holland, who owned land and engaged in lumbering and other businesses in the same area and somewhat northward, also appears in these suits. Others were an innkeeper, farmers, an owner of a tanning yard, and "mechanics."[31] The census records indicate different religious affiliations, but the only case that clearly involved religion – intra-Presbyterian disputation – was Church of Scotland minister Donald Fraser's suit against the radical, strict Presbyterian leader Norman McLeod for accusing Fraser of bigamy.[32]

Only one woman was a party, recently married Anne Crawley, who with her husband Henry sued merchant Thomas Forrester in 1823 for malicious prosecution and slander. Forrester had evidently attempted unsuccessfully to prosecute her for something.[33] Henry's father was a Cape Breton naval captain and surveyor general. A few years later, Henry's Sunday skating touched off a small tempest, as recounted in Chapter 5. Henry's brother Edmund, newly admitted to the bar, practiced with James W. Johnston, one of the lawyers who represented Anne and Henry. Anne Crawley's witnesses, one being William Sawers, were notable members of Halifax society, which may signal a concern with preserving respectability in those circles. The other cases look more like strategic moves in neighbor disputes. The scarcity of women in my sample is consistent with Julian Gwyn's findings about women in civil cases generally and defamation in particular from 1749 to 1830.[34]

---

[31] See the 1827 and 1838 Nova Scotia census returns, available at novascotia.ca/archives/census/; Dawson, *Nova Scotia's Lost Highways*, 55; Tratt, "Holland, Anthony Henry."

[32] See Campey, *After the Hector*, 15, 110–12; MacPherson, *Watchman against the World*; Patterson, *History of Pictou*, 316–19; Robinson, *To the Ends of the Earth*.

[33] Forrester was prosecuted in 1825 for a letter alleging a conspiracy among the members of Halifax's business community to defraud certain London insurers.

[34] Gwyn finds that no more than 5 percent of Nova Scotia civil suits from 1749 to 1801 had female parties. Only 3.3 percent of the cases involving women (25 cases) were for

The libel cases suggest the significance of newspapers as conduits for defamation, and hint at the growing sense that newspapers and courts were emerging as fora for engaging public judgment. Of the eight cases, two arose from a letter: two brothers sued someone, who might have been a justice of the peace, for alerting another person that they had fled their apprenticeship and one had stolen money from their father. The other four early libel cases involved the *Acadian Recorder*, essentially the only newspaper that published controversial matters. The seventh libel case arose from John Flohr's prosecution for obscene libel: Flohr placed notices in newspapers that implied that David Fletcher had manufactured the obscenity case against him. The eighth arose from mutual name-calling among newspapermen, plaintiff Edmund Ward and defendants John English and Hugh Blackadar. Just as *R. v. Wilkie* and *R. v. Howe* arose from political criticism, five of the civil cases – *Fraser v. Holland*, *Fraser v. Patterson*, *Bowes v. Holland*, *Fletcher v. Flohr* and *Ward v. English and Blackadar* – started with a published appeal to the public's judgment.

The centrality of newspapers in libel suits and the mixture of plaintiff motivations – some cases apparently being retribution against neighbors and others aimed more at clearing one's name – emerge in Massachusetts as well.

Massachusetts

Table 6.2 summarizes the Massachusetts cases. People of modest means sued, but the cases reveal no sign of African American or Indigenous parties. A very few may have been recent immigrants, especially in Boston – one woman complained of being called a "damned Irish whore" and a thief, and at least one man was Irish-born – but the vast majority were native-born Americans of the broad, white middle tier of society. Farmers and yeomen – some prosperous, some less so – were less common as parties than their numbers in Worcester would seem to warrant, and men of higher social status are more so. Possibly such people's words did more harm, but their

---

defamation, the vast majority being for debt. In other work that extends his study to 1830, Gwyn identifies seven slander suits involving female parties in the NSSC between 1754 and 1830. Gwyn, "Female Litigants," 313, 323; Gwyn, "Women As Litigants," 296.

TABLE 6.2 Civil cases in the Massachusetts sample. Dates are of the first hearing in CP. "L" means libel.

Dates & Places	Causes of Action	Allegations	Plaintiffs	Defendants
Suffolk 1820–25, plus two CP 1819 (18 cases)	3 newspaper libel 1 pamphlet libel 14 slander	1 medical malpractice (L) 1 public servant misconduct (L) 1 maliciously prosecuting (L) 9 theft (1L) 1 theft & housebreaking 1 theft & lying 1 theft & fornication 2 adultery/fornication 1 fraud	1 physician (L) 1 customs official (L) 1 gentleman 3 gentlemen/isenglass maker (same plaintiff in 3 cases) 2 merchants/traders (1L) 3 skilled tradesmen (1L) 1 yeoman 1 mariner 1 constable's wife (& husband) 1 laborer's wife (& husband) 1 minor (young man, guardian a mason) 1 single woman 1 unclear	2 "esquire" (1L) 1 auctioneer (L) 7 merchants/traders (2L) 1 master mariner 1 mariner 1 innholder 1 brewer 2 widows 1 gentleman's wife (& husband) 1 ropemaker's wife (& husband)

(continued)

TABLE 6.2 (*continued*)

Dates & Places	Causes of Action	Allegations	Plaintiffs	Defendants
Suffolk 1826–30 (12 cases)	2 newspaper libel 1 libel for a notice of some sort 1 libel for a letter 8 slander	1 misconduct by public official (L) 1 having violent, domineering tendencies (L) 1 lying, blasphemy, hypocrisy (L) 6 theft (1L) 1 attempt to defraud 1 false swearing 1 adultery & lying	1 lawyer/newsman (D.L. Child) (L) 1 prison official (L) 1 gentleman 2 merchant/traders (1L) 1 boardinghouse keeper (L) 2 skilled tradesmen 1 tragedian 2 wife of "esquire" (& husband – same people in 2 cases) 1 minor (male)	1 physician (L) 2 gentlemen (1L) 2 newspaper editors (both L) 3 merchants/traders 2 skilled tradesmen 2 single women shopkeepers
Suffolk 1831–35 (8 cases)	1 libel – probably letter 7 slander	1 keeping a dirty inn (L) 1 mutiny 2 theft 2 fraud/cheating 2 fornication/adultery	1 company agent/ "esquire" 1 master mariner 3 boardinghouse-/ innkeepers (1 woman) (1L) 2 skilled tradesmen 1 minor (female)	1 gentleman (L) 1 master mariner 1 trader 3 skilled tradesmen 1 stabler 1 wife of trader (& husband)

(*continued*)

Suffolk 1836–40 (4 cases)	2 newspaper libel 1 pamphlet libel 1 slander	2 job misconduct/incompetence (1L) 1 perjury (L) 1 conspiring to lure women into prostitution (L)	1 gentleman (L) 1 master mariner (L) 1 boardinghouse keeper (L) 1 skilled tradesman	1 gentleman (L) 1 newsmen (L) 1 trader (L) 1 master builder
Worcester 1820–25 (12 cases, plus one begun with wrong writ)	1 libel – public notice 1 libel – copy of affidavit 10 slander (wrong writ case is unclear if oral or written)	2 theft (1L) 1 false swearing 1 suborning perjury 1 bestiality 5 adultery/fornication 1 incest (L) 1 drunkenness (wrong writ case pertains to sexual impropriety)	3 ministers (2 cases have same plaintiff) 2 "esquire"/gentlemen (1L) 1 boardinghouse keeper/merchant 3 yeomen (1L) 1 wife of yeoman (& husband) 1 woman domestic worker 1 widow (wrong writ case is a single woman)	2 ministers 4 "esquire"/gentlemen (1L) 1 trader (L) 3 yeomen 1 wife of yeoman (& husband) 1 widow (wrong writ case is a trader)

(continued)

TABLE 6.2 (*continued*)

Dates & Places	Causes of Action	Allegations	Plaintiffs	Defendants
Worcester 1826–30 (5 cases)	5 slander	1 theft 1 theft & false swearing 1 false swearing 1 bankrupt bigamist 1 lying minister	1 Congregational minister 2 yeoman 2 women domestic workers	1 gentleman 4 yeoman
Worcester 1831–35 (9 cases)	9 slander	5 theft 1 forging credential 1 adultery 1 murder 1 drunkenness	1 Congregational deacon 1 physician 1 "esquire" 2 yeoman 1 cordwainer 1 temperance lecturer 2 women domestic workers	1 retired minister 1 physician 1 "esquire" 1 gentleman alias yeoman 2 yeomen 1 wife of gentleman (& husband) 1 bookseller 1 blacksmith
Worcester 1836–40 (5 cases)	4 slander 1 slander & malicious prosecution	2 theft 1 false swearing 1 poisoning animals 1 wasting estate	1 gentleman 3 yeomen 1 widow	2 gentlemen 3 yeomen

(*continued*)

Other counties 1820–25 (9 cases)	1 libel – church complaint 1 libel – report to school committee 1 libel – letter 6 slander	1 theft 4 adultery/fornication (one with getting abortion) (1L) 1 pugilism (L) 1 false swearing (L) 2 unclear	1 physician (L) 1 gentleman 1 farmer (L) 2 schoolteacher (one person, two cases) (1L) 1 minor (female) 3 unclear	1 minister (L) 3 gentlemen (1L) 1 wife of yeoman (& husband) 4 unclear (L)
Other counties 1826–30 (11 cases)	11 slander	1 calling a minister a liar/knave/rascal 1 attempted rape & lawyerly misconduct 1 forging a note 1 bribery 1 fraud 2 election fraud (same plaintiff) 4 fornication/adultery (2 same defendant)	1 minister 2 lawyer/"esquire" 1 masonic lodge treasurer 1 yeoman 1 almshouse keeper 1 almshouse worker 2 skilled tradesman (same plaintiff) 1 teacher 1 single woman	1 physician 3 gentlemen (1 was defendant in two cases) 2 lawyer/"esquire" 2 yeomen 1 trader 2 skilled tradesmen

(*continued*)

TABLE 6.2 (*continued*)

Dates & Places	Causes of Action	Allegations	Plaintiffs	Defendants
Other counties 1831–35 (8 cases)	1 newspaper libel 1 poster libel 1 slander & malicious prosecution 5 slander	1 caricature of court martial (L) 1 child abuse (L) 4 theft 1 fornication 1 unclear	1 military judge (L) 1 master of school (L) 1 trader 1 journeyman 1 single woman 3 unclear	1 newsmen (L) 1 yeoman 2 traders (1L) 4 unclear
Other counties 1836–40 (4 cases)	4 slander	1 theft 2 adultery 1 unclear	1 physician 1 minister 1 farmer 1 unclear	1 merchant 2 yeoman/farmer 1 unclear

affluence and other entanglements probably also drew them into disputes for which legal redress beckoned.

The Suffolk parties had a greater variety of careers than those from elsewhere, and libel cases tend to skew to involve more socially prominent or affluent people, and newspaper editors and publishers, especially as defendants. Outside of Suffolk, Congregationalism's turmoil is evident: six cases have ministers and one a deacon as plaintiffs; three acting and one retired minister appear as defendants.[35] All were Congregational. They sued over allegations of adultery, misusing church resources and lying, reputations for honesty being essential for the clergy.

Four plaintiffs and three defendants were physicians. Three of the plaintiffs sued over allegations touching on their fitness to practice medicine, and the fourth over an allegation of adultery.[36] Lines of affiliation run among the parties and witnesses in these cases and the criminal ones: Ferdinand Andrews, sued by the Congregational deacon, printed George Cheever's temperance tract; Azor Phelps, whose medical credentials were impugned by another doctor, sympathized with the Worcester farmer who accused the new, young minister Charles Goodrich of embezzling money. Phelps had also attracted the ill will of Abner Phelps, one of the Boston-based reformers allied with antimasonry and Garrison.[37]

As with the criminal cases discussed in Chapter 4, just over half of the Massachusetts cases in which the subject matter is clear were brought by men suing over allegations of dishonesty about themselves – theft, embezzlement, false swearing, suborning perjury, self-dealing in a public office and so forth.[38] Unlike male plaintiffs in

---

[35] On *Goodrich v. Child*, which emerged out of Congregationalist tensions in Worcester, see Lawes, *Women and Reform*, 9–22; Lincoln, *History of Worcester*, 161–62; and *Origin and Progress of the Late Difficulties in the First Church*. On *Russell v. Howe*, see *Trial of the Action in Favor of the Rev. Samuel Russell*; Russell, *Review of a Pamphlet*. William Wesson's suits against John Fiske and Thomas Snell are discussed in Chapter 4.

[36] On the professionalization of medicine and contestation over medical knowledge, see Wiebe, *Opening of American Society*, 161–63; Hatch, *Democratization of American Christianity*, 28–29; *Comm. v. Samuel Thompson* [sic].

[37] See Vaughn, *Antimasonic Party*, 115; Garrison, *William Lloyd Garrison*, 279; "Meeting of Citizens," *Boston Morning Post*, December 6, 1837.

[38] Massachusetts actions brought in the closely related tort of malicious prosecution also often arose over prosecutions brought for acts of dishonesty, such as uttering a forged promissory note or theft.

eighteenth-century New Haven, no one in my sample complained of damage to his reputation for creditworthiness.[39] Two men had been accused of endangering or abusing children or young adults in their care. Only one of the male plaintiffs was a minor – he sued over an accusation of theft.[40] Ten of the 81 cases over harm to men's reputations arose from allegations of sexual misconduct, one of incest, one of sexual assault, one of bestiality and seven of adultery (two by William Wesson[41]).

Women were somewhat more commonly parties in these Massachusetts defamation suits than they were in Cornelia Hughes Dayton's sample from the New Haven courtroom from 1760 to 1789 or in Abraham Lincoln's law practice, as described by Mark Steiner.[42] Of the cases with women plaintiffs, twenty-three were for slander, one was for libel and one – Maria Goffe's – was brought with the wrong writ. Eleven plaintiffs appear to have been between age eighteen and twenty-four, including Goffe. Five were minors and one was widowed. Unmarried women in this age group in Massachusetts frequently lived and worked in domestic service in homes away from their parents, which made them vulnerable to charges of fornication and theft. Seven of these young women sued over allegations of sexual improprieties, three over allegations of theft (one of these with perjury as well), and one over both. As well, two unmarried women of twenty-nine brought three cases (one for libel) over allegations related to sex. In four of these fourteen cases the circumstances are unclear, but six cases were brought by women living away from their parents, either employed as domestics or helping care for young relatives. Paulina Whiting and

---

[39] See Dayton, *Women before the Bar*, 287.
[40] The defendant brewer said that the plaintiff, William Simonds, was being harbored by one Ambrose Salisbury, who had introduced his version of the velocipede to curious Bostonians a month or so before. See Verlihy, *Bicycle*, 39.
[41] See Chapter 4.
[42] Steiner says that women brought twenty-one of Abraham Lincoln's ninety-two slander suits (23 percent): *Honest Calling*, 88–89. Dayton says women brought 19 percent of New Haven slander suits from 1760 to 1789: *Women before the Bar*, 289, 304. Women are twenty-three of the eighty-six slander plaintiffs in my Massachusetts sample (27 percent), and they appear as defendants in twelve suits, one of which was for libel. (In nine cases, one being for libel, women appear on both sides.) Only one of the nineteen libel cases had a female plaintiff. Leaving aside Maria Goffe's case, women therefore appeared as parties in 26 percent of the 105 Massachusetts defamation suits in my sample and were plaintiffs in 23 percent.

Sophia Bodwell (twice) sued over allegations of sexual misconduct aimed at depriving them of employment as teachers.

Five of the eleven female plaintiffs who were over thirty brought actions on their own, all over allegations that in some way disrupted their ability to support themselves. Lydia Oakes objected to an allegation that she was having an affair with the married keeper of the almshouse where she worked. Charlotte Hunt had been accused of adultery with a boarder. Betsey Bacon was a resident housekeeper accused by her employer's estranged wife of sleeping with him. Sarepta Hix was accused of stealing yarn from neighbors, which jeopardized her ability to hire a man to work in her fields. Betsey Ammidown was accused of wasting her deceased's husband's estate.

Courts evidently accepted the legitimacy of women's engagement in the paid economy. This finding departs somewhat from Dayton's observations about eighteenth-century New Haven. In both places, women who lived outside of male-headed households – widows, orphaned boarders and the like – were particularly vulnerable to slander. In New Haven, however, young white women sued over sexual slander, which impaired their marriageability, but they almost never sued over allegations of cheating or incompetence in their work. They claimed damage for social ostracism, not lost income, even though their work was economically important and depended on social networks.[43] Only Betsey Bacon emphasized social ostracism in her pleadings. Differences in pleadings can reflect legal as well as social rules and priorities, and younger Massachusetts women, like their elders, typically identified vulnerability to criminal prosecution as their main form of harm, but Whiting and Bodwell emphasized the harm to their economic stability, as did three of the five older women who sued on their own. As well, although lawyers appear not to have thought of domestic work as an actual job, the economic threat to a woman employed as a domestic and accused of theft was obvious.

These claims reflected women's presence in the paid workforce in Massachusetts. Young women, especially, commonly worked as teachers, textile workers and domestic workers.[44] Historians have

---

[43] Dayton, *Women before the Bar*, 308–9, 316–17, 323–27.
[44] By 1837, perhaps one in five New England–born women had taught school, and it was common for young women, in particular, to work for wages. On women's attitudes to their work, see Hansen, *Very Social Time*, 15–51. See also Leonard,

identified a "cult of domesticity" arising in the mid-1830s, premised on the idea that women and men should work in separate places, with respectable women finding fulfillment at the fireside; however, before the early 1830s – and organized resistance to Fanny Wright's assault on religion and marriage – doubt had not yet arisen that young women could legitimately participate in the rapidly developing market economy by moving out and supporting themselves.[45] As I describe below, courts in the 1820s and 1830s awarded substantial damages for harm to a reputation for trustworthiness in work, as well as to sexual reputation.[46] Women's suits could also be part of larger conflicts, as cases like *Miller v. Parish* show.

The other six cases with women plaintiffs were brought by five married women with their husbands. Three of these cases arose from allegations of sexual misconduct, two of theft, and one of being an Irish whore who had stolen an apron. The very young widow, Laura Howe, and the married woman who sued twice, Abigail Fales, were the two affluent women in this sample. Howe complained of stories being told by a local rumormonger who claimed that before her marriage, when she worked in someone else's home, the man's son had often slept with her, infecting her with the French pox.[47] Fales sued two women shopkeepers for saying she has stolen from them. Her husband, Samuel, was a prominent Boston merchant, whose mother's ancestry ran directly back to William Bradford of the *Mayflower*, the second governor of the Plymouth Colony. Born in Windsor, Nova Scotia, Abigail's family pedigree ran back to the Middle Ages; Sir Walter Scott was a relative, as was Thomas Chandler Haliburton, the rising Nova Scotian lawyer, writer and reformer. Perhaps Abigail really did steal, or perhaps she stood out somehow, for her wealth or perhaps her hauteur or her accent.

News for All, 19; Bernard and Vinovskis, "Female School Teacher," 332–33; Porter, "Victorian Values in the Marketplace," 23–30.

[45] See Ryan, *Empire of the Mother*, 41; Porter, "Victorian Values in the Marketplace"; Ginzberg, "Hearts of Your Readers"; Kelly, *In the New England Fashion*, 3.

[46] Dayton has observed that in Connecticut "as the colonial period progressed, a woman's honor rested almost entirely on her sexual reputation – at least among those for whom a county court suit mattered": *Women before the Bar*, 308.

[47] Lyman B. Howe's probate record is available on the website of the New England Historic Genealogical Society, americanancestors.org.

The two shopkeepers sued by the Fales were among only twelve women whose words formed the basis for defamation actions, with one of those women having apparently jointly with her husband drafted the complaint to their church's disciplinary body. The shopkeepers and three others – widows – were sued alone, while the others were sued with their husbands. In just three cases men sued for damage done by women's words, in each case suing a woman and her husband. The allegations were bestiality, theft and shopbreaking, and false swearing. Of the nine cases brought by women plaintiffs over women's words, two pertained to theft (Abigail Fales's cases), six to sexual improprieties, and the last to the allegation of being an apron-stealing Irish whore. Six came from Boston, and the larger context is unclear, but the cases, including the Fales', seem like low-stakes skirmishes between irritated neighbors. Worcester County's Sally Putnam probably simply disliked Maria Thayer and did not want her to marry a young relative: she told another relative that Maria's sister had chased her out of the sister's house with a carving knife for sleeping with Maria's brother-in-law, but Sally quickly regretted her words and said she would deny saying such things. Sena Swan supported and promulgated allegations of sexual improprieties that a local notable, Benjamin Osgood, had submitted to the local school committee to discourage it from rehiring Sophia Bodwell as a teacher. Alice Holbrook was probably focused on convincing the community that her estranged husband was committing adultery, damage to housekeeper Betsey Bacon's reputation being basically collateral. Suing women – especially if husbands could not be sued as well – seems not generally to have been worthwhile, possibly because their words did little harm, possibly because they seldom had the assets to satisfy a judgment or possibly because they tended not to be entangled in the other kinds of disputes with their male neighbors that led to defamation proceedings.

A methodological comment is required. At least one of the women plaintiffs whose pleadings described her as a "singlewoman" was in fact married, with a husband living nearby. Sarepta Hix complained that Joel Drury, a prosperous "yeoman," had accused her of stealing cotton yarn out of his house six years earlier and using it to pay him for work he did for her. Hix's witnesses' evidence was that she had entered the empty Drury home that Sunday morning to retrieve her shoes, en

route to church, and that the bundle she was carrying was a child, not
the Drurys' yarn. In Massachusetts, witnesses who lived more than
thirty miles from the courthouse could give evidence through
depositions rather than appear in person, so the Worcester court
files – more so than the Suffolk ones – are frequently thick. The *Hix
v. Drury* file contains some 100 depositions. Hix's character was
a central issue. She and her husband had come to the Athol area in
1819 or 1820. Josiah Hix moved out soon after, leaving Sarepta to
support several children on the farm for around four years. He
returned for about two years and another child was born. By the time
of the trial, he had been gone for another year and a half. The
depositions contain references to a rumor that Sarepta had killed
Josiah, which no one actually believed, but no one mentioned
divorce. Josiah lived nearby with his sister or sister-in-law, who was
deposed. Between the trial and Drury's appeal, in September 1827,
Sarepta sued Josiah for arrears of child support.[48] Evidently Drury's
lawyers, Lewis Bigelow and Aaron Brooks Jr., did not raise
a coverture-related objection but, presumably, understood Hix to be
entitled to sue as a single woman because that was how she lived.

The impact of coverture was raised head-on six years later in *Bacon
v. Holbrook*. Alice Holbrook had been spreading rumors that Bacon
was sleeping with Alice's husband Willard, for whom Bacon worked as
a housekeeper. Bacon sued both Holbrooks, but Willard took no part
in the defense. In CP, Pliny Merrick defended the Holbrooks before
a jury. Losing, they appealed to SJC. However, when the case was
called, Bacon appeared but Willard did not. Merrick asked for leave to
represent Alice alone. Chief Justice Shaw refused and heard evidence
on damages only. The legal question was then put forward to the whole
bench, where Alice Holbrook was disappointed and Betsey Bacon was

[48] *Sarepta Hix v. Josiah Hix* (C.P. Worc., Sept. 1827). An absolute divorce was available
for adultery or impotency of either party, and a divorce from bed and board (i.e.
a legal separation) was available for extreme cruelty or utter desertion by either party,
or when the husband, being able to maintain the wife, "grossly or wantonly, and
cruelly" refused or neglected to do so: *Revised Statutes of Massachusetts*, c. 76, ss.
5 & 6 (1836). Charlotte Hunt, who sued Parnel and James Flahaven in slander, may
also have been married. She described herself simply as a boardinghouse keeper. The
defamatory allegation was that in the late 1820s Hunt had cohabited with a boarder
while both of them had living spouses. Perhaps her husband had died by 1835, when
she sued, but perhaps not.

ordered to recover her damages. Although the majority of appeals to the full bench were reported, this one was not. The strictness of the rules of coverture in Massachusetts courts, then, must be treated as unsettled, and perhaps changing, in the 1820s and 1830s: from this distance, the practice looks like "don't ask, don't tell."

Damages and Costs: The Incentives and Disincentives to Litigation

The strategic opportunities offered by the writ of attachment and the greater accessibility of courts and lawyers in Suffolk and Worcester, compared to Halifax and, more so, Pictou and Yarmouth, are factors that undoubtedly contributed to the greater prevalence of defamation cases in Massachusetts. As well, a plaintiff's odds of a windfall were greater, and the costs of starting an action and dropping it were likely to be lower.

Nova Scotia

Table 6.3 summarizes the outcomes of the Nova Scotia cases. Unlike Massachusetts, where cases began in CP and often moved to SJC, in Nova Scotia cases were brought at one level of court only, the NSSC in Halifax and Pictou, although probably also in the ICCP elsewhere in Nova Scotia. Plaintiffs prevailed more often than defendants. One clear pattern emerges: special juries made considerably larger awards than regular petit juries did. However, the highest damages were awarded after a sheriff's inquiry, in favor of an aggrieved Church of Scotland clergyman over a rival's allegations of bigamy. The prevalent attitudes in the Pictou area toward the defendant, Norman McLeod, are likely evident in this award. Awards of costs were also considerably higher when they included a special jury. Claims brought before special juries were evidently larger than those brought before petit juries, but – perhaps because the writ of attachment was not in use – the amount of the claim was frequently omitted from the records.

Some additional information will put these figures in perspective. The Commissioners' Courts, established in 1817, could address claims up to ten pounds. Their costs awards were generally well under one pound. Philip Girard characterizes debts between five and ten pounds as "medium-sized." Two shillings bought vegetables for

TABLE 6.3 Outcomes of the Nova Scotia cases

Case name	Jury	Claim	Outcome	Damages*	Costs
Crawley v. Forrester	special	unclear	P by jury†	£100	
Bowes v. A. Holland	special	£1,000	P by jury	£50	38..0..4‡
Fletcher v. Flohr	special	unclear	P by jury	£45	54..7..4
Ward v. English	special	unclear	P by jury	£40	29..13..8
Campbell v. McKay	likely petit	unclear	P by jury	£15	22..5..8
Hosking v. Thompson	petit	unclear	P by jury	£3	21..2..1
J. Heffler v. Maxner	petit	unclear	P by jury	40 s	20..4..6
McKenzie v. Ross	petit	£200	P by jury	40 s	17..6..4
Keating v. Sullivan	petit	unclear	P by jury	40 s	11..2..5
C. Heffler v. Goff	petit	unclear	P by jury	1 s	
Plummer v. Davie	petit	unclear	P by jury		0..5..0
Fraser v. McLeod		unclear	P: D's plea failed – sheriff's inquiry on damages	£250	12..11..7
Anderson v. Reid		unclear	P: D "says nothing" – sheriff's inquiry on damages	£1	13..6..10
Doyle v. Hefler		unclear	P: D admitted liability	5..6..8	12..19..7
Fraser v. A. Holland	special	£5,000	D by jury		31..19..3
Fraser v. Patterson	special	unclear	D by jury		56..5..0

(*continued*)

W. Thomas v. Philips	petit	£500	D – P nonsuit	6..16..6
D. Thomas v. Philips	petit	£500	D – P nonsuit	6..16..6
W. Holland v. Kenty	petit	£500	D – P nonsuit	6..5..1
Dore v. McLennan	petit	unclear	D – P nonsuit	5..13..6
Walker v. Scott	petit	unclear	hung jury	
Bissett v. Hawthorn	petit	unclear	discontinued	
Hobson v. Hobson	petit	unclear	unclear	

* Halifax currency was used for record-keeping although no actual notes or coins represented it. Before 1834, £1 sterling bought £1.11 in Halifax currency. In 1834, by statute £1 sterling was pegged at £1.25, Halifax currency (£1, 5s). A variety of coins circulated. See McCullough, *Money*, 142–51, 289–92 and Curtis, "History of the Canadian Currency."

† The record book entries for *Crawley v. Forrester* and *Bowes v. Holland* both note a subsequent motion to set aside the verdict unless certain evidence was produced within a few days. The case file for *Bowes v. Holland* indicates that costs were ordered, and Bowes's lawyer (R.J. Uniacke) entered the case on the record, so that appeal evidently failed. As the *Crawley v. Forrester* case file has not survived, it is unclear whether or not Anne and Henry Crawley recovered damages or what costs were ordered.

‡ Thirty-eight pounds, 0 shillings, 4 pence. This is the notation in the court records.

a couple of days. Subscriptions to most newspapers cost between five and twenty shillings. In 1828, taking the stage from Halifax to Pictou cost two pounds.[49] Damage awards of under five pounds, then, were small. On the other hand, the chief justice's salary was £850 sterling from London plus substantial fees, which came to around £1,400 in Halifax currency in the early 1830s.[50] A damage award of £50 was a tidy sum, but only Reverend Fraser's award was really substantial.

Awards of costs added considerably to a defendant's risk, especially before a special jury, and could exceed damages if a regular jury heard the case or if no jury was involved. Each document created and each service performed had a price.[51] Lawyers' fees were included at least to some extent. After 1825, special jurors were normally paid five shillings per trial, while regular jurors were paid only one.[52] Trials with special juries tended to hear more witnesses, whose fees could be higher than jurors'. Apparently even plaintiffs who won less than forty shillings' damages might receive full costs, although Charles Heffler in my sample did not.[53] Defendants who did not contest liability kept their cost awards at around thirteen pounds.

What if a plaintiff initiated a suit and then dropped it? Nonsuited plaintiffs were subjected to costs in the range of six pounds. Currency valuation is complex, but these cost awards appear to have been worth about twenty-six dollars, more than the highest of the recorded cost awards made against Massachusetts plaintiffs nonsuited in CP. On the

---

[49] Records of the Court of Commissioners for the Summary Trial of Actions [misidentified as Halifax Supreme Court, Court of Commissioners for the Summary Trial of Actions], vol. 23, RG 39 M, NSA; Girard, Patriot Jurist, 161–62; A Housekeeper [pseud.], letter to the editor, *Novascotian* (Halifax), August 16, 1827; Patterson, *History of Pictou*, 391. Newspapers noted their prices on their mastheads.

[50] See Phillips and Miller, "Too Many Courts and Too Much Law," 94–95.

[51] For example, the costs for an 1834 nondefamation trial (*Crawford v. Cowan*) included ten shillings for the retainer, three for the warrant and *praecipe*, a six-shilling fee for the first term of court in which the case was addressed and an additional six shillings each time the case was continued to a new term (which happened seven times), three shillings for an affidavit, £1..3..4 for the examination of a witness, £1..14 for the chief justice's fee, £2..10 for the prothonotary's, £1..4 for two separate juries, £3..6 each for three notices of trial, £2..6..8 for the "counsel fee," and additional items. The total was £19..14..8: 1834 Supreme Court Attorney General, Lawyers' and Court Costs (Miscellaneous) file, Supreme Court Halifax, Lawyers' Costs & Accounts, Bills, etc., 1834–81, vol. 36, RG 39 M, NSA.

[52] *An Act Relating to Special Juries*, S.N.S. 1825, c. 24.

[53] See letter to the editor, *Colonial Patriot* (Pictou), June 4, 1828.

whole, in Nova Scotia, damages were seldom enormous; even defaulting defendants apparently did not pay the whole claim, as sheriffs would conduct inquiries on damages. Costs of suit were an important consideration for both parties as they decided how to proceed.

Massachusetts

Massachusetts claims ranged from $20 to $10,000.[54] Of the thirteen claims for less than $1,000 one came from Worcester and one from Norfolk. The two smallest claims were for $20, the maximum jurisdiction of the Suffolk Justices' Court, from which they were appeals. In another five cases, also all from Suffolk, the claim was for $70. Constables' jurisdiction may be the key determinant: they could serve writs in their own towns in personal actions for up to $70 and may have been more readily available than sheriffs.[55] All of these smallest-stakes cases resulted in default judgments, and the cost awards, regardless of which party defaulted, ranged from none to over $21. Two of the other six cases – both from Suffolk – resulted in default judgments at CP; the other four went on to SJC, where one ended in default, one went to referees and two to juries.

The most commonly claimed amount was also the median, $2,000. No inflationary pattern is evident in the data overall or when examined according to the gender of the plaintiff: large and small claims are scattered throughout the period, even for the reported cases. Leaving aside the very small Suffolk claims, there is no discernible relationship between the claim and the likelihood that the case would go to a jury; claims of all sizes were addressed outside the courtroom. However, the claims in appealed, and especially reported, cases tended to be higher than the claims overall.[56]

---

[54] I have the claims for ninety cases.
[55] Sheriffs' and constables' fees were $0.30 for uncomplicated service and $0.50 where the service involved attaching property or arresting someone. Travel costs were additional. See *Revised Statutes of Massachusetts*, c. 15, s. 71 and c. 122, ss. 5 & 8 (1836).
[56] I have the claim in twenty of the thirty reported cases (two being reported on the decision on costs and for which I do not have the claim). The median and mode is $2,000 in these cases as well, but the lowest claim was $500 (one case), and the highest $5,000 (four cases). In eight cases the claim was for more than $2,000, and in

Pots of Gold: Damages Awarded by Juries

Although plaintiffs tended to win defamation suits in both places, in
Nova Scotia damage awards were more predictable, generally smaller,
and strongly conditioned on the type of jury employed. The chance of
hitting the jackpot was higher in Massachusetts.

In both places, plaintiffs usually won before juries. In the thirteen
Nova Scotia cases whose results before juries are decisive and clear,
only one plaintiff lost: Simon Fraser, who lost two suits over
allegations he mistreated immigrants on one of his ships. Similarly, in
all the jury trials in both courts in Suffolk and Worcester, plaintiffs
won at least thirty and probably thirty-one and defendants seven;
referees awarded damages to plaintiffs in four.

Plaintiffs' claims always substantially exceeded their awards.
Winning one-third of the claim was a great success in
Massachusetts, and many plaintiffs won much less. The largest
award went to Peter Fay – $2,000 over an allegation of incest –
but he had claimed $10,000. When James Clark was awarded half
of his $2,000 claim against Amos Binney – a higher proportion
than any other plaintiff – Binney appealed, arguing that the jury
must have been *"inflamed by public prejudice"* against him, as an
evidently unpopular naval agent. In this case and others in the mid-
1820s, the SJC declined to interfere with the verdict, indicating that
only "flagrantly outrageous" verdicts that obviously showed the
jury's partiality might be overturned.[57] The SJC similarly refused
to reduce the second-highest award in my Massachusetts sample, of
$1,400 to the young Essex teacher Sophia Bodwell, or the awards
of $707.50 and $591.67 to Isaac Shute and Lydia Oakes, accused
by a local notable of adulterous cohabitation while running an
almshouse. The awards stood, despite the defendant's argument

---

five it was for less. In the cases overall for which I have the claims, thirty-one were for
more than $2,000 and thirty-three for less. Of the six appealed cases that were not
reported, three had claims for less than $2,000, two for $2,000, and one for $10,000.
The Suffolk and Worcester cases show the same pattern: thirteen cases went to
appeal, for which I have the claim in twelve. The median and mode is $2,000, with
three claims for smaller amounts (two at $1,000, one at $1,500) and five for larger
(two each for $3,000 and $5,000, one for $6,000). In none of the reported appealed
cases from Suffolk and Worcester was the claim for less than $2,000.

[57] *Clark v. Binney*, 19 Mass. (2 Pick.) 113, 119 (1824), emphasis in original.

that Oakes was too unrefined to have suffered reputational damages of that magnitude. Juries maintained and exercised this discretion throughout the 1820s and 1830s, evaluating who was responsible for what had happened, how much harm had occurred, and what the defendant should pay.

Table 6.4 compares the Massachusetts and Nova Scotia damage awards.[58]

In Massachusetts, the median award was $300; over half the Nova Scotia awards were below $50. The highest and lowest Massachusetts jury awards were for libel: the allegation of incest against Peter Fay arose from a court filing that had circulated more broadly than necessary; at the other extreme, an Essex jury contemptuously awarded $1 to Alfred Pike, the preceptor of a school, against the editors of the *Boston Morning Post* over articles charging Pike with grossly neglecting a child in his care.[59]

---

[58] All the awards in my sample are represented, whether or not they were superseded by later events such as appeals or defaults, and whether or not the jury also determined liability. As noted, £1 Halifax currency was pegged by statute at £0.90 sterling. Conversion rates between the British pound sterling and the American dollar can be well established from 1791 on, according to www.measuringworth.com, which cites as the author Lawrence H. Officer of the Department of Economics at the University of Illinois at Chicago. One pound sterling was worth US$4.76 in 1830, making £1 Halifax currency equivalent to US$4.284. The explanation of the conversion rate is as follows:

For 1791–1912 the exchange rate data pertain to what was called a 'sight' (or 'demand') bill of exchange. This meant that the buyer of British pounds paid in dollars immediately, but received the pounds after shipping the bill across the Atlantic and "presenting" it in London. Until 1879, in fact, "time" bills were the basis of exchange transactions. For example, a sixty-day bill would involve an additional sixty-three-day lag before receiving pounds – sixty days inherent in the bill itself plus three "days of grace." The time-bill data (1791–1878) are converted to a sight-bill basis by eliminating the interest-component associated with the additional lag beyond that for a hypothetical sight bill.

For an additional point of comparison, in Halifax in 1830, four American dollars were treated as equivalent to £1 Halifax currency. It is difficult to know whether to use the 4:1 ratio, which takes no account of the buying power of one American dollar in the United States or the vicissitudes of Haligonian uses of various coins, or the conversion rates based on trade through London. I have chosen the latter, as seeming more stable.

[59] "Alfred Pike v. Charles G. Greene," *Boston Investigator*, December 11, 1835.

TABLE 6.4 Comparison of damage awards in Massachusetts and Nova Scotia

Court	$0–$49	$50–99	$100–$199	$200–$299	$300–$399	$400–$499	$500–$599	$600–$699	$700–$799	$800–$899	Above $900
Mass. CP	4	1	0 or 1	2	3	1	1				2 ($1,200, $2,000)
Mass. SJC	7	5	3	2	5	3	4	2	2	1	3 ($1,000, $1,250 & $1,400)
NSSC	6	1	2	1		1					

These ranges are broadly comparable to those Andrew King has found mentioned in reported cases from 1800 to 1830, but King notes a somewhat smaller portion of low-value awards and a higher proportion of higher-value ones.[60] Similarly, of the eighteen appealed cases for which I have damage awards, half involved damage awards of $500 and more, which is the same ratio as among the fourteen of these cases that are reported.

The only Nova Scotian damage award comparable to the highest Massachusetts awards was £250 (worth about $1,071), awarded to Reverend Donald Fraser by a Pictou-based sheriff's inquiry. It lay at the low end of the high Massachusetts awards. The other sheriff's inquiry in the Nova Scotia sample, also held in Pictou, determined damages at one pound. Massachusetts referees' awards, similarly, ranged from $40 to $225, below the median of jury awards. On the whole, then, a would-be Massachusetts plaintiff could hope for a larger award of damages than could a similarly situated Nova Scotian.

The Costs of Stopping: Massachusetts versus Nova Scotia

Not only was the jackpot bigger in Massachusetts, but the costs of initiating a suit and dropping it were lower. Table summarizes the results as the Suffolk and Worcester cases passed through the courts. In Common Pleas in Massachusetts, pleadings were tested, juries sometimes heard trials and cases were occasionally sent to referees. Most jury trials took place in Supreme Judicial Court, and some cases then went to appeal. Table 6.5 demonstrates the progress of the cases through the court system.

Less than half of the seventy-four cases ended with jury or referee verdicts. The majority ended when one party did not take a necessary next step. In a large minority of cases, notations in the records indicate that an agreement accompanied a nonappearance or default judgment. Steiner's findings about Lincoln's law practice are echoed here: the vast majority of Lincoln's defamation cases ended

---

[60] In a sample of seventy-five awards, King finds 24 percent for $99 or less, 57 percent between $100 and $999; and 19 percent for more than $1,000: "Law of Slander in Early Antebellum America," 22.

TABLE 6.5 Progress of Worcester and Suffolk cases through Massachusetts courts. Plaintiff successes begin with the letter P in the Outcome column; defendant successes begin with the letter D. The cases in the last four rows terminated in ways that were not clearly favorable to one side or the other and begin with the letter S, for stalemate. Italics indicate that the case involved an appeal on the law. Shading indicates that the parties chose the outcomes themselves, through discontinuing the proceedings, failing to appear in court or coming to an agreement. Rows without shading indicate outcomes determined by outsiders, such as judges, juries or referees. (W is Worcester; S is Suffolk)

# cases & county	Claim	Final level of court	Outcome	Damages	Costs
1W	$1,000	CP	P: D defaulted, papers not filed		
6S	$20–$1,000	CP	P: D defaulted, judgment issued	$0.01–$70	$0–$21.55
3W, 8S	$20–$5,000	CP	D: P nonsuit/default	$0	$0.01–$21.15
1W	$5,000	CP	D: P wrong writ, case continued on costs	0	unclear
2W	$1,000, $2,000	CP	P by referees	$225, $200	$50.04, $85.95
2W, 3S	$1,000–$10,000	CP	P by jury	$5–$2000	unspecified to $45.93
0		CP	D by jury		
1W	$1,000	SJC	P: P on demurrer in CP, appeal entered, stopped	[$1,000*]	unspecified
0		SJC	P: P on demurrer in CP, D defaulted		

(continued)

1W, 2S	$1,000–$3,000	SJC	P: D on demurrer in CP, D defaulted	$0.01–$50	$0–$51.36
3W, 4S	$300–$5,000	SJC	D: D on demurrer in CP, appeal entered but P nonsuit/default/ discontinued	0	$9.09–$143.49
1S	$2,000	SJC	D: P on demurrer in CP, P nonsuit/default/discontinued	0	$262.27
2W	$6,000,	SJC	*– nonsuit upheld on appeal/ appeal discontinued*		$100.80,
	$1,000				*unstated*
1S	$1,000	SJC	D: D by jury in CP, P nonsuit in SJC	0	$68.06
1W	*$1,000*	SJC	*P: P by jury in CP, D defaulted, default upheld on appeal*	*$307.05*	$203.79
1W	$3,000	SJC	P: P on demurrer in CP, agreement in SJC	$157.61	0
1W, 1S	$2,000, $500	SJC	P: P on demurrer in CP, P by referees in SJC	$100, $200	$109.60, $109.25
4W, 5S	$2,000– $10,000	SJC	P: D on demurrer in CP, P by jury in SJC	$15–$600	$3.75– $281.39

(continued)

TABLE 6.5 (continued)

# cases & county	Claim	Final level of court	Outcome	Damages	Costs
1 W, 2S	$2,000, $3,000		– verdict upheld on appeal	$512.16–$1,015	$68.39–$376.75
1 W	$5,000		– D successful appeal but P won second jury trial too	$450	$176.13
2 W, 2S	$1,000, $2,000	SJC	P by jury in both courts	$55.18–$350	$69.83–$246.37
0			P: D by jury in CP, P by jury in SJC		
1 W, 1S	$1,000–$3,000	SJC	P on demurrer in CP, P by jury in SJC	$89.50–$775	$48.38–$85.60
1 W	$2,000		– verdict upheld on appeal	$307.70	$172.13
1S	$300	SJC	D on demurrer in CP, D by jury	0	$35.46
1 W	$1,500		– verdict upheld on appeal	0	$97.23
1 W	$5,000	SJC	D by jury in CP, D by jury in SJC, P successful appeal but D won before second jury too	0	$188.31
1S	$2,000	SJC	D: P on demurrer in CP, D by jury	0	unspecified

(continued)

$_2$S	$5,000	SJC	S: P on demurrer in CP, apology accepted in SJC	o	o
$_1$S	$3,000	SJC	S: D on demurrer in CP, P by jury in SJC, new trial ordered, stopped		
$_1$W	unclear	SJC	S: D on demurrer in CP, D by jury in SJC, new trial ordered, stopped		
$_1$S	unclear	SJC	S: hung jury, stopped		

* The plaintiff likely settled for less.

well short of trial.[61] Harmonious relations may have been restored (Steiner observes that Lincoln emphasized his role as a peacemaker), but the strategic ends that defamation suits – and the writ of attachment – could serve were presumably addressed as well when parties decided to end suits themselves.

A party who decided not to continue faced an order of costs. Statutes periodically amended the law of costs throughout the period, to discourage frivolous appeals and to encourage parties with small claims to turn to justices of the peace rather than CP. Modest allowances were set for attorneys' fees, and these were lower if no issue was joined – if, for example, a party defaulted or apologized. Limits were placed on costs awarded for attending court and for traveling. Costs were taxed – formally assessed – by the court clerk.[62]

It was of course generally cheaper to default earlier in the proceedings, in CP rather than SJC. Orders of costs bore no relation to the amount of the claim but were determined by the steps taken in the case, as adjusted through negotiation. The lowest award of costs made against a defaulting plaintiff in SJC was $29.50 against a litigious character called Eliakim Davis in Worcester; Davis and his sons figured in several cases in the early 1820s so likely used the courts strategically. The highest recorded award of costs made against a defaulting plaintiff was $262.27, a sum to which the parties apparently agreed. Another large award, $143.49, was made in *Clark v. Bishop*: a Havana-based merchant sued a Boston mariner over accusations the mariner made in Belfast. Probably witnesses abroad were deposed, which would have been expensive.

---

[61] Unless at least one party appeared, the court record books do not describe what the case was about, so such cases are generally missing from my sample. Because Steiner works from Lincoln's own records from 1836 to 1860, his sample contains these cases: in Lincoln's practice, only five of the thirty-seven slander suits initiated by plaintiffs actually went to trial. The others were dismissed, disappeared from the court docket, reached settlement in a consent judgment, were determined on demurrer, or ended when a party failed to take a necessary step. Only two default judgments were entered against plaintiffs. See Steiner, *Honest Calling*, 97–100.

[62] By an act of 1795, the party recovering costs in a civil cause was entitled to $2.50 as an attorney's fee in SJC when "an issue of law or fact [was] joined," and $1.25 otherwise. In CP, the corresponding allowances were $1.50 and $1.00. Parties themselves were allowed $0.33 for each day's attendance in court and $0.33 for every ten miles traveled. Each witness was owed a dollar for attending plus compensation for travel. See *Revised Statutes of Massachusetts*, c. 121, ss. 27, 28 & 32 and c. 122, s. 10 (1836).

Although awards of costs against defaulting plaintiffs were high in SJC, defaulting in CP was cheaper than in the NSSC.[63] In CP these awards ranged from $6.16 to $21.15, versus about $26 in NSSC. Not only, therefore, were potential damage awards larger in Massachusetts, but launching a suit and then dropping it before it reached court was cheaper than in Nova Scotia. People were incentivized to bring defamation claims to court; the strategic lure of the writ of attachment undoubtedly encouraged high estimates of damages.

Rational defendants should have defaulted more often than they did. The cost awards made against the three Nova Scotia defendants who defaulted ranged from twelve pounds to fourteen pounds, and they either confessed damages or had them assessed on a sheriff's inquiry: they did not simply pay the plaintiff's full claim. If they defended and faced a regular jury, their damages and costs could be lower than they would have been on default, but if they faced a special jury both damages and costs rose substantially. Most defendants lost before juries, paying costs if the plaintiff was awarded damages of at least forty shillings. Defaulting looks, at this distance, like the most sensible economic option for defendants, but few did so. Perhaps there was shame in defaulting or, in the heat of battle, they overestimated their odds of success.

Massachusetts defendants had similar prospects and acted similarly. In only two cases did plaintiffs win the full amount of their claims, for $20 and $70, along with costs of $21.55 and $6.91, respectively. In the other four defendant-default cases in which an order was made, the total award ranged from $0.01 to $50. Notes in the record books suggest that the very low cost awards ($0 or $0.01) reflect agreements. In SJC as well, agreements are noted in three cases in which defendants defaulted, with the total award ranging from $25 to $157.61. Although no sign of agreement is apparent, Nehemiah Kittredge, defaulting, was ordered to pay $0.01 in damages and $28.25 in costs. The only case in which a really large award of costs ($203.79) was made against a defaulting defendant was *Bacon v. Holbrook*, which had two juries and an appeal on the law. Betsey Bacon

---

probably had no reason to settle with Alice Holbrook on a smaller award.

These cases suggest, then, that as in the NSSC, a defendant who defaulted in CP was unlikely to face a large award of damages and might well negotiate over costs, which would in any case likely be smaller than in the NSSC. Waiting until SJC to default could raise the costs above the Nova Scotia level, but agreements could be made there too. Nonetheless, most defendants kept going. Before the doctrinal considerations that likely influenced parties' calculation are considered – especially the truth defense – the effects of geography and gender on how suits passed through the court system in Massachusetts require attention.

Variations on the Theme: Geography and Gender

Suffolk versus Worcester

CP was used somewhat differently in Suffolk and Worcester. In this section, I consider the passage through the CP in those counties of the forty-two defamation cases in which decisions are recorded in the record books for selected years.[64] Judges in CP heard appeals from the Suffolk Justices' Court, tried actions with juries, and ruled on the pleadings in cases that would go on to SJC. Nineteen of these cases came from Worcester and twenty-three from Suffolk. Table 6.6 summarizes the outcomes for these cases.

Default judgments were entered in all seven of the lowest-value cases in Suffolk, for twenty dollars and seventy dollars. The records hint at some kind of negotiated outcome in three of these cases; in four the cost awards are substantial enough to suggest that the defaulting party simply did not appear. The Worcester CP passed more cases through to SJC for trial. Lawyers may be a factor: they are more evident in the Worcester records and may have been more energetic about inserting themselves into disputes – and probably once one party got a lawyer, the other did too. The Suffolk CP records, although

---

[64] Worcester: all terms for 1825, 1830, 1835 and 1840 plus two terms from 1820 to 1821; Suffolk: all of 1825, 1830 and 1835 plus one term of 1820. I include the case begun with the wrong writ, in which Maria Goffe attempted to bring a slander claim against a third party who was reputedly holding the defendant's assets to protect them from creditors. The court ruled against her, and the case continued on costs.

TABLE 6.6 Outcomes in Common Pleas

County	Default/nonsuit	Referees	Jury	Pleadings
Worcester	4*	2	3	10
Suffolk	14	0	3	6

* Two cases were sent to referees but ended in default judgments.

perhaps simply less fulsome, seem to contain more self-represented plaintiffs beginning and dropping suits.[65] Perhaps greater proximity to the courthouse in Suffolk meant parties chose not to employ lawyers and managed cases themselves at CP. In both counties, around one-third of the cases were decided by the parties themselves at SJC: these cases had generally passed through CP on the pleadings, so lawyers would presumably normally have been involved.[66]

Gender

Women were far more often parties to defamation suits in Massachusetts than in Nova Scotia. Nova Scotia had Anne Crawley; Massachusetts had twenty-five women plaintiffs and nine women defendants, of whom four were sued on their own and five with their husbands.[67] Their actions suggest the strategic effects of their dependence on men – their husbands, guardians *ad litem* and lawyers – their vulnerability to reputational harm as participants in the paid workforce and in other capacities, and their belief that the

[65] Although counsel were usually not noted in Suffolk default cases, they may sometimes have been present anyway: in *Weafer v. Parker*, although Samuel D. Parker was not mentioned in the main record of the case, in a separate note he acknowledged receipt of damages as counsel for Weafer. In two cases, the defendant defaulted but the court order (for $0.01 damages in both cases and $0.01 in costs in one case and none in the other) referred to the consent of the parties.

[66] The Suffolk record books less often deliberately record the lawyers' names, but sometimes they are mentioned as having signed off on receipt of damages or costs: likely the court clerk was more assiduous in Worcester and lawyers often simply went unmentioned in Suffolk. No particular pattern is evident in the outcomes of the cases that note lawyers versus those that do not.

[67] I include here Maria Goffe, who sued using the wrong writ. Sophia Bodwell sued for libel; the other women sued for slander. Benjamin Crosby and William Tolman sued women for slander; Ezekiel Remington sued for libel.

legal system should provide a remedy for reputational harm they suffered and its consequences.

The range of claims women brought over harm from other women's words was broadly similar to the range of claims over men's words, but the damages juries awarded were smaller, ranging from $5 to $320, and the only jury award against a woman who was apparently single was for $25, against a widow named Sally Putnam. Only three men sued over women's words, alleged to have damaged the men's reputations, and all sued married couples; in *Remington v. Congdon*, the libel – a complaint to a church – had been signed by both spouses. Perhaps married women's speech was more harmful, or perhaps single women seldom had the assets to satisfy a judgment. Most likely, however, men sued women to attack their husbands too, at least sometimes because of abiding conflicts: *Remington v. Congdon* arose from another conflict, and Susanna Williams probably did not, out of nowhere, suddenly allege that William Tolman had sodomized a cow: a jury awarded him $225 in damages.[68]

Table 6.7 shows claims over reputational harm to women as a proportion of the total number of claims I have of each magnitude.

Women's claims tended to be lower than men's, largely due to outliers. Three of the seven lowest-value claims had women plaintiffs, and all four of the highest-value claims were brought by men claiming damage for harm done by other men. Otherwise, four women brought claims below the median ($2,000) and seven above it.

TABLE 6.7 Massachusetts women's claims and their frequency

County	$20 / $70	$300 / $500	$1,000 / $1,500	$2,000*	$3,000 / $4,000	$5,000 / $6,000	$10,000	Total
Suffolk	3/7	1/4	0/5	1/9	0/3	3/8	0/2	8/38
Worcester	0	0/1	2/9	5/10	1/4	1/6	0/1	9/31
Other	0	0/1	1/4	4/6	0/4	2/4	0/1	7/20

* Median and mode. I lack the claim in one Suffolk case.

[68] Benjamin Crosby was nonsuited, and I lack the award in *Remington v. Congdon*.

Women who sued on their own tended to claim higher damages and be more likely to take their cases before juries than did women who sued with their husbands or guardians, all of whom were men. Women were less likely to sue alone in Suffolk than in the other counties. Table 6.8 summarizes women's claims. "WM" refers to a woman who sued with her husband or guardian. Parentheses indicate the number of plaintiffs in the category who were minors (no defendants were minors).

Of the ten cases in which a woman sued with a man (for one of which I lack the claim), eight did not reach juries. In my dataset, only Abigail and Samuel Fales settled for apologies in their two suits against women shopkeepers in Boston. The frequency of default judgments resembles that in the dataset overall: the four lowest-value Suffolk CP cases and one median claim from Worcester ended in defaults. Seven cases in the whole dataset were ordered to be sent to referees, and referees decided five of these, of which two had women plaintiffs and one a woman defendant. All three women were accompanied by men in their actions. The other two cases were brought by men against men. The damages referees awarded ranged from $40 to $225 – below the median ($300) – and the damages women suing with men won when defendants defaulted were $20, $50 and a single penny.

Neither of the women who sued with men and whose cases reached juries was awarded damages above the median.[69] Women's cases mainly reached juries if the women were suing on their own; if they did so, their damages tended to be higher. Seven of the nine cases brought by women alone in Suffolk (2) and Worcester (5) reached juries. Two finished in CP and five in SJC (male plaintiffs were less likely to stop at CP).[70] Women acting alone, then, were less likely than men to negotiate resolutions out of court or to turn to referees, looking to courts instead for final judgments. The more common practice of

[69] *Miller v. Parish* ($300) and *Sanborn v. Lane* ($200).

[70] In Suffolk and Worcester, twenty-one adult male plaintiffs and one male minor, all suing men, took their cases through to SJC juries, sometimes also appealing on the law. Only three men's cases stopped with juries at CP. I include *Bacon v. Holbrook* in the cases that ended with jury verdicts at SJC because although the case formally ended in a default owing to Willard Holbrook's nonappearance, both Betsey Bacon and Alice Holbrook were prepared to argue the case, and the jury assessed damages. It was not a negotiated ending.

TABLE 6.8 Claims of women who sued alone versus those of women accompanied by men

	$20 / $70	$300 / $500	$1,000 / $1,500	$2,000	$3,000 / $4,000	$5,000 / $6,000	$10,000	Total
Suffolk								
WM v WM*								0
WM v M	2 (2)							2 (2)
WM v W	1	1				2		4
W v M						1		1
W v WM				1				1
W v W								0
Worcester								
WM v WM								0
WM v M				2 (1)				2 (1)
WM v W								0

(continued)

	$20/$70	$300/$500	$1,000/$1,500	$2,000	$3,000/$4,000	$5,000/$6,000	$10,000	Total
W v M			1	3		1†		5
W v WM		1						1
W v W				1				1
Other Counties								
WM v WM								0
WM v M			1 (1)	1 (1)				2 (2)
WM v W								0
W v M				2		2		4
W v WM				1				1
W v W								0
Total	3(2)	1	3 (1)	11 (2)		6		24(5)

* I lack the claim for *Sanborn v. Lane*.
† *Goffe v. Preston*, begun with the wrong writ

retaining lawyers in Worcester may well have left its fingerprints on
these cases.

Women suing alone – especially young women whose careers were
jeopardized – had considerable success before juries; indeed, some
male defendants appealed these verdicts as patently unreasonable.
The appellate judgments in these cases were reported, sending
a signal to lawyers and similarly situated clients. As well as the seven
jury verdicts from Suffolk and Worcester, my sample contains five
cases brought by women alone in other counties that went to juries.
One was for $1,000, seven were for $2,000, one was for $3,000, and
three were for $5,000. All of these plaintiffs won, but the damages
awarded in the cases that were appealed and reported were greater
than the damages in the other cases. In the six unreported cases, all
from Suffolk and Worcester, three awards exceeded the overall median
($320, $500 and $1,200) versus four in the six reported cases
($591.67, $866, $1,250 and $1,400). Three of the five Massachusetts
damage awards for over $900 were awarded to women.

Two of these highly successful plaintiffs were teachers who sued
over allegations of sexual indiscretions that threatened their
employment. Paulina Whiting was in her early twenties and Sophia
Bodwell, who sued twice, was twenty-nine. Bodwell was awarded only
$150 against Sena and Caleb Swan. Sena had evidently been spreading
rumors, but it was Benjamin Osgood – against whom Bodwell was
awarded $1,400 in damages – who wrote the school committee as part
of a systematic campaign to have her removed from her post. Karen
V. Hansen estimates that Bodwell might have earned perhaps nine
dollars a month teaching.[71] Represented by two of the most
prominent lawyers of the time, Leverett Saltonstall and Daniel
Webster, Osgood unsuccessfully appealed the damages. Justice
Samuel Wilde held that the damages, though large, did not warrant
interference: "[t]he plaintiff being an unprotected female, having
nothing whereon to depend but an unblemished reputation, and the
defendant being a man of wealth and influence."[72] After the reported
judgments in this case, plus Whiting's in 1831 and the wealthy young
widow Laura Howe's in 1834 for $1,250 over a local gossipmonger's

---

[71] Hansen, *Very Social Time*, 130.
[72] *Bodwell v. Osgood*, 20 Mass. (3 Pick.) 379, 385 (1825).

allegations of sexual improprieties, the courts' signal that large awards were available to women was clear.

Other women who brought claims over allegations made in the context of work were also notably successful, especially if they were young. Although they tended not to plead that they had lost means of self-support doing domestic work for nonrelatives, the claims of at least nine women (two minors) arose in this context. One of the five who were under twenty-five, Suffolk minor Hannah Hardy, was nonsuited, and the case brought by the other minor, Louisa Sanderson, went to referees who awarded Sanderson $100. Juries awarded Mary Hayden $300 over an allegation of theft, Lucy Barrows $500 over allegations of theft and perjury, and Mary Knowlton $1,200 over an allegation that she had slept with her married employer.[73] Of the four older women who sued for harm in this kind of context, one won only $5 in damages (the jury probably guessed that something was going on between Charlotte Hunt and her boarder even if it could not be proven), but juries awarded the other three more substantial sums: almost $600 to the almshouse-worker Lydia Oakes and $300 each to Sarepta Hix and Betsey Bacon. By contrast to these and the three teacher cases, in the ten cases in which women's claims did not evidently arise in the context of work for nonrelatives, smaller damages and default verdicts were more common.[74]

These working women's successes before juries in the 1820s and 1830s – and especially the large awards made to Whiting, Bodwell and Oakes between 1825 and 1831 – signal a level of acceptance of women as workers that has not been emphasized in previous work on other places and times. By the 1820s in Massachusetts – but not Nova Scotia – women were generally literate and were moving into textile mills, teaching and paid writing. They were also active in voluntary associations, increasingly aimed at abolition, social reform and at times women's rights. In Nova Scotia, some women supported themselves, but the Nova Scotia scholarship does not suggest that it

[73] The contexts for *Glezen v. Draper* and *Weafer v. Kelly* are unknown. Mary Hayden's age is unclear, but the contextual evidence strongly suggests that she should be included in this group.
[74] Maria Thayer was awarded $25 against an older widow, Sally Sanborn and her husband were awarded $175, and Jennett Miller was awarded $300. Abigail and Samuel Fales accepted apologies, and four other cases ended in default judgments. The wealthy young widow Laura Howe is the notable exception: she won $1,250.

was common for young women to work for pay, and women's
voluntary associations were charitable and not sites of rights
activism.[75] There were no mills and few schools outside Halifax, and
most of these, at least, were conducted by male teachers.[76] Whiting,
Bodwell and Osgood brought their cases when most young women – or
at least their mothers – had worked outside their homes at some point
in their lives, often as teachers, and before the backlash against "Fanny
Wrightism" really took hold and the "cult of domesticity" pulled and
pushed young women to seek fulfillment and safety at the fireside.[77]

As well, Massachusetts women, like men, evidently saw courts as
sites for redress for reputational harm and perhaps tactical

[75] Criticism of married women's rights appeared in print very rarely, and these articles
often treated the matter as entertainment: see e.g. "Law of Divorce in England,"
Wesleyan (Halifax), September 24, 1838; "Authority of Husbands," *Yarmouth
Herald*, August 10, 1838; M.M. [pseud.], "Law to the Ladies," *Novascotian*
(Halifax), July 6, 1826. Other articles reminded and reassured readers of English
women's exalted status: see e.g. "The Women of England," *Novascotian* (Halifax),
January 10, 1828. On aspects of the struggle for women's rights in Massachusetts, see
Avery and Konefsky, "Daughters of Job."

[76] Historians generally agree that by 1830 the literacy rate for white men and women
approached 100 percent in New England. See Gilmore, *Reading Becomes a Necessity*,
116–17; Sklar "Schooling of Girls," 511; Horowitz, *Rereading Sex*, 44. Julian Gwyn,
in a study of court records from the second half of the eighteenth century, notes that
female literacy seemed relatively high in Shelburne, where many Americans had
settled, low in Lunenburg, where there were few schools, and in between in
Halifax: "Female Litigants before the Civil Courts," 318. Schooling was patchy in
Nova Scotia, better in Halifax and urban areas than elsewhere. Although reforming
voices argued for change, schooling beyond the primary levels was accessible chiefly
to the sons of the elite, although Halifax had some small private schools for girls,
often run by women, that advertised teaching reading, composition, grammar, arith-
metic, geography, history, and not infrequently branches of natural philosophy,
botany and other sciences, as well as needlework, drawing, French and other orna-
mental subjects. See Verette, "The Spread of Literacy," 170; Cuthbertson, *Old
Attorney General*, 85–86; Murdoch, *Epitome of the Laws of Nova-Scotia*, 1:201–2;
Fingard, "Attitudes towards the Education of the Poor," 17–18; Winks, *Blacks in
Canada*, 135–37; Maximilian [pseud.], "Education," *Colonial Patriot* (Pictou),
January 18, 1828.

[77] Mary P. Ryan locates the rise of notions of feminine delicacy and the cult of domesticity between 1830 and 1850: *Empire of the Mother*, 41. Similarly, Susan L. Porter's
study of the life paths of four cohorts of orphaned Massachusetts girls who passed
through the Boston Female Asylum suggests a temporary rise between about 1825
and 1840 in the acceptability of young women moving out on their own and supporting themselves through skilled labor. See Porter, "Victorian Values in the
Marketplace." Thomas Leonard remarks that most New England women in the
early republic probably "worked for pay and lived in other people's households at
some point in their lives": *News for All*, 19. Women made up over half of the

opportunism as well. Courts' recognition of women as economic actors would have reinforced women's sense that they were right to bring such claims. The differences between women's usage of courts in Suffolk and Worcester, too, seems to hint that lawyers played a role in bringing women's claims to court and taking them through to trial. All of these factors contributed to bringing more Massachusetts than Nova Scotia women into courtrooms.

Defendants' Choices and the Lure of Truth

Although many Massachusetts defendants evidently settled out of court or abandoned their cases, more carried on than would seem warranted given their success rates and the damages and costs they faced if they lost. Perhaps they relished having their day in court, the chance to prove, through witnesses, that they had not said or meant what the plaintiff claimed or – most importantly – that they were justified by the circumstances or especially the truth of the allegations. Plaintiffs were not the only ones whose dignity was at stake in defamation cases.

It was an article of constitutional faith in Massachusetts that everyone had a right to express the truth with good motives and justifiable ends. However, as discussed in Chapter 4, beginning in 1818, judges made truth risky to plead and argue, because the special plea undermined defenses available under the general denial and could increase damages rather than mitigate them, a possibility that Chief Justice Parsons had introduced in 1807. Judges evaded the Massachusetts legislature's efforts to protect defendants. Even the legislature's elimination of special pleading in 1836 did not completely work, because judges continued to require defendants to supply details and make assertions that functioned like a special plea. Defendants had to assert and prove that the allegations were true. Juries were not to be invited to blame plaintiffs for contributing to their own woes. No comparable difficulties arose in Nova Scotia with respect to the truth plea.

Massachusetts teaching force by 1834 and a greater proportion by 1850: Bernard and Vinovskis, "Female School Teacher," 332–33.

How useful was the truth defense? First, it could be a bad strategy. Especially in Worcester, on their first appearance in court, lawyers continued to seek permission to plead double until special pleading was abolished, even though the protection it offered was dubious. These notations in the courts' record books – and their absences – hint at lawyers' consideration and rejection of the truth defense in specific cases. In the twenty-seven cases begun in CP in Worcester before 1836, permission to plead double was sought in at least nineteen and granted in all but one, *Hix v. Drury*, in which uncertainty about the new statute may have played a role. Defendants appear to have decided not to apply to plead double when the allegations were unprovable or the defendant already knew they were false. For example, John Burbank presumably realized that the man courting his daughter was neither bankrupt nor a would-be bigamist, much as Burbank evidently disliked him. Moses Child appears to have realized quickly that Reverend Charles Goodrich had not actually embezzled church money. Alice and Willard Holbrook certainly could not admit that Willard had committed adultery with Betsey Bacon. Signaling an intention to plead truth was unnecessary and probably would have raised tensions further. In a few other cases, defendants got leave to plead double but then decided not to raise a truth defense, probably for similar reasons. Sally Putnam, for example, did not attempt to prove that Maria Thayer had been sexually involved with her brother-in-law.

The much-vaunted truth defense was made in about half of the Worcester and Suffolk cases that reached juries before 1836, and it failed well over half of the time. Truth was pleaded in six Worcester and five Suffolk cases, and in one other case in each county the defendant was allowed to give evidence of truth under the general issue. Defendants prevailed before juries in two of each county's cases, probably because of the truth defense: there was no question in these cases of privilege, or of ambiguities in the meaning of the allegations, their application to the plaintiff, or other questions that might have absolved the defendant. Similarly, among the cases from the other counties for which I have the records, the defendant prevailed in one case out of seven in which truth was raised in defense.

This rate of success for a truth defense is similar to Abraham Lincoln's: his defendants were wholly successful only four times in the twenty-one cases in which the plea was raised. Steiner thinks that the evidence of truth may have mitigated damages in several other cases.[78] Judges in Massachusetts, led by Charles Jackson, attempted to curtail this possibility, but what probably actually happened is that the plea aggravated the damages when the jury thought it unfounded but mitigated them when it left the jury with doubts. Damages against Benjamin Osgood were likely increased because he had investigated Sophia Bodwell's sexual history but then not argued truth, which the judge suggested raised the inference that Osgood knew his allegations were false when he made them. However, truth was argued before at least seven of the seventeen juries that awarded damages of less than $100. In all of these cases it seems likely that the evidence introduced through the truth defense – of adultery, unethical behavior and attempted sexual assault – raised enough doubt about the plaintiffs' innocence to inspire low awards of damages. It is difficult to assess how such evidence affected jury awards in the midrange cases, but if the oral evidence in *Hix v. Drury* did not clarify what emerges from the enormous stack of surviving depositions, that jury was likely uncertain: Hix's award of $300 may have reflected a kind of sympathetic compromise.

Even though truth pleas usually failed, the evidence led under them could reduce the damages awarded, at times to an amount less than what a plaintiff would have been likely to consent to or referees to order. And a truth defense was still a defendant's best bet: of the twelve juries that found for defendants, four heard truth defenses, one heard truth introduced under the general issue, two heard privilege defenses and five heard neither. Under such circumstances, it is understandable that defendants convinced of the rightness of their allegations would have gone ahead with the case, despite the law's tilt in favor of the plaintiff.

Procedure and law incentivized individuals in both places to bring defamation claims, but the incentives were stronger in Massachusetts, where the costs awarded against a plaintiff who dropped a suit or lost were lower (undoubtedly at least partly because the parties bore their own lawyers' costs in Massachusetts) and the odds of a windfall higher. Such actions could be used to punish proud older men who

[78] *Honest Calling*, 93–94.

threw their weight around, to redeem the reputations of ordinary people, to salvage finances, and to raise the stakes and complicate the proceedings in other actions in which the parties were engaged. In both places defendants seem to have contested the claims against them less out of carefully calculated economic self-interest than out of a desire to fight the fight, probably often feeling that truth was on their side and would help them more than it usually did. The truth defense usually failed, but it was often their best shot, at least reducing damages, despite the (confused) law on this point. Occasionally a failed truth defense aggravated the damages.

Conclusion: Rights Claims and Courts

In Massachusetts and Nova Scotia, plaintiffs in defamation suits tended to come from the broad middle tier of white society. These suits were often entangled with other disputes. Libel claims were less common than slander and usually involved newspapers. Women were far more often parties in Massachusetts. Men settled their suits more often than did women, possibly because men's suits were more often strategic in the first place. Women were more likely to take their cases to juries and win large awards of damages when they retained lawyers on their own than when they were represented by husbands or guardians.

The importance of reputation was not the key to the different litigation rates over defamation in these places. The discourse of the 1820s and 1830s reveals no disagreements over the importance of reputation or individual dignity in the two places. Men sued over the same types of harm, with law contributing to this convergence by dictating the classes of slander that were actionable per se. Allegations of behavior tainted with dishonesty inspired the majority of suits in both places. Massachusetts women claimed to be entitled to function as economic actors without being waylaid by defamation. Newspapers' harder-edged criticism probably inspired some men to bring criminal rather than civil proceedings. The desire to be seen to be seeking redemption rather than money probably played a role as well.

A similar ambivalence about litigation characterized the two places. Andrew King has suggested that the revolutionary ideology of equal rights undergirded a broad sense of an entitlement to sue over reputation.[79] However, news and ideology flowed freely across the border, and in Nova Scotia, which lacked much socioeconomic stratification, the constitutional rights of Englishmen offered the same promises.

Rivalry between journalists and lawyers in both places complicates the interpretation of attitudes to courts: journalists often thought lawyers had too much political influence.[80] However, participants and onlookers seldom evinced distrust or dislike of the system's treatment of civil defamation in either place. Importantly, though, those of African descent, Indigenous people and linguistic minorities are conspicuous by their entire absence from cases in both places. The joy that Black spectators expressed when Robert Morris, a young African American lawyer, won his first case, representing a Black man suing a white man for services rendered, strongly suggests that such sights were uncommon.[81]

Both places acknowledged the need for courts while being concerned about unnecessary litigation. Nova Scotian legislation of the 1830s aimed to reduce the costs of bringing small claims and discourage appeals, to increase the accessibility of courts, to simplify cross-actions, to ease evidentiary requirements, and to reduce the number of judges required to hear cases on circuit.[82] Evidently legislators thought litigation was too expensive, not that there was too much of it. As Jim Phillips and Bradley Miller

---

[79] "Law of Slander in Early Antebellum America," 7–8.

[80] For example, Benjamin Austin was a leader in the 1790s movement to curtail lawyers' influence over the legal system, and after 1800 the Republican party was split by tensions between these two groups; his nephew, James Trecothick Austin, became attorney general of Massachusetts. Similarly, while quoting the pronouncement of Scottish Whig politician, jurist and historian James Mackintosh about the constitutional importance of the press, Joseph Howe declared himself pleased to see a lawyer plowing his own field and thus conferring a benefit on society. See Pasley, *"Tyranny of Printers,"* 271–72; "Eastern Rambles," *Novascotian* (Halifax), July 13, 1831; Ottawalta [pseud.], "Fiat Justitia Ruat Coelum," *Novascotian* (Halifax), September 14, 1836.

[81] Horton and Horton, *Black Bostonians*, 56. For an expression of confidence in the system, see Farmer, *Report of a Trial*, 39–40.

[82] See e.g. *An Act for Reducing the Expenses of Suits at Law, in Certain Cases*, S.N.S. 1832, c. 53; *An Act for Preventing the Multiplicity of Law Suits*, S.N.S. 1833, c. 58; *An Act to Lessen the Expense of the Proof of Written Documents, in Actions*

demonstrate, the legislative debates about courts in the 1820s and 1830s similarly reveal that the main concerns were judicial fees and salaries, the superfluity of the ICCP, and the chief justice's membership in the colonial council. These debates had some Jacksonian overtones – concerns about judges living as local aristocrats, and lawyers coveting these plumb appointments – and some argued that judicial fees impeded access to justice for the poor. These concerns also dovetailed with broader ones about the power of the legislative assembly. Outside the legislature, some argued that having two court systems promoted litigation, as courts, reliant on fees, competed for business.[83] On the whole, though, Nova Scotians did not assert that litigation was per se a bad thing but that institutional reforms were needed to reduce the cost and increase democratic accountability. It was neither attitudes to reputation nor to litigation that produced the far lower rate of defamation cases in Nova Scotia.

Courts provided stronger incentives to sue in Massachusetts. The range of damages a plaintiff might recover was wider, higher and less predictable. Launching a suit offered the strategic attractions of the writ of attachment, and dropping a suit once matters were settled was less expensive than in Nova Scotia. The salience of the truth defense in constitutional rights discourse (and possibly in lawyerly advice) probably gave many defendants undue confidence in their legal position and kept them from settling. In some parts of Nova Scotia, court use was discouraged by religious dictates, linguistic barriers and the inaccessibility of courts and lawyers. Massachusetts women were more substantially engaged in commercial and public life, which both increased the likelihood that they would experience quantifiable economic harm from

---

Depending [sic] in Any of the Courts within this Province, S.N.S. 1833, c. 13; An Act Respecting the Trial of Issues in the Supreme Court, and for Regulating the Times of Holding the Circuits of the said Court in the Several Counties and Districts of this Province, S.N.S. 1834, c. 4.

[83] Phillips and Miller, "Too Many Courts and Too Much Law." Greg Marquis finds similar concerns in New Brunswick: "that lawyers' political involvement threatened to corrupt public life and that their professional monopoly perpetuated an outdated, cumbersome, expensive and sometimes oppressive justice system": "Anti-Lawyer Sentiment," 165.

defamation and, apparently, assured them that courts were available to them for redress. Attitudes to court usage in Massachusetts and Nova Scotia aligned with the incentive structures that courts, as institutions, offered to people thinking about using defamation law to fight their fights.

7

Conclusion

In the long wake of the revolutionary period, fundamental battles about the shape of the republic and the democracy to the north took place in the context of cases about expression, cases fought in – and about – both courts and legislatures. Then, as now, Nova Scotia and Massachusetts were both distinct and connected. The arguments that shaped the law and legal institutions of these places flowed around the Atlantic in idiosyncratic paths, through the travels of people, books and journals. The uptake of English common law was neither automatic nor unproblematic: law is grounded in daily life. These were dynamic places, full of ideas, conviction and optimism. One person's excellent idea could, to another, portend disaster – hence the story that James T. Austin used fireplace tongs to exorcise Maria Child's antislavery *Appeal in Favor of that Class of Americans Called Africans* from his premises. Circulating among the literate – almost everyone in Massachusetts and growing numbers in Nova Scotia – were legal and constitutional doctrines; birth control manuals; political and theological opinion; childrearing advice; texts on astronomy, paleontology and chemistry; literature; and, perhaps, pornography. Publishing was vibrant, controversial and vigorous in Massachusetts; in Nova Scotia it was more restrained but disputes were increasingly waged in newspapers. Law books – like other kinds of books – were tapped for the arguments they contained, which were mustered to support the arguments lawyers and their clients wanted to make, which could vary with local concerns. An author's presentation of the law could be reworked to fit, sometimes awkwardly, into different analytical frameworks. For example, making those who reprinted libelous texts liable for harms they could not anticipate because of their distance from the source seemed problematic; the rule was regarded warily in Nova Scotia and was murky and often ignored in Massachusetts – even when all the publishing action took place in Boston. Massachusetts jurists took the English law presented in the treatises of Francis Ludlow Holt and Thomas Starkie, raggedly snipped out lingering monarchism and adapted the law to fit their understandings of the needs of republicanism, as they worked through the implications of this constitutional theory. Nova Scotian commentators portrayed the British House of Commons as more restrained and respectful of subjects' rights than it was. Of course, if a given book or legal idea had not yet arrived in a certain place, the people there addressed conflicts with the legal tools and frameworks they had.

Occasionally the law was marshaled to address threats to social stability posed by texts likely to stir up the subordinate. As the arguments in and around *Whitmarsh* show, the extent to which common law criminal libel should have been considered a legitimate part of Massachusetts law is debatable, but after 1791 it was there nonetheless. Blasphemous libel and statutory variants were old causes of action, responding, like sedition, to challenges to the bonds of allegiance that were understood to stabilize the minimalist state. Obscene libel was new, a response to attacks that threatened not simply hierarchy but the moral order upon which the state was thought to rest. Challengers to religious and moral orthodoxy were active in Massachusetts by the 1820s and 1830s, with Frances Wright the most disruptive of all. In Nova Scotia, controversies about religion were more about political power than religious or moral order. In Massachusetts, other disruptive personalities were subjected to defamatory libel proceedings, although not always over their most contentious expression: abolitionists appeared remarkably often as lawyers and parties in the criminal libel cases of the mid-1830s. These people's ideas threatened to destabilize relations of power and authority, including those within the family. These cases were political, even if they no longer appear that way to us. Criminal defamatory libel was the charge of choice: seditious libel was impolitic and understood to be inconsistent with republican government. Seditious libel was, however, used in Nova Scotia twice. It may have been thought broadly justified in Wilkie's case, but Howe's inspired indignation and, soon afterward, the end of magisterial government in Halifax. Overall, the slander and libel cases of Massachusetts and Nova Scotia provide a reminder of the mutually constitutive nature of legal and social cultures: social and political anxieties and irritations shaped legal choices, but at the same time lawyers and the aggrieved structured their understandings of their experiences and their options through legal categories and alternatives.

The development of these bodies of law in the early decades of the nineteenth century shows the importance of strategic choices in an environment in which claims about freedom of conscience and the democratization of knowledge and expertise were increasingly made in Massachusetts. Unitarians, Universalists, abolitionists and Free Thinkers all bore the standard of freedom of conscience. These concerns were expressed more quietly in Nova Scotia. Beamish Murdoch and John George Marshall ignored the increasing scope of English blasphemy law. S.G.W. Archibald and Brenton Halliburton agreed with Joseph Howe that skating on Sunday should be overlooked. Howe, Jotham Blanchard and their correspondents increasingly insisted that newspapers had a legitimate role in keeping politics honest.

Navigating this shifting legal, philosophical, religious and political environment, lawyers experimented with forms of pleading, their practices sometimes varying regionally. Their indignation and their uncertainty about what the law actually required showed in their drafting of indictments against purveyors of *Fanny Hill* and *Fruits of Philosophy*. Charles Knowlton appears to have been prosecuted on the basis of a prospectus alone. In Boston, James T. Austin and Samuel D. Parker stood for a moral consensus that favored Unitarians and the orthodox (who were locked in an uneasy standoff) and was determined to uphold paternalistic and patriarchal power arrangements. Although the moral consensus over blasphemy, obscenity and criminal defamatory libel cases often dissolved over time, in the short term reformers like David Lee Child, William J. Snelling, George Cheever and Samuel D. Greene and representatives of upstart faiths like the Methodists found it difficult to succeed in these cases, whether they were defending their own statements or taking on a more conservative opponent who had defamed them. In a pattern we may recognize today, criminal defamatory libel was frequently used in these disputes over authority, both public and patriarchal, and the SJC shaped the law – especially the so-called truth defense – to keep such people in their place.

The law of libel and slander was also used in the name of repairing injured reputations through financial redress. Libel actions – civil and criminal – tended to arise from allegations in newspapers, which were far more numerous in Boston than anywhere else, with Halifax next. Slander was, by this point, strictly a civil matter in both Nova Scotia and Massachusetts, although in earlier times the common law had recognized criminal slander. A defamatory printed or written allegation could attract either civil or criminal proceedings. In Nova Scotian criminal cases, the defendant could not rely on truth, a strategic situation that could have both advantages and disadvantages for someone interested in attracting public sympathy, as truth could be hard to prove. In Massachusetts, because truth was increasingly understood to be admissible and (eventually) a defense if one's intentions and goals were good, truth was probably less of a consideration in the decision to sue or prosecute. Truth was admissible in civil cases, but suing always raised the risk of appearing to be seeking financial gain from being defamed. Of course, another difficulty with criminal proceedings was that an aggrieved individual had to convince a prosecutor to pursue the case. Joseph Howe remarked that S.G.W. Archibald disliked prosecutions of the press, which may have been a factor in the scarcity of such prosecutions in Nova Scotia. In Boston, the Russian consul wrote to James T. Austin in 1824, urging Austin not to abandon any of the counts against Joseph T. Buckingham.[1] Austin may well have signaled that he did not relish the cause. He had been Suffolk's county attorney in 1811, when Perez Morton and Daniel Davis identified well over 200 actionable libels in newspapers but secured a mere three convictions for their efforts. Although Austin did bring libel prosecutions as county attorney and attorney general, he does not seem to have been as energetic as his

---

[1] Eustaphieve to Austin, Feb. 1, 1824, James Trecothick Austin papers, Ms. N-1789, Massachusetts Historical Society.

successor as county attorney, Samuel D. Parker. In Worcester county, criminal defamatory libel cases were rare, brought only once in my sample, by Davis against Thomas Snell and Daniel Tomlinson for their attack on William Wesson's suitability for the ministry – and then dropped when a new statute made truth a defense. The case against Abner Kneeland – based on three passages drawn from the same issue of the *Boston Investigator* – suggests that at some point someone decided enough was enough and it was time to prosecute Kneeland. A similar fate probably befell William J. Snelling, who found himself subjected to three prosecutions in short order. In a different way, Samuel D. Greene's decision to retain Benjamin Franklin Hallett – or perhaps Hallett's eagerness to insert himself in an antimason's case – suggests that the prosecutor and the aggrieved individual did not necessarily agree about what issues were important or how the case should be prosecuted. The case was exceptional, however: generally the prosecutors ran the show alone.

In these small worlds, personalities and relationships mattered. When David Lee Child appeared in court, everyone knew his wife had written *The Frugal Housewife* – about how to make ends meet on a husband's small income – as well as her *Appeal* on behalf of African Americans. When Samuel G.W. Archibald decided to introduce evidence of truth despite not having pleaded it, his younger counterpart James W. Johnston let him, probably calculating, correctly, that his preparations would allow him to turn this breach of procedure to his advantage. Both parties and lawyers made strategic choices about how to proceed. Women's reputations were not treated as matters of public interest – only one criminal proceeding was launched to clear a woman's name, and she was dead by the time the case reached the courtroom. As women strategized, they may have been drawn by the potential financial returns of a civil suit, as well as the prospect of punishing the defendant and setting the record straight. Certain lawyers, like Worcester's Pliny Merrick and Rejoice Newton, may have been particularly supportive. Women in Massachusetts likely settled their cases less often than men did, which may suggest that their suits were less often brought to gain leverage in other local disputes and more often brought to attempt to provide redress for real reputational harm. The *Miller v. Parish* affair, however, underlines the ways that women's and men's actions could be entangled. The absence of Indigenous people and racialized and linguistic minorities from civil cases in both places underlines courts' roles as upholders of existing power arrangements.

Unlike criminal actions, civil suits were not considered repressive but merely protective of reputational rights. Defamation cases and all types of libel cases were far more common in Massachusetts than in Nova Scotia, however. Segments of Nova Scotia had little real contact with courts or lawyers, which lowered the overall figures on court usage, although lawyers and court sittings were spreading out through the province in the 1820s and 1830s. The risk–reward calculation in Nova Scotia was different too: the likelihood of a windfall for a successful plaintiff was comparatively low, and the costs to be borne by a plaintiff who began and then dropped a suit were higher. Indeed, legislators were making efforts to reduce the costs of litigation in Nova Scotia in this period. The harassment possibilities offered by the writ of attachment in Massachusetts made slander suits more attractive than they were in Nova Scotia after that writ ceased to be available against defendants who – in other kinds of suits involving the parties – posed no flight risk. Nothing in the discourse around the civil cases suggests that, on the whole, Massachusetts citizens valued their reputations more highly than Nova Scotians, were more offended by allegations of untrustworthiness or other slurs, or even consciously regarded litigation as a more socially acceptable pursuit, but institutional differences – the structures that had developed over time – made Massachusetts courts more enticing.

Women's much greater participation in Massachusetts cases may arise in part because other impediments to litigation in Nova Scotia – poor roads, scarcity of lawyers, court sittings, specie, ministerial discouragement – affected them more acutely than they did men. Massachusetts lawyers advocated for women clients more effectively than their husbands and guardians *ad litem* did. It also seems likely, however, that Massachusetts women's greater participation in economic life prepared them to see courts as available to them for redress for reputational injury – or, at times, for revenge. With women commonly teaching school or working in textile mills for at least short periods in their lives, courts proved receptive to claims that powerful men had deliberately sabotaged women's efforts to support themselves. At least one Massachusetts woman in these cases, Sarepta

Hix, was married but sued in her own name, with no objection raised by Joel Drury or his lawyers. Alice Holbrook's effort to defend a suit on her own despite her estranged husband's lack of involvement was rebuffed by the SJC, but these cases, taken together, remind us that unless counsel raised the issue of coverture, it was not considered. One wonders whether women's participation in defamation cases and the likelihood of winning large awards began to fall in the 1840s, as the specter of Fanny Wright was conjured to encourage women to devote their energies to the home. It is possible that the law, having recognized women's entitlements, continued to protect them; but it is also possible that juries became more reluctant to see lost wages as a real, undeserved injury to a woman who ought not to have been doing that kind of work anyway.

The common law in this environment was – as it always is – a work in progress, with local power arrangements, the opinions of earlier jurists, the realities of social life and individual interests, legal traditions, and contested constitutional principles all brought to bear on disputes over the proper limits of expression, as embodied in the diverse set of rules drawn together and given the appearance of conceptual coherence by Holt and Starkie. Most fundamentally, around the turn of the century the law on libels turned into libel law: from a type of object that could attract punishment through a variety of causes of action in courts and legislatures, "libel law" became conceptualized as a body of law that was the purview of courts, where procedural rules applied; actions taken by legislatures came to look illegitimate because of their lack of procedural protection for individuals. The common law was reshaped to fit evolving theories of sovereignty and government in the two places, even as it was also evolving in England to accommodate the political winds that were shifting dramatically between 1790 and 1835. There, showcase trials made legal processes – and the individual's vulnerability to oppressive state power – highly visible.

American politicians in the 1790s fixed on the ethically satisfying idea that a republican citizen should not and could not be punished for speaking truth, but the truths of politics and religion were often not self-evident. In Massachusetts, the legal question of whether or not good intent should absolve a libeler from criminal responsibility took decades to address. At first it seemed that it could, and that evidence of truth could be admitted to show good intent, since bad intent was thought to be a necessary element of the prosecution's case. However, once moral reformers and members of upstart religious groups began to assert truths about alcohol, slavery and the misdeeds of those holding the strings of power, good intent ceased to be a defense unless truth accompanied it and vice versa. As the cases unfolded, it became clear that courts thought some characters deserved the searching beam of truth more than others, which shaped the meaning of good motives and justifiable ends. Reformers – with abolitionists conspicuous among them – were a particular target, especially as antiabolitionist pressure rose in the early 1830s; they mostly lost as complainants, defendants and counsel. At the same time, Starkie's analytical framework, which distinguished legal from actual malice, was absorbed into Massachusetts law, to be employed in both truth and privilege cases. Although Peter Thacher in the municipal court refused twice to order the defense to help the prosecution make its case, Lemuel Shaw, sympathizing with James T. Austin and Samuel Parker in their efforts to clear the name of an elderly police magistrate, was persuaded to throw together a judgment that gave them what they needed: a right to particulars of the case the defense intended to put forward. Truth, thus safely contained, became a full defense. Truth was also vexing in civil cases. Judges were wary and limited its admissibility and use. It was defendants' best hope, and the idea of proving truth likely lured many on when they should have settled, but the defense usually failed. Special pleading was slain on this altar, but the difficulties with pleading and proving truth remained. As the common law was adapted and tweaked by statutory amendments, Massachusetts republican citizens' right to speak contested truths – especially to power – was shakier than they often proclaimed it to be.

Not all the challenging literature promulgated by reformers and religious renegades in Massachusetts was amenable to prosecution for defamation, as some of it was aimed at beliefs or social problems. In the mid-1830s, in a climate of rising majoritarian danger, new arguments emerged in and out of court based on individual conscience and the dubious pedigree of the law of libel. The trials of Abner Kneeland, Charles Knowlton and George Cheever demonstrated judges' impatience with the idea of a constitutional right to express unpopular views. Peter Thacher excluded witnesses,

evidence and jurors on suspect grounds. In return, the opinionated
newsmen Charles G. Greene and Benjamin Franklin Hallett attacked
both libel law and the judiciary, making a solid but unsuccessful
argument that common law prosecutions for criminal libel were
inconsistent with the state constitution and had not been brought in
Massachusetts until well after the Revolution. The judges hung onto
the common law and slightly reshaped blasphemy law in Kneeland's
case to make more room for honest expressions of belief while
continuing to prohibit wanton attacks on others' beliefs –
particularly the beliefs of the religious majority, since profanity and
blasphemy had theological content. Despite his avowed concern with
individual belief, however, Greene joined the majority of Boston
editors in asserting that a respectable mob should have been called
out to suppress the insult to law offered by African Americans and their
advocates who rescued two women from a slavecatcher in
a courtroom: freedom of expression and majoritarianism hung in an
uneasy balance. Nova Scotians rejected majoritarianism as an aspect of
the flawed republican thinking that was bringing disaster upon the
Canadas. Lacking the pressure of such arguments, the insult to
majority opinion offered by abolitionists, Free Thinkers and the like,
and a written constitution that made judges into central constitutional
arbiters, Nova Scotia did not see disputes over the expression of
individual conscience.

Truth is a content-based defense to a libel action, with good
intention wrapped around and through it. This work emphasizes the
importance of another, widely neglected way of thinking about rights
to self-expression, a long-established tradition of framing rights
through the institutions that protected them. The United States,
starting anew with written constitutions, settled on republican
sovereignty and then gradually worked out the implications for
individual rights, but it was clear that courts were the forum for
addressing them and that legislators' privileges should be confined to
their particular sphere, however defined. In Britain and Nova Scotia,
matters were more complicated. Parliamentarians could speak their
minds in debate, but until the late eighteenth century parliamentary
debate took place behind closed doors. Only a House could discipline
members for what they said, but their speeches stayed in the House and
its records. Once newspapers began reporting its doings and as tempers

and fears rose after the French Revolution, the jurisdictional immunities safeguarded through privilege became a problem. The old constitutional uncertainty over the power of the Commons flared again. The Nova Scotia assembly assumed the privileges of rejecting petitions, expelling members, disciplining the press and initiating money bills in the 1820s and 1830s.

It was through a reworked understanding of privilege that the extent of freedom of expression was addressed through the common law in this period. The seed was the guarantee, set out in the English Bill of Rights, that speech under certain institutional conditions – in parliamentary debate – could not be the subject of court actions. The principle spread fairly smoothly to protect most of what was said in court proceedings. The individual houses of Parliament could address their members' inappropriate comments in order to protect the dignity of each House. Although the Crown was the old threat to the Commons, official parliamentary reporting enabled critique to emerge in the world outside, without any breach of secrecy. As they long had done, the Houses continued to use their contempt powers to punish those who impugned their dignity, whether inside or outside – but could they? Blackstone said yes: a House acted in accordance with the *lex parliamenti*, of which it alone was cognizant. This law was higher than the common law, just as Parliament was higher than the common law courts – indeed the House of Lords was the highest appellate court. King's Bench and the other common law courts could not determine parliamentary law and, furthermore, could not question a House's decision, even on its jurisdiction. A House, then, could be at one time complainant, judge and jury. John Wilkes, Brass Crosby and Sir Francis Burdett, among others, felt its wrath and fought back, with Burdett's case against the Speaker constituting an important step along the way of limiting the power of the Commons and strengthening King's Bench as the protector of individual rights. Jurisdictional tensions between these two "courts" were a quiet but mammoth problem of constitutional theory in the early nineteenth century, which came to a head in the late 1830s.

The colonial period familiarized Americans with abuses of legislative privilege, and in the 1790s they were still occupied with the problem, as Jefferson's *Manual of Parliamentary Practice* suggests. In 1808, in *Coffin v. Coffin*, Chief Justice Theophilus

Parsons moved to contain these powers. Legislators did not require the protections that shielded British parliamentarians from the Crown, so Massachusetts legislators needed only to be protected against legal proceedings that would disrupt their ability to serve their constituents. Courts could safely limit the legislature's jurisdiction and, guided by a written constitution, evaluate individual rights claims. When the Massachusetts House considered disciplining David Lee Child for short remarks in his newspaper, the members who had to take the measure of the House's privileges had to grapple with the conundrum of claiming the traditions of the English House of Commons, which Child depicted as a bastion of tyranny. In the end, the perturbed House declared him deserving of censure, and he resigned his seat. The privileges of the legislature remained tempting but suspect and increasingly disconnected from what happened in court. Legislative libel proceedings seemed absurd to Charles Greene, as precedents showing the acceptance of the common law of libel in Massachusetts in the context of the *Whitmarsh* case – but Peter Thacher relied on them as he upheld the constitutionality of this body of law, despite its dubious pedigree.

If legislative privilege was troubling in Massachusetts, it was much harder to limit constitutionally in Britain, especially given the claims of the House of Commons to be the true defenders of the people against the Crown. In colonial Nova Scotia, reformers sought greater power for the legislature and insisted on its privileges at the expense of the Crown and its cliquish appointees. When the Nova Scotian legislature took steps to discipline newspaper editors and a recalcitrant member in 1829 and 1830, reformers tended to overlook the threat to the freedom of the press; it was conservatives who protested the infringements of the rights of the English subject and argued that this undignified body of colonials subject to London's guiding hand bore little resemblance to the Commons. The NSSC upheld the validity of the Speaker's warrant and ruled that the assembly had the powers it claimed, including the power to imprison a member for contempt or disobedience. In this, Justice Brenton Halliburton showed considerably less concern about presuming to assess the assembly's powers than Chief Justice Ellenborough had demonstrated in Sir Francis Burdett's case. Halliburton ruled for the assembly, but he probably cared as little about preserving its privileges as he did about protecting Barry's liberty.

In the climate of political repression of early nineteenth-century Britain, it was the doctrine of privilege that expanded to protect speakers and writers who gave their honest, nonmalicious opinions in situations in which a person had an ethical duty to do so. There is irony in this, but also, I suspect, a quiet strategy mounted by the ever-so-careful Thomas Starkie (with the complex figure of Lord Ellenborough behind him) to frame protections of speech and the press through categories that sounded traditional and uncontroversial. Out of the spotlight, through mundane civil claims brought by beer dealers and the like, the word privilege crept over to attach itself to the emerging common law category of expression for which no liability could arise because of the circumstances in which it had been uttered or published, even as the unboundedness of parliamentary privilege claims was becoming problematic. The law began, in the eighteenth century, by providing protections to those who were disappointed in their servants, although other assorted circumstances could excuse a defendant from liability as well. The obligations of candor in business required that those sorts of communications be protected. Privilege was addressed under the general issue, through which the truth or falsity of the allegation was kept carefully out of view. This idea that a communication could be privileged, subject to rebuttal through proof of malice, did make its way to Massachusetts and was set out by Chief Justice Shaw in *Bradley v. Heath*, but the signal importance of the truth defense rendered privilege a minor and often confusing thread in Massachusetts jurisprudence. Qualified privilege could potentially protect false statements made with good intent, which reformers like William J. Snelling seemed all too likely to utter. A defense that sounded like qualified privilege was among those run by Samuel G. Archibald as he defended Anthony H. Holland in the early 1820s, and Joseph Howe put forward a fully fledged defense of this sort in 1835, but the NSSC declined to extend it to newspapers. Acquitted, Howe proclaimed that his jury had brought free speech to Nova Scotia by protecting the freedom of the press. Howe's acquittal left the law of libel officially unchanged but it mattered on the ground, as it reassured newspaper editors, perhaps more than it should have. A few years later, however, in *Ward v. Blackadar and English*, the solicitor general, acting for Edmund Ward, acknowledged that privilege was a valid defense.

Privilege was the lens for understanding the relationship of individuals to state power, but more commonly raised were concerns about the institutional context for criminal cases, chiefly the *ex officio* information and jury selection processes but also the form of the Speaker's warrant when the Commons moved to arrest. Awareness of these controversies is hinted at in discussions in Nova Scotia but not Massachusetts. Structuring the procedure and the institutions so that they could operate in an unbiased way – so that prosecutorial discretion would not undermine individual liberty – was central to reformers' projects in Britain and Nova Scotia, a function of the longstanding British constitutional tradition of looking to the proper functioning of institutions to protect individual rights against the executive.

In the republican United States of the early nineteenth century – but also in Britain – courts were taking over this role. Violence was also always a possible mode of redress, less significant in Nova Scotia – where violence was simply an affront to order – than in Massachusetts, where it could be given meaning and legitimacy as an expression of majority will, specifically the majority's concern to preserve the union and profitable relations with the South. Courts were not always seen as up to the job – and their impartiality could be doubted, though they tended to be biased in the same direction as those who resorted to collective action. William Lloyd Garrison narrowly escaped from a Boston mob, George Cheever was beaten on the street, and William Snelling complained of threats and police magistrate Benjamin Whitman's inability or unwillingness to address them. The specter of violence, not just excused but explicitly threatened by the respectable, spurred abolitionists and others to insist that they had an individual right to voice their beliefs, regardless of the majority's views. The death of abolitionist editor Elijah Lovejoy at the hands of a mob pushed into sometimes uneasy alliance those who sought to eliminate slavery, those concerned about a right to individual expression, and those who insisted that collective violence was unacceptable, that order must be maintained through the enforcement of constitutionally valid laws passed by legislatures and recognized by courts. The majoritarianism embedded in the idea that sovereignty lay in the people had to be reoriented to accommodate individual expression, if the republic were not to devolve into mob rule.

The questions of the centrality of courts as fora for addressing disputes and the extent to which they could be the site for the repression of expression were entangled. Under the Massachusetts constitution, courts were made the arbiters of individual rights, which meant, among other things, that it was appropriate to limit the reach of legislative privilege and the protections legislators enjoyed in favor of allowing subjects to sue one another over reputational harms. Criminal prosecutions lay for expression that impugned the dignity of the legislature or its members. In England, both criminal prosecutions and contempt actions by the houses of Parliament arose from these kinds of attacks. In Nova Scotia in the 1820s and 1830s (at least after *Wilkie*, who targeted so many), the assembly took action itself when aggrieved, rather than turning to the attorney general – Richard Uniacke was not a friend. Civil proceedings were brought in much greater numbers in Massachusetts than in Nova Scotia. Although reputation was important in both places and there was similar ambivalence about excess litigation, courts and lawyers were more widely available in Massachusetts and more often in the news – and the incentives offered to plaintiffs were stronger. As to the profusion of criminal libel prosecutions in Massachusetts – chiefly Boston – these cases may reflect a greater inclination to see courts as the proper place to address disruption and disputes, but personalities – Parker's and Austin's – and the greater sense of order under threat in Boston likely played an even greater role. Prosecutions probably had a snowball effect: once one aggrieved person found a receptive ear in a prosecutor, others came forward as well. In responding to violence, Nova Scotians insisted that courts were the proper way of resolving disputes, but – whether because they lacked Fanny Wright and David Lee Child or because of the different structure of sociocultural tensions – they seldom used criminal libel. Legislative proceedings were more significant, but the only institutional structure for sorting out the jurisdictional tensions that arose on that front was the Judicial

Committee of the Privy Council, and none of these disputes got that far.

In both Nova Scotia and Massachusetts, it was a matter of fundamental importance for people that they had the right to speak on matters of public importance, but the development of the law and legal institutions was conditioned by diverging constitutional traditions as well as the social conditions that developed after the revolutionary period of the late eighteenth century. Defending reputational interests in civil cases was unproblematic in either place, but courts were more inviting in Massachusetts. Criminal cases, in which the state's power was marshaled against an individual, drew vigorous defenses based on truth, conscience and privilege. The earlier idea that seditious libel could be used against challengers to social and political stability had been rejected in Massachusetts, but new tools developed instead. In Nova Scotia, while reformers saw a need to change political structures, challenging the existing institutions in the name of gaining more power for the assembly was complicated by the risk of being called disloyal and, indeed, republican, as Jotham Blanchard was in the late 1820s and as Howe was when he responded with understanding to the Canadian rebellions in the winter of 1837–38. Persuasive arguments against unrestricted expression were present in both places: the union would fail, domestic order would break down, souls would be lost, the rights of Englishmen would be replaced by the violent instability of republicanism. Libel law changed as the social, institutional and constitutional footing upon which it stood changed as well, in ways that both shaped and responded to the different social, legal and constitutional pressures in two kindred places.

Appendix A: Sources

Archives

Unpublished court records are the core of this research. They are found at the Nova Scotia Archives ("NSA") in Halifax, at the Massachusetts Judicial Archives in Boston ("MJA") and on the microfilm reels in the library of the Church of Jesus Christ of Latter-Day Saints ("LDS"). Other legal sources include legislative records, legal treatises, magistrates' manuals, statutes and other law books. This work draws heavily on contemporary newspapers and also on legal and literary periodicals published in the United States, Nova Scotia and Britain; diaries, disciplinary files, and records from church archives in Nova Scotia and Massachusetts; pamphlets on libel cases and publishers' book catalogues kept originally mainly by the American Antiquarian Society ("AAS") in Worcester and now often available online; and surviving catalogues of private libraries and collections, personal correspondence and miscellaneous records housed at the Massachusetts Historical Society ("MHS"), the Bostonian Society and the NSA. I have also made heavy use of the genealogical resources of the New England Historic and Genealogical Society ("NEHGS") and of the LDS, often cross-referencing town records of births, deaths and marriages against census records in order to identify relationships between families and neighbors.

Massachusetts Sample

My sample contained all of the reported cases for 1820 through 1840 from the Massachusetts SJC that I could locate through online searches of Westlaw and LexisNexis, as well as those from the Boston municipal court that Peter Oxenbridge Thacher reported in his *Reports of Criminal Cases*. I also reviewed all of the record books of the SJC for Suffolk and Worcester counties for that period; the record books of the municipal court of Boston for 1820–26, 1830, 1835 and January through April 1840; the record books of the Suffolk Court of Common Pleas ("CP") for January 1820 and all of 1825, 1830 and 1835; and the record books of the Worcester CP for September and December 1820, March and June 1821, and all of 1825, 1830, 1835 and 1840. A shortcoming of this strategy is that cases that did not produce judgments are often omitted from the record books. Another problem is that the Worcester CP record books do not include entries for the criminal terms that began to be held in May 1835. For all three of these courts, I also sought out and read the lower court records of cases I had identified through the SJC records, and I obtained court records on some cases I had come across in pamphlets and newspapers. All court records for Massachusetts are held at the MJA, and microfilmed versions of many are held by the LDS.

Nova Scotia Sample

The Nova Scotia court records have not survived as well as those from Suffolk and Worcester. For the Supreme Court ("NSSC") sitting at Halifax, I examined the Proceedings Books for 1820–21 and the Minutes of Civil Causes for 1821–40, which disclose civil causes of action. Unfortunately the volume for 1834–38 has been lost, but I went through the judgment books for that period and for various other years as well. I also reviewed the surviving case files, although they too are incomplete. Nonetheless, the overlapping coverage of these various documents leaves me confident that I have found practically every civil defamation suit heard in the NSSC at Halifax from 1820 to 1840. The records of the Halifax Inferior Court of Common Pleas ("ICCP") for the period disclose no defamation suits.

For the NSSC sitting at Pictou on civil matters, I read the judgment books for the whole period and also those for the ICCP for 1832–40. These show only one case dealing with expression, although in most terms of each court there were one or two actions for "trespass on the case" that did not specify for what. Slander and libel were possibilities, but other indirect torts like nuisance and malicious prosecution could also have been pleaded as trespass on the case.

The NSSC did not begin sitting at Yarmouth until 1834, having previously served Yarmouth through sittings at Shelburne. Since the NSSC sat only once a year in the Yarmouth area and the ICCP twice, in two widely separated locations (Tusket and Cape Forchu), and since only three civil trials took place in Yarmouth from 1835 through 1839, it seems reasonable to conclude that Yarmouth's residents used courts less often than those of Halifax and Pictou, which had 102 and 69 civil trials, respectively, in the same period.[1] Population alone does not

[1] *An Act Respecting the Trial of Issues in the Supreme Court, and for Regulating the Times of Holding the Circuits of the Said Court in the Several Counties and Districts of this Province*, S.N.S. 1834, c. 4; *An Act for the Better Regulating the Manner of*

account for the disparity: according to the 1838 census, Yarmouth had a population of 9,189, Pictou's was a bit more than twice that, and the combined population of the city and district of Halifax was about three times larger.[2] The NSSC in Shelburne heard no suits for trespass on the case or defamation from 1820 to 1834, and there are no signs of such actions in Yarmouth after that date. Indeed, there was only one trial for any kind of trespass in either the NSSC or the ICCP in Yarmouth between 1835 and 1839.[2] The paucity of civil cases in Yarmouth must therefore be assessed.

The grand jury books for Halifax have survived for 1820 through 1840; all of the criminal cases appear to be represented there. All of those indicted for libel in Halifax were prosecuted in the NSSC. Pictou's records of indictments have not survived, but the records of the Sessions for 1820–30 reveal no prosecutions for speech-related offenses. A newspaper did allude to one indictment for "insulting a public officer" and "being 'an habitually wicked and malicious slanderer'" – perhaps some action was taken in the Sessions, although the case seems to have been a poor one.[3] There were six criminal trials in the Supreme Court in Pictou from 1835 to 1839 and one in Yarmouth, and only nine trials for misdemeanors in the whole province (one of which must have been Howe's), so it seems unlikely that there were more than a couple of criminal libel trials, if any, in Pictou or Yarmouth in those years.[4] The records of the Sessions and grand jury of Yarmouth during the 1820s and 1830s (a district until 1833 and a county thereafter) are not as fulsome as one would like, but they do reveal two occasions on which the grand jury refused to indict for libel, once in 1825 and once in 1829. There tended only to be four or five cases in the Sessions per term.

Jurisdiction of Massachusetts Courts

In Massachusetts, summary civil jurisdiction was set at up to twenty dollars in 1808.[5] From 1820 to 1840, the jurisdiction of the Court of Common Pleas appears to have begun at above that amount. Smaller claims, which could include slander and libel, lay in the jurisdiction of justices of the peace outside Boston; in Boston, the Justices' Court for the County of Suffolk

Holding the Inferior Court of Common Pleas and General Sessions of the Peace, in the District of Yarmouth and Argyle, in the County of Shelburne, S.N.S. 1817, c. 24, as amended; Nova Scotia House of Assembly, *NS Journals*, 1841, A22–102.

[2] Supreme Court, Halifax, Return of Civil Causes Tried throughout the Province in 1835–39, A.8, RG 39 C, NSA.

[3] James Dawson to W.Q. Sawers, *Novascotian* (Halifax), April 30, 1835.

[4] *NS Journals*, 1841, A22–103.

[5] An Act in Addition to an Act, Entitled, 'An Act Describing the Power of Justices of the Peace, in Civil Actions;' Passed the Eleventh day of March, Seventeen Hundred and Eighty-Four, ch. 122, 1808 Mass. Acts 358.

heard these smaller claims. Two Boston cases were appeals from the Justices Court: *John Ham and Jerusha Ham v. Patience Russell* (Suffolk CP, January term 1825) and *Hannah Hardy v. Levi Melcher* (Suffolk CP, July term 1830).[6]

Capital and certain other offenses were prosecuted in the SJC. Noncapital but serious criminal cases, such as for libel, were normally initiated in the municipal court of Boston or, outside Boston, in the SJC before July 1831 and in the CP after that time.[7] Very minor criminal offenses, such as profane swearing or minor assaults, could, by statute, be brought before a justice of the peace outside of Suffolk or the Boston police court, with an appeal lying to CP or the municipal court, as the case might be.[8]

Jurisdiction of Nova Scotia Courts

Jurisdiction over minor civil matters was the subject of legislative renovation on several occasions between 1807 and 1822. Various configurations of

---

[6] A magistrates' manual published in 1810 included sample language for slander suits, as it was one of those that "most commonly come under the cognizance of Justices of the Peace": Freeman, *Massachusetts Justice*, at 39, 46–47, 50.

[7] See An Act to Give Criminal Jurisdiction, Except in Capital Cases, to the Court of Common Pleas, ch. 113, 1831 Mass. Acts 658. All the criminal libel prosecutions brought outside Boston before 1832 were brought in the Supreme Judicial Court, except for *Comm. v. Holmes* (tried in 1819), in which the jurisdiction of the Circuit Court of Common Pleas was an issue on appeal. An Act to Establish a Court of Common Pleas for the Commonwealth of Massachusetts, ch. 79, 1821 Mass. Acts 545 purported to give to the various county Courts of Common Pleas the jurisdiction that had previously resided in the Circuit Courts of Common Pleas, including criminal jurisdiction, but libel cases outside Boston were nevertheless initiated in Supreme Judicial Court until about 1832. Indeed, An Act Enlarging the Jurisdiction of the Court of Common Pleas in Criminal Cases, and Regulating the Appointment and Duties of Prosecuting Officers, ch. 130, 1832 Mass. Acts 396 gave exclusive original jurisdiction over noncapital crimes and misdemeanors to Common Pleas outside of Suffolk, with appeals to the Supreme Judicial Court (for capital crimes, indictments were returned to Common Pleas, but the case was then transferred to the higher court). This statute also divided the state outside Suffolk into four districts and established the office of district attorney to conduct cases for the Commonwealth in those districts. In 1835, different terms were established for civil and criminal business in Worcester County, with the existing terms being used for civil business and three new terms (starting at the end of May, in mid-September and in late January) being established for criminal business: see *Revised Statutes of Massachusetts*, c. 82, ss. 41–42 (1836), incorporating An Act Establishing Additional Terms of the Court of Common Pleas in the County of Worcester, ch. 116, 1835 Mass. Acts 466.

[8] See Freeman, *Massachusetts Justice*, 58–59, 65, 231–33; An Act to Regulate the Administration of Justice within the County of Suffolk, and for Other Purposes, ch. 109, 1822 Mass. Acts 727; Griffith, *Annual Law Register*, 488–94; *Revised Statutes of Massachusetts*, c. 85, c. 87, and c. 130, s. 16 (1836). By 1836, Salem, Lowell, Newburyport and New Bedford also had police courts, which were composed of justices of the peace (*ibid.*).

magistrates were empowered to hear small claims up to various thresholds. A statute of 1817 authorized the creation of Commissioners' Courts in every county and district, to hear civil claims for up to ten pounds, including slander claims for up to five pounds. These commissioners, who did not necessarily have legal training, would meet two days a month to hear trials without juries. Appeals lay to the NSSC for judgments worth more than five pounds.[9] Philip Girard notes that, judging from the rapid decline in the number of judgments rendered in the ICCP for Halifax County after 1818, the Commissioners' Court probably "rapidly became the forum of choice for the recovery of medium-sized debts (those between £5 and £10), favored because of its summary procedure and low costs."[10] William Wilkie, however, thought that justice there was still too expensive for the poor.[11] Fifteen years later Joseph Howe complained of execution taking eighteen months.[12]

Outside of Halifax, Commissioners' Courts did not really catch on. In 1818, the 1817 legislation regarding Commissioners' Courts was continued for Halifax only; elsewhere single justices of the peace had jurisdiction over the smallest of these debts and Commissioners' Courts composed of two or three justices could hear debts for three to ten pounds. These justices and commissioners lost their jurisdiction to hear actions for "words" (slander) and other trespass actions.[13] In 1822, the jurisdiction of Commissioners' Courts outside Halifax was divided between justices of the peace and the superior courts.[14] Outside Halifax, therefore, in the 1820s and 1830s, suits for slander and libel could only be heard in the NSSC on assize or in the ICCP for each county. In Halifax, it was theoretically possible to bring a defamation suit for up to ten

---

[9] *An Act for the Summary Trial of Actions*, S.N.S. 1817, c. 11.

[10] Patriot Jurist, 161–62. Unfortunately, few records of the Halifax Commissioners' Court survive. The Nova Scotia Archives have a box of writs of executions, which are undoubtedly only a subset of those created at the time, and the records of the occasional case that was appealed to the NSSC or ICCP. Unfortunately, neither provides any information about the cause of action. Of the hundreds of surviving writs of execution, however, not a single one is for costs only, which suggests that costs were only granted to plaintiffs who won their cases. On appeal, some victors did receive judgments for costs only. See Halifax Court of Commissioners for the Summary Trial of Actions, vol. 34, RG 39 M, NSA; Supreme Court at Halifax Judgment Books (Easter term 1833 – Michaelmas term 1833), vol. 37, RG 39 J, at 81, 100, 226, 227, 408, 463, 479. The volume of the court's work from 1827 to 1837 can be assessed from an 1837 legislative report. The court issued twenty executions in March 1827 and reached a high of eighty-nine in November 1834. By 1836 the numbers had dropped into the teens and single digits: Nova Scotia House of Assembly, *NS Journals*, 1837, 1st sess., A81-174–76.

[11] *Letter to the People of Halifax*, 9–10.

[12] *Trial for Libel, on the Magistrates of Halifax*, 59–60. See also Girard, "Rise and Fall of Urban Justice," 60.

[13] *An Act for the Summary Trial of Actions*, S.N.S. 1818, c. 10.

[14] *An Act for the Summary Trial of Actions*, S.N.S. 1822, c. 30.

pounds – five pounds after 1824[15] – if one were willing to set such a value upon one's reputation. Unfortunately the records do not disclose whether anyone actually ever brought such a suit.

The NSSC and ICCP had concurrent jurisdiction in civil matters, although the courts' workloads were differently distributed in different parts of the province.[16] Halifax, for instance, had four sittings annually of the NSSC. The Halifax ICCP, on the other hand, sitting as frequently, heard no trials at all from 1835 through 1839; from 1820 to 1840 its judgment books disclose no contested cases and only seventy-six judgments in total, with none at all in several years and a high of seventeen in 1834.[17] Pictou in the 1820s and 1830s, on the other hand, had sittings of the NSSC in May or June and September and of the ICCP in January and July,[18] which yielded forty-five trials in the NSSC and twenty-four in the ICCP from 1835 through 1839.[19] From 1824 on, sittings of the ICCP had to include at least one legally trained justice, the "First-Justice of the Inferior Court of Common Pleas." The province outside of Halifax was divided into three districts (as well as Cape Breton), each of which had one of these officials.[20] The sittings of each of the divisions of the ICCP moved around within the districts, so that by the early 1830s the major towns were served about twice a year.[21]

While jurisdiction over serious criminal matters lay with the NSSC, lesser criminal offenses were brought before the General Sessions of the Peace in each county or district. Criminal libel, a misdemeanor, could theoretically be prosecuted in the Sessions or in the NSSC, but was in fact

---

[15] *An Act Relating to the Court of Commissioners at Halifax*, S.N.S. 1824, c. 36, s. 5.

[16] It was possible to seek *certiorari* in Supreme Court to rectify errors in the ICCP, but such cases were exceedingly rare: I encountered two such cases over twenty years in the courts of Halifax, Pictou and Shelburne. On the history and reform of the ICCPs, see Phillips and Miller, "Too Many Courts and Too Much Law."

[17] *NS Journals*, 1841, A22–102. The judgment books for 1820 through 1840 are archived as vol. 25, nos. 4 & 5, RG 37 HX, NSA. Most of these cases were for *indebitatus assumpsit*, and in all of these the defendant confessed judgment or (less often) "said nothing." C.H. Belcher's 1835 *Nova Scotia Temperance Almanac* identified one of the ICCP's magistrates, the aging John Howe, senior (59–60). The terms of the various courts in Halifax as of about 1832 appear in Murdoch, *Epitome of the Laws of Nova-Scotia*, 3:54–55, 61.

[18] This pattern continued after Pictou was converted from a district of Halifax County into a separate county by *An Act to Divide the County of Halifax, and to Regulate the Representation thereof*, S.N.S. 1834–35, c. 37.

[19] *NS Journals*, 1841, A22–102.

[20] *An Act to Make Further Provision for the Equal Administration of Justice in the Province of Nova-Scotia*, S.N.S. 1824, c. 38. Cape Breton had a similar structure, created under separate legislation.

[21] See Murdoch, *Epitome of the Laws of Nova-Scotia*, 3:61–64.

prosecuted only in the NSSC in Halifax and probably was not prosecuted at all in Pictou or Yarmouth. The same men may frequently have sat both in the Sessions and the ICCP, at least outside Halifax.[22] As well, the First Justices of the ICCP doubled as "President or First-Justice of the Court of Sessions."[23]

[22] That outside of Halifax throughout the period the same people sat as magistrates in the Sessions and the ICCP is suggested by the statutes that established the courts' schedules: these statutes consistently scheduled the sittings of the Sessions and the ICCP for the same few days of each year. Although the preamble to a Halifax statute of 1812 asserted that it was inconvenient to have the Sessions and the ICCP meet at the same time, they likely did anyway. See *An Act to Alter the Time of the Sitting of the Inferior Court of Common Pleas, for the County of Halifax*, S.N.S. 1812, c. 12.

[23] *An Act to Make Further Provision for the Equal Administration of Justice in the Province of Nova-Scotia*, 4 & 5 Geo. IV, S.N.S. 1824, c. 38.

Appendix B: Cases

Nova Scotia

Halifax

Civil

> *William [?] Hobson v. Joseph Hobson*, Supreme Court, Hilary term 1820, Proceedings Book 1817–21, v. 121, RG 39 J, NSA, p. 174.
>
> *Donald A. Fraser v. Norman McLeod*, Supreme Court, Hilary term 1820, Judgment Book, v. 26, RG 39 J, NSA, p. 265; Proceedings Book 1817–21, v. 121, RG 39 J, NSA, p. 176; case file, 1820 (Fo–J), box 159, RG 39 C, NSA.
>
> *John Dore v. Fred McLennan*, Supreme Court, Trinity term 1820, Judgment Book, v. 27, RG 39 J, NSA, p. 170; Proceedings Book 1817–21, v. 121, RG 39 J, NSA, pp. 204–5.
>
> *Davidson [?] Walker v. John Scott*, Supreme Court, Trinity term 1820, Proceedings Book 1817–21, v. 121, RG 39 J, NSA, pp. 208–9.
>
> *James Doyle v. John Hefler*, Supreme Court, Michaelmas term 1820, Judgment Book, v. 27, RG 39 J, NSA, p. 255.
>
> *Simon Fraser v. Anthony H. Holland*, Supreme Court, Easter term 1821, Judgment Book, v. 28, RG 39 J, NSA, p. 25; Minutes of Civil Causes Book 1821–26, v. 118A, RG 39 J, NSA, p. 6; case file, 1820 (A–H), box 163, RG 39 C, NSA.
>
> *James Plummer v. John Davie*, Supreme Court, Trinity term 1821, Minutes of Civil Causes Book, v. 118A, RG 39 J, 1821–26 NSA, p. 14.
>
> *George Hosking v. James Thompson*, Supreme Court, Hilary term 1822, Judgment Book, v. 28, RG 39 J, NSA, p. 337; Minutes of Civil Causes Book 1821–26, v. 118A, RG 39 J, NSA, p. 40.

William Bowes v. Anthony H. Holland, Philip J. Holland & Edward A. Moody, Supreme Court, Hilary term 1822, Judgment Book, v. 29, RG 39 J, NSA, p. 2; Minutes of Civil Causes Book 1821–26, v. 118A, RG 39 J, NSA; case file, 1820 (A–C), box 165, RG 39 C, NSA.

Simon Fraser v. Robert Patterson, Supreme Court, Easter term 1822, Judgment Book, v. 29, RG 39 J, NSA, p. 21; Minutes of Civil Causes Book 1821–26, v. 118A, RG 39 J, NSA, p. 56.

John McKenzie v. William Ross, Supreme Court, Easter term 1823, Minutes of Civil Causes Book 1821–26, v. 118A, RG 39 J, NSA, p. 123; case file, 1823 (L–Z & Misc.), box 168, RG 39 C, NSA.

Henry W. Crawley & Anne Crawley v. Thomas Forrester, Supreme Court, Easter term 1823, Minutes of Civil Causes Book 1821–26, v. 118A, RG 39 J, NSA, pp. 125, 130.

William Holland v. John Kenty, Supreme Court, Trinity term 1823, Judgment Book, v. 30, RG 39 J, NSA, p. 24; Minutes of Civil Causes Book 1821–26, v. 118A, RG 39 J, NSA, p. 140; case file, 1823 (A–K), box 167, RG 39 C, NSA.

David Thomas v. Alexander Philips, Supreme Court, Michaelmas term 1824, Judgment Book, v. 30, RG 39 J, NSA, p. 288; Minutes of Civil Causes Book 1821–26, v. 118A, RG 39 J, NSA, p. 195; case file, 1824 (H–Z), box 169, RG 39 C, NSA.

William Thomas v. Alexander Phillips, Supreme Court, Michaelmas term 1824, Judgment Book, v. 30, RG 39 J, NSA, p. 289; Minutes of Civil Causes Book 1821–26, v. 118A, RG 39 J, NSA, p. 195; case file, 1824 (H–Z), box 169, RG 39 C, NSA.

John Heffler v. Henry Maxner/Mixner, Supreme Court, Trinity term 1825, case file, 1825 (A–Z), box 170, RG 39 C, NSA.

Jos. Bissett v. __ D. Hawthorn, Supreme Court, Michaelmas term 1825, Minutes of Civil Causes Book 1821–26, v. 118A, RG 39 J, NSA, p. 227; case file, 1825 (A–Z), v. 170, RG 39 C, NS.

Charles Heffler v. John Goff, Supreme Court, Hilary term 1832, Minutes of Civil Causes Book 1827–33, v. 118B, RG 39 J, NSA, pp. 139–40.

Thomas Keating v. Pierce Sullivan, Supreme Court, Easter term 1834, Judgment Book, v. 38, RG 39 J, NSA; case file, 1834 (D–Z), box 178, RG 39 C, NSA.

David Fletcher v. John H. Flohr, Supreme Court, Hilary term 1836, Judgment Book, v. 40, RG 39 J, NSA, p. 27.

Edmund Ward v. John English and Hugh Blackadar, Supreme Court, Easter term 1840, Judgment Book, v. 42, RG 39 J, NSA, p. 27; Minutes of Civil Causes Book 1839–46, v. 118C, RG 39 J, NSA, pp. 23–24.

Criminal

R. v. William Wilkie, indicted Apr. 5, 1820; Halifax County Grand Jury
Book, Court of General Sessions, 1811–28, P. 8, RG 34–312, NSA.

R. v. Thomas Forrester, indicted Dec. 14, 1824; Halifax County Grand Jury
Book, Court of General Sessions, 1811–28, P. 8, RG 34–312, NSA.

R. v. John H. Flohr, indicted Dec. 14, 1832; Halifax County Grand Jury
Book, Court of General Sessions, 1828–34, P. 13, RG 34–312, NSA.

R. v. Joseph Howe, indictment proceedings Feb. 17 and 20, 1835; Halifax
County Grand Jury Book, Court of General Sessions, 1835–43, P. 14,
RG 34–312, NSA.

R. v. Thomas Gilfoyle, Jan. 8, 1838; Halifax County Grand Jury Book,
Court of General Sessions, 1835–43, P. 14, RG 34–312, NSA.

Pictou

Civil

Andrew Anderson v. John Reid, Supreme Court, May term 1820, Pictou
Judgment Book, Jun. 1816–Sept. 1820, v. 2, Series 1363, RG 39, NSA,
p. 214.

James Campbell v. Donald McKay, Supreme Court, Sept. term 1820, Pictou
Judgment Book, Jun. 1816–Sept. 1820, v. 2, Series 1363, RG 39, NSA,
p. 237.

Yarmouth

Criminal

R. v. David McConnet, General Sessions for Yarmouth and Argyle,
Sept. term 1825, Sessions Book, 1816–28, v. 3, RG 34–324 P, NSA,
p. 176. (No bill in indictment for libel.)

R. v. Prince Kinney, General Sessions for Yarmouth and Argyle, May term
1829, Sessions Book, 1828–55, v. 4, RG 34–324 P, NSA, p. 15. (No bill
in indictment for libel.)

Massachusetts

Significant Cases prior to 1820

Samuel Larned v. Samuel Buffinton, Supreme Judicial Court, Suffolk, 3
Mass. (2 Tyng) 546 (Nov. 1807).

Comm. v. William Clap, Supreme Judicial Court, Suffolk, 4 Mass. (3 Tyng) 163 (Mar. 1808).

William Coffin v. Micajah Coffin, Supreme Judicial Court, Suffolk, 4 Mass. (3 Tyng) 1 (Mar. 1808).

Patty W. Jackson v. Lebbeus Stetson and Sally Stetson, Supreme Judicial Court, Suffolk, 15 Mass. (14 Tyng) 48 (Mar. 1818).

Suffolk

Civil

William Simonds, minor, by Aaron Wells v. John Cooper, Common Pleas, Jul. 1819; Supreme Judicial Court, Nov. term 1820, SJC Record Books, 42, MJA.

Andrew Sanborn and Sally Sanborn v. Henry Lane and Elizabeth Lane, Common Pleas, Oct. 1819; Supreme Judicial Court, Nov. term 1820; SJC Record Books, 39, MJA.

Benjamin Crosby v. John Dogan and Abigail Dogan, Common Pleas, Jan. term 1820; Record Books, 139v, MJA m/f 903896.

Nathaniel Niles v. Benjamin Russell, Common Pleas, Oct. 1820; Supreme Judicial Court, Mar. term 1821; SJC Record Books, 143, MJA.

Isaac Waters v. William C. Hall, Common Pleas, Jul. 1822; Supreme Judicial Court, Mar. term 1825; SJC Record Books, 291, MJA.

James Clark v. Amos Binney, Common Pleas, Jan. 1823; Supreme Judicial Court trial Nov. 1823, appeal Mar. term 1824, SJC Record Books, 95, MJA; 19 Mass. (2 Pick.) 113.

Ferdinand Clark v. Hutson Bishop, Common Pleas, Jan. 1823; Supreme Judicial Court, Nov. 1824; SJC Record Books, 29, MJA.

Willard Badger v. William Phillips, Common Pleas, Oct. 1823; Supreme Judicial Court, Nov. 1824; SJC Record Books, 42, MJA.

Mary Hayden v. John Creamer [Cramer], Common Pleas, Jul. 1824; Supreme Judicial Court, Nov. term 1824; SJC Record Books, 229, MJA.

John Ham and Jerusha Ham v. Patience Russell, Common Pleas, Jan. term 1825; Record Books, 93v, MJA.

David Coleman v. Samuel Harding, Common Pleas, May 1824; Supreme Judicial Court, Mar. term 1825; SJC Record Books, 215, MJA.

George Taylor v. Daniel Tucker, Common Pleas, Apr. term 1825; CP Record Books, 11, MJA; Supreme Judicial Court, Nov. term 1825; SJC Record Books, 561v, MJA.

Phillip Curtis v. George Jones, Common Pleas, Jul. term 1825; Record Books, 425v, MJA.

Michael Ronayne and Ellen Ronayne v. Mary Kimball, Common Pleas, Oct. term 1825; Record Books, 112v, MJA.

William Hall v. Daniel Tucker, Common Pleas, Oct. term 1825; Record Books, 136, MJA.

William Hall v. Daniel Tucker [#2], Common Pleas, Oct. term 1825; Record Books, 137v, MJA.

William Hall v. Horatio Snow, Common Pleas, Oct. term 1825; Record Books, 138, MJA.

Aaron Isaacs v. Nathaniel H. Whitaker, Common Pleas, Oct. term 1825; CP Record Books, 164, MJA; Supreme Judicial Court, Nov. term 1825; SJC Record Books, 459v, MJA.

Nathaniel Dockham v. Michael Shute, Common Pleas, Oct. term 1826; Supreme Judicial Court, Nov. term 1826; Record Books, 291, MJA.

Samuel R. Johnson v. David Lee Child, Common Pleas, Oct. term 1828; Supreme Judicial Court, Nov. term 1828; Record Books, 204, MJA.

Samuel Fales and Abigail Fales v. Martha M. Soren, Common Pleas, Jan. term 1829; Supreme Judicial Court, Nov. term 1829; Record Books, 223v, MJA.

Samuel Fales and Abigail Fales v. Elizabeth O. Lane, Common Pleas, Jan. 1829; Supreme Judicial Court, Nov. term 1829; Record Books, 225v, MJA.

Charles C. Richardson v. George Homer, Common Pleas, Jan. term 1830; Record Books, 3, MJA.

Kendall F. Edgell v. Edward Thompson, Common Pleas, Apr. term 1830; Record Books, 1, MJA.

Hannah Hardy (minor) v. Levi Melcher, Common Pleas, Jul. term 1830; Record Books, 48, MJA.

Miles Farmer v. Dr. David Humphreys [Humphries] Storer, Common Pleas, Jul. term 1830; CP Record Books, 89, MJA; Supreme Judicial Court, Mar. term 1831; Record Books, 60, MJA; review of costs 28 Mass. (11 Pick.) 241 (Mar. 1831).

David Lee Child v. William Beals, James Lee Homer and George A. Otis Jr. [deceased], Common Pleas, Oct. term 1830; CP Record Books, 29, MJA; sub. nom. *David Lee Child v. William Beals and James Lee Homer*, Supreme Judicial Court, trial Oct. term 1832, appeal Mar. term 1833; 30 Mass. (13 Pick.) 503.

William S. Carlton v. Dean Willis, Common Pleas, Oct. term 1830; CP Record Books, 196, MJA; Supreme Judicial Court, Nov. term 1831; Record Books, 49, MJA.

Andrew Somerby v. Israel Brown, Common Pleas, Oct. term 1830; Record Books, 272, MJA.

William Pelby v. Walter James, Common Pleas, Oct. term 1830; Record Books, 43, MJA.

Timothy Gay v. David Homer, Common Pleas, Oct. term 1831; Supreme Judicial Court trial Nov. term 1831, appeal Mar. term 1833; SJC Record Books, 53, MJA; 30 Mass. (13 Pick.) 535.

Ephraim C. Loud v. Nehemiah Kittredge, Common Pleas, Oct. term 1833; Supreme Judicial Court, Nov. term 1834; SJC Record Books, 251, MJA.

Charlotte Hunt v. James Flahaven and Parnel Flahaven, Common Pleas, Jan. term 1835; Record Books, 42, MJA.

Harriet Weafer, minor, by James Weafer v. William Kelly, Common Pleas, Jan. term 1835; Record Books, 95, MJA.

Silas Wessen v. J.D.E. Vander Heyden, Common Pleas, Jul. term 1835; Record Books, 54, MJA.

Robert H. Stewart v. Thomas S. Jones, Common Pleas, Jul. term 1835; Record Books, 157, MJA.

John D. Howard v. William D. Bell, Common Pleas, Oct. term 1835; Record Books, 151, MJA.

William M. Hatstat v. John Hancock, Common Pleas, Oct. term 1835; Record Books, 217, MJA.

John Cassidy v. Josiah Barker, Common Pleas, Jul. term 1836; Supreme Judicial Court, Nov. term 1836; SJC Record Books, 407, MJA.

Ebenezer Howes Jr. v. William Halstat, Common Pleas, Oct. term 1837; Supreme Judicial Court, Nov. term 1837; Record Books, 586, MJA.

Azell Snow v. John Ford and John S. Sleeper, Supreme Judicial Court, 25 Apr. 1838; *Trial for Libel before the Supreme Judicial Court, Apr. 25, 1838.*

John H. Tebbets v. Otis G. Randall and William Trumbull, Common Pleas, Jul. term 1838; Supreme Judicial Court, Nov. term 1839; Record Books, 352, MJA.

Criminal

Comm. v. Thomas Boardman, Charles Willis, Jun. & John Minchin, Municipal Court, May term 1820; Record Books, v. 8, 268, MJA.

Comm. v. Thomas Farnam, Municipal Court, Mar. term 1821; Record Books, v. 9, 48, MJA.

Comm. v. Lorenzo Hall [#1 – naval agent Amos Binney], Municipal Court, Nov. term 1822; Record Books, v. 10, 502, MJA.

Comm. v. Joseph T. Buckingham [#1 – Maffit], Municipal Court, Dec. term 1822; Record Books, v. 10, 497, 517, 526, MJA.

Comm. v. Lorenzo Turner Hall [#2 – obscene libel, re disclosing the location of brothels], Municipal Court, Dec. term 1822, Record Books, v. 10, 531, MJA.

Comm. v. Lorenzo T. Hall [#3 – engraver Abel Bowen], Municipal Court, Jan. 1824, Record Books, v. 11, 172, MJA; Supreme Judicial Court, Nov. term 1824, SJC Record Books, 412, MJA.

Comm. v. Joseph T. Buckingham [#2 – Eustaphieve re. U. Stuffy and parenting allegations], Municipal Court, Jan. term 1824, Record Books, v. 11, 175, MJA; Thach. Crim. Cas. 29; Municipal Court, Mar. term

1824 [#2a – Eustaphieve re fighting at a ball]; Record Books, v. 11, 175, 220, MJA; Thach. Crim. Cas. 51. Supreme Judicial Court, Nov. term 1824 [re. #2a], SJC Record Books, 386, MJA; Supreme Judicial Court, Mar. term 1827 [two nolles entered], SJC Record Books, 2v, MJA.

Comm. v. *Theodore Lyman*, Supreme Judicial Court, Nov. term 1828 [hung jury], Nov. term 1829 [nol. pros.]; SJC Docket Book Nov. term 1828, 131; SJC Docket Book Nov. term 1829, 48, MJA.

Comm. v. *Origen Bacheler [Origen Batchelder/Orregen Baccheller]*, Municipal Court, Mar. term 1829; Record Books, v. 17, 80, MJA; Thach. Crim. Cas. 191.

Comm. v. *Frederick S. Hill*, Municipal Court, Jun. term 1831; case file MJA, nol. pros'd.

Comm. v. *Charles W. Moore & Edwin Sevey*, Municipal Court, Jul. term 1833; Record Books, v. 21, 300, 470, MJA.

Comm. v. *William J. Snelling* [#1 – police magistrate Whitman], Municipal Court, Jul. term 1833; BMC Record Books, v. 21, 473, MJA; Thach. Crim. Cas. 318; Supreme Judicial Court, Mar. term 1834; SJC Record Books, 126, MJA; 32 Mass. (15 Pick.) 321.

Comm. v. *William J. Snelling* [#2 – Harrison and Allen], Municipal Court, Jul. term 1833; BMC Record Books, v. 21, pt. 2, MJA; Supreme Judicial Court, Mar. term 1834; SJC Record Books, 123; 32 Mass. (15 Pick.) 337.

Comm. v. *William J. Snelling* [#3 – Susan Munroe], Municipal Court, Aug. term 1833; BMC Record Books, v. 21, 513, MJA; Supreme Judicial Court, Nov. term 1833; SJC Record Books, 311, MJA.

Comm. v. *Aaron Guild*, Municipal Court, Aug. term 1833; BMC Record Books, v. 21, 678, MJA; Thach. Crim. Cas. 329.

Comm. v. *Abner Kneeland*, Municipal Court, Jan. term 1834; Thach. Crim. Cas. 346; Supreme Judicial Court trial #1 Mar. term 1834, trial #2 Nov. 1834, trial #3 Nov. 1835, appeal argued Mar. 1836, appeal judgment delivered Mar. term 1838; SJC Record Books, 6; 37 Mass. (20 Pick.) 206.

Comm. v. *Benjamin F. Bond*, Municipal Court, Feb. term 1835; Record Books, v. 23, 127, MJA.

Comm. v. *Edward C. Purdy*, Municipal Court, Feb. term 1835; Record Books, v. 23, 148, MJA.

Comm. v. *John W. [H.?] Stevens*, Municipal Court, Apr. term 1835; Record Books, v. 23, 231–33, MJA. No bill in indictment for selling obscene libels and indecent songs.

Comm. v. *Edward Stearns*, Municipal Court, Jun. term 1835; Record Books, v. 23, 401, MJA.

Comm. v. *Joseph A. Whitmarsh*, Municipal Court, Jul. term 1836; BMC Record Books, v. 24, 465, MJA; Thach. Crim. Cas. 441; Supreme Judicial Court, Nov. term 1837; Record Books, 435, MJA.

Comm. v. Samuel Thompson [i.e. Thomson], Municipal Court, Mar. term
1839; BMC Record Books, v. 27, 367, MJA; Supreme Judicial Court,
Nov. term 1839; Record Books, 461, MJA.

Worcester

Civil

Charles Augustus Goodrich v. Moses N. Child, Common Pleas, Jun. 1820;
Supreme Judicial Court, Apr. term 1821; SJC Record Books, v. 5, 296,
LDS m/f 2200258

William Tolman v. Samuel Williams and Susanna Williams, Common
Pleas, Dec. term 1820; Record Books, v. 51, 260, LDS m/f 894990.

Mary Knowlton v. Artemas Parker, Common Pleas, Feb. term 1821;
Record Books, v. 51, 581, LDS m/f 894990.

John Macoumber and Anna Macoumber v. Jonas Bemis, Common Pleas,
Mar. term 1821; Record Books, v. 52, 60, LDS m/f 894990.

Peter Fay v. Temple Parker, Common Pleas, Mar. term 1825; Record
Books, v. 60, 33, LDS m/f 894994.

Eliakim Davis v. Philip F. Cowden, Common Pleas, Jun. term 1825; Record
Books, v. 60, 205, LDS m/f 894994; Supreme Judicial Court, Apr. term
1827, SJC Record Books, v. 7, 10, LDS m/f 2200259.

William B. Wesson v. Thomas Holt, Common Pleas, Aug. term 1825; CP
Record Books, v. 61, 28, LDS m/f 894994; Supreme Judicial Court, Oct.
term, 1826, SJC Record Books, v. 6, 621, LDS m/f 2200259.

William B. Wesson v. John Fisk, Common Pleas, Aug. term 1825; CP
Record Books, v. 61, 31, LDS m/f 894994; Supreme Judicial Court, Oct.
term, 1826, SJC Record Books, v. 6, 624, LDS m/f 2200259.

Nathaniel Pike v. John R. Bowles, Common Pleas, Aug. term 1825; Record
Books, v. 61, 48, LDS m/f 894994.

Maria Goffe v. Amariah Preston, Common Pleas, Aug. term 1825; Record
Books, v. 61, 54, LDS m/f 894994.

Eli Wheelock v. Daniel Gilbert, Common Pleas, Dec. term 1825; CP Record
Book, v. 61, 258, LDS m/f 894994; Supreme Judicial Court, Apr. term
1827; Record Book, v. 7, 17, LDS m/f 2200259.

Sumner Swain v. Elijah A. Gould, Common Pleas, Dec. term 1825; Record
Books, v. 61, 264, LDS m/f 894994.

Maria Thayer v. Sally Putnam, Common Pleas, Dec. term 1825; CP Record
Books, v. 61, 426, LDS m/f 894994; Supreme Judicial Court, Aug. term
1826; SJC Record Books, v. 6, 531, LDS m/f 2200259.

Sarepta Hix v. Joel Drury, Common Pleas, Mar. term 1827; CP Record
Books, v. 64, 25, LDS m/f 894995); Supreme Judicial Court trial Apr.

term 1827, appeal Oct. term, 1827, SJC Record Books, v. 7, 121, LDS m/f 2200259; 22 Mass. (5 Pick.) 296.

Lucy Barrows v. John Paige, Common Pleas, Dec. term 1827; CP Record Books, v. 65, 293, LDS m/f 894996; Supreme Judicial Court trial Apr. term 1828, appeal Sept. term 1828; SJC Record Books, v. 7, 309, LDS m/f 2200259.

Jonathan Sibley v. Thomas Marsh, Common Pleas, Dec. term 1827; CP Record Books, v. 65, 326, LDS m/f 894996; Supreme Judicial Court trial Apr. term 1828, appeal heard Sept. 1828 and new trial ordered Oct. 1828, 24 Mass. (7 Pick.) 38; second trial Apr. 1829; SJC Record Books, v. 7, 377, LDS m/f 2200259.

Samuel Russell v. John Howe II, Common Pleas, Dec. term 1829; CP Record Books, v. 70, 56, LDS m/f 894999; Supreme Judicial Court trial Oct. 1830, appeal Apr. term 1831; SJC Record Books, v. 9, 289, LDS m/f 2200259.

Erasmus Clark Jr v. John Burbank, Common Pleas, Dec. term 1830; Record Books, v. 73, 30, LDS m/f 897501.

Azor R. Phelps v. William Workman, Common Pleas, Mar. term 1831; CP Record Books, v. 73, 401, LDS m/f 897501; Supreme Judicial Court, Apr. term 1831, SJC Record Books, v. 8, 296, LDS m/f 2200259.

James G. Carter v. Ferdinand Andrews, Common Pleas, Dec. term 1832; CP Record Books, v. 76, 238, LDS m/f 897502; Supreme Judicial Court when plaintiff nonsuit Apr. term 1833, appeal Sept. term 1834; SJC Record Books, v. 9, 221, LDS m/f 2200260; 33 Mass. (16 Pick.) 1.

Betsey Bacon v. Willard Holbrook and Alice M. Holbrook, Common Pleas, Dec. term 1833; CP Record Books, v. 78, 503, LDS m/f 897503; Supreme Judicial Court trial when Willard Holbrook defaulted Apr. term 1834, appeal Sept. term 1834, SJC Record Books, v. 9, 252, LDS m/f 2200260.

Levi Lewis v. Asa Packard, Common Pleas, Mar. term 1834; CP Record Books, v. 79, 1, LDS m/f 897504; Supreme Judicial Court, Sept. term 1834; SJC Record Books, v. 9, 235, LDS m/f 2200260.

Jotham Peckham v. John Clark, Common Pleas, Jun. term 1835; Record Books, v. 81–82, 496, LDS m/f 897505.

Daniel Frost Jr. v. Larned Marcy, Common Pleas, Dec. term 1835; Record Books, v. 83, 263, LDS m/f 897506.

Louisa Sanderson by her next friend, William Mann v. John W. Weston, Common Pleas, Dec. term 1835; CP Record Books, v. 83, 273, LDS m/f 897506; Supreme Judicial Court, Apr. term 1837; Record Books, v. 10, 24, LDS m/f 2200260.

Ephraim Covell v. John Chandler, Common Pleas, Dec. term 1835; CP Record Books, v. 83, 282, LDS m/f 897506; Supreme Judicial Court, Apr. term 1836; Record Books, 522, LDS m/f 2200260.

William Bains v. Nathaniel Green, Common Pleas, Dec. term 1835; Record Books, v. 83, 334, LDS m/f 897506.

David McFarland v. Calvin Marcy, Common Pleas, Mar. term 1837; CP Record Books, v. 86, 180, LDS m/f 897507; Supreme Judicial Court, Apr. term 1837, SJC Record Books, v. 10, 207, LDS m/f 2200260.

Betsey Ammidown v. Adolphus Ammidown, Larkin Ammidown, Otis Ammidown, and Eldridge Ammidown, Common Pleas, Dec. term 1837; Record Books, v. 87, 629, LDS m/f 897508; Supreme Judicial Court, Apr. term 1838; SJC Record Books, v. 10, 207, LDS m/f 2200260.

Eliphalet Stone v. Joseph Clark, Common Pleas, Mar. term 1837; CP Record Books, v. 86, 62, LDS m/f 897507; Supreme Judicial Court trial [Mar. term 1838?], appeal Oct. term 1838; 38 Mass. (21 Pick.) 51; Supreme Judicial Court neither party appeared, Oct. term 1839; SJC Record Books, v. 10, 484, LDS m/f 2200260.

Joseph Clark v. Eliphalet Stone, Common Pleas, Mar. term 1837; CP Record Books, v. 86, 183, LDS m/f 897507; Supreme Judicial Court, Apr. term 1837; SJC Record Books, v. 10, 67, LDS m/f 2200260.

Harvey Hartwell v. Emery Tafts [Taft], Common Pleas, Dec. term 1838; CP Record Books, v. 89, 284, LDS m/f 897509; Supreme Judicial Court, Apr. term 1839; SJC Record Books, v. 10, 394, LDS m/f 2200260.

Criminal

Comm. v. Stillman Howe, Supreme Judicial Court, Apr. term 1820; Record Books, v. 5, 209, LDS m/f 2200258.

Comm. v. Stillman Howe [#2], Supreme Judicial Court, Apr. term 1820; Record Books, v. 5, 210, LDS m/f 2200258.

Comm. v. Peter Holmes, Common Pleas, Dec. 1819; CP Record Books, v. 49, 283, 609; Supreme Judicial Court trial Oct. 1820, appeal Oct. 1821; SJC Record Books, v. 5, 430, LDS m/f 2200258; 17 Mass. (16 Tyng) 336.

Comm. v. Thomas Snell and Daniel Tomlinson, Supreme Judicial Court, Apr. term 1827; Record Books, v. 7, 63, LDS m/f 2200259.

Comm. v. Cyrus Stockwell and Chester Sessions, Supreme Judicial Court trial Apr. 1827, released after pardon Apr. term 1828, Record Books, v. 7, 233, LDS m/f 2200259.

Berkshire

Civil

Alderman v. French, Common Pleas, Sept. term 1821; Supreme Judicial Court trial May 1822, appeal Sept. 1822, judgment read May term 1823; 18 Mass. (1 Pick.) 1.

Grotius Bloss v. Augustus Tobey, Common Pleas; Supreme Judicial Court
    trial Sept. 1823 [?], appeal Sept. 1824; 19 Mass. (2 Pick.) 320.
Ezekiel Remington v. William Congdon and Seneca Congdon, 19 Mass. (2
    Pick.) 310 (Sept. term 1824).
Daniel D. Stone v. Levi Crocker, 41 Mass. (24 Pick.) 81 (Sept. term 1832).
John Sperry v. Reuben Wilcox, 42 Mass. (1 Met.) 267 (Sept. term 1840).
Franklin O. Sayles v. Peter Briggs, 42 Mass. (1 Met.) 291 (Sept. term
    1840).

Bristol

Civil

Jonathan Allen v. Robert Hillman, Common Pleas, Mar. term 1829;
    Supreme Judicial Court when plaintiff nonsuit Nov. term 1830, appeal
    Oct. term 1831; SJC Record Books, v. 5, 96, LDS m/f 905542; 29 Mass.
    (12 Pick.) 101.
Joseph H. Allen v. Henry I. Perkins, Common Pleas, Mar. term 1834;
    Supreme Judicial Court trial Apr. term 1835, appeal Oct. term 1835; SJC
    Record Books, v. 5, 199, LDS m/f 905542; 34 Mass. (17 Pick.) 369.

Criminal

Comm. v. Charles Knowlton, Supreme Judicial Court, Apr. term 1832;
    Record Books, v. 5, 133, LDS m/f 905542.

Essex

Civil

Sophia W. Bodwell v. Caleb Swan and Sena Swan, Common Pleas, Sept.
    term 1824; Supreme Judicial Court trial Apr. term 1825, appeal Apr.
    term 1826; SJC Record Books, v. M, 212, MJA; 20 Mass. (3 Pick.) 376
    (reported judgment says case decided in Nov. term 1825, but court
    records indicate this is incorrect).
Sophia W. Bodwell v. Benjamin Osgood, Common Pleas, Sept. term 1824;
    Supreme Judicial Court trial Nov. term 1824, appeal Nov. term 1825;
    SJC Record Books, v. M, 96, MJA; 20 Mass. (3 Pick.) 379.
John A. Bodwell v. Jacob W. Eastman, Common Pleas, Sept. term 1825;
    Record Books, v. 61, 48, LDS m/f 877730.
Samuel Wonson v. Daniel Sayward, 30 Mass. (13 Pick.) 402 (Nov. term
    1832).

Alfred W. Pike. v. William Beals and Charles Greene, Common Pleas, Sept. term 1835; Record Books, v. 81, 46, LDS m/f 877743; Supreme Judicial Court trial Nov. term 1835, appeal Nov. term 1836; SJC Record Books, v. Q, 27, MJA.

John Brickett v. William Davis, Common Pleas, Mar. term 1837; CP Record Books, v. 84, 41, LDS m/f 877743; Supreme Judicial Court appeal Nov. term 1838, 38 Mass. (21 Pick.) 404 (judgment delivered Apr. term 1839).

Criminal

Comm. v. George B. Cheever, Common Pleas, Jun. term 1835; Record Books, v. 80, 307, MJA, LDS m/f 877742

Comm. v. Dudley Phelps and Ferdinand Andrews, "Salem Police," *Boston Morning Post*, Feb. 19, 1835. Case nol. pros'd.

Franklin

Civil

Alpheus Harding v. William Brooks, Common Pleas, Nov. term 1826; Supreme Judicial Court trial Apr. term 1827, appeal Apr. term 1828; SJC Record Books, v. 3, 27, LDS m/f 901090, 22 Mass. (5 Pick.) 244 (reported judgment says case decided in Sept. term 1827, but court records indicate this is incorrect).

Laura Howe v. Benjamin Perry, Common Pleas, Aug. term 1834; Supreme Judicial Court trial Sept. term 1834, appeal Sept. term 1834; SJC Record Books, v. 4, 11, LDS m/f 901091; 32 Mass. (15 Pick.) 506.

Criminal

Comm. v. Roswell Shepard, Common Pleas, Aug. term 1835; Record Books, v. 11, 244, MJA.

Comm. v. Charles Knowlton, Common Pleas, Aug. term 1835; Record Books, v. 11, 245, MJA.

Hampshire

Civil

Jennett Miller, minor, by her uncle Linus Bagg v. Daniel Parish, Common Pleas, Nov. term 1828; CP Record Books, v. 24, 16v, LDS m/f 893026; Supreme Judicial Court trial Apr. term 1829, appeal Sept. term 1829; SJC Record Books, v. 4, 361, LDS m/f 1579060; 25 Mass. (8 Pick.) 384.

Horace Miner v. Hiram Bagg, Common Pleas, Nov. term 1828; CP Record
Books, v. 24, 33v, LDS m/f 893026; Supreme Judicial Court, Apr. term
1829; SJC Record Books, v. 4, 345, LDS m/f 1579060.

Daniel Parish v. Hiram Bagg, Common Pleas, Mar. term 1829; CP Record
Books, v. 24, 91, LDS m/f 893026; Supreme Judicial Court, Apr. term
1829; SJC Record Books, v. 4, 338, LDS m/f 1579060.

William Swan v. Samuel Luce, Common Pleas, Mar. term 1829; CP Record
Books, v. 24, 96v, LDS m/f 893026; Supreme Judicial Court, Apr. term
1829; SJC Record Books, v. 4, 342, LDS m/f 1579060.

Middlesex

Civil

Call Tufts v. Herbert Marsten [Marstin], Common Pleas, Mar. term 1820; CP
Record Books, Mar.–Jun. 1820, 56, LDS m/f 0901521; Supreme Judicial
Court, Mar. term 1820, Record Book 1820–24, 64, LDS m/f 878216.

Catherine Glezen, minor, by her father Reuben Glezen v. James Draper,
Common Pleas, Mar. term 1820; CP Record Books, Mar.–Jun. 1820,
134, LDS m/f 0901521.

Isaac Shute v. William Barrett, Common Pleas, Sept. term 1826; CP Record
Books, Sept–Dec. 1826, 28, LDS m/f 901524; Supreme Judicial Court trial
Oct. term 1827, appeal Oct. term 1828; SJC Record Books, 1820–24,
LDS m/f 878216; reported with *Oakes v. Barrett*, 24 Mass. (7 Pick.) 82.

Lydia [Lidia] Oakes v. William Barrett, Common Pleas, Sept. term 1826;
Record Books, Sept–Dec. 1826, 25, LDS m/f 901524; Supreme Judicial
Court trial Oct. term 1827, appeal Oct. term 1828; SJC Record Books,
1820–24, LDS m/f 878216; reported with *Shute v. Barrett*, 24 Mass. (7
Pick.) 82.

Abijah Ellis v. Moses Kimball, Common Pleas, Dec. term 1832; Supreme
Judicial Court trial Oct. term 1833, appeal Oct. term 1834; SJC Record
Books, 1830–34, 503, LDS m/f 878217; 33 Mass. (16 Pick.) 132.

Newell C. Pond v. David Hartwell, 34 Mass. (17 Pick.) 269 (Oct. term
1835).

John Abbott v. Benjamin B. Wiley, 34 Mass. (17 Pick.) 321 (Oct. term
1835).

Criminal

Comm. v. David L. Child, Supreme Judicial Court trial, Oct. term 1828,
appeal Oct. term 1832; Record Books, 1830–34, 259, LDS m/f 878217;
30 Mass. (13 Pick.) 198. See also 27 Mass. (10 Pick.) 252 (Oct. 1830).

Comm. v. John Knowlton alias John Smith [Charles Knowlton], Common Pleas, Dec. term 1832; Record Books, Sept.–Dec. 1832, 533, MJA, LDS m/f 901528.

Norfolk

Civil

Ziba Cook v. Abraham Darling, 19 Mass. (2 Pick.) 605 (Oct. term 1824).

Paulina S. Whiting v. Draper Smith, Common Pleas, Apr. term 1829; Supreme Judicial Court trial Feb. term 1830, appeal Feb. term 1831; SJC Record Books, v. 9, 18, LDS m/f 878207; 30 Mass. (13 Pick.) 364 (opinion delivered Oct. 1832).

Benjamin Bradley v. Benjamin Goddard, Common Pleas, Dec. term 1829; Supreme Judicial Court, Feb. term 1830; Record Books, v. 8, 586, LDS m/f 878207.

Benjamin Bradley v. Ebenezer Heath, Common Pleas, Dec. term 1829; Supreme Judicial Court trial Feb. 1830 [?], appeal Nov. 1831; SJC Record Books, v. 9, 81, LDS m/f 878207; 29 Mass. (12 Pick.) 163.

Moses Thacher [Thatcher] v. Gen. Preston Pond, Common Pleas, Dec. term 1837; Record Books, v. 35, 494, LDS m/f 886866.

Plymouth

Criminal

Comm. v. James Blanding, 20 Mass. (3 Pick.) 304 (Oct. 1825). The SJC sat at Plymouth for the counties of Plymouth, Barnstable, Bristol and Dukes. Although this case gives every appearance of having arisen in Bristol, it does not appear in the SJC Record Books for Plymouth or Bristol. A case of the same name was continued in Nov. 1825 in Bristol. The innkeeper, Enoch Fowler, brought other actions in Bristol during this time.

Malicious Prosecution Actions

John Gibbs, minor, by his father Gill Gibbs v. Joseph Davis, Worcester Common Pleas, Sept. term 1820; Record Books, v. 51, 75, LDS m/f 894990.

Jeduthan M. Gibbs, minor, by his father Gill Gibbs v. Eliakim Davis, Worcester Common Pleas, Sept. term 1820; Record Book, v. 51, 79, LDS m/f 894990.

Boylston Fullum v. David Fullum and Cyrus Bruce, Suffolk Common Pleas, Supreme Judicial Court, Nov. term 1821; SJC Record Books, 135, Nov. 1821, MJA.

Thomas Darling v. Liber Cook, Worcester Common Pleas, Dec. term 1820; Record Books, v. 51, 244, LDS m/f 894990.

John Peters v. Simon Gillet, Suffolk Common Pleas, Oct. term 1825; Record Books, 80v, MJA.

Peter Williams v. Isaiah Atkins, Suffolk Common Pleas, Jan. term 1826; Supreme Judicial Court, Nov. term 1826; SJC Record Books, 245, MJA.

Jacob Dickman [Dickenson] v. Jason Chamberlain, Worcester Common Pleas, Mar. term 1830; CP Record Books, v. 71, 35, LDS m/f 895000; Supreme Judicial Court, Apr. term 1830, further proceedings Apr. term 1833; SJC Record Books, v. 8, 75 & v. 9, 36, LDS m/f 2200259.

Ezekiel Wood v. Almira Thayer, minor, by Enoch Thayer and Simon White, Worcester Common Pleas, Dec. term 1830; Record Books, v. 73, 82, LDS m/f 897501.

Ezekiel Mason v. George Jones, Suffolk Common Pleas, Oct. term 1830; Record Books, 274, MJA.

Enos Wilder v. George Holden, Suffolk Common Pleas, Oct. term 1831; Supreme Judicial Court trial, Nov. term 1832, appeal Mar. term 1833; SJC Record Books, 94, MJA; 41 Mass. (24 Pick.)8.

Daniel D. Stone v. Levi Crocker, 41 Mass. (24 Pick.) 81 (Berkshire, Sept. term 1832). (This case was also brought in slander.)

Joseph Clark v. Eliphalet Stone, Worcester Common Pleas, Mar. term 1837; Record Books, v. 86, 183, MJA; Supreme Judicial Court, Apr. term 1837; Record Books, v. 10, 67 LDS m/f 2200260. (This case was also brought in slander.)

John Emerson & Samuel P. Kent v. John S. Kimball, Common Pleas, Oct. term 1839; Supreme Judicial Court, Mar. term 1840; SJC Record Books, 271, MJA.

Phineas Drew v. William H. Hoogs, Common Pleas, Oct. term 1839; Supreme Judicial Court, Nov. term 1840; Record Books, 496, MJA.

Bibliography

Secondary Sources

Abzug, Robert H. *Cosmos Crumbling: American Reform and the Religious Imagination*. New York: Oxford University Press, 1994.

Armstrong, John Russell. "The Exchange Coffee House and St. John's First Club." *Collections of the New Brunswick Historical Society* 7 (1907): 60–78.

Austin, John. "The Collection as Literary Form: Sedgwick's *Tales and Sketches* of 1835." In *Catharine Maria Sedgwick: Critical Perspectives*, edited by Lucinda Damon-Bach and Victoria Clements, 158–70. Boston: Northeastern University Press, 2003.

Avery, Dianne, and Alfred S. Konefsky. "The Daughters of Job: Property Rights and Women's Lives in Mid-Nineteenth-Century Massachusetts," *Law and History Review* 10, no. 2 (1992): 323–56.

Bacon, Edwin M. *Rambles around Old Boston*. Boston: Little, Brown, and Company, 1914.

Bacon, Margaret Hope. "By Moral Force Alone: The Antislavery Women and Nonresistance." In *The Abolitionist Sisterhood: Women's Political Culture in Antebellum America*, edited by Jean Fagan Yellin and John C. Van Horne, 275–97. Ithaca, NY: Cornell University Press, 1994.

Bailyn, Bernard. *The Ideological Origins of the American Revolution*. Cambridge, MA: Belknap Press of Harvard University Press, 1967.

Barker, Hannah. "Stockdale, John." Oxford Dictionary of National Biography, www.oxforddnb.com.

Bartlett, Irving H. "The Persistence of Wendell Phillips." In *The Antislavery Vanguard: New Essays on the Abolitionists*, edited by Martin Duberman, 102–22. Princeton: Princeton University Press, 1965.

Basch, Norma. "Marriage and Domestic Relations." In *The Long Nineteenth Century (1789–1920)*. Cambridge History of Law in America, edited by Michael Grossberg and Christopher L. Tomlins, 245–79. Cambridge: Cambridge University Press, 2008.

Beck, J. Murray. "Archibald, Samuel George William." Dictionary of Canadian Biography Online, www.biographi.ca.

Beck, J. Murray. "Blanchard, Jotham." Dictionary of Canadian Biography Online, www.biographi.ca.

Beck, J.M. "'A Fool for a Client': The Trial of Joseph Howe." *Acadiensis* 3, no. 2 (174): 27–44.

Beck, J. Murray. *The Government of Nova Scotia*. Toronto: University of Toronto Press, 1957.

Beck, J. Murray. "Howe, Joseph." Dictionary of Canadian Biography Online, www.biographi.ca.

Beck, J. Murray. *Joseph Howe*. Vol. 1, *Conservative Reformer 1804–1848*. Kingston: McGill-Queen's University Press, 1982.

Beck, J. Murray. "Nugent, Richard." Dictionary of Canadian Biography Online, www.biographi.ca.

Beck, J. Murray. "Rise and Fall of Nova Scotia's Attorney General: 1749–1983." In *Law in a Colonial Society: The Nova Scotia Experience*, edited by Peter Waite, Sandra Oxner and Thomas Barnes, 125–42. Toronto: Carswell Company, 1984.

Beck, J. Murray. "Robie, Simon Bradstreet." Dictionary of Canadian Biography Online, www.biographi.ca.

Beck, J. Murray. "Young, George Renny." Dictionary of Canadian Biography Online, www.biographi.ca.

Beedell, A.V. "John Reeves's Prosecution for a Seditious Libel, 1795–6: A Study in Political Cynicism." *Historical Journal* 36, no. 4 (1993): 799–824.

Bell, D.G. "Allowed Irregularities: Women Preachers in the Early 19th-Century Maritimes." *Acadiensis* 30, no. 2 (2001): 3–39.

Bell, D.G. "Paths to the Law in the Maritimes, 1810–1825: The Bliss Brothers and Their Circle." *Nova Scotia Historical Review* 8, no. 2 (1988): 6–39.

Bell, D.G. "Religious Liberty and Protestant Dissent in Loyalist New Brunswick." *University of New Brunswick Law Journal* 36 (1987): 146–62.

Bell, D.G. "Sedition among the Loyalists: The Case of Saint John, 1784–1786." *University of New Brunswick Law Journal* 44 (1995): 163–78.

Bell, D.G. "Yankee Preachers and the Struggle for the New Brunswick Christian Conference, 1828–38." In *Revivals, Baptists, & George Rawlyk: A Memorial Volume*, edited by Daniel C. Goodwin, 93–112. Wolfville, NS: Acadia Divinity College, 2000.

Bentham, Jeremy. *On the Liberty of the Press, and Public Discussion*. London: printed for William Hone, 1821.

Benton Jr., Josiah H. *A Notable Libel Case: The Criminal Prosecution of Theodore Lyman Jr. by Daniel Webster in the Supreme Judicial Court of Massachusetts November Term 1828*. Littleton, CO: Fred B. Rothman & Co., 1985.

Bernard, Richard M., and Maris A. Vinovskis. "The Female School Teacher in Ante-bellum Massachusetts." *Journal of Social History* 10, no. 3 (1977): 332–45.

Bezanson, Randall P. *Taxes on Knowledge in America: Exactions of the Press from Colonial Times to the Present*. Philadelphia: University of Pennsylvania Press, 1994.

Billias, George Athan. *Elbridge Gerry: Founding Father and Republican Statesman*. New York: McGraw-Hill Book Company, 1976.

Billington, Ray Allen. *The Protestant Crusade 1800–1860: A Study of the Origins of American Nativism*. Chicago: Quadrangle Books, 1964.

Bird, Wendell. Freedoms of Press and Speech in the First Decade of the U.S. Supreme Court. D. Phil. diss., Oxford University, 2011.

Bird, Wendell. "New Light on the Sedition Act of 1798: The Missing Half of the Prosecutions." *Law and History Review* 34, no. 3 (2016): 541–614.

Bird, Wendell. *Press and Speech under Assault: The Early Supreme Court Justices, the Sedition Act of 1798, and the Campaign against Dissent*. New York: Oxford University Press, 2016.

Bitterman, Rusty. "Farm Households and Wage Labour in the Northeastern Maritimes in the Early 19th Century." In *Labour and Working-Class History in Atlantic Canada: A Reader*, edited by David Frank and Gregory S. Kealey, 9–40. St. John's, NF: Institute of Social and Economic Research, 1995.

Blakeley, Phyllis R. "Blowers, Sampson Salter." Dictionary of Canadian Biography Online, www.biographi.ca.

Blakeley, Phyllis R. "Cunard, Sir Samuel." Dictionary of Canadian Biography Online, www.biographi.ca.

Bloch, Ruth H. "Inside and Outside the Public Sphere." *William and Mary Quarterly*, 3rd ser., 62 (2005): 99–106.

Bonney, Margaret Atherton. "The Salubria Story." *The Palimpsest* 56, no. 2 (1975): 34–45.

Bonomi, Patricia U. *Under the Cope of Heaven: Religion, Society, and Politics in Colonial America*. New York: Oxford University Press, 1986.

Booth, Alan. "'The Memory of the Liberty of the Press': The Suppression of Radical Writings in the 1790s." In *Writing and Censorship in Britain*, edited by Paul Hyland and Neil Sammells, 107–22. London and New York: Routledge, 1992.

Boylan, Anne M. *The Origins of Women's Activism*. Chapel Hill: University of North Carolina Press, 2002.

Brewer, Holly. "The Transformation of Domestic Law." In *The Cambridge History of Law in America*. Vol. 1, *Early America (1580–1815)*, edited by

Michael Grossberg and Christopher L. Tomlins, 288–323. Cambridge: Cambridge University Press, 2008.

Briggs, Asa. *A History of Longmans and Their Books 1724–1990: Longevity in Publishing*. London: British Library, and New Castle, DE: Oak Knoll Press, 2008.

Brown, George S. *Yarmouth, Nova Scotia: A Sequel to Campbell's History*. Boston: Rand Avery Company, 1888.

Brown, Kate Elizabeth. "Rethinking *People v. Croswell*: Alexander Hamilton and the Nature and Scope of 'Common Law' in the Early Republic." *Law and History Review* 32, no. 3 (2014): 611–45.

Brown, R. Blake. *A Trying Question: The Jury in Nineteenth-Century Canada*. Toronto: University of Toronto Press for the Osgoode Society, 2009.

Buckner, Phillip. "Chipman, Ward." Dictionary of Canadian Biography Online, www.biographi.ca.

Buggey, S. "Mortimer, Edward." Dictionary of Canadian Biography Online, www.biographi.ca.

Bullock, Steven C. *Revolutionary Brotherhood: Freemasonry and the Transformation of the American Social Order, 1730–1840*. Chapel Hill: University of North Carolina Press, 1996.

Bumsted, J.M. *The People's Clearance: Highland Emigration to British North America, 1770–1815*. Winnipeg: University of Manitoba Press, 1982.

Bunting, William Franklin. *History of St. John's Lodge, F. & A.M. of Saint John, New Brunswick, Together with Sketches of All Masonic Bodies in New Brunswick, from A. D. 1784 to A. D. 1894*. Saint John, NB: J. & A. McMillan, 1895.

Burkholder, Robert E. "Emerson, Kneeland, and the Divinity School Address." *American Literature* 58, no. 1 (1986): 1–14.

Bussiere, Elizabeth. "Trial by Jury as Mockery of Justice: Party Contention, Courtroom Corruption, and the Ironic Judicial Legacy of Antimasonry." *Law and History Review* 34, no. 1 (2016): 155–98.

Cahill, Barry. "*Habeas Corpus* and Slavery in Nova Scotia: *R. v. Hecht Ex Parte Rachel*, 1798." *University of New Brunswick Law Journal* 44 (1994): 179–209.

Cahill, Barry. "*Howe* (1835), *Dixon* (1920) and *McLachlan* (1923): Comparative Perspectives on the Legal History of Sedition." *University of New Brunswick Law Journal* 45 (1996): 281–307.

Cahill, Barry. "*R. v. Howe* (1835) for Seditious Libel: A Tale of Twelve Magistrates." In *Canadian State Trials*. Vol. 1, *Law, Politics, and Security Measures, 1608–1837*, edited by F. Murray Greenwood and Barry Wright, 547–75. Toronto: University of Toronto Press for the Osgoode Society, 1996.

Cahill, Barry. "Sedition in Nova Scotia: *R. v. Howe* and the 'Contested Legality' of Seditious Libel." *University of New Brunswick Law Journal* 51 (2002): 95–140.

Cahill, Barry. "Sedition in Nova Scotia: *R. v. Wilkie* (1820) and the Incontestable Illegality of Seditious Libel before *R. v. Howe* (1835)." *Dalhousie Law Journal* 17, no. 2 (1994): 458–97.

Cahill, Barry. "The Sedition Trial of Timothy Houghton: Repression in a Marginal New England Planter Township during the Revolutionary Years." *Acadiensis* 24, no. 1 (1994): 35–58.

Cahill, Barry. "Slavery and the Judges of Loyalist Nova Scotia." *University of New Brunswick Law Journal* 43 (1994): 73–135.

Cahill, Barry. "The Treason of the Merchants: Dissent and Repression in Halifax in the Era of the American Revolution." *Acadiensis* 26, no. 1, 52–70.

Cahill, Barry, and Jim Phillips. "The Supreme Court of Nova Scotia: Origins to Confederation." In *The Supreme Court of Nova Scotia, 1754–2004: From Imperial Bastion to Provincial Oracle*, edited by Philip Girard, Jim Phillips and Barry Cahill, 53–139. Toronto: University of Toronto Press for the Osgoode Society, 2004.

Cairns, John W. "Hume, David." Oxford Dictionary of National Biography, www.oxforddnb.com.

Calhoun, Craig. "Introduction: Habermas and the Public Sphere." In *Habermas and the Public Sphere*, edited by Craig Calhoun, 1–48. Cambridge, MA: MIT Press, 1992.

Caller, James M., and M.A. Ober. *Genealogy of the Descendants of Lawrence and Cassandra Southwick of Salem, Mass.* Salem, MA: J.H. Choate & Co., 1881.

Campbell, John Richard. *A History of the County of Yarmouth Nova Scotia.* Saint John, NB: J. & A. McMillan, 1876.

Campbell, Lyndsay. "The 'Abolition Riot' Redux: Voices, Processes." *New England Quarterly* 94, no. 1 (2021): 7–46.

Campbell, Lyndsay. "Licence to Publish: Joseph Howe's Contribution to Libel Law in Nova Scotia." *Dalhousie Law Journal* 29, no. 1 (2006): 79–116.

Campbell, Lyndsay. "Race, Upper Canadian Constitutionalism and 'British Justice.'" *Law and History Review* 33, no. 1 (2015): 41–91.

Campbell, Lyndsay. "Starkie's Adventures in North America: The Emergence of Libel Law." In *The Grand Experiment: Law & Legal Culture in British Settler Societies*, edited by Hamar Foster, Benjamin L. Berger and Andrew Buck, 196–207. Vancouver: UBC Press, 2008.

Campbell, Lyndsay. "Truth and Privilege: Libel Treatises and the Transmission of Legal Norms in the Early Nineteenth-Century Anglo-American World." In *Law Books in Action: Essays on the Anglo-American Legal Treatise*, edited by Angela Fernandez and Markus D. Dubber, 165–80. Oxford: Hart Publishing, 2012.

Campey, Lucille H. *After the Hector: The Scottish Pioneers of Nova Scotia and Cape Breton, 1773–1852.* Toronto: Natural Heritage Books, 2004.

Ceplair, Larry. *The Public Years of Sarah and Angelina Grimké.* New York: Columbia University Press, 1989.

Chafee Jr., Zechariah. *Free Speech in the United States*. Cambridge, MA: Harvard University Press, 1942.

Chambers-Schiller, Lee. "'A Good Work among the People': The Political Culture of the Boston Antislavery Fair." In *The Abolitionist Sisterhood: Women's Political Culture in Antebellum America*, edited by Jean Fagan Yellin and J. C. Van Horne, 249–74. Ithaca, NY: Cornell University Press, 1994.

Chisholm, Joseph A. "The King v. Joseph Howe: Prosecution for Libel." *Canadian Bar Review* 13, no. 8 (1935): 584–93.

Chroust, Anton-Hermann. *The Rise of the Legal Profession in America*. Vol. 2, *The Revolution and the Post-Revolutionary Era*. Norman: University of Oklahoma Press, 1965.

Clark, J.C.D. *The Language of Liberty 1660–1832: Political Discourse and Social Dynamics in the Anglo-American World*. Cambridge: Cambridge University Press, 1994.

Clark, S.D. *Church and Sect in Canada*. Toronto: University of Toronto Press, 1948.

Clarke, Ernest A., and Jim Phillips. "Rebellion and Repression in Nova Scotia in the Era of the American Revolution." In *Canadian State Trials*. Vol. 1, *Law, Politics, and Security Measures, 1608–1837*, edited by F. Murray Greenwood and Barry Wright, 172–220. Toronto: University of Toronto Press, 1996.

Clarke, James Freeman. "The Antislavery Movement in Boston." In *The Memorial History of Boston, Including Suffolk County, Massachusetts, 1630–1880*. Vol. 3, *The Revolutionary Period, The Last Hundred Years, Part I*, edited by Justin Winsor, 369–400. Boston: Ticknor and Company, 1881.

Clarke, Mary Patterson. *Parliamentary Privilege in the American Colonies*. New York: Da Capo Press, 1971, originally published in 1943.

Cmiel, Kenneth. *Democratic Eloquence: The Fight over Popular Speech in Nineteenth-Century America*. New York: William Morrow & Co., 1990.

Cochran, Peter. "Hobhouse, John Cam, Baron Broughton." Oxford Dictionary of National Biography, www.oxforddnb.com.

Colley, Linda. *Britons: Forging the Nation 1707–1837*. London: Pimlico, 2003.

Commager, Henry Steele. "The Blasphemy of Abner Kneeland." *New England Quarterly* 8, no. 1 (1935): 29–41.

Comstock, C.B. *Some Descendants of Samuel Comstock of Providence, R.I., Who Died about 1660*. New York: Knickerbocker Press, 1905.

Conrad, Margaret. *Recording Angels: The Private Chronicles of Women from the Maritime Provinces of Canada, 1750–1950*. Ottawa: Canadian Research Institute for the Advancement of Women, 1982.

Conroy, David W. *In Public Houses: Drink and the Revolution of Authority in Colonial Massachusetts*. Chapel Hill: University of North Carolina Press, 1995.

Cooley, Thomas M. *A Treatise on the Constitutional Limitations which Rest upon the Legislative Power of the States of the American Union.* Boston: Little, Brown, and Company, 1868.

Cowley, Charles. *Illustrated History of Lowell.* Boston: Lee & Shepard, 1868.

Craton, Michael, and Gail Saunders. *Islanders in the Stream: A History of the Bahamian People.* Vol. 1, *From Aboriginal Times to the End of Slavery.* Athens: University of Georgia Press, 1999.

Creighton, Donald. *A History of Canada: Dominion of the North*, rev. ed. Boston: Houghton Mifflin, 1958.

Cressy, David. *Dangerous Talk: Scandalous, Seditious, and Treasonable Speech in Pre-Modern England.* Oxford: Oxford University Press, 2010.

Curry, Thomas J. *The First Freedoms: Church and State in America to the Passage of the First Amendment.* New York: Oxford University Press, 1986.

Curtis, C.A. "History of the Canadian Currency." Quebec History, http://faculty.marianopolis.edu/c.belanger/quebechistory/encyclopedia/CanadianCurrency-CurrencyinCanada.htm, reprinted from *The Encyclopedia of Canada.* Vol. 2, edited by W. Stewart Wallace, 159–67. Toronto: University Associates of Canada, 1948.

Curtis, Michael Kent. *Free Speech, "The People's Darling Privilege": Struggles for Freedom of Expression in American History.* Durham, NC: Duke University Press, 2000.

Cushing, John D. "Notes on Disestablishment in Massachusetts, 1780–1833." *William and Mary Quarterly* 26, no. 2 (1969): 169–90.

Cuthbertson, Brian. *Johnny Bluenose.* Halifax, NS: Formac Publishing, 1994.

Cuthbertson, Brian. *The Old Attorney General: A Biography of Richard John Uniacke.* Halifax, NS: Nimbus Publishing, 1980.

Cuthbertson, B.C.U. "Place, Politics and the Brandy Election of 1830." *Collections of the Royal Nova Scotia Historical Society* 41(1982): 5–19.

Davidson, Cathy N., and Jessamyn Hatcher, eds. *No More Separate Spheres! A Next Wave American Studies Reader.* Durham, NC: Duke University Press, 2002.

Davis, Michael T. "Tooke, John Horne." Oxford Dictionary of National Biography, www.oxforddnb.com.

Davis, William T. *Bench and Bar of the Commonwealth of Massachusetts.* 2 vols. Boston: Boston Publishing Company, 1895.

Davis, William T. *History of the Judiciary of Massachusetts, Including the Plymouth and Massachusetts Colonies, the Province of the Massachusetts Bay, and the Commonwealth.* Boston: Boston Book Co., 1900.

Dawson, Joan. *Nova Scotia's Lost Highways: The Early Roads That Shaped the Province.* Halifax, NS: Nimbus Publishing, 2009.

Dayton, Cornelia Hughes. *Women before the Bar: Gender, Law, and Society in Connecticut, 1639–1789.* Chapel Hill: University of North Carolina Press, 1995.

Dennis, Donna. "Obscenity Law and the Conditions of Freedom in the Nineteenth-Century United States." *Law & Social Inquiry* 27, no. 2 (2002): 369–99.

d'Entremont, H. Leander. "Father Jean Mande Sigogne, 1799–1844." *Collections of the Nova Scotia Historical Society* 23 (1936): 103–15.

Dickerson, Donna Lee. *The Course of Tolerance: Freedom of the Press in Nineteenth-Century America.* New York: Greenwood Press, 1990.

Dublin, Thomas. *Women at Work: The Transformation of Work and Community in Lowell, Massachusetts, 1826–1860.* New York: Columbia University Press, 1979.

Ducharme, Michel. *The Idea of Liberty in Canada during the Age of Atlantic Revolutions, 1776–1838,* translated by Peter Feldstein. Montreal: McGill-Queen's University Press, 2014.

Dumond, Dwight Lowell. *Antislavery: The Crusade for Freedom in America.* Ann Arbor: University of Michigan Press, 1961.

Duniway, Clyde Augustus. *The Development of Freedom of the Press in Massachusetts.* Cambridge, MA: Harvard University Press, 1906.

Dunlop, Allan C. "Albro, John." Dictionary of Canadian Biography Online, www.biographi.ca.

Dunlop, Allan C. "Dickson, Thomas." Dictionary of Canadian Biography Online, www.biographi.ca.

Dunn, Susan. *Jefferson's Second Revolution: The Election Crisis of 1800 and the Triumph of Republicanism.* Boston: Houghton Mifflin, 2004.

Eamon, Michael. *Imprinting Britain: Newspapers, Sociability, and the Shaping of British North America.* Montreal: McGill-Queen's University Press, 2015.

Eckhardt, Celia Morris. *Fanny Wright: Rebel in America.* Cambridge, MA: Harvard University Press, 1984.

Edwards, Laura. "Status without Rights: African Americans and the Tangled History of Law and Governance in the Nineteenth-Century U.S. South." *American Historical Review* 112, no. 2 (2007): 365–93.

Eldridge, Larry D. "Before Zenger: Seditious Speech in Colonial America, 1607–1700." *American Journal of Legal History* 39, no. 3 (1995): 337–58.

Evans, R.D. "Stage Coaches in Nova Scotia, 1815 to 1867." *Collections of the Nova Scotia Historical Society* 24 (1938): 107–34.

Farish, James C. *Yarmouth 1821.* Yarmouth, NS: Yarmouth County Historical Society, 1971.

Fingard, Judith. "Attitudes towards the Education of the Poor in Colonial Halifax." *Acadiensis* 2, no. 2 (1973): 15–41.

Fingard, Judith. "The 1820s: Peace, Privilege, and the Promise of Progress." In *The Atlantic Region to Confederation: A History,* edited by Phillip A. Buckner & John G. Reid, 263–83. Toronto: University of Toronto Press, 1994.

Finkelman, Paul, ed. *A Brief Narrative of the Case and Tryal of John Peter Zenger: Printer of the New York Weekly Journal*. St. James, NY: Brandywine Press, 1997.

French, Roderick S. "Liberation from Man and God in Boston: Abner Kneeland's Free-Thought Campaign, 1830–1839." *American Quarterly* 32, no. 2 (1980): 202–21.

French, Roderick S. The Trials of Abner Kneeland: A Study in the Rejection of Democratic Secular Humanism. Ph.D. diss., George Washington University, 1971.

Gallaher, Ruth A. "Abner Kneeland – Pantheist." *The Palimpsest* 20, no. 7 (1939): 209–25.

Garner, John. *The Franchise and Politics in British North America 1755–1867*. Ottawa: University of Toronto Press, 1969.

Garrison, Wendell Phillips. *William Lloyd Garrison 1805–1879, The Story of His Life, Told by His Children*. Vol. 1. New York: Century, 1885.

Gawalt, Gerard Wilfred. Massachusetts Lawyers: A Historical Analysis of the Process of Professionalization, 1760–1840. Ph.D. diss., Clark University, 1969.

Gilman, Alfred. "Lowell." In *History of Middlesex County, Massachusetts, Containing Carefully Prepared Histories of Every City and Town in the County, by Well-Known Writers* [etc.], edited by Samuel Adams Drake, 53–113. Boston: Estes and Lauriat, 1880.

Gilmore, William J. *Reading Becomes a Necessity of Life: Material and Cultural Life in Rural New England, 1780–1835*. Knoxville: University of Tennessee Press, 1989.

Ginzberg, Lori D. "'The Hearts of Your Readers Will Shudder': Fanny Wright, Infidelity, and American Freethought." *American Quarterly* 46, no. 2 (1994): 195–226.

Girard, Philip. "'I Will Not Pin My Faith to His Sleeve': Beamish Murdoch, Joseph Howe, and Responsible Government Revisited." *Journal of the Royal Nova Scotia Historical Society* 4 (2001): 48–69.

Girard, Philip. *Lawyers and Legal Culture in British North America: Beamish Murdoch of Halifax*. Toronto: University of Toronto Press for the Osgoode Society, 2011.

Girard, Philip V. Patriot Jurist: Beamish Murdoch of Halifax, 1800–1876. Ph.D. diss., Dalhousie University, 1998.

Girard, Philip. "The Rise and Fall of Urban Justice in Halifax, 1815–1886." *Nova Scotia Historical Review* 8, no. 2 (1988): 57–71.

Girard, Philip. "Themes and Variations in Early Canadian Legal Culture: Beamish Murdoch and His Epitome of the Laws of Nova Scotia." *Law and History Review* 11, no. 1 (1993): 101–44.

Goodwin, Daniel C. *Into Deep Waters: Evangelical Spirituality and Maritime Calvinistic Baptist Ministers, 1790–1855*. Montreal: McGill-Queen's University Press, 2010.

Grant, John N. "The Canso Riots of 1833: 'The Lawlessness of These People Is Truly Beyond Comprehension." *Nova Scotia Historical Review* 14, no. 2 (1994): 1–19.

Greco, Clara. "The Superior Court Judiciary of Nova Scotia, 1754–1900: A Collective Biography." In *Essays in the History of Canadian Law.* Vol. 3, *Nova Scotia*, edited by Philip Girard and Jim Phillips, 42–79. Toronto: University of Toronto Press for the Osgoode Society, 1990.

Green, Samuel A. *An Account of the Lawyers of Groton, Massachusetts* [etc.]. Cambridge, MA: John Wilson and Son, 1892.

Green, Thomas A. "The Jury, Seditious Libel, and the Criminal Law." In *Juries, Libel, & Justice: The Role of English Juries in Seventeenth- and Eighteenth-Century Trials for Libel and Slander*, edited by R.H. Helmholz and Thomas A. Green, 37–91. Los Angeles: Williams Andrew Clark Memorial Library, University of California, Los Angeles, 1984.

Greene, Evarts Boutell. *The Provincial Governor in the English Colonies of North America.* New York: Russell & Russell, 1966.

Greene, Jack P. *The Constitutional Origins of the American Revolution.* Cambridge: Cambridge University Press, 2011.

Greenwood, F. Murray, and Barry Wright, eds. *Canadian State Trials.* Vol. 1, *Law, Politics, and Security Measures, 1608–1837.* Toronto: University of Toronto Press, 1996.

Greenwood, F. Murray, and Barry Wright, eds. *Canadian State Trials.* Vol. 2, *Rebellion and Invasion in the Canadas, 1837–1839.* Toronto: University of Toronto Press, 2002.

Greenwood, F. Murray, and Barry Wright. "Parliamentary Privilege and the Repression of Dissent in the Canadas." In *Canadian State Trials.* Vol. 1, *Law, Politics, and Security Measures, 1608–1837*, edited by F. Murray Greenwood and Barry Wright, 409–49. Toronto: University of Toronto Press, 1996.

Gregory, Winifred, ed. *American Newspapers 1821–1936: A Union List of Files Available in the United States and Canada.* New York: H.W. Wilson, 1937.

Griffith, William. *Annual Law Register of the United States.* Vol. 3. Burlington, NJ: David Allinson, 1822.

Grossberg, Michael. *Governing the Hearth: Law and Family in Nineteenth-Century America.* Chapel Hill: University of North Carolina Press, 1985.

Guildford, Janet. "Separate Spheres: The Feminization of Public School Teaching in Nova Scotia, 1838–1880." In *Separate Spheres: Women's Worlds in the 19th-Century Maritimes*, edited by Janet Guildford and Suzanne Morton, 119–43. Fredericton, NB: Acadiensis Press, 1994.

Gwyn, Julian. "Female Litigants before the Civil Courts of Nova Scotia, 1749–1801." *Histoire Sociale/Social History* 36 (2003): 311–46.

Gwyn, Julian. "Imports and the Changing Standard of Living in Nova Scotia, 1832–1872." *Nova Scotia Historical Review* 11, no. 2 (1991): 43–64.

Gwyn, Julian. "Women as Litigants before the Supreme Court of Nova Scotia, 1754–1830." In *The Supreme Court of Nova Scotia, 1754–2004: From Imperial Bastion to Provincial Oracle*, edited by Philip Girard, Jim Phillips and Barry Cahill, 294–320. Toronto: University of Toronto Press for the Osgoode Society, 2004.

Habermas, Jürgen. *The Structural Transformation of the Public Sphere: An Inquiry into a Category of Bourgeois Society*, edited by Frederick Lawrence, translated by Thomas Burger. Cambridge, MA: MIT Press, 1991.

Hales, J.G. *Map of Boston in the State of Massachusetts*. Boston: Library of Congress, 1814. www.loc.gov/resource/g3764b.wd000501/.

"Hallett, Benjamin." In *Appleton's Cyclopedia of American Biography*, edited by James Grant Wilson and John Fiske, Vol. 3. New York: D. Appleton & Company, 1888.

Hamburger, Philip. "The Development of the Law of Seditious Libel and the Control of the Press." *Stanford Law Review* 37, no. 3 (1985): 661–765.

Hamburger, Philip. *Separation of Church and State*. Cambridge, MA: Harvard University Press, 2002.

Hansen, Karen V. *A Very Social Time: Crafting Community in Antebellum New England*. Berkeley: University of California Press, 1994.

Harland-Jacobs, Jessica L. *Builders of Empire: Freemasonry and British Imperialism, 1717–1927*. Durham, NC: University of North Carolina Press, 2007.

Harling, Philip. "The Law of Libel and the Limits of Repression, 1790–1832." *Historical Journal* 44, no. 1 (2001): 107–34.

Harper, John Paull. "Be Fruitful and Multiply: Origins of Legal Restrictions on Planned Parenthood in Nineteenth-Century America." In *Women of America: A History*, edited by Carol Ruth Berkin and Mary Beth Norton, 244–69. Boston: Houghton Mifflin, 1979.

Harvey, D.C. "The Civil List and Responsible Government in Nova Scotia." *Canadian Historical Review* 28, no. 4 (1947): 365–82.

Harvey, D.C. "Early Public Libraries in Nova Scotia." *Dalhousie Review* 14 (1934–35): 429–43.

Harvey, D.C. "The Intellectual Awakening of Nova Scotia." *Dalhousie Review* 13 (1933): 1–22.

Hatch, Nathan O. *The Democratization of American Christianity*. New Haven: Yale University Press, 1989.

Hay, Douglas. "Contempt by Scandalizing the Court: A Political History of the First Hundred Years." *Osgoode Hall Law Journal* 25, no. 3 (1987): 431–84.

Hay, Douglas. "Property, Authority and the Criminal Law." In *Albion's Fatal Tree: Crime and Society in Eighteenth-Century England*, by Douglas Hay, Peter Linebaugh, John G. Rule, E.P. Thompson and Carl Winslow, rev. ed., 17–63. London: Verso, 2011.

Helmholz, R.H. "Civil Trials and the Limits of Responsible Speech." In *Juries, Libel, & Justice: The Role of English Juries in Seventeenth- and Eighteenth-Century Trials for Libel and Slander*, edited by R.H. Helmholz and Thomas A. Green, 1–36. Los Angeles: Williams Andrew Clark Memorial Library, University of California, Los Angeles, 1984.

Hempton, David. *Methodism: Empire of the Spirit*. New Haven: Yale University Press, 2005.

"Henshaw, David, 1791–1852." Library of Congress Name Authority File, id. loc.gov/authorities/names/n88002077.html.

Hill, Kay. *Joe Howe: The Man Who Was Nova Scotia*. Toronto: McClelland & Stewart, 1980.

Himes, Norman E. *Medical History of Contraception*. New York: Schocken Books, 1970.

Hobson, Barbara Meil. *Uneasy Virtue*. Chicago: University of Chicago Press, 1987.

Hoffer, Peter Charles. *The Free Press Crisis of 1800: Thomas Cooper's Trial for Seditious Libel*. Lawrence: University Press of Kansas, 2011.

Hoffman, Nicole Tonkovich. "Sarah Josepha Hale (1788–1874)." *Legacy* 7, no. 2 (1990): 47–55.

Holdsworth, W.S. *A History of English Law*. Vol. 1. London: Methuen & Co., 1903.

Holman, H.T. "Palmer, James Bardin." Dictionary of Canadian Biography Online, www.biographi.ca.

Horowitz, Helen Lefkowitz. *Rereading Sex: Battles over Sexual Knowledge and Suppression in Nineteenth-Century America*. New York: Knopf, 2002.

Horton, James Oliver, and Lois E. Horton. *Black Bostonians: Family Life and Community Struggle in the Antebellum North*. New York: Holmes & Meier Publishers, 1979.

Horwitz, Morton. *The Transformation of American Law, 1780–1860*. New York: Oxford University Press, 1992.

Howes, Frederick G. *History of the Town of Ashfield, Franklin County, Massachusetts from Its Settlement in 1742 to 1910; Also a Historical Sketch of the Town Written by Dr. Thomas Shepard in 1834*. Ashfield, CA. 1910.

Hulsebosch, Daniel J. *Constituting Empire: New York and the Transformation of Constitutionalism in the Atlantic World, 1664–1830*. Chapel Hill: University of North Carolina Press, 2005.

Hunt, Alan. *Governing Morals: A Social History of Moral Regulation*. Cambridge: Cambridge University Press, 1999.

Hunt, Lynn. *Inventing Human Rights: A History*. New York: W.W. Norton, 2007.

Hunter, Ian, David Saunders and Dugald Williamson. *On Pornography: Literature, Sexuality and Obscenity Law*. Houndsmills, UK: Macmillan, 1993.

Hunter, James Davison. *Culture Wars: The Struggle to Define America*. New York: Basic Books, 1991.

Hurd, D. Hamilton. *History of Bristol County, Massachusetts, with Biographical Sketches of Many of Its Pioneers and Prominent Men*. Vol. 1. Philadelphia: J.W. Lewis & Co., 1883.

Hurd, D. Hamilton. *History of Worcester County, Massachusetts, with Biographical Sketches of Many of Its Pioneers and Prominent Men.* Vol. 1. Philadelphia: J.W. Lewis & Co., 1889.

Isenberg, Nancy. *Sex and Citizenship in Antebellum America.* Chapel Hill: University of North Carolina Press, 1998.

James, Charles P. *The Power of Congress to Punish Contempts and Breaches of Privilege.* Washington, DC: W.H. & O.H. Morrison, 1879.

Johnson, Richard R. "'Parliamentary Egotisms': The Clash of Legislatures in the Making of the American Revolution." *Journal of American History* 74, no. 2 (1987): 337–62.

Johnson, Whittington B. *Race Relations in the Bahamas, 1784–1834: The Nonviolent Transformation from a Slave to a Free Society.* Fayetteville: University of Arksansas Press, 2000.

Jones, David Lewis. "Hansard, Thomas Curson." Oxford Dictionary of National Biography, www.oxforddnb.com.

Kamensky, Jane. *Governing the Tongue: The Politics of Speech in Early New England.* New York: Oxford University Press, 1997.

Karcher, Carolyn L. *The First Woman in the Republic: A Cultural Biography of Lydia Maria Child.* Durham, NC: Duke University Press, 1994.

Kelley, Mary. *Learning to Stand & Speak: Women, Education, and Public Life in America's Republic.* Chapel Hill: University of North Carolina Press, 2006.

Kelly, Catherine F. *In the New England Fashion: Reshaping Women's Lives in the Nineteenth Century.* Ithaca, NY: Cornell University Press, 1999.

Kennedy, Joan E. "Jane Soley Hamilton, Midwife." *Nova Scotia Historical Review* 2, no. 1 (1982): 6–29.

Kerber, Linda K. "Separate Spheres, Female Worlds, Woman's Place: The Rhetoric of Women's History." *Journal of American History* 75, no. 1 (1988): 9–39.

Kerber, Linda K. *Toward an Intellectual History of Women: Essays by Linda K. Kerber.* Chapel Hill: University of North Carolina Press, 1997.

Kielbowicz, Richard B. "The Law and Mob Law in Attacks on Antislavery Newspapers, 1833–1860." *Law and History Review* 24, no. 3 (2006): 559–600.

King, Andrew. "The Law of Slander in Early Antebellum America." *American Journal of Legal History* 35, no. 1 (1991): 1–43.

Kornblith, Gary J. "Becoming Joseph T. Buckingham: The Struggle for Artisanal Independence in Early-Nineteenth-Century Boston." In *American Artisans: Crafting Social Identity, 1750–1850*, edited by Howard B. Rock, Paul A. Gilje and Robert Asher, 123–34. Baltimore: Johns Hopkins University Press, 1995.

Koschnik, Albrecht. "Young Federalists, Masculinity, and Partisanship during the War of 1812." In *Beyond the Founders: New Approaches to the Political History of the Early American Republic*, edited by Jeffrey L. Pasley, Andrew

W. Robertson and David Waldstreicher, 159–79. Chapel Hill: University of North Carolina Press, 2004.

Kramer, Larry D. *The People Themselves: Popular Constitutionalism and Judicial Review*. New York: Oxford University Press, 2004.

Labaree, Leonard Woods. *Royal Instructions to British Colonial Governors 1670–1776*. 2 vols. New York: Octagon Books, Inc., 1967.

Lane, J.P. *Historical Sketches of the First Congregational Church, Bristol, R.I., 1687–1872*. Providence, RI: Providence Press Company, 1872.

Lane, Roger. *Policing the City: Boston 1822–1885*. Cambridge, MA: Harvard University Press, 1967.

Langbein, John H. "The Prosecutorial Origin of Defence Counsel in the Eighteenth Century: The Appearance of Solicitors." *Cambridge Law Journal* 58, no. 2 (1999): 314–465.

Laurence, William H. "Acquiring the Law: The Personal Law Library of William Young, Halifax, Nova Scotia, 1835." *Dalhousie Law Journal* 21, no. 2 (1998): 490–515.

Laurence, William H. "Process and Particulars: The Informational Needs and Sources of a Nineteenth-Century Nova Scotian Sheriff." *Épilogue* 12, no. 1 (1997): 1–22.

Laurie, Bruce. "'Spavined Ministers, Lying Toothpullers, and Buggering Priests': Third-Partyism and the Search for Security in the Antebellum North." In *American Artisans: Crafting Social Identity, 1750–1850*, edited by Howard B. Rock, Paul A. Gilje and Robert Asher, 98–119. Baltimore: Johns Hopkins University Press, 1995.

Lawes, Carolyn J. *Women and Reform in a New England Community, 1815–1860*. Lexington: University Press of Kentucky, 2000.

Leonard, Thomas C. *News for All: America's Coming-of-Age with the Press*. New York: Oxford University Press, 1995.

Levy, Leonard. "The 'Abolition Riot': Boston's First Slave Rescue." *New England Quarterly* 25, no. 1 (1952): 85–92.

Levy, Leonard W. *Blasphemy: Verbal Offense against the Sacred, from Moses to Salman Rushdie*. New York: Knopf, 1993.

Levy, Leonard. *Blasphemy in Massachusetts: Freedom of Conscience and the Abner Kneeland Case, A Documentary Record*. New York: Da Capo Press, 1973.

Levy, Leonard W. "Did the Zenger Case Really Matter? Freedom of the Press in Colonial New York." *William and Mary Quarterly* 17, no. 1 (1960): 35–50.

Levy, Leonard W. *Emergence of a Free Press*. New York: Oxford University Press, 1985.

Levy, Leonard W. *The Law of the Commonwealth and Chief Justice Shaw*. Cambridge, MA: Harvard University Press, 1957.

Levy, Leonard W. *Legacy of Suppression: Freedom of Speech and Press in Early American History*. Cambridge, MA: Belknap Press of Harvard University Press, 1960.

Lieberman, David. "The Mixed Constitution and the Common Law." In *The Cambridge History of Eighteenth-Century Political Thought*, edited by Mark Goldie and Robert Wokler, 317–46. Cambridge: Cambridge University Press, 2006.

Lincoln, William. *History of Worcester, Massachusetts: From Its Earliest Settlement to September 1836* [etc.]. Worcester: Charles Hershey, 1862, originally published in 1837.

Lobban, Michael. "Brougham, Henry Peter." Oxford Dictionary of National Biography, www.oxforddnb.com.

Lobban, Michael. "From Seditious Libel to Unlawful Assembly: Peterloo and the Changing Face of Political Crime c1770–1820." *Oxford Journal of Legal Studies* 10, no. 3 (1990): 307–52.

Lobban, Michael. "Holt, Francis Ludlow." Oxford Dictionary of National Biography, www.oxforddnb.com.

Lobban, Michael. "Law, Edward." Oxford Dictionary of National Biography, www.oxforddnb.com.

Logan, J.D. "Plays and Players in Halifax – A Hundred Years and More." In Scrapbook on Nova Scotia, Vol. 36, MG 9, Nova Scotia Archives, Halifax.

Longley, J.W. *Joseph Howe*. Toronto: Morang & Co., 1909.

Longworth, Israel. *Life of S.G.W. Archibald*. Halifax, NS: S.F. Huestis, 1881.

Lynch, Peter. "Early Reminiscences of Halifax – Men Who Have Passed from Us." *Collections of the Nova Scotia Historical Society* 16 (1912): 171–204.

Macdonald, James S. *Annals North British Society, Halifax, Nova Scotia*. Halifax, NS: McAlpine Publishing Company, 1905.

Mackey, Philip English. "Reverend George Barrell Cheever: Yankee Reformer As Champion of the Gallows." *Proceedings of the American Antiquarian Society* 82, no. 2 (1972): 323–42.

Macleod, John. "The Library of Richard John Uniacke." In *History of the Book in Canada*. Vol. 1, *Beginnings to 1840*, edited by Patricia Lockhart Fleming, Gilles Gallichan and Yvan Lamonde, 209–10. Toronto: University of Toronto Press, 2004.

MacPherson, Flora. *Watchman against the World: The Story of Norman McLeod and His People*. Toronto: Ryerson, 1962.

Madison, James H. "The Evolution of Commercial Credit Reporting Agencies in Nineteenth-Century America." *Business History Review* 48, no. 2 (1974): 164–86.

Maier, Pauline. "Popular Uprisings and Civil Authority in Eighteenth-Century America." In *American Law and the Constitutional Order: Historical Perspectives*, edited by Lawrence M. Friedman and Harry N. Scheiber, enlarged edition, 69–84. Cambridge, MA: Harvard University Press, 1988.

Maitland, F.W. *The Constitutional History of England*. Cambridge: Cambridge University Press, 1965, originally published in 1908.

Manchester, Colin. "A History of the Crime of Obscene Libel." *Journal of Legal History* 12, no. 1 (1991): 36–57.

Mancke, Elizabeth. Two Patterns of New England Transformation: Machias, Maine and Liverpool, Nova Scotia, 1760–1820. Ph.D. diss., Johns Hopkins University, 1989.

Marquis, Greg. "Anti-lawyer Sentiment in Mid-Victorian New Brunswick." *University of New Brunswick Law Journal* 36 (1987): 163–74.

Marsh, Joss. *Word Crimes: Blasphemy, Culture, and Literature in Nineteenth-Century England.* Chicago: University of Chicago Press, 1998.

McCoy, Ralph Edward. Banned in Boston: The Development of Literary Censorship in Massachusetts. Ph.D. diss., University of Illinois, 1956.

McCullough, A.B. *Money and Exchange in Canada to 1900.* Toronto: Dundurn Press, 1984.

McCutcheon, Marc. *The Writer's Guide to Everyday Life in the 1800s.* Cincinnati: Writer's Digest Books, 1993.

McDonald, R.H. "Nova Scotia Newspapers View the United States, 1827–1840." *Nova Scotia Historical Quarterly* 6, no. 1 (1976): 1–16.

McInnis, Marvin. "The Population of Canada in the Nineteenth Century." In *A Population History of North America*, edited by Michael R. Haines and Richard H. Steckel, 371–432. Cambridge: Cambridge University Press, 2000.

McKay, Ian. "Lawson, Alexander." Dictionary of Canadian Biography Online, www.biographi.ca.

McNairn, Jeffrey L. *The Capacity to Judge: Public Opinion and Deliberative Democracy in Upper Canada, 1791–1854.* Toronto: University of Toronto Press, 2000.

Miller, Russell E. *The Larger Hope: The First Century of the Universalist Church in America 1770–1870.* Boston: Unitarian Universalist Association, 1979.

Miller, William Lee. *Arguing about Slavery: The Great Battle in the United States Congress.* New York: Knopf, 1995.

Minot, George Richards. *Continuation of the History of the Province of Massachusetts Bay, from the Year 1748. With an Introductory Sketch of Events from Its Original Settlement.* Boston: Manning & Loring, 1798.

Mitchell, Paul. *The Making of the Modern Law of Defamation.* Oxford: Hart Publishing, 2005.

Moody, Barry M. "Crawley, Edmund Albern." Dictionary of Canadian Biography Online, www.biographi.ca.

Moir, John S. *Early Presbyterianism in Canada.* Gravelbourg, SK: Laverdure & Associates, 2003.

Morison, Gene. "The Brandy Election of 1830." *Collections of the Nova Scotia Historical Society* 30 (1954): 151–83.

Muir, Elizabeth Gillian, and Marilyn Färdig Whiteley, eds. *Changing Roles of Women within the Christian Church in Canada.* Toronto: University of Toronto Press, 1995.

Muir, James. *Law, Debt, and Merchant Power: The Civil Courts of Eighteenth-Century Halifax*. Toronto: University of Toronto Press for the Osgoode Society, 2016.

Mullane, George. "Old Inns and Coffee Houses of Halifax." *Collections of the Nova Scotia Historical Society* 22 (1933): 1–23.

Mullane, George. "A Sketch of Lawrence O'Connor Doyle, a Member of the House of Assembly in the Thirties and Forties." *Collections of the Nova Scotia Historical Society* 17 (1913): 151–95.

Myers, Robin. "Hansard, Luke." Oxford Dictionary of National Biography, www.oxforddnb.com.

Neem, Johann N. *Creating a Nation of Joiners: Democracy and Civil Society in Early National Massachusetts*. Cambridge, MA: Harvard University Press, 2008.

Nelson, William E. *Americanization of the Common Law: The Impact of Legal Change on Massachusetts Society, 1760–1830*. Cambridge, MA: Harvard University Press, 1975.

Newman, Richard. "Protest in Black and White: The Formation and Transformation of an African American Political Community during the Early Republic." In *Beyond the Founders: New Approaches to the Political History of the Early American Republic*, edited by Jeffrey L. Pasley, Andrew W. Robertson and David Waldstreicher, 180–204. Chapel Hill: University of North Carolina Press, 2004.

Newmyer, R. Kent. "Harvard Law School, New England Legal Culture, and the Antebellum Origins of American Jurisprudence." *Journal of American History* 74, no. 3 (1987): 814–35.

Newton, Judith L., Mary P. Ryan and Judith R. Walkowitz. *Sex and Class in Women's History*. London: Routledge & Kegan Paul, 1983.

Norton, Mary Beth. "Gender and Defamation in Seventeenth-Century Maryland." *William and Mary Quarterly*, 3rd ser. 44, no. 1 (1987): 3–39.

Novak, William J. *The People's Welfare: Law and Regulation in Nineteenth-Century America*. Chapel Hill: University of North Carolina Press, 1996.

Nye, Russel B. *Fettered Freedom: Civil Liberties and the Slave Controversy 1830–1860*. East Lansing: Michigan State University Press, 1963.

Olbertson, Kristin. Criminally Impolite: Speech Transgressions & Social Order in Massachusetts, 1690–1776. Ph.D. diss., University of Michigan, 2005.

Parker, George L. "Ward, Edmund." Dictionary of Canadian Biography Online, www.biographi.ca.

Pasley, Jeffrey L. *"The Tyranny of Printers": Newspaper Politics in the Early American Republic*. Charlottesville: University of Virginia Press, 2001.

Patterson, George. *A History of the County of Pictou Nova Scotia*. Belleville, ON: Mika Studio, 1972.

Perry, George D. "'The Grand Regulator': State Schooling and the Normal School Idea in Nova Scotia, 1838–1855." *Acadiensis* 32, no. 2 (2003): 60–83.

Phelps, A.A. *The Sabbath*, 2nd ed. New York, 1842.

Phillips, Jim. "A Low Law Counter Treatise? 'Absentees' to 'Wreck' in British North America's First Justice of the Peace Manual." In *Law Books in Action: Essays on the Anglo-American Legal Treatise*, edited by Angela Fernandez and Markus D. Dubber, 203–19. Oxford: Hart Publishing, 2012.

Phillips, Jim, and Bradley Miller. "'Too Many Courts and Too Much Law': The Politics of Judicial Reform in Nova Scotia, 1830–1841." *Law and History Review* 30, no. 1 (2012): 89–133.

Porter, Susan L. "Victorian Values in the Marketplace: Single Women and Work in Boston, 1800–1850." In *Women of the Commonwealth: Work, Family, and Social Change in Nineteenth-Century Massachusetts*, edited by Susan L. Porter, 43–61. Amherst: University of Massachusetts Press, 1996.

Portrait and Biographical Record of Shelby and Moultrie Counties, Illinois. Containing Biographical Sketches of Prominent and Representative Citizens of the Counties, Together with Biographies of All the Governors of the State, and of the Presidents of the United States. Chicago: Biographical Publishing Co., 1891.

Poser, Norman S. *Lord Mansfield: Justice in the Age of Reason.* Montreal: McGill-Queen's University Press, 2013.

Post, Robert C. "Censorship and Silencing." In *Censorship and Silencing: Practices of Cultural Regulation*, edited by Robert C. Post, 1–12. Los Angeles: Getty Research Institute for the History of Art and Humanities, 1998.

Post, Robert C. "Defaming Public Officials: On Doctrine and Legal History." *American Bar Foundation Research Journal [Law & Social Inquiry]* 12, no. 2/3 (1987): 539–57.

Pothier, Bernard. "Sigogne, Jean-Mandé." Dictionary of Canadian Biography Online, www.biographi.ca.

Punch, Terence. "Halifax Town: The Census of 1838." *Nova Scotia Historical Quarterly* 6, no. 3 (1976): 233–58.

Putnam, John. "The Excommunication of Nathaniel Clark." *Pikes Peak Genealogical Society Newsletter* 28 (2008): 1, 4–6.

"Quincy, Josiah. " Dictionary of Unitarian and Universalist Biography, www.uua.org/uuhs/duub/articles/josiahquincy.html.

Rabban, David M. "The Ahistorical Historian: Leonard Levy on Freedom of Expression in Early America." *Stanford Law Review* 37, no. 3 (1985): 795–856.

Rabban, David M. *Free Speech in Its Forgotten Years.* Cambridge: Cambridge University Press, 1997.

Rand, John C. "Moses Everett Ware." In *One of a Thousand: A Series of Biographical Sketches of One Thousand Representative Men Resident in the*

Commonwealth of Massachusetts A. D. 1888-'89, 630–31. Boston: First National, 1890.

Reichardt, Mary R. "Snelling, William Joseph." American National Biography Online, www.anb.org.

Rice, James C., and C.K. Brewster. *History of the Town of Worthington, from Its First Settlement to 1874*. Springfield, MA: Clark W. Bryan & Company, 1874.

Richards, Leonard L. *"Gentlemen of Property and Standing": Anti-Abolition Mobs in Jacksonian America*. New York: Oxford University Press, 1970.

Riegel, Robert E. "The American Father of Birth Control." *New England Quarterly* 6, no. 3 (1933): 470–90.

Robinson, Neil. *To the Ends of the Earth: Norman McLeod and the Highlanders' Migration to Nova Scotia and New Zealand*. Auckland: HarperCollins, 1998.

Rosenberg, Norman L. *Protecting the Best Men: An Interpretive History of the Law of Libel*. Chapel Hill: University of North Carolina Press, 1986.

Rudé, George F.E. "The Gordon Riots: A Study of the Rioters and Their Victims." *Transactions of the Royal Historical Society*, 5th ser., 6 (1956): 93–114.

Rudé, George. *Revolutionary Europe 1783–1815*, 2nd ed. Oxford: Blackwell, 2000.

Ryan, Mary P. *Civic Wars: Democracy and Public Life in the American City during the Nineteenth Century*. Berkeley: University of California Press, 1997.

Ryan, Mary P. *The Empire of the Mother: American Writing about Domesticity 1830–1860*. New York: Institute for Research in History and Haworth Press, 1982.

Ryan, Mary P. *Women in Public: Between Banners and Ballots, 1825–1880*. Baltimore: Johns Hopkins University Press, 1990.

Schauer, Frederick. *Free Speech: A Philosophical Enquiry*. Cambridge: Cambridge University Press, 1982.

Schauer, Frederick F. *The Law of Obscenity*. Washington, DC: Bureau of National Affairs, 1976.

Schlesinger Jr., Arthur M. *The Age of Jackson*. Boston: Little, Brown, 1945.

Schultz, Nancy Lusignan. "Introduction." In *Veil of Fear: Nineteenth-Century Convent Tales*, by Rebecca Reed and Maria Monk, vii–xxxiii. West Lafayette, IN: NotaBell Books, 1999.

Scobie, Charles H.H., and John Webster Grant, eds. *The Contribution of Methodism to Atlantic Canada*. Montreal: McGill-Queen's University Press, 1992.

Shapin, Steven. *A Social History of Truth: Civility and Science in Seventeenth-Century England*. Chicago: University of Chicago Press, 1994.

Shields, David S. *Civil Tongues and Polite Letters in British North America*. Chapel Hill: University of North Carolina Press, 1997.

Shuger, Debora. "Civility and Censorship in Early Modern England." In *Censorship and Silencing: Practices of Cultural Regulation*, edited by Robert C. Post, 89–110. Los Angeles: Getty Research Institute for the History of Art and Humanities, 1998.

Singer, Joseph. "The Legal Rights Debate in Analytical Jurisprudence from Bentham to Hohfeld." *Wisconsin Law Review*, no. 6 (1982): 975–1059.

Sklar, Kathryn Kish. "The Founding of Mount Holyoke College." In *Women of America: A History*, edited by Carol Berkin & Mary Beth Norton, 177–201. Boston: Houghton Mifflin, 1979.

Sklar, Kathryn Kish. "The Schooling of Girls and Changing Community Values in Massachusetts Towns, 1750–1820." *History of Education Quarterly* 33, no. 4 (1993): 511–42.

Smith, James Morton. *Freedom's Fetters: The Alien and Sedition Laws and American Civil Liberties*. Ithaca, NY: Cornell University Press, 1956.

Sprague, Alan B. "Some American Influences on the Law and Lawcourts of Nova Scotia, 1749–1853." *Nova Scotia Historical Review* 12, no. 2 (1992): 1–31.

Steiner, Mark E. *An Honest Calling: The Law Practice of Abraham Lincoln*. DeKalb: Northern Illinois University Press, 2006.

Stern, Simon. "*Fanny Hill* and the 'Laws of Decency': Investigating Obscenity in the Mid-Eighteenth Century." *Eighteenth-Century Life* 43, no. 2 (2019): 162–87.

Sutherland, David A. "Forrester, Thomas." Dictionary of Canadian Biography Online, www.biographi.ca.

Sutherland, D.A. "Johnston, James William." Dictionary of Canadian Biography Online, www.biographi.ca.

Sutherland, David A. "Voluntary Societies and the Process of Middle-Class Formation in Early-Victorian Halifax, Nova Scotia." *Journal of the Canadian Historical Association* 5, no. 1 (1994): 237–63.

Sutherland, D.A. "Wallace, Michael." Dictionary of Canadian Biography Online, www.biographi.ca.

Tarr, Alan G. *Understanding State Constitutions*. Princeton: Princeton University Press, 1998.

Taylor, George Rogers. *The Transportation Revolution, 1815–1860*. Armonk, NY: M.E. Sharpe, 1951.

Thomas, Donald. *A Long Time Burning: The History of Literary Censorship in England*. New York: Frederick A. Praeger, 1969.

Thompson, E.P. *Customs in Common*. New York: New Press, 1991.

Thompson, E.P. *The Making of the English Working Class*. New York: Vintage Books, 1966, originally published in 1963.

Tiffany, Nina Moore. *Samuel E. Sewall: A Memoir*. Boston: Houghton, Mifflin and Company, 1898.

Tocqueville, Alexis de. *Democracy in America*, edited by Richard D. Heffner. New York: Signet Classics, 2001, first published 1835.

Tratt, Gertrude. "Holland, Anthony Henry." Dictionary of Canadian Biography Online, www.biographi.ca.

Tratt, Gertrude E.N. *A Survey and Listing of Nova Scotia Newspapers 1752–1957 with Particular Reference to the Period before 1867*. Halifax, NS: Dalhousie University Libraries, 1979.

Tulloch, Judith. "Tonge, William Cottnam." Dictionary of Canadian Biography Online, www.biographi.ca.

Tyler, Alice Felt. *Freedom's Ferment: Phases of American Social History from the Colonial Period to the Outbreak of the Civil War*. New York: Harper & Brothers, 1944.

Tyrrell, Ian R. *Sobering Up: From Temperance to Prohibition in Antebellum America, 1800–1860*. Westport, CT: Greenwood Press, 1979.

Ulrich, Laurel Thatcher. *A Midwife's Tale: The Life of Martha Ballard, Based on Her Diary, 1785–1812*. New York: Vintage Books, 1991.

Vaughn, William Preston. *The Antimasonic Party in the United States: 1826–1843*. Lexington: University Press of Kentucky, 1983.

Verette, Michael. "The Spread of Literacy." In *History of the Book in Canada*. Vol. 1, *Beginnings to 1840*, edited by Patricia Lockhart Fleming, Gilles Gallichan and Yvan Lamonde, 165–72. Toronto: University of Toronto Press, 2004.

Verlihy, David V. *Bicycle: The History*. New Haven: Yale University Press, 2004.

Vickery, Amanda. "Golden Age to Separate Spheres? A Review of the Categories and Chronology of English Women's History." *Historical Journal* 36, no. 2 (1993): 383–414.

Waddams, S.M. *Sexual Slander in Nineteenth-Century England: Defamation in the Ecclesiastical Courts, 1815–1855*. Toronto: University of Toronto Press, 2000.

Waldrep, Christopher. *The Many Faces of Judge Lynch: Extralegal Violence and Punishment in America*. New York: Palgrave Macmillan, 2002.

Waldstreicher, David. *In the Midst of Perpetual Fetes: The Making of American Nationalism, 1776–1820*. Chapel Hill: University of North Carolina Press, 1997.

Waldstreicher, David. "Two Cheers for the 'Public Sphere' ... and One for Historians' Skepticism." *William and Mary Quarterly* 62, no. 1 (2005): 107–12.

Wallace, James M. "The Feminization of Teaching in Massachusetts: A Reconsideration." In *Women of the Commonwealth: Work, Family, and Social Change in Nineteenth-Century Massachusetts*, edited by Susan L. Porter, 43–61. Amherst: University of Massachusetts Press, 1996.

Warren, Charles. *A History of the American Bar*. New York: Howard Fertig, 1966.

Whitehill, Walter Muir. *Boston: A Topographical History*, 2nd ed. Cambridge, MA: Belknap Press of Harvard University Press, 1959.

Wiebe, Robert H. *The Opening of American Society: From the Adoption of the Constitution to the Eve of Disunion.* New York: Alfred A. Knopf, 1984.

Wiebe, Robert H. *The Segmented Society: An Introduction to the Meaning of America.* New York: Oxford University Press, 1975.

Wiebe, Robert H. *Self-Rule: A Cultural History of American Democracy.* Chicago: University of Chicago Press, 1995.

Willard, Joseph. "History of Worcester County: History of Lancaster." *Worcester Magazine and Historical Journal* 2, no. 5 (1826): 257–344.

Williams, Carolyn. "The Female Antislavery Movement: Fighting against Racial Prejudice and Promoting Women's Rights in Antebellum America." In *The Abolitionist Sisterhood: Women's Political Culture in Antebellum America*, edited by Jean Fagan Yellin and John C. Van Horne, 159–77. Ithaca, NY: Cornell University Press, 1994.

Williams, E. Neville. *The Eighteenth-Century Constitution 1688–1815.* Cambridge: Cambridge University Press, 1965.

Williams, H. Clay. *Biographical Encyclopedia of Massachusetts in the Nineteenth Century.* Vol. 2. Boston: Metropolitan Publishing and Engraving Company, 1883.

Winks, Robin. *The Blacks in Canada: A History.* New Haven: Yale University Press, 1971.

Wright, Barry. "The Gourlay Affair: Seditious Libel and the Sedition Act in Upper Canada, 1818–19." In *Canadian State Trials.* Vol. 1, *Law, Politics, and Security Measures, 1608–1837*, edited by F. Murray Greenwood and Barry Wright, 487–504. Toronto: University of Toronto Press, 1996.

Wright, Barry. "Sedition in Upper Canada: Contested Legality." *Labour / Le Travail* 29 (1992): 7–57.

York, Robert M. *George B. Cheever, Religious and Social Reformer 1807–1890.* Orono, ME: University Press, 1955.

Zagarri, Rosemarie. "Women and Party Conflict in the Early Republic." In *Beyond the Founders: New Approaches to the Political History of the Early American Republic*, edited by Jeffrey L. Pasley, Andrew W. Robertson and David Waldstreicher, 107–28. Chapel Hill: University of North Carolina Press, 2004.

Primary Sources

The Acts and Resolves, Public and Private, of the Province of the Massachusetts Bay: To which are Prefixed the Charters of the Province. Vol. 1. Boston: Wright & Potter, 1869.

Adair, James. *Discussions of the Law of Libels as at Present Received* [etc.]. London: printed for T. Cadell, 1785.

Akins, Thomas B. *History of Halifax City.* Halifax, NS, 1895.

Appeal to Common Sense and the Constitution, in behalf of the Unlimited Freedom of Public Discussion: Occasioned by the Late Trial of Rev. Abner Kneeland, for Blasphemy. Boston, 1834. Reprinted in Levy, *Blasphemy in Massachusetts*, 293–306.

Archbold, John Frederick. *A Summary of the Law Relative to Pleading and Evidence in Criminal Cases; with Precedents of Indictments, &c. and the Evidence Necessary to Support Them.* London: Pheney, Sweet and Dublin: Millikin, 1822.

Articles of Faith, Plan of Church Government, and Covenant, Proposed by the General Convention of Universalists, in the Year of Our Lord, 1803. Charlestown, MA: Caleb Rand, 1844.

Austin, James T. *An Address Delivered before the Massachusetts Society for the Suppression of Intemperance, May 27, 1830.* Boston: John H. Eastburn, 1830.

Austin, James T. "Annual Report of James T. Austin, Esq., Attorney-General of Massachusetts; Made to the Legislature of that State, at the January Session Thereof, 1837." *American Jurist* 17, no. 34 (July 1837): 482–83.

Austin, James T. *The Life of Elbridge Gerry. With Contemporary Letters* [etc.]. 2 vols. Boston: Wells & Lilly, 1829.

Bacheler, Origen. *Discussion on the Existence of God, between Origen Bacheler and Robert Dale Owen.* London: J. Watson, 1840.

Bacheler, Origen. *Review of the Trial of Origen Bacheler, Editor of the Anti-Universalist, for an Alleged Libel; And of the Report of that Trial.* Boston: Whitcomb & Page, 1829.

Bacon, Matthew. *A New Abridgement of the Law.* Vol. 3. London, 1740.

Ballou, Hosea. *A Series of Letters, in Defence of Divine Revelation; In Reply to Rev. Abner Kneeland's Serious Inquiry into the Authenticity of the Same. To Which is Added, a Religious Correspondence, between the Rev. Hosea Ballou, and the Rev. Dr. Joseph Buckminster and Rev. Joseph Walton, Pastors of Congregational Churches in Portsmouth, N.H.* Boston: Henry Bowen, 1820.

Belcher's Farmer's Almanack for the Year of Our Lord, 1833 [etc.]. Halifax, NS: C.H. Belcher, 1833.

Belcher's Farmer's Almanack for the Year of Our Lord, 1838 [etc.]. Halifax, NS: C.H. Belcher, 1838.

Blackstone, William. *Commentaries on the Laws of England.* 4 vols. Oxford: Clarendon Press, 1765–70.

Borthwick, John. *A Treatise on the Law of Libel and Slander: As Applied in Scotland, in Criminal Prosecutions and in Actions of Damages: With an Appendix, Containing Reports of Several Cases Respecting Defamation, which Have Not Been, Hitherto, Published.* Edinburgh: W. & C. Tait and London: J. and W.T. Clarke, 1826.

Boston Female Anti-Slavery Society. *Annual Report of the Boston Female Anti-Slavery Society, With a Sketch of the Obstacles Thrown in the Way of Emancipation by Certain Clerical Abolitionists and Advocates for the Subjection of Woman, in 1837.* Boston: Isaac Knapp, 1837.

Boston Trade Sale. Catalog of Books to be Sold to Booksellers Only, on Tuesday, August 7, 1827. [BDSDS 1827F, AAS.]

"Bracton on the Laws and Customs of England." Bracton Online. Harvard Law School Library, bracton.law.harvard.edu/.

Brougham, Henry. "Liberty of the Press and Its Abuses: Rev. of Thomas [*sic*] Ludlow Holt, *The Law of Libel [etc.]*" *Edinburgh Review* 27, no. 53 (1816): 102–44.

Buckingham, James Silk. *Canada, Nova Scotia, New Brunswick, and the Other British Provinces in North America, with a Plan of National Colonization.* London: Fisher, Son, & Co., 1843.

Buckingham, Joseph T. *Personal Memoirs and Recollections of Editorial Life.* 2 vols. Boston: Ticknor, Reed, and Fields, 1852.

Buckingham, Joseph T. *Specimens of Newspaper Literature.* 2 vols. Boston: Little & Brown, 1852.

Burdett, Francis. *Speech of Sir Francis Burdett, Bt. Delivered in the House of Commons On the 28th March, 1811, Upon a Motion of Lord Folkestone, to Examine into the Practice of Ex-Officio Informations, Filed by the Attorney-General, in Cases of Libel.* London: J. Morton, 1811.

Burn, Richard. *The Justice of the Peace, and Parish Officer*, edited by Charles Durnford and John King, 21st ed. 5 vols. London: A. Strahan for T. Cadell et al., 1810.

Burn, Richard. *The Justice of the Peace, and Parish Officer*, edited by Thomas D'Oyly and Edward Vaughan Williams, new ed. 5 vols. London: T. Cadell et al., 1836.

Carpenter, William. "A Letter to the Right Hon. Lord Brougham." In *Political Letters and Pamphlets [etc.].* London: William Carpenter, 1830–31.

Catalogue of Books for Sale by C. H. Belcher, July, 1837. Halifax, NS: C.H. Belcher,1837.

Catalogue of Books, in the Law Library at Halifax. Michaelmas Term, 1835. Halifax, NS: J.S. Cunnabell, 1835.

Catalogue of Books to be Sold at Auction On Thursday, March 13th, 1823. At 9 & 3 o'clock, at Blake & Cunningham's Office, No. 5 Kilby-Street. Boston: Blake & Cunningham, 1823.

Catalogue of the Library of the Hon. Theophilus Parsons. To be Sold by Auction March 1st 1814, at the Store of Francis Amory, No. 41, Marlboro' Street. Boston: Francis Amory, 1814.

Catalogue of the Library of the Late Chief Justice Sewall, to be Sold at Auction Sep. 2, 1814, at the Store of Whitwell & Bond, No. 5, Filry Street, Boston. Cambridge: Hilliard & Metcalf, 1814. Channing, William E. *Slavery.* Boston: James Munroe and Company, 1835.

Channing, William E. *The Works of William E. Channing, D.D.*, new ed. Boston: American Unitarian Association, 1875.

"Characters of Law Books and Judges." *American Jurist* 12, no. 23 (1834): 5–66.

Cheever, George B. *Defence in Abatement of Judgment for an Alleged Libel in the Story Entitled "Inquire at Amos Giles' Distillery." Addressed to the Hon. Chief Justice Shaw, at the Session of the Supreme Judicial Court of Massachusetts Held in Salem, Dec. 4, 1835.* New York: Leavitt, Lord, & Co., 1836.

Cheever, George B. *The Dream, or, The True History of Deacon Giles's Distillery and Deacon Jones's Brewery: Reported for the Benefit of Posterity.* New York, 1843.

Cheever, George B. *The True History of Deacon Giles' Distillery. Reported for the Benefit of Posterity.* New York, 1844.

Child, David Lee. *The Despotism of Freedom: Or, The Tyranny and Cruelty of American Republican Slave-Masters: Shown to be the Worst in the World in a Speech Delivered at the First Anniversary of the New England Anti-Slavery Society, 1833.* Boston: Boston Young Men's Anti-Slavery Association, 1833.

Child, David Lee. *An Oration Pronounced before the Republicans of Boston, July 4, 1826, the Fiftieth Anniversary of American Independence.* Boston: Josiah B. Clough, 1826.

Child, David Lee. *Report of the Case of Alleged Contempt, and Breach of the Privileges of the House of Representatives of Massachusetts: Tried before Said House, on Complaint of William B. Calhoun, Speaker, against David L. Child, a Member, with Notes by the Latter.* Boston: Carter and Hendee, 1832.

Child, Lydia Maria. *An Appeal in Favor of that Class of Americans Called Africans*, edited by Carolyn Karcher. Amherst: University of Massachusetts Press, 1996.

Child, Lydia Maria. *The First Settlers of New-England: Or, Conquest of the Pequods, Narragansets and Pokanokets. As Related by a Mother to Her Children.* Boston: Munroe & Francis, 1829.

Child, Lydia Maria. *Letters of Lydia Maria Child*, with a biographical introduction by John G. Whittier and an appendix by Wendell Phillips. Boston: Houghton, Mifflin and Company, 1883.

Child, Lydia Maria. *Lydia Maria Child: Selected Letters, 1817–1880*, edited by Milton Meltzer, Patricia G. Holland and Francine Krasno. Amherst: University of Massachusetts Press, 1982.

Christian, Edward. *A Concise Account of the Origin of the Two Houses of Parliament: With an Impartial Statement of the Privileges of the House of Commons, and of the Liberty of the Subject.* London: T. Cadell & W. Davies, 1810.

Cleland, John. *The Memoirs of Fanny Hill, A Woman of Pleasure. With Plates, Engraved by a Member of the Royal Academy. Written by Herself.* Halifax,

Novia Scotia [*sic*]: G. Fendon for W.H.S. Fillman, 1820. (This book is an illicit copy of the original.)

Coffin, R.S. *The "Boston Bard" to the Citizens of Boston.* Boston: John Putnam, 1826.

Coffin, R.S. *Epistle to Joseph T. Buckingham, Esq. by R. S. Coffin, the "Boston Bard."* Boston, 1826.

Cooper, Thomas. *An Account of the Trial of Thomas Cooper, of Northumberland; on a Charge of Libel against the President of the United States* [etc.]. Philadelphia: John Bioren, 1800.

Cooper, Thomas. *A Treatise on the Law of Libel and the Liberty of the Press; Showing the Origin, Use, and Abuse of the Law of Libel: With Copious Notes and References to Authorities in Great Britain and the United States* [etc.]. New York: G.F. Hopkins & Son, 1830.

A Cosmopolite [David Henshaw]. *A Review of the Prosecution of Abner Kneeland, for Blasphemy.* Boston, 1835. Reprinted in Levy, *Blasphemy in Massachusetts*, 343–74. (Page references are to Levy's text.)

Cunningham, Joseph. *Catalogue of Law Books. To be Sold on Thursday, June 13, 1827, at Cunningham's Auction Room, Corner of Milk and Federal Streets.* [BDSDS 1827, AAS.]

Cunningham, J.L. *Second Boston Trade Sale. Catalogue of Books to be Sold to Booksellers Only, on Tuesday, July 22, 1828.* [BDSDS 1828 F, AAS.]

Cunningham, J.L. *Second Catalogue of the Second Boston Trade Sale. July 22, 1828.* [BDSDS 1828 F, AAS.]

Cunningham, J.L. *Second Catalogue of the Third Boston Trade Sale, July 21, 1829.* [BDSDS 1829 F, AAS.]

Cushing, L.S. *A Practical Treatise on the Trustee Process, or Foreign Attachment of the Laws of Massachusetts and Maine; With an Appendix, Containing the Statutes of Massachusetts, Connecticut, Rhode Island, New Hampshire, Vermont, and Maine, on that Subject.* Cambridge, MA: Brown, Shattuck and Co., 1833.

Dane, Nathan. *A General Abridgement and Digest of American Law, with Occasional Notes and Comments.* Vol. 3. Boston: Cummings, Hilliard & Co., 1824.

Davis, Daniel. *A Practical Treatise upon the Authority and Duty of Justices of the Peace in Criminal Prosecutions.* Boston: Cummings, Hilliard & Co., 1824.

de Lolme, Jean Louis. *The Constitution of England, or, An Account of the English Government, in which it is Compared with the Republican Form of Government, and Occasionally with the Other Monarchies in Europe*, new ed. London: G. Kearsley and J. Ridley, 1777.

Dunlap, Andrew. *A Speech Delivered before the Municipal Court of the City of Boston, in Defence of Abner Kneeland, on an Indictment for Blasphemy. January Term, 1834.* Boston, 1834. Reprinted in Levy, *Blasphemy in Massachusetts*, 45–174. (Page references are to Levy's text.)

Dyer, George. *An Address to the People of Great Britain, on the Doctrine of Libels, and the Office of Juror.* London, 1799.

East, Edward Hyde. *Pleas of the Crown.* London: Professional Books Limited, 1972, originally published in 1803.

Elrington, Thomas. *A Reply to John Search's Considerations on the Law of Libel, as Relating to Publications on the Subject of Religion.* Dublin: Richard Milliken and Son, 1823.

Erskine, Thomas. *The Speeches of the Hon. Thomas Erskine, (Now Lord Erskine), When at the Bar, on Subjects Connected with the Liberty of the Press; Against Constructive Treasons, and on Miscellaneous Subjects.* New York: Eastburn, Kirk & Co., 1813.

Everett, L.S. *An Exposure of the Principles of the "Free Inquirers."* Boston: Benjamin B. Mussey, 1831.

Farmer, Miles. *Report of a Trial: Miles Farmer, versus Dr. David Humphreys Storer, Commenced in the Court of Common Pleas, April Term, 1830* [etc.]. Boston, 1831.

Freeman, Samuel. *The Massachusetts Justice: Being a Collection of the Laws of the Commonwealth of Massachusetts Relative to the Power and Duty of Justices of the Peace* [etc.], 3rd ed. Boston: Thomas & Andrews, 1810.

A Friend to the Constitutional Rights of the Citizen [pseud.], *Letter to Messrs. John C. Cook, Foreman; Richard Bartlett, Thomas Chamberlain, John P. Coolidge, Joseph H. Cotton, David Eckley, John F. Elliot, Daniel Goodnow, James Goddard, John T. Heard, Ridgeway E. Holbrook, All of Boston; and Henry Slade of Chelsea; Jurors Empannelled [sic] to Try the Indictment against John A. Whitmarsh, for an Alleged Crime of Libel.* Boston: Beals & Greene, 1838.

Garrison, William Lloyd. *A Brief Sketch of the Trial of William Lloyd Garrison, for an Alleged Libel on Francis Todd, of Massachusetts.* Boston: Garrison and Knapp, 1834.

Garrison, William Lloyd. "Triumph of Mobocracy in Boston." In *Selections from the Writings and Speeches of William Lloyd Garrison*, 373–83. New York: Negro Universities Press, 1968. Reprinted from *The Liberator* (Boston), November 7, 1835.

Garrison, William Lloyd. *Selections from the Writings and Speeches of William Lloyd Garrison.* New York: Negro Universities Press, 1968.

The General Laws of Massachusetts, from the Adoption of the Constitution, to February, 1822 [etc.], compiled by Asahel Stearns and Lemuel Shaw, edited by Theron Metcalf. 2 vols. Boston: Wells & Lilly and Cummings & Hilliard, 1823.

George, John. *A Treatise on the Offence of Libel: With a Disquisition on the Rights, Benefits, and Proper Boundaries of Political Discussion.* London: Taylor and Hessey, 1812.

Greene, Samuel D. *Appeal of Samuel D. Greene, in Vindication of Himself against the False Swearing of Johnson Goodwill, a Morgan Conspirator, in*

the Case of Commonwealth v. Moore & Sevey, Editors of the Masonic
Mirror, for a Libel on Said Greene. Boston, 1834.

Greene, Samuel D. *The Broken Seal; Or, Personal Reminiscences of the
Morgan Abduction and Murder*, 3rd ed. Boston: Carter & Pettee, 1872.

Greenleaf, Simon. "Sketch of the Law School at Cambridge." *American Jurist*
13, no. 25 (1835): 107–30.

Griffith, William. *Annual Law Register of the United States*. Vol. 3.
Burlington, NJ: David Allinson, 1822.

Grimké, Sarah. *Letters on the Equality of the Sexes, and the Condition of
Woman: Addressed to Mary S. Parker, President of the Boston Female Anti-
Slavery Society*. Boston: Isaac Knapp, 1838.

H [pseud.]. "The Law of Libel." *Law Magazine or Quarterly Review of
Jurisprudence* 11, no. 2 (1834): 432–47.

Haliburton, Thomas Chandler. *The Attaché, or Sam Slick in England*. Paris:
Baudry's European Library, 1843.

Haliburton, Thomas Chandler. *The Clockmaker; Or The Sayings and
Doings of Sam Slick, of Slickville* [etc.]. Paris: Baudry's European
Library, 1839.

Hall, Basil. *Travels in North America in the Years 1827 and 1828*. Edinburgh:
Cadell and Co., 1829.

Hamilton, Thomas. *Men and Manners in America*. New York: Augustus
M. Kelley, 1968, originally published in 1833.

Hansard, T.C. *The Parliamentary Debates from the Year 1803 to the Present
Time* [etc.]. London: Longman, Hurst, Rees, Orme, and Brown, various
dates.

Harvard University. *A Catalogue of the Law Library of Harvard University in
Cambridge, Massachusetts*. Cambridge: Folsom, 1834.

Harvard University. *A Catalogue of the Law Library of Harvard University in
Cambridge, Massachusetts*. Cambridge: Folsom, Wells, and Thurston,
1841.

Harvard University. *Catalogue of the Library of the Law School of
Harvard University*. Cambridge, MA: University Press – Hilliard &
Metcalf, 1826.

Hawkins, William. *A Treatise of the Pleas of the Crown; Or, A System of the
Principal Matters Relating to that Subject, Digested under Proper Heads*,
edited by Thomas Leach, 7th ed. 4 vols. London: S. Sweet et al., 1795.

Hawkins, William. *A Treatise of the Pleas of the Crown; Or, A System of
the Principal Matters Relating to that Subject, Digested under Proper
Heads*, edited by John Curwood, 8th ed. 2 vols. London: S. Sweet et al.,
1824.

Hayward, John. *New-England and New-York Law-Register, for the Year
1835* [etc.]. Boston: John Hayward, 1834.

Highmore, Anthony. *Reflections on the Distinction Usually Adopted in
Criminal Libel Prosecutions for Libel; and on the Method, Lately*

Introduced, of Pronouncing Verdicts in Consequence of Such Distinction. London: T. Farnworth for J. Johnson, 1791.

Hilliard, Gray & Co. *Catalogue of Law Books for Sale by Hilliard, Gray & Co. Boston*, ca. 1831. [BDSDS 1830F, AAS.]

Hilliard, Gray & Co. *Catalogue of Law Books for Sale by Hilliard, Gray & Co. Boston*, ca. 1832. [BDSDS 1830 F, AAS.]

Holt, Francis Ludlow. *The Law and Usage of Parliament in Cases of Privilege and Contempt: Being an Attempt to Reduce Them within a Theory and System.* London: W. Reed and Dublin: P. Phelan, 1810.

Holt, Francis Ludlow. *The Law of Libel: In which is Contained, a General History of this Law in the Ancient Codes, and of its Introduction, and Successive Alterations, in the Law of England* [etc.]. New York and London: Garland Publishing, 1978. Reprinted from the London, 1812 edition.

Holt, Francis Ludlow. *The Law of Libel: In which is Contained A General History of this Law in the Ancient Codes, and of its Introduction, and Successive Alterations, in the Law of England* [etc.], 2nd ed. London: Butterworth & Son, 1816.

Holt, Francis Ludlow. *The Law of Libel: In which is Contained A General History of this Law in the Ancient Codes, and of its Introduction, and Successive Alterations, in the Law of England* [etc.], 1st Amer. ed. New York: Stephen Gould, 1818.

House of Commons (UK). "Copy of the Reply of the Inspectors of Prisons for the Home District, with Regard to the Report of the Court of Aldermen, to whom it was Referred to Consider the First Report of the Inspectors of Prisons, so far as Relates to the Gaol of Newgate." *Parliamentary Papers*, No. 486, 1836.

Howe, Joseph. *Trial for Libel, on the Magistrates of Halifax, the King v. Joseph Howe, Before the Chief Justice and a Special Jury, Supreme Court – Hilary Term.* Halifax, NS, 1835.

Howe, Joseph. *The Speeches and Public Letters of Joseph Howe (Based upon Mr. Annand's Edition of 1858)*, edited by Joseph A. Chisholm, new ed. 2 vols. Halifax, NS: Chronicle Publishing Company, 1909.

Howell, T.B. *A Complete Collection of State Trials and Proceedings for High Treason and Other Crimes and Misdemeanors from the Earliest Period to the Present Time* [etc.]. Vol. 14, A.D. *1700–1708*. London: T.C. Hansard and others, 1812.

"Instructions for Our Trusty and Wellbeloved Arthur Dobbs Esqre Our Captain General and Governor in Chief in and over Our Province of North Carolina in America." In *The Colonial Records of North Carolina.* Vol. V, *1752 to 1759*, edited by Walter L. Saunders, 1107–44. Raleigh: Josephus Daniels, 1887.

"Instructions to Governor Carleton, 1768." In *Documents Relating to the Constitutional History of Canada 1759–1791*, Vol. 1, edited by Adam

Shortt and Arthur G. Doughty, 2nd ed., 301–24. Ottawa: J. de L. Taché, 1918.

"Instructions to Governor James Murray." In *Canadian Constitutional Development: Shown by Selected Speeches and Despatches, with Introductions and Explanatory Notes*, edited by Hugh Edward Egerton and William Lawson Grant, 1–21. London: John Murray, 1907.

Jefferson, Thomas. *A Manual of Parliamentary Practice: For the Use of the Senate of the United States*. Washington City: Samuel Harrison Smith, 1801.

Jervis, John, ed. *Archbold's Summary of the Law Relative to Pleading and Evidence in Criminal Cases: with Precedents of Indictments, &c. and the Evidence Necessary to Support Them*, 3rd Amer. ed. from 5th London ed. New York: Gould, Banks and Co., 1835.

Journal of Debates and Proceedings in the Convention of Delegates, Chosen to Revise the Constitution of Massachusetts, Begun and Holden at Boston, November 15, 1820, and Continued by Adjournment to January 9, 1821. Boston: Boston Daily Advertiser, 1821.

Kimball, Edmund. *Reflections Upon the Law of Libel in a Letter Addressed to "A Member of the Suffolk Bar."* Boston: Wells & Lilly, 1823.

Knapp, Samuel L. *The Genius of Masonry, or A Defence of the Order* [etc.]. Providence, RI: Cranston & Marshall, 1828.

Kneeland, Abner. *An Introduction to the Defence of Abner Kneeland, Charged with Blasphemy; before the Municipal Court, in Boston, Mass. at the January Term, in 1834.* Boston: Kneeland, 1834. Reprinted in Levy, *Blasphemy in Massachusetts*, 3–43. (Page references are to Levy's text.)

Kneeland, Abner. *A Review of the Trial, Conviction, and Final Imprisonment in the Common Jail in the County of Suffolk, of Abner Kneeland, for the Alleged Crime of Blasphemy.* Boston: George A. Chapman, 1838. Reprinted in Levy, *Blasphemy in Massachusetts*, 461–592. (Page references are to Levy's text.)

Kneeland, Abner. *Speech of Abner Kneeland, Delivered before the Full Bench of Judges of the Supreme Court, in his Own Defence, for the Alleged Crime of Blasphemy. Law Term, March 8, 1836.* Reprinted in Levy, *Blasphemy in Massachusetts*, 375–418. (Page references are to Levy's text.)

Kneeland, Abner. *Speech of Abner Kneeland, Delivered before the Supreme Court of the City of Boston, in his Own Defence, on an Indictment for Blasphemy. November Term, 1834.* Boston: J.Q. Adams, 1834. Reprinted in Levy, *Blasphemy in Massachusetts*, 307–41. (Page references are to Levy's text.)

Kneeland, Abner, and W.L. McCalla. *Minutes of a Discussion on the Question "Is the Punishment of the Wicked Absolutely Eternal? Or Is It Only a Temporal Punishment in this World, for Their Good, and to be Succeeded by Eternal Happiness after Death?" Between Rev. Abner*

Kneeland and Rev. W. L. M'Calla [etc.], taken in shorthand by R.L. Jennings. Philadelphia, 1824.

Knowlton, Charles. *Elements of Modern Materialism: Inculcating the Idea of a Future State, in which All Will Be More Happy, under whatever Circumstances They May be Placed than if They Experienced No Misery in this Life.* Adams, MA: A. Oakey, 1829.

Knowlton, Charles. *Fruits of Philosophy: Or The Private Companion of Young Married People,* 2nd ed. Boston, 1833.

Knowlton, Charles. *A History of the Recent Excitement in Ashfield.* [Boston?], 1834.

Knowlton, Charles. *Two Remarkable Lectures Delivered in Boston, by Dr. C. Knowlton, on the Day of His Leaving the Jail at East Cambridge, March 31, 1833, Where He Had Been Imprisoned, for Publishing a Book.* Boston: A. Kneeland, 1833.

The Law of Libel: Report of the Trial of Dr. Samuel Thomson, the Founder of the Thomsonian Practice, for an Alleged Libel in Warning the Public Against the Impositions of Paine D. Badger, as a Thomsonian Physician Sailing Under False Colors, Before Judge Thacher, in the Municipal Court of Boston, April Term, 1839. Boston: Henry P. Lewis, 1839.

List of Books Belonging to the Estate of the Late Hon. R.J. Uniacke to be sold THIS DAY, Monday at 11 o'clock, by W. M. Allan. Halifax, NS: W.M. Allan, ca. 1830.

Little & Brown. *A Catalogue of Law Books Published and For Sale by Charles C. Little and James Brown.* Boston: Freeman and Bolles, 1837. [Book Dealers Cats. Litt., AAS.]

Locke, Charles H. *Trial of Moore & Sevey for a Libel on Samuel D. Greene, in the Municipal Court, Boston, July Term, 1833.* Boston: Moore & Sevey, 1833.

Maddock, Henry. *A Vindication of the Privileges of the House of Commons, in Answer to Sir Francis Burdett's Address.* London: W. Clarke and Sons, 1810.

Maffit's Trial; or, Buckingham Acquitted, on a Charge of Slander against the Character of John N. Maffit, Preacher in the Methodist Episcopal Society. New York: C.N. Baldwin, 1831.

Marshall, John George. *The Justice of the Peace, and County & Township Officer, in the Province of Nova Scotia. Being a Guide to Such Justice and Officers in the Discharge of Their Official Duties.* Halifax, NS: Gossip & Coade, 1837.

Massachusetts Anti-Slavery Society. *Sixth Annual Report of the Board of Managers of the Massachusetts Anti-Slavery Society. Presented January 24, 1838.* Boston: Isaac Knapp, 1838.

Massachusetts Register and United States Calendar for the Year of Our Lord 1829 [etc.]. Boston: Richardson & Lord and James Loring, 1829.

The Massachusetts Sheriff: Being a Digest of the Principal Decisions of the Supreme Judicial Court of the Commonwealth of Massachusetts, Relative to the Power, Duty and Responsibility of Sheriffs, Their Deputies, Coroners and Constables, in the Execution of Civil Process. To Which is Prefixed, Several Important Statute, Defining the Duties of Those Officers. Boston: R.P. and C. Williams, 1814.

May, Samuel J. *Some Recollections of Our Anti-slavery Conflict.* Boston: Fields, Osgood & Co., 1869.

May, Thomas Erskine. *A Treatise upon the Law, Privileges, Proceedings and Usage of Parliament.* London: Charles Knight & Co., 1844.

Mence, Richard. *The Law of Libel.* London: Pople, 1824.

Merrick, Pliny. *A Letter on Speculative Free Masonry* [etc.]. Worcester, MA: Dorr and Howland, 1829.

Monk, Maria. *Awful Disclosures of the Hotel Dieu Nunnery of Montreal.* New York, 1836.

Mr. Blake's Speech, Relative to the Privileges of the House of Commons, Delivered at a Meeting of the Freeholders of Middlesex, on Friday, June 8, 1810. London: J.J. Stockdale, 1810.

Murdoch, Beamish. *The Epitome of the Laws of Nova-Scotia.* 4 vols. Halifax, NS: Joseph Howe, 1832 (vols. 1 & 2), 1833 (vols. 3 & 4).

New Brunswick House of Assembly. *Journal of the House of Assembly of the Province of New-Brunswick, from Tuesday the 9th Day of December, 1828 to Tuesday the 10th Day of February, 1829.* Fredericton: George K. Lugrin, 1829 ["NB Journals, 1829"].

New Brunswick House of Assembly. *Journal of the House of Assembly of the Province of New-Brunswick, from Monday, the 7th day of February, to Thursday, the 31st day of March, 1831.* Fredericton: John Simpson, 1831 ["NB Journals, 1831"].

New Brunswick House of Assembly. *Journal of the House of Assembly of the Province of New-Brunswick, from Thursday, the 19th Day of January, to Friday, the 9th Day of March, 1832.* Fredericton: John Simpson, 1832 ["NB Journals, 1832"].

New Brunswick House of Assembly. *Journal of the House of Assembly of the Province of New Brunswick, from the Twentieth Day of January to the Sixteenth Day of March.* Fredericton: John Simpson, 1836 ["NB Journals, 1836"].

New Brunswick House of Assembly. *Journal of the House of Assembly of the Province of New Brunswick, from the Twentieth Day of December to the First Day of March. Being the Fourth Session of the Eleventh General Assembly.* Fredericton: John Simpson, 1837 ["NB Journals, 1837"].

New Brunswick House of Assembly. *Journal of the House of Assembly of the Province of New Brunswick, from the Fifteenth Day of January to the Twenty Third* [sic] *Day of March, Being the Second Session of the Twelfth General Assembly.* Fredericton: John Simpson, 1839 ["NB Journals, 1839, 2nd sess."].

Nova Scotia House of Assembly. *Journal and Proceedings of the House of Assembly.* Halifax, 1808 ["NS Journals, 1807"].

Nova Scotia House of Assembly. *Journal and Proceedings of the House of Assembly.* Halifax, 1818 ["NS Journals, 1818"].

Nova Scotia House of Assembly. *Journal and Proceedings of the House of Assembly.* Halifax, 1827 ["NS Journals, 1827"].

Nova Scotia House of Assembly. *Journal and Proceedings of the House of Assembly.* Halifax, 1829 [NS Journals, 1829"].

Nova Scotia House of Assembly. *Journal and Proceedings of the House of Assembly,* 1st sess. Halifax: King's Printer, 1830 ["NS Journals, 1830, 1st sess."]

Nova Scotia House of Assembly. *Journal and Proceedings of the House of Assembly, 1837.* Halifax, 1837 ["NS Journals, 1837"].

Nova Scotia House of Assembly. *Journal and Proceedings of the House of Assembly, 1841.* Halifax: R. Nugent, 1841 ["NS Journals, 1841"].

Nova Scotia Temperance Almanac, for the Year of Our Lord 1835. Halifax: C.H. Belcher, 1835.

Origin and Progress of the Late Difficulties in the First Church in Worcester, Mass. Containing All the Documents Relating to the Subject. To Which is Added the Result of a Mutual Ecclesiastical Council, Convened May, 1820, to Investigate Certain Charges Exhibited to the Church Against Rev. Charles A. Goodrich, Pastor of Said Church. Worcester: Manning & Trumbull, 1820.

Otis, Harrison Gray. *A Letter to the Hon. Josiah Quincy, Judge of the Municipal Court, in the City of Boston, on the Law of Libel, as Laid Down by Him in the Case of Commonwealth vs. Buckingham.* Boston: Wells & Lilly, 1823.

Owen, Robert Dale. *Moral Physiology; Or, A Brief and Plain Treatise on the Population Question,* 6th ed. New York: Wright & Owen, 1831.

Paine, Thomas. *The Trial of Thomas Paine, For a Libel, Contained in the Second Part of Rights of Man. Before Lord Kenyon, and a Special Jury, at Guild Hall, December 18, 1792. With the Speeches of the Attorney General and Mr. Erskine at Large.* Boston, 1793.

Phillips, Richard. *On the Powers and Duties of Juries, and on the Criminal Laws of England.* London: Sherwood, Neely and Jones, 1811.

Plan of the City of Boston. Boston: Charles Stimpson, 1829. Norman B. Leventhal Map Center at the Boston Public Library, maps.bpl.org/id/12254.

Pollock, Frederick, R. Campbell and O.A. Saunders, eds. *The Revised Reports: Being a Republication of Such Cases in the English Courts of Common Law and Equity, from the Year 1785, as are Still of Practical Utility.* Vol. 5, 1799–1801. London: Sweet and Maxwell, 1892.

Pond, Preston. *The Reviewer Reviewed: Or Strictures and Testimony on Moses Thacher's Review of His Own Case and Conduct.* Boston, 1838.

Ponsonby, George. *The Speech of Mr. Ponsonby on the Question Relative to the Privileges of the House of Commons, as Connected with the Committal of Sir Francis Burdett and Gale Jones.* London: R. Dutton, 1810.

Prince Edward Island House of Assembly. *Journal of the House of Assembly of His Majesty's Island Prince Edward, Third Session of the Twelfth General Assembly.* Charlottetown: King's Printer, 1827 ["PEI Journals, 1827"].

Prince Edward Island House of Assembly. *Journal of the House of Assembly of Prince Edward Island Anno Primo Regis Gulielmi IV: First Session of the Thirteenth General Assembly.* Charlottetown: James D. Haszard, 1831 ["PEI Journals, 1831"].

Prince Edward Island House of Assembly. *Journal of the House of Assembly of Prince Edward Island Anno Secundo Regis Gulielmi IV: Second Session of the Thirteenth General Assembly.* Charlottetown: James Douglas Haszard, 1832 ["PEI Journals, 1832"].

Prince Edward Island House of Assembly. *Journal of the House of Assembly of Prince Edward Island Anno VII Gulielmi IV Regis: Fourth Session of the Fourteenth General Assembly.* Charlottetown: John Henry White, 1837 ["PEI Journals, 1837"].

Publicola [Robert Harding Evans]. *Letter to the Freeholders of the County of Middlesex.* London: J. Morton, 1810.

Putnam, Samuel. "Charge to the Jury in the Trial of Abner Kneeland on Appeal from a Conviction of Blasphemy: Supreme Judicial Court of Massachusetts, Boston May 16, 1834." Reprinted in Levy, *Blasphemy in Massachusetts*, 289–91. (Page references are to Levy's text.)

Rayner, John [A Gentleman of the Inner Temple]. *A Digest of the Law Concerning Libels: Containing All the Resolutions in the Books on the Subject, and Many Manuscript Cases* [etc]. London: H. Woodfall and W. Strahan, 1765.

Reed, Rebecca Theresa. *Six Months in a Convent; Or, the Narrative of Rebecca Theresa Reed, who was under the Influence of the Roman Catholics about Two Years, and an Inmate of the Ursuline Convent on Mount Benedict, Charlestown, Mass., Nearly Six Months, in the Years 1831–2.* Boston: Odiorne & Metcalf, 1835.

Report of the Arguments of the Attorney of the Commonwealth, at the Trials of Abner Kneeland, for Blasphemy, in the Municipal and Supreme Courts, in Boston, January and May 1834. Boston: Beals, Homer & Co., 1834. Reprinted in Levy, *Blasphemy in Massachusetts*, 177–269. (Page references are to Levy's text.)

Review of the Case of Moses Thacher versus Preston Pond, in Charging the Plaintiff with the Crime of Adultery: Including Letters of Mrs. Jerusha Pond, the Main Witness in the Defence. Boston, 1838.

Review, of the Report of the Case of the Commonwealth versus David Lee Child: For Publishing in the Massachusetts Journal a Libel on the Honorable John Keyes. Boston: J.H. Eastman, 1829.

Revised Statutes of the Commonwealth of Massachusetts, Passed November 4, 1835 [etc.], prepared by Theron Metcalf and Horace Mann. Boston: Dutton & Wentworth, 1836.

Rice, C. Duncan. "Enlightenment, Evangelism, and Economics: An Interpretation of the Drive towards Emancipation in British West India." *Annals of the New York Academy of Sciences* 292, no. 1 (1977): 123–31.

Roberton, John. *On the Generative System: Being an Anatomical and Physiological Sketch of the Parts of Generation, and a Treatise on Their Diseases* [etc.], 4th ed. London: J.J. Stockdale, 1817.

Russell, Samuel. *Review of a Pamphlet, Entitled 'Trial of an Action in Favor of the Rev. Samuel Russell of Boylston, Against John Howe of Boylston, for Defamation at the Supreme Judicial Court, Holden at Worcester, April, A. D. 1831.'* Boston: Peirce & Parker, 1831.

Sargent, Lucius M. *Temperance Tales*. Boston: Whipple and Damrell, 1837.

Snelling, William J. *Exposé of the Vice of Gaming, as It Lately Existed in Massachusetts: Being a Series of Essays and Reports Originally Published in the New-England Galaxy, with Notes and Emendations*. Boston: William J. Snelling, 1833.

Snelling, William J. *A Brief and Impartial History of the Life and Actions of Andrew Jackson, President of the United States*. Boston: Stimpson and Clapp, 1831.

Starkie, Thomas. *A Practical Treatise on the Law of Evidence, and Digest of Proofs, in Civil and Criminal Proceedings*. 3 vols. London: J. & W.T. Clarke, 1824.

Starkie, Thomas. *A Practical Treatise on the Law of Evidence, and Digest of Proofs, in Civil and Criminal Proceedings*, edited by Theron Metcalf, 1st Amer. ed. 3 vols. Boston: Wells and Lilly, 1826.

Starkie, Thomas. *A Practical Treatise on the Law of Evidence, and Digest of Proofs, in Civil and Criminal Proceedings*, edited by Theron Metcalf and Edward D. Ingraham, 2nd Amer. ed. 3 vols. Boston: Wells and Lilly, 1828.

Starkie, Thomas. *A Practical Treatise on the Law of Evidence, and Digest of Proofs, in Civil and Criminal Proceedings*, edited by Theron Metcalf and Edward D. Ingraham, 3rd Amer. ed. 3 vols. Philadelphia: P.H. Nicklin & T. Johnson, 1830.

Starkie, Thomas. *A Practical Treatise on the Law of Evidence, and Digest of Proofs, in Civil and Criminal Proceedings*, edited by Theron Metcalf and Edward D. Ingraham, 4th Amer. ed. 3 vols. Philadelphia: P.H. Nicklin & T. Johnson, 1832.

Starkie, Thomas. *A Practical Treatise on the Law of Evidence, and Digest of Proofs, in Civil and Criminal Proceedings*, 2nd English ed. 3 vols. London: J. & W.T. Clarke, 1833.

Starkie, Thomas. *A Treatise on Criminal Pleading: With Precedents of Indictments, Special Pleas, &c., Adapted to Practice*. 2 vols. London: W. Clarke and Sons, 1814.

Starkie, Thomas. *A Treatise on Criminal Pleading: With Precedents of Indictments, Special Pleas, &c., Adapted to Practice*, 2nd English ed. 2 vols. London: J. & W.T. Clarke, 1822.

Starkie, Thomas. *A Treatise on Criminal Pleading: With Precedents of Indictments, Special Pleas, &c., Adapted to Practice*, 1st Amer. ed. Exeter, NH: Gerrish & Tyler, 1824.

Starkie, Thomas. *A Treatise on the Law of Slander, Libel, Scandalum Magnatum, and False Rumours; Including The Rules Which Regulate Intellectual Communications Respecting the Characters of Individuals and the Interests of the Public, With a Description of the Practice and Pleadings in Personal Actions, Informations, Indictments, Attachment for Contempts, &c. Connected with the Subject*. London: W. Clarke and Sons, 1813.

Starkie, Thomas. *A Treatise on the Law of Slander, Libel, Scandalum Magnatum, and False Rumours* [etc.], edited by Edward D. Ingraham, 1st Amer. ed. New York: G. Lamson, 1826.

Starkie, Thomas. *A Treatise on the Law of Slander and Libel, and Incidentally of Malicious Prosecutions*, 2nd English ed. 2 vols. London: J. and W.T. Clarke, 1830.

Starkie, Thomas. *A Treatise on the Law of Slander, Libel, Scandalum Magnatum, and False Rumours* [etc.], edited by Thomas Huntington, 2nd Amer. ed. New York: Collins and Hannay, 1832.

Starkie, Thomas. *A Treatise on the Law of Slander and Libel, and Incidentally of Malicious Prosecutions*, edited by John L. Wendell. Albany, NY: C. Van Benthuysen and Co., 1843.

Stimpson's Boston Directory; Containing the Names of the Inhabitants, their Occupations, Places of Business, and Dwelling Houses, and the City Register [etc.]. Boston: Charles Stimpson, Jr., 1835.

Story, Joseph. *Commentaries on the Constitution of the United States; with a Preliminary Review of the Constitutional History of the Colonies and States, before the Adoption of the Constitution*. Boston: Hilliard, Gray, and Company, 1833.

Story, Joseph. *Commentaries on the Constitution of the United States: A Preliminary Review of the Constitutional History of the Colonies and States before the Adoption of the Constitution*, 5th ed., edited by Melville M. Bigelow. 2 vols. Buffalo, NY: William S. Hein & Co., 1994, originally published in 1891.

Thacher, Peter Oxenbridge. *Charge to the Grand Jury of the County of Suffolk, for the Commonwealth of Massachusetts, at the Opening of the Municipal Court of the City of Boston, on the First Monday of December, A. D. 1831*. Boston: Samuel N. Dickinson, 1832.

Thacher, Peter O. *A Charge to the Grand Jury of the County of Suffolk, for the Commonwealth of Massachusetts, at the Opening of the Municipal*

Court of the City of Boston... Dec. A. D. 1832. Boston: Stimpson & Clapp, 1832.

Thacher, Peter. "Charge to the Jury in the Trial of Abner Kneeland on an Indictment for Blasphemy: Municipal Court of Boston, January, 1834." In Levy, *Blasphemy in Massachusetts*, 271–88. (Page references are to Levy's text.)

Thacher, Peter Oxenbridge. "A Charge to the Grand Jury of the County of Suffolk, for the Commonwealth of Massachusetts, at the Opening of the Municipal Court of the City of Boston, on the First Monday of December, A. D. 1834." *American Jurist and Law Magazine* 13 (1835): 229–30 [excerpt].

Thacher, Peter. "Incendiary Publications." *American Jurist and Law Magazine* 8, no. 15 (1832): 66–69.

Thacher, Peter Oxenbridge. *Reports of Criminal Cases, Tried in the Municipal Court of the City of Boston*, edited by Horatio Woodman. Boston: Charles C. Little and James Brown, 1845 ["Thach. Crim. Cas."].

Tocqueville, Alexis de. *Democracy in America*. New York: Signet Classic, 2001. First published 1835.

Tremaine, John. *Pleas of the Crown in Matters Criminal and Civil* [etc.], revised by John Rice, translated by Thomas Vickers. 2 vols. Dublin: printed by H. Watts, 1793.

Trenchard, John, and Thomas Gordon. *Cato's Letters: Essays on Liberty, Civil and Religious, and Other Important Subjects*, 6th ed. 4 vols. London, 1755.

Trial: Commonwealth vs. J. T. Buckingham, On an Indictment for a Libel, Before the Municipal Court of the City of Boston, December Term, 1822. Boston, 1823.

Trial for Libel before the Supreme Judicial Court, April 25, 1838. Chief Justice Shaw, Presiding: Azell Snow, vs. John Ford and John S. Sleeper. Boston: printed by Cassady and March, 1838.

Trial for Libel, on the Magistrates of Halifax, The King vs Joseph Howe, Before the Chief Justice and a Special Jury. Supreme Court – Hilary Term. Halifax, NS: Joseph Howe, 1835.

Trial of the Action in Favor of the Rev. Samuel Russell of Boylston against John Howe of Boylston, for Defamation, at the Supreme Judicial Court, Holden at Worcester, April, A.D. 1831. Worcester, MA: Spooner & Church, 1831.

Trial of William Beals & Charles G. Greene, for an Alleged Libel, Published in the Boston Morning Post, on Alfred W. Pike, Preceptor of the Topsfield Academy, at the November Term of the Sup. J. Court, at Salem, before His Honor Judge Putnam. By the Reporter of the Boston Morning Post. Boston: Beals & Greene, 1835.

Trial of William J. Snelling for a Libel on the Honorable Benjamin Whitman, Senior Judge of the Police Court. Commonwealth vs. Snelling. Supreme

Judicial Court of Massachusetts, December 27th, 1833. Before the Hon. Samuel Putnam, Justice. Boston, 1834.

Upham, Charles Wentworth. *Salem Controversy. Pamphlets and Extras, Containing the Articles of Unitarian* [sic]. Salem, 1834.

Vital Records of Sutton, Massachusetts, To the End of the Year 1849. Worcester, MA: Franklin P. Rice, 1907.

Whately, Richard [John Search]. *Considerations on the Law of Libel, as Relating to Publications on the Subject of Religion.* London: James Ridgeway, 1833.

White, Joseph Blanco. *The Law of Anti-Religious Libel Reconsidered, in a Letter to the Editor of the Christian Examiner, in Answer to an Article of that Periodical against a Pamphlet Entitled "Considerations, &c." by John Search.* Dublin: Richard Milliken and Son, 1834.

Whitman, John W. *Report of a Trial in the Supreme Judicial Court, Holden at Boston, Dec. 16th and 17th 1828, of Theodore Lyman, Jr., for an Alleged Libel on Daniel Webster, a Senator of the United States, Published in the Jackson Republican* [etc.]. Boston: Putnam and Hunt, 1828.

Whitman, John W. *Trial of the Case of the Commonwealth versus David Lee Child, for Publishing in the Massachusetts Journal a Libel on the Honorable John Keyes, before the Supreme Judicial Court, Holden at Cambridge, in the County of Middlesex. October Term, 1828.* Boston: Dutton and Wentworth, Printers, 1829.

Whitman, John W. *Trial of the Commonwealth, versus Origen Bacheler, for a Libel on the Character of George B. Beals, Deceased, at the Municipal Court, Boston, March Term, A. D. 1829. Before Hon. P. O. Thacher, Judge.* Boston: John H. Belcher, 1829.

Whitmarsh, Joseph A. *To the Members of the "First Free Church," Boston.* Boston, 1838.

Wilkie, William. *A Letter to the People of Halifax, Containing Strictures on the Conduct of the Magistrates* [etc.]. Halifax, NS: Anthony Henry Holland, 1820.

Wilson, James. *Collected Works of James Wilson,* edited by Kermit L. Hall and Mark David Hall. 2 vols. Indianapolis: Liberty Fund, 2007.

Winslow, Hubbard. *Rejoice with Trembling: A Discourse Delivered in Bowdoin Street Church, Boston, on the Day of Annual Thanksgiving, November 30, 1837.* Boston: Perkins & Marvin, 1837.

Woodman, Horatio. "Preface." In *Reports of Criminal Cases, Tried in the Municipal Court of the City of Boston, before Peter Oxenbridge Thacher, Judge of that Court from 1823 to 1843,* iii–vi. Boston: Little and Brown, 1845.

Wright, Frances. *Views of Society and Manners in America: In a Series of Letters from that Country to a Friend in England, During the Years 1818, 1819, and 1820.* London: Longman, Rees, Orme, and Brown, 1821.

Index

Fanny Hill (Cleland), 28, 234, 236, 237, 238, 239, 240, 241, 242, 243, 258, 309, 310, 380. *See also pornography*
Farnam, Thomas, 240
Fay v. Parker, 241
Fay, Peter, 241, 352, 353
Federalists, 63, 64, 68, 72, 75, 106, 189, 190, 219, 229
First Amendment, xii, 18, 19, 62, 63, 64, 65
First Free Church of Boston, 224
Fiske, John, 197, 198, 341
Fletcher, David, 243, 334
Fletcher, Richard, 195, 196, 279
Flohr, John H., 243, 334
Forrester, Thomas, 136, 329, 333
Fox, Charles, 24, 45
Fox's Libel Act (1792), 24, 67, 138, 146, 153, 155, 194
Fraser v. Holland, 139, 140, 141, 142, 143, 145, 176, 334
Fraser v. McLeod, 333
Fraser v. Patterson, 140, 334
Fraser, Donald, 333, 350, 355
Fraser, Simon, 139, 140, 141, 144, 176, 352
Free Enquirer, 248, 263, 264
Free Press, 85, 90, 91, 92, 94, 97, 100, 103, 145
Free Thought movement, 232, 234, 236, 245, 249, 275, 283, 308, 380, 386. *See also religion; women*
freedom of conscience, 3, 6, 28, 166, 219, 232, 233, 247, 252, 253, 262, 263, 264, 268, 270, 271, 272, 273, 274, 282, 286, 293, 299, 300, 302, 303, 310, 311, 380, 390
freedom of debate. *See legislatures*
freedom of religion, 2, 192, 253, 266, 269, 271, 287
freedom of speech, press, expression, discussion, 1, 2, 5, 10, 17, 19, 25, 30, 33, 62, 63, 64, 66, 69, 84, 88, 93, 130, 131, 144, 146, 159, 161, 183, 187, 194, 195, 196, 223, 225, 232, 233, 247, 252, 253, 274, 279, 280, 286, 287, 294, 300, 302, 303, 311, 387, 390. *See also majoritarianism*
Freeman, Colonel, 90, 91
Freeman, Edmund, 66, 278, 290, 297
freemasonry, 13. *See also antimasonry*

French Revolution, ii, 2, 4, 66, 76, 310, 387
French, Thomas, 220
Frugal Housewife, The (L.M. Child), 202, 204, 230, 382
Fruits of Philosophy (Knowlton), xiii, 230, 250, 256, 257, 258, 259, 260, 261, 264, 310, 380

Gardiner, Thomas, 148
Gardiner, William, 193, 194, 196, 212
Garrison, William Lloyd, 107, 165, 202, 203, 251, 280, 281, 282, 285, 286, 292, 308, 310, 341, 390
Gazette, 139
Gazetteer, 262
Genius of Universal Emancipation, The, 251
George, John, 8
Gerry, Elbridge, 71, 72, 74, 184, 190, 202, 229
Girard, Philip, 160, 245, 328, 347, 397
Glezen v. Draper, 369
Goff, John, 333
Goffe, Maria, 342, 359, 363
Goodrich, Charles, 328, 341, 372
Goodwill, Johnson, 216, 218
Gordon, Thomas, 65
Gospel Visitant, The, 262
Gough, Patrick, 90
government
    criticism of, 8, 64, 75
    public interest in, 16
    stability of, 33
    structure of, 45, 52, 72
Gray, James, 151
Greene, Charles G., 158, 216, 222, 255, 272, 279, 285, 292, 294, 386, 388
Greene, Samuel D., 215, 227, 380, 382
Grimké, Angelina, 249, 251
Grimké, Sarah, 251, 293
Grosvenor, Mason, 259, 260, 261
Guild, Aaron, 219, 220, 228
Gwyn, Julian, 333, 370

habeas corpus, 37, 38, 42, 43, 44, 46, 48, 95, 104
Habermas, Jürgen, 110
Hale, Matthew, 76
Haliburton, Thomas Chandler, 86, 87, 89, 91, 93, 99, 101, 245, 344

Index 463

Moore, Charles, 215, 228
Moral Physiology (Owen), 230, 250,
    256, 258
Morgan, William, 200, 216, 296
Mormonism, 292
Morris, Robert, 375
Morton, Marcus, 144, 196, 197, 212,
    305, 307, 312
Morton, Perez, 73, 123, 164, 179, 187,
    201, 381
Muir, James, 320
Munroe, Susan, 212
Murdoch, Beamish, 104, 137, 152, 160,
    243, 244, 320, 328, 380
Murray, George, 99
Murray, James, 98

Negro Hill, 165, 198, 204, 238, 241
NEHGS (New England Historic and
    Genealogical Society), 393
Nelson, William, 33
New Brunswick, 92, 102, 103, 136, 137,
    146, 148, 149, 156, 299, 376
New England Anti-Slavery Society, 165,
    203, 204
New-England Galaxy, 180, 181, 184,
    188, 200, 201, 204, 214, 219, 298
newspapers
    and duty to the public, 82
    and editors' responsibility, 157
    as partisan, 6, 87
    as politically engaged, 11
    significance of, 181, 334, 374, 378
    variety of, 181
Newton, Rejoice, 164, 202, 239, 327,
    328, 382
Norton, Mary Beth, 322
Nova Scotia
    access to courts in, 7
    and common law, 56, 163
    and infrequent civil defamation
        cases, 10
    and perceptions of the United States,
        254, 299, 386
    and race, 302, 330
    and skating, 245, 246
    and women, 10
    civil cases sample, 331
    colonial situation of, 10, 56, 89, 95,
        98, 103
    compared to England, 149

connections to Massachusetts, 11
constitutional thought, 4, 6, 30, 55, 86,
    89, 91, 93, 97, 101, 102, 103, 104,
    106, 148, 150, 153, 156, 159
demographics, 324, 326
frequency of cases in, 165, 314, 322,
    330, 347, 394
lawyers in, 11, 326, 327, 328, 329,
    330
legal influences on, 135, 159
litigants, 331, 333
litigants' complaints, 330
money bills, 89, 96, 97, 98, 100
New England lawyers in, 153
newspapers in, 11, 84, 87, 88, 180
political tensions, 83
reform movements in, 145, 156, 232
religion in, 234, 245, 246, 324, 325
revenues for, 96
riots in, 94, 95, 254, 300, 301, 302
road-building, 85, 91
travel within, 324
use of privilege in, 84, 86, 91, 109
Nova Scotia legislature. *See also*
    legislatures
    criticism of, 89
    jurisdiction of, 83
    powers of, 86, 97, 101, 104
    suspension from, 91
Novascotian, 18, 86, 88, 93, 99, 100, 102,
    148, 151, 152, 158, 160, 246,
    300, 329
Noyes, George, 303
NSA (Nova Scotia Archives), 393
Nugent, Richard, 158, 329

Oakes, Lydia, 343, 352, 369
obscene libel, 9, 13, 28, 32, 77, 78, 79, 81,
    158, 184, 185, 225, 233, 234, 237,
    238, 239, 240, 241, 242, 243, 250,
    255, 257, 258, 259, 260, 261, 264,
    265, 268, 269, 271, 291, 305, 306,
    309, 379. *See also blasphemy*;
    Commonwealth v. Holmes;
    Commonwealth v. Kneeland;
    Commonwealth v. Knowlton; *porn-
    ography*; R. v. Flohr; *verbatim
    passages*
On the Generative System (Roberton), 61
On the Powers and Duties of Juries
    (Phillips), 145, 147. *See also malice*

women (cont.)
  involvement in civil cases, 7, 10, 22,
    315, 316, 330, 333, 342, 363, 365,
    371, 374, 383
  married suing as single, 345, 346
  married women, 248, 263, 344, 364, 365
  reported cases, 368
  reputation of, 344
  single women, 345
  suing alone, 343, 365, 368
  use of courts, 7, 10, 315
  women's words, 345, 364

Wright, Frances (Fanny), 231, 245, 247,
  248, 249, 250, 256, 265, 272, 309,
  310, 344, 379, 384, 391. *See also
  women*
Wright, John, 58

Yarmouth Herald, 147, 299,
  300
Young, George, 85, 86, 87, 88
Young, John, 85

Zenger, John Peter, 65, 67, 68

Publications of the Osgoode Society for Canadian Legal History

2021   Daniel Rûck, *The Laws and the Land: The Settler Colonial Invasion of Kahnawà:ke in Nineteenth-Century Canada*
Lyndsay Campbell, *Truth and Privilege: Libel Law in Massachusetts and Nova Scotia, 1820–1840*
Colin Campbell and Robert Raizenne, *Income Tax in Canada: Laying the Foundations, 1917–1948*
Martine Valois, Ian Greene, Craig Forcese and Peter McCormick, eds. *The Federal Courts at Fifty: Equity,* Droit, *Admiralty*

2020   Heidi Bohaker, *Doodem and Council Fire: Anishinaabe Governance through Alliance*
Carolyn Strange, *The Death Penalty and Sex Murder in Canadian History*

2019   Harry Arthurs, *Connecting the Dots: The Life of an Academic Lawyer*
Eric Reiter, *Wounded Feelings: Litigating Emotions in Quebec*

2018   Philip Girard, Jim Phillips and Blake Brown, *A History of Law in Canada. Volume 1: Beginnings to 1866*
Suzanne Chiodo, *The Class Actions Controversy*

2017   Constance Backhouse, *Claire L'Heureux-Dube: A Life*
Dennis G. Molinaro, *An Exceptional Law: Section 98 and the Emergency State, 1919–1936*

2016   Lori Chambers, *A Legal History of Adoption in Ontario, 1921–2015*
Bradley Miller, *Borderline Crime: Fugitive Criminals and the Challenge of the Border, 1819–1914*
James Muir, *Law, Debt, and Merchant Power: The Civil Courts of Eighteenth-Century Halifax*

2015   Barry Wright, Eric Tucker and Susan Binnie, eds., *Canadian State Trials. Volume IV: Security, Dissent and the Limits of Toleration in War and Peace, 1914–1939*
David Fraser, *"Honorary Protestants": The Jewish School Question in Montreal, 1867–1997*
C. Ian Kyer, *A Thirty Years War: The Failed Public /Private Partnership That Spurred the Creation of the Toronto Transit Commission, 1891–1921*

2014   Christopher Moore, *A History of the Ontario Court of Appeal*

Dominique Clément, *Equality Deferred: Sex Discrimination and British Columbia's Human Rights State, 1953–84*

Paul Craven, *Petty Justice: Low Law and the Sessions System in Charlotte County, New Brunswick, 1785–1867*

Thomas Telfer, *Ruin and Redemption: The Struggle for a Canadian Bankruptcy Law, 1867–1919*

2013 Roy McMurtry, *Memoirs and Reflections*

Charlotte Gray, *The Massey Murder: A Maid, Her Master and the Trial That Shocked a Nation*

C. Ian Kyer, *Lawyers, Families, and Businesses: The Shaping of a Bay Street Law Firm, Faskens 1863–1963*

G. Blaine Baker and Donald Fyson, eds., *Essays in the History of Canadian Law. Volume 11: Quebec and the Canadas*

2012 R. Blake Brown, *Arming and Disarming: A History of Gun Control in Canada*

Eric Tucker, James Muir and Bruce Ziff, eds., *Property on Trial: Canadian Cases in Context*

Shelley A.M. Gavigan, *Hunger, Horses, and Government Men: Criminal Law on the Aboriginal Plains, 1870–1905*

Barrington Walker, ed., *The African-Canadian Legal Odyssey: Historical Essays*

2011 Robert J. Sharpe, *The Lazier Murder: Prince Edward County, 1884*

Philip Girard, *Lawyers and Legal Culture in British North America: Beamish Murdoch of Halifax*

John McLaren, *Dewigged, Bothered and Bewildered: British Colonial Judges on Trial*

Lesley Erickson, *Westward Bound: Sex, Violence, the Law, and the Making of a Settler Society*

2010 Judy Fudge and Eric Tucker, eds., *Work on Trial: Canadian Labour Law Struggles*

Christopher Moore, *The British Columbia Court of Appeal: The First Hundred Years*

Frederick Vaughan, *Viscount Haldane: The Wicked Step-Father of the Canadian Constitution*

Barrington Walker, *Race on Trial: Black Defendants in Ontario's Criminal Courts, 1850–1950*

2009 William Kaplan, *Canadian Maverick: The Life and Times of Ivan C. Rand*

R. Blake Brown, *A Trying Question: The Jury in Nineteenth-Century Canada*

Barry Wright and Susan Binnie, eds., *Canadian State Trials. Volume 3: Political Trials and Security Measures, 1840–1914*

Robert J. Sharpe, *The Last Day, the Last Hour: The Currie Libel Trial*

2008   Constance Backhouse, *Carnal Crimes: Sexual Assault Law in Canada, 1900–1975*

Jim Phillips, R. Roy McMurtry and John Saywell, eds., *Essays in the History of Canadian Law. Volume 10: A Tribute to Peter N. Oliver*

Gregory Taylor, *The Law of the Land: Canada's Receptions of the Torrens System*

Hamar Foster, Benjamin Berger and A.R. Buck, eds., *The Grand Experiment: Law and Legal Culture in British Settler Societies*

2007   Robert Sharpe and Patricia McMahon, *The Persons Case: The Origins and Legacy of the Fight for Legal Personhood*

Lori Chambers, *Misconceptions: Unmarried Motherhood and the Ontario Children of Unmarried Parents Act, 1921–1969*

Jonathan Swainger, ed., *The Alberta Supreme Court at 100: History and Authority*

Martin Friedland, *My Life in Crime and Other Academic Adventures*

2006   Donald Fyson, *Magistrates, Police and People: Everyday Criminal Justice in Quebec and Lower Canada, 1764–1837*

Dale Brawn, *The Court of Queen's Bench of Manitoba 1870–1950: A Biographical History*

R.C.B. Risk, *A History of Canadian Legal Thought: Collected Essays*, edited and introduced by G. Blaine Baker and Jim Phillips

2005   Philip Girard, *Bora Laskin: Bringing Law to Life*

Christopher English, ed., *Essays in the History of Canadian Law. Volume 9: Two Islands, Newfoundland and Prince Edward Island*

Fred Kaufman, *Searching for Justice: An Autobiography*

2004   John D. Honsberger, *Osgoode Hall: An Illustrated History*

Frederick Vaughan, *Aggressive in Pursuit: The Life of Justice Emmett Hall*

Constance Backhouse and Nancy Backhouse, *The Heiress versus the Establishment: Mrs. Campbell's Campaign for Legal Justice*

Philip Girard, Jim Phillips and Barry Cahill, eds., *The Supreme Court of Nova Scotia, 1754–2004: From Imperial Bastion to Provincial Oracle*

2003   Robert Sharpe and Kent Roach, *Brian Dickson: A Judge's Journey*
        George Finlayson, *John J. Robinette: Peerless Mentor*
        Peter Oliver, *The Conventional Man: The Diaries of Ontario Chief Justice Robert A. Harrison, 1856–1878*
        Jerry Bannister, *The Rule of the Admirals: Law, Custom and Naval Government in Newfoundland, 1699–1832*
2002   John T. Saywell, *The Law Makers: Judicial Power and the Shaping of Canadian Federalism*
        David Murray, *Colonial Justice: Justice, Morality and Crime in the Niagara District, 1791–1849*
        F. Murray Greenwood and Barry Wright, eds., *Canadian State Trials. Volume 2: Rebellion and Invasion in the Canadas, 1837–38*
        Patrick Brode, *Courted and Abandoned: Seduction in Canadian Law*
2001   Ellen Anderson, *Judging Bertha Wilson: Law As Large As Life*
        Judy Fudge and Eric Tucker, *Labour before the Law: Collective Action in Canada, 1900–1948*
        Laurel Sefton MacDowell, *Renegade Lawyer: The Life of J. L. Cohen*
2000   Barry Cahill, *"The Thousandth Man": A Biography of James McGregor Stewart*
        A.B. McKillop, *The Spinster and the Prophet: Florence Deeks, H.G. Wells, and the Mystery of the Purloined Past*
        Beverley Boissery and F. Murray Greenwood, *Uncertain Justice: Canadian Women and Capital Punishment*
        Bruce Ziff, *Unforeseen Legacies: Reuben Wells Leonard and the Leonard Foundation Trust*
1999   Constance Backhouse, *Colour-Coded: A Legal History of Racism in Canada, 1900–1950*
        G. Blaine Baker and Jim Phillips, eds., *Essays in the History of Canadian Law. Volume 8: In Honour of R.C.B. Risk*
        Richard W. Pound, *Chief Justice W.R. Jackett: By the Law of the Land*
        David Vanek, *Fulfilment: Memoirs of a Criminal Court Judge*
1998   Sidney Harring, *White Man's Law: Native People in Nineteenth-Century Canadian Jurisprudence*
        Peter Oliver, *"Terror to Evil-Doers": Prisons and Punishments in Nineteenth-Century Ontario*
1997   James W. St. G. Walker, *"Race," Rights and the Law in the Supreme Court of Canada: Historical Case Studies*
        Lori Chambers, *Married Women and Property Law in Victorian Ontario*

Patrick Brode, *Casual Slaughters and Accidental Judgments: Canadian War Crimes and Prosecutions, 1944–1948*

Ian Bushnell, *The Federal Court of Canada: A History, 1875–1992*

1996   Carol Wilton, ed., *Essays in the History of Canadian Law. Volume 7: Inside the Law – Canadian Law Firms in Historical Perspective*

William Kaplan, *Bad Judgment: The Case of Mr. Justice Leo A. Landreville*

Murray Greenwood and Barry Wright, eds., *Canadian State Trials. Volume 1: Law, Politics and Security Measures, 1608–1837*

1995   David Williams, *Just Lawyers: Seven Portraits*

Hamar Foster and John McLaren, eds., *Essays in the History of Canadian Law. Volume 6: British Columbia and the Yukon*

W.H. Morrow, ed., *Northern Justice: The Memoirs of Mr. Justice William G. Morrow*

Beverley Boissery, *A Deep Sense of Wrong: The Treason, Trials and Transportation to New South Wales of Lower Canadian Rebels after the 1838 Rebellion*

1994   Patrick Boyer, *A Passion for Justice: The Legacy of James Chalmers McRuer*

Charles Pullen, *The Life and Times of Arthur Maloney: The Last of the Tribunes*

Jim Phillips, Tina Loo and Susan Lewthwaite, eds., *Essays in the History of Canadian Law. Volume 5: Crime and Criminal Justice*

Brian Young, *The Politics of Codification: The Lower Canadian Civil Code of 1866*

1993   Greg Marquis, *Policing Canada's Century: A History of the Canadian Association of Chiefs of Police*

Murray Greenwood, *Legacies of Fear: Law and Politics in Quebec in the Era of the French Revolution*

1992   Brendan O'Brien, *Speedy Justice: The Tragic Last Voyage of His Majesty's Vessel* Speedy

Robert Fraser, ed., *Provincial Justice: Upper Canadian Legal Portraits from the* Dictionary of Canadian Biography

1991   Constance Backhouse, *Petticoats and Prejudice: Women and Law in Nineteenth-Century Canada*

1990   Philip Girard and Jim Phillips, eds., *Essays in the History of Canadian Law. Volume 3: Nova Scotia*

Carol Wilton, ed., *Essays in the History of Canadian Law. Volume 4: Beyond the Law – Lawyers and Business in Canada 1830–1930*

Patrons of the Osgoode Society

For EU product safety concerns, contact us at Calle de José Abascal, 56–1°, 28003 Madrid, Spain or eugpsr@cambridge.org.

www.ingramcontent.com/pod-product-compliance
Ingram Content Group UK Ltd.
Pitfield, Milton Keynes, MK11 3LW, UK
UKHW010248140625
459647UK00013BA/1727